DECOLONIAL VOICES

DECOLONIAL VOICES

Chicana and Chicano Cultural Studies in the 21st Century

ARTURO J. ALDAMA *and*
NAOMI H. QUIÑONEZ, *editors*

INDIANA
University Press
Bloomington & Indianapolis

This book is a publication of

Indiana University Press
601 North Morton Street
Bloomington, IN 47404-3797 USA

http://iupress.indiana.edu

Telephone orders 800-842-6796
Fax orders 812-855-7931
Orders by e-mail iuporder@indiana.edu

The paper used in this publication meets the minimum requirements of American National Standard for Information Sciences—Permanence of Paper for Printed Library Materials, ANSI Z39.48-1984.

Manufactured in the United States of America

Library of Congress Cataloging-in-Publication Data

Decolonial voices : Chicana and Chicano cultural studies in the 21st Century / edited by Arturo J. Aldama and Naomi H. Quiñonez.
p. cm.
Includes bibliographical references and index.
ISBN 978-0-253-34014-6 (cloth : alk. paper) — ISBN 978-0-253-21492-8 (paper : alk. paper)
1. Mexican Americans—Intellectual life. 2. Mexican Americans—study and teaching. 3. Mexican Americans—Social conditions. 4. Mexican American arts. 5. American literature—Mexican American authors. 6. Postcolonialism—United States. 7. Decolonization—United States. 8. Mexican-American Border Region—Social conditions. 9. Mexican-American Border Region—Civilization. I. Aldama, Arturo J., date. II. Quiñonez, Naomi Helena.

E184.M5 D34 2002
305.868'72073—dc21

2001039495

2 3 4 5 6 12 11 10 09 08 07

CONTENTS

PART I. DANGEROUS BODIES

PART II. DISMANTLING COLONIAL/ PATRIARCHAL LEGACIES

PART III. MAPPING SPACE AND RECLAIMING PLACE

FOREWORD

The present anthology, *Decolonial Voices: Chicana and Chicano Cultural in the 21st Century,* edited by Arturo J. Aldama and Naomi Quiñonez, provides us with a splendid collection of essays exploring a broad range of issues affecting Chicano/a society, particularly along the United States–Mexican border, in the first decade of the twenty-first century. Issues of the racialized body, of globalization, immigration, and the question of gender, are problematized through multiple perspectives in this volume. Significant in the area of border violence and immigration are the essays by Arturo J. Aldama and Jonathan Xavier Inda. Aldama's "Millennial Anxieties: Borders, Violence, and the Struggle for Chicana and Chicano Subjectivity" traces landmark studies related to the border by such renowned border critics as Emily Hicks, José Saldívar, Alfred Arteaga, and Leo Chávez, and proceeds to explore the continuing problems Mexicans and Chicanos/as encounter along the two thousand or so miles of the U.S.-Mexican border. Violence along the *frontera* (border) is not new. Nevertheless, for those of us who believe in "progress" and the continuing development of the human spirit in keeping with a modernist tradition, it is profoundly disappointing to witness the cyclical violence predicted by René Girard in his book *Violence and the Sacred* (1984). Girard states in this book that if humans do not examine their lives and their actions in a critical manner they will continue to repeat the violence inherent in the birthing of nations through acts of war. The United States acquired the Southwest, including the states of Texas, New Mexico, Arizona, Colorado, Utah, California, and Nevada and parts of Oregon, through a violent act of war against a weaker nation—Mexico in 1848. The violence continued during the Gold Rush period with the lynching and murdering of *Californio,* Mexican, and Latin American miners, ranchers, and others who got in the way of the new colonization process. Violence was ever present in the dispossession of thousands of acres of land from the Mexican and *Californio* landowners. Indeed, the taking of these lands is brilliantly chronicled by the *Californiana* writer Amparo Ruiz de Burton in her two novels, *Who Would Have Thought It* (1872) and *The Squatter and the Don* (1882).

Nevertheless, the great expanses taken from Mexican Americans in the various southwestern states needed strong bodies to work the land, to develop the land, to make the land productive. Bridges had to be built, irrigation projects had to be instituted, railroad tracks had to be laid, and acres and acres of land had to be tilled, plowed, planted, irrigated, and harvested. Hundreds of thousands of Mexicans—indeed, millions of Mexicans—throughout the past 152 years have been recruited to do this arduous work.

In spite of the great need the United States has had for Mexican labor and the concerted efforts to recruit Mexican workers by the U.S. government, as was the case in the Bracero Program (1942–1964), and by agribusiness, farmers, and other employers, violence has erupted off and on against Mexican nationals migrating to the United States. Jonathan Xavier Inda explores how in the past decade an alarming trend has taken place both in Europe and the United States regarding the flow of politically displaced refugees, immigrant workers, and other exiled groups. Inda points out how "First World" nations view the flow of migrants from Third World nations as undesirable, parasitic, threatening the nation-state at the level of both its geopolitical boundaries and its cultural contours. The essay perceptively applies postmodern theories from Derrida and Foucault as they pertain to biopolitics and the pathological tangent given immigrants. Within this biopolitical conceptualization, immigrants are framed within the discourse of disease and pathogens. They are perceived to be the harbingers of all social ills and seen "as parasites intruding the body of the host nation." Viewed in such dehumanizing terms, it is no wonder that immigrants become the easy targets of racist, angry, alienated youth. A recent report by the *Los Angeles Times* (July 18, 2000, pp. A3 and A24) headlined "7 Teens Arrested in Hate-Crime Attack on Elderly Migrants." The teenagers, ranging in age from fourteen to seventeen, attacked the elderly Mexican workers living in "a makeshift camp in a desolate canyon," according to police. And although the teenagers were not linked to any organized hate group such as the neo-Nazis or the Ku Klux Klan, the *Los Angeles Times* describes how some of the suspects had been seen frequently near a "dilapidated shack where racist and Nazi literature and anti Latino graffiti were later found" (ibid.).

The teenagers, of course, ape what adults say and do. Anti-immigrant sentiment was brazenly expounded in a lengthy column published by the *Santa Barbara News-Press* (July 16, 2000, pp. G1–G2) and written by Diana Hull, president of Too Many People, a California organization. In this extended diatribe against "illegal aliens," Latinos, and Hispanics, Hull bemoans the fact the racial and cultural Anglo-Saxon landscape is changing to a brown hue. She applauds the ranchers in Arizona who according to her propagandistic essay "are arming to keep thousands of Mexican nationals from crossing their property, cutting their fences and breaking into their houses." Of course, she does not substantiate all of the above charges with any concrete data. She advises the federal government to do what Francis Parkman demanded it do against the Native Americans—the Dakotas in 1846—and that was to bring military force and military law against them. According to Hull, Parkman noted that the Dakotas were becoming "more insolent and exacting in their demands" and that "each demand acceded to, they become more presumptuous and rapacious. Any timorousness on the part of the settlers creates a very dangerous situation that mounts to a higher pitch with each concession—after which the Indians threaten them with more destruction or kill them." Since the Anglo settlers were the immigrants, Diana Hull's thinking is completely muddled. Are the contemporary immigrants supposed to behave like the Anglo immigrants of 1846 and bring military force against the original inhabitants? I do not think that is what Ms. Hull had in mind!

Fortunately for us, the Aldama-Quiñonez anthology is characterized by a compendium of expertly researched essays, clearly written and cogently argued. In Part II, "Dismantling Colonial/Patriarchal Legacies," the essays focus on gender issues. The six excellent studies explore from the vantage point of literary creations Chicana writers' contestation of patriarchal domination and oppression. Naomi Quiñonez's essay, for example, zeroes in on the La Malinche paradigm to expose Chicano/Mexicano gender oppression. She deftly demonstrates how Chicanas have not been silent victims but have articulated their discomfort with the male status quo. Her analysis of Chicana creative cultural production underscores the insistent voice that refuses to be subjugated.

Amelia María de la Luz Montes, on the other hand, explores the complexities of race and gender as exhibited by the writings of Amparo Ruiz de Burton in her nineteenth-century novel *Who Would Have Thought It?* Ruiz de Burton in this novel critiques the hypocrisy of white New Englanders who were ostensibly abolitionists but harbored racism toward the young Mexican woman, Lola, a character in the novel. Ruiz de Burton, a *Californiana* of Mexican descent, was from the California aristocracy who considered themselves superior to Indians, mestizos, and blacks. In spite of the contradictions inherent in Ruiz de Burton's work, Montes underscores her importance in teasing out both racial and gender issues in nineteenth-century American and Mexican American society.

Other essays, such as those by Cordelia Candelaria, Anna Sandoval, and Sarah Ramirez, offer splendid incursions in the feminist-oriented cultural production of Chicana writers. Cordelia pointedly examines the writings of the recently deceased Estela Portillo Trambley, who was one of the earliest writers of the Chicano renaissance and who valiantly wrote on feminist issues such as those presented in her short story "The Paris Gown." The El Paso, Texas, writer also wrote about lesbian issues such as the ones expounded on in the play *The Day of the Swallows.* Portillo Trambley was ahead of her time both for being among the first Chicanas to be widely published in the early 1970s and due to her defiant venturing into taboo subjects. Candelaria makes a significant contribution in her analysis of Portillo Trambley's work.

In Part III of this outstanding anthology, the essays focus on the border as a magical place where things happen. The cultural production at this site is intense, original, energizing, riveting. Literature, theater, art, politics, and other issues explode under the intense rays of the *frontera*'s sun. Chicano music, literature, and art in particular are areas of cultural production; they are constantly in evidence in Chicano/a border artists. Pancho McFarland provides us with a seminal essay on Chicano rap and its political ramifications. Chicano rap, influenced by African American rap, retains the bite and sting of its predecessor. Its originality lies not only with its musical composition, but also with the political themes it covers. Chicano rap focuses on institutionalized racism against peoples of color and in particular Chicanos within a context of world globalization. The *migra* (the U.S. Immigration and Naturalization Service) and the police are perceived to be the archenemies of Mexican Americans and it is in this role that they are portrayed. Chicano rap, therefore, becomes a cultural weapon of resistance and affirmation for young alienated youth.

Anthologies such as this one are important venues for discussing contemporary issues affecting our society. The issue of violence, for example, is one that is grabbing headlines since senseless attacks on people seem to be on the rise. The *Los Angeles Times* reported a 12 percent increase in hate crimes in California in 1999. The newspaper describes how "[t]he state's 1,962 hate crimes, occurring at a rate of more than five a day last year, represent an increase of 12% over the previous year. The total is the second highest since California began keeping track in 1994" (July 28, 2000, p. A3). The *Los Angeles Times* further reports that "60% were motivated by race or ethnicity, with more than half of those crimes directed at blacks" (p. A28). Furthermore, 14 percent of hate crimes targeted Latinos. These unfortunate statistics are alarming because, as the California attorney general, Bill Lockyer, commented, "Each hate crime is an attack on the victim's personal identity or beliefs, leading to an on-going fear of repeated attacks . . . the perpetrators view their victims as lacking full human worth due to their skin color, language, religion, sexual orientation or disability" (p. A3). It is only with a firm commitment to continue critically analyzing our human condition that we will be able to move toward an appreciation and a respect for our differences. Aldama and Quiñonez are to be congratulated for bringing together such an outstanding collection of essays in this anthology. They have made an excellent contribution toward addressing the social, cultural, and political border issues confronting our nation in this decade.

María Herrera-Sobek
University of California–Santa Barbara

ACKNOWLEDGMENTS

We would like to acknowledge our friends, colleagues, and mentors and recognize their support in helping us complete the *Decolonial Voices* volume. We are especially grateful to the Center for Chicano Studies at UC Santa Barbara for the financial and administrative support during the 1999–2000 academic year. The warmth and encouragement of Carl Gutiérrez-Jones, the acting Director, and the rest of the UCSB Chicano Studies Department was very motivating. In specific, we are grateful to Maria Herrera-Sobek for making time in her busy schedule to write the foreword. At Arizona State University, we are in debt to the Department of Chicana and Chicano Studies for their vibrancy, collegiality, and support. In specific, we would like to thank Vicki Ruiz, a fearless scholar and a wonderful mentor, and Cordelia Candelaria for her insights, support, and intellectual generosity. We also want to acknowledge Loida Gutiérrez for her commendable administrative and Spanish proofing efforts.

We thank the publishers for permission to republish the following essays and chapters: Norma Alarcón, "Anzaldúa's Frontera: Inscribing Gynetics," in *Displacement, Diaspora, and Geographies of Identity*, ed. Smadar Lavie and Ted Swedenburg (Durham, N.C.: Duke University Press, 1996), 41–53; and José David Saldívar, "On the Bad Edge of the Frontera," in *Border Matters: Remapping American Cultural Studies* (Berkeley: University of California Press, 1997), 95–130.

Finally, we want to thank the outside readers—especially the first report for its rich comments and important suggestions—as well as the editorial staff at Indiana University Press. In specific, we want to thank Joan Catapano for her vision and leadership and Michael Lundell for his follow-through, warmth, and attention to detail. Also, we would like to thank the managing editor, Jane Lyle, and the copyeditor, Susanna Sturgis, for their speed, thoroughness, and professionalism. Finally, we want to thank the contributors for sharing their inspiring, rigorous, and provocative work. We dedicate this work to the *compañeras* and *compañeros* throughout the history of colonialism in the Américas whose voices have been cut short by the literal violence of the U.S./México border.

DECOLONIAL VOICES

¡PELIGRO! SUBVERSIVE SUBJECTS: CHICANA AND CHICANO CULTURAL STUDIES IN THE 21ST CENTURY

Arturo J. Aldama and Naomi H. Quiñonez

> The decolonial imaginary embodies the buried desires of the unconscious, living and breathing in between that which is colonialist and that which is colonized. Within that interstitial space, desire rubs against colonial repressions to construct resistant, oppositional, transformative, diasporic subjectivities that erupt and move into decolonial desires.
>
> —Emma Pérez, *The Decolonial Imaginary* (1999)

THE U.S.-México border zone is a site that is lived and expressed by those who reside in the physical/discursive margins generated by the edge of two nation states. As Gloria Anzaldúa (1999) reminds us, "The U.S.-Mexican border *es una herida abierta* where the Third World grates against the first and bleeds . . . the lifeblood of two worlds merging to form a third country—a border culture" (25). In discussing the aesthetics of "border culture" in relation to juridical, linguistic, and political tensions produced by the U.S.-México border, Alfred Arteaga (1997) analyzes how the "cultural politics of hybridization" are grounded "in the material space" of the militarized borderlands. Arteaga argues how Chicana and Chicano subjects are "coming to be amid the competing discourses of nation" (91). This collection of essays reflects how the multidimensional nature of the border fosters unique forms of Chicana and Chicano cultural productions and informs complex cultural frameworks. As "residents" of the borderlands before and after 1848, Chicana and Chicano scholars and artists are expanding the contours of a geopolitical and geocultural space that holds many ramifications for the new millennium. Although we, as editors, recognize the growing population of Latinas and Latinos along the borderlands and praise their contributions to American culture, we have chosen to focus on Chicana and Chicano cultural studies and gauge our development "works in progress" since that historic date of 1848, when Mexican citizens were forced to become part of the United States.

With the struggle for the cultural and intellectual liberation of Chicana and Chicano border subjects, new dimensions of perception, focus, and analysis have emerged since the social and cultural gatherings of the 1960s and 1970s. Many scholars have been compelled to offer visions and disclosures of a dynamic and distinctive cultural aesthetic that reaches back into precolonial México. The resulting representations and articulations of this growing terrain of cultural expression/production incorporate and extend the impact of gender, sexuality, ethnicity, and class, and shed light on the possibilities and complexities of Chicana and Chicano culture. The matrix of cultural collisions, disjunctures, cohesions, and hybridizations on which Chicana and Chicano culture is grounded has triggered a new wave of mestiza/o cultural workers. These "seers" into the world of "mestizaje consciousness" deconstruct, reinvent, and affirm the multiple subjectivities of a dynamic cultural contextualization. *Decolonial Voices: Chicana and Chicano Cultural and Literary Studies in the 21st Century* is about the messages issued by those voices. They are voices that sing praises and question authorities; that recover subjugated histories and knowledge(s); that critique and contradict master narratives of racial and patriarchal orders; and finally, that (re)claim space and place for Chicana and Chicano cultural discourses. Most significantly, they are voices engaged in extracting meaning from a cultural aesthetic that has long been omitted from Euro-Western cultural canons, signaling new directions in Chicana and Chicano cultural studies.

Decolonial Voices: Chicana and Chicano Cultural Studies in the 21st Century offers a range of interdisciplinary essays that discuss racialized, subaltern, feminist, and diasporic identities and the aesthetic politics of hybrid and mestiza/o cultural productions. In doing so, it pulls together a body of theoretically rigorous interdisciplinary essays that articulate and expand the contours of Chicana and Chicano cultural studies. Our collection continues the prerogatives of *Living Chicana Theory* (1998), edited by Carla Trujillo, and *Criticism in the Borderlands: Studies in Chicano Literature, Culture and Ideology* (1991), edited by Héctor Calderón and José David Saldívar. This collection makes central the struggle to "live Chicana theory" by putting into practice a resistance to the multiplicity of oppression. We also want to continue Saldívar's and Calderón's commitment to provide a sustained forum for "Chicano/a theory and theorists in our global borderlands: from ethnographic to post-modernist, Marxist to feminist" (6). In this collection, the contributors were asked to reflect on what the new millennium means for them as critics given the 500-year legacy of colonial and neocolonial subjugation and resistance in México and the Americas and the 150-year history of the Treaty of Guadalupe Hidalgo (1848). They were also asked to consider how their work responds to the current rise of transnational and predatory global capitalism. The majority of the essays represent new unpublished work by major and emerging scholars in Chicana and Chicano cultural studies.

Decolonial Voices seeks to reflect several key directions in the field: first, it charts how subaltern cultural productions of the U.S.-Mexico borderlands (film, art, music, lit, pop culture, and alternate historiographies) speak to what Walter Mignolo (2000) considers the intersections of "local," "hemispheric," and "globalized" power relations of the border imaginary. Second, this collection excavates and recovers the Mexican women's and Chicana literary and cultural heritages (from the 1850s to the present) that have been ignored and suppressed by Euro-American canons and patriarchal exclusionary practices (see Montes, Candelaria, and Quiñonez). Our collection also seeks to expand the field in postnationalist directions by creating an interethnic, comparative, and transnational dialogue between Chicana and Chicano, African American, Mexican feminist, and U.S. Native American cultural vocabularies (see McFarland, Penn-Hilden, Sandoval, D. Ruiz, V. Ruiz, and Johnson).

In charting these discursive movements of this growing and heterogeneous field, there is a commitment to understand how Chicana and Chicano cultural productions articulate a resistance to the multiplicity of oppression across race, class, gender, and sexuality and perform a cultural mestizaje and hybridity in the age of transnational globalizations. It is our hope that the precedent to consider the politics of cultural production in comparative, interethnic, and postnationalist terms will encourage further alliances with U.S. Latina and Latino work, especially the Afro-Caribbean diaspora (Flores, 1998), the "tropicalization" of urban space (Aparicio, 1997), and the rise of exile-descendant Central American literary and cultural voices.

Part I, "Dangerous Bodies," considers how Chicana and Chicano cultural production maps, enunciates, and (re)claims discourses, technologies, and spaces of the "body." Working within feminist, postcolonial, and Chicana theorizations of the "body" (Butler, Mohanty, Alarcón), these essays contribute to an understanding of how Chicana and Chicano bodies are "performed" in a variety of cultural texts and social spaces. For example, Arturo Aldama's essay on borders and violence attempts to ground the florescence of border theory and discourses of the "abject" (Kristeva) to the materiality of state violence on the bodies of Mexican border crossers and Chicana and Chicano youth. Laura Pérez's "Writing on the Social Body" examines how such Chicana artists as Diane Gamboa, Yolanda López, and Ester Hernández decorate, dress, and manipulate Chicana bodies to articulate a politics of erotic ownership by critiquing the prescripts of sexist and heterosexist gender roles. In similar terms, Ramón García examines how recent Chicana-authored videos enact a feminist and queer agency by parodying the martyrs in traditional Catholic culture, which in the case of *Lupe Velez* creates a counter-Hollywood diva and saint icon for the multiply marginalized queer Chicana/o and Mexicana/o communities.

Frederick Luis Aldama's "Penalizing Chicano/a Bodies in Edward J. Olmos's *American Me*" provides a unique perspective on the issues of machismo, criminalization, and the construction of masculinity in the film *American Me*, by reading male sexual violence as a re-enactment of Spanish conquest violence in the Américas. Jonathan Inda's "Biopower, Reproduction, and the Migrant Woman's Body" considers how nativist discourse and the "biopolitics" of the state (under former California governor Pete Wilson) combine to construct migrant workers as pathogen carriers that contaminate the "healthy citizenry" and "purity" of the nation. Finally, Norma Alarcón's "Anzaldúa's *Frontera:* Inscribing Gynetics" interrogates racialist and masculinist apparatuses of representation and material domination(s) in the U.S.-Mexico borderlands. In specific, Alarcón discusses how Anzaldúa (re)centers and unshames desire for sexual and cultural decolonization into the "everyday resistance" of the lived, the living, and the present.

Part II, "Dismantling Colonial/Patriarchal Legacies," builds on feminist and postcolonial theories and strategies to identify and challenge the multiple legacies of colonialism and its effects on Chicana and Native women. "Talking back" to the Eurocolonial narratives that have marginalized them and often rendered them "invisible," these Chicana and Native scholars marshal their analytical forces to reveal, explore, and dismantle the patriarchal structures that have historically attempted to silence them. Turning the light switch on patriarchy's power allies—racism and classism—these scholars dare to reveal not only the dichotomized relationship between the racialized other and the Eurocolonial power structure, but also how colonialism seeps into and colors the fragile relationships between and among the subaltern communities of the borderlands. Consequently, intercultural, interethnic conflicts and tensions between men and women, men and men, and women and women provide complex ramifications and challenges for the twenty-first century. Also in this section borders are defined and redefined, dismantled and re-invented. Spaces along and within the border are mapped to identify sites of oppression and struggle, but also to create locations of hope, healing, and strategies for material and spiritual opposition and resistance.

"Re(Riting) the Chicana Postcolonial," by Naomi Quiñonez, draws parallels between Malintzín Tenepal (La Malinche) and "first-wave" (1960s–1970s) Chicana writers. Both became "interpreters" for their culture, one during the Spanish Conquest, the other during the Chicano Movement. Quiñonez enacts an autoethnography to chart how her early poetic consciousness linked organically with first-wave Chicana poets and cultural activists to articulate a consciousness of race, class, gender, and sexuality. Patricia Penn-Hilden sheds light on a more shadowy side of the postcolonial condition in "How the Border Lies." Weaving together threads of narrative from newspapers, anecdotes, poetry, colonial texts, and postcolonial discourse from the sixteenth century to the present, Penn-Hilden examines how the border between the Eurocolonial and the racialized "other" often becomes transposed to form borders between Chicanos and Native Americans. Amelia María de la Luz Montes analyzes the contradictory subject positions of María Amparo Ruiz de Burton's recently recovered historic novel *Who Would Have Thought It?* (1995), which on one hand condemns the ideologies of racial superiority in the New England society of the 1870s and on the other "animalizes" indigenous and African peoples.

Cordelia Candelaria offers readers an appreciation of the feminist legacy left by fiction writer Estela Portillo Trambley and gives a thorough understanding of the writer's ability to identify and resolve race, class, and gender struggles through her central female characters. Anna Sandoval offers a necessary comparison between Chicana and Mexicana writing that crosses the border. Along the space of border feminism, Sandoval explores the similar strategies used by Chicana and Mexicana writers in responding to systems of patriarchal control over gender and sexuality. In the work of Sarah Ramírez, decolonization and the effects of Chicano cultural nationalism provide the framework to analyze the work of artist Alma López. Ramírez examines how Lopez's digital photography creates a Chicana aesthetic space rooted in indigenous spirituality. The essays in this section surface the often dysfunctional consequence of the attitudes and behaviors of the subaltern condition. Yet by bringing them to light, these scholars lay the groundwork for mending, healing, changing and transcending a legacy of colonialism and patriarchy.

Part III, "Mapping Space and Reclaiming Place," seeks to discuss how Chicana and Chicano cultural productions enter into what Michel de Certeau calls the "the practice of everyday" resistance to negotiate space and time (Lefebvre, 1991) in racialized and sexist political and discursive economies. Fusing Chicana feminist theory (Chabram-Dernersesian) and critical pedagogy issues (Giroux), Alejandra Elenes theorizes a "border pedagogy" that critiques the limited access to nonracist and nonsexist institutional "spaces" of educational empowerment for the linguistically diverse Chicano-Mexicano communities. In doing so, Elenes addresses how schools and normative pedagogy perpetuate the paradoxical spaces of "belonging" and "not-belonging" for Chicanas and Chicanos. As it sideswipes Los Angeles, José David Saldívar's geopolitical border is a porous, living entity given breath by organic cultural visionaries such as Helena María Viramontes, John Rechy, and Los Illegals. Saldívar utilizes these visionaries to present a view of *La Frontera* as a space that not only separates but also frames a postmodern montage of fragmentations and artistic interstices. Issues of citizenship, disempowerment, dislocation, militarization, and sociopolitical transformations are contained "On the Bad Edge of *La Frontera.*"

In similar terms, Pancho McFarland analyzes how Chicano and Latino rap and hip-hop bands like Psycho Realm and Cypress Hill provide counternarratives to the effects of globalization on "the social restructuring" of "nonwhite majorities" in urban barrios and communities of color. To outline a coalitional politics between working-class African Americans and Latinos, Gaye Johnson charts a history of "Afro-Latino collaborations" in development of salsa, jazz, and blues (Dizzy Gillespie and Carlos Santana). Then, Johnson examines how the recent band Ozomatli, a multiethnic urban ensemble (Latino, African American, Asian American, and Jewish) formed to raise money for a working-class youth job center in Los Angeles, reflects the possibilities of pan-ethnic coalition whose political concerns are both local and global.

Citing Noam Chomsky's ethical challenge toward socially responsible scholarship, Alberto Ledesma seeks to expand the boundaries of Chicana and Chicano cultural studies to include further attention to cultural and literary productions of "undocumented" subjects, calling into question the privileged albeit liminal status of Chicana and Chicano criticism. The essay titled "*Teki Lenguas del Yollotzín* (Cut Tongues from the Heart)" aptly describes Delberto Dario Ruiz's project. His implication of colonialism in the theft of not only land and resources, but also language, underscores the need to recognize the recovery of indigenous languages as an integral aspect of both personal and collective mestiza and mestizo identities. Both Ledesma and Ruiz expand the internal vocabularies of Chicana and Chicano cultural studies by decolonizing further the relationships between cultural and legal citizenship, and by pointing to the heterogeneity of our indigenous ancestry that expands beyond the Aztecs of central Mexico. In specific, Ruiz and Ledesma expand the field of border studies to consider both the *recién llegados,* the newly arrived émigrés, and the indigenous communities whose ancestral landbase is literally split by the U.S.-Mexico border (Yaqui, Tohono O'Odham, Pima, and Kickapoo, to name a few).

Rolando Romero "remembers the Alamo" and considers how this historical monument functions as a trope for Texas nationalism and continues to contribute to a "brown panic" about non-assimilationist Mexicans in Texas. His work excavates an alternate historiographic space that uncovers a manipulation and interpretation of events that are "ahistorical" and yet serve the historical purpose of legitimizing white supremacy and anti-Mexican violence in Texas.

Vicki L. Ruiz's end essay, "Color Coded: Reflections at the Millennium," emphasizes a dramatic resurgence of nativism in the United States and traces how nativist ideologies fuel public opinion and public policy. Examples such as the campaign for Proposition 187 and the abusive 1997 Chandler, Arizona, INS/police deportation raid are contrasted with current accurate and realistic statistical information on immigration patterns. Ruiz uses the idea of "suburban legends" to show how a white privileged class justifies a frenzied fear of the "colored" masses, which in turn validates vigilante and "legal" actions taken against Latina/o immigrants, especially women. Ruiz encourages readers to not become apathetic to the current tide of anti-immigrant violence and reminds those interested in cultural studies to keep grounded in the material intersections of racial and sexual violence in our globalized borderlands.

Although our collection is specific to the field of Chicana and Chicano cultural studies, we share the aims of feminist and postcolonial work committed to analyzing the complex relationships between subalternity, globalization, nation-states, and the "performance" of culture and identity in the multiple margins of racial, class, sexual, and gender *différance.* As such this collection seeks to create alliances with other cultural, postcolonial, and feminist studies collections: for example, *Between Woman and Nation: Nationalisms, Transnational Feminisms, and the State,* edited by Caren Kaplan, Norma Alarcón, and Minoo Moallem (1999), and the recent work of Chandra Mohanty and Jacqui Alexander (1997).

Finally, it is important to discuss the nature of our collaboration in putting this collection together. *Arturo:* It is an honor to work with Naomi Quiñonez, a poet, feminist scholar, and cultural activist whose poetic consciousness is tied to the first wave of Chicana cultural workers. *Naomi:* It has been an especially enriching experience to work in collaboration with Arturo Aldama. As a child of Mexico City's working class who has spent most of his life in the United States, his astute and incisive observations of borderland culture have contributed greatly to the depth and texture of this book. I am fortunate to have him as a *colega* and a friend.

WORKS CITED

Anzaldúa, Gloria. *Borderlands / La Frontera: The New Mestiza.* 2nd ed. San Francisco: Aunt Lute Press, 1999.

Arteaga, Alfred. *Chicano Poetics: Heterotexts and Hybridities.* Los Angeles and Cambridge: Cambridge University Press, 1997.

Mignolo, Walter. *Local Histories / Global Designs: Coloniality, Subaltern Knowledges and Border Thinking.* Princeton, N.J.: Princeton University Press, 2000.

Peréz, Emma. *The Decolonial Imaginary: Writing Chicanas into History.* Bloomington: Indiana University Press, 1999.

PART I

DANGEROUS BODIES

1 MILLENNIAL ANXIETIES: BORDERS, VIOLENCE, AND THE STRUGGLE FOR CHICANA AND CHICANO SUBJECTIVITY

Arturo J. Aldama

The events of 1836 brought forth charges of Mexican depravity and violence, a theme which became pervasive once Anglos made closer contact with the state's Hispanic population following the war. In the crisis of the moment, firebrands spoke alarmingly of savage, degenerate, half-civilized, and barbarous Mexicans committing massacres and atrocities at Goliad and the Alamo.

—Arnoldo de León, *They Called Them Greasers: Anglo Attitudes toward Mexicans in Texas, 1821–1900* (1983)

We were thrown out of just about everywhere, but what really made me feel bad was when we tried to go into a restaurant or a restroom downtown, and we were told, "No you can't use it." The police would always come and say, "This is a public place, you have to get out, you're not allowed here."

—Maria Elena Lucas, *Forged under the Sun / Forjada bajo el Sol* (1993)

CHICANA/O BORDER studies, devoted to understanding the complex dialectics of racialized, subaltern, feminist, and diasporic identities and the aesthetic politics of hybrid mestiza/o cultural production, is at the vanguard of historical, anthropological, literary, cultural, artistic, and theoretical inquiry.[1] This essay is an invitation to situate the diverse practices of critical U.S.-Mexican borderland inquiry in the historical moment of 2000. We hang at the precipice of the next millennium with all of the promises and anxieties that it produces. For our inquiry, one of the most important of these anxieties is the unkept promise that ensued from the signing of the Treaty of Guadalupe Hidalgo over 150 years ago. This treaty signed at the end of the U.S.-Mexican war resulted in the formation of the U.S.-Mexico border and the forced purchase of northern México for fifteen million dollars (California, New Mexico, Texas, Arizona, Nevada, Utah, and parts of Colorado, Oklahoma, and Kansas), as well as the supposed protection of property and civil, cultural, and religious rights of Chicanos and Mexican peoples.[2] Disturbed and outraged by the continued prevalence of historical patterns of criminalization, marginalization, dispossession, civil rights violations, and torture in Chicana/o and other subaltern communities, my essay seeks to contribute to the field of critical border studies by exploring the relationship between discourses of otherization crystallized by the U.S.-México border (racial, sexual, ideological) and state-enforced acts of violence (Immigration and Naturalization Service [INS], paramilitary, and police) on the bodies of Mexicana/o and Latina/o immigrants and Chicana/o youth.

"Shifting Borders, Free Trade, and Frontier Narratives: U.S., Canada, and México" (1994), by Pamela Maria Smorkaloff, summarizes the movement of critical border studies as it responds to specific geopolitical locations. Smorkaloff considers the ways in which theorists, writers, and performance artists map transfrontier social space challenging monologic sociopolitical forces that maintain national borders: "Transfrontier writers and theorists are developing a kind of syncretism of the first and third worlds in their writing that captures not only the complex reality of the border zone, but also a more profound understanding of the contemporary US and the Latin America living within" (97).

In similar terms, *Border Writing: The Multidimensional Text* (1991) by D. Emily Hicks examines the dialectics of transfrontier identity and border writing. Hicks uses the concept of border crossings as a metaphor and a tool to analyze the heterogeneity of identity in Latin American writing. Even though the bulk of the text focuses on two major Argentinean writers, Julio Cortázar and Luisa Valenzuela, Hicks begins the study by discussing the U.S.-Mexico border region, and concludes it by returning to Chicano and Mexicano writing in the U.S.-Mexico border regions.

Hicks argues that border writing "emphasizes the differences in reference codes between two or more cultures" (xxv), expressing the "bilingual, bi-cultural, bi-conceptual reality" of border crossers. However, Hicks is emphatic in positing that border writing is about crossing cultural borders and not physical borders. This leads to her disturbing characterization of the U.S.-Mexico border as a theater of "metaphors" where "actors"—*pollos* (undocumented border crossers), *la migra* (INS), and *coyotes* (contractors who bring undocumented people over the border)—act their daily "dramas." Hicks creates a universalizing model that moves beyond concrete historical understandings of subaltern Latina/o "border-crossers" as "real people" responding to "real" geopolitical social realities and understands their experiences as a type of carnivalesque and postmodern theater. In doing so, Hicks deracinates the individuality of people—their/our specific histories, and family and community ties—who negotiate the often violent border crossing for such reasons as poverty, hunger, political persecution, the desire to reunite with loved ones, or a simple curiosity to see life *al otro lado* (on the other side).[3]

The foundational anthology, *Criticism in the Borderlands: Studies in Chicano Literature, and Ideology* (1991), edited by Héctor Calderón and José David Saldívar, grounds the discussion of transfrontier ideology in a concrete geopolitical zone. This anthology challenges the exclusionary practices of the American literary academy and the formation of the canon by recovering "neglected authors and texts" in the "Southwest and the American West." The work also provides a forum for diverse theoretical perspectives: "Chicano/a theory and theorists in our global borderlands: from ethnographic to post-modernist, Marxist to feminist" (6). What renders the anthology even more significant to the growth of critical border studies is the argument by its contributors that Chicano theoretical analyses can move from a regional understanding of relations of power to a global one without denying the historical specificities of each geopolitical locale.

In an earlier essay, "Limits of Cultural Studies" (1990), Saldívar articulates the cultural and border studies imperative in more detail, arguing that cultural studies must be both regional and global: "Finally, cultural studies, a border zone of conjunctures, must aspire to be regionally focused, and broadly comparative, a form of living and of travel in our global borderlands" (264). In this essay, Saldívar critiques both the subjectifying forces which inferiorize and homogenize non-Western peoples in the social relations of power and how scholarly practices replicate these forces. Saldívar shares in the British cultural studies understanding of culture as a dynamic and heterogeneous site where tensions of domination and resistance compete, linking these principles to forge a greater understanding of borders, resistance, and mestizaje. By studying the "subordinate and dominant cultures like public schoolchildren in Great Britain or low riders and *cholos* in East Los Angeles," Saldívar argues that cultural studies is committed to "transforming any social order which exploits people on the grounds of race, class, and gender." Cultural studies and border theory challenge "the authority of canon theory and emergent practice" and the relations of power which sustain this authority (252). After setting up his critique of monologic tendencies in anthropological practices, Saldívar surveys several key border writers, "native informants" Rolando Hinojosa, Gloria Anzaldúa, Guillermo Gómez Peña, and Renato Rosaldo. Saldívar argues that these writers offer counternarratives to the master narratives of nations that attempt to normalize identity and totalize cultural heterogeneity. Saldívar summarizes their writings as "cultural work" that "challenges the authority and even the future identity of monocultural America" (264).

Border Matters: Remapping American Cultural Studies (1997) by José Saldívar, a dazzling and impressive study of border writers, artists, musicians, theorists, and scholars, dramatically builds on this critique of the master-narratives that author the hegemonization of "monocultural America." Saldívar argues that

> U.S. Mexico border writers and activist intellectuals have begun the work of exploring the terrains of border crossing and diaspora amid the debris of what El Vez calls our "national scar" of manifest destiny and the cultures of the U.S. imperialism. . . . The history of migration, forced dispersal in the Américas as represented in the

> vernacular border cultures, challenges us to delve into the specific calculus of the U.S.-Mexico border crossing condition. (197)

In similar terms "Beasts and Jagged Strokes of Color: The Poetics of Hybridization on the US Mexican Border," by literary scholar and Chicano poet Alfred Arteaga (1994), addresses the multidimensional intersection of real and discursive forces along the U.S.-Mexico border—the border patrol and Tex-Mex *caló,* for example—by discussing the formation of the Chicana/o subject in relation to tensions produced by the border. With reference to Chicano poet Juan Felipe Herrera's "Literary Asylums," a heteroglossia of voices subjectified by and resistant to competing discourses of the nation-state, Arteaga states:

> "Literary Asylums" and other Chicano poems play in a poetics of hybridization that calls to mind the quotidian cultural politics of hybridization in the material space of the frontier. What is at play is the formation of a Chicano subject coming to be amid the competing discourses of nation. (1)

Arteaga continues his discussion of Chicano poetics of hybridization or dialogic poetics by grounding the discussion in the material border. Arteaga considers the purpose of the border as intended by the nations at stake—the United States and México:

> Consider the border: in the imagining of nation, it is the infinitely thin line that truly differentiates the US from México. The absolute certainty of its discrimination instills confidence in national definition, for it clearly marks the unequivocal edge of the nation. Its perceived thinness and keenness of edge are necessary for the predication of national subjectivity, which defines itself as occurring inside its border and not occurring outside. (2)

Arteaga observes how "[t]he thin borderline cleaves two national narratives, two national monologues of ideal and finalized selves" (2). Central to Arteaga's argument is the tension between the monologic tendencies of national narrative and the dialogic, interlingual, and hybridizing impulses of Chicana/o subjects and their literary expression. Arteaga locates the border zone as a site that is lived and expressed by those marginalized by nationalizing forces and who reside in the physical/discursive interstices and margins generated by the border.

The border for Arteaga is a site of power that selectively privileges and marginalizes, reinforcing social hierarchies along axes of race, class, nationality, and sexuality. He compares the experience of elite Mexican bourgeois Octavio Paz—who knows himself to be fully Mexican when crossing the border, a line that reinforces his imagined singular self—with that of

Chicana-Tejana lesbian theorist and writer Gloria Anzaldúa, who argues that "[b]orders are set up to define the places that are safe and unsafe, to distinguish us from them. The prohibited and the forbidden are its inhabitants" (5).[4]

However, to consider the experience of Mexican immigrants or émigrés crossing the border from the south, I assert a series of propositions that add to Arteaga's discussion of the multivalent nature of the U.S.-Mexico border. At the outset, I need to clarify that these assertions on the effects of the border for Mexicans traveling north reflect the socioeconomic conditions of peoples who do not enjoy the privilege of such national subjects as Paz and other bourgeois elite who can demonstrate to the visa-granting embassy in Mexico City, Ciudad Juárez, or Tijuana, that they have sufficient economic ties to Mexico—bank accounts, businesses, and high-status occupations. As border performance artist and poet Gerardo Navarro states in his reference to the "apartheid" of the border, the Tortilla Curtain operates like "a valve that is closed or opened by the invisible hands of the market in accord with the fluctuations in Wall Street and in the global market" (1994, 4). My propositions are as follows:

1. The border serves as a "free zone" for U.S. citizens and U.S. corporations (U.S. border crossers). The free zone applies, among others, to weekend tourists crowding the bars, drinking cheap beers, and seeking male and female prostitutes, and to U.S. companies exploiting "cheap" labor and lax environmental regulation controls.[5]

2. Contrary to the free zone where all Euro-American taboos drop, the border is also a free zone of violence, a barrier to those trying to cross from the south—as evidenced by the Border Patrol, weekend vigilantism, bandits, and *coyotes* who after collecting their fees rob, rape, and denounce border crossers.

3. Even though the border is selectively open to those whose class positions confirm their tourist and student status, it forces a discourse of inferiorization on Mexicans and other Latinos, especially those whose class position, ethnicity, and skin color emerges from the *campesina/o* and urban proletariat groups.

4. Finally, once crossed, the border is infinitely elastic and can serve as a barrier and zone of violence for the Mexican or Latino/a who is confronted by racialist and gendered obstacles—material and discursive—anywhere s/he goes in the United States. This means that the immigrant continually faces crossing the border even if s/he is in Chicago (or wherever in the United States)—a continual shifting from margin to margin.

In no way do these propositions give breadth to the infinite variety of experiences and struggles for Mexicans and other Latin American immigrants moving across and through this infinitely elastic border to the United States. The immediate questions that the border poses are these: How can we chart the multiple vectors of forced liminalities produced by the U.S.-Mexico border? Is it enough to say that "no matter where a Mexican travels or lives in the United States, he or she always inhabits an economic, racial and discursive status that is automatically secondary and perpetually liminal?"[6]

In *Shadowed Lives: Undocumented Immigrants in American Society* (1992), an important study of contemporary Mexican immigration, Leo R. Chávez understands liminality as a state of living in the shadows. Chávez illustrates the liminality in concrete terms with the following description of a family trying to visit Disneyland from San Diego: "Undocumented immigrants frequently told me that because of their illegal status they were not free to enjoy life, often citing as an example the fact that they were unable to take their children to Disneyland because of the immigration checkpoint at San Clemente" (14).

On February 1, 1997, the Rocky Mountain regional conference of the National Association of Chicana and Chicano Studies took place in downtown Phoenix, Arizona. The event was an inspirational gathering of scholars from a wide variety of disciplines, Chicana/o studies department chairs, community leaders and activists, cultural workers and students dedicated to promoting the interdisciplinary and multifaceted field of Chicana/o studies, as well as to re-igniting further consciousness regarding the marginalized and uneven status of the Chicana/o communities. My participation in this rich *encuentro* of scholarly and political knowledge made me question further the roles of critics and scholars dedicated to Chicana/o studies as we begin the new millennium.

Specifically, I balance the wonderful gains that the field of Chicana/o Studies has witnessed—a proliferation of interdisciplinary scholarship, an increased focus on issues of gender and sexuality, the recent establishment of the Chicana/o Studies Department at Arizona State University, an increased enrollment of Chicana/o students at all levels, and further support for Chicana/o graduate students—with the realization and recognition that there are still negative constants facing the Chicana/o community.[7] Examples of these constants are: (1) continued economic marginalization, (2) substandard housing, schooling, and general public services, (3) extremely high incarceration rates,[8] and (4) an increase in the sophistication and deployment of violence especially toward Chicana/o youth and Mexicana/o immigrants, including those residents and citizens of Mexican descent unfortunate enough to get caught in immigration or *migra* sweeps. Regarding Chicana/o youth, their style of dress, music, and art is categorically demonized and criminalized by the dominant culture, thus continuing hegemonic patterns of demonization and the concomitant violation of youth seen most dramatically during the "Zoot Suit Riots" (1940s) and the repression of Chicana/o youth believed to be associated with the Brown Berets (1970s), and in the treatment of the youth suspected of being involved in gangs (1940s–present), who are now called "urban and domestic terrorists."[9]

Also, there is a continuing increase in the sophistication of methods of surveillance, weaponry, capture, and detainment in the Chicana/o communities by such state and federal agencies as the Immigration and Naturalization Service and state and county police and sheriffs. Growing technological sophistication coupled with a continuance of brute force and strategies of deception are evidenced by the use of infrared technologies, video surveillance, impenetrable bulletproof vests, assault rifles, and laser tracking devices, as well as such vulgar ruses as informing alleged "illegals" that they need to show up at a warehouse to claim their televisions and cars—prizes that they supposedly won by lottery—only to be captured, detained, and deported.[10]

I ask these unsettling questions: What does it mean for me to write as a Chicano in the cusp of the new millennium, 508 years after the full-scale invasion of the Américas—the usurpation of lands, the wholesale rape and slaughter of indigenous peoples, the forced importation and brutal enslavement of African peoples, and the institutionalized criminalization and marginalization of the Chicana/o community, etc.? What is my responsibility to the past, to the present, and to the future, and to the practice of representation? What does it mean for me to enter into the practice of methodologies that empower peoples who have not only been physically colonized—the "other," the "marginal," the "subaltern"—but also intellectually colonized by apparatuses of representation that reify their status as savage with all of the connotations of barbarism, inferiority, and child-like innocence that accompany such an identification?[11]

We celebrate the epistemological shifts that feminist, multiethnic, postmodernist, and postcolonial discourse provides us scholars, writers, activists, and theorists.[12] We rally together with freedom to discuss and analyze the social formations of the subject, and the hybridity of forces that impinge upon and constitute the subject.[13] The epistemological shifts in the politics and practice of ethnography, literary criticism, and cultural studies free us up to discuss the micro- and macro-politics of how subjects are formed, positioned, and represented in both social and discursive economies. We challenge each other to implement interdisciplinary methods that embrace the heterogeneous nature of social reality.

As critics, writers, and theorists of communities and histories that are our own, we, as insiders and outsiders, call for the questioning of borders and an end to neocolonialism, to racism, to sexism, and to homophobia as well as to the devastation of ecosystems through agribusiness, mining, and the timber industry. At the same time, however, in even the seconds, minutes, hours, and days that I write and think about this project and about ways to discuss subaltern peoples in liberating terms, funds are being transferred electronically. The funds pass into the "borderless" global free-trade market, legalized by such international accords as the General Agreement on Tariffs and Trade (GATT) and the North American Free Trade Agreement (NAFTA); yet travel for subaltern peoples—Mexicanos and other Latinos, for example—is highly restricted by militaristic border patrol agents. If the travelers and refugees cannot prove sufficient economic ties to their home country, they have to run like *pollos* (a slang term which literally means "chickens" and refers to border crossers)—hungry, stressed, and avoiding robbery, assaults, and rape by a variety of predatory groups, and human rights abuses by the INS—to cross the border into *el Norte*, or *el otro lado* (the other side), where they will live in fear of deportation and racial harassment, and suffer extreme exploitation. Put simply, money travels; people can't (well, at least some people).[14] For example, consider the following depiction of the potential hazards of crossing the U.S.-Mexico border (referred by many as the Tortilla Curtain) in *Across the Wire / Life and Hard Times on the Mexican Border* (1993) by Luis Alberto Urea:

> Now say that you are lucky enough to evade all these dangers on your journey. Hazards still await you and your family. You might meet white racists, complimenting themselves with the tag 'Aryan.' They 'patrol' the scrub in combat gear, carrying high-powered flashlights, rifles, and bats. . . . And of course there is the Border Patrol (*la migra*). (17)

Labor-intensive sweat factories, *maquiladoras*, are built in the "free-trade zones" of Mexico, Central America, and Southeast Asia to take advantage of extreme inequities in global pay scales. Mexican, Salvadoran, and Filipino women and children are hired not only because they are the most exploitable in local economies, but also because they are perceived to have nimble fingers and rapid hand-eye coordination. Thankful to have some job in a crippling economic crisis, they race to meet their production quotas in fourteen-hour days, with two strictly enforced bathroom breaks of ten minutes each, so that U.S., Arab, Japanese, and European consumers, as well as the bourgeois consumers of each producing country, can buy Gap clothes and Nike shoes at ever greater discounts, and with greater variety of styles.[15]

In trying to understand the larger patterns of race, class, and gender oppression, as well as movements of capital on the global stage that inform a given historical moment and contextualize a given literary, cultural, and social text, the importance of specific peoples and individuals affected by these plays of power is easily overlooked. To do this, discourses and movements of oppression and resistance need to be analyzed at the level of the body and personhood to illustrate how they have "real" consequences for "real" people. I say this aware that statements on the "real," the "individual," and the "person" could imply that I am recapitulating notions of the fixed, stable autonomous subject—a concrete, knowable, a priori subject—so idealized by Western metaphysics. To do this would disregard or repress what poststructural, postcolonial, and radical feminist thought has taught us regarding the social construction of subjects.[16]

However, I ask: How is the diverse play of heterogeneous discourses that constitute human subjectivity (re)understood when subjects are shot at, chased, detained, raped, and incarcerated because they are of a certain ethnic group, sexuality, and gender; or, with respect to Mayan, Kenyan, and Mexican workers, for example, because they are demanding some kind of protection for their labor; or, in the case of Chicana/o youth, because they are walking home from school and get caught in an INS sweep? Perhaps, the dialectic that drives discursive practices of inferiorization and materialist practices of repression is precisely that: the "play" of human subjectivity is handcuffed, imprisoned, deported, and violated in acts of containment and repression by monologues of dominance and denial which state and enforce: "You are Other . . . You are Alien . . . You are Messican . . . You have no rights . . . You are unnatural . . . You are a beast." In *Borderlands / La Frontera: The New Mestiza* (1987), Gloria Anzaldúa eloquently speaks to the violent otherization of Chicana/os and other peoples marginal to the dominant Euro-American culture:

> Gringos in the U.S. Southwest consider the inhabitants of the borderlands transgressors, aliens—whether they possess documents or not, whether they're Chicanos, Indians or Blacks. Do not enter, trespassers will be raped, maimed, gassed, shot. The only "legitimate" inhabitants are those in power, the whites and those who align themselves with whites. Tension grips the inhabitants of the borderlands like a virus. Ambivalence and unrest reside there and death is no stranger. (4)

A dramatic example of how anti-Mexican immigrant discourses of otherization and dehumanization translate into acts of state-enforced physical violence was the brutal April 2, 1996, Riverside County sheriff beatings of Mexican immigrants, called by many "another Rodney King beating" because of the extreme and brutal nature of the physical batterings. To recount the dramatic footage, a truck full of Mexicanas/os and Latinas/os, alleged "undocumented" subjects, is being vigorously pursued by, first, Border Patrol agents and then Riverside County sheriffs through "parts of Riverside, San Bernardino and Los Angeles counties before ending on Pomona Freeway about 20 miles east of Los Angeles" (*CNN Interactive,* Web post 11:05 A.M., April 2, 1996). The truck is so old and worn that it literally starts deconstructing. At the height of the pursuit, pieces of the fenders and siding start to fly off onto the freeway; the truck motor is shaking, and the suspension is pushed to its ultimate limits. A large group of people grip what is left of the shell on the back. After the truck veers to the side, those who can escape flee into the nearby brush, but the situation is much different for those left in the cab. Video footage clearly shows how one sheriff swings his baton at least six times with full force on the male driver, who offers absolutely no resistance, and more dramatically, both sheriffs repeatedly strike a woman on the passenger seat with their batons, even though Alicia Sotero-Vásquez offers no physical resistance and literally goes limp as a rag doll. One of the sheriffs viciously "pulls her to the ground by the hair" (CNN, 1996). This disturbing event illustrates the absolute unambiguity in the violation of the civil and human rights of these suspected "illegals" and asks the following question: Does having the status of "illegal alien" ascribed to you because of your physical and linguistic characteristics and your appearance legalize violence against your person and community?[17] I ask: Will these actions, which speak so directly to the impunity with which state-enforced violence occurs and which nakedly reflect the brutality of the relationship between the United States and Mexican immigrants, be the ones that set the tone for race relations in the twenty-first century?[18]

In the case of police, paramilitary, and INS bullets shooting "Others" (as well as fatal violence from other coercive agents of the dominant culture such as neo-Nazi vigilante groups or thugs hired by *finca* owners), the historicity and vitality of subaltern subjects are stopped and driven into annihilation by the monologism of the state. Persons whose bodies are violated and nullified—and who are characterized in such abject terms as "greaser," the "drunken Indian," the "Black gang-banger," "Jap stealer of jobs," or "Castro-loving *indio*"—are remembered only in the collective consciousness of each person's family and community. The impunity with which these deaths and violence occur only reinforces the subaltern and abject status of these subjects and communities.

Powers of Horror: An Essay on Abjection (1982), by the prolific psychoanalytic feminist scholar Julia Kristeva, argues that abjection, the most extreme form of otherization, is the process that expulses, then mutilates, defiles, and desecrates anything that is deemed alien and opposed to the "I" of the Self: "Abjection, on the other hand, is immoral, sinister, scheming and shady: a terror that dissembles, a hatred that smiles, a passion that uses the body for barter instead of inflaming it, a debtor who sells you up, a friend who stabs you" (4). To illustrate the politics of abjection further, Kristeva reflects on her visit to the halls of the Auschwitz museum where she observes "a heap of children's shoes" and "dolls" under a "Christmas tree" (4). Kristeva eloquently observes: "The abjection of Nazi crime reaches its apex when death, which, in any case, kills me, interferes with what, in my living universe, is supposed to save me from death: childhood, science, among other things" (4).

Bodies that are marked as "Other" because of race, class, gender, sexuality, ethnicity, religion, and political affiliation become sites where power brands subjects, turning them into social abjects: invisible, subversive (un- . . .), libidinal, and violent, and in the case of slavery, branded objects to be bartered, sold, and literally worked to death. An example in classic American literature comes to mind: Nathaniel Hawthorne's *The Scarlet Letter,* where the letter "A," cut from crimson cloth, "brands" Hester Prynne, marking her body as "Other" for transgressing the sexual taboos and cultural mores of puritan society. Another instance where power literally brands subjects—turning them into social abjects—is the yellow cloth stars and serial numbers worn by and engraved on the arms of Jewish peoples in Germany and Europe during World War II. These violently engraved "signs" of otherization and abjection compare to the literal hot-iron branding of the skin of African and indigenous slaves in the Américas (and other areas of colonial conquest) that marked their bodies not only as Others, but also as property or commodities of the colonial overlords.[19]

The Conquest of America: The Question of the Other (1984), by Bulgarian linguist and critic Tzvetan Todorov, is a landmark study of the ideological justifications and methods of the conquest of the Américas which resulted in the horrific genocide of over 90 percent of the indigenous populations: Over seventy million died between 1500 and 1650 due to direct murder and warfare, slavery and work conditions, and the "microbe shock" of diseases unknown in the Americas, smallpox, syphilis, and cholera (133–137). Todorov recalls Vasco de Quiroga's description of the slave traffic and the practice of branding indigenous peoples by, first, the royal seal of Spain, and then the individual brands of the Spanish *encomenderos* or royally appointed overlords in the "New World":

During the first years after the conquest, the slave traffic flourished, and slaves often changed master. "They are marked with brands on the face and in their flesh are imprinted the initials of the names of those who are successfully their owners; they pass from hand to hand, and some have three or four names, so that the faces of these men who were created in God's image have been, by our sins, transformed into paper" (137). Todorov analyzes further the physical consequences of enslavement and observes the horrific effects of the Spanish abjection and desecration of the indigenous Other to a literal "trunk" of "flesh":

> Enslavement, in this sense of the word, reduces the other to the status of an object, which is especially manifested in conduct that treats the Indians as less than men: their flesh is used to feed the surviving Indians or even the dogs, they are killed in order to be boiled for grease . . . all their extremities are cut off, nose, hands, breasts, tongue, sexual organs, thereby transforming them into shapeless trunks. (175)

Nez Perce historian and cultural studies critic Patricia Penn-Hilden calls the Anglocentric cultural hegemony, among others imposed by the colonizing forces in the Américas, the "overculture" or the *überculture* (1997). This term resonates directly with the fascist culture of dominance in wartime Germany. I can't help but recall that at the height of the Nazi genocide of Jews, gays, and Romanian Gypsies, officers of the Third Reich loved to show off the lamps made from stretched Jewish skin.[20] In trying to understand how Euro-American, Spanish, and even Mexican *übercultures* (as with all nation-states) operate in multidimensional ways—power circulates and disperses on multiple fronts, layers, and vectors—I argue that the trajectories of an overculture end only to then regenerate themselves in the complete abjection and desecration of the Other. To illustrate this process of abjection, desecration, and regeneration in the history of the U.S.-Mexico borderlands, one needs only to examine the consequences of figures who were perceived as threats to the race- and gender-coded social order of the United States. For example, in the case of the renowned social bandit of the 1850 California Gold Rush, Joaquín Murieta, who after being persecuted, ambushed, and executed, was decapitated, after which his head was pickled and put on a traveling display; or the case of the shrunken head of Mexican revolutionary leader Pancho Villa, a prized collector's item among prominent Western capitalists.[21] Consider the reprint of an 1853 poster (Fig. 1.1) advertising the traveling exhibition of the "The Head of the Renowned Bandit! Joaquín!"[22]

According to the *The Life and Adventures of Joaquin Murieta, the Celebrated California Bandit* (1854) by Yellow Bird (or John Rollin Ridge, a Cherokee-Anglo crossblood), Captain Love, the commissioned California Ranger who captured Joaquín Murieta, was paid much more than the "sum of one thousand dollars," the reward money posted for the capture of the "bandit, dead or alive" by the governor of California: "And subsequently, on the fifteenth day of May 1854, the legislature of California, considering that his truly valuable services in ridding the country of so great a terror—were not sufficiently rewarded, passed an act granting him an additional sum of five thousand dollars" (158).

In addition, perhaps the starkest example of legalized vigilante violence in the California Gold Rush years aimed at the Mexicana/o community in general, and women in specific, is the barbaric lynching of Josefa Vasquez, a pregnant woman from Sonora, Mexico. In 1851, Josefa, popularly known as Juanita de Downieville, in an attempt to defend herself against vile verbal abuse and rape in her own home stabbed and killed Fred Cannon, a well-liked Anglo-American miner. By four o'clock that afternoon, when a kangaroo trial "proved" that Juanita was an "antisocial prostitute" and Cannon was a "peaceful" and "honest" man, Josefa was lynched. *Occupied America: A History of Chicanos* (1988), by Rodolfo Acuña, a Chicano historian, evokes this tragic and brutal moment:

> Senator John B. Weller was in town but he did nothing to stop the hanging. Weller was an ambitious politician who was later to become governor, and one voteless Mexican made no difference. Over 2000 men lined the river to watch Josefa hang at the bridge. After this, lynching became commonplace and Mexicans came to know Anglo-American democracy as "Linchocracia." (119)

I mentioned the conquest of the Américas and the violent aftermath of the U.S.-Mexico war for the Mexicana/o community in the United States, as well as the violence of state repression and the violence of hyper-exploitation, in order to ground the discussion of identity in the "real" world of contemporary social relations where, I argue, the lives of the "Others"—Chicanas/os, Latinas/os, Mayan women, Salvadoran campesinas, Turks, Tunisians, Asians, gays and lesbians, to name a few—still have

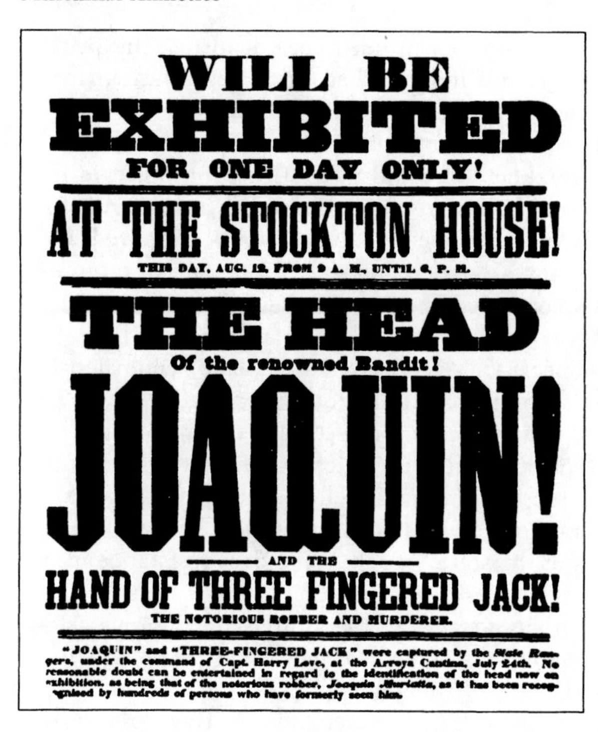

Figure 1.1. The first known poster advertising the exhibition, in Stockton, California, August 12, 1853, of the bandits' remains.

little meaning within cultures of dominance (the *überculture*s). In the case of the Américas, the torture of individuals—inquisitions of the late twentieth century—is now called interrogation or intelligence gathering. To induce a confession, CIA-refined science uses techniques of pain dating back to the Spanish Inquisition, developed by the infamous fifteenth-century inquisitor Tomás de Torquemada, as well as the most advanced surgical, electrical, and video technologies. The modus operandi includes electrocutions and incisions, which are extremely painful but show little on the skin, as well as violent beatings, among other things. In addition to these practices, individuals are subjected to audiovisual recreations or simulations of loved ones and comrades being tortured or confessing to their crimes against the state with the goal of inducing and intimidating the insurgent "subjects" into admitting to whichever crime/s the state has decided they committed. These "scientific" techniques, along with other methods of repression, are taught by U.S. military advisors to the members of a given military regime who are fighting, in the words of both groups, "the communist terrorists" (in, e.g., El Salvador, Nicaragua, or Guatemala), or they are taught in a more systematic way to officers of a given military regime in Latin America "lucky" enough to attend the "School of the Americas" whose campus is at Fort Benning, Georgia.[23] The scrivener's pen of the Inquisition is now replaced by ready-to-sign typewritten forms and the video cameras that film the subject's "confession." These victims of torture are dressed in clean shirts and made up with cake powder to cover bruises and swollen faces.[24] Videotapes of torture are prized commodities on the underground market that circulates "snuff films," child pornography, and materials about bestiality and necrophilia.

In cases of imperial conquests, counterinsurgency, repression, and torture, the body is literally broken apart and reconstituted: people are imprisoned, starved, and beaten; bones are broken; muscles are ripped; skin is flayed and burned; body hair is ripped out by the roots or shaved with a rusty razor; women and men are raped and sodomized; and in more extreme cases, bodies are dismembered and decapitated. The following questions are crucial in engaging these realities: What is the relationship between the body and the subject? Can a subject, enveloped by conditions of intense physical domination by the state, maintain a sense of his or her own subjectivity while the body is being repressed and tortured? Or is torture and repression precisely the point at which subjectivity is reconstituted via the channels of the body? The Other, the insurgent subject, is obliterated, used to obliterate others, or made into a model citizen, obedient to the laws and morals of the state.[25] I ask: What does resistance mean within these conditions?

In the contemporary urban context of the United States, I ask: How do we theorize about or respond to such acts of power on the body, which are an all too familiar sight in poor neighborhoods in the United States, where Chicanas/os, Latinas/os, African Americans, Native Americans, Southeast Asians, and the homeless—the Others of Anglo-American society—are bent over with their cuffed hands pulled back or are lying facedown with arms spread, each like a fallen crucifix? As a visual semiotic what is the "language" of an arrest scenario? When an officer has somebody cuffed, bent over, or facedown in order to search for drugs or weapons, the way in which that officer intervenes into the body of a "suspect" betrays a violent posture of invasion. In the case of male officers collapsing the body of male suspects, there is a homoerotics possibly in denial of itself that underpins heterosexist and patriarchal culture.[26] What do the bodies of both the officer and "suspect" become in these situations? Are they "texts" where the micro- and macro-physics of power can be read? Are the police and military the agents of master narratives whose discourse and practice suppress the Other as a countertext?

Furthermore, what does "resistance" (in the cultural studies sense of the word) mean in these situations where people are severely beaten or killed because, in the words of an officer, they "resisted arrest"? In fact, as I wrote these words, a young Chicano from Oakland was lying in the hospital in a coma because he had resisted arrest. The story that circulated on the local Spanish-speaking stations recounted that officers, at the request of the victim's family, came to arrest him because he was drunk. When he staggered because of his intoxication, his body was interpreted as resisting arrest. Police threw the young man down with such force that he received a severe concussion, putting him in a coma.

In the United States, a rise of theories, testimonials, and histories is empowering the marginal, the Other, the people of color, the poor, and is mounting political challenges to create a fair and just multicultural society. All of this, however, is tempered by the implementation of cuts in federal aid for education, welfare for single mothers, and job training; the end of affirmative action; increasing prison, police, and border patrol budgets; and the enforcement of laws against sodomy and other "unnatural" sexual relationships. For people of color in general, and for Chicanas/os in particular, more police translates into more harassment, more beatings, and more unexplained deaths.[27] More prisons, more police, fewer educational opportunities, and no job training means that more disenfranchised youth—*cholos/as* and "homeys"—will act out the rage of racism, alienation, and poverty by shooting and raping each other for their *clicas,* their sets, their streets, and their colors—red or blue.[28] Meanwhile, "Middle America" retreats farther into fortified suburban ethnic enclaves, buying guns, locking the doors to their houses and cars, fearing robbery, assault, and carjacking. At the same time, people glue themselves to their TV sets to watch the "heroic regulators" of postmodern society confirm their worst fears of the Other in such prime-time hits as the filmed-on-location *COPS* or *LAPD,* further denigrating subaltern peoples, especially African Americans and Spanish-speaking Latinas/os, and normalizing police brutality. As we close this century and enter a new millennium, to be a witness, a victim, and a participant requires from us a state of alarm—that we write, teach, resist, and act with urgency!

Linguistic violence—the creation of the Other—interanimates violence on the body. However, the present work engenders further questioning. For example, taking into account the scenarios mentioned above, how do we theorize on the social text of violence? Is it a language of social relations? If so, what is the *langue* and *parole* of violence? Is violence both the fringe and the center of social relations, as well as the enforcer of the social order in a given historical and cultural context? How does the consideration of physical violence impact conceptions of race, class, ethnicity, gender, and sexuality? In general, future analyses need to focus directly on the interrelationship of discourse, violence, resistance, and the body. Specifically, they must aim to understand further how Chicana/o bodies are "raced," "sexed," and "Othered" by discourses and practices of abjection, as well as how Chicanas/os reclaim our bodies, enunciate our subjectivities, and articulate a resistance of the spirit and the flesh.

I end this essay by considering the death of Julio Valerio, a sixteen-year-old Chicano teenager from Phoenix, Arizona, whose violent and brutal killing provoked an emotional and focused panel at the NACCS, as well as other acts of community support around issues of police violence and racism. According to the *Arizona Republic,* "Six officers fired a total of 25 rounds—20 from 9mm handguns, five from shotguns" (November 17, 1996). Six fully armed, non-Hispanic officers with impenetrable bullet vests, extensive training in arrest procedures, and whose collective physical weight was easily over a thousand pounds were not able to subdue the slim and distressed youth without the use of lethal force. When the Phoenix police force faced public outcry, Mike Pechtel, president of the Phoenix Law Enforcement Association, responded as follows: "'For their efforts, these officers are being vilified by opportunist politicians, whose support for a dope selling, dope smoking gang member is disgusting," drawing upon the rhetoric of the War on Drugs as a way to validate the appalling use of violence on youth (*Arizona Republic,* November 26, 1996). Thus, the vicious police execution of this Chicano teenager, gainfully employed at a furniture factory and with dreams of owning his own home and taking care of his family, was justified because he was perceived as a "drug crazed knife wielding gangbanger." However, the knife Julio carried was in all probability so dull that it could have been a butter knife.

NOTES

1. José Saldívar, Vicki Ruiz, Sonya Saldívar-Hull, Ramon Gutiérrez, Teresa McKenna, Norma Alarcón, Alfred Arteaga, Gloria Anzaldúa, Rolando Romero, Homi Bhabha, and James Clifford have made substantial contributions to critical border studies. I am especially indebted to Dr. Vicki Ruiz and Dr. Manuel de Jesus Hernández-Gutierrez at Arizona State University for their insightful comments on this essay.

2. This border was established after the defeat of General Santa Anna through the Treaty of Guadalupe Hidalgo in 1848. This border is literally a straight line over 2,300 miles long which has no respect for natural ecosystem formations or tribal territories. Yet this arbitrary and intentionally rigid line has immense consequences for both nations. See David Gutiérrez, *Walls and Mirrors: Mexican Americans, Mexican Immigrants, and the Politics of Ethnicity* (Berkeley and Los Angeles: University of California Press, 1995).

3. For a critique of Hicks's often-cited work, see Juan Bruce-Novoa and María Cordoba in "Remapping the Border Subject," a key collection of essays in a special issue of *Discourse,* ed. Rolando J. Romero, vols. 1 and 2 (Fall–Winter, 1995–96): 32–54, 146–169.

4. See Gloria Anzaldúa's *Borderlands / La Frontera: The New Mestiza* (1987), which catalyzed the rise of border theory and discourse in the late 1980s.

5. For a discussion of how border cultures resist and subvert these tendencies, see Guillermo Gómez-Peña's consideration of hybridity and carnival along the border, "Border Culture: A Process of Negotiation towards Utopia" (in *The Broken Line / La Línea Quebrada,* a Border Arts publication, San Diego/Tijuana, Year 1, No. 1 [May 1986]), as well as his book *Warrior for Gringostroika: Essays, Performance Texts, and Poetry* (St. Paul, Minn.: Graywolf Press, 1993).

6. As a term, the word "immigrant" is problematic in understanding Mexican people. What is the status for Mexicans who lived in Mexican territories before they were annexed by the Treaty of Guadalupe Hildalgo in 1848? For a discussion of identity for recent immigrants see Rouse and Rosaldo, both of whom discuss cultural invisibility for undocumented workers in the United States.

7. See David Maciel and Isidro D. Ortiz, eds., *Chicanas / Chicanos at the Crossroads* (Tucson: University of Arizona Press, 1996).

8. See Vicki Ruiz, "'And Miles to Go . . .': Mexicans and Work, 1930–1985," which charts systematically low wage earnings of Chicanas, in *Western Women, Their Land, Their Lives,* edited by Vicki Ruiz, Janice Monk, and Lillian Schlissel (Albuquerque: University of New Mexico Press, 1988). For discussion of criminalization of the Chicano community and the resultant incarceration rates, see Antoinette Sedillo López, ed., *Criminal Justice and Latino Communities* (New York: Garland Press, 1995).

9. For discussion of the systemic and historic criminalization of the Chicana/o

community from the Treaty of Guadalupe Hidalgo to the present, see Alfred Mirandé, *Gringo Justice* (Notre Dame, Ind.: University of Notre Dame Press, 1987), and Larry Trujillo, "La Evolución del 'Bandido' al 'Pachuco': A Critical Examination and Evaluation of Criminological Literature on Chicanos," *Issues in Criminology* 9 (1974): 43–67. For studies that attempt to understand Chicana/o youth cultural expression on its own terms, see Brenda Jo Bright and Liza Bakewell, eds., *Looking High and Low: Art and Cultural Identity* (Tucson: University of Arizona Press, 1995), as well as Rubén Martinez, *The Other Side: Notes from the New L.A., México City and Beyond* (1993)

10. The deceptive tactic of the INS was brought up in a talk by Dr. Lisa Magaña on the dual roles of the INS, given at Arizona State University, Spring 1997.

11. For discussion of the savage in European colonial imagination, see Lewis Hanke (1959) and Hayden White (1978); for how the idea of the savage was used to justify the colonization of non-European peoples in general, see Robert C. Young, *Colonial Desire: Hybridity in the Theory, Culture and Race* (London and New York: Routledge, 1995): 1–29; and for the savagization of Chicanas/os in specific, see Mirandé (1987) and De León (1983).

12. My use of "we" is a strategically essentialist act (see Gayatri Chakravorty Spivak, *In Other Worlds: Essays in Cultural Politics* [London and New York: Routledge, 1988]) of imagining a community (see Benedict Anderson, *Imagined Communities: Reflections on the Origin and Spread of Nationalism* [London: Verso, 1983]) of cultural studies scholars, writers, and activists who are concerned with challenging racism, homophobia, sexism, and colonialism in our scholarly and theoretical work and the larger academic and non-academic communities.

13. For good summaries of the social construction of the subject from a wide range of critical trajectories, see Paul Smith, *Discerning the Subject* (Minneapolis: University of Minnesota Press, 1988), and Linda Alcoff, "Cultural Feminism versus Post-Structuralism: The Identity Crisis in Feminist Theory," *Signs* 13 (1988): 405–436. For discussion of the postcolonial hybrid subject, see Homi K. Bhabha, *The Location of Culture* (London: Routledge, 1994), and Robert C. Young (1995). For discussion of social constructivism in feminist thought, see Diana Fuss, *Essentially Speaking: Feminism, Nature and Difference* (New York: Routledge and Kegan Paul, 1989).

14. See Saskia Sassen, "Why Migration?" *Report on the Americas*, "Special Issue on Immigration," vol. 26, no. 1 (1992): 14–48.

15. See the National Labor Committee Education Fund in Support of Worker and Human Rights in Central America, investigation updates of the Gap clothing company in El Salvador, October 1995; also see their video, *Zoned for Slavery / The Child behind the Label.*

16. See the following: Firdous Azim, *The Colonial Rise of the Novel: From Aphra Behn to Charlotte Brontë* (London and New York: Routledge, 1993), 1–34; Sidonie Smith, *Subjectivity, Identity and the Body* (Bloomington: Indiana University Press, 1993), 3–14; and Caren Kaplan, "Resisting Autobiography: Out-law Genres and Transnational Feminist Subjects," in *De/colonizing the Subject*, ed. Sidonie Smith and Julia Watson (Minneapolis: University of Minnesota Press, 1991), 115–139.

17. To appreciate further this act of racially coded nation-state violence re-enacted in the form of a quicktime video clip, visit the following Web site: <http://cnn.com/US/9806/12/immigrant.beating/index.html>.

18. Although Alicia Sotero-Vásquez and Enrique Funes Flores, hospitalized for the vicious beatings by Riverside County Deputy Tracy Watson and Deputy Kurtis Franklin, will share a $740,000 settlement provided by the Riverside County, California Sheriffs Department, these officers will not face any indictments for civil rights violations. See <http://cnn.com/US/9806/12/immigrant.beating/index.html>.

19. See Ronald Takaki, *Iron Cages* (1990), and Jack Forbes, *Columbus and Other Cannibals* (1992).

20 See Daniel Goldhagen, *Hitler's Willing Executioners: Ordinary Germans and the Holocaust* (New York: Alfred A. Knopf, 1996).

21. See Paul J. Vanderwood and Frank N. Samponaro, *Border Fury: A Picture Postcard Record of Mexico's Revolution and U.S. War Preparedness, 1910–1917* (Albuquerque: University of New Mexico Press, 1988), which in general details how the Mexican Revolution became a spectator sport for Euro-Americans who would sit on bleachers next to the Rio Grande, and in specific shows how any memorabilia of General Pancho Villa became highly sought-after collector's items after his death.

22. Downloaded from <http://www.calweb.com/~rbbusman/outlaws/murhead.gif>.

23. See the documentary *School of the Americas, School of Assassins* (Maryknoll World Productions, VHS, 1994).

24. Much of my commentary is informed by the following testimonies: María Teresa Tula, *Hear My Testimony: María Teresa Tula, Human Rights Activist of El Salvador* (1994), and Rigoberta Menchú, *I, Rigoberta Menchú: An Indian Woman in Guatemala* (1993).

25. See Elaine Scarry, *The Body in Pain: The Making and Unmaking of the World* (Oxford: Oxford University Press, 1985).

26. A most poignant example of this type of violence is case of the Haitian immigrant Abner Louima, who was viciously tortured and sodomized with a toilet plunger by officers Schwarz, Volpe, Bruder, and Weise of the New York Police Department, August 9, 1997. See the following CNN Web site: <http://cnn.com/US/9709/08/police.torture/index.html>.

27. Examples of this are two police killings of "dubious" circumstances that come straight to mind. See "The Mendocino Murders," *San Francisco Bay Guardian,* June 7, 1995, 15–18, which recounts how Leonard Davis, a tribal person from the Round Valley Reservation, was "mistakenly" shot dead by an M-16-toting sheriff's deputy. Also, I think of Aaron Williams, a local African American who died due to police brutality. See "12 S.F. Cops Accused by Chief of Lying," *San Francisco Chronicle,* November, 27 1995, A-1, which discusses how seven officers are accused of covering up their brutality, which unjustifiably killed Aaron Williams.

28. Chicano/Latino gangs in San Francisco are split by *Norte* (north), symbolized by the color red, and *Sur* (south), symbolized by the color blue, paralleling splits in the African American gangs: the Bloods (red) and the Crips (blue). However, I refer to an event that has troubled many activists who work with Chicano/Latino youth in the Mission area of San Francisco, where two adolescent girls were abducted, gang-raped, and sodomized by the opposing gang (North: Red).

BIBLIOGRAPHY

Acuña, Rodolfo. *Occupied America: A History of Chicanos.* 3rd ed. New York: Harper & Row, 1988.

Anzaldúa, Gloria. *Borderlands / La Frontera: The New Mestiza.* San Francisco: Spinsters / Aunt Lute, 1987.

Barrera, Mario. *Race and Class in the Southwest.* South Bend, Ind.: University of Notre Dame Press, 1979.

Clifford, J., and G. Marcus, eds. *Writing Culture: The Poetics and Politics of Ethnography.* Berkeley: University of California Press, 1986.

Drinnon, Richard. *Facing West: The Metaphysics of Indian-Hating and Empire-Building.* New York: Schocken Books, 1990.

Forbes, Jack. *Columbus and Other Cannibals.* New York: Automedia, 1992.

Galeano, Eduardo. *Memory of Fire I: Genesis.* Trans. Cedric Belfrage. New York: Pantheon Books, 1985.

Hanke, Lewis. *Aristotle and the American Indians: A Study in Race Prejudice in the Modern World.* New York and Chicago: H. Regnery Co., 1959.

Hicks, D. Emily. *Border Writing: The Multidimensional Text.* Minneapolis and Oxford, England: University of Minnesota Press, 1991.

Jonas, Susanne. *The Battle for Guatemala: Rebels, Death Squads, and U.S. Power.* Latin American Series. Boulder, Colo.: Westview Press, 1991.
Kristeva, Julia. *Powers of Horror: An Essay on Abjection.* Trans. Leon S. Roudiez. New York: Columbia University Press, 1982.
Martínez, Rubén. *The Other Side: Notes from the New L.A., México City, and Beyond.* Los Angeles and New York: Vintage Books, 1993.
Menchú, Rigoberta. *I, Rigoberta Menchú: An Indian Woman in Guatemala.* Ed. Elizabeth Burgos-Debray. Trans. Ann Wright. London: Verso, 1993.
Rosaldo, Renato. "Ideology, Place, People without Culture." *Cultural Anthropology* 3, no. 1 (1988): 77–87.
Rouse, Roger. "Mexican Migration and the Social Space of Postmodernism." *Diaspora* 1 (1991): 8–23.
Saldívar, José David. *Border Matters: Remapping American Cultural Studies.* Berkeley and Los Angeles: University of California Press, 1997.
——. "Limits of Cultural Studies." *American Literary History* 2, no. 2 (1990): 251–66.
Saldívar, José David, and Héctor Calderón, eds. *Criticism in the Borderlands: Studies in Chicano Literature and Ideology.* Durham, N.C.: Duke University Press, 1991.
Scarry, Elaine. *The Body in Pain: The Making and Unmaking of the World.* Oxford: Oxford University Press, 1985.
Slotkin, Richard. *Regeneration through Violence: The Mythology of the American Frontier, 1600–1860.* Middletown, Conn.: Wesleyan University Press, 1973.
Smorkaloff, Pamela María. "Shifting Borders and Frontier Narratives: US, Canada and Mexico." *American Literary History* 6, no. 1 (1994): 88–102.
Takaki, Ron. *Iron Cages: Race and Culture in the Nineteenth Century.* Oxford: Oxford University Press, 1990.
Todorov, Tzvetan. *The Conquest of America: The Question of the Other.* Trans. Richard Howard. New York: Harper & Row, 1984.
Tula, María Teresa. *Hear My Testimony: María Teresa Tula, Human Rights Activist of El Salvador.* Trans. and ed. Lynn Stephen. Boston: South End Press, 1994.
White, Hayden. *Tropics of Discourse: Essays in Cultural Criticism.* Baltimore: John Hopkins University Press, 1978.

2 WRITING ON THE SOCIAL BODY: DRESSES AND BODY ORNAMENTATION IN CONTEMPORARY CHICANA ART

Laura E. Pérez

> Through body decoration, concepts of social order and disorder are depicted and legitimized, or specific power and class structures confirmed or concealed. In all cultures body art also expresses the normal and the abnormal, stability and crisis, the sacred and the profane.
> —Elizabeth Reichel-Dolmatoff, "Foreword" to *Body Decoration*

WHETHER THEY attempt to appear natural within a given culture or to create a spectacle of difference within it, as Dick Hebdige described the politics of subcultural styles (1987 [1979]: 102), clothing[1] and body decoration signal the nature of membership within a given culture, whether it be normal, privileged, marginal, in opposition, or ambiguous. In themselves, dressing and other forms of decorating the body (e.g., cosmetics and other forms of body painting, tattooing, piercing, and scarification) are cultural practices that produce, reproduce, interrupt, or hybridize (and thus produce new) cultural values. The use or representation of dress and body ornamentation in visual, installation, or performative art practices is, similarly, both symbolic and productive. In contemporary culture in the United States, dresses remain particularly charged symbols that mark, and produce, gender identities, whether these be normative or historically newer forms of constructing and representing femaleness, femininity, or the undecidability of gender, and whether these are worn by females or males.

Dresses, like other forms of dress and body ornamentation, are props in racialized constructions of identities as well.[2] Thus, in the United States, for example, where the majority of domestic workers are Latina or African American and racist assumptions about the inherent or cultural inequality of people of color continue to circulate, the uniform of the servant or nanny is likely to connote women of color in particular, while the power suit for women is more likely to call up images of Euro-American women of particular classes.[3] Indeed, the body itself may be thought of as a social garment.[4] From pigment to physical build to comportment, the presentation and reception of the body is, following Butler, part of the performance that reinscribes or interrupts social roles attributed as normal to racialized and gendered bodies, whether these be "white" male bodies or those of women "of color."[5] Thus clothing and ornamentation in cross-dressing, passing (e.g., for "white"), voguing, and subcultural styles transgress expectations according to gender, racial, and class roles.[6] Within the metaphor of the social body as text, dress and body ornamentation are writings on and about the body. Body, dress, and body ornamentation speak, in this sense, both of how they are inscribed within the social body and how they, in turn, act upon it.[7] Dress and body decoration in the Chicana art of the 1980s and 1990s examined in this chapter calls attention to both the body as social, and to the social body that constitutes it as such, specifically through gendered and racialized histories of dress, labor (in domestic service and the garment industry), immigration, urban dwelling, academic discourse, art production, and religious belief. In so doing, the work of Yolanda López, Ester Hernández, Amalia Mesa-Bains, Diane Gamboa, and Yreina D. Cervántez flesh out the numerous and conflicting ways in which socially and culturally invisible, or ghostly, bodies matter in the United States in the 1980s and 1990s—particularly those of women of color.[8]

HISTORIES OF RACIALIZATION AND THE DOMESTIC UNIFORM: YOLANDA LÓPEZ'S *THE NANNY*[9]

"The clothing of humanity is full of profound significance," Carl Kohler wrote over one hundred years ago in *A History of Costume,* "for the human spirit not only builds its own body but also fashions its own dress, even though for the most part it leaves the actual construction to other hands. Men and women dress themselves in accordance with the dictates of that great unknown, the spirit of the time"[10] (quoted in *Parabola:* 43). In *Margaret S. Stewart: Our Lady of Guadalupe* (1978), San Francisco–based artist Yolanda López focused precisely on the great unknown of women's socially and economically invisible labor as seamstresses.[11] In her 1994 installation, *The Nanny* (fig. 2.1), López endeavored to illuminate the material effects of that other great unknown, the spirit of a time. If this spirit is understood to be embodied in the social, cultural, and economic practices of a time, then these can, in turn, be traced in the dictates of dress within a given culture and historical moment. *The Nanny* succeeds in such a project, bringing into view the power differentials among women of different classes and ethnicities, through an exploration of dress and media representation of the relationship between women positioned differently by ethnicity and class.

At the heart of the installation, as the title suggests, is the theme of subservience as a constant factor in terms of how relations between Indigenous Latina women and European and Euro-American women have been, and continue to be, historically constituted. The nanny's uniform hangs between enlarged, actual advertisements for airline travel (Eastern

Figure 2.1. *The Nanny,* Yolanda López.
Courtesy of the artist.

Airlines, in a 1961 *National Geographic* magazine) to Mexico and for the wool industry (in a 1991 *Vogue* magazine). López chooses to contextualize her study of domestic labor, gender, cultural difference, and ethnicity in the visual language of actual media materials that stage the historical asymmetry of power relations between the so-called First and Third Worlds. The advertisements mediate this asymmetry through the discourse of tourism. The wool industry advertisement announces that "wool feels new" and implies that the newness of this experience is like exotic travel. The off-the-shoulder, "Latin flavor," clinging wool dress and large hoop earrings worn by a model posed in high heels, with legs wide apart, suggest "Mexican Spitfire" adventures as well. This Euro-American or European tourist is clearly meant to appear as free, chic, and desirable, in clear contrast to the Indigenous woman, who is literally in the other's shadow. Her clothing is both worn and simple, and she does not appear to have been physically groomed for the photograph. She is pictured static, where the other is dynamic. This same visual strategy, of using the woman of color as a foil against which to contrast a "latinized" European woman as desirable, functions in the travel poster, as well. Cultural appropriation and consumption are also visualized in this ad, through the folkloric costume that the blond tourist affects and the flowers she bends over to receive. Here, the gaze of the woman of color is fixed on the tourist who does not return her gaze, but rather focuses on what is presumably her purchase, while the viewer-as-consumer's gaze is drawn to the visually dominating image of the tourist, and then to the other objects symbolizing the exotic and sensual allure of travel to Latin America (e.g., watermelon and flowers).

In both corporate advertisements, the women of color are vendors, as the domestic worker is of her labor, and are made to represent racialized relations of subservience, as the nanny uniform does in the United States, where the majority of domestic workers are women of color. The nanny's dress hangs on a white folding screen, over a hamper containing laundry and indigenous clay figurines, near toys and a potted cactus. Particularly because of the items that speak of house cleaning and personal service work in addition to child care, López's installation suggests that behind the appearance of the specific job description "nanny" lie troubling relations of exploitation by one woman of another, as sociologist Mary Romero has documented in her 1992 study, *Maid in the U.S.A.* Indeed the second chapter of her study of U.S.-born Chicana women engaged in domestic service work is titled, as is López's ongoing series of which *The Nanny* forms a part, *Women's Work Is Never Done.* "Housework is ascribed on the basis of gender," Romero writes, "and it is further divided along class lines, and in most cases, by race and ethnicity. Domestic service accentuates the contradiction of race and class in feminism, with privileged women of one class using the labor of another woman to escape aspects of sexism" (Romero, 1992: 15).

The white folding screen in the installation alludes to middle-class conventions of hiding washers and the like behind screens or doors, and thus to a carefully tended culture of appearances, whereby cleansers, laundry, garbage disposal, kitchen, and domestic service itself are veiled to the degree possible, thus erasing all evidence of the labor and "dirty work" behind the seemingly effortless impeccable wife and home, an illusion that interestingly is still at work today. The potted cactus calls to mind two other artworks by López: the installation *Cactus Hearts / Barbed Wire Dreams: Media, Myths and Mexicans* (1988), produced in collaboration with Ricardo Reyes and Larry Herrera, and the video *When You Think of Mexico: Commercial Images of Mexicans* (1986), where she explored the history of stereotypes about Mexicans and Mexican Americans as represented in films, corporate advertising, souvenirs, clothing, and house and garden ornaments. Thus, along with the uniform of the domestic servant (and this includes the nanny), the potted cactus can be read as a symbol of the Mexican or Chicana nanny's effacement by Euro-American employers whose sense of superior identity and empowerment derives, in part, from internalizing cultural stereotypes of Mexicans and domestic workers as culturally or socially inferior. "Hiring a woman from a different class and ethnic background to do the household labor," Romero writes, "provides white middle-class women with an escape from both the stigma and the drudgery of the work" and helps to veil the unpaid kinds of psychological and symbolic work that the Chicana domestic is commonly called upon to perform as well (43).

The theme of cultural and ethnic (or "racial") difference, staged in the travel and wool industry advertisements, is represented differently in the installation, through focusing instead on the dress of the "invisible" woman of color. The otherwise nondescript blue-gray domestic uniform is adorned, beneath the scalloped white collar, with the gray silk-screened necklace of hands, hearts, and skulls of Coatlicue, a pre-Columbian goddess of balanced dualities that include life and death. This decoration implies the power of the nanny, certainly over the child in her care. A colored image of the plumed serpent Quetzalcoátl, the Toltec man-God of philosophy, technology, and the arts, is drawn above the right pocket of the uniform, and speaks of the nanny's interior space. In the other pocket is a clear baby bottle in which is inserted a dollar bill. Between the two pockets, in the pelvic area, is stenciled a photograph of a nude mestizo baby. On the back of the dress are photos of Latina/o children and a Coatlicue image. The Native American deities imagery and the photographic images on the uniform work to present the subjectivity of the nanny, against the objectification of her that is symbolized, and in part produced, by the uniform. Both sets of imagery call attention to a culturally different system of meaning and values that may be operative in an empowering fashion for the installation's imagined Chicana domestic, and to the contrast between how she is seen—and not seen—in her own household and ethnic culture and those of her employer. The pre-Columbian figurines thrown in with the laundry point to what may be the more subversive effect of the nanny's cultural difference, namely, the effect on the children. López's concern with the agency of the nanny brings to mind Laura Alvarez's multimedia *The Double Agent Sirvienta [Servant]* series,[12] featuring the servant as "an undercover agent posing as a maid on both sides of the border" (Artist's Statement).

The image of the infant, the basket of laundry, and the toys in *The Nanny* together suggest that indeed the work of women as nannies engaged in other kinds of household service is never done, for their own homes must be cleaned and their children cared for, after they have relieved other men and women of these gendered and highly racialized duties. López's *The Nanny* suggests that the beauty, vitality, freedom, and pursuit of adventure that the travel and wool industry advertisements represent as the desirable cultural difference of European/Euro-American women is made possible "domestically," as well as abroad, by the economic and gender exploitation of women by women. Thus, in an ironic twist, advertisements exploiting and reinscribing power differentials between "First World" and "Third World" women, are renarrativized in the installation as troubling and apt images of what is happening "back home." By decorating a representation of the middle-class domestic space with marketing advertisements articulated through a discourse of tourism that is rooted in histories of imperialism, López allows us to see that these same intertwined interests are at work in the relations between women in familial and national domestic spaces. The juxtaposition of the two domestic spheres (familial and national), as imbricated in common economic and historical relations,

Figure 2.2. *Immigrant Woman's Dress*, Ester Hernández. Courtesy of the artist.

examines unquestioned cultural stereotypes about both dominant and "minority" cultures and thus works toward the denaturalization of racialized relations between women and, between peoples of "First World" and "Third World" origins.

THE SEAMS OF THE GHOSTLY: ESTER HERNÁNDEZ'S *IMMIGRANT WOMAN'S DRESS*

"I often wonder what I would take with me if I had to pick up my life and carry it with me—to be scattered like a seed in the wind," Ester Hernández wrote in an artist's statement accompanying her *Immigrant Woman's Dress* installation (fig. 2.2), originally shown as part of the Oakland Museum's 1998 exhibition *Day of the Dead: Traditions and Transformations.*[13] The dress and baggage she created to imagine the geographical, cultural, and psychic journey of her grandmother, who fled from the Mexican Revolution to the United States with her husband and the artist's mother, who was then six years old, is a transparent, pearl-colored silk organza dress. The fabric is stamped with images of the Virgin of Guadalupe and the dismembered Coyolxauhqui, in white ink that is barely perceptible against the pale fabric. The dress is lined with images of Mexican and U.S. coins of that period as well, referring to the habit of safekeeping valuables that her grandmother practiced throughout her life, and that must have served her well during the dangerous period of her exodus and immigration. To one side, resting next to the dress in a patch of sand, the artist placed a small, chestlike basket, with a shawl and two small bags of corn and *chile,* symbolizing nourishment and protection lying over it.

In the installation, the translucency of the immigrant woman's dress was lit from behind, creating a ghostly effect that expressed the idea of the barely visible, gendered history to which the piece's title referred. The dress's styling—high neckline, sober collar, long sleeves, and full-length, layered skirts—and its installation within an island of sand evoked the transitory process of the turn-of-the-century journey. The pale and barely perceptible Coyolxauhqui and Guadalupe stamps functioned ambiguously, suggesting a cultural legacy in the very fiber of the immigrant's being, yet also a low visibility that could be read as a gradual disappearance.

The tension between the modest tailoring of the dress and the fabric that hides nothing effectively embodies a different tension as well, around the limited movement of women within patriarchal cultures, and their vulnerability. This uncertain place of the Indian and Mexican female lineage in history and religion is told in the very fabric of a garment that is barely visible. What it perhaps symbolizes most is the yearning for a time and a place where clothing can be taken to speak, like the gigantic vestments of branches and feathers in Mesa-Bains's work, of the honor in which the powerful female body it clothes is held.

INVESTITURES OF POWER: AMALIA MESA-BAINS'S *VENUS ENVY CHAPTER III*[14]

From the 1980s to the present, Amalia Mesa-Bains has used dress and "*domesticana*"[15] to explore the spaces of women's gendered, and transgressive, social and cultural activities in her altar-based installations. Perhaps the culmination of the altar-installation genre that she has explored in more than thirteen major pieces since 1975, *Venus Envy Chapter I: Or, the First Holy Communion, Moments before the End* (1993), *Venus Envy Chapter II: The Harem and Other Enclosures* (1994), and *Venus Envy Chapter III: Cihuatlampa, the Place of the Giant Women* (1997)[16] might be read as the carefully researched and meditated study of the social and cultural institutions, and the public and domestic spaces and practices that have shaped Latina female subjectivity, from the autobiographical present, across ancestral cultural histories, into the ancient past of prepatriarchal myth uncovered by feminist archaeology, and projecting forward through the present to postpatriarchal futures.[17] As the third title indicates, it is also imagining the mythic Cihuatlampa, the place of heroic women, in contemporary terms.

All three "chapters" of the *Venus Envy* installations utilize dresses and gender-specific domestic or public spaces as organizing structures from which to consider the artist's own, and other women's, shaping by and shaping of their social and cultural environments. *Chapter I,* for example, explores the gendered narratives of religious and social discourses symbolized by the dresses of First Holy Communion, marriage, and religious orders in Roman Catholic Mexican and Mexican American cultures, and the interpenetration between domestic and religious spaces, as symbolized, for example, by the juxtaposition of the vanity table and the altar of religious ritual. *Chapter II* continues exploring spaces of feminine enclosure and sociality as the first installation did, but now featuring recreations of a "harem" and Sor Juana Inés de la Cruz's convent study, where laboratory and writing desk once again recall the altar and its invocation of the sacred, power, and *ofrenda* (offering/sacrifice). Here, the desk-as-altar figures the predicament, sacrifice, and heroic accomplishment of brilliant women such as Sor Juana under the patriarchal, religious, and social institutions of seventeenth-century colonial Mexico, while the altar-as-desk speaks to how cultures are "written" or constructed through the gendering of religious practice and experience. As part of the second "chapter" of the trilogy, the desk-altar resemanticizes the vanity table–altar of the first installation, interrogating the degrees of relation among the vanity table, the altar, and the desk, particularly from the point of view of how spatial (e.g., domestic, public) segregation and the social limitations of day-to-day, as well as occupational or vocational, practices produce and enforce gender and other social identities.

On the level of the use of dress, a similar circulation and interrogation of meaning is set in motion. Thus, the first Holy Communion dress, wedding gown, nun's habit, and the implied priest's cassock of *Chapter I* are set in dialogue with the dresses of the Goddess-Virgin in *Closet of the Goddess*; with the multiple and culturally varied bodies-as-garments of the women connoted by the harem; and finally, with the religious habit donned by the intellectual, creative writer, and feminist Juana Ramírez, who found through the convent the most social freedom her time and culture would allow an unmarried woman-loving woman. The semantic function of dress—and undress—seemingly clear in the case of the wedding gown, cassock, nun's habit, and harem garb, is blurred as these commingle visually and conceptually in the disparate closet of *Venus Envy* as potentially exchangeable costumes that upset the social codes of dress and the social status and identity (i.e., sexual, gender, class, "racial") they are meant to enact when worn according to social propriety. Thus, the dress and undress connoted by the simulation of the harem and nun's habits both signify sexualities—enforced sexualities, among other possibilities—and social disempowerment. However, the reference to Sor Juana speaks to the spectacular possibilities heroically achieved by women, in spite of social inequity and enforced subordination. In this sense, the juxtaposition of various forms of dress, across the gender, historical, and cultural specificities of their normative usage, recalls Marjorie Garber's insightful discussion of transvestism as practices of dress that signal transgressive crossings, or "category crises" along various social vectors, pointing to the insufficiency of the social sign, including dress, to either define or delimit gender, sexual, class or racialized identities. "If transvestism offers a critique of binary sex and gender distinctions," she writes, "it is not because it simply makes such distinctions reversible but because it denaturalizes, destabilizes, and defamiliarizes sex and gender *signs*" (Garber, 1993: 147).

To the degree that the harem and the convent are gynosocial spaces, *Chapter III: Cihuatlampa, the Place of the Giant Women* is, like them, situated in an imagined place both within and without patriarchal history. Cihuatlampa is the Mexica ("Aztec") heaven of heroines who died as a result of their first childbirth, as the artist has explained. *Cihuatlampa,* the installation, however, is populated by the memory and projection (into the past and future) of women, including the artist, whose acknowledged creativity is not consigned primarily to biological reproduction, and who otherwise exceed the gendered social roles and expectations of their time.[18] An exhibition statement for the installation's opening in 1997 reads:

> Amalia Mesa-Bains uses *Cihuatlampa* as a metaphor for her own experience of being too large for society. It is a critique of the restriction of those womyn who refuse to keep their proscribed place in the patriarchy. In *Cihuatlampa,* these giant womyn live beyond the roles that men traditionally assign to them. *Cihuatlampa* is a place of counterpoint to a patriarchy that tames womyn, purportedly to ensure social order and to guarantee sexual reproduction on male terms. *Cihuatlampa* is the mythical and spiritual place that enables Amalia Mesa-Bains to cite/site her collective exploration through cultural material, memory, and the interrogation of sexuality and gender. (Steinbaum Krauss Gallery, 1997)

The props in this willful projection of the larger-than-patriarchal-cultures' possibilities for women and society are *The Amazona's Mirror;* the sensually reclining sculpture, *Cihuateotl* (*Woman of Cihuatlampa*);[19] numerous hanging iris prints; an *Archaeology Table;*[20] *Der Wunderkammer. The Room of Miracles;* a shelf of feminist and art history books; a miniature perfume garden; and two spectacular pieces of clothing, *Vestiture . . . of Branches,* a copper-mesh dress, nearly twelve feet in height, and *Vestiture . . . of Feathers,* a twenty-foot cape of red, green, and white feathers (fig. 2.3); and a giant pair of high heels. It is to the *Cihuateotl* sculpture (fig. 2.4), the mirror, and the two garments that I wish to turn now in my discussion of body, dress, and body ornamentation.

On one level, the gigantic *Cihuateotl (Woman of Cihuatlampa),* covered as it is in green moss, engraved with pre-Columbian figures, and sprinkled with withering Days of the Dead *cempaxochitl* flowers, seems to represent nothing less than "Mother Earth," from Indigenous and other pre-Christian "pagan" perspectives wherein both "feminine" and "masculine" energies are considered common to all of nature.[21] Like the Empress in the *Motherpeace* (1981) feminist tarot deck by Karen Vogel and Vicki Noble, Earth is represented as abundant and sensual. She is posed as an "Odalisque," but she visibly enlarges the Western art historical tradition

Figure 2.3. *Vestiture . . . of Branches,* Amalia Mesa-Bains. Courtesy of the artist.

Figure 2.4. *Cihuateotl,* Amalia Mesa-Bains. Courtesy of the artist.

of the reclining female nude. Giorgione's *Venus Resting* (c. 1508–1510), Velásquez's *The Toilet of Venus* ("The Rokeby Venus," c. 1650), and J. A. D. Ingres's *La Grande Odalisque* (1814), for example, represent women as sexually desirable and available objects, as Roszika Parker and Griselda Pollack have shown (1981). More recently, Carol Duncan has pointed to the continuity and preponderance of this representation of women in modernist and modern art. She writes that "[t]he women of modern art," as represented through museum selection and exhibition strategies, "regardless of who their real life models were, have little identity other than their sexuality and availability, and often, their low social status" (1995: 111).[22] In its very mass as a sculpture over eight feet long that at its widest is three feet and seven inches, Mesa-Bains's *Cihuateotl* is made to outweigh masculinist Western painting, displacing its Eurocentric construction of what constitutes the female, and the sexually desirable in women.

If what is perceived as feminine—i.e., related to women or supposedly womanlike—in patriarchal cultures has been historically divested of social, intellectual, creative, sexual, and spiritual power, as the artist's three-"chapter" installation suggests, then what the artist's archaeological sifting of the material culture of the past also reveals is what can only be the "Venus Envy," or "estrus envy" (Garber, 1992: 120), of patriarchal heterosexist cultures.[23] What is instead divested of authority in the amazonian province of *Cihuatlampa* are patriarchal, Eurocentric discourses, and women are (once again) invested with power, as the titles of the two regal robes underscore. *Venus Envy III*, like *I* and *II*, is characterized by an aesthetic that reflects the archaeological operation necessary to such investitures and divestitures. Layering, juxtaposition, the impression of images onto mirrors, the use of tables/altars as sites of accumulation, and the repeated use of dress (a layering over the body), all might be read to mimic, and thus signal, a feminist archaeological effort that rejects Western male-centered discourses of knowledge as tautological creation of the Western male discourses of knowledge that reflect nothing so much as their own masculinist imagination, to put a feminist spin on Edward Said's thesis in *Orientalism* (1978).

In addition to presenting a feminist rereading of art history, history, and anthropology, the artist is rethinking psychological discourse, as the title of her trilogy suggests. Mesa-Bains appears to ironically appropriate and undermine Jacques Lacan's theory of the mirror stage in the development of the psyche (i.e., as a sign of the birth of social identity as split and founded on a sense of loss). An immense "hand mirror," measuring over seven feet in height, indeed reflects the separation from the mother, but as the historical and cultural loss to patriarchal Eurocentric Christian cultures. Imprinted upon *The Amazona's Mirror*, the Virgin of Montserrat, one of numerous culturally enigmatic black madonnas throughout Europe and Latin America, indeed reflects a lost wholeness, and the psychic, cultural split from the female, African, and other "dark" peoples that plagued Freud, whom Lacan elaborates, and Jung.[24] The artist instead would seem to concur that the black madonnas "are not 'psychological symbols of the dark side of the mother of Christ'—or not solely, or originally. They are solid iconic remains of the ancient time when the religion of the Black Goddess ruled Africa, and from thence, much of the rest of the world" (Sjöö and Mor, 1987: 32).[25] But, beyond this idea of Christian Virgins as vestiges of pre-Christian or pagan goddesses, the Goddess-Virgin in *Venus Envy III* (as in the other two installations) leads beyond a politics of feminist recovery of what is supposedly distinctively feminine, to nondualist notions of gender, sexuality, and spirituality. *The Amazona's Mirror*, like the artist's other scraped and imprinted mirrors in the trilogy, suggests that the surface of cultural beliefs must be worked at to uncover what lies beneath biased projections.

Other images function as signs of the layered and masked historical identities of women and what is perceived as feminine as well, particularly in the iris prints, hanging throughout the installation, produced as they are through digital manipulation, and the gigantic robes. Through their titles and stunning fabrication, these garments most directly confront the issue of the social empowerment and disempowerment of women. Mesa-Bains's extravagant use of fantasy reflects a sizable desire to transcend culturally limited notions of identity, truth, and power. The ideological work of these costumes is perhaps therefore to be found in the construction of a nonpatriarchal mythos—a modern-day Cihuatlampa—from which to redress the split psyche of patriarchal cultures. *Vestiture . . . of Branches,* a towering garment with branches spraying out from the neck and the arms, suggests that the forest itself is the god/dess-like wearer's frock. A large seashell and the interlocking circles that are the symbol of atomic energy lie dwarfed at the robe's feet, like a child's ball. Giant, jeweled metal high heels lie nearby. On the other side of the *Cihuateotl* sculpture hangs the twenty-foot red, green, and white feathered *Vestiture . . . of Feathers.* Like the glyphs inscribed in the moss-covered sculpture, the feathers, and their color, refer to pre-Columbian Mexica ("Aztec") tradition of featherworking and to the exquisite post-contact "paintings" made of feathers. Both garments and the sculpture offer suitable replies to the playful, yet socially suggestive question, how does one dress a god/dess? Sensual, beautiful, regal garments made with abundant use of precious materials, and named in etymologically rare terms, magnificently bespeak power. Garments styled like these would indeed create the impressive spectacle the artist did at the opening reception of the installation, in a black translucent robe with a very high collar framing her head.

Within the context of the rest of the installation, the superhuman dimensions and cosmic allusions of the "vestitures" symbolize transcendence of social gender, and indeed, their androgynous styling would appear to confirm this. Fit for genderbending amazons, priest/esses,[26] or god/desses, *Vestiture . . . of Branches'* wide copper weave of metal and air, like Hernández's *Immigrant Woman's Dress,* speaks to the reality and power of that which is partially disembodied, on the level of the social (e.g., females, queers, and "minorities"), the intellectual (e.g., nonpatriarchal histories), and the religious (e.g., non-Christian and nonpatriarchal spiritualities). These garments, as the ellipses in the titles of the *Vestiture* pieces underscore, point to the unarticulated, indeed to that which exceeds what we think we expect and believe we know. They flash us with social and spiritual beyonds that do indeed seem like the Cihuatlampas of s/heroes.

AMBIVALENT MIMICRY:[27] DIANE GAMBOA'S PAPER FASHIONS

As early as 1972, ASCO, the East Los Angeles art group, was producing performance costumes made partly from paper and cardboard. Patssi Valdez, one of the four founding members, traces the concept of paper fashions, however, to fellow ASCO member, Gronk, in a fashion show he organized in 1982, limiting the group of Chicana/o artists he invited, including Diane Gamboa, to the use of paper.[28] Diane Gamboa's fascination with the possibilities of paper fashions dates from that show through the present. Her wearable paper art is characterized by elaborately created, high-fashion-styled clothing and accessory art pieces, that are, in terms of design, as wildly imaginative as the most indulgent of haute couture, and that like it, are largely throwaway, though for clearly different reasons. Unlike high fashion, Gamboa's paper fashions are, first, crafted by the artist herself (rather than assigned to others for assembly), and second, constructed from inexpensive materials such as butcher paper, tissue, wire, and glitter. "The paper fashions stem," Gamboa was quoted as saying in 1986, "from playing with paper dolls as a little girl and always having the fantasy of being glamorous and wearing an original. But because of my economic bracket, it's very rare for me to even be able to go out and buy a dress. But I figure even if you only have 50 cents in your pocket, you should be able to look great" (Burham, 1986). At this point, Gamboa has produced seventy-five paper fashions, of which some sixty-four are dresses, including three cross-gender dresses; and eleven other outfits for males. In addition, she has produced "purse art" and hats, and painted on pre-existing jackets, some of which accessorize her paper fashions. Alongside this art form, she has produced an immense body of paintings and drawings, photography, and other work, such as set designs.

The struggle to survive has remained a constant in Gamboa's work, in spite of her establishment as a major Chicana artist, in the Chicana/o art community, and the sporadic and brief attention that the mainstream media (*Los Angeles Times*) and art publications (*High Performance; Journal, A Contemporary Art Magazine*) gave her work in the 1980s. This theme generates powerful tensions in her paper fashion work, as well as in her spectacular usage of dense, ornate design decorating bodies and rooms in her drawings and paintings. Rather than the horror of the void that modernist thinkers read into baroque and related aesthetics, Gamboa's characteristic love of ornamentation can be seen as "the incarnation of a seam that never mends," that is, "of the incarnation of desire" (Taylor, 1997: 123, 129). The desire her work registers in a gender-, ethnic-, and class-specific way, is for that which is inaccessible economically and culturally to her, as a woman of working-class, Mexican American origins, and others like her. Her work registers a politically significant yearning for the material beauty, glamour, and creativity expressed in clothing, domestic space, and other parts of the social landscape that the social elite appropriate as innately characteristic to them. Gamboa's work makes clear that creativity is restricted only in terms of the tools and the labor that are economically within reach for its production. Her paper fashions cite the function of clothing as symbols of social status and, in their highly eroticized, glamorous, and ornate construction, exhibit longing for more fulfilling and creative social intercourse.

As artwork, Gamboa's paper fashions ironically reflect upon the art world (i.e., museums, galleries, publications, academia) as the machinery that produces art as ephemeral fashion, and that is ruled by class and economic interests, behind the pretenses of economic disinterestedness and innate cultural taste. As art pieces built through dressmaking, they call attention to the highly gendered and racialized fields of both dressmaking (globally, women of "Third World" origin predominate in the assembly "home work," factory, and sweatshop fabrication of the garment industry) and art (European/Euro-American men's work continues to constitute the bulk of what is purchased, exhibited, and taught as art).[29] They suggest that the historically constructed elitist class-, gender-, and racially biased divide between craft (e.g., dressmaking) and art is anything but natural. Particularly from these perspectives, Gamboa's appropriation of glamour and high-fashion design as signifiers of cultural capital, as Bourdieu defined it (1984; 1979 French original),[30] display an ambivalent mimicry on her part that records her aesthetic and identity formation through popular cultural media such as film noir, fashion magazines, and celebrity journalism. Lavish detail, mimicry of a high-fashion aesthetic, and the fairy-tale wearability of her designs coexist with the irony toward the ideologies embedded in these, and within herself.

The ambivalent mimicry of Gamboa's paper fashions functions with respect to desire for the glamour of the worlds represented through these media, and in particular to how gendered social and erotic desires are constructed. A good number of Gamboa's paper fashions (and their titles) sardonically comment on the constraining and gender-producing absurdity of fashion for women, while inscribing herself as the artist and models (whether female or male) within that problematic economy of desire. At the same time, her paper fashions, as well as her other similarly structured and thematized work, attempt to reclaim the terrains of the erotic and the fantastic as spaces of creativity and freedom. *Cutting Through,* for example, was worn by the artist to the release party of *Sí,* the short-lived Los Angeles–based Latino magazine (fig. 2.5). A black, strapless, very short, tight-bodiced, wide-skirted dress, black gloves to the elbow, fake-jewel-encrusted headdress, heavy "diamond" earrings and necklace, makeup that included eyebrows that ended in ornate curls, permanent tattoos on both upper arms, and a huge papier-mâché "jeweled" sword completed the outfit. The fantasy, wit, and sexiness of the piece aptly spoke to the challenging but welcome project of launching a publication dedicated to commentary on Latina/o arts and cultural life.

The ludicrous and purely fantastic styling of *Butterscotch Twist* recalls "real" designer evening wear whose symbolic function seems to be the display of nonutilitarian clothing as economic and social capital, and where women are presented as expensive ornaments. *Butterscotch Twist* goes one step further, presenting the woman model as nothing more than a superfluous sweet (fig. 2.6). Gamboa's "rip-off" of high-fashion design style is a politically oppositional reversal of elite designers' 1980s and 1990s ransacking of street and "ethnic" and, in an all-time low, of "homeless" "fashions." Her show-stopping paper fashions dispel the delusion—(re)produced through fashion, the acquisition of art, and discourse—that "pure" fantasy and creativity are found among the "aristocracies" (i.e., historical, economic, and social) of the world. Instead, the high-fashion style of Gamboa's paper fashions, like her "urban royalty" work to be examined

Figure 2.5. *Cutting Through,* Diane Gamboa. Courtesy of the artist.

Figure 2.6. *Butterscotch Twist,* Diane Gamboa. Courtesy of the artist.

in the next section, *show* that "higher rank" is enacted through creativity in thought, art, and social action (Gamboa, 1999b).

Like high fashion, the design of pieces such as *Mother and Child* and *In the Heat of the Night* far exceeds cultural norms of propriety and utility for clothing. As "garments," they function as ornamental excess, insisting upon the high social value of the wearers. Pieces like the sadomasochistic-themed *In Charge* and *Don't Touch,* as well as the already mentioned *Cutting Through,* are even more specific in their statement about the imaginative paucity of social roles and thus dress, for women—and men—who exceed sexual, social, artistic, and cultural norms. Painted, pre-existing jackets like *Off My Back* and *Falling Angel* and handbags like *A Night Out* and *Box Bag* display clothing and dress as social language, by making visible, through what is pictured upon them, the attitudes, obsessions, and desires with which we dress. When viewed from her position as a Chicana artist from East Los Angeles—recognized within the Chicana/o art community yet all but invisible in the dominant cultural art world—Diane Gamboa's paper fashions in general function like voguing and drag, appropriating and enacting supposedly class-specific and "racial" attributes signified by clothing and demeanor, through cross-class, cross-"racial," and cross-gender dressing (e.g., *She on He; He Wares Her Well; Boy Blue as Girl*).

Gamboa's formidable talents render her appropriation and elaboration of the design language of high fashion an indisputable "class act." Her ambitions, however, subvert those of high fashion to decorate the socially and economically powerful in ways that uniquely signal and enact their power. Painted paper, molded papier-mâché, rhinestone jewelry, and glitter self-consciously mark the illusion of wealth with which the paper fashions play, and suggest that the pretensions of the socially and economically powerful to innate cultural, intellectual, and spiritual gifts are also paper-thin. Gamboa's dollar-store originals also mark the contradictions and limits of the fairy-tale lives of glamour, opulence, and power told by the media and signaled by designer originals. From this perspective, Gamboa's complex paper fashions speak to the desire for beauty, creative expression, and empowerment—however these are culturally understood—that such fairy tales also figure.

INSCRIBING EXCESSIVE SOCIAL DESIRES: DIANE GAMBOA'S "URBAN ROYALTY" DRAWINGS AND PAINTINGS

"I take on the 'urban warrior' mode when I am on the streets of Los Angeles. Conflict is experienced in a blink of an eye in the urban landscape. As I find my way into the studio setting and out of the mass public I go into what I call 'urban royalty' mode. I feel a higher rank on the [level] of the mind. I also use the term urban royalty as a form of expression for creative thinkers, creative art makers, and the powerful creative changers

Figure 2.7. *Little Gold Man,* Diane Gamboa. Courtesy of the artist.

of our time," writes Diane Gamboa (1999b). Paintings such as *Tame a Wild Beast,* her numerous India ink drawing series (e.g., *In the Name of Love; Pinch Me; PIN-UP; Pin Down*), and silk-screen prints such as *Little Gold Man* and *Altered States* further elaborate the imaginative social setting for such a "futuristic urban royalty."[31]

In the drawings, paintings, and prints mentioned, however, the "flesh" of nearly nude, androgynous bodies is directly ornamented, as are the private interiors in which they are pictured and that function as extensions of the decorated body, in some cases as emotional prosthesis. In *Little Gold Man,* curtains, sofas, and rugs, clothing and bodies are all highly decorated, but it is the decoration of the bodies rather than that of the furnishings that most creates a surreal effect (fig. 2.7). Pink, lavish spiral designs adorn several bodies, while another figure wears sutures on her arms, torso, and forehead. Images of human and monstrous (i.e., three-eyed, double-headed, zipper-mouthed) free-standing sculptures outstrip in their expressiveness—or compensate for—the coolly composed images of alienated, hip urbanites. In *Pinch Me* and in *Altered States,* the distinction between human and object surfaces is blurred (figs. 2.8 and 2.9). From the sofa in *Pinch Me,* for example, hang the kinds of tassels that decorate the nipples and brassieres of androgynous bodies in other pieces. A female or transgender body[32] is decorated like an object, with drawings of jewels on the arms and a floral-and-heart-patterned trellis on one leg. Like Patssi Valdez's psychically intense interiors and palette of the mid-1980s through the mid-1990s, Gamboa's representation of spatial interiors as animated renders the energy of human relationships palpable through color, line, application technique of paint, and composition. However, in Gamboa's urban royalty world, reversals between the human and the inanimate are part of the dense and obsessive décor. And while paintings by Valdez such as *The Watermelon, Broken,* or *Volcanic Sunday* express anxiety around the repressed violence of domestic or familial space, primarily through cracked and impaled surfaces, skewed perspectives in composition, and the use of bloody reds, Gamboa's urban royalty work expresses anxiety

Figure 2.8. *Pinch Me,* Diane Gamboa. Courtesy of the artist.

Figure 2.9. *Altered States,* Diane Gamboa. Courtesy of the artist.

through the *desencuentros* ("disencounters," i.e., bad encounters) between people in emotionally strained or hellish, densely decorated party or sex scenes.

Clothing for both females and males in *Madonna Whore Complex* (fig. 2.10), *Pinch Me,* and *Altered States* is little more than bikini bottoms or breast tassels, and as such it draws attention to body decoration as dress, but also to the body itself as social skin. The bodies represented in pieces like these wear both their scars and their desire, through obsessive decoration as already mentioned, but also more explicitly through Sacred Heart and other heart-and-dagger imagery. Sacred Heart imagery is a culturally specific iconography that is particularly appropriate since its history in the Americas dates back to the Spanish invasion of Native America and re-

Figure 2.10. *Madonna Whore Complex,* Diane Gamboa. Courtesy of the artist.

cords the code-switching and hybridity that resulted from the colonial encounter of (at least) two different visual cultures, the Spanish and the Mesoamerican.[33] In *Little Gold Man,* a pierced heart worn as a necklace says more than the shirtless pretty boy's closed-face expression would allow. In *Madonna Whore Complex,* the sadomasochistic-themed, topless Virgin is tattooed from arm to arm across her/his chest with a double helix of thorns and a chain necklace of a stylized heart, itself decorated with an image of an anatomical heart. The scepter the androgynous, downcast-eyed figure holds is also crowned with a heart. Here, it seems that it is human desire itself which is sacrificed and heroic, but it is an ironic deification, since it is Christian culture that represses the body and prohibits nonreproductive and nonmarital sexual practices. In *Altered States,* a magenta wall that horizontally occupies half the print is decorated with a pattern elaborated around flaming Sacred Hearts. Heartlike bulbs appear throughout the decoration of the interior space and the bodies within it. Heart imagery derived from both sacred and profane traditions powerfully functions to render the ambiguities of sexual and emotional liaisons. In spite of the dominatrix's harsh expression and the lover's bondage, the abundance of hearts and the overwhelming pink palette speak of the inextricability in this scenario of love and pain. Perhaps most radically, Gamboa pictures a zone where liminal erotic and spiritual experiences cross. On a more general level, it can be said that the figures in these pieces wear their hearts on more than just their sleeves, and thus are inscribed visibly at least as much by their desires as they are by their alienation and other wounds.

The visible tensions in the work discussed in this section are generated by the contrast between decorative abundance on highly eroticized bodies and interior spaces, and the closed, distant, pained, or malevolent expressions that the figures wear. In Gamboa's urban royalty work, erotic bodies visibly "wear" emotional and physical scars and desires alongside properly aesthetic ornamentation that nonetheless speaks of countercultural identifications (e.g., punk, sadomasochistic, neotribal). What Gamboa writes about her "PIN UP" series may be said of the larger group of works mentioned: the work "incorporates notions related to the urban experience as a form of social and personal absurdist commentary" and "focuses on the distortion of ego as a method of surviving the adverse conditions of the urban environment." Her work "presents the extreme dramas of the unconscience [*sic*] as a spectacle of the cultural netherworld of 'outsiders' who have chosen to include themselves into their own world where they can be dominant as well as fashionable. Fashion is the metaphor for the temporal nature of what it is to be 'normal'" (Gamboa, 1999c).

The decorative excess of Gamboa's highly ornamented bodies in the drawings and paintings discussed, which thus far has characterized her oeuvre as a whole, figures the extreme of unrequited social desires of the ambivalent s/heroes of her urban warriors/urban royalty.

DEFAMILIARIZING THE RACIALIZED BODY: YREINA D. CERVÁNTEZ'S *SELF-PORTRAIT*

In Western and westernized cultures, tattooing has historically marked social marginality, including criminal status (Mifflin, 1997; Chinchilla, 1997; Taylor, 1997). Since the colonial encounters of the late fifteenth and early sixteenth centuries, painting of the body (especially parts other than the face), tattooing (a process of incision and inking), and scarification have traditionally been viewed from upper-class Eurocentric perspectives, as markers of the culturally and historically primitive. Since the nineteenth-century rise and circulation of modernist aesthetic discourses of Europe and the United States, excess with respect to decoration of the body, the home, and the public sphere have been both consciously and unconsciously linked to the culturally and historically primitive, inferior, and vulgar (Taylor, 1997: 97–103). Tattooing and the other forms of body decoration explicitly viewed as transgressive may continue to function not only to interrupt normative, middle-class discourses, as they have throughout their modern-history usage in the United States and Europe, but also to disrupt Eurocentric discourses of aesthetic, moral, and cultural superiority. To some extent, these culturally hybrid practices of body decoration reflect the increasingly interracial, multicultural identities and cultural practices of global cities such as Los Angeles, San Francisco, Miami, and New York.[34] However, the failure of many viewers to perceive the fictional and performative aspects of Guillermo Gómez-Peña and Coco Fusco's 1992 performance of "liv[ing] in a golden cage for three days, presenting ourselves as undiscovered Amerindians from an island in the Gulf of Mexico that had somehow been overlooked by Europeans for five centuries" (Fusco, 1995: 39), suggests that in spite of the effects of cultural globalization upon both "First Worlders," and "Third Worlders," Latina/o neotribals might—depending on how "ethnic" (i.e., non-European) they look—still be mistaken, as Gómez-Peña and Fusco were, for the "authentic," "primitive" Indians.

Particularly in view of the widespread chic of tattoos among celebrities, the rich, and the middle class in the United States, it is clear that tattooed, pierced, scarified bodies occupy different social registers and have different cultural meanings, as well as specific iconographic repertoires. That is, not all tattooed, pierced, or scarified bodies read the same way. In Mexican American communities, images of the Virgin of Guadalupe, particular versions of the Sacred Hearts of Jesus, Mary, or Guadalupe, crosses, and tears, for example, have histories that date at least to the pachucos of the 1940s. From the perspective of a mainstream that by definition is normalizing, tattooing on the already devalued bodies of women, people "of color," the (presumably) identifiable transgender, gay, and lesbian, or of the working class doubly marks these as culturally and socially marginal, and possibly criminal.

It is within the complex parameters and ambiguities of these considerations that Yreina D. Cervántez's self-portrait, *Big Baby Balam,* a work in progress since 1998, needs to be approached (fig. 2.11). If Frida Kahlo's self-portraits inscribe—with the help of her discovery by U.S. feminists and Chicana/o artists in the 1970s—the indigenous mestiza and androgynous presence into male, Eurocentric art histories, Cervántez's recent self-portraits deconstruct the visual language of western portraiture and the racialization of identity (as signified in the body) in which it is embedded. Through it, Cervántez, a student of self-portraiture since the 1960s, has developed visual tactics that defamiliarize an image of the gendered and racialized self. In *Big Baby Balam,* facial tattooing defamiliarizes what darkly pigmented skin and non-European facial features, particularly in combination, signify in cultures where the particularities of skin and bones are read through discourses of idealized, Eurocentric national identity (see Fanon, 1967).

The Cervántez's repertoire of masks, tattoos, and other facial decorations in her self-portraits in watercolor and prints is drawn, and reworked, from various pre-Columbian genres, pictographic conventions, and images (e.g., glyphs, sculptures, murals, codices), in addition to those of Western visual culture. In *Danza Ocelotl* ("Jaguar Dance"), for example, the artist superimposes a symbolic sun mask, decorated with symbols representing Nahua concepts of duality, over an image of her face. Out of a third eye emerges the *ollin* glyph, representing continuous and harmonious change.[35] A hand that holds up the mirror/mask is sheathed in a transpar-

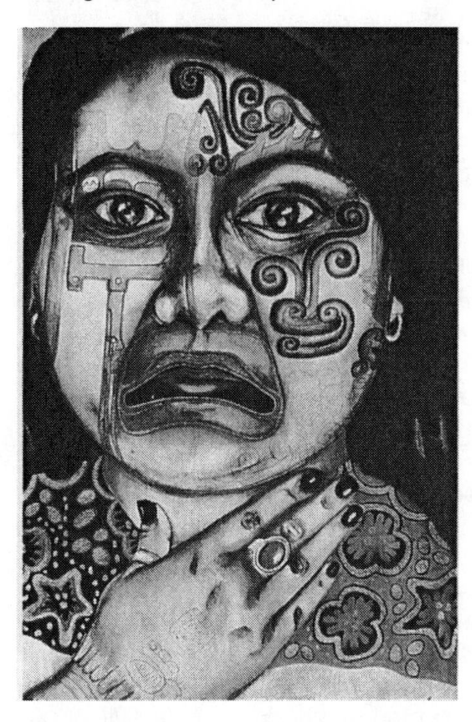

Figure 2.11. *Big Baby Balam,* Yreina D. Cervántez. Courtesy of the artist.

ent glove that recalls Mexica spring rituals. The ritual flaying and wearing of human skins in honor of the god Xipe Totec suggest that the flesh itself is a costume, a mask, and a sacrifice. This serigraph charts Cervántez's early (1983) efforts to develop alternative visual significance for the brown, Indigenous body in the genre of self-portraiture and to hybridize contemporary Western visual art languages through the use of Mesoamerican glyphs or glyph-based symbols, spatial conventions, and color palettes. But perhaps most crucially, *Danza Ocelotl* and, after it, *Mi Nepantla* are shaped by Indigenous views about the fluidity of human identity, particularly in relation to the natural world. What the artist is perhaps most interested in rendering is the changing, and transformative, nature of the self, rather than static, limiting, and objectifying notions of the self overly identified with the social and material world.

Big Baby Balam (fig. 2.11) represents the self as a tattooed surface, and as such inescapably pictures the fact of the body as a text inscribed with social meaning. But it also represents the self through markings that allude to the animal self, in her case, the jaguar. Thus, around her mouth the artist paints the stylized mouth of a jaguar from Mesoamerican art history, and the spotted pattern of her clothes follows a traditional representation of the jaguar, through its skin. The artist thus represents herself as both animal and human, that is, the unsocialized, natural self and the socially constructed self. But the self-portrait has an uncanny effect because the artist captures herself as a twilight between these two selves, in a moment of transformation between them. The image of this self has the effect of displacing the racializing semiotics of skin color and features. The artist shows herself to be another social self through covering herself in the unfamiliar signs of the self outside of human society, the jaguar. Identity is represented as process, and as a zone between the known and the social unknown. The spiritual self represented by the animal double is one such social unknown, but so are a host of other enactments of the self that belie dehumanizing gendered, cultural stereotypes.

In this sense, Cervántez's notion of subjectivity shares a great deal with poststructuralist notions of the uncertainty of identity, but the artist's idea of identity as fluid and changeable is rooted in traditional Indigenous worldviews that understand the human self as a spiritual being, in fundamental relation and identity with a natural environment imbued with such energy and consciousness as well. Thus, the artist's face is also tattooed with glyphs for water, corn, and other natural elements, making plain the stuff she is made of. Cervántez's self-portrait is a portrait of our time as well. It powerfully speaks of a cultural as well as an individual self, balancing very different perspectives about identity and thus truth, in general. It captures a moment best lived through receptivity to the change that is natural to social identity, culture, and history. Her self-portrait models such struggle for the self-realization that beckons in the face of the social gaze that may lock us into its perceptions.

COSMETIC DECORATION OR TATTOO? THE LOCUS OF CHICANA ART IN THE SOCIAL BODY

What meanings are produced—or silenced—through the kinds of circulation and receptions available—or not—to the artists and their works? What impact does their work have and in what communities? If gender and ethnic identity politics is passé, as some theorists would have it, are we to assume that their work has met with dominant cultural, mainstream, or feminist critical, if not economic, success? How has their work been received in the dominant cultural art world? What does their work finally tell us about the social body upon which it writes? Within the metaphor of the social body, where does Chicana Art fit? Is it mere decoration, a (no longer) fashionable but still exoticized "flavor of the month," as the Latin American- and U.S. Latino–themed major museum shows of the 1980s and early 1990s[36] now seem to Chicana/o artists other than the handful who got through the door that cracked open then?

López, Hernández, Mesa-Bains, Gamboa, and Cervántez are respected, active artists whose reputations were "established" early in their careers within the Chicana/o and, in some cases, the U.S. Latina/o art world of galleries, museums, publications, arts education curriculum, and, to some degree, art history. It must be said, however, that though they have all presented their work in Chicana/o studies or ethnic studies departments or programs in universities and community colleges, art remains marginalized for the most part in these would-be "havens." The art of Chicanas, however, is even less visible in mainstream art history departments. López, Hernández, and Mesa-Bains, like most of the other Chicana artists roughly of their generation, have received some recognition from mainstream feminist and multicultural art histories.[37] Lucy R. Lippard's *Mixed Blessings: New Art in a Multicultural America* notably included the work of twelve Chicana artists and the muralist group Mujeres Muralistas, including the work of all of the artists discussed here except Cervántez. Some have been included in California art histories (Goldman, 1989). They have also received some attention in Latin American and/or U.S. Latina/o art histories, exhibition catalogs, and compilations.[38] Shifra Goldman's excellent curatorial, scholarly, and journalistic writing on Chicana (and Chicano) art, grounded in an equally pioneering (for the United States, that is) expertise in modern Latin American art history, has been both extensive and sustained. Along with Goldman's work, the most exposure these artists have received has been through numerous Chicana/o or U.S. Latina/o group shows, exhibition catalogs, and scholarship.[39] Overall, however, the attention their work has received in art venues, media publications, and scholarship has been scant and, with few exceptions, of limited scholarly or intellectual depth. No doubt this is due to the same reason Goldman (1994: 318) found the curatorial practices and essays of the mentioned Latin American and/or U.S. Latina/o exhibitions of the late 1980s so seriously lacking in rigor and judgment: "Critics—to say nothing of art historians—know very little about Latin American art"—let alone about Chicana/o or other U.S. Latina/o art, I would add.

Of the artists discussed in this chapter, López's *Portrait of the Virgin of Guadalupe* triptych, Mesa-Bains's altar installations, and Hernández's *Sun Mad* and *La Ofrenda* are perhaps best known in mainstream feminist art writing.[40] With the exception of Mesa-Bains, who is represented by the Steinbaum Krauss Gallery in New York City, their work has been predominantly shown in such venues as Chicana/o community centers, galleries, and museums and, in Latin American and/or U.S. Latina/o international exhibitions, and mainly through group shows. All have had one-woman shows, but none at mainstream public museums. To date, mainstream and U.S. Latina/o museums and collectors have most often purchased prints of their work; again, Mesa-Bains is the exception.[41] Tellingly, López's groundbreaking Guadalupe triptych, perhaps the best known of all Chicana art images, remains in her private collection because she has never been approached for its purchase. For the most part, their work is sold through Chicana/o or U.S. Latina/o galleries and museums, and acquired by the latter.

All of them, like other Chicana artists, have been asked to curate and/or participate in Days of the Dead exhibitions at mainstream museums. This, however, raises the question of why their work does not appear more regularly in these venues on other occasions. Chicana artists have played a key role in recirculating, and redefining, Indigenous cultural worldviews through the Days of the Dead celebrations, and creating an art form of the domestic altar tradition. But, inviting them to install altars solely at these or other "Hispanic" events runs the risk of folklorizing their contemporary art forms, and reinscribing them in the margins of an ostensibly multicultural museum in ethnically prescriptive ways. That art by Chicana women in general, and the work of these powerful artists in particular, remains generally unintegrated in art histories of the United States—even in some recent California art histories—is due as much to the ongoing absence of Chicana/o art curricula and artists within departments of art history and university-produced art journals as to a general, ongoing neglect within the mainstream professional art world of museums, galleries, and related publications. As Carol Duncan recently observed in her feminist study of major public art museums in the United States, Europe, and Australia,

> For many, the entire art world—its art schools, critics, dealers, and especially its summit museum spaces—has seemed organized to maintain a universe precisely structured to negate the very existence of all but white males (and a few token "exceptions"). (1995: 128)

Art by most Chicana artists, like that of most Chicano men, apparently continues to represent cultural, and therefore intellectual, challenges to Eurocentric canons regarding appropriate or interesting formal and thematic concerns. Part of the solution lies in the in-depth study of Chicana/o art in art history departments and art publications. Another part lies in abandoning facile and unlearned generalizations about Chicana/o art's essentially politically activist nature, which maintain that if you have seen one piece, you have seen it all. Art by Chicana artists such as those studied here, like all vital art meant to do more than decorate the homes or vaults of the wealthy, engages issues having to do with our lived reality and the productive re-examination of our belief systems. The generalization that Chicana/o art is mainly activist is as uninformative and dull an observation as saying that German expressionist, French Surrealist, or Mexican Muralist artists were "merely" political.

The National Association of Latino Arts and Culture (NALAC) report on the status of Latino arts and cultural organizations in the United States found that "[d]espite the emergence of several thousand Latino art and culture organizations from 1965 to 1995, most have folded" (1996: xx). It also found that demographics had everything to do with where Latina/o arts and cultural organizations existed—and were funded, such that "sizable populations have made it easier to advocate for Latino art and culture."

However, even where "La Raza constitutes a quarter or more of the population . . . there has not been strong support for Chicano/Latino art and culture institutions" (ibid.: 100). Cynthia Orozco, the researcher of the Southwest section of the national report, pointedly observes in an updated version of her portion of the NALAC report:

> Arts and media groups receive public funds to which all taxpayers contribute, among them Chicanos and Latinos, whether immigrants or U.S. citizens. But financial support of art and culture has historically gone to Eurocentric institutions controlled and dominated by European Americans. . . . These larger, white institutions are favored over those controlled by people of color. Latino institutions do not receive equitable funding. (Orozco: 103)

What indeed does writing on the social body mean if art by most Chicanas, like the artists whose work I study here, is institutionally marginalized at every level of the mainstream art and academic worlds, and effectively barred by racialized and gendered misunderstandings? The gravity of the question is only compounded by the significant funding inequities experienced by the local Chicana/o and Latina/o art venues that have almost exclusively supported their work to date. Like Cervántez's self-portrait in facial tattoo, against its general social invisibility, Chicana art like that studied here captures national art histories and identities in a moment of their natural transformations, and in so doing, it contributes to a greater alignment of U.S. culture's "face and soul."

NOTES

1. Following Bourdieu, dress may be read as one of the numerous and mundane forms of displaying cultural capital or its lack. Zoot suits in the 1940s and *chola/o* urban styles in the 1970s, punk attire in the 1970s and 1980s, African urban styles of the 1980s and 1990s, all of these styles of dress speak of specific historical moments in the United States, of different forms of cultural alterity and oppositional cultural politics with respect to mainstream norms of dress, behavior, and beliefs. In addition, all of these moments in an alternative history of costume of the United States have contested, and to some degree transformed, mainstream and dominant cultures, even as they have been partially absorbed or exploited by these. On zoot suits see Cosgrove (1989 [1984]) and Sánchez Tranquilino and Tagg (1991). On punk styles of England see Dick Hebdige, *Subculture: The Meaning of Style* (London: Methuen, 1979).

2. Consider, for example, Austrian architect Adolf Loose's declaration in his 1908 "Ornament and Crime": "I have discovered the following truth and present it to the world: cultural evolution is the equivalent to the removal of ornament from articles in daily use" (quoted in Taylor, 1997: 101). Writing on domestic service in the United States in 1992, Mary Romero discusses the importance of the appearance of domestic workers for their employers. For some employers, the color of the domestic worker, like the requirement that uniforms be worn, boosts their own status, in their own eyes and socially, to the degree that a community is based on race and identity (1992: 111–113).

3. "In South Carolina, employers typically expect to hire African American

women as domestics; in New York, employers may expect their domestics to be Caribbean immigrants; however, in Los Angeles and Chicago they can expect to hire undocumented Latin American immigrants. Racial, class, and gender stratification so typifies domestic service that social expectations may relegate all lower-class women of color to the status of domestic" (Romero, 1992: 71).

4. "The idea of the body as 'garment' was a widespread metaphor in antiquity," writes Stuart Smithers in an issue of *Parabola* on clothing, "suggesting a metaphysics of clothing that can be traced back to the Genesis account of God clothing Adam and Eve in 'garments of skin'" (Smithers, 1994: 7). "Strip away layer after fashionable layer and you discover not an unadorned body but a body that has become fashionable. With virtually everyone strapped to exercise machines that future generations of archeologists will surely see as direct descendants of medieval torture devices, it should be obvious that the body is no more natural than the clothes it wears" (Taylor, 1997: 185). Performance art since the 1960s points to the body itself as socially constructed in explicit ways. The Paris-based performance artist Orlan, for example, films and displays herself before, during, and after cosmetic surgery and exhibits the flesh removed in the process (Hirschhorn, 1996: 110–134; Taylor, 1997: 139–143).

With respect to the racialized garment of the skin, Susan S. Bean writes of the importance of dress in Gandhi's politics and charts his journey in political and spiritual consciousness through his attire. She writes that after trying to dress correctly as a gentleman by English colonial standards in South Africa, "it had becomes clear [to him] that the color of one's skin was as much a part of one's costume as a frock coat, and this fundamental Indianness Gandhi would not have changed even if he could." The loincloth and shawl that most remember him by today, "[h]is satyagrahi garb[,] was his own design, and expressed simplicity, asceticism, and identity with the masses." "By appearing in this eccentric fashion," Bean concludes, "he forced his colleagues to notice and accommodate his view of a truly Indian nationalism. He deliberately used costume not only to express his sociopolitical identity, but to manipulate social occasions to elicit acceptance of, if not agreement with, his position" (Bean, 1994: 30–31).

5. "[P]erformativity must be understood not as a singular or deliberate 'act,' but, rather, as the reiterative and citational practice by which discourse produces the effects that it names" (Butler, 1993: 2). "Performativity . . . is always a reiteration of a norm or set of norms, and to the extent that it acquires an act-like status in the present, it conceals or dissimulates the conventions of which it is a repetition" (ibid.: 12).

6. "[C]lass, gender, sexuality, and even race and ethnicity—the determinate categories of analysis for modern and postmodern cultural critique—are themselves brought to crisis in dress codes and sumptuary regulation. . . . the transvestite is the figure of and for that crisis, the uncanny supplement that marks the place of desire" (Marjorie Garber, *Vested Interests: Cross-dressing and Cultural Anxiety* [New York: Routledge, 1992], p: 28).

7. "For many working-class women, women of color, and women of the middle and upper classes, the application of makeup serves as a daily ritual in which the woman, either consciously or not, has a hand in authoring or defining the image that she presents to the world. Cosmetics and dress remain, for some women, their only vehicle of self-expression and self-definition. For women of color, the factors that limit their individual potential are written in the color, ethnic features, and gender of their own faces and bodies. Makeup and other forms of masking sometimes are used to protect themselves against the harsh judgments of a society that deems them invisible or unacceptable" (Gutiérrez Spencer, 1994: 69). My thanks to Juliana Martínez for bringing this essay to my attention.

8. The use of the phrase "bodies that matter" draws upon both Judith Butler's *Bodies That Matter* and Avery Gordon's *Ghostly Matters: Haunting and the Sociological Imagination.* Butler's discussion of bodies that are socially devalued and discursively marginal and Avery's discussion of the social significance of that which haunts because it is improperly or inappropriately buried within the social psyche, so to speak, provide

particularly useful ways to think about the socially haunting presence of the gendered and racialized bodies of women of color in the United States.

9. My thanks to the artist for our conversation, on November 10, 1999, clarifying aspects of the installation.

10. Kohler, 1963.

11. For an image and discussion of this piece see Yvonne Yarbro-Bejarano, "Gloria Anzaldúa's *Borderlands / La Frontera*: Cultural Studies, 'Difference,' and the Non-Unitary Subject," *Cultural Studies* (Fall 1993), pp. 5–28; Angie Chabram-Dernersesian, "I Throw Punches for My Race, but I Don't Want to Be a Man: Writing Us—Chica-nos (Girl, Us) / Chicanas into the Movement Script," in *Cultural Studies*, ed. Lawrence Grossberg, Cary Nelson, and Paula Treichler (New York and London: Routledge, 1992), and Pérez (1999). On gender and the garment industry, see Cynthia Enloe, *Bananas, Beaches, and Bases: Making Feminist Sense of International Politics* (Berkeley and Los Angeles: University of California Press, 1999 [1989]), and Andrew Ross, ed., *No Sweat: Fashion, Free Trade, and the Rights of Garment Workers* (New York and London: Verso, 1999 [1997]).

12. See chapter 5 of my forthcoming book, *Altarities: Chicana Politics, Art, and Spirituality.*

13. The dress was reinstalled for the artist's one-woman show, *Transformations: The Art of Ester Hernández*, guest curated by Holly J. Barnett, at MACLA, San Jose Center for Latino Arts, 1998.

14. Installed at the Whitney Museum of American Art at Philip Morris, in New York City, which represents the artist, February 15 through March 15, 1997. *Cihuateotl (Woman of Cihuatlampa)* and *The Amazona's Mirror*, both from *Venus Envy Chapter III*, were shown as part of the group show *Memorable Histories and Historic Memories*, an all-woman show curated by Alison Ferris, at the Bowdoin College Museum of Art, September 25 through December 6, 1998.

15. "*Chicana rasquache (domesticana)*, like its male counterpoint [i.e., *rasquachismo*], has grown not only out of both resistance to majority culture and affirmation of cultural values, but from women's restrictions within the culture. A defiance of an imposed Anglo-American cultural identity, and the defiance of restrictive gender identity within *Chicano* culture has inspired a female *raquacheism* [*sic*]. *Domesticana* comes as a spirit of Chicana emancipation grounded in advanced education, and to some degree, Anglo American expectations in a more open society. With new experiences of opportunity, *Chicanas* were able to challenge existing community restrictions regarding the role of women. Techniques of subversion through play with traditional imagery and cultural material are characteristic of *domesticana*" (Mesa-Bains, 1995: 160).

16. Installed at the Whitney Museum at Philip Morris, New York City, in 1993; Williams College in 1994, and the Steinbaum Krauss Gallery, New York City, in 1997, respectively.

17. *Chapter I* is situated within the historical spaces of autobiography and family genealogy, and within the cultural spaces of contemporary Catholic Mexican and Chicana/o cultures and explores the gender-forming socialization of females through the metaphor of the bride (in First Holy Communion, marriage, and the taking of religious vows). *Chapter II* references the cultural history of the subjugation of women in the Muslim legacy of Hispanic cultures and in the colonial Mexico of the intellectual and poet, Sor Juana Inés de la Cruz.

18. Steinbaum Krauss Gallery (1997).

19. "[H]er giant Cihauteotl [*sic*] . . . is 'both a kind of archeological history and a mythic inventory,' Mesa-Bains said.

20. "The second part of the exhibition, subtitled 'The Room of Miracles,' extends the notion of spiritual revisionism towards the material evidence of a long-lost past . . . What is striking about this collection of tagged specimens interspersed with magnifying mirrors and sample mounts is the way in which it carries the notion of the acquisition of culture through direct observation. Meaningfully, as the viewer identifies individual

elements within the artwork such as a small statue of the Virgin of Guadalupe, a packet of seeds, a starfish, visually and discursively what is conveyed is a pragmatic recasting of Latin American art and culture as a diverse collection of obscured fragments whose importance lies in situating a space beyond intellectual verification" (Douglas, 1997: 57).

21. For one reviewer of the exhibition, Susan Douglas, "*Cihuateotl* (Woman of Cihuatlampa) (1997) is a key work. In the figure of a sleeping woman, it suggests ancient burial mounds, thus the home of the mythical Amazonas, warriors of legend" (Douglas, 1997: 57). For Alison Ferris, "On one level, Mesa-Bains reclaims women's association with nature in this work, an idea that some feminists reject because this association keeps women from being active participants in the creation of history and culture. However *Cihuateotl* is also marked with cultural symbols in the form of Aztec designs which balance the association with nature. Her body is the corpus of migration and displacement in the struggle for land experienced by generations of Mexicans within the continent." And also, "[o]ne could understand *Cihuateotl* as Mesa-Bains ironically offering herself as the 'nature' of cultural analysis. By providing the context in which her work is to be understood through myth, metaphor, and history, she allows neither her work nor herself to be reduced to evidence" (Ferris, 1998: 27).

22. "The reclining female nude since the Renaissance—one of the central images in Western painting—raises the question of the male gaze in more acute form than perhaps any other artistic stereotype. The woman is almost invariably shown as completely passive, an object for contemplation" (Chicago and Lucie-Smith, 1999: 100). In the coffee-table-style book he recently co-edited with Judy Chicago, Edward Lucie-Smith unfortunately neutralizes to some degree the feminist insights he otherwise appropriates, given that the more relevant issue is not whether images are created for contemplation, but rather whether these reproduce through the artist's, the ideal male viewer's, and the female representation's gazes unequal, gendered, power relations. See Parker and Pollock's chapter, "Painted Ladies," and Duncan's "The Modern Art Museum: It's a Man's World," from which the citations of their work in the text are taken.

23. On the tautology of Freudian thought: "Penis envy *is* phallus envy, phallus envy *is* fetish envy. It is not clear that it is possible to go 'beyond ideology' here; the ideology of the fetish is the ideology of phallocentrism, the ideology of heterosexuality" (Garber, 1993: 119). And elsewhere, "phallocentrism is *loss* of estrus. . . . And Freud's attempt to make the fetish part of the *female* body is both denial and displacement" (ibid.: 120).

24. See Sjöö and Mor, pp. 21–32. On the repression of the "primitive" and the occluded contributions of a female theorist to psychoanalytic theory, see "Distractions" (Gordon, 1997: 31–60). Torgovnick observes that "for Jung on the eve of his nervous breakdown and subsequent travels in Africa, the 'terrible mother' played the same role he would later attribute to Africa and to the primitive in general: like Africa, the mother is forever an attractive, desired site of the undifferentiated; but she is also feared as the potential absorber and destroyer of the self. This kind of thinking, this kind of intuitive association, is surprisingly common in male or male-identified primitivist thinking, even when it presents itself as historical or scientific rather than as purely imaginative" (Torgovnick, 1997: 40).

25. "[N]one of the societies most often cited as authentic Goddess cultures actually conforms to our expectations. Not a single one provides clear evidence of a single, supreme female deity; not a single one exhibits the signs of matriarchal rule, or even of serious political power-sharing between the sexes; not a single one displays with any surety the enlightened attitudes towards social egalitarianism, nonviolent interpersonal and interstate relations, and ecological sensitivity which we have been led to anticipate. In each of these cases, the story of the Goddess is a fabrication in defiance of the facts" (Davis, 1998: 83–84). See also Cynthia Eller, *The Myth of Matriarchal Prehistory: Why an Invented Past Won't Give Us a Future* (Boston: Beacon Press, 2000).

26. Copper and mirrors and shells were all found in the huge burial mounds of a

people called Sarmations that are believed by Jeannine Davis-Kimball, their discoverer, to very possibly be the Amazons from the eastern steppes described by Herodotus. Some of these huge mounds (60 feet high by 350 feet in diameter) were believed to belong to priestesses, for in them were found small clay or stone altars, bronze mirrors, bronze spoons, and seashells (David Perlman, "Evidence of Long-Lost Amazon Tribes Uncovered," *San Francisco Chronicle*, January 28, 1997: pp. A1 and A5). Provided by the artist's gallery as part of her promotional materials.

27. The idea of "ambivalent mimicry" is informed by Judith Butler's fruitful ideas of performativity in the social sphere and, more specifically, her discussion of "ambivalent drag" (Butler, 1993: 124), as well as upon the poststructuralist idea of ambivalent subject positions and Homi Bhabha's reflections on the ambivalence of colonial mimicry (Bhabha, 1994: 85–92).

28. Telephone conversation with Valdez, August 7, 2000. Victoria Delgadillo, of the Mexican Spitfires, recalled several paper fashion shows, including one by Sean Carrillo, also part of that first paper fashion show. See Porelli 1982 for press coverage of the March 1982 "Moda Chicana" show. My thanks to Delgadillo for sending me a copy.

29. On the garment industry, see Sassen, 1998: 84. On art, see Duncan, 1995: 102–132.

30. Bourdieu's sociological study of the concept and ideological function of cultural taste in France led him to formulate a complex notion of capital as three variably interrelated forms of "actually usable resources and powers—economic capital, cultural capital, and also social capital" (Bourdieu, 1998 [1984]: 114). The concept of cultural capital takes into account what is inherited from one's class background, such as table manners and distinctive forms of taste with respect to music, art, and behavior, as well as what is acquired (and/or unlearned) through education, or other forms of self-fashioning. "[T]he exchange rate of the different kinds of capital is one of the fundamental stakes in the struggles between class fractions whose power and privileges are linked to one or the other of these types. In particular, this exchange rate is a stake in the struggle over the dominant principle of domination (economic capital, cultural capital or social capital), which goes on at all times between the different fractions of the dominant class" (ibid.: 125) Of taste, Bourdieu observes, "[t]hose whom we find to our taste put into their practices a taste which does not differ from the taste we put into operation in perceiving their practices" (ibid.: 243).

31. Telephone conversation with the artist, March 31, 1999.

32. Whether they appear to be more female than male, or the opposite in other pieces, Gamboa's drawings repeatedly suggest androgyny, that is, the undecidability of whether we are looking at individuals that appear androgynous because if women, they exceed gender expectations, or because they also could be read as bodies in gender drag, with large breasts the results of hormones, and bikini bottoms indicating the possibility of all forms of transgendered identities. But even if Gamboa's figures are taken to represent "straight" women, they are transgendered identities as well, in that the kind of desire, sexuality, and power represented in these bodies is transgressive of heterosexual idealizations and limitations of female-to-male desire.

33. Chicana/o and Mexican artists have extensively explored Sacred Heart imagery. See, for example, the exhibition catalog, *El Corazón Sangrante / The Bleeding Heart* (1991). New Mexico–based artist Delilah Montoya has also written on its history in an unpublished catalog accompanying her "El Sagrado Corazón" series: "Even the skillfully conceived Baroque Heart would not have become a dominant icon in the Americas, had it not been kept alive in principle and intuition by the native legacy of the yollotl. . . . Expressing the European concept of passion as well as the Nahua understanding of the soul, it is simultaneously the Nahua sacrificial heart and Mary's heart reflecting the heart of Christ. El Corazón Sagrado expresses a vision shared between two cultures" (Delilah Montoya, unpublished essay on the Sagrado Corazón, 1994: 7, 8). See the artist's website for more on this series: <http://sophia.smith.edu/~dmontoya/ArtistStatement.html>.

34. "The space constituted by the global grid of cities, a space with new economic and political potentialities, is perhaps one of the most strategic spaces for the formation of transnational identities and communities. This is a space that is both place centered in that it is embedded in particular and strategic locations; and it is transterritorial because it connects sites that are not geographically proximate yet are intensely connected to each other. As I argued earlier, it is not only the transmigration of capital that takes place in this global grid, but also that of people, both rich (i.e., the new transnational professional workforce) and poor (i.e., most migrant workers) and it is a space for the transmigration of cultural forms, for the reterritorialization of 'local' subcultures. An important question is whether it is also a space for new politics, one going beyond the politics of culture and identity, though at least partly likely to be embedded in it" (Sassen, 1998: xxxii). Also see Hall for earlier observations on "the erosion of the nation-state and the national identities that are in association with it" (Hall, 1991: 25).

35. This and some of the other descriptions pertaining to this piece are from an unpublished interview of the author with the artist, in Los Angeles, on February 23, 1996, and subsequent conversations.

36. See, for example, Goldman (1994: 317–343) and Ramírez (1996).

37. See, for example, Goldman (1988; 1989), Lippard (1990), LaDuke (1992), Broude and Garrard (1994), Shohat (1998), and Chicago and Lucie-Smith (1999).

38. For example, Museum of Contemporary Hispanic Art, *The Decade Show* (1990); Garduño and Rodríguez (1992); Arceo-Frutos et al. (1993); Sullivan (1996); Goldman (1994); and Henkes (1999).

39. See, for example, *Imagine, International Chicano Poetry Journal* 3, nos. 1 and 2 (summer-winter 1986); Sánchez Tranquilino and Tagg (1991); *Le Demon des Anges: 16 Artistes "Chicanos" al Volant de "Los Angeles"* (Centre d'Art Santa Monica, Barcelona, November-December 1989); and Gaspar de Alba (1998).

40. The Broude and Garrard (1994) anthology includes the works of López, Hernández, and Mesa-Bains in three essays, one of which is co-authored by López herself, another by Gloria Feman Orenstein, and the third by Suzanne Lacy that includes a conversation with Chicana artist Judy Baca. LaDuke (1992) includes essays on and images by López and Chicana artist Patricia Rodríguez. Lippard (1990) includes the work or discussion of the works of López, Hernández, Mesa-Bains, and Gamboa, along with that of nine other Chicana artists.

41. Based on collections information in their résumés and conversations with the artists.

WORKS CITED

Arceo-Frutos, René, Juana Guzmán, and Amalia Mesa-Bains. *Art of the Other México: Sources and Meanings.* Chicago: Mexican Fine Arts Center Museum, 1993.

Bean, Susan S. "The Fabric of Independence." *Parabola* 19, no. 3 (August 1994): 29–33.

Bhabha, Homi. "Of Mimicry and Man: The Ambivalence of Colonial Discourse." In *The Location of Culture,* 85–92. London and New York: Routledge, 1994.

Bourdieu, Pierre. *Distinction: A Social Critique of the Judgement of Taste.* Trans. Richard Nice. Cambridge: Harvard University Press, 1984. Originally published in French (Paris: Les Editions de Minuit, 1979).

Broude, Norma, and Mary D. Garrard. *The Power of Feminist Art: The American Movement of the 1970s, History and Impact.* New York: Harry N. Abrams, 1994.

Burnham, Linda. "Art with a Chicano Accent." *High Performance* #35, vol. 9, no. 3 (1986).

Butler, Judith. *Bodies That Matter: On the Discursive Limits of "Sex."* New York and London: Routledge, 1993.

Cervántez, Yreina D. Unpublished interview with the artist by the author, February 23, 1996, Los Angeles.

Chicago, Judy, and Edward Lucie-Smith. *Women and Art: Contested Territory.* New York: Watson-Guptill, 1999.

Chinchilla, Madame. *Stewed, Screwed, and Tattooed.* Mendocino, Calif.: Isadore Press, 1997.

Cosgrove, Stuart. "The Zoot Suit and Style Warfare." In *Zoot Suits and Second Hand Dresses,* ed. Angela McRobbie, 3–22. Boston: Unwin Hyman, 1989. Originally published in the *History Workshop Journal* (1984).

Davalos, Karen Mary. "Exhibiting Mestizaje: The Poetics and Experience of the Mexican Fine Arts Center Museum." In *Latinos and Museums: A Heritage Reclaimed,* ed. Antonio Río-Bustamante and Christine Marin (Malabar, Fla.: Krieger, 1998), pp 39–66.

Douglas, Susan. "Amalia Mesa-Bains." *Parachute* 87 (July–September 1997): 57.

Duncan, Carol. *Civilizing Rituals. Inside Public Art Museums.* London and New York: Routledge, 1995.

Fanon, Frantz. *Black Skin, White Masks.* New York: Grove Press, 1967. Originally published by Editions de Seuil, Paris, 1952.

Ferris, Alison. "Amalia Mesa-Bains." In *Memorable Histories and Historic Memories,* 24–27. Brunswick, Maine: Bowdoin College, 1998.

Fusco, Coco. *English Is Broken Here: Notes on Cultural Fusion in the Americas.* New York: New Press, 1995.

Gamboa, Diane. "Altered State." Produced and distributed by the artist. Terminal Annex, P.O. Box 861868, Los Angeles, CA 90086. 1999.

———. "The Brush Off, the Ink Blot, and the Right Angle." Diane Gamboa 1999 Art Notes. Produced and distributed by the artist: Terminal Annex, P.O. Box 861868, Los Angeles, CA 90086. 1999.

———. "The Nature of the Works of Diane Gamboa." Produced and distributed by the artist: Terminal Annex, P.O. Box 861868, Los Angeles, CA 90086. 1999.

Garduño, Blanca, and José Antonio Rodríguez. *Pasión por Frida.* Mexico: Instituto de Bellas Artes, 1992.

Gaspar de Alba, Alicia. *Chicano Art: Inside Outside the Master's House.* Austin: University of Texas Press, 1998.

Goldman, Shifra M. "Dimensions of the Americas." In *Art and Social Change in Latin America and the United States.* Chicago and London: University of Chicago Press, 1994.

———. "Mujeres de California: Latin American Women Artists." In *Yesterday and Tomorrow: California Women Artists,* 202–229. New York: Midmarch Arts Press, 1989.

———. "'Portraying Ourselves': Contemporary Chicana Artists." In *Feminist Art Criticism: An Anthology,* ed. Arlene Raven et al., 187–205. Ann Arbor: UMI Press, 1988.

Gordon, Avery F. *Ghostly Matters: Haunting and the Sociological Imagination.* Minneapolis: University of Minnesota Press, 1997.

Gutíerrez Spencer, Laura. "Mirrors and Masks: Female Subjectivity in Chicana Poetry." *Frontiers* 15, no. 2 (1994): 69–86.

Hall, Stuart. "The Local and the Global: Globalization and Ethnicity." In *Culture, Globalization and the World System,* ed. Anthony D. King, 19–39. London: Macmillan Education, 1991.

Henkes, Robert. *Latin American Women Artists of the United States: The Works of 33 Twentieth-Century Women.* Jefferson, N.C., and London: McFarland and Company, 1999.

Hernandez, Ester. "Immigrant Woman's Dress." Day of the Dead: Traditions and Transformations Exhibition, Oakland Museum, Oakland, California, 1998. One page.

Hirschhorn, Michelle. "Orlan: Artist in the Post-human Age of Mechanical Reincarnation: Body As Ready (to Be Re-)Made." In *Generations and Geographies in the Visual Arts: Feminist Readings,* ed. Griselda Pollock, 110–134. New York and London: Routledge, 1996.

Kohler, Carl. *A History of Costume.* Edited and augmented by Emma Von Sichart. Trans. Alexander K. Dallas. New York: Dover Publications, 1963.

LaDuke, Betty. *Women Artists: Multi-Cultural Visions.* Trenton, N.J.: Red Sea Press, 1992.

Lippard, Lucy R. *Mixed Blessings: New Art in a Multicultural America.* New York: Pantheon Books, 1990.

Mesa-Bains, Amalia. "*Domesticana:* The Sensibility of Chicana *Rasquache.*" In *Distant Relations / Cercanías Distantes / Clann I gCéin,* 156–163. New York: Smart Art Press, 1995.

———. "Amalia Mesa-Bains. Venus Envy Chapter III: *Cihuatlampa,* the Place of the Giant Women." New York: Steinbaum Krauss Gallery, 132 Greene Street, New York City 10012. One page.

Mifflin, Margot. *Bodies of Subversion: A Secret History of Women and Tattoo.* New York: Juno Books, 1997.

The Museum of Contemporary Hispanic Art, the New Museum of Contemporary Art, and the Studio Museum of Harlem. *The Decade Show: Frameworks of Identity in the 1980s.* New York: Museum of Contemporary Hispanic Art, New Museum of Contemporary Art, and Studio Museum of Harlem, 1990.

The National Association of Latino Arts and Culture. *Latino Arts and Cultural Organizations in the United States. A Historical Survey and Current Assessment.* San Antonio, Tex.: National Association of Latino Arts and Culture, 1998.

Orozco, Cynthia E. "Chicano and Latino Art and Culture Institutions in the Southwest: The Politics of Space, Race, and Money." In *Latinos and Museums: A Heritage Reclaimed,* 95–107. Malabar, Fla.: Krieger Publishing Company, 1998.

Parker, Rozsika, and Griselda Pollock. *Old Mistresses: Women, Art, and Ideology.* New York: Pantheon Books, 1982. (Originally published London: Routledge and Kegan Paul, 1981).

Pérez, Laura. "*El Desorden,* Nationalism, and Chicana/o Aesthetics." In *Between Women and Nation: Nationalisms, Transnational Feminisms, and the State,* 19–46. Durham, N.C.: Duke University Press, 1999.

———. "Spirit Glyphs: Reimagining Art and Artist in the Work of Chicana *Tlamatinime.*" *Modern Fiction Studies* 44, no. 1 (Spring 1998): 36–76.

Ramírez, Mari Carmen. "Beyond 'the Fantastic': Framing Identity in US Exhibitions of Latin American Art." In *Beyond the Fantastic: Contemporary Art Criticism from Latin America.* Cambridge: MIT Press, 1996. Originally published by the Institute of International Visual Arts, London, 1995.

Reichel-Dolmatoff, Elizabeth. "Foreword." In *Body Decoration. A World Survey,* ed. Karl Groning, 12–15. New York: Vendome Press, 1998.

Ríos-Bustamante, Antonio. "Summary of the 1991–1992 National Survey of Latino and Native American Professional Museum Personnel." In *Latinos in Museums: A Heritage Reclaimed,* 131–139. Malabar, Fla.: Krieger Publishing Company, 1998.

Romero, Mary. *Maid in the U.S.A.* New York and London: Routledge, 1992.

Sánchez Tranquilino, Marcos, and John Tagg. "The Pachuco's Flayed Hide: The Museum, Identity, and *Buenas Garras.*" In *Chicano Art. Resistance and Affirmation, 1965–1985,* ed. Richard Griswold del Castillo, Teresa McKenna, and Yvonne Yarbro-Bejarano, 97–108. Los Angeles: Wight Art Gallery, University of California, 1991.

Sassen, Saskia. *Globalization and Its Discontents: Essays on the New Mobility of People and Money.* New York: New Press, 1998.

Shohat, Ella, ed. *Talking Visions. Multicultural Feminism in a Transnational Age.* New York: MIT Press, 1998.

Sjöö, Monica, and Barbara Mor. *The Great Cosmic Mother: Rediscovering the Religion of the Earth.* San Francisco: Harper and Row, 1987.

Smithers, Stuart. "Bodies of Sleep, Garments of Skins." *Parabola* 19, no. 3 (August 1994): 6–10.

Sullivan, Edward J. *Latin American Art in the Twentieth Century.* London: Phaidon Press, 1996.

Taylor, Mark C. *Hiding.* Chicago: University of Chicago Press, 1997.

Torgovnick, Marianna. *Primitive Passions. Men, Women, and the Quest for Ecstasy.* New York: Alfred A. Knopf, 1997.

3 NEW ICONOGRAPHIES: FILM CULTURE IN CHICANO CULTURAL PRODUCTION

Ramón Garcia

THIS ESSAY examines Chicana/o cultural work whose citation of international film movements and various cinematic iconographies index a resistance to oppressive regimes of representation. While contesting the dominant culture's abject markings, these same cinematic reflections introduce a significant critique of gender, national, sexual, and cultural norms in contemporary Chicana/o culture. My argument is that film culture has been central to a critique of dominant culture while it has provided a way of interrogating a homogeneous Chicana/o subject. I will identify two currents in contemporary Chicano cultural work: Chicana/o literature which uses a cinematic apparatus, and what I define as Chicana/o counter-cinema and video.

Chicano cultural work, which reflects on new Chicana/o subjectivities through a citation of cinema, operates within very specific geographical, historical, and ethnic networks and simultaneously highlights the localization and internationalization of Chicano/Mexicano cultures in the Southwest. In contemporary Chicano literature, a citation of cinematic icons, images, and themes has strongly inflected Chicana feminist and queer literary production. Through a reflection of a cinematic imaginary, Chicana/o writers have created a space from which to construct a form of political agency for subjects that occupy multiple subject positions. This project is directly related to earlier nationalist and monolithic Chicano subject formations in that it makes artificial those universalizing foundational mythologies concerning a return to origins, heroism, or nativism. What marks this new form of identity formation is its irony and the interrogation of community and sexuality as it relates to specific forms of feminist and queer agency.

Mexican films and Mexican film stars play a central role in defining the feminist agency of characters in various short stories from Sandra Cisneros's celebrated collection of short stories *Woman Hollering Creek.* In Ana Castillo's short story "Subtitles," in her collection *Loverboys,* a Chicana writer in Europe imagines herself as an exotic and "literary" star living inside of a foreign film. Denise Chávez, in the short story "The McCoy Hotel," recounts the childhood experiences of two adolescents visiting the McCoy Hotel in El Paso, Texas, with their mother. It is in the transitory space of the hotel and from the viewing of classic Mexican films that the young girls learn about sexuality, men, romantic ideals, and gendered expectations. Mexican cinema, for Cisneros and Chávez, is the political/cultural structure that binds heterosexual romance, romantic expectations, and patriarchal morality.

In Chicana theater, the significance of cinema to the construction of sexual identity is evident in Cherríe Moraga's *Giving Up the Ghost.* Corky, one of the main characters in *Giving Up the Ghost,* defines her butch identity in terms of cinematic role-playing:

> *[W]hen I was a real little kid I usta love the movies*
> *every Saturday you could find me there*
> *my eyeballs glued to the screen*
> *then later my friend Arturo 'n' me*
> *we'd make up our own movies*
> *one was where we'd be out in the desert*
> *'n' we'd capture these chicks 'n' hold 'em up for ransom*
> *we'd string 'em up 'n' make 'em take their clothes off*
> *"strip" we'd say to the wall all cool-like*
> *funny . . . now when I think about how little I was at the time*
> *and a girl but in my mind I was big 'n' tough 'n' a dude*
> *in my mind I had all their freedom.*[1]

In this scene Corky is reflecting upon the origin of her butch identity, which is to be located in the childhood role-playing of macho male characters in movies. The male role in cinema affords an erotic agency and a sense of freedom through its artificial reconstruction in the form of play. This is the framework that has been analyzed in the context of what Judith Halberstam terms "female masculinity."[2] For Corky, the sense of heroic freedom is one that is adapted from the male's violent aggressiveness on the screen. The internalization of cinematic male models of masculinity foregrounds a framework for the construction of a lesbian-butch identity, what Halberstam terms a "masculinity without men."

In reconstituting the myths of cinema as a critique of gender and sexual matters, cinematically based Chicano cultural work has entailed a radical departure from a unified, centered, and totalizing Chicano subject, what Angie Chabram-Dernersesian has defined as "the splitting of the Chicano subject."[3] "I want movies till death do us part," states Marisela Norte in a poem entitled "Act of the Faithless,[4] in one stanza undoing heterosexual romance, decoding it as cinematic, as mythic, as artificial. For writer/*performera* (performance artist) Aida Salazar, the genre of 1940s Mexican *cabaretera* films and *Siglo de Oro* (golden age) Mexican film stars are a mode of reflecting on contemporary Chicana/Mexicana contradictions. In an interview I conducted with Salazar, she comments on what she defines as the "indigenous chic," which she bases on the representations of the "Indian" by Mexican film stars Emilio "El Indio" Fernández, María Félix, Pedro Armendariz, and Dolores Del Río. She views this cinematic aesthetic as a hybrid form: "The indigenous chic. . . . It's completely comfortable with its own hybridity. It's comfortable because, you know, it's got these . . . yes, I've got these crazy features, you know, that are not necessarily . . . purely Indian, but they're mestizo, they're more mestizo, and I'm glamorous about it, fuck yea, why not. And I think it's more real. It's just more real. . . . " As she remarked, "I get bored when I see corn," unless "it's on a stick." According to Salazar, "corn goddess" mythology is a limited perspective because it lacks the conscious hybridity that she strives for in her writing and performances.[5]

Salazar is interested in the urban myths of Mexican cinema, exemplified by the 1945 Indio Fernández/Gabriel Figueroa film *Salon México,* which Salazar references in her writing. Salazar comments that she is interested in recuperating the problematic and contradictory mythology of gender in classic Mexican film, what she refers to as "the femme-fatales with *trenzas.*" Like many Chicana writers, Salazar engages with the myths of classic Mexican film by reinscribing their sexual and cultural contradictions and making them contemporary.

CHICANO COUNTER-CINEMA

Chicano cinema has been defined as an alternative, oppositional cinema, and a film practice that counters a hegemonic Hollywood market and a dominant, colonizing North American culture. Rosa Linda Fregoso, in *The Bronze Screen,* critiques and extends the seminal essays on Chicano film by Francisco X. Camplis[6] and Jason C. Johansen[7] by defining Chicano cinema as a film practice "by, about and for Chicanas and Chicanos."[8] The decisive question in this definition of Chicano cinema remains: by, about, and for which Chicanas and Chicanos? This question is what Chicana/o filmmakers Juan Garza, Berta Jottar, and Rita González specify and politicize in their video work. According to Fregoso, "The project of Chicano cinema may succinctly be summed up as the documentation of social reality through oppositional forms of knowledge about Chicanos."[9] While the video work of Juan Garza, Berta Jottar, and Rita González remains within the political project of Chicano cinema,[10] their deconstruction of "documentary" forms and their particular presentation of localized oppositional knowledges locate Chicana/o counter-cinema at the crux of many contingencies—cinematic, national, geographical, sexual, ethnic, and material.

By Chicano counter-cinema, I mean Chicana/o film practices that utilize what Chela Sandoval has defined as "a method of oppositional consciousness in the postmodern world."[11] I locate Chicana/o counter-cinema on the margins of Chicano cinema, avant-garde art, and Third World cinema. While Chicana/o counter-cinema belongs within the above-mentioned cinematic and artistic projects, its particular form of oppositional consciousness makes it a mobile and contingent cinema, institutionally unstable and strategically critical of the forms which have provided its own material and aesthetic base. Chicana counter-cinema is, fundamentally, an oppositional and self-critical art practice.

Chicano counter-cinema resists the co-opted mythologies of Hollywood Chicano cinema and the Eurocentrism of North American avant-garde art. Rosa Linda Fregoso has commented, "The adoption of the Hollywood model by Chicano cultural producers signals the transformation of Chicano cinema from an alternative form into a genre within dominant cinema."[12] Fregoso has identified certain conservative mythologies, the motif of the mother in particular, which have been reproduced in Hollywood Chicano film. The Chicano counter-cinema of Berta Jottar and Rita González has opposed generic reinscriptions and dominant cinematic ideologies by constructing what Barthes once defined as "artificial"[13] myths in opposition to myths which have dehistoricized Chicano identity. Likewise, the Chicana/o literature that has used cinematic tropes has introduced a localized critique of gender and Chicano identity while constructing contemporary, critical, and complex counter-myths devoid of nostalgia and idealization. In this context, Rosaura Sánchez has offered a materialist proposal in opposition to the revival and recovery of dehistoricized and idealized myths. Sánchez states, "The experiences and struggles of Chicanas since 1848 offer ample opportunities for research without the need to resort to the idealization of ancestors or a glorious past. . . . "[14] Jottar's and González's videos investigate neglected, overlooked, or trivialized icons by performing them as contradictory markers of community, gender, history, and identity.

THE CHICANO NEW WAVE

In Juan Garza's 1984 video entitled "Gronk's Tormenta," a group of self-conscious dressed-up people whisper incongrous and mysterious things. Things like "Who is she?" and "She can, but she can't." A man carrying a tray of hors d'oeuvres (played by Gronk) whispers the name of a mysterious woman who never reveals her face, just a gorgeous backside framed by an elegant black dress in the midst of a set identifiably Gronk, circa mid-1980s. "Tormenta," he whispers, in a sophisticated voice that resonates with pretentiousness. Tormenta, as a voice-over at the beginning of the video reveals, has an identity problem: "She was young, she was rich, she was beautiful, but she didn't know who she was." The video presents a commentary about identity, one that foregrounds identity's artificiality and reliance on fashion and *chisme.* "Tormenta" is not about identity in any "deep" sense, but about identity as a product of a cinematic gendering of artifice. Tormenta, the woman whose personality is concentrated in her backside, recalls the backsides of many divas in classic Hollywood cinema.

Tormenta, the woman with the perfect backside, has a sister, Isela Boat (a name inspired by Mexican actress and 1970s sex symbol Isela Vega), a jealous hunchback "dancer," played by poet Marisela Norte. Isela Boat, sporting two cone-shaped polka-dotted objects on her hands, proceeds to

Figure 3.1. Tormenta and doomed revelers aboard the *Titanic* in Gronk's *Tormenta.* Courtesy of the artist.

dance an esoteric dance announced as "the rite of the cone." The glamorous onlookers look on in wonder at the enigmatic sister of Tormenta, the talented but strange Isela Boat, interpreting a ritualistic existential 1980s New Wave dance. The spectators of Isela Boat's dance are victims of their incommunicable existential void. Their glamour is the sign of their cluelessness.

The glamorous people turn out to be a group aboard a very low budget *rasquache* Titanic, and their whispers resonate with the impending doom of their existentially tormented but fashionable condition. *Tormenta* is a B-video version of the late 1950s–early 1960s French New Wave, a distinctly European cinema that was popular in the United States and Mexico via art houses and cineclubs in the 1960s and 1970s. In Mexico, the French New Wave and its literary counterpart, the new novel, were pivotal influence for writers and filmmakers in the 1960s and 1970s, influencing a generation of Mexican writers and critics and culminating in films such as *Los Bienamados* (1966) with scripts written by Juan García Ponce and Carlos Fuentes.

A product of postwar French existentialism and European fashion, the New Wave was fashion masquerading as politics; its look and glamour were its most distinct visual and narrative structures. Carlos Monsiváis recognized this in a 1973 essay on Mexican actress turned pro-Zapatista politician Irma Serrano, popularly known as "La Tigresa." Referring to Mexican cultural politics in the 1970s, Monsiváis ironized the Alan Resnais–Marguerite Duras film, *Hiroshima, Mon Amour* by stating, "Oh, the seventies. The intrigues of History against a reality dressed-up like a premiere gala. *Hiroshima, Mon Glamour.*"[15] The American film critic Pauline Kael also recognized the duplicity of this type of European filmmaking by calling it "The Come Dressed-As-the-Sick-Soul-of-Europe Parties."[16] *Tormenta* could be subtitled "The Come-Dressed-As-the-Sick-Soul-of-Los-Angeles Party," for Gronk's canvas Titanic that carries the sick souls of formally attired Angelinos is about to sink. The party is obviously happening in the 1980s, the look is very "Decade of the Hispanic" and the

Figure 3.2. Marisela Norte as Isela Boat, the hunchback sister of the enigmatic Tormenta. From Gronk's *Tormenta.* Courtesy of the artist.

Figure 3.3. Isela Boat, played by Marisela Norte, performs a strange existential 1980s "New Wave" dance. From Gronk's *Tormenta.* Courtesy of the artist.

age of Reaganomics. But *Tormenta* is fashion masquerading as politics; it does not pretend to be anything else. The party is about to end; the symbolic sinking of the Titanic will be realized with the L.A. uprising of 1992.

Historian Vicki Ruiz has argued that "conforming to popular fashion and fads cannot be construed as a lack of ethnic or political consciousness."[17] Harry Gamboa Jr., in discussing the politics of ASCO, has commented, "Fashion was a response to fascism."[18] In *Tormenta* fashion and faddishness are what construct a political consciousness and various political positionings. *Tormenta,* although an ironic and humorous work, radically undermines Euro-seriousness, perhaps the strongest form of cultural hegemony. *Tormenta,* through its overly aestheticized dialogue, its high fashion posturing and existential gesturings, cites Alan Resnais's 1961 film *Last Year at Marienbad,* a terribly pretentious piece of French New Wave filmmaking that should be camp but has not been, except in this Chicano video version from 1984. While a lot of Chicano cultural work in the 1990s has been plagued by facile parody, *Tormenta* references the defining elements of the French New Wave, the films of Antonioni, the French new novel, and their Mexicanized versions, through a subtle and oblique satirization of their original seriousness.

Tormenta, the video, is emblematic of the materialist foundation of Chicana/o counter-cinema. While Chicana/o counter-cinema and video recycle Hollywood iconography and utilize strategies from international and alternative cinemas, their budgets and modes of production require cooperatives of friends, associates, and artistic fellow travelers. The appropriation of cinematic fashion, media, and Hollywood culture in *Tormenta* is satiric resistance to cultural domination. The parody of European art films is not a strategy of assimilation or a pastiche recycling. *Tormenta* deauthorizes and de-legitimizes modern European cinema's power as "serious" and "high" art, derailing its value as a high art commodity in postmodern culture.

THE MASKED WOMAN AND LUPE VÉLEZ

The recuperation and recycling of cinematic and pop cultural icons in Berta Jottar's 1991 video *Border Swings* and Rita González's 1998 video *The Assumption of Lupe Vélez* is not arbitrary; specific icons and myths are recuperated in order to reinscribe them with a politics previous representations denied them. In *Lupe,* the hyperbolic performance of gender is reconnected to Lupe Vélez's "Mexicanness"—a connection that her star persona in Hollywood naturalized and depoliticized. By acknowledging and reflecting upon Lupe Vélez's ethnic markings and her gendered perfomativity, the myth of Lupe Vélez, the Mexican spitfire, is decoded and politicized.

Unlike conventional Chicano cinema, whether it adopts documentary or Hollywood melodramatic forms, *The Assumption of Lupe Vélez* and *Border Swings* document community from a critically feminist and queer space. In *Lupe,* documentary and Hollywood melodrama styles are not presented as "real," but as the problematic and the artificial in the construction of Lupe Vélez's iconography, her quasi-religious "assumption." The "assumption" in the title of the piece refers to Lupe Vélez's iconographic status as "saint" or "martyr" in a queer hagiography in which movie stars and their drag queen impersonators occupy the Catholic narrative of saint's lives. Like many Catholic saints, extraordinary glory, tragedy, and consequent adoration marked Lupe Vélez's life. In Catholic liturgy, the "assumption" refers to Mary's ascent to heaven and her escape from bodily decomposition after death due to her immaculate virginity.[19] The Catholic myth of Mary's assumption as it is attributed to Lupe Vélez implies the star's preservation and glorification/adoration by the community coalesced in the memory of her glory and glamour. The video reflects on the production of iconicity, as Lupe Vélez is reconstructed as a legend of saintly proportions, an Evita Peron or Selena for a queer countercultural community.

National, gender, or cinematic binaries do not contain the contemporary assumption of her identity by a community. Lupe Vélez, the icon, is

Figure 3.4. From Rita González's *The Assumption of Lupe Vélez.* Courtesy of the artist.

representative of a community at the limits of multiple marginalities. González's *Lupe,* like Jottar's Enigma in *Border Swings,* is a communal icon, crossing multiple political and aesthetic borders by invalidating the normative expectations of cinematic and nationalist purities.

But what is the subject of *The Assumption of Lupe Vélez*? While the video pretends to be a pseudobiography of actress Lupe Vélez, via a re-enactment of the cinematic and biographical strategies which have made her an underground legend, the "real" subject of the video is the production of the video itself and the construction of Lupe Vélez as icon. Those who were involved in the making of *Lupe* are also in front of the camera, their voices are heard through voice-overs, and their faces appear in screen tests. *Lupe* is as much about a cinematic icon as it is about a community which finds that icon representative of contemporary Latino dilemmas.

Lupe is a collage of sequences and segments related to each other through oblique references to pre-existing representations of Lupe Vélez. The very first image, for example, is a direct quotation of Andy Warhol's 1965 film *Lupe,* in which the very last reel is a double image of Edie Sedgwick with her head resting on a toilet bowl, a dramatic recreation of Lupe Vélez's suicide. The rest of the video is a series of citations of a Hollywood Babylon repertoire (scandals, *chismes,* lies, imagined biography, found footage) and avant-garde representations of the Lupe icon. In the middle of the video appears a trailer for a film that does not exist: dancing to soundtracks from María Móntez B-movies, a contemporary Echo Park drag queen, La Lupe, drinks martinis and imagines herself a star. In another sequence, a drag queen impersonating Warhol superstar Mario Móntez is interviewed by the director off-camera. The dialogue is a dramatization of an interview with Mario Móntez that appeared in *Film Culture* in the 1960s.[20] All images in *Lupe* are simulations of pre-existing Lupe Vélez images, and are reconstituted in terms of a contemporary community in Los Angeles. There is nothing originary in the various images which construct a communal "portrait" out of localized and recontextualized cinematic images from "the ubiquitous periphery of Hollywood."[21]

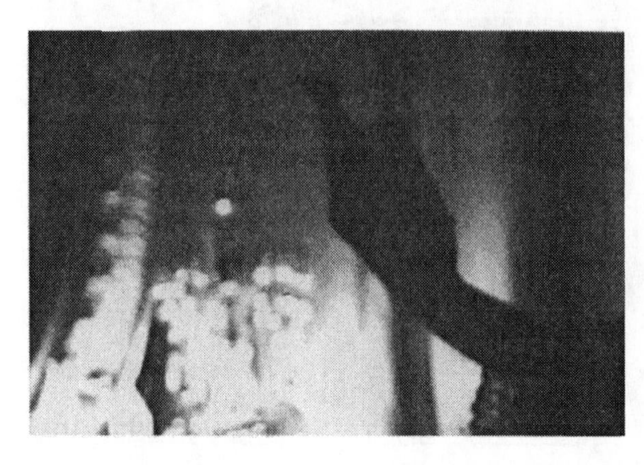

Figure 3.5. From Rita González's *The Assumption of Lupe Vélez.* Courtesy of the artist.

González's quotations of cinema are directly related to ASCO's interrogations of dominant cinematic apparatuses. According to Ondine C. Chavoya, ASCO's No-Movies comment on the absence of Chicanos in the media.[22] As in ASCO's No-Movies, *Lupe* appropriates the Hollywood studio system in order to underscore the exclusion of Mexican/Chicano subjectivity from its structuring effects. *Lupe* interrogates both the absence and the hyperbolic ethnic "presence" symbolized by Lupe Vélez, the "Mexican Spitfire." *Lupe* occupies not only the absenting space of Latino cinematic exclusion, but also the ghostly hyperpresence of Lupe Vélez's glamour and abjection which defined her specular currency in Hollywood and the American underground.

While ASCO's No-Movies appropriated images from Hollywood and international cinema, González's *Lupe* appropriates, more specifically, the images of Latina movie stars (Lupe Vélez, María Móntez) and the avant-garde's own appropriations of ethnic stardom. González's appropriation of Warhol's *Lupe* and Jack Smith's writings are appropriations to the second degree: they are appropriations of appropriations.

The reperformance of Jack Smith's appropriations of Latino kitsch exotica, which José Muñoz refers to as Jack Smith's "Third World ethnoscapes," is a way of mediating and recircumventing the queer and empowering possibilities of avant-garde practices for a specific community. This strategy is what José Muñoz defines as "disidentification," a mode of "transfiguration and reorganization on the level of identification."[23] *Lupe* transfigures the overdetermined details of Lupe Vélez's biography in order to reorganize a queer form of disidentification with her image:

> Disidentification is about recycling and rethinking encoded meaning. The process of disidentification scrambles and reconstructs the encoded message of a cultural text in a fashion that both exposes the encoded message's universalizing and exclusionary machinations and recircuits its workings to account for, include, and empower minority identities and identifications. Thus, disidentification

> is a step further than cracking open the code of the majority; it proceeds to use this code as raw material for representing a disempowered politics of positionality that has been rendered unthinkable by the dominant culture.[24]

Disidentification is the process which Muñoz theorizes by focusing on the "performance of politics" in the performance work of various artists of color. In the work of Rita González and Berta Jottar, video is a medium for the performance of politics. *Lupe* is a response to images of Latinas and other "exotics" in Hollywood and "Latino" images in American avant-garde filmmaking. This response is in the form of disidentificatory performances which cite the stereotypes, excesses, and abject nuances of Lupe Vélez's mythification in Hollywood and in the American underground. The drag queen performance of the Mexican spitfire stereotype which Lupe Vélez made famous and the performative recreation of her tragic suicide enable a "rethinking" of their "encoded meaning." This is neither a break from nor a rejection of the majoritarian Lupe Vélez images, but a reflection and a performance of their base significations. The minoritarian performance in *Lupe* creates, in Muñoz's words, "worlds of transformative politics and possibilities" that engender "worlds of ideological potentiality that alter the present and map out a future."[25] The ideological potentialities in *Lupe* are located in the performative politics of community and the cognitive mapping of queer worlds. This is a resistance, in disidenticatory fashion, of both the dominant culture's alienation and the normative demands of the gay "community" itself.[26]

Border Swings, by U.S.-born Chilanga video artist Berta Jottar, is a feminist work that concerns gender, identity, and women's labor on the U.S.-Tijuana border. Enigma, an *enmascarado/a,* is a literal border swinger —bilingual, possibly bisexual, and adept at dancing the *quebradita* while investigating the "disappearance" of a woman artist/activist in Tijuana. While the disappearance of the artist's work is signified by her missing body, what is implied is the disappearance and misrecognition of woman's work and activism in an artistic field, specifically on the U.S.-Mexican border.

While Berta Jottar and Rita González are the auteurs of *Border Swings* and *The Assumption of Lupe Vélez,* their functions within the production of the videos are not limited by their auteurship or filmmaking personality. The "directors" Jottar and González make their presence known within the structure of the video and the production values, as highlighted by each director's physical presence and/or voice in the video itself. Berta Jottar was a member of Comadres, a group of Mexican/Chicana artists in Tijuana in the late 1980s and early 1990s. In *Border Swings* Enigma, the *enmascarada* detective, is investigating the "missing body," a woman whose cultural work is associated with the Comadres artistic collective. In *The Assumption of Lupe Vélez,* the voice of the director is heard twice; at the beginning of the twenty-minute video, simulating a commentary by

Warhol superstar Edie Sedgwick, on Warhol's discovery of Lupe Vélez's suicide in a book entitled *Hollywood R.I.P.* and as the off-camera interviewer in the re-enactment of the *Film Culture* interview with Warhol drag superstar Mario Móntez.

Border Swings and *The Assumption of Lupe Vélez* enter a global network of recycled images via a critique and politicization of their signification within the very systems of signification which have mythified them. In *Border Swings,* gender, border politics, and artistic recognition on the U.S.-Mexican border are inscribed into the *enmascarado*'s familiar B-movie narrative. The subject of Jottar's *Border Swings* is also a local Tijuana–San Diego community. According to Rita González, Jottar's iconographic figure Enigma symbolizes the multinational and gendered identity of a historical community, represented by a cinematic and political icon, the masked wrestler. González states, "What Jottar conceptualizes of as 'a politics of the possible' is the terms of individual actions constituting a change within a collective identity. The possible has much to with the creation of collective identity made possible by a shifting of location (the crossing back and forth over the border) and is determined by the interplay of personal and public personas."[27] The recodification of a familiar icon from popular culture is a form of political agency that begins to represent the resistances and collective possibilities of displaced and disenfranchized communities.

Ana M. López has criticized the national privileging of Hollywood in mainstream star studies; taking Dolores Del Río as a case study, López has demonstrated the transnationality of Dolores's star persona and her indeterminacy within Hollywood and Mexican cinema.[28] Like López's study of Dolores Del Río, Jottar's and González's treatment of the *enmascarado* wrestler and Lupe Vélez resist what Josébe Martinez has defined as "Hollywood's continuity." *Border Swings* and *The Assumption of Lupe Vélez* make evident the multinationality, the raciality, and the gendered artificiality which previous and more conservative representations of the *enmascarado* and Lupe Vélez tried to naturalize, purify, and contain. What is countered and decoded in *Border Swings* and *Lupe* are the naturalization of racial, national, and gendered notions of Chicano/Mexican mythographies in cinema and in history. The very last scene in *Lupe* is emblematic of this denaturalization of Mexican/Chicano mythologies. A woman's face is seen with tears streaming down her face. It is a melancholy image, both glamorous and uncanny. But it is not a "real" woman: it is the face of Sophia Loren, her wax museum version at the Hollywood Believe it or Not Museum. The image is ambiguous about its wanting the viewer to believe it or not. This is the disturbance at the core of this image as Chavela Vargas sings, "No soy de aquí, Ni soy de allá, No tengo edad ni porvenir y ser feliz es mi color de identidad" (I am from neither here nor there, I am without age or future and to be happy is the color of my identity). The ambiguous song and that last uncanny image of Lupe encapsulate the unstable subject of the video and the project of Chicano counter-

Figure 3.6. From Rita González's *The Assumption of Lupe Vélez.* Courtesy of the artist.

cinema. *Ni de aquí ni de allá* (neither from here or there), neither male nor female, neither recognizably Chicano or Mexican, yet geographically and historically localized as both; gendered and nationally mobile—*Lupe* is representative of a Chicano counter-cinema at the margins of various cinemas and political histories. In essence false documentaries, *Lupe* and *Border Swings* are works interrogating the main codifiers of Mexican/Chicano performativity—culture, nation, community, gender, and violence.

As nationalist Chicano icons become increasingly more monumental or static with the Americanization of Mexico and the performative Mexicanization of Chicanos, Chicana feminist literature and Chicano counter-cinema engage in a radical recycling of neglected icons that have been robbed of their politics and their contradictions. By politicizing kitsch icononography and gender contradictions, cinematically based Chicana/o literature and Chicana/o counter-cinema are constructing a differential consciousness that enacts new forms of collective agency in a postmodern world.

NOTES

1. Cherríe Moraga, "Giving Up the Ghost," in *Literatura Chicana 1965–1995: An Anthology in Spanish, English, and Caló,* ed. Manuel de Jesús Hernández-Gutiérrez and David William Foster (New York: Garland Publishing, 1997), 303–304.

2. Judith Halberstam, *Female Masculinity* (Durham, D.C., and London: Duke University Press, 1998).

3. In Angie Chabram-Dernersesian, "And, Yes . . . the Earth Did Part: On the Splitting of Chicana/o Subjectivity," in *Building with Our Hands: New Directions in Chicana Studies,* ed. Adela De La Torre and Beatríz M. Pesquera (Berkeley: University of California Press, 1993).

4. Marisela Norte's "Act of the Faithless" appears on the CD *Norte Word* (Lawndale, Calif.: New Alliance Records, 1991).

5. Aida Salazar, interview with author, April 10, 1999.

6. Francisco X. Camplis, "Towards the Development of a Raza Cinema," in *Chicanos and Film: Representation and Resistance,* ed. Chon A. Noriega (Minneapolis: University of Minnesota Press, 1992).

7. Jason C. Johansen, "Notes on Chicano Cinema," in *Chicanos and Film: Rep-*

resentation and Resistance, ed. Chon A. Noriega (Minneapolis: University of Minnesota Press, 1992).

8. Rosa Linda Fregoso, *The Bronze Screen: Chicana and Chicano Film Culture* (Minneapolis: University of Minnesota Press, 1993), xiv. For a comprehensive overview of Chicano cinema, see also Chon Noriega's introduction and his essay "Between a Weapon and a Formula: Chicano Cinema and Its Contexts," in *Chicanos and Film: Representation and Resistance,* ed. Chon A. Noriega (Minneapolis: University of Minnesota Press, 1992).

9. Fregoso, xiv–xv.

10. The work of underground Chicana/o video artists continues the decolonizing project of earlier Chicano filmmaking. Camplis (1992) proposed that Chicano cinema should be "a decolonizing cinema; a film of disruption." "Our films must decolonize in a different way. . . . Our films must be provocative," Camplis stated. Camplis's arguments resonate quite forcefully in the video work that I am discussing.

11. Chela Sandoval, "U.S. Third World Feminism: The Theory and Method of Oppositional Consciousness in the Postmodern World," *Genders* 10 (1991): 1–24.

12. Rosa Linda Fregoso, "The Mother Motif in *La Bamba* and *Boulevard Nights,*" in *Building with Our Hands: New Directions in Chicana Studies,* ed. Adela De La Torre and Beatriz M. Pesquera (Berkeley: University of California Press, 1993), 131.

13. Roland Barthes, *Mythologies* (New York: Hill and Wang, 1972), 135.

14. Rosaura Sánchez, "The History of Chicanas: A Proposal for a Materialist Perspective," in *Between Borders: Essays on Mexican/Chicana History,* ed. Adelaida R. Del Castillo (Encino, Calif.: Floricanto Press, 1990).

15. Carlos Monsiváis, "Irma Serrano: Entre apariciones de la venus de fuego," in *Amor perdido* (Mexico, D.F.: Ediciones Era, 1977), 297.

16. Pauline Kael, "The Come-Dressed-As-the-Sick-Soul-of-Europe Parties: *La Notte, Last Year at Marienbad, La Dolce Vita,*" in *I Lost It at the Movies* (New York: Bantam Books, 1966).

17. Vicki Ruiz, "Star Struck," in *Building with Our Hands: New Directions in Chicana Studies,* ed. Adela De La Torre and Beatriz M. Pesquera (Berkeley: University of California Press, 1993).

18. Harry Gamboa Jr. made this remark on an ASCO panel at California State University at Long Beach on April 9, 1999. Also on the panel were Patssi Valdez, Gronk, and Willie Herrón. The session was videotaped by Roberto Oregel.

19. John A. Hardon, S.J., *Pocket Catholic Dictionary* (New York: Image Books, Doubleday, 1985), 32. See also Marina Warner, *Alone of All Her Sex: The Myth and Cult of the Virgin Mary* (New York: Random House, 1983).

20. "The Superstar: An Interview with Mario Móntez," *Film Culture,* no. 17 (1968).

21. Ondine C. Chavoya, "Pseudographic Cinema: ASCO's No-Movies," *Performance Research* 3, no. 1 (1998): 4. Chavoya states, "As pseudographic film stills the No-Movies circulated as examples of 'authentic' Chicano produced motion pictures, creating the specious illusion of an active body of Chicano cinema being produced from the ubiquitous geographical periphery of Hollywood." ASCO was a performance group that flourished in East Los Angeles in the 1970s. Its "No-Movies" were faked stills from Chicano films that were never made.

22. Chavoya: "No-Movies were both a critical assault on and an evasion of the Hollywood studio system, denouncing the absence of Chicano access to and participation in mass media."

23. José Esteban Muñoz, *Disidentifications: Queers of Color and the Performance of Politics* (Minneapolis: University of Minnesota Press, 1999), 41. Jack Smith, the legendary New York avant-garde artist of the 1960s and 1970s, was a devotee of Dominican B-movie actress María Móntez. See the preface to Muñoz.

24. Muñoz, 31.

25. Muñoz, 195.

26. Muñoz, 34. Muñoz, in discussing Marga Lopez's performances and her vision of community life, states that Marga Gomez's piece *Marga Lopez Is Pretty, Witty and Gay,* offers a critical perspective on community gay life: "Marga's look toward the mystery and outlaw sensibility of *the life* is a critique of a sanitized and heteronormativized *community*. . . . More than that, we see a desire to escape the claustrophobic confines of 'community,' a construct that often deploys rhetorics of normativity and normalization, for a life."

27. Rita González, "Unmasking Performance: Berta Jottar's *Vaivenes Fronterizos/ Border Swings,*" in *Cine Estudiantil* 96: International Chicano/Latino/Native American Student Film and Video Festival, program, San Diego/Tijuana, March 7–16, 1996.

28. Ana M. López, "From Hollywood and Back: Dolores Del Río, a Trans (National) Star," *Studies in Latin American Popular Culture* 17 (1998).

4 PENALIZING CHICANO/A BODIES IN EDWARD J. OLMOS'S *AMERICAN ME*

Frederick Luis Aldama

FIVE-PLUS centuries after the European conquest and colonization of the Americas, its violent racist and heterosexist legacy continues to cut deeply into the minoritarian subject's body and soul. In the year or so leading up to the new millennium, New York Police Department officers were found guilty of beating and sodomizing (with a toilet plunger) Haitian émigré Abner Louima; then several months later, a couple of white supremacists dragged the wheelchair-ridden African American James Byrd Jr. to his death in Texas; and, in Riverside, California, four of L.A.'s finest boys 'n blue unloaded dozens of bullets into the African American teenager Tyisha Miller. Six months later, L.A.'s special task force bum-rushed a modest house in Compton, filling Mario Paz's sixty-four-year-old brown body with lead. Of course, these individual acts simply point to larger acts of genocide committed against peoples of color as we enter the new millennium. With state legislation passing incarcerate-don't-educate public policies—California's three-strike rule and the legalizing of racial profiling, for example—Chicano/Latino and African American men are more likely to see the grays of a jail cell wall than a college textbook. So, while the techniques might differ from their colonial/*conquistador* forefathers, today's new millennial neocolonialists' exploitative labor laws, racist immigration policy, urban redlining, and glass-ceiling employment, to name a few strategies, effect the same end: today as much as yesterday, communities of color struggle to survive in a U.S. mainstream out to violently erase difference.

In response to these *fin-de-siglo* genocidal acts, Chicano actor Edward James Olmos (bankrolled by Universal Pictures' distribution department) released his directorial debut, *American Me* (1992). As the film unfolds, Olmos (as director and the story's protagonist) begins to cut new turf in Chicano cinema by bringing to the surface those everyday (neo)colonialist systems of surveillance that control from within and without the Chicano/a subject in today's so-called "New World Order."

In *American Me* Olmos opens mainstream eyes to the multilayered terrain—psychological, sexual, social, political—that makes up the East L.A. barrio-dwelling Chicano gang-banger's modus vivendi. His interweaving of connotative and denotative[1] detail at the level of both the story (plot, characters, events, themes) and the telling (cinematic narrator's use of music, mise-en-scène, editing, voice-over narration[2]) make for a film that is both implicitly critical of the type of white-associated, neocolonialism that restricts our quotidian reality and is critical of the brown (especially male) subject's reproduction of such oppressive, hegemonic tactical strategies—*joto* (gay male)- and woman-directed—within the Chicano/a community (*nuestra comunidad*). *American Me* as a cinematic gestalt deeply resonates with ur-narratives of the Euro-Spaniard's colonial/*conquistador* model of desiring and fearing, indulging in and controlling the New World subject/object.

Briefly, *American Me* (scripted by Floyd Mutrux) unfolds as follows: We first meet the protagonist Santana (Edward James Olmos) as the bars slam and he enters Folsom State Pen.[3] The story begins to unfold as Olmos recalls (his interior monologue-as-voice-over fills the film's narrative diegetic space) the complicated contours of his past. A series of flashbacks first takes the audience back to his inception—the brutal rape of his mother, Esperanza (Vira Montes), by white Navy sailors on the night of the Zoot Suit Riots (June 3, 1943).[4] Then Santana's voice-over leads the audience into his life as an estranged teenager in the late fifties, forming his gang, "*la primera*," in East Los Angeles; after several sequences that show gang camaraderie between Santana and his "number one crime partners," white-boy-cum-*Chicon* J.D. and big-eyed Mundo, the audience soon finds them behind bars in Juvenile Hall. Here Santana knives in the jugular the much-feared, sodomizing white rapist, which fast-tracks him into Folsom State Prison.[5] The audience catches up with Santana and his *clica* eighteen years later. La Primera has transformed into "*la eme*"—the factually based Chicano mafia that today controls most of the pushing, pimping, and gambling that goes on inside California state penitentiary walls. In the late seventies, Santana and J.D. are paroled and struggle to adapt to a very transformed outside world. In an act of desperation that seals Santana's fate—he orders the sodomitical rape and murder of an incarcerated Italian, the son of his archcompetitor, the 90210-villa-owning Italian drug lord—along with Santana's inability to be re-formed—he sodomitically rapes love-interest Julie (Evilinda Fernandez)—Santana is swept back to the pen. Diegetically speaking, as the film comes to a close, we are closest in story time to the moment when we first meet Santana at the film's start. The story's tragic denouement—six members of *la eme* stab then tier-drop Santana because he showed "weakness"—the film story comes full circle.[6] However, while the film's story is centrally focalized through Santana's consciousness, it nonetheless gives over a little extra diegetic time to Julie and to Santana's younger brother, Paulito (Jacob Vargas). Namely, after Santana's death (which is logically the place where the film story should cease), the camera-narrator continues to tell the story: Julie is described as leaving the barrio and on her way to night school, and Paulito sniffs glue with another *chavalito* and, behind the wheel of a '56 Chevy, fires a bullet at some innocents.

There's more than the break-the-cycle moral to this tale of redemption. As Santana experiences a 180-degree turn to his sense of self and community—his encounter with Julie (who identifies him, not so incidentally, as an oxymoronic, bifurcated man-infant) opens his eyes to his own participation in the genocide of his community—we see him struggle symbolically to break away from a deep-seated Euro-Spaniard supermacho legacy. Santana's struggle, finally, is about how he breaks free of age-old binaries—colonizer vs. colonized, bully vs. sissy, male vs. female, *activo* vs. *pasivo,* buggerer vs. *maricón,* hole maker and holed one—that continue to inform and control from within the Chicano/mestizo subject today.

The film centralizes Santana's internalized violence and consequent genocidal acts at the level of the story—to a deeply disturbing degree. The film's major shifts in plot line occur after the story's three rape events, The first, the rape of Esperanza, his mother, marks Santana a proverbial *hijo de la chingada* (as did Cortés et al.'s rape of the Maya and Aztec peoples); as a result of the rape, his taciturn father, Pedro (Sal Lopez), cuts him off emotionally, so Santana turns to the streets and forms his alternative male-male social matrix. The second and third rapes take place in the same temporal moment. The camera-narrator uses an increasing jump-cut tempo to juxtapose Santana's sodomitical rape of Julie in an apartment with that of the sodomitical rape and murder of the Italian in prison by Santana's American henchmen, Puppet (Danny De La Paz), Mundo (Pepe Serna), and El Japo (played by Asian American actor Cary-Hiroyuki Tagawa). This event leads to a small apocalypse in the barrio and alienates Santana from Julie. As a result, Santana questions his raison d'être; he shows weakness.

However, the rape scenes work as more than kernel events that shift the plot. Director Olmos's use of the rape scenes creates a film that, on the one hand, uncritically reproduces the anal encounter as abnormal and perverse—as an act of physical violence that leads to the mass destruction of the heterosexual matrix. For example, in a post-anal-rape repentive moment just before his death, Santana writes in a letter to Julie, "Here in this cage . . . behind these bars, I can read, I can learn, I can *make love,* but it's distorted." And, of course, when the double-anal-rape scene leads to an apocalypse in the barrio, one can't help but read this against our AIDS-panicked mass culture that associates anal intercourse (men "taking it like a woman") with suicide and disease, especially in poor ethnic enclaves. Other examples abound. For example, as soon as the character Little Puppet gets out of the male-male-only pen, homosexual panic sets in; he swiftly marries. And, while same-sex encounters are suggested (some to greater degrees than others, as with Santana's open declaration that he can make love in prison), it is only to assert the heterosexual encounter. For example, when J.D (William Forsythe) gets paroled and struts his stuff down the pen's tier, the character Mundo says, "Get laid out there for me"—as if "getting laid" can happen only in the civilian, heterosexually coded world.[7]

The film's machismo complex, it would seem, rechannels the homosexualization of desire back toward the heterosexual object. In her essay "Inside/Out" (1991) Diana Fuss maintains:

> For heterosexuality to achieve the status of the "compulsory," it must present itself as a practice governed by some internal necessity. The language and law that regulates the establishment of heterosexuality as both an identity and an institution, both a practice and a system, is the language and law of defense and protection: heterosexuality secures its self-identity and shores up its ontological boundaries by protecting itself from what it sees as the continual predatory encroachments of its contaminated other, homosexuality. (2)

Heterosexuality swallows all that threatens an economy built on male-female biological reproduction and that ensures the safe passage of power from father to son. Even though the prison system functions to sexualize Santana's desire as anal-directed, for the civilian system to work this must be considered only as a means to a better, heterosexual end. In a post-anal encounter scene, Julie reproduces this heterosexist tendency when, angrily resisting Santana's *apología,* she likens his death drive ("you'd kill me") to anal sex ("No, you'd fuck me in the ass"), thus reproducing the oppositional model: life is heterosexual (vaginal); sex and death are homosexual (anal).

Certainly, however, *American Me* does interrogate the Chicano macho/bully paradigm—the hyperexaggerated machismo of the male inmates calls attention to varying shades of the same impulse many Chicano men evince, such as Santana's taciturn, fly-off-the-handle father, Pedro, and their violence against women and children. The camera-narrator identifies Santana's macho behavior as the origin for the series of events that leads to the Italian godfather's circulating uncut coke that kills off dozens of Chicanitos. And the film is critical of Santana's self-victimization—a self-identification that transforms his initial alienation from the Father and society (his non-citizen status as a Chicano) into a subject firmly entrenched in the very power that alienates peoples of color. Through the camera-narrator's critical lens, we see how the drive to acquire power as a way to authenticate the Chicano-self-in-nation only leads to Santana's internalizing of a will-to-bully that destroys more than saves his family. Conversely, however, the camera-narrator's deconstruction of the machismo complex also functions to naturalize the constructed hetero-ethnosocioeconomic paradigm that normalizes the same-sex encounter as de facto "*contra natura.*"

Along with the film's denotation of the sodomitic act as perverse, the sodomitic rape scenes carry an equally strong connotation of the colonial encounter. Namely, not so unlike the erstwhile *conquistadores,* Santana penetrates and, according to the heterosexist code, humiliates the unknown subject/object—or Julie and heterosexual love. While their love-making begins in the heterosexualized *missionary* position, he's confused; something deep within is triggered—a legacy of Euro-Spanish sexual domination of the *indio/a.* To control and synthesize the "exotic" female qua new virgin territory, he violently turns Julie over on her face, humiliates, and penetrates. Here the act of buggering (undesired by the bottom and thus a rape) connotes much. Importantly, it speaks to a history of trans-atlantic *colon*ial libido that penetrated (anally, orally, and vaginally) the New World Other. As José Piedra claims in his seminal essay "Nationalizing Sissies," the *conquistador*/colonizer's construction of a discourse that prohibited racial mixing to maintain the purity of the Euro-Spanish blood-line was simply a way for the colonizer to justify the buggering, or "sissifying," of the New World Amerindian men and women. In other words, like the colonial fear/desire for the New World male hole (mostly), the drive was always ultimately to maintain the purity of the Euro-Spaniard heterosexual lineage. José Piedra contends that the women remained "the hidden object of desire enacted by the sissy who operates in her stead just enough to save the bully from admitting to a gay connection" (371). And, in the big fear/desire dialectical scheme of things, Piedra informs, the "sissy becomes less of a man or a lesser man and more than a woman. In a parallel fashion, the bully becomes more of a man upon treating a lesser man as a woman" (371–372). This is to say, the machismo complex isn't new. The double rape is simply a modern-day version of the colonizer's violent penetration, humiliation, annihilation of *los indigenas*—this time, however, enacted by the very progeny that *came* of the anal-to-vagina slippage during the conquest.[8]

Furthermore, the sodomitical act in *American Me* resonates with narratives seen in the early *conquistador* and colonizer texts that, by describing the New World other as "sodomites," "pederasts," hybrid hypergenitalized men/women-animals, justified Euro-Spaniards' realization of their own closeted transgendering desire. José Piedra writes of colonial take-over as the colonizer (whom he calls "bully") keeping the New World subject (whom he calls "sissy") in a "suspended libidinal state," between, he maintains, "maleness and femaleness, hetero- and homosexuality, or 'worse.' Fantasized as androgyny, hermaphroditism, virginity, or celibacy, the sissy's 'in-betweenness' serves as the ultimate butt of macho rhetorical inscription, physical intervention, or both" ("Nationalizing Sissies," 371–372). In other words, while Olmos invents a filmscape that questions the naturalization of macho codes of conduct that work to control and contain women and children, the film also speaks to the process of internalizing the colonial model of other-controlling and self-releasing in the act of sodomizing the exotic subject/object.

The rape sequences and Santana's apparent turn toward heterosexual norms in the post-anal encounter (he seems to visually repent with furrowed brow and head bowed low after he violates Julie) lend themselves to yet another reading. The film is being more critical of the sodomy-as-rape code than we see at first glance. Rather than uncritically reproducing the *conquistador*'s *indio*-as-hole-to-be-filled ur-narrative, if we consider the camera-narrator's heavy gesture toward revealing the more complicated pre-Columbian cultural terrain, the film also works to denaturalize the normalization narratives used by the *conquistador*/colonizer to justify the anal, oral, and vaginal penetrating of the New World subject-as-perversely-genitalized-object. Set against this, then, we can reread Santana's rape-cum-repentance less as his sexualization in terms of *lacking* the "correct" hole (vagina), but rather as his move into a sexual in-between zone that threatens the male-male power structure of *la eme.* Santana's "weakness," then, identifies his move into a more ambiguous top/bottom, *activo/pasivo,* strong/weak identification that, by resisting age-old binaries (macho vs. sissy), threatens *la eme*'s male-male, teleologically heterosexual goal-directed, capitalist economy.[9]

Santana's story is complex, revealing both the construction of his internalized colonialism and consequent violence against Chicanas and the tragedy of his *coming* into a more complicated sexual zone not confined by binary oppositions. As a result, he's penetrated to death by six of the male-male, macho initiates. When mestizo-identified masculine desire is versatile and/or ambiguous, it threatens the system—national, sexual, racial—founded on constructed dichotomies that function to contain, to control, and to uphold (even if cloaked as Raza-emancipating, like *la eme*) the white, heterosexist, middle-class status quo.

It's not so much, then, that Santana must be annihilated because of his show of the dreaded detumescent "weakness" felt in his heterosexualized postlapsarian blues. Rather, it's his coming into an unfixity of subject identity that leads to his annihilation. In *Tendencies* Eve Sedgwick celebrates just such an in-between sexual identity as one that is an "open mesh of possibilities, gaps, overlaps, dissonances and resonances, lapses and excesses of meaning" (8). And Gloria Anzaldúa similarly celebrates a ethno-queer-sexual-borderland identity inhabited by "the prohibited and forbidden," "*los atravesados* . . . those who cross over, pass over, or go through the confines of the 'normal'" (8); such an ethnosexual, unfixed identity threatens the status quo precisely because it is uncontainable and, in its crossover movements, invisible to even the best of panoptic, ethnosexual surveillance structures. Santana's "weakness," then, is also his strength. As he crosses from *activo* to *pasivo* he inhabits that threatening borderland identity that, as Sedgwick writes of the sexual crisscrosser, no longer exists to "signify monolithically" (8). I assert that the camera-narrator, along with character portrayal, betrays a not-so-heterosexualized, vagina-redirected Santana, but rather a character who comes into an in-between ethnosexual identity that is both bully/top (the heterosexed macho anal penetrator) and also sissy/bottom (anally penetrated). Of course, this is all connotative and subtextual within the film—and in this silver-screen day and age, subtext it would have to be. With less celebratory zeal than Anzaldúa and Sedgwick, David L. Eng reminds one of the forced liminality the ethnic queer (particularly Asian) inhabits: "In this particular ordering of the social sphere [lack of political membership and impossibility of full social recognition], to 'come out' is precisely and finally never to *be* 'out'—a never-ending process of constrained avowal, a perpetually deferred state of achievement, an uninhabitable domain. Suspended between an 'in' and 'out' of the closet—between origin and destination, and between private and public space—queer entitlements to home and a nation-state remain doubtful as well" (1997: 32).

FILLING THE WRONG FILMIC HOLES

I've briefly laid out the so-called surface (denotative) and deep (very connotative) structures that make up the various messages readable in *American Me.* It isn't so surprising that the film carries several, even conflictive messages. Films, we know, are as open to multiple layers of interpretation as, say, novels; this is partly the result of the filmic text's lack of a time-present, that responding interlocutor (unlike the real-time of uttered quotidian speech) that would, according to one's response (conditioned by society, race, sex, or gender), shape the outcome of the story/exchange.[10] Of course, this isn't to say that *American Me* is a tabula rasa open to all sorts of interpretive squiggles. Indeed, the camera-narrator's auditory and visual channels and the story itself intertwine (intentionally or not) and cluster around certain nodes of meaning. It's not completely out of left field, then, to read Santana's ultimate show of "weakness" as the move into an unfixed identity zone informed by a legacy of anal-colonization when, for example, the film story begins with the Navy gang-rape sequence that spins the audience's mind into allegorical re-memories of the sexual conquest of the New World.

However, this Raza-informed audience frame doesn't necessarily guarantee a postcolonial reading of the film. For example, take the case of Raza patriarch Luis Valdez. Valdez, who has championed the Chicano/a (mostly Chicano) cause since the sixties with his Maya/Aztec-informed *teatro campesino* and film productions, told a reporter for the *San Jose Mercury News* just after *American Me* hit the big screen: "My response then was that it was a diatribe against Latinos. . . . This is a genre (street-crime movies) that's been offered to me many times. It's not what I relate to. I believe in the cinema of triumph" (Lovell, 1). Valdez wasn't alone. Other Chicanos/as in Los Angeles and throughout California more vehemently attacked the film for its negative portrayal of the Chicano community.

Few reviewers and critics picked up on anything but the film's ghetto/gang-banger code, leading either to extreme pans or extreme celebrations; of course, there were few peeps about the film's complicated meddling with sexual middle grounds. For example, in the March issue of the *New*

Republic, Stanley Kauffmann took it as an opportunity to wax negative, writing that *American Me* is just "one more story of boys being led by ghetto conditions into drugs and crime, of gangs as the only available validation of self, of consequent prison, of crime in prison" (26). And that same month, and seemingly with the same breath, Brian D. Johnson commented on how "Hollywood's most visible crusader of Hispanic causes" (Olmos) failed to "rehabilitate the tired formula of the prison movie" (51). Johnson doesn't hold back here, writing, "The violence, which is both visceral and frequent, verges on exploitation. And the movie becomes a vicarious excursion into underworld exotica" (51). Might the use of "visceral," "exploitation," and "vicarious excursion into underworld exotica" betray something more than Johnson's dislike of the sculpted, brown male body?

American Me certainly is a film that focuses on gangs and prison life; the camera-narrator announces at the beginning the film's self-proclaimed affiliation with the prison-flick genre: prison doors clank, keys jangle, and an unidentifiable voice commands, "Open mouth . . . lift up your nut sack . . . bend over . . . grab your ass and give me two good coughs." However, Kauffmann et al. seem to be stuck in their own preconceptions of how a prison-flick story unfolds; they've missed the many complicated, often contradictory, codes that make *American Me* more than a simple rehabilitation of "the tired formula of the prison movie."

TURNING HOLES INSIDE OUT

Chicano/a critics are also very critical of *American Me,* reading it as a film that simplistically reproduces the machismo complex. Kathleen Newman concludes her essay "Reterritorialization in Recent Chicano Cinema" by proclaiming *American Me* a failed attempt to "deterritorialize" the U.S. patriarch-serving nation-state (95); because of its violence toward Chicanas, she informs, it fails to "reterritorialize the State . . . as a neutral site of equality and justice for all citizens" (104). Newman interprets the double-rape scenes "as actants" that simply move "the narrative to a conclusion wherein gender is disconnected from character and redeployed in the service of epic" (99). Rosa Linda Fregoso attacks *American Me* in her important book *The Bronze Screen* because, like other gangxploitation flicks, it re-inscribes patriarchal politics of gender instead of promoting a non-gender-essentialized cultural nationalism. Sergio de la Mora maintains that

> The various inserts of male rape in prison—functioning visually and narratively to both interrupt and punctuate the emotional texture of the heterosexual coupling—reinforce Hollywood's narrow conceptualization of sodomy (whether straight or gay) as an apparent act which is all about domination and submission. Julie's sod-

> omitic rape, thus, highlights Santana's deviant and pathological sexuality because it falls outside the narrow constructs of heterosexual reproductive norms. (14)

While Newman's, Fregoso's, and de la Mora's observations are well taken, the rape scene and subsequent character "epiphany"—read against a homophobic and colonialist backdrop—reveal a less clear-cut sodomy-as-psychopathology narrative.[11] Indeed, more than the rape functioning to reproduce a normative biologically progenerative heterosexuality (to be made whole by hole-ing the holy vagina), Santana enters (conscious or not) into an in-between, in-flux sexuality that complicates those heterosexed vs. homosexed identity codes. For this reason, Santana steps on *straight* and *bent* feet.

TUMBLING TOPS AND BOTTOMS

The camera-narrator first introduces the filmgoer to Santana as he enters Folsom State Pen just before his grand, multiple-knife-penetrated death—and just before his "autoethnographic" (Pratt) story unfolds as a series of analepses.[12] Before story time begins (the series of flashbacks), then, we have an imagistic impression of the protagonist—Edward James Olmos as a solemn, older, macho character. We glean this from the series of "focal character" shots (Santana's perspective) the camera-narrator uses to open the film:[13] camera pans down from gray wall with "Palm Hall" stenciled in black letters to medium shot of back of prisoner's head as prison door opens and the body walks forward and guard follows. Cut to frontal shot, medium long shot with character's head and chest framed by prison door barred window. The character walks forward into the shot (with red-lettered "Exit" inscribed above doorway) and into a medium shot. The audience can now identify the character as actor Edward James Olmos. At the level of discourse, the camera-narrator mixes in with noises of door opening and closing a guard's voice: "bend over, grab your ass, give me two good coughs." Then, as the film's thematic music score begins, an accented woman's voice (which later we identify as Julie's) enters at the level of the discourse (voice-over): "you are like two people: One is like a kid, doesn't know how to dance, doesn't know how to make love. The one I cared about. The other one I hate, the one who knows, who has this rap down, who kills people."

Olmos as the macho protagonist, however, isn't so surprising. When Olmos appears in a film, he carries with him clusters of adjectives accumulated by his previous roles. Olmos's tough-guy image (Lieutenant Castillo in the TV series *Miami Vice,* the bad-ass pachuco in Valdez's *Zoot Suit,* the great Chicano *patriarca* in *Mi Familia* and *Selena,* and the hybrid Hispano-Asian detective in *Blade Runner*) has acquired a stable meaning—a kind of quintessence of the top/buggerer. Not surprisingly, then, audiences are apt to resist the recodification of Olmos as not just a top, but as a bottom as well. So, while the rape scene disturbs, there is an equal amount of confusion and discomfort when the actor who signifies machismo suddenly turns over for us. This shift between top and bottom should be of little surprise. It's a myth that in same-sex relationship patterns sexual preference and role-playing behavior are etched in stone as a binary oppositional. The film's denouement arrives when Olmos-as-Santana is stabbed to death and becomes the receptor (unlike Julie, he is willing here) to the *clica*'s penetrating blades.

While the death scene certainly brings into high relief the subtextual politics of prison same-sex identity (penetrations and humiliations that depose tops for bottoms), as the film unfolds, the filmgoer witnesses not only Santana's transformation into a top, but how even an identity as a top isn't so clear-cut. There's the story of Santana's socialization into a top/*activo*. As the older Santana-as-narrator rhymes, "I thought I knew it all . . . ended up in Juvey Hall and the shit got even deeper"—literally. Santana flashbacks to the night in Juvenile Hall when a white boy, just after sodomizing Santana, threatens, "Say one word about this and they'll be shit on my knife, not on my dick." The knife conflates phallus with violence and humiliation (we see this throughout). In the postcoital moment, Santana jumps the white boy from behind, wrestles him to the bed, and, as he takes the knife and plunges it into the white boy's body (a very sexualized scene where the boy's eyes roll up as his mouth opens and he gasps ecstatically and blood spurts sporadically), becomes the top. However, for Santana there's more than just posturing as a tough guy for the other men. He's a top with a hard-core exterior, but whose small gestures and off-handed comments betray a love (romantic even) for his "number one crime partner," J.D., as well as desire (physical mostly) for the hard-bodied, chisel-jawed Asian inmate (played by a puppy-eyed Cary-Hiroyuki Tagawa).

Like many homosocial exclusive cliques (including the most homophobic of male gangs, sport teams, and Greek fraternities), ass-slapping, crotch-grabbing, and "fag"-identifying labels betray a complicated fear of and *desire for* dialectic that informs the male-male identity. Considering Santana and J.D. belong to a *clica*, then, their open signs of affection betray a similar dialectic. J.D. often calls Santana "chavala" (in Spanish this is slang for sweetheart, or fiancée, and is sometimes used to identify a *pasivo/maricón*). However, there's more here than meets the eye. While we never see them cross those lines that define Hollywood heterosexual romance (no tongue kissing, no romantic scores, and no candle lighting), you can see them struggle with an intimacy that wants to push across such lines. Of course, J.D. and Santana (and Mundo) set in motion the male-male desire as teenagers when they needle (tattoo)[14] each other in the closetlike space of a mausoleum.[15] As adults, J.D. and Santana show acceptable signs of affection, such as little pecks on the cheek—even longing glances. For example, the camera-narrator pauses to describe a long scene wherein a newly paroled J.D. looks deep into Santana's eyes just before he leaves Folsom State Pen; and, perhaps more obviously, once on the outside and living that heterosexual lifestyle much desired in prison (Mundo tells J.D., "Get laid *out there* for me"), they exchange longing glances across a courtyard while dancing with their respective love interests. At one point, too, the camera-narrator describes a prison scene with J.D. fighting back tears for Santana just before his death—tears that betray a push across those lines that traditionally separate the macho from the *maricón.*

For all of Santana's macho presence, the camera-narrator rarely shows him alone in prison. Either J.D. or the Asian character *fill* the mise-en-scène when Santana is in the spaces of the prison yard and storage rooms. However, Santana's interaction (gestures, dialogue, bodily exchanges) differs for each, depending on context. For example, it is unclear even who is top and who is bottom when the camera-narrator describes Santana with J.D.; they both manifest hard and soft qualities when together. Yet it is J.D. who, in the end, remains purely *activo* by effectively signing Santana's death warrant.

While it seems clear that Santana is the *activo* with the Asian character, the Asian himself in a different context (the rape of the Italian) can switch roles. Importantly, one context that determines the type of *activo/pasivo* interaction between Santana and his male lovers, subtextually speaking of course, is race. For the *güero* J.D., who is phenotypically marked as "white," his final interaction with Santana—signing his death warrant—is one that de facto aligns whiteness with the *activo* role. On the other hand, Santana's engagement with the Asian character, El Japo, plays into confining stereotypical images of the Asian as bottom/sissy in hierarchies of erotic images (especially seen in U.S. white-ga(y)zed porn). El Japo is hard-bodied and without a voice. He's physically strong, but without an agency unhitched from Santana's über-*activo* will to power. He hovers around Santana as an obedient bottom. Once El Japo comes to exist sans Santana (Santana's paroled), his will and action are tied to Santana, but no longer as a mute, passive bottom. As one of the rapists who forcefully sodomize the Italian (under Santana's direction, admittedly), codes of behavior turn upside down. El Japo transforms from the submissive "Rice Queen" (pejorative label used in gay porn) to a violent top who shows not only how context shapes sexual behavior, but how sexuality shifts refract the traditional hierarchies of power that would normally confine the Asian on the outside. The Italian-as-white (a symbolic stand-in for globalized, capitalist, white-based power) versus the Asian-as-subaltern (symbolic of those without power and lacking fundamental claim to turf in the nation-state), he's accepted by like-subalternized subjects, the Chicanos. As he ties down the Italian, gags him with a ripped-open bag of rice (scribbled with red and black Asian ideographs), then sodomitically rapes him, the Asian not only inhabits a different sexual identity (*activo*), but reverses age-old racial hierarchies of power.

This isn't to say that I condone violence if it subverts racial and sexual oppression. Rather, I delineate the characters' more fluid *activo*-to-*pasivo* roles as determined by context—a context that resonates beyond the confines of the story world and spills into master narratives of race and sexuality. Santana, then, role-shifts according to context (racial, inside/outside spatial) and so, too, do the male love interests. Santana role-plays the *activo* with the Asian—the camera-narrator describes the Asian as somewhat adoring—and plays a softer role—*una chavala*—with J.D.; we even get a glimmer of jealousy in Santana's eye when he sees J.D. dancing with a woman. And J.D. and the Asian character do not conform to an either *activo* or *pasivo* role type; they, too, shift according to context.

A REPOSITORY OF TRADITION BETWEEN THE CRACK

Of course, all of the characters' movement between the macho and sissy roles belies the friction that generates character arcs and epiphanies, but does not lead to the traditional cinematic denouement: the white heterosexual coupling and promise of biological reproduction. What Santana's interactions with his love interests leave the audience with is his story—a story generated out of the rape of his mother, punctuated by his being raped, then becoming a rapist, but ultimately sustained by his male-male interactions. Certainly there is much in the film that directs our reading of Santana's nonbiologic reproduction as a deficiency. After all, in one of the film's penultimate sequences he concludes his autobiographic letter to Julie, "You Julie . . . were the door to another life, where my seed might have been reaffirmed." Stereotypes of women as repository aside, that his melancholia gravitates around his inability to have his "seed" affirmed strongly lends to a reading that positions male-male sexual interaction as *lack*. This is further emphasized when, addressing his male-male environs as a void, he continues to write, "I've brought back to this *hole* some life which I'm trying to use." However, while it is certainly his encounter with Julie that functions as the impetus to the writing of his autobiography, it is nonetheless an autobiography that speaks to homosocial (and homosexual) socialization. Namely, his story is the surrogate offspring of his male-male interactions. His story, with its mnemonic devices and circular (analeptic and paraleptic) patterns, is the concrete product of male-male intercourse (that which sustains and even generates the story) that will survive Santana. So, while women play an important role in Santana's evolution of self, it is ultimately his story that acts as his lineage (just consider the screen time given to the men and also how the kernel events turn around the male characters).

Of course, while Santana's nonbiologically procreative presence threatens the heterosexual codes and leads to his annihilation, his nonbiological scion survives him; the letter to Julie and the film itself (his voice-over narration) function in the form of recorded testament as a surrogate lineage. Like his namesake, Saint Anna, Santana is biologically barren. Unlike Saint Anna, whose narratives worked as convincing supplications to the heavenly Father and who soon found herself impregnated with the

Virgin Mary, Santana's narrative leads to a biological (heterosexual) reversal of his fortune. While his story isn't of the biological reproductive kind, it does exist as an alternative savior narrative intended to save future generations of Chicanos/as from self-destruction.

Not only does Santana represent an alternative, nonbiologically produced savior narrative that dialogues with and subverts Judeo-Christian religious paradigms, but his coming into his role as a storyteller who leaves behind the concrete artifact of his written story/testimony for future generations positions Santana within a long line of asexual, bisexual, and homosexual spiritual figures traditionally responsible for holding together communities before and during the conquest. (The Zuni Indian bisexual "berdaches" were similarly revered as the repository of tribal tradition.) For example, in the late fifteenth century Fray Ramón Pané wrote in his proto-ethnographic study of the Arawak Indians that "hay algunos hombres que *practican entre ellos,* y se les dice behiques (there are some men who practice among themselves and are called *behiques*)" (quoted in Piedra, 392; emphasis mine). While the Euro-Spanish, Catholic ideologue certainly had good reason for constructing the indigenous medicine man as a sexual other ("hombres que practican entre ellos")—a foolproof conversion/genocide justification narrative—José Piedra recovers similar evidence from native records that suggest the *behiques* were not only revered as keepers of Arawak tradition, medicine men, and tellers of stories, but were also queer. Piedra's research reveals the close link between the *behiques* and the age-old myth of the Guaganaona, popularly known in the Afro-Hispanic Caribbean as "The-One-Without-Male-Ancestry." According to historical and present Hispano-Caribbean language and lore, the mythic Guaganaona, not so unlike the *behiques,* is "transgendered."

Santana's inhabitation of that sexualized in-between storytelling zone lends itself to a transposing of the Guaganaona myth-template. José Piedra briefly classifies the sexualized symbolic spaces the Guaganaona inhabits: "First, this entity is the Being of the Yucca, a 'female' root fetishized as the penis—and more specifically, a penis engaged in a male self-satisfying, masturbatory action. Second s/he is the Sea, a female power that once held the transatlantic male voyagers in the palm of her hand. Third, s/he is 'The-One-Without-Male-Ancestry,' an originating force with no male models or need for phallic instruction or introduction—a less-than-traditional phallic 'resolution'" (393). First, Santana functions symbolically as female and male: he's a quintessential Chicano macho who brings home the money and physically protects *la familia*—and he is the community storyteller (a position in Latino culture traditionally inhabited by women and/or asexualized, old, and impotent *curanderos*). Too, while on the one hand Santana's story functions to save his community (as his voice-over spills out into the discourse for the audience to hear), on the other, materially it is a story penned as a letter in the confines of his prison cell; his story contains that inherent quality of the epistolary form: the masturbatory, s/he autoerotic. He's the Being of the Yucca. Second, Santana comes into a more fluid sense of self, not so coincidentally, just after his first splash in the Pacific Ocean. (The camera-narrator weighs this scene as a kind of New World baptism, but with a precolonial spiritual tinge.) It is after his tryst with heterosexual love interest Julie at the beach that, while standing knee-deep in the ocean, the "she" coded storytelling act passes symbolically from Julie to Santana; after this sequence, Santana becomes a storyteller, writing his autoethnography from prison.

As Santana crisscrosses gendered roles in the act of penning his autoethnography, he disrupts the hierarchical economy of (neo)colonial desire that genitalizes the presence of subaltern identities in U.S. mainstream culture. In a symbolic sense he becomes Piedra's identified "s/he . . . Sea" that can powerfully turn upside down, even destroy, those transatlantic male Euro-Spanish voyagers. This is to say that Santana fulfills the criteria by becoming a modern-day avatar of the Guaganaona/*behique.* He comes to inhabit a transsecting sexual and gender (even a trans-Chicano/Latino/Carib) identity that, like "The-One-Without-Male-Ancestry" entity, exists as an alternative "originating force" to the traditional vagina/penis binary system.

(NEO)COLONIAL BACKDOORS

Santana's coming into a complicated in-between sexual and racial identity as he tells his story is the subtext to *American Me.* Interestingly, while film critic Rita Kempley negatively reviewed the film for what she termed its "cruddy, *K-Y-jelly-coated* look into the prison house" that "spares few anatomical details" and where inmates "become ethnically *cannibalistic,*" she unwittingly reproduces in film review guise the *conquesta*'s narratives that perversely genitalized the New World Other (*Washington Post,* March 13, 1992). Of course, her comment (neocolonial and all) speaks, albeit without intending to, to those denotative codes that allow, for example, the audience to transpose the Zoot Suit Riots of 1943 onto the brutal conquest of the Americas. Of course, as a result of the work of Gloria Anzaldúa, José Piedra, and others, we now know that for the Euro-Spaniards to justify their conquest and genocide of Amerindian peoples, they genitalized and made "perverse" the Other; this act also allowed the Euro-Spaniards to set up a convenient libidinal system that would legitimate their frictive synthesis, sans biological miscegenation, of the sexualized Other.[16] This violent penetration and violent synthesis of the hypergenitalized Other (Amazonas, pederasts, queer men and women) didn't always take place along heterosexual vectors of desire.[17] As José Piedra maintains, "many Spaniards secretly adopted sodomy to provide human contact and sexual release while skirting the dangers of miscegenation. . . . In the end, sodomy and homosexuality become transatlantic forms of birth control as well as metonymic expressions of male-centered elitism and imperialism on both sides of the Atlantic, as well as a unifying macho-saving feature of transatlantic colonialism" (397–398).

Importantly, as Piedra boldly identifies, the conquest included not only the Euro-Spaniard's sodomizing the Other, but also the macho, elite indigenous male's sodomitical desire. The camera-narrator doesn't exactly equalize Pedro's macho behavior (the male tattoo artist penetrates and stains Pedro's arm) with that of the belligerent white sailors, but both coexist in the same sequence, and both represent different degrees of macho behavior that hides a same-sex desire. (With whom do the sailors really share their fluids?) Recall, too, that Bernal Diaz's gifting of his much-favored boy-page, Orteguilla, to Moctezuma was more than just a token of his friendship. It was a *warped* expression of his desire to exchange fluids with the elite male Other. There's much subtextual evidence to suggest that Moctezuma and Cortez shared fluids across Orteguilla's body. According to Diaz's journals, Orteguilla was referred to as a female (often referred to as *la malinche,* the name used to identify Cortez's female mistress, Dona Marina) and a *pasivo.* Orteguilla is the hole that is filled (textually and physically) by both macho elites as they engage in a same-sex desire perverted by their heteronormative, *conquista* ideological baggage. This is to say, the film not only sets up an easy time/space transposition of the 1943 rape and consequent marking off of Santana as a bastard (the product of the U.S. military's violent penetration of the barrio as New-World-hole-in-need-of-filling) with the *conquista* encounter, but also delineates the heterosexual machos' (white and brown) violently twisting up of a deep desire for the anus.

UTOPIC SLITS AND DYSTOPIC HOLES

The film continues to make explicit the conflation of vagina with anus in a heterosexist, neocolonial twisting up of desire—especially when it comes to Santana's buying into an economy of power built on the in- and outflow of drugs and capital from within the *pinta.* Not so unlike the white, sailor-boy rapists, Santana internalizes the he-who-controls-the-hole-has-the-power model. Women's holes are used in this economy as a way to ensure citizen-like rights to Chicanos; the women are used by the men to make prison environs homelike. For example, the camera-narrator's auditory channel plays the song "Slipping into Darkness" by the '70s band War while the visuals describe the following: an above, tilt-angled medium long shot of an unnamed white woman character (previously seen with J.D. in the prison visiting room) lifting up her dress, sitting on a toilet, then removing a balloonlike object from her vagina that she then flushes down the toilet. Cut to close-up of black sewer pipe and a rapid pan left as flush sound continues. Cut to close medium close shot of pipe as the camera follows it vertically downward. The shot pauses with a shot of a half-naked inmate fishing out shit and the balloonlike object with his hand. The scene ends with a medium shot of the inmate (now identifiable as the character Puppet) opening the balloon, tasting white powder, sealing it, then squeezing K-Y jelly onto it and visibly inserting it into his anus. The flow of cocaine from vagina to anus to mouth/nose promises the inmates inside a momentary, albeit imaginative, escape to the outside. Santana peddles drugs that promise to make the inmate feel whole in a hole full of men that is coded in the popular imaginary as lacking. By controlling the flow, Santana participates in the reproduction of a desiring system that marks off the prison as the place inhabited by the fragmented, lacking subject. He mistakenly believes that his acting as valve controller to the opening and closing of the flow of desire in and out of various bodily pipes and holes will allow him to emancipate himself and his *compañeros.* On one occasion, he informs Julie, "before if somebody wanted something from you like your manhood and they were stronger than you, they just took it. We changed all that."

For Santana, controlling the flow of power—shit, semen, vaginal discharge—is to effect an end: to create a sense of belonging not just in the prison, but in an outside world that alienates. The power to be the *activo* (after all, when he tells Julie "we changed all that," he's really saying he acquired the power to choose who to bugger), then, is implicated in this move to create a sense of belonging for his fellow Chicano gang-bangers, his Chicano/a community outside the prison's walls, and finally the nation. In *Tendencies* Eve Sedgwick calls attention to the fact that all "chromosomal sexed" and "socially gendered"—and, I would add, socially racialized—people in the modern nation-state must, as she writes, "be seen as partaking of what we might (albeit clumsily) call a "habitation/nation system" (147) The "habitation/nation system" would be the set of discursive and institutional arrangements that mediate between the physical fact that each person inhabits, at a given time, a particular geographical space, and the far more abstract, sometimes even apparently unrelated organization of what has emerged since the late seventeenth century as one's national identity, as signalized by, for instance, citizenship (147). However, if like Santana, his criminal status disallows him from participating in a system that requires one to "be seen as partaking" in a "habitation/nation system," then even while one might have a handle on the flusher of power, one will always remain an outsider. Namely, while the heterosexual, *white*-collar breadwinner can exploit the system (S&L-style) because his whiteness gives him a de facto visibility (with the concomitant power to be invisible at will) as a participant in the "habitation/nation" system, Santana, as he realizes finally at the end, will never experience that long-sought-after citizen status. He's visible only as a racial, sexual, class outlaw; like Chicanos/as in general, he's an invisible citizen of the nation. In a telling, postsodomitical moment, Santana caustically asks Julie, "What do you want from me *esa*? To start over . . . become a citizen?"

FINAL REMARKS

By taking into account the *American Me* as a film-text with surface structures—the internalized colonialism that leads to violence against Chicanas

—as well as a film-text with precolonial and colonial deep-structures—Santana's coming into an ambiguous sexuality that threatens the order of things—we can read *American Me* as a film that reveals the many layers at work in our violently racist and heterosexist new-millennial social matrix. Finally, *American Me* remains controversial and problematic as a Chicano text precisely because it reveals (unwittingly or not) the everyday violence that prevents Chicanos/as (straight and bent) the possibility of feeling at "Home" in a white, middle-class, male-coded, heterosexualized nation-state.

NOTES

1. In *Film Language* Christian Metz points out, " . . . the filmed spectacle already had its own expressiveness, since it was after all a piece of the world, which always has a meaning" (76). He sums up: "[L]iterature and the cinema are by their nature condemned to connotation, since denotation always precedes their artistic enterprise" (76).

2. Seymour Chatman writes in *Coming to Terms*, "The cinematic narrator is not to be identified with the voice-over narrator. A voice-over may be one *component* of the total showing, one of the cinematic narrator's devices, but a voice-over narrator's contribution is almost always transitory; rarely does he or she dominate a film the way a literary narrator dominates a novel—that is by informing every single unit of semiotic representation" (134).

3. Floyd Mutrux takes the screenplay's title, *American Me*, from Beatrice Griffith's sociologically informed book on post–World War II U.S. gangs. The title and content have now been retooled by Mutrux, who focuses less on Griffith's original taxonomy of the male pathological type and more on developing a complex characterization of the biographical Chicano gangster Cheyenne, a founding member of the Mexican mafia, who was killed in prison in 1972.

4. Santana's narrative works as a subversive re-memory of historical events. During the time of the so-called "Zoot Suit Riots" (June 3–6, 1943) newspapers failed to report that it was indeed a battery of white sailors who hired dozens of taxis to drive into the barrio. Here, the Marines—legitimated as penile extensions of the white phallus—brutally raped, maimed, and killed without having to field any of the blame.

5. The Folsom State Prison warden denied Olmos's first request to film on site; the warden feared that it might incite a riot. Considering California's incarcerate-don't-educate policy making—I'm thinking particularly of ex-governor Pete Wilson's three-strikes law and his disavowal of urban and rurally underfunded school districts while dumping big cash into building newly improved for the '90s panopticons—this should come as little surprise. Evelyn Nieves reports for the *New York Times* (Saturday, November 7, 1998) of the increase from twelve prisons in 1988 to house 31,000 inmates to thirty-three prisons to house 160,000 inmates in 1998. Of the San Joaquin Valley's Corcoran State Prison, Nieves says, "I[I]n October, five prison guards at Corcoran were indicted on state charges of conspiracy, accused of having an inmate rape another inmate in 1993." He continues, "The prison's security housing units, or super-maximum prisons within prisons, where most of the shootings have taken place, were built so that one or two guards with high-powered rifles could watch over a yard with dozens of the most troublesome prisoners." Director of corrections C. A. Terhune responds, "The design, the staffing, and many of the factors that go into the program operations of the California prison system were based on having lethal force as a control mechanism." Olmos was finally granted permission to *shoot* on site, filming within Folsom State Pen's walls for nearly three weeks.

6. Including Santana, the group makes up seven. This resonates with symbolic

significance. Rafael Pérez-Torres writes that according to legend, "Aztlán names the Mexican homeland—the land of seven caves (Chicomostoc), the palace of the Twisted Hill (Colhuacán), the place of whiteness (Aztlán)—from which the Mexica migrated south toward the central plateau in A.D. 820" (229).

7. I will henceforth refer to "code" not in the sense of Barthes's wedges into deciphering a text's ideological structures, the now-famous four cardinal codes: proairetic, paradigmatic, syntagmatic, and hermeneutic. Rather I will use "code" simply to refer to that system of norms and rules used to produce a message form/shape that will carry meaning to its audience/receiver. Namely, I use "code" more linguistically to refer to those rules of utterance that ensure the production and reception of the denotative and connotative contours of the conveyed message.

8. Importantly, much of what we know of the Amerindian other hails from *conquista*/discoverer/colonizer accounts. As Michel De Certeau writes in *Heterologies:* "[T]he written discourse that cites the speech of the other is not, cannot be, this discourse of the Other. On the contrary, this discourse, in writing the Fable that authorizes it, alters it" (78).

9. Switching of *activo* and *pasivo* roles is commonplace in Mexico. Writer Reinaldo Arenas, however, reveals in his *Antes que Anochezca* the complicated social repercussions of switching from *activo* to *pasivo* in a macho-complexed society. He picks up an athletic youth (physically the *activo*) and recollects how "Once inside my home, [he] surprisingly asked me to play the role of the man. . . . I fucked him and he enjoyed it like a convict. Then, still naked, he asked me, 'And if anybody catches us here, who is the man?' He meant who fucked whom. I replied, perhaps a little cruelly, 'Obviously, I am the man, since I stuck it into you.' This enraged the young man, who was a judo expert . . . " (103).

10. See the famed film semiotician Christian Metz's *Film Language* for more on film-audience interpolation, especially pp. 80–90.

11. In queering *American Me* I do not intend to displace Newman's and Fregoso's important feminist critiques, but rather to read the film as a spectacle that "disidentifies" (José Muñoz Jr.'s term to describe the strategy of recycling dominant images and structures to form a politics of resistance from within centers of patriarchal power) pervasive domination/subordination colonialist master narratives. See José Esteban Muñoz's *Disidentifications: Queers of Color and the Performance of Politics,* where he makes visible the complex interrelations of race and non-normative sexuality that inform queer Latino visual culture today.

12. In her book *Under Imperial Eyes,* Mary Louise Pratt uses the term "autoethnography," which refers to "instances in which colonized subjects undertake to represent themselves in ways which engage with the colonizer's own terms. If ethnographic texts are a means in which Europeans represent to themselves their (usually subjugated) others, autoethnographic texts are those the other construct in response to or in dialogue with the metropolitan representations" (6–7).

13. In *Narrative Discourse* Gerard Genette usefully distinguishes between the narrative presentation associated with the character who perceives, or "reflector character," and who orients the narrative perspective (189–190). For the purposes of *American Me,* the camera-narrator uses a "fixed focalization" to filter the story events.

14. See Ben Olguín's article "Tattoos, Abjection, and the Political Unconscious: Toward a Semiotics of the *Pinto* Visual Vernacular," in *Cultural Critique* (1997). Here Olguín theorizes the tattoo as counterhegemonic in its validation of the collective self and subversion of society's marking of the brown other as "illegal." According to Ben Olguín's semiotics of the *tatuaje,* the tattoo allows Chicano prisoners to "expose the distinctly racialized and inherently classist nature of the hegemonic notions of 'criminality' and 'normalcy' that inform various permutations on the War on Crime" (163). I would add, too, that the act of body piercing requires the same collective effort as killing and male-male sex in prison. All of the above are deemed illegal and require a point man in order for the event (penetration) to occur.

15. While I will continue to make references that graft the conquest narratives onto the text of *American Me,* I want to make it clear that the conquest and colonialist texts are by no means the unmediated voices of the Amerindian other. It's not so much that I want to draw an analogy between Santana, Mundo, and J.D.'s act of body piercing (tattooing) and the Amerindian male's piercing, as that I want to draw attention to the film's reproduction (and sometime subversion) of the Euro-Spaniard's original representation of the other as a body with holes open to being filled. Amerigo Vespucci writes in his *Letter II* (1502): "The men are accustomed to make *holes* in their lips and cheeks and in those *holes* they *put bones* or stones, and you must not think they are *small ones,* for most of the men have no fewer than three holes (and some seven, and even nine), in which they place stone of green and *white alabaster,* which are half a span long and *big* as Catalan plums, so that they appear something utterly *unnatural.* . . . it is a bestial thing" (emphasis mine; 32). (He repeats this description again in *Letter V* where he adds the description of how the men's "members swell to such thickness that they look ugly and misshapen" [49]). Unnatural, bestial acts of filling holes with bones and long, hard white objects smacks of something more than innocent taxonomization. It might help our reformulation of the *conquistador*/discoverer's fetishizing *phantasia* to know that in *Letter VI* Vespucci writes that New World men "were so well built that they were a beautiful thing to behold" (83). And there's more than simple mediation when the twenty-something Cortés writes in 1519 how "some pierce their ears and put very large and ugly objects in them . . . giving a most deformed appearance" (30). Objectification of the New World other? Yes. Sodomitical desire for the New World other? Absolutely.

16. José Piedra writes in "Loving Columbus" how the early New World taxonomies—islands populated sans men, Amazonas, *bestías grandisimas,* women with fish-tails, men-men eating rituals, and so on—worked to translate into reality and into cash "classical and Renaissance projections and fantasies of the existence of a world beyond the known, not to mention a Third Sex or Gender able to fulfill the full range of the Self's libidinal expectations" (243). Of the cannibalizing of the New World male, citing Hernan Pérez de Oliva's account of "estos numbrauan caribes que . . . no comían las mujeres," Piedra theorizes such descriptions as the Euro-Spaniard male's displaced desire for the exoticized male. He carefully delineates the process, writing how the Native Caribes were theorized as cannibals that ate "mostly other males for the sake of love of the ancestors and/or for the sake of hate of the neighbor. . . . Consequently they symbolically and factually recreate procreation—passing on digestively rather than genetically precious knowledge chiefly from male to male" (246).

17. In *Sodometries* Jonathan Goldberg discusses the early *conquista* texts and the Euro-Spaniards' coding of the New World other—a carry-over from representations of the Moors—not just as cannibals, but as sodomitical bodies that need to be effaced; the representations were used to justify genocide by bringing the natives as ontologically low as the animal in the European reader's mind. Goldberg cites Cortés's diary of 1519, wherein he wrote of the Veracruzianos "They are all sodomites," as well as Tomás Ortiz's 1552 account that described the Caribs not just as *cannibals* but as "sodomites" (193). Goldberg also quotes Pedro da Cieza's 1553 account of "giant" Peruvian men who were "inspired by the demon" and "practiced the unspeakable and horrible sin of sodomy" (185).

REFERENCES

Anzaldúa, Gloria. *Borderlands / La Frontera: The New Mestiza.* San Francisco: Spinsters / Aunt Lute, 1987.

Arenas, Reinaldo. *Antes que Anochezca* Barcelona: Tusquets Editores. Translated into English as *Before Night Falls* (New York: Viking, 1993).

Chatman, Seymour. *Coming to Terms: The Rhetoric of Narrative in Fiction and Film.* Ithaca, N.Y.: Cornell University Press, 1990.

De Certeau, Michel. *Heterologies: Discourse on the Other.* Minneapolis: University of Minnesota Press, 1986.

de la Mora, Sergio. "Giving It Away: *American Me* and the Defilement of Chicano Manhood." *Cine-Estudiantil '95*, March 7–11, 1995, 14.

Eng, David L. "Out Here and Over There." *Social Text* 15 (1997): 31–52.

Fregoso, Rosa Linda. *The Bronze Screen: Chicana and Chicano Film Culture.* Minneapolis: University of Minnesota Press, 1993.

Fuss, Diana. "Inside/Out." In *Inside/Out: Lesbian Theories/Gay Theories*, 1–10. New York: Routledge, 1991.

Genette, Gerard. *Narrative Discourse Revisited.* Trans. Jane E. Lewin. Ithaca, N.Y.: Cornell University Press, 1988.

Goldberg, Jonathan. *Sodometries: Renaissance Texts, Modern Sexualities.* Stanford, Calif.: Stanford University Press, 1992.

Johnson, Brian. Review. *Maclean*, March 23, 1992.

Kauffmann, Stanley. Review. *New Republic*, March 30, 1992.

Kempley, Rita. Review. *Washington Post*, March 16, 1992, F6.

Lovell, Glenn. "Hispanic Film's Brutality Stirs Praise, Outrage." *San Jose Mercury News*, February 29, 1992.

Metz, Christian. *Film Language: A Semiotics of the Cinema.* Chicago: University of Chicago Press, 1974.

Muñoz, José Esteban. *Disidentifications: Queers of Color and the Performance of Politics.* Minneapolis: University of Minnesota, 1999.

Newman, Kathleen. "Reterritorialization in Recent Chicano Cinema: Edward James Olmos's *American Me* (1992)." In *The Ethnic Eye: Latino Media Arts*, ed. Chon Noreiga and Ana Lopez. Minneapolis: University of Minnesota Press, 1996.

Olguín, Ben. "Tattoos, Abjection, and the Political Unconscious: Toward a Semiotics of the *Pinto* Visual Vernacular." *Cultural Critique* 37 (1997): 159–213.

Pérez-Torres, Rafael. *Movements in Chicano Poetry: Against Margins, Against Myths.* New York: Cambridge University Press, 1995.

Piedra, José. "Loving Columbus." In *Hispanic Issues*, vol. 19: *Amerindian Images and the Legacy of Columbus*, ed. René Jara and Nicholas Spadaccini, 230–265. Minneapolis: University of Minnesota Press, 1992.

———. "Nationalizing Sissies." In *Entiendes: Queer Readings, Hispanic Writings*, ed. Emile L. Bergmann and Paul Julian Smith, 307–409. Durham, N.C.: Duke University Press, 1995.

Pratt, Mary Louise. *Under Imperial Eyes: Travel Writing and Transculturation.* New York: Routledge, 1992.

Sedgwick, Eve. *Tendencies.* Durham, N.C.: Duke University Press, 1993.

Vespucci, Amerigo. *Letters from a New World: Amerigo Vespucci's Discovery of America.* Trans. David Jacobson. New York: Marsilo Publishers.

5 BIOPOWER, REPRODUCTION, AND THE MIGRANT WOMAN'S BODY

Jonathan Xavier Inda

> "They keep coming," a voice intones as the television ad opens with black-and-white footage of about a dozen "undocumented" immigrants running between cars at the California-Mexico border in San Ysidro. The words "Border Crossing, Interstate 5, San Diego County" are inscribed on the lower left corner of the screen. "Two million illegal immigrants in California," the voice continues. "The federal government won't stop them at the border, yet requires us to pay billions to take care of them."

THIS AD of illegal immigrants scurrying across the border, which ran as part of former governor Pete Wilson's 1994 Republican gubernatorial primary campaign, dramatizes nicely one of the most prevalent concerns of Californians during the 1990s: the "problem" of illegal immigration. The picture and the words carry the ominous message that foreigners are streaming into California to take things that properly belong to legal California residents—jobs, services, and tax dollars. As such, the ad is reflective of the highly charged political rhetoric that has developed around the issue of immigration over the past decade. It is a rhetoric in which "Third World" migrants, Mexicans in particular, have been blamed for many of the socioeconomic ills of the United States—unemployment, crime, deteriorating schools, deficiencies in social services. It is also a rhetoric in which these immigrants have been construed as posing a threat to the national unity of the nation because they are culturally different.[1] The fear seems to be that the masses of foreigners, with their plurality of languages, experiences, and histories, will soon overwhelm the dominant culture of the United States, transforming it beyond recognition. This ad, then, epitomizes the assumption, prevalent throughout the 1990s, that immigrants posed a threat to the general welfare of California and the nation.

The political effects of this sort of rhetoric have not been insignificant, for it has given rise to and legitimated numerous efforts to exclude the immigrant from the body politic (e.g., fortification of the border, denial of health care). The logic here is rather simple: since the migrant population threatens the common good, its exclusion or elimination is seen as necessary in order to guard the well-being of the nation. The repudiation of the immigrant is thus justified in the name of protecting the welfare of the social body. One way to interpret these practices of exclusion is in terms of what Michel Foucault called biopower.[2] This term describes a technology of power whose main concern is "the welfare of the population, the improvement of its condition, the increase of its wealth, longevity, health, etc." ("Governmentality": 100). The focus of biopower, in other words, is the control of the species body and its reproduction. It is a regulatory power whose highest function is to thoroughly invest in life in order to produce a healthy and vigorous population. There is an underside to biopower, however, since it is often the case that "entire populations are mobilized for the purpose of wholesale slaughter in the name of life necessity. . . . It is as managers of life and survival, of bodies and the race, that so many regimes have been able to wage so many wars, causing so many men to be killed" (*History:* 137). Simply put, then, biopower does not just foster life; it also routinely does away with it in order to preserve it. This means that the counterpart of the power to secure an individual's continued existence is the power to expose an entire population to death (or at least to multiplying its risk of death). It is thus possible under regimes of biopower to simultaneously protect life and to authorize a holocaust.

It is in this biopolitical space that I would like to situate the contemporary repudiation of the migrant in the United States. Thus the purpose of this chapter is to explore how the state, in order to fortify the health of the population, routinely aims to eliminate those influences that are deemed harmful to the biological growth of the nation. It will show how the exclusion of the immigrant—as well as his/her exposure to the risk of death—is codified as an essential and noble pursuit necessary to ensure the survival of the social body. This exclusion will be explored primarily through the state's repeated attempts to deny undocumented immigrants access to prenatal care. In other words, the paper will concentrate mainly on the body of the undocumented immigrant woman as an important terrain of struggle, particularly as it pertains to the regulation of her capacity to reproduce. In the end, the essay will suggest that these attempts to exclude the immigrant from the body politic convey the implicit message that illegal lives are expendable—that the lives of undocumented immigrants and their children are not quite worth living. We begin with a fuller discussion of Foucault's notion of biopower.

BIOPOWER AND THE VALUE OF LIFE

"For a long time," Foucault notes, "one of the characteristic privileges of sovereign power was the right to decide life and death" (*History:* 135).[3] For instance, if an external enemy sought to overthrow him, the sovereign could justly wage war, requiring his subjects to fight in defense of the state. So, without directly proffering their death, the sovereign was sanctioned to risk their life. In this case, he exercised "an indirect power over them of life and death" (135). However, if someone hazarded to rebel against him and violate his laws, the sovereign could exert a direct power over the transgressor's life, such that, as penalty, the latter could be put to death. The right to life and death, then, was somewhat dissymmetrical, falling on the side of death: "The sovereign exercised his right to life only by exercising his right to kill, or by refraining from killing; he evidenced his power over life only through the death he was capable of requiring. The right which was formulated as the 'power of life and death' was in reality the right to *take* life or *let* live" (136). As such, this type of power, Foucault observes, was wielded mainly as a mechanism of deduction, making it "essentially a right of seizure: of things, time, bodies, and ultimately life itself" (136). That is, power was fundamentally a right of appropriation—the appropriation of a portion of the wealth, labor, services, and blood of the sovereign's subjects—one that culminated in the right to seize hold of life in order to subdue it.

This power of appropriation or of deduction, Foucault suggests, is no longer the principal form of power in the West. Since the classical age, the mechanisms of power there have undergone a radical transformation. Power now works "to incite, reinforce, control, monitor, optimize, and organize the forces under it"; it is "a power bent on generating forces, making them grow, and ordering them, rather than one dedicated to impeding them, making them submit, or destroying them" (*History:* 136). Thus, in contrast to a power organized around the sovereign, modern "power would no longer be dealing simply with legal subjects over whom the ultimate dominion was death, but with living beings, and the mastery it would be able to exercise over them would be applied at the level of life itself; it was the taking charge of life, more that the threat of death, that gave power its access even to the body" (142–143). In short, political power has assigned itself the duty of managing life. It is now over life that power establishes its hold and on which it seeks to have a positive influence.

This power over life, which Foucault calls biopower, is most apparent in the emergence of "population" as an economic and political problem in the eighteenth century.[4] This "population" is not simply a collection of individual citizens. We are not dealing, as Foucault notes, with subjects, or even with a "people," but with a composite body "with its specific phenomena and its peculiar variables: birth and death rates, life expectancy, fertility, state of health, frequency of illness, patterns of diet and habitation" (*History:* 25). The "population," in other words, has its own form of order, its own energy, traits, and dispositions. The management of this "population," principally of its health, Foucault suggests, has become the primary commitment as well as the main source of legitimacy of modern forms of government:

> It's the body of society which becomes the new principle [of political organization] in the nineteenth century. It is this social body which needs to be protected, in a quasi-medical sense. In place of the rituals that served to restore the corporeal integrity of the mon-

> arch, remedies and therapeutic devices are employed such as the segregation of the sick, the monitoring of contagions, the exclusion of delinquents. ("Body/Power": 55)

The concern of government, then, is to produce a healthy and productive citizenry. Its commitment is to the protection and enhancement of the health of particular bodies in order to foster the health of the composite body of the population. This means, according to Foucault, that "biological existence" has now come to be "reflected in political existence" (*History:* 142). As such, biopower ultimately designates "what brought life and its mechanisms into the realm of explicit calculations" (143), its main overall concern being the life of the population, that is, of the species body—the body that functions as the foothold of biological processes pertaining to birth, death, health, and longevity. Simply put, the species body and the individual as a simple living being have become what are at stake in a state's political tactics, marking the politicization of life, turning politics into biopolitics and the state into a biopolitical state.

The important thing here is that the governing of bodies and the calculated management of life has supplanted the old power of death that typified sovereign power. This does not mean, however, that the right of death has altogether disappeared. Rather, it has experienced a shift, or at least, Foucault suggests, "a tendency to align itself with the exigencies of a life-administering power and to define itself accordingly" (*History:* 136). The awesome power of death "now presents itself as the counterpart of a power that exerts a positive influence on life, that endeavors to administer, optimize, and multiply it, subjecting it to precise controls and comprehensive regulations" (137). Wars, for example, are no longer conducted on behalf of the sovereign. They are waged in defense of the population. It is thus "as managers of life and survival . . . that so many regimes have been able to wage so many wars, causing so many men to be killed" (137). If genocide is an effect of modern power, this is not by virtue of the restitution of the sovereign right to kill, but because power is located and practiced at the level of life. What is at stake in war is not the existence of the sovereign, but the biological well-being of a population. The same thing could be said about the death penalty. As Foucault notes:

> Together with war, it was for a long time the other form of the right of the sword; it constituted the reply of the sovereign to those who attacked his will, his law, or his person. Those who died on the scaffold became fewer and fewer, in contrast to those who died in wars. But it was for the same reasons that the latter became more numerous and the former more and more rare. As soon as power gave itself the function of administering life, its reason for being and the logic of its exercise—and not the awakening of humanitarian feelings—made it more and more difficult to apply the death penalty. How could power exercise its highest prerogatives by putting

> people to death, when its main role was to ensure, sustain, and multiply life, to put this life in order? For such a power, execution was at the same time a limit, a scandal, and a contradiction. (138)

The only reason, at least according to Foucault, that capital punishment continues to be practiced in the modern state is that it calls attention less to the atrocity of the crime itself than to the aberrance and incorrigibility of the criminal—that is, to the danger he/she presents to society. The practice of capital punishment can thus be maintained and justified today only to the extent that its aim is to safeguard the welfare of the population. It is in order to nurture life—the life of the population—that life can be disallowed. As in the case of war, then, what is of concern here is not the existence of the sovereign but the well-being of the population. "The ancient right to *take* life or *let* live," Foucault suggests, "has [thus] been replaced by a power to *foster* life or *disallow* it to the point of death" (138). This means that while the right to life and death continues to be asymmetrical, it now falls on the side of life. It is to life that power must attend. As such, the modern state—that is, the biopolitical state—can legitimately take life only in the name of life itself.

One important result of this inclusion of man's natural life in the calculations and mechanisms of power is that it becomes possible, according to Foucault, to simultaneously protect life and authorize a holocaust. The politicization of life, in other words, necessarily implies a judgment regarding the threshold beyond which life stops being politically pertinent and can as such be eliminated without penalty. The biopolitical logic of the modern state necessitates a decision on the value or non-value of life. Every society necessarily makes a distinction between those lives that deserve to be lived and those that do not. The logic here is that the death of the other, the death of those lives unworthy of being lived, will make life in general more healthy and pure. This death does not have to be direct death (or the literal act of putting to death). It could also be indirect death: the act of exposing to death, of multiplying for some the risk of death, or simply political death, expulsion, rejection, or exclusion. In any case, the modern biopolitical state routinely aims to fortify the health of the population through the elimination of those lives that putatively harm the biological growth of the nation. Thus, when life becomes the ultimate political value, the logic of war—that one must be capable of killing to keep on living—seems to become the principle of states. The care of the health of the population is indistinguishable from the fight against (and the necessity of eliminating) the enemy.[5]

An essential characteristic of modern biopolitics, then, is the necessity of establishing a threshold in life that distinguishes what is inside from what is outside, separating those bodily interests that can be represented in the polity from those which cannot, from those adverse to the social order it embodies. This biopolitical rationality is perhaps nowhere best embodied than in the Nazi State. The basic goal of the Nazis, to put it rather simply, was to create a new, and better, social order. For them, this meant fostering the life of the species body through the preservation of racial health—that is, through the propagation of those who were considered to be of healthy German stock. This goal was perhaps most clearly articulated in a booklet of National Socialist ideology published by Otmar von Vershuer, one of the most authoritative German specialists in matters of health and eugenics: "'The new State knows no other task than the fulfillment of the conditions necessary for the preservation of the people.' These words of the Führer mean that every political act of the National Socialist state serves the life of the people. . . . We know today that the life of the people is only secured if the racial traits and hereditary health of the body of the people [*Volkskörper*] are preserved" (quoted in Agamben: 147). Pragmatically, this preservation of the health of the social body entailed not only the cultivation of the lives of those of healthy German racial stock, but also the containment, or elimination, of any unhealthy elements. It was only through the systematic selection and elimination of the unhealthy that the propagation of healthy stock could take place. It was thus that the Jews came to be designated as enemies of the social body and targeted for elimination. They were typically characterized as a diseased race, as a cancer in the body of the German Volk. One physician, for example, described Jews in the following terms: "There is a resemblance between Jews and tubercle bacilli: nearly everyone harbors tubercle bacilli, and nearly every people of the earth harbors the Jews; furthermore, an infection can only be cured with difficulty" (quoted in Proctor: 173). What the Nazis did then, according to Zygmunt Bauman, was "split human life into worthy and unworthy: the first to be lovingly cultivated and given *Lebensraum*, the other to be 'distanced', or—if the distancing proved unfeasible—exterminated" (67–68). It was in the name of the preservation of life that Nazi Germany was able to massacre millions of Jews. This makes the Nazi state the perfect embodiment of modern biopolitical rationality. For it shows that when the life of the species becomes a political issue, it becomes possible to simultaneously protect life and to authorize a holocaust.

It is not just totalitarian states, however, that operate according to biopolitical rationality. Foucault argues that the play between the affirmation of life and the right to kill (or at least to disallow life to the point of death) operates to some extent in all modern states ("Faire vivre"). The Nazi state represents only the most radical and horrific extension of a power centered on life. More generally, in the modern state, biopower works to create a wedge between the normal and the pathological, conferring aberrance on individual or collective bodies and casting certain abnormalities as dangers to the body politic. That is, it simply functions as a mechanism for distinguishing those bodily interests that can be represented in the polity from those which cannot, from those against whom society must be defended. Biopower thus implies nothing specific about what is to be done with those bodies construed as dangerous. One possibility, of course, is extermination. However, more typical of the modern state is the practice of multiplying for some the risk of death or of subjecting dangerous bodies to marginalization, expulsion, and rejection. The logic, in both cases, is the same: the exclusion and/or elimination of certain bodies secures the protection of others. Social death, as much as the literal act of putting to death, serves to safeguard the social body. So whether a modern state practices mass extermination or simply increases the risk of death for certain bodies, it is likely to be operating according to biopolitical logic.

Following from this, the rest of the paper focuses on the biopolitical rationality of the United States. In particular, it explores how certain bodies, namely immigrant bodies, are discursively construed as posing a danger to the body politic and must therefore resolutely be eliminated or excluded. In other words, it will focus on how anti-immigrant discourses construct immigrants as unsuitable participants in the body politic and thus codify their exclusion as a noble pursuit necessary to ensure the well-being and survival of the social body.

REPRODUCTION AND THE MIGRANT WOMAN'S BODY

In the United States, the best place to explore the biopolitical logic of anti-immigrant discourse is the state of California. Over the past three decades, California has witnessed a major demographic transformation, changing from predominantly white and U.S.-born to increasingly Latino and foreign-born.[6] A major symptom of this metamorphosis has been the rise of nativism, producing, particularly during the 1990s, a political and cultural climate that has been distinctly hostile toward immigrants. Much of this hostility has centered on the economic consequences of migration, that is, on the economic costs and benefits of these newcomers.[7] In 1994, for instance, Governor Pete Wilson filed a series of lawsuits against the federal government in which he sought to have California reimbursed for the cost of providing emergency health care, prison facilities, and education to illegal immigrants. The claim was that the economic and political burden of serving illegal immigrants was so great that California had been denied its sovereign right to shape its own destiny, and thus that the presence of so many illegal immigrants in the state amounted to a foreign invasion the federal government was constitutionally obligated to resist: "The massive and unlawful migration of foreign nationals . . . constitutes an invasion of the state of California against which the United States is obligated to protect California" (quoted in Weintraub: A3).[8]

What's more, in the same year, the voters of California approved Proposition 187, a grassroots initiative that sought to deny undocumented immigrants access to welfare, education, and health-care services.[9] The main premise behind the proposition was that undocumented immigrants were costing California millions of dollars a year in public services, depleting the state of scarce financial resources and precipitating a decline in the general "health" of the state: "The people of California have suffered for too long from the impact of illegal immigration, specifically in the areas of crime and from the costs of health, education and welfare for illegal aliens. The time has come to stop rewarding illegal aliens for breaking our laws. With California's budget deficits spiraling out of control, the taxpayers of this state must conserve their scarce financial resources for the benefit of citizens and legal immigrants" (Citizens for Legal Immigration: n.p.). The hope was that the denial of public benefits would reduce, if not altogether stop, the flow of undocumented immigrants, as well as force those who were already inside the state to leave the country: "Many of the hundreds of thousands of illegals who arrive every year will be discouraged from coming. Many of the more than two million illegals already here will be encouraged to leave" (ibid.). The state would thus be relieved of a major drain on its coffers, paving the way for a healthier and more prosperous California: "Prop 187 will save taxpayers billions of dollars. . . . California's public services (health, education, and welfare) won't be depleted by funding illegals. With more money available for citizens and legal residents, the quality of services will improve" (ibid.).

In general, then, undocumented immigrants have been construed as enemies who threaten the well-being of the body politic. They have been figured as hostile foreign bodies, as dangerous beings who only bring malaise to the nation. This makes it imperative for the state to control and eliminate the flow of these threatening foreigners into the social body. The nation can only be cured if the enemy is eliminated. The nation can only be healed if the body of the immigrant is expunged. The name of the game here is to preserve the health or well-being of the population. It is on behalf of the population, as a composite body with the singular state of "health," that the attempts to exclude the immigrant from the nation are justified. The idea of the "population" functions as a mechanism for distinguishing those bodily interests that can be represented in the polity from those which cannot, from those that need to be eliminated in order to preserve the health of the nation. The care and governing of the population thus becomes one with the fight against the enemy. This is the rationality of the biopolitical state. The political entity needs to eliminate its enemies in order to guard the safety of its population.

The story does not end here, however. For it is not simply that the state has attempted to expel or exclude immigrants from the body politic in the name of preserving the welfare of the population. It has done so (or made an effort to do so) in ways that have (or would have) increased the risk of death for immigrants. The state, in other words, has pursued various policy measures in which the lives of immigrants have implicitly been judged as not worthy of being lived or at least as not worthy of being lived as U.S. citizens. One such measure has been the effort to regulate the reproductive capacity of migrant women, particularly Mexicans, by denying them access to prenatal care. The rest of the paper will concentrate on this issue, that is, on the regulation of the migrant woman's body, highlighting how the life of the migrant has been deemed, in some ways, expendable.

For over a decade, under federal and California state law, undocumented women have been eligible to receive state-financed checkups, nutritional supplements, fetal monitoring, and other prenatal aid.[10] The rationale for providing this care seems to be pragmatic in nature: "Prenatal care saves money by reducing the number of sickly infants who, if born in the United States, are citizens any way" ("Cutoff of Prenatal Care": A28). All the same, critics contend that providing such assistance is unwise, for it acts as a magnet for illicit immigration (McDonnell, "Ruling Delays": A24). The scenario they paint is one in which "poor immigrant women are drawn to the United States to give birth in publicly financed county hospitals, allowing their children to be born as U.S. citizens and subsequent recipients of taxpayer supported medical care, public assistance, and education. Immigrants and their children constitute a growing underclass, draining education and medical resources in the United States" (Hondagneu-Sotelo: 173). Moreover, they argue that it is not really fair for illegal immigrants to receive free prenatal care since most citizens of California are not eligible for this benefit (McDonnell, "State Delays Ban": A29).

The most vociferous of these critics has been former governor Pete Wilson. While in office, he took it upon himself to block undocumented women from having access to prenatal care. The governor first tried to end prenatal care for undocumented immigrants in 1994, right after California voters overwhelmingly adopted Proposition 187. One of the main aims of the ballot measure was the elimination of non-emergency medical care for those in the country illegally. From the perspective of the governor, this meant, among other things, barring undocumented women from access to prenatal care. However, a federal court blocked the execution of most of the proposition, so the governor was not able to implement his plan. This failure did not seem to discourage the governor. A couple of years later, he again moved to end prenatal care for illegal immigrants. This time Governor Wilson found justification for his plan in Congress's 1996 revision of U.S. welfare law. This revision incorporated many issues formerly enunciated in Proposition 187, one of them being that states were generally prohibited from providing non-emergency aid to illegal immigrants. For Governor Wilson, this meant, as the previous time, denying women access to prenatal care. The governor's move, however, was again blocked. In March of 1998, a Los Angeles Superior Court judge issued an injunction preventing Governor Wilson from denying prenatal care to undocumented women (McDonnell, "Ruling Delays": A24). The rationale for this injunction was that while Congress did prohibit states from providing non-emergency aid to undocumented immigrants, it also guaranteed that poor immigrants, of whatever status, would retain access to publicly financed diagnosis and care of transferable diseases. Congress reasoned that to bar immigrants from such aid would have compromised the public health. For the court, the treatment and diagnosis of communicable diseases in pregnant women couldn't be disassociated from prenatal care.[11] This meant that Pete Wilson could not deny illegal immigrants prenatal care.

Governor Wilson was never able to carry out his plan. And now that there is a new governor of California,[12] providing prenatal care for immigrant women no longer seems to be an issue. But the fact that prenatal care was an issue is in and of itself highly significant. One of the main reasons most often given for the efforts to deny immigrant women access to prenatal care is that it encourages illegal immigration. But one could also argue that it is really an attempt to govern the reproduction of an undesirable population.[13] In other words, since undocumented immigrants are deemed to pose an uncontrollable threat to the nation's economic, cultural, and political health, any law that would bar them from using reproductive health services can be seen as an effort to discourage them from reproducing and thus to control their numbers, sending a "powerful message about who is worthy to add their children to the future community of citizens" (Roberts: 205). Such "population" policies demonstrate how the American nation-state seeks to regulate the reproductive capacity of unworthy segments of the general population in defense of the interests of the nation-state. These policies thus seem to be formulated and to exist in direct relation to any group's perceived value within the polity. They are designed to foster the health of the nation through the elimination or exclusion of those bodies deemed dangerous.

This effort to discourage or to prevent the propagation of unworthy segments of the population is of course not a new phenomenon in the United States. The regulation of the migrant woman's body is only the latest in a long string of policies aimed at fostering the health of the population through the elimination of the unfit. During the first half of the twentieth century, for example, the eugenics movement proffered a theory stipulating that intelligence and other character traits were genetically conditioned and thus inherited (Roberts: 212–214). This theory drove a campaign to redress America's social problems by guarding against biological degeneracy. Eugenicists thus promoted such policies as compulsory sterilization to prohibit people "likely" to produce defective offspring from reproducing.[14] Their thinking was so influential that by 1917 sixteen states had enacted involuntary sterilization laws aimed at those considered burdens on society: habitual criminals, the mentally retarded, epileptics, and various categories of the insane (Porter 170). And their influence did not stop there. It extended even to the U.S. Supreme Court. In a 1927 decision, *Buck v. Bell,* the Court upheld the constitutionality of a Virginia involuntary sterilization law. Reflecting the majority opinion, Oliver Wendell Holmes expressed the eugenicist tenor of this decision:

> It would be strange if it could not call upon those who already sap the strength of the state for these lesser sacrifices, often not felt to be such by those concerned, in order to prevent our being swamped by incompetence. It is better for all the world, if instead of waiting

> for their imbecility, society can prevent those who are manifestly unfit from continuing their kind. The principle that sustains compulsory vaccination is broad enough to cover cutting the Fallopian tubes. . . . Three generations of imbeciles is enough. (Quoted in Collins: 272)

The basic view of eugenicists, then, was that social problems were technical problems amenable to biological solutions. The control of reproduction was thus crucial to their project.[15] For it was only through regulating the propagation of the unfit that the future prosperity and security of the population could be ensured. As such, the eugenicist project can be seen as a precursor to contemporary efforts to control the reproduction of immigrants. In both cases the objective is the same: to control the reproduction of those deemed a burden to society. They are both manifestations of a politics aimed at fostering the well-being of the population.

What is going on here, then, from a biopolitical perspective, is that reproduction ceases to be a "fact of Nature" and becomes instead a social-technical object, a manageable social practice (Horn: 66). Thus, in order to ensure the health of the social body, the body of the migrant woman is turned into an object of ongoing surveillance and management. The point of these biopolitical policies is to govern the proper form of species reproduction. Here the fight against the enemy takes place on the terrain of the migrant woman's body, the aim being to eliminate the enemy through controlling its capacity to reproduce. The biopolitical rationality of the state thus takes the form of a social-technical intervention designed to transform the procreative practices of undocumented migrants. The reproduction of the immigrant has to be managed and regulated for the greater good of all.

What is also going on, implicitly, is that some lives are judged worthy of being lived while others are not. The logic of this argument goes as follows. If Wilson's plan had gone into effect and undocumented women had been denied access to prenatal care, it would have led, medical experts warned, to an increase in infant mortality, birth abnormalities, and illness (McDonnell, "Judge Upholds": A49). For example, Dr. Brian D. Johnston, speaking as president of the Los Angeles County Medical Association, noted that "cutting prenatal care for pregnant women will cause unwarranted suffering, avoidable birth complications, sicker, smaller babies and needless disability" (quoted in McDonnell, "Plan to End": A3). Similarly, Dr. Jack Lewin, speaking as executive vice president of the group, stated that the denial of prenatal care to undocumented women "will cause an epidemic of low-birth-weight babies and expectant mothers presenting late to emergency rooms" (A3). The position of such medical authorities, then, is that prenatal care is crucially important to the well-being of a pregnant woman and her child; and that, if we truly want to have a healthy society, such care should be provided irrespective of a woman's legal status. Despite the suggestions of medical experts, however, Governor Wilson maintained that limited state funds should go to legal residents and not to illegal immigrants (McDonnell, "State Delays Ban": A3). The act of denying such care, I maintain, would have been tantamount to exposing the immigrant child and mother to death, or, at least, to multiplying their risk of death. Governor Wilson thus established a fundamental division between those who must live (or whose lives must be fostered) and those who must die (or whose lives can be disallowed to the point of death). This division pivots around the legal/illegal axes, sending the message that illegal lives are expendable, that the lives of undocumented immigrant women and their children are not worth living. Such is the rationality of the biopolitical state. The sovereign right to kill appears here "as an excess of 'biopower' that does away with life in the name of securing it" (Stoler: 84). As such, the biopolitical state proposes to foster the health of the population through the elimination of those lives unworthy of being lived—those lives that putatively harm the health of the nation. It sets up a confrontation between life and death, giving credence to the idea that the elimination of the enemy will make the body politic stronger and more vigorous. In short, then, in order to nurture life, the biopolitical state must disallow it. In this case, it is the life of the migrant that becomes expendable.

It is thus in this space between life and death that it is possible to locate the present-day rejection of the migrant. The logic of anti-immigrant politics is such that it aims to fortify the health of the population through the elimination of those influences that are deemed harmful to the well-being of the nation. The exclusion of the immigrant and the control of the immigrant woman's reproduction are thus judged as necessary to ensure the survival of the social body. If this is the logic of anti-immigrant politics, then what we are dealing with is nothing other than biopower. This concept, as noted before, describes a technology of power whose main object is to foster the welfare of the population. As such, the function of biopower is to regulate the species body and its reproduction; its highest function being to invest in life through and through. However, as Jennifer Terry points out, "under the guise of health and welfare, the administrative state turns politics into biopolitics, where decisions and choices are constructed in terms of preserving life and determining benevolent destruction" (33). It is possible, then, under regimes of biopower—that is, in a biopolitical state—to simultaneously protect life and authorize a holocaust. The correlate of the power to safeguard an individual's lasting existence is the power to expose a whole population to death. This is not to suggest that the repudiation of the migrant in the United States is tantamount to a holocaust. However, the logic in both cases is the same: it is that of biopower. It is a logic that posits that in order to protect life one must disallow it to the point of death.

NOTES

1. For an in-depth analysis of this political rhetoric in Europe, see Stolcke 1–24.

2. Foucault discusses biopower most notably in *The History of Sexuality*, "Body/Power," "Governmentality," and "Faire vivre et laisser mourir."

3. For two works that influenced my interpretation of Foucault, see Agamben and Stoler.

4. The concern over "population" or the species body is actually only one pole of biopower. The other pole is centered on the body as machine. Here the body is approached as an object to be manipulated and controlled. The object is to forge a "docile body that may be subjected, used, transformed, and improved" (Foucault, *Discipline:* 198).

5. Foucault ("Faire vivre") views this fight against the enemy as a form of racism. For him, however, as Diane Nelson notes, "racism is not just the assignment of hierarchical value to a range of phenotypic expressions such as hair, skin color, and nose shape . . . Foucault sees racism instead as a grid of intelligibility, a grammar that is not necessarily about any particular group of people but about a more generalized division within a body politic. He connects racism to a pervasive sense of threat from internal enemies whose identities vacillate. Racism, understood as the constant war against these threats to the health and happiness of this body politic, promises a common good—it is not merely a negative or repressive discourse" (94).

6. In 1970 the foreign-born accounted for 8.8 percent of the population of California, while in 1995 the statewide total was 24.4 percent. As for the Latino population, the numbers went from 8 percent to 27 percent (Cleeland: A22). These demographic transformations have a lot to do with the changing nature of the U.S. economy. As industrial production has moved overseas, to take advantage of wage differentials, the traditional U.S. manufacturing base has deteriorated and been partly replaced by a downgraded manufacturing sector, one characterized by an increasing supply of poorly paid, semiskilled or unskilled production jobs. The economy has also become more service oriented. Financial and other specialized service firms have replaced manufacturing as the leading economic sectors. This new core economic base of highly specialized services has tended to polarize labor demand into high-skill and low-skill categories. The upshot of all this, then, is that these changes in the economy, particularly the creation of low-skill jobs, have created the conditions for the absorption of vast numbers of workers. For a longer exposition on these economic transformations, see Calavita, pp. 284–305.

7. A second locus of anti-immigrant sentiment, which is not dealt with here, targets the detrimental cultural consequences of immigration. This focus, which I call cultural nativism, is most visible in the current antipathy toward the use of non-English languages, much of it derived from the fear that linguistic difference will fragment the American nation. For a discussion of cultural nativism see Mirón, Inda, and Aguirre, pp. 659–681.

8. The suit based was based on Article IV, Section 4, of the Constitution, which states: "The United States shall guarantee to every state in this union a republican form of government, and shall protect each of them against invasion . . . " (quoted in Weintraub: A3).

9. Although the measure was overwhelmingly approved (59 percent to 41 percent) by the voters of California, it never went into effect. Its main provisions were declared unconstitutional.

10. For a more thorough legislative history, see California Primary Care Association.

11. What you have here, really, are two competing biopolitical projects. They both aim to foster the health of the population. However, they define the population differently. For one the population includes illegal immigrants; for the other it does not.

12. A new governor, Gray Davis, was elected in November of 1998.

13. For a more general treatment of population policies aimed at poor women and women of color, see Collins, pp. 266–282.

14. Eugenicists also urged for restrictions on the immigration of inferior races (e.g., Jews, Italians) as a means of protecting the nation from genetic contamination (Roberts: 212–213).

15. In *The History of Sexuality,* Foucault notes that, as the practice of modern gov-

ernment came to center upon population as its object, reproduction, as well as sexual conduct more generally, became an important target of management and intervention. It was important for the state to administer the reproduction of individuals, for this could affect the health and future prosperity, eugenics, and security of the population.

WORKS CITED

Agamben, Giorgio. *Homo Sacer: Sovereign Power and Bare Life.* Stanford, Calif.: Stanford University Press, 1998.

Bauman, Zygmunt. *Modernity and the Holocaust.* Ithaca, N.Y.: Cornell University Press, 1989.

Calavita, Kitty. "The New Politics of Immigration: 'Balanced-budget Conservatism' and the Symbolism of Proposition 187." *Social Problems* 43, no. 3 (1996): 284–305.

California Primary Care Association. *Position Statement on Prenatal Care Funding for Non-Citizens.* Retrieved January 13, 1999, from the World Wide Web: http://www.cpca.org/prenatalpos.htm.

Citizens for Legal Immigration/Save Our State. *Proposition 187: The "Save Our State" Initiative: The Questions and the Answers.* Orange Country, Calif.: Citizens for Legal Immigration/Save Our State, n.d.

Cleeland, Nancy. "Making Santa Ana Home." *Los Angeles Times,* August 4, 1997, A1+.

Collins, Patricia Hill. "Will the 'Real' Mother Please Stand Up? The Logic of Eugenics and American National Family Planning." In *Revisioning Women, Health, and Healing: Feminist, Cultural, and Technoscience Perspectives,* ed. Adele E. Clarke and Virginia L. Olesen, 266–282. New York and London: Routledge, 1999.

"Cutoff of Prenatal Care for Illegal Immigrants Allowed." *Los Angeles Times,* November 13, 1994, A28.

Foucault, Michel. *Discipline and Punish: The Birth of the Prison.* New York: Vintage Books, 1979.

——. *The History of Sexuality. Volume I: An Introduction.* New York: Vintage Books, 1980.

——. "Body/Power." In *Power/Knowledge: Selected Interviews and Other Writings, 1972–1979,* ed. Colin Gordon, 55–62. New York: Pantheon Books, 1980.

——. "Governmentality." In *The Foucault Effect: Studies in Governmentality,* ed. Graham Burchell, Colin Gordon, and Peter Miller, 87–104. London: Harvester/Wheatsheaf, 1991.

——. "Faire vivre et laisser mourir: La naissance du racisme." *Les temps modernes* 46 (1991): 37–61.

Hondagneu-Sotelo, Pierrette. "Women and Children First: New Directions in Anti-Immigrant Politics." *Socialist Review* 25, no. 1 (1995): 169–190.

Horn, David G. *Social Bodies: Science, Reproduction, and Italian Modernity.* Princeton, N.J.: Princeton University Press, 1994.

McDonnell, Patrick J. "Plan to End Funding for Prenatal Care Is Assailed." *Los Angeles Times,* October 17, 1996, A3+.

——. "State Delays Ban on Prenatal Care for Immigrants." *Los Angeles Times,* July 10, 1997, A3+.

——. "Judge Upholds Wilson Ban on Prenatal Care." *Los Angeles Times,* December 18, 1997, A3+.

——. "Ruling Delays Prenatal Care Ban Decision." *Los Angeles Times,* June 12, 1998, A3+.

Mirón, Louis F., Jonathan Xavier Inda, and JoAnne K. Aguirre. "Transnational Migrants, Cultural Citizenship, and the Politics of Language in California." *Educational Policy* 12, no. 6 (1998): 659–681.

Nelson, Diane M. *A Finger in the Wound: Body Politics in Quincentennial Guatemala.* Berkeley: University of California Press, 1999.

Porter, Dorothy. *Health, Civilization, and the State: A History of Public Health from Ancient to Modern Times.* London: Routledge, 1999.
Proctor, Robert N. "The Destruction of 'Lives Not Worth Living.'" In *Deviant Bodies: Critical Perspectives on Difference in Science and Popular Culture,* ed. Jennifer Terry and Jacqueline Urla, 170–196. Bloomington: Indiana University Press, 1995.
Roberts, Dorothy E. "Who May Give Birth to Citizens? Reproduction, Eugenics, and Immigration." In *Immigrants Out! The New Nativism and the Anti-Immigrant Impulse in the United States,* ed. Juan F. Perea, 205–219. New York: New York University Press, 1997.
Schwartz, Stacey M. "Beaten Before They Are Born: Immigrants, Their Children, and a Right to Prenatal Care." *Annual Survey of American Law* 3 (1997): 695–730.
Stolcke, Verena. "Talking Cure: New Boundaries, New Rhetorics of Exclusion in Europe." *Current Anthropology* 36, no. 1 (1995): 1–24.
Stoler, Laura Ann. *Race and the Education of Desire: Foucault's History of Sexuality and the Colonial Order of Things.* Durham, N.C.: Duke University Press, 1995.
Terry, Jennifer. "Medical Surveillance of Women as Reproducers." *Socialist Review* 19, no. 2 (1989): 13–43.
Weintraub, Daniel M. "Wilson Sues U.S. over Immigrants' 'Invasion.'" *Los Angeles Times,* September 23, 1994, A3+.

6 ANZALDÚA'S *FRONTERA*: INSCRIBING GYNETICS

Norma Alarcón

THE INSCRIPTION OF THE SUBJECT

In our time the very categorical and/or conceptual frameworks through which we explicitly or implicitly perceive our sociopolitical realities and our own subjective (private) contextual insertion are very much in question. There is a desire to construct our own (women of color) epistemologies and ontologies; and to obtain the interpretive agency with which to make claims to our own critical theory. Theoretically infused writing practices as those found in anthologies such as *This Bridge Called My Back: Writings by Radical Women of Color*, edited by Cherrie Moraga and Gloria Anzaldúa (1981); *All the Women Are White, All the Blacks Are Men, but Some of Us Are Brave*, edited by Gloria Hull, Patricia Bell Scott and Barbara Smith (1982); and *Making Face, Making Soul / Haciendo Caras*, edited by Gloria Anzaldúa (1990), are salient testaments to that desire for inscription in a different register—the register of women of color.

The self that writes combines a polyvalent consciousness of "the writer as historical subject (who writes? and in what context?), but also writing itself as located at the intersection of subject and history—a literary and sociological practice that involves the possible knowledge (linguistical and ideological) of itself as such. . . . " Self-inscriptions, as focal point of cultural consciousness and social change . . . weave into language the complex relations of a subject caught between the contradictory dilemmas of race, gender, ethnicity, sexualities, and class, transition between orality and literacy and the "practice of literature as the very place where social alienation is thwarted differently according to each specific context" (Trinh, 1990, 245).

Self-inscription as "focal point of cultural consciousness and social change" is as vexed a practice for the more "organic/specific" intellectual, as it is for the "academic/specific" intellectual trained in institutions whose business is often to continue to reproduce his hegemonic hold on cognitive charting and its (political) distribution in the academy itself. As a result, it should be no surprise that critics of color, in a different context than that of *Bridge* and thus differently articulated, nevertheless critique through their exclusion, their absence or displacement in the theoretical production and positions taken by Euroamerican feminists and African Americanists: "The black woman as critic, and more broadly as the locus where gender-, class-, and race-based oppression intersect, is often invoked when Anglo-American feminists and male Afro-Americanists begin to rematerialize their discourse" (Smith, 1989, 44). Thus cultural/national dislocations also produce cognitive ones as the models which assume dominance increasingly reify their discourse through the use of non-revised theories thus resembling more and more so-called "androcentric criticisms." In other words, Smith says, "when historical specificity is denied or remains implicit, all the women are presumed white, all the blacks male. The move to include black women as historical presences and as speaking subjects in critical discourse may well then be used as a defense against charges of racial hegemony on the part of white women and sexist hegemony on the part of black males" (Smith, 44–45). Thus the "black woman" appears as "historicizing presence," which is to say that as the critical gaze becomes more distanced from itself as speaker it looks to "black women" as the objective difference that historicizes the text in the present, signaling the degree to which such theorists have ambiguously and ambivalently assumed the position of Same/I as mediated by current critical theories. In this circuitous manner, the critical eye/I claims Same/Not Same, an inescapability that itself is in need of elaboration through the narratives that incorporate the historical production of differences for the purpose of exclusion, repression, and oppression. The inscription of the subject takes place in a polyvalent historical and ideological context that demands larger frames of intelligibility than that of a self/other duality.

Insofar as the critical discourses of Euroamerican feminists transform white patriarchal thought via the critical infusion of gender and sexuality, and racialized men challenge a white supremacist patriarchy via the critical infusion of race, women of color who are minimally intersected by these are excluded from what become accepted critical discourses in institutions. Though it is no small critical achievement to transform conceptual frames of intelligibility through the inclusion of a culturally produced category of difference, the fact remains that women of color by our mere existence and self-inscription continue to question those critical hermeneutics that silence the very possibility of another critical practice that does not foreclose inclusion or at least reveal awareness of the exclusions that make the construction of our work possible. The work of women of color emerges through the critical and material gap produced by multiple exclusions, in the silences of the text which further may implicitly suggest inclusion such that we *appear* to be working together in opposition to the "Name of the Father and the Place of the Law." Are we?

Smith goes on to affirm that as black feminist theorists emerge they challenge "the conceptualizations of literary study and concern themselves increasingly with the effect of race, class, and gender on the practice of literary criticism" (46–47). My intention here is not so much to produce a "literary criticism" for Chicanas, nor do I want to be limited by the reach of what are perceived as "literary texts." I want to be able to hybridize the textual field so that what is at stake is not so much our inclusion or exclusion in literary/textual genealogies and the modes of their production, which have a limited, though important critical reach, but to come to terms with the formation and displacement of subjects, as writers/critics/chroniclers of the nation, and the possibility that we have continued to recodify a family romance, an oedipal drama in which the woman of color in the Américas has no "designated" place. That is, she is elsewhere. She is simultaneously presence/absence in the configurations of the nation-state and its narrative representation. Moreover, the moment she emerges as a "speaking subject in process" the heretofore triadic manner in which the modern world has largely taken shape becomes endlessly heterogeneous and ruptures the "oedipal family romance" that is historically marked white in the United States. That is, the underlying structure of the social and cultural forms of the organization of Western societies, which further have been superimposed through administrative systems of domination—political, cultural and theoretical; and which subsequent counter nation-making narratives have adapted, is, in the Americas, disrupted by the voice of writers/critics of color such as Chicanas, so that we must "make familia from scratch."

In an earlier essay "Chicana Feminisms: In the Track of the Native Woman" (1990), I appropriated as metonym and metaphor for the referent/figure of the Chicana, the notion of the "differend" from Lyotard which he defines as "a case of conflict, between (at least) two parties that cannot be equitably resolved for lack of rule of judgment applicable to both arguments. One side's legitimacy does not imply the other's lack of legitimacy." In part her conflictive and conflicted position emerges, as Smith affirms, when the oppositional discourses of "White" Women and "Black" Men vie for her "difference" as historical materialization and/or a shifting deconstructive maneuver of Patriarchy, "The name of the Father and the place of the Law." Yet one must keep in mind that Lyotard's disquisition on the term doesn't negotiate well the transitions between textual representation and political/juridical representation. As Fraser has noted, "There is no place in Lyotard's universe for critique of pervasive axes of stratification, for critique of broad-based relations of dominance and subordination along lines like gender, race and class" (Fraser, 1989, 23). Relations of dominance and subordination arise out of the political economy and the ways in which the nation has generated its own self-representation in order to harness its population towards its own self-projection on behalf of the elite; as such the formation of political economies in tandem with the making of nations provides the locations from which historical material specificity arises generating its own discourses which philosophically may or may not coincide with theories of textual representation which may be held hostage through a discipline. The shift from theories of symbolic self-representation to juridical and phenomenological ones is not seamless, indeed the interstice, discontinuity, and gap is precisely a site of textual production—the historical and ideological moment in which the subject inscribes herself contextually. In other words the located historical writing subject emerges into conflictive discourses generated by theories of representation, whether it be juridical or textual/symbolic. Each is rule-governed by different presuppositions, and a Chicana may have better fortunes at representing herself or being represented textually than legally as a Chicana. That is the juridical text is generated by the ruling elite who have access to the state apparati through which the political economy is shaped and jurisprudence is engendered, while representation in the cultural text may include representations generated by herself. However, insofar as the latter are, as it were, "marginalia" they not only exist in the interstices, they are produced from the interstices. She, akin to Anzaldúa's "Shadow Beast," sends us in as "Stand-ins," reinforcing and ensuring the interstitiality of a differend, as the very nonsite from which critique is possible. Her migratory status which deprives her of the "protection" of "Home," whether it be a stable town or a nation-state, generates an "acoherent" though cogent discourse that is our task to revise and inscribe.

It is, I believe, in the spirit of the above remarks which are as much produced by my reading of Gloria Anzaldúa as hers are produced by her "hunger of memory," and for a coming into "being" which Anzaldúa understands to be both the truth and a fiction. A truth as the "Shadow Beast" who is continually complicit with and resistant to the stand-in, conscious will, and who "threatens the sovereignty" of conscious rulership (Anzaldúa, 16). The "Shadow Beast," ultimately, undermines a monological self-representation, because it kicks out the constraints and "bolts" "at the least hint of limitations" (Anzaldúa, 16).

INSCRIBING GYNETICS

Gloria Anzaldúa is a self-named Chicana from Hargill, Texas, a rural town in what is known as El Valle, the Valley. It is an agricultural area notorious for the mistreatment of people of Mexican descent, African Americans, and displaced indigenous peoples. Indeed, many of the narratives that emerge from that area tell of the conflictive and violent relations in the forging of an anglicized Texas out of the Texas-Coahuila territory of New Spain; as well as of the eventual production of the geopolitical border between Mexico and the United States. These borderlands are spaces where, as a result of expansionary wars, colonization, juridico-immigratory policing, coyote exploitation of emigrés and group-vigilantes, formations of violence are continuously in the making. These have been taking place, as misogynist and racialized confrontations, at least since the Spanish began to settle Mexico's (New Spain) "northern" frontier of what is now the incompletely Angloamericanized Southwest. Subsequently, and especially after the end of the Mexican-American War in 1848, these formations of violence have been often dichotomized into Mexican/American which actually have the effect of muting the presence of indigenous peoples yet setting "the context for the formation of 'races' . . . " (Montejano, 1987, 309).

Consequently, the modes of autohistoricization in and of the borderlands often emphasize or begin with accounts of violent racialized collisions. It is not surprising, then, that Anzaldúa should refer to the current US/Mexican borderline as an "open wound" from Brownsville to San Diego, from Tijuana to Matamoros where the former are considerably richer than the latter and the geopolitical line itself artificially divides into a two-class/culture system; that is, the configuration of the political economy has the "third" world rub against the "first." Though the linguistic and culture systems on the border are highly fluid in their dispersal, the geopolitical lines tend to become univocal, i.e., "mexican" and "anglo."

Of Hargill, Texas and Hidalgo County and environs Gloria Anzaldúa says, "This land has survived possession and ill-use by five powers: Spain, Mexico, the Republic of Texas, the United States, the Confederacy, and the U.S. again. It has survived Anglo-Mexican blood feuds, lynchings, burnings, rapes, pillage" (Anzaldúa, 1987, 90). Hidalgo is the "most poverty stricken county in the nation as well as the largest home base (along with Imperial Valley in California) for migrant farmworkers." She continues, "It was here that I was born and raised. I am amazed that both it and I have survived" (Anzaldúa, 98).

Through this geographic space, then, people displaced by a territorialized political economy, whose juridical centers of power are elsewhere, in this case Mexico, D.F. and Washington, D.C., attempt to reduce the level of material dispossession through the production of both counter- and disidentificatory discourses. That is, the land is repossessed in Imaginary terms, both in the Lacanian and Althusserian sense. I shall return below to a more elaborate discussion of this proposition, which I will further also characterize as dialogically paradigmatic and syntagmatic respectively, yielding a highly creative heteroglossia.

However, before turning to Anzaldúa's attempt to repossess the borderlands in polyvalent modes, let's quickly review one area of counter-identificatory or oppositional discursive productions which are based on a self/other dualistic frame of intelligibility. Thus, for example, Américo Paredes and now his follower José E. Limón claim El Valle as the site where the Corrido originated. That is, in the Américas in the Valley of a landmass now named Texas a completely "new" genre emerged, the corrido. As such Limón strategically moves the emergence towards a disengagement from claims of the corrido's origins in the Spanish romance—Spain's own border ballads. The Paredes-Limón move could be contextualized as a racialized-class-culture-based one, where "people" of Mexican descent mediate their opposition to Anglos via the corrido. The trans(form)ation and trans(figure)ation in raced class-crossing remains unexplored (Limón, 1992, chap. 1). That is, the metamorphoses of the Spanish ballad form are induced by the emergence of an oppositional hero in the U.S.-Mexico border whose raced-class position is substantially different from Spanish ballad heroes who are often members of the aristocracy. Limón's strategy is in contradiction to that of María Herrera-Sobek's in her book *The Mexican Corrido: A Feminist Analysis* where she aligns the corrido with the Peninsular origins theory where border ballads also emerged in the making of Spain. Herrera-Sobek's lack of desire to disengage the formal origins from Spain in its Spanish language form and relocalize them in Texas could be a function of an implicit feminist position; the representation of women, be it in the romance or the corrido, reenacts a specularly Manichean or romantic scenario in patriarchal tableaus. Why claim a "new" genre, when what we have is a "new" dispossessed figure with claims to becoming a hero for "his" people in a different formation—people of Mexican descent, Chicanos.

The point of my analysis, however, is to call attention to the need to "repossess" the land, especially in cultural nationalist narratives, through scenarios of "origins" that emerge in the selfsame territory, be it at the literary, legendary, historical, ideological, critical or theoretical level—producing in material and imaginary terms "authentic" and "inauthentic," "legal" and "illegal" subjects. That is the drive to territorialize/authenticate/legalize and deterritorialize/deauthenticate/delegalize is ever present, thus constantly producing "(il)legal"/(non)citizen subjects both in political and symbolic representations in a geographical area where looks and dress have become increasingly telling of one's (un)documented status (Nathan, 1991). It should be no surprise then, that the Corrido in the borderlands makes a paradigmatic oppositional hero of the persecuted in the figuration of the unjustly Outlaw(ed), the unjustly (un)documented, in Gloria's terms, Queers.

Thus, also, in Anzaldúa's terms the convergence of claims to proper ownership of the land "has created a shock culture, a border culture, a third country, a closed country" (Anzaldúa, 11) where the "detribalized" and dispossessed population is not only comprised of "females, . . . homosexuals of all races, the darkskinned, the outcast, the persecuted, the marginalized, the foreign" (Anzaldúa, 38), but is also possessed of the "faculty," a "sensing," in short, a different consciousness which as we shall see is represented by the formulation of the consciousness of the "new mestiza," a reconceptualized feminist consciousness that draws on cultural and biological miscegenation.

If, however, Gregorio Cortés becomes a paradigmatic oppositional corrido figure of Texas-Mexican ethno-nationalism, given new energy after the publication of Paredes' *With His Pistol in His Hand* (1958), Gloria Anzaldúa crosscuts masculine-coded "Tex-Mex" nationalism through a configuration of a borderland "Third Country" as a polyvocal rather than univocal Imaginary and Symbolic. She says, "If going home is denied me then I will have to stand and claim my space, making a new culture—*una cultura mestiza*—with my own lumber, my own bricks and mortar and my own feminist architecture" (Anzaldúa, 22). To the extent that she wavers in her desire for reterritorialization à la Gregorio Cortés' oppositional paradigm, the "third country" becomes a "closed country," bounded; to the extent that she wants to undercut the "Man of Reason," the unified sovereign subject of philosophy, she constructs a "crossroads of the self," a *mestiza consciousness.* Anzaldúa's conceptualization, of the *mestiza* as a produced vector of multiple culture transfers and transitions, resonates simultaneously with Jameson's version of the Lacanian pre-individualistic "structural crossroads." That is, "in frequent shifts of the subject from one fixed position to another, in a kind of optional multiplicity of insertions of the subject into a relatively fixed Symbolic Order" (Jameson, 1991, 354). It has resonance with Cornelius Castoriadis' version as well: "The subject in question is . . . not the abstract moment of philosophical subjectivity; it is the actual subject traversed through and through by the world and by others. . . . It is the active and lucid agency that constantly reorganizes its contents, through the help of these same contents, that produces by means of a material and in relation to needs and ideas, all of which are themselves mixtures of what it has already found there before it and what it has produced itself" (Castoriadis, 1987, 106). Notwithstanding the different locations of each theorist, Anzaldúa, Jameson, and Castoriadis, the resonance is inescapable (as is the resonance with Trinh Minh-ha, cited at the beginning of this essay).

That transversal simultaneity is that one where the speaking subject in process is both traversed "by the world and by others" and takes hold so as to exercise that "lucid agency that constantly reorganizes . . . contents" and works in what the subject has produced herself. Now, the relatively fixed Symbolic Order that Anzaldúa's text crosscuts is differently reorganized as Anzaldúa shifts the targets of engagement. It is now cutting across eurohegemonic representations of Woman, now Freudian/Lacanian psychoanalysis ("I know things older than Freud" [Anzaldúa, 26]), through Jungian psychoanthropology, and the rationality of the sovereign subject as she in non-linear and non-developmental ways shifts the "names" of her resistant subject positions—Snake Woman, La Chingada, Tlazolteotl, Coatlicue, Cihuacoatl, Tonantsi, Guadalupe, La Llorona. . . . The polyvalent name-insertions in *Borderlands* is a rewriting of the feminine, a feminist reinscription of gynetics. Of such revisionary tactics, Drucilla Cornell says, in another context, that they work "in affirmation, as a positioning, as a performance, rather than of Woman as a description of reality" (Cornell, 1992). Since the category of Woman in the case of Chicanas/Latinas and other women of color has not been fully mapped, nor rewritten across culture-classes, the multiple-writing, multiple-naming gesture must be carried out given the absence of any shared textualization. Thus, a text such as Anzaldúa's is the racialized "ethnic" performance of an implicitly tangential Derridean deconstructive gesture which "must, by means of a double gesture, a double science, a double writing, practice an *overturning* of the classical opposition *and* a general *displacement* of the system" (Derrida, 1982, 329; his italics). That is, through the textual production of, and the speaking position of, a "*mestiza consciousness,*" and the recuperation and recodification of the multiple names of "Woman,"

Anzaldúa deconstructs patriarchal ethnonational oppositional consciousness on the one hand, and its doublet, "the Man of Reason." An oppositional consciousness, which as stated earlier, is given shape through the dualism of self (raced male subject) and other (white male subject).

Insofar as Anzaldúa implicitly recognizes the power of the nation-state to produce "political subjects" who are now legal, now illegal, deprived of citizenship, she opts for "ethnonationalism" and reterritorialization in the guise of a "closed/third country." While she rejects a masculinist ethnonationalism that would exclude the Queer, she does not totally discard a "neonationalism" (i.e., the "closed/third" country) for the reappropriated borderlands, Aztlán. However, it is now open to all of the excluded, not just Chicanos, but all Queers. That is the formation of a newer imaginary community in Aztlán would displace the ideology of the "holy family"/"family romance" still prevalent in El Valle and elsewhere in the Southwest which makes it possible for many to turn away from confronting other social formations of violence.

The imaginary utopic community reconfirms from a different angle Liisa Malkki's (1992) claim that our confrontation with displacement and the desire for "home" brings into the field of vision "the sedentarist metaphysic embedded in the national order of things" (31). That is, the counterdiscursive construction of an alternate utopic imagined community reproduces the "sedentarist metaphysic" in (re)territorialization. Malkki continues, "sedentarist assumptions about attachment to place lead us to define displacement not as a fact about sociopolitical content, but rather as an inner, pathological condition of the displaced" (32–33). Anzaldúa has clear recognition of this in the very concept of a "*mestiza consciousness*" as well as in her privileging of the notion of migratoriness, the multiplicity of our names, and the reclamation of the borderlands in feminist terms that risk the "pathological condition" by representing the non-linearity and the break with a developmental view of self-inscription: "We can no longer blame you nor disown the white parts, the male parts, the pathological parts, the queer parts, the vulnerable parts. Here we are weaponless with open arms, with only our magic. Let's try it our way, the mestiza way, the Chicana way, the woman way" (Anzaldúa, 88). Indeed the hunger for wholeness—el sentirse completa—guides the chronicles, and that hunger is that same desire that brings into view both the migratoriness of the population and the reappropriation of "Home." That is, in the Américas today, the processes of sociopolitical empire and nation-making displacements over a 500-year history are such that the notion of "Home" is as mobile as the populations, a "home" without juridically nationalized geopolitical territory.

THE "SHADOW BEAST" MOVES US ON

The trope of the "Shadow Beast" in the work of Gloria Anzaldúa functions simultaneously as a trope of a recodified Lacanian unconscious, "as the discourse of the Other" and as an Althusserian Imaginary through which the real is grasped and represented (Lacan, 1977; Althusser, 1971). That is the "Shadow Beast" functions as the "native" women of the Américas, as a sign of savagery—the feminine as a sign of chaos. The speaking subject as stand-in for the "native" woman is already spoken for through the multiple discourses of the Other, as both an unconscious and an ideology. Thus, the question becomes what happens if the subject speaks through both simultaneously, and implicitly grasping her deconstruction of such discursive structures, proposes the New Consciousness: "This almost finished product seems an assemblage, a montage, a beaded work with several leitmotifs and with a central core, now appearing, now disappearing in a crazy dance" (Anzaldúa, 66). "It is this learning to live with *la coatlicue* that transforms living in the borderlands from a nightmare into a numinous experience. It is always a path/state to something else" (Anzaldúa, 73).

The Lacanian linguistic unconscious sets in motion a triangulated paradigmatic tale of mother/daughter/lesbic lover. The Althusserian Imaginary, on the other hand, sets in motion syntagmatic conjunctions of experience, language, folklore, history, Jungian psychoanthropology, and political economy. Some of these are authorized by "academic" type footnotes, that go so far as to appeal to the reader for the authorizing sources that will "legitimate" the statement. Some of these conjunctions in effect link together multiple ideologies of racist misogyny as it pertains to indian/mestizas. Simultaneously the Shadow Beast is metonymically articulated with Snake Woman, Coatlicue, Guadalupe, La Chingada, et al. and concatenated into a symbolic metaphor through which more figures are generated to produce the axial paradigm—the totalizing repression of the lesboerotic in the fabulation of the nation-state. The chronicle effect, however, is primarily produced through the syntagmatic movement of a collective text one may call "panmexican," yet relocated to the borderlands, thus making the whole of it a Chicano narrative. The indigenous terms and figurations have filtered through the Spanish-language cultural text, the code switching reveals the fissures and hybridity of the various incomplete imperialist/neocolonial projects. The terms and figurations preserved through the oral traditions and/or folktalk/streettalk coexist uneasily with "straight/talk," i.e., Standard Spanish and Standard English, all of which coexists uneasily with scholarly citations. The very "Symbolic Order" that "unifies" in Anzaldúa's text, the production, organization, and inscription of *mestiza consciousness* is granted the task of deconstruction of other symbolic structures.

In short, then, Coatlicue (or almost any of her metonymically related sisters) represents the non(pre)-oedipal (in this case non[pre]-Columbian) mother, who displaces and/or coexists in perennial interrogation of the "Phallic Mother," the one complicitous in the Freudian "family romance." Coatlicue is revised and released as non(pre)-oedipal and non-Phallic Mother: "And someone in me takes matters into our own hands, and eventually, takes dominion over serpents—over my own body, my sexual activity, my soul, my mind, my weaknesses and strength. Mine. Ours. Not the heterosexual white man's or the colored man's or the state's or the culture's or the religion's or the parents'—just ours, mine. . . . And suddenly I feel everything rushing to a center, a nucleus. All the lost pieces of myself coming flying from the deserts and the mountains and the valleys, magnetized toward that center. Completa" (Anzaldúa, 51).

Anzaldúa resituates Coatlicue through the process of the dreamwork, conjures her from non-conscious memory, through the serpentine folklore of her youth. The desire to center, to originate, to fuse with the feminine/maternal/lover in the safety of an Imaginary "third country," the borderlands disidentified from the actual site where the nation-state draws the juridical line, where formations of violence play themselves throughout miles on either side of the line: "she leaves the familiar and safe homeground to venture into the unknown and possibly dangerous terrain. This is her home / this thin edge of / barbwire" (Anzaldúa, 13). The sojourner is as un-documented as some maquila workers in southern California. In this fashion the syntagmatic narratives, as an effect in profound structural complicity with ideologies of the nonrational "Shadow Beast," contribute to the discursive structuration of the speaking subject who links them to figures (like Coatlicue) of paradigmatic symbolicity recodified for ethical and political intent in our time, engaged in the search, in Anzaldúa's vocabulary, for the "third space." Anzaldúa destabilizes our reading practices as autobiographical anecdotes, anthropology, ideology, legend, history and "Freud" are woven together and fused for the recuperation which will not go unrecognized this time around. In a sense reconstitution of completeness for the subject is a reweaving of the subject through "interdisciplinary" thinking, or its inverse "disciplinary" thinking has produced a fragmentation of the most excluded subject in the Symbolic Order. The (im)possibility that Anzaldúa presents is the desire for wholeness or is it a totalization for Queers?

When Anzaldúa says she knows "things older than Freud," notwithstanding the whispering effect of such a brief phrase, she is, I think, announcing her plan to re(dis)cover what his system, and in Lacanian terms the patronymic legal system, displaces. This is so especially with reference to the oedipal/family-romance drama. The Freudian/Lacanian systems are contiguous to rationality, the "Man of Reason," the subject-conscious-of-itself-as-subject, insofar as such a subject is its point of their departure (Lacan, 1977). Thus the system that displaces the Maternal Law, substitutes it with the concept of the "unconscious" where the so-called "primal repression" is stored so that consciousness and rationality may be privileged especially as the constituted point of departure for the discovery of the "unconscious," further it constitutes itself as the science-making project displacing what will thereafter be known as mythological systems, that is the "unconscious-as-the-discourse-of-the-Other"'s multiple systems of signification, to which the maternal/feminine is also imperfectly vanished. In a sense Anzaldúa's eccentricity—effected through non-Western folk/myth tropes and practices as recent as yesterday in historical terms, through the testimonies textually conserved after the conquest, and more recently excavated in 1968 by workmen repairing Mexico City's metro—constructs a tale which is feminist in intent. It is feminist insofar as through the tropic displacement of another system she re(dis)covers the mother and gives birth to herself as inscriber/speaker of/for *mestiza consciousness.* In Julia Kristeva's (1980) words, "Such an excursion to the limits of primal regression can be phantasmatically experienced as a 'woman-mother'." However it is not as a "woman-mother" that Anzaldúa's narrator actualizes the lesboerotic "visitation" of Coatlicue but as daughter and "queer." Kristeva gives us a sanitized "homosexual facet of motherhood" as woman becomes a mother to recollect her own union with her mother. Though in her early work Kristeva posited the semiotic "as the disruptive power of the feminine that could not be known and thus fully captured by the masculine symbolic" . . . she has "turned away from any attempt to write the repressed maternal or the maternal body as a counterforce to the Law of the Father" (Cornell, 1992, 7). We are left instead with a theorization of the "maternal function" in the established hierarchy of the masculine symbolic (Cornell, 7). Anzaldúa's narrator, however, represents the fusion without the mediation of the maternal facet itself. In Kristeva's text the "sanitization" takes place on the plane of preserving rather than disrupting the Freudian/Lacanian oedipal/ family-romance systems, not to mention the triadic Christian configuration (Kristeva, 1980, 239).

Anzaldúa's rewriting of the feminine through the polyvalent Shadow Beast is an attempt to reinscribe what has been lost on the one hand through colonization—she says, "Let's root ourselves in the mythological soil and soul of this continent" (68), and on the other, to reinscribe it as the contemporaneous codification of a "primary metaphorization" as Irigaray has posited—the repressed feminine in the Symbolic Order of the Name of the Father and the Place of the Law as expressed in the Lacanian rearticulation of Freud and the Western metaphysic (Butler, 1990). According to Irigaray the psychic organization for women under patriarchy is fragmented and scattered so that this is also experienced as dismemberment of the body, that is "the nonsymbolization" of her desire for origin, of her relationship to her mother, and of her libido, acts as a constant to polymorphic regressions [due] to "too few figurations, images of representations by which to represent herself" (Irigaray, 1985, 71). I am not citing Irigaray so that her work can be used as a medium for diagnostic exercises of Anzaldúa's work as "polymorphic regressions." On another plane of interpretation this could be understood as a representation symptomatic of the histories of dismemberment and scattering which have their own polyvalence in the present for Chicanas. Anzaldúa's work is simultaneously a complicity with, a resistance to, and a disruption of Western psychoanalysis through systems of signification drastically different from those of Irigaray herself, for example. Yet the simultaneity of conjunctures is constitutive of Anzaldúa's text itself. Indeed what Irigaray schematizes as description is the multiple ways in which the "oedipal/family-romance," whatever language-form it takes, makes women sick even as it tries to inscribe their resistance as illness already. The struggle for representation is not an inversion per se; rather the struggle to heal through rewriting and retextualization yields a borrowing of signifiers from diverse potentially monological discourses as Anzaldúa does in an effort to push towards the production of another signifying system that not only heals through remembering the paradigmatic narratives that recover iconographic figures, memory and history, but also rewrites and codifies the heterogeneity of the present. The desire is not so much a counterdiscourse as that for a disidentificatory one that swerves away and begins the laborious construction of a new lexicon and grammars. Anzaldúa weaves self-inscriptions of mother/daughter/lover which if unsymbolized as "primary metaphorization" of desire will hinder "women from having an identity in the symbolic order that is distinct from the maternal function and thus prevents them [us] from constituting any real threat to the order of Western metaphysics" (Irigaray, 71) or, if you will, the national/ethnonational "family romance." Anzaldúa is engaged in the recuperation and rewriting of that feminine/ist "origin" not only in the interfacing sites of various symbolizations but on the geopolitical border itself—El Valle (Saldívar-Hull, 1991).

Anzaldúa's "Shadow Beast," intratextually recodified as Snake Woman, La Llorona, and other figurations, sends her stand-in forth as an Outlaw, a Queer, a "mita y mita," a fluid sexuality, deployed through a fluid cultural space, the borderlands, which stand within sight of the patronymic LAW, and where many except those who possess it are Outlaws, endlessly represented as alterities by D.C. and D.F. *Borderlands / La Frontera* is an "instinctive urge to communicate, to speak, to write about life on the borders, life in the shadows . . . the preoccupations with the inner life of the subject, and with the struggle of that subject amidst adversity and violation with the 'unique positionings consciousness takes at these confluent streams' of inner/outer. An outer that is presented by the Texas-U.S., Southwest/Mexican border. . . . and the psychological borderlands, the sexual and spiritual borderlands" (Anzaldúa, preface). A self that becomes a crossroads, a collision course, a clearinghouse, an endless alterity who once she emerges into language and self-inscription, so belated, appears as a tireless peregrine collecting all the parts that will never make her whole. Such a hunger forces her to recollect in excess, to remember in excess, to labor to excess and produce a text layered with inversions and disproportions, which are effects of experienced dislocations, vis-à-vis the text of the Name of the Father and the Place of the Law. Chicanas want to textualize those effects.

The contemporaneous question then is how can this continue to be rewritten in multiple ways from a new ethical and political position and what might it imply for the feminine in our historical context, especially for women of Mexican descent and others for whom work means migrations to the electronic, high-tech assembly work on both sides of the U.S.-Mexican border.

WORKS CITED

Alarcón, Norma. 1990. "Chicana Feminisms: In the Tracks of the Native Woman." *Cultural Studies* 4, no. 3 (October 1990): 248–256.

Althusser, Louis. 1971. *Lenin and Philosophy and Other Essays.* Trans. Ben Brewster. New York: Monthly Review Press.

Anzaldúa, Gloria. 1987. *Borderlands / La Frontera: The New Mestiza.* San Francisco: Spinsters / Aunt Lute.

Butler, Judith. 1990. "Gender Trouble, Feminist Theory, and Psychoanalytic Discourse." In *Feminism/Postmodernism,* ed. Linda J. Nicholson, 324–340. New York: Routledge.

Castoriadis, Cornelius. 1987. *The Imaginary Institution of Society.* Trans. Kathleen Blamey. Cambridge: MIT Press.

Cornell, Drucilla. 1991. *Beyond Accommodation: Ethical Feminism, Deconstruction and the Law.* New York: Routledge.

Derrida, Jacques. 1982. *Margins of Philosophy.* Trans. Alan Bass. Chicago: University of Chicago Press.

Fraser, Nancy. 1989. *Unruly Practices: Power, Discourse, and Gender in Contemporary Social Theory.* Minneapolis: University of Minnesota Press.

Fraser, Nancy, and Linda J. Nicholson. 1990. "Social Criticism without Philosophy: An Encounter between Feminism and Postmodernism." In *Feminism/Postmodernism,* ed. Fraser and Nicholson, 19–38. New York: Routledge.

Herrera-Sobek, María. 1990. *The Mexican Corrido: A Feminist Analysis.* Bloomington: Indiana University Press.

Irigaray, Luce. 1985. *Speculum of the Other Woman.* Trans. Gillian C. Gill. Ithaca, N.Y.: Cornell University Press.

Jameson, Fredric. 1991. *Postmodernism, or, The Cultural Logic of Late Capitalism.* Durham, N.C.: Duke University Press.

Kristeva, Julia. 1980. *Desire in Language: A Semiotic Approach to Literature and Art.* Ed. Leon S. Roudiez; trans. Thomas Gora, Alice Jardine, and Leon S. Roudiez. New York: Columbia University Press.

Lacan, Jacques. 1977. *Ecrits.* Trans. Alan Sheridan. New York: W. W. Norton.

Limón, José E. 1992. *Mexican Ballads, Chicano Poems: History and Influence in Mexican-American Social Poetry.* Berkeley: University of California Press.

Lyotard, Jean-François. 1988. *The Differend: Phrases in Dispute.* Minneapolis: University of Minnesota Press.

Malkki, Liisa. 1992. "National Geographic: The Rooting of People and the Territorialization of National Identity among Scholars and Refugees." In *Cultural Anthropology: Space, Identity, and the Politics of Difference,* ed. James Ferguson and Akhil Gupta, 7(1): 24–44.

Montejano, David. 1987. *Anglos and Mexicans in the Making of Texas, 1836–1986.* Austin: University of Texas Press.

Nathan, Debbie. 1991. *Women and Other Aliens: Essays from the U.S.-Mexican Border.* El Paso, Tex.: Cinco Puntos Press.

Paredes, Américo. 1971. *With a Pistol in His Hand: A Border Ballad and Its Hero.* Reprint. Austin: University of Texas Press.

Saldívar-Hull, Sonia. 1991. "Feminism on the Border: From Gender Politics to Geopolitics." In *Criticism in the Borderlands: Studies in Chicano Literature, Culture, and Ideology,* ed. Héctor Calderón and José D. Saldívar, 203–220. Durham, N.C.: Duke University Press.

Smith, Valerie. 1989. "Black Feminist Theory and the Representation of the 'Other.'" In *Changing Our Own Words: Essays on Criticism, Theory, and Writing by Black Women,* ed. Cheryl A. Wall, 38–57. New Brunswick, N.J.: Rutgers University Press.

Trinh T. Minh-ha. 1990. "Not You / Like You: Post-Colonial Women and the Interlocking Questions of Identity and Difference." In *Making Face, Making Soul / Haciendo Caras: Creative and Critical Perspectives by Women of Color,* ed. Gloria Anzaldúa, 371–375. San Francisco: Aunt Lute Foundation.

PART II

DISMANTLING COLONIAL/ PATRIARCHAL LEGACIES

7 RE(RITING) THE CHICANA POSTCOLONIAL: FROM TRAITOR TO 21ST CENTURY INTERPRETER

Naomi H. Quiñonez

Anima

The fog in my mirror / slowly unveils
a woman of bronze, earth fire.
The clouding of mystery / a shrouded face
breasts that Picasso had seen and painted.
An eye dark as shadows / that bury the temples
deep in the image of reflected haze.
Still wet from waters of Aztec baptismal
an ancient face lingers at the edge of my soul.
Suspended in time I wait in suspense
for the mirror to reveal a forgotten woman.
And slowly the cheekbones of India take form
Rough-hewn forehead, lips full and quiet
two eyes turn inward to see what is born . . . [1]

I FIRST recited poetry in elementary school when my second grade teacher asked me to participate in a talent show. It was a simple poem about ducks, willow trees, and ponds—elements of nature to which I had little exposure in the urban clutter of Los Angeles. How or why I began to write poetry, I cannot recall. My family had its fair share of musicians, my mother and grandmother were seasoned storytellers, and my father often plied us with his World War II experiences. Although I know that all of this had something to do with my desire to write, no one that I knew of wrote poetry. Poetry just seemed to appear, it landed on my shoulder like a colorful bird and I found myself interpreter, antenna, and catalyst for words that helped give meaning to my young life. Later in high school, poetry became a sacred and secret place for my innermost feelings, something separate from the scrutiny of adults and parental authority. Poetry recorded the personal and social struggles common to many adolescents. However, political issues fueled by the power of the social protest movement of that time pushed me to record my bewilderment and my awe.

During the height of the Chicano Movement, the days seemed filled with the excitement of conferences, meetings, and rallies where people discussed and debated. I found myself with hundreds of other students, parents, and community members filling the chamber of the Los Angeles

Board of Education to demand improved education. I attended youth conferences where we discussed issues of identity and the need for social activism. Members of the UMAS (United Mexican American Students) chapter of a local college addressed my classes and encouraged Chicano students to enroll in college. Community organizations encouraged participation in an emerging La Raza Unida Party. Although I was uncertain about everything occurring around me, it proved difficult to remain detached from the heady, almost tumultuous tenor of those times. Writing poetry provided a kind of order for the hundreds of questions that surfaced in my mind as a result of this "revolution." It seemed as if everyone—students, teachers, school administrators, parents, politicians, my entire world—were caught by surprise by the wave of change that so intensely challenged the ways in which we thought about ourselves and our society.

While I was a student at California State College–Los Angeles, poetry provided me the strength to accept the consequences of my new life. I became involved in community volunteer programs such as Head Start, joined protest marches and rallies, and embraced the term "Chicana." Later, as a student at San Jose State College, community activism shaped and informed my muse. I joined the United Farmworkers Union boycott, initiated an Ethnic Pride volunteer program for students, and taught remedial skills at the Neighborhood Youth Corps—a War on Poverty program. I also attended MEChA (Movimiento Estudiantil Chicano de Aztlan) meetings and argued with my peers about cultural nationalism and Marxist Leninism. I embraced a Chicano identity while questioning the marginalization of women from the Chicano Movement, which, in turn, aided me in understanding the importance and necessity of feminism.

All during this time, I wrote and wrote. Majoring in English and journalism I applied my skills to writing about Chicano issues. My interest in journalism led to a job reporting for the Model Cities Program—another War on Poverty organization. But poetry was the expression that came most naturally. A turning point in my life occurred when I took a Chicano literature class with Dr. Felipe Ortego at San Jose State College. After I shared with him a sampling of my poetry, he encouraged me to write more. He became my first editor and an invaluable supporter of my art. Later in the semester, he organized a Chicano issues conference, Cantos y Gritos de Mi Liberación, named after a book by Ricardo Sánchez. Ortego invited me to recite poetry at the conference and I refused, scared to death of airing my personal thoughts in public. He coaxed me to no avail and then gently backed off. Two weeks later, a friend of mine excitedly waved a program for that conference at me, and pointed to my name. I was outraged! How dare Ortego include me when I had so adamantly refused? I marched to his office, where he explained that he hoped that I would change my mind. However, if I did not want to take the responsibility of sharing my art for the sake of the struggle, he understood perfectly and would not press me. Shrewdly, Ortego managed to coax me into reciting at the conference, which I did, knees knocking and sweat pouring, for a full twenty minutes. The response was overwhelmingly positive and I have been reciting poetry ever since. I had no idea at that time that I was part of an entire generation of Chicana writers cresting on the cultural wave the Chicano Movement generated.

FIRST WAVE CHICANA WRITERS DEFINED

A substantial body of Chicana literature was produced during this period. The works of Pat Mora, Ana Castillo, Bernice Zamora, Adaljiza Sosa-Riddell, Estela Portillo, Gina Valdes, and Denise Chávez represent only a sampling of a larger group of writers that initially dotted the landscape of first wave Chicana literature.[2] In defining this group I maintain that the first wave was motivated to write as a result of increased political awareness and a commitment to the cultural ideals of the Chicano Movement. These ideals included linking the purpose of art and culture to the struggle for socioeconomic and political change.[3] First wave Chicana literature incorporates issues of race, class, and gender by addressing the experiences of poor and working-class Mexican and Mexican American women. This analysis is not meant to exclude Chicanas whose writing may share the same sociopolitical impetus as that of the first wave. However, writers after this period may not have the close connection to the Chicano movement. In addition, they may not share the urgency to construct or establish feminist discourse or to insert their image after a long historical period of invisibility. This "second wave," if you will, may possess other motives for writing that are not central to ideas of the Chicano/a movement. In fact, some younger writers indicate that they work to *be* writers and not necessarily for the advancement of social change.

THE CHICANO CULTURAL MOVEMENT

When cultural nationalism was declared, the essential foundation for social and political action, Chicano activists saw the possibility of culture in all its manifestations. Through the mediums of art, poetry, music, and theater, Chicano artists could encourage, reaffirm, and mirror efforts toward social change. My own experiences reflect this desire. I wrote poetry while at antiwar rallies, during class discussions about capitalism, at Cinco de Mayo celebrations, at the unveiling of murals, and at Santana concerts. Sit-ins, teach-ins, walk-outs, the silent assemblies after bomb threats, all provided the spaces to consider the possibilities of social change. Those possibilities pushed, shoved, and thrust artists like myself toward creating the cultural movement that emerged. Full-length murals appeared almost overnight, Chicano musicians seemed to perform everywhere, Chicano theaters sprung up in the middle of barrios, and poetry flourished as the uncontested word of *"la gente—la palabra del movimiento."* Throughout California and most of the Southwest *centros culturales* (cultural centers) sprang to life and became major venues for developing artists. This cultural movement became an essential component of the Chicano movement for identifying and asserting symbols of inspiration and unity. If cultural nationalism served as an ideological framework for social change, the cultural movement provided a strategy to achieve that goal.

Chicano and Chicana artists contributed by developing the movement's cultural wing. They saw themselves as cultural workers and eschewed a Euro-Western "art for art's sake" credo. Cultural workers created and shared their work to advance cultural pride, to identify types of oppression, or to educate others about historical and social issues important to Chicano identity. Cultural workers also provided the organizational skills to produce cultural presentations and became a powerful force in the recruitment of people into the movement.[4] Representation figured prominently into the Chicano movement as the need for signifiers that could attract and unify activists along common lines took on greater importance. El Teatro Campesino—a direct cultural by-product of the farmworkers' movement—and its use of the black eagle and the Virgen de Guadalupe proved to be instrumental in identifying, advancing, and inserting cultural symbols that could unify Chicanos.[5]

Rooted in similar principles, Chicano poetry emerged. Chicano theater and poetry are so linked that several Chicana/o writers developed from that medium. Lorna Dee Cervantes joined the Teatro del Barrio at San Jose State College before she began to recite her poetry solo. Dorinda Moreno formed a performance troupe, Las Cucarachas (The Cockroaches), based on poetry. My own participation in the Teatro de la Gente in San Jose, reciting poetry between acts, fostered my development as an oral presenter.

Poetry functioned as an oral practice as well as a written one. Orality became central to Chicano poetry because of a number of factors. Tomas Ybarra-Frausto notes that early Chicano poets helped to establish the emphasis on poetry as a spoken art. "The Chicano poet writes for an audience that is not predominantly a reading audience. . . . Chicano poets assume that their audience will not ponder individual lines. . . . A Chicano audience is more likely to hear the poem, perhaps only once, and must comprehend it as it is sung or spoken. This focus on public comprehension calls for rhythmic patterning, a strong narrative line, and frequent use of the vernacular to reinforce 'orality.' Such poetry represents an attempt to reverse the tradition of private poets who elaborate a personal hermetic world in their verse."[6] Although Ybarra-Frausto examines the more recent impetus for Chicano poetic orality, the influence of a strong oral tradition in Mexican culture also proved to be a strong influence on Chicana/o writers.

Chicana/o poets reclaimed and adopted the ancient Mexican idea of *flor y canto* (flower and song), which achieved high value in pre-Columbian society as a public presentation of dramatic poetry accompanied by music. *Flor y canto* became an appropriate vehicle for Chicano poets to reach larger audiences. Thus, the oral significance of Chicano poetry has its roots in an indigenous Mexican tradition.[7]

While cultural workers served as catalysts for the advancement of culture, poetry developed into a political act defined as the edge to the blade of Chicano culture.[8] Tomás Rivera perceived this process as integral to the creation of a Chicano community. "Clearly, the impetus to document and develop the Chicano community became the essential raison d'être of the Chicano Movement itself and of the writers who tried to express that."[9] Rivera goes further to emphasize that as Chicano writers documented the community they helped to "decolonize the mind," which in turn led to intellectual emancipation.[10]

FIRST WAVE CHICANA WRITERS: NEGOTIATING BETWEEN CULTURAL NATIONALISM AND FEMINISM

Although most Chicano writers during this time may have possessed a strong sense of their role in this "decolonization," the perceptions of what this actually signified differed between women and men.[11] For a Chicana feminist/writer, decolonizing the mind led to a deeper understanding of the effects of racial/class oppression as well as gender oppression. For example, although I benefited greatly from the Mexican history previously denied me in public school, my eventual exposure to this "new" information prompted me to ask: "Where are the women in this history?" Writing poetry became a way to initiate a search. In 1972 I wrote a poem entitled "Anima" or *the haunting shadow.* This proved to be my first venture into searching for the women missing from the books. Understanding the process of decolonization showed me that just because a people is absent from the history books of the dominant culture does not mean they do not exist. The same held true for women. In "Anima," I ask, "Where am I in this history?" These questions were as much a part of the process of discovery as recovery. Through this poem I invoked and invented the woman, and in finding her, I made her eternal in my mind.

I open my eyes / the mirror is clouded
from ages of living / breathing and dying
Eyes Hollow sockets / loins dry as bone
but my soul / strong and fertile
will give birth to my children.[12]

This poem helped connect me to other women because without a "feminine/feminist" history, I was confronted with a feeling of isolation. In fact, other Chicana writers proved to be engaged in similar work, inventing, reinventing, and deconstructing similar feminine archetypes. The number of poems on La Malinche, La Llorona, and mothers and grandmothers written by different Chicana writers during this time are testaments to a larger process at work.[13] For example, an early poem by Adaljiza Sosa-Riddell looks at the Malinche dynamic in "Como Duele."

Malinche, pinche, forever with me;
I was born out of you, / I walk beside you,
bear my children with you, for sure I'll die alone with you,
. . . Pinche, como duele ser Malinche. / Pero sabes, ese,
what keeps me from shattering / into a million fragments?
It's that sometimes / you are el hijo de la Malinche too.[14]

This 1973 poem reflects the dilemma Chicana feminists confronted. In the writer's struggle to find her identity she is subjected to "Malinche baiting" by Chicano men. The refrain, "pinche como duele ser Malinche" (damn, how it hurts to be Malinche), is not a rejection of Malinche but an acceptance. For the writer understands the contradiction Chicano men must experience in order to gain a sense of self while being exposed to the trappings of assimilation. This poem reveals that her search is not unlike his, that men also must admit their likeness to Malinche. The poem helps turn Malinche-baiting on its head, since rather than feel shame, the poet unabashedly relates and accepts her identity as synonymous with Malinche.

In Lorna Dee Cervantes's 1975 poem "Beneath the Shadow of the Freeway" the figures of grandmother and mother prove to be pivotal to the author's identity. The poem illustrates the harsh life of her woman-centered family and calls attention to the tough, survival-driven independence of struggling women in counterbalance to the poet's desire to maintain a sense of self and sensitivity.

Grandma from the hills of Santa Barbara,
I would open my eyes to see her stir mush
in the morning, hair in loose braids / sucked close around her
head with a yellow scarf. / Mama said, "it's her own fault
getting screwed by a man for that long,
Sure as shit wasn't hard," / soft she was / soft . . .
. . . and in time, I will plant geraniums.
I will tie up my hair into loose braids / and trust only
what I have built / with my own hands.[15]

Within the subtle texture of her lines, Cervantes takes on both the softness of her grandmother—the braids, the geraniums—and the tough exterior of her mother, which compels her to trust only what she herself constructs.

The common themes and archetypes inherent in first wave Chicana writing serve as responses to the process of decolonization. According to Tey Diana Rebolledo, since women live under the dictates of male patriarchal systems that advance values and myths that attempt to control their behavior, "women may create new role models for themselves or choose existing models but imbue them with different (sometimes radically different) traits and characteristics.[16] Rebolledo examines how "Chicana writers choose, define, and image their myths and heroines." In *Women Singing in the Snow* Rebolledo deconstructs the most identifiable archetypes in Chicana poetry: the Aztec goddess Tonantzín and her syncretic mirror, the Catholic Virgen de Guadalupe; La Llorona, the phantom woman accused of murdering her children; the Bruja/Curandera (witch/healer); and the Adelita (the female soldier of the Mexican Revolution), to name a few. In doing so, she shows how Chicana writers transcend the virgin/whore dichotomy to which these archetypes are linked. Additionally, she illuminates how they have been historically utilized to exert control over Chicana behavior. In the interpretations and reconstructions of Chicana writing, these archetypes lose their moralistic hold and are transformed into symbols that reflect the complexity, the problematic social circumstances, and the humor of the Chicana experience.[17] Thus the manifestations of archetypes, so central to Chicana literature, are reconstructed by the writers' experiences and points of view.

INVISIBILITY

If first wave Chicana writers expressed a common feeling of isolation in their artistic endeavors, that feeling proved to be directly related to the dynamics of cultural nationalism and its effects on Chicana feminists in the cultural movement. Writing appeared to be a male construct. The contradiction emerged in the form of rejecting Western literary traditions and ideas of poetry while perpetuating a very Western gender bias that recognized men as the creator/artist.[18] Hence, the male face of the larger Chicano movement became expressed in the male voice of the cultural movement. Around me I heard the words of Alurista, José Montoya, Luis Valdez, Corky Gonzales, and Abelardo Delgado, or I read their work in quality, well-distributed Chicano literary publications. Although I had been invited to recite poetry at many events during this time, I often found myself the only woman on the program.

Angie Chabram-Dernersesian's critique of sexism in the Chicano literary movement emphasizes how representation served to manipulate the community gaze to focus on male writers. Her analysis of the title of a well-known Chicano literary journal, *El Espejo / The Mirror*, takes issue with the masculine face of this metaphor. Referring to the *Mirror's* statement that describes its editors as "those who needed no other reflection other than themselves, thus the *Mirror*," Chabram-Dernersesian poses a searing question: "Who is this subject so empowered with literary capital as to know itself, not once, but many times, doubling incessantly within the tasty banquet of alternative literary production?"[19] Her answer is prefaced by a look at Chicano literature's most celebrated thematic heroes and critics, all male, and all espousing the dynamics of the Chicano experience. With this, Chabram-Dernersesian points out that "[t]extually within the very same Chicano vernacular which challenged the Eurolingocentrism of English and Spanish by crossing their borders in illegal codes that would elicit charges of "illiteracy," Chicano identity is written with linguistic qualifiers, *-o/os,* which subsume the Chicana into a universal ethnic subject that speaks with the masculine instead of the feminine and embodies itself in a Chicano male.[20] Chicana writers, like most Chicana activists, were rendered *invisible.* Invisible within the larger circle of the Chicano movement, and invisible even to themselves.

My own question in the early seventies, "Where are the Chicana voices?" led me to a certain paradox. The great din created by the Chicano cultural movement drowned out the voices of Chicana writers. Although active in our art and in the community, we were relegated to the fringes of the cultural movement. It would be several years before we found each other. My eventual exposure to other Chicana writers of this period not only proved to be inspiring, but made me more aware than ever that something was wrong with the mirror that did not reflect the totality of the Chicano Movement. Absent from that reflection was the feminine face.

The same strategies that drove a wedge between Chicano Movement activists and Chicana feminists also separated male and female artists, creating different cultural representations based on gender. According to Chabram-Dernersesian:

> Without the possibility of uninterrupted self-duplication, without the possibility of inscribing viable Mexican/Chicana female subjects with which to identify at the center of Chicana/o practices of resistance, Chicanas were denied cultural authenticity and independent self-affirmation. Yet, both these elements were central to a movement dedicated to altering the negative configurations of Chicanas/os at the hands of others who had for centuries blocked any possibility of legitimate self-representation to Americanas/os of Mexican descent. (83)

Chabram-Dernersesian continues, "[I]f Chicanas wished to receive the authorizing signature of predominant movement discourses and figure within the record of Mexican practice of resistance in the U.S., then they had to embody themselves as males, adopt traditional family relations, and dwell only on their racial and/or ethnic oppression."[21] Of course feminist Chicana writers did not care to be men, and so for about ten years, between 1970 and 1980, Chicanas wrote in the margins of the dominant culture and on the margins of the Chicano movement.

Even when Chicana writers gained some recognition through the few publications that would carry their work, the overall presentation proved to be devoid of feminist analysis. In 1973, *El Grito* published one of the first collections of Chican*a* literature. Estela Portillo, the contributing editor for this issue, begins her introduction with a traditionally feminine perspective of women's literature. "The voice of a woman—does it belong to a particular time and place? Is it not something much more eternal? Like the womb? Is it a soft, gentle fertility of instinct?"[22] Portillo's analysis clearly shows that before Chicanas embraced and re-inscribed a feminist analysis, women proved to be susceptible to qualifying themselves in traditional terms, even if they were doing something quite revolutionary.

It is ironic that at this same time Chicano males who ascribed to a literal sense of cultural nationalism were engaged in what became known as "Malinche baiting." Seen as a traitor to her own culture for allegedly aiding the Spanish conquest of Mexico, La Malinche became a symbol used to taunt and denigrate Chicana feminists who challenged the sexism of the Chicano movement. Relegated to subordinate roles that encouraged women to take on domestic activities during the movement, women who wanted more active roles as leaders in the public realm were susceptible to being labeled a "Malinche."

Nonetheless, Chicanas continued to take active roles in their communities, and writing took on more importance as a political act. Hence, many Chicanas produced poetry and prose as part of a larger feminist discourse. Very few critics could predict or imagine the profusion of Chicana literature that would explode during the 1980s. Yet, despite the obstacles, Chicana writing burst on the scene due to several factors. The politicization of Chicanas created a critical mass of writers who desired and needed to express their ideas and viewpoints. As a political act more Chicanas took pen to page throughout the late seventies and early eighties, and did not stop. They relentlessly and consistently shared and transmitted their work, no matter the odds. Within a context of a dominant hegemonic society, first wave Chicana writers negotiated between their service to the Chicano movement, their relative invisibility within that movement, and their feminist values. As such they could have languished in discouragement. Instead, as is surmised in *Breaking Boundaries,* they gained strength. "It is possible to envisage the debilitation of the Latina subject as a result of continually having to struggle with tokenism, holding the fabric of many lives together, denouncing injustices in the worlds they inhabit, and eking out a living between the cracks or in the fractures of two systems. Rather, as she affirms her Self, the Latina writer engages in a dialectic and dynamic process, transforming those aggressions directed at her into her own strength."[23]

Elizabeth Ordóñez explains that although Chicana writers shared a common sociopolitical condition with their brothers, they also walked "a cultural tightrope somewhere between women's culture and the general culture." Ordóñez goes on to describe Chicana writing as a "double-voiced discourse . . . She makes the invisible visible, gives voice to the muted." Expanding on this polarization, Norma Alarcón sees Chicana poets as "umpires" mediating between a past Chicano patriarchal interpretation of culture, which holds the potential for locking them into "crippling traditional stereotypes," and a future that can be equally limiting within an "Anglo American feminist promise."[24] The roles of mediator, umpire, and interpreter are crucial features of first wave Chicana writers as they identify, define, and reconcile cultural displacements and resist hegemonic control. Early on, Chicana writers not only traversed the uncertain political grounds between their brothers and Anglo women, they captured those dilemmas and consequential insight in their literature, and helped to create the discourse on which Chicana feminism became rooted.

HIJAS DE LA MALINCHE: INTERPRETERS AND POSTCOLONIAL WRITERS

As first wave Chicana writers traversed uncertain social and political terrain, they documented their experiences in the form of literature and engaged in a feminist discourse from a cultural position. In so doing, they pulled the personal and unspeakable out of the shadows and threw light on generally proscribed subjects such as sexuality, family violence, and social injustice. As a personal commentary on living the "legacy of conquest," the tensions between Mexican traditions and American values, conquest and colonization, feminism and patriarchy, sexuality and repression, and power and dispossession provided the source and inspiration for literary themes. The decentering of Euro-dominant discourse, the defiance of patriarchal traditions, and the assertion of new identities displaced old stereotypes of Chicana and Mexican women that became important elements of their cultural production. First wave Chicana writers began to create a literature that privileged the margins by asserting themes and language use that authenticated and validated their experiences.

As a literature of resistance, the work of first wave Chicana writers challenges dominant discourse which either commodifies or renders Chicanas invisible. Additionally, these writers tend to adopt and modify the language and literary tools of the dominant culture in order to redefine themselves. In this sense, the role of first wave Chicana writers may be compared to that of La Malinche, who, as interpreter during the conquest, possessed the skill of adaptation during a time of intense cultural upheaval. Hence the often-ambiguous role of the interpreter becomes part of postcolonial discourse. Cordelia Candelaria affirms this comparison in her observation that Malinche's position "might be read as an account of the prototypical Chicana feminist. La Malinche embodies those personal characteristics—such as intelligence, initiative, adaptability, and leadership—which are most often associated with Mexican American women unfettered by traditional restraints against activist public achievement. By adapting to the historical circumstances thrust upon her, she defied traditional social expectations of a woman's role."[25] Adaptation, interpretation, and resistance are key elements of postcolonial literature.

In expounding on the significant role language played in the conquest of the Americas, the authors of *The Empire Writes Back* reflect upon Tzvetan Todorov's analysis of the first contact between the Spanish and the Aztecs.[26] One of Hernán Cortés's chief concerns at the onset of the conquest was to acquire an interpreter for the purpose of communicating with the people. However, his desire was driven by a need to control language in order to exert control over the indigenous population. The authors surmise that as mediator between language and communication, the role of interpreter during first contact must have been "profoundly ambiguous. . . . The interpreter always emerges from the dominated discourse. The role entails radically divided objectives: It functions to acquire the power of the new language and culture in order to preserve the old, even [while] it assists the invaders in their overwhelming of that culture." Their analysis prompts them to conclude, "the role of the interpreter is like that of the postcolonial writer, caught in the conflict between destruction and creation."[27]

Discussion of the Spanish conquest of Mexico establishes a relevant entry into an examination of Chicana postcolonial writing since it serves as the historical turning point in the creation of "mestizaje" (mixed race). Within this context a major Mexican historical figure, that of Malintzín Tenepal, surfaces. Her precarious position as first interpreter renders her controversial even to this day. Malintzín, more commonly known as La Malinche, bears the dubious distinction of linguist, interpreter, diplomat, and traitor. Sold into slavery by her mother at the age of eight, she was given to Cortés as one of twenty slaves at the age of fourteen. Malinche distinguished herself by her facility with language and became his interpreter and concubine.[28] Malinche's upbringing within the noble class of the Nahuatl hierarchy and her knowledge of the people made her an adept diplomat. She was both respected and despised by her own people; her intervention did not always save certain enclaves of people but did help to save others. Her strongest claim to infamy emerges in the aftermath of a violent conquest when her name becomes associated with the bitter defeat and is uttered as a curse by the conquered Mexicanos who perceive La Malinche as culpable for the dire turn of events in Mexican history.[29] Malinche is also known to have borne mestizo children from the indigenous/Spanish union. However, the union, originating in force, is perceived as betrayal to the Aztecs. Consequently, La Malinche is often referred to as "La Chingada" or the "violated woman," a term Mexican writer Octavio Paz exploits and perpetuates in his examination of La Malinche. Paz attempts to show that this notion (which developed over the last four centuries) constitutes a national self-perception of Mexicans as products of a whore/mother, or *"hijos de la Chingada,"* children of the violated woman.[30] Her descendants, Mexican and Chicano alike, become implicated in this tragic self-perception. However, Malinche represents the root cause of defeat and bears the blame. Although feminist scholarship has attempted to revise and reinterpret La Malinche, her name continues to evoke intense feelings. The idea of "La Chingada" functions not only as a curse, but as a reminder of the power of the interpreter, even five hundred years after the conquest.[31]

In their discussion of the "ambiguous" role of the first interpreter, the authors of *The Empire Writes Back* imply a significant ramification for the relationship between Malinche and her descendants. "The post-colonial writer, whose gaze is turned in two directions, stands already in that position which will come to be occupied by an interpretation. For he/[she] is not the object of an interpretation, but the first interpreter."[32] Historically, La Malinche appears to be among the first interpreters in the Americas. Theoretically, first wave Chicana writers serve as first interpreters for their culture. Given this relationship, La Malinche can be viewed as the mother of first wave Chicana writers, who represent "hijas de La Malinche." Todorov makes a valuable reference to the position of current Chicano postcolonial writers in his summation of Malinche's role. "La Malinche glorifies mixtures to the detriment of purity—Aztec and Spanish—and the role of intermediary. She does not simply submit to the other; she adopts the other's ideology and serves it in order to understand her own culture better, as is evidenced by the effectiveness of her conduct.[33] The function of interpreter within the context of conquest requires the ability to negotiate between native and dominant cultures and languages, which can alter perceptions and values.

Nigerian writer Chinua Achebe describes the tenuous position postcolonial writers straddle on the borders of conflicting cultures: "The crossroads does have a certain dangerous potency; dangerous because a man [woman] might perish there wrestling with multiple-headed spirits, but also [s/he] might be lucky and return . . . with the boon of prophetic vision."[34] As interpreters, postcolonial writers are heirs to a range of interpretive choices depending on how they perceive their relationship to the dominant culture. This is why some choose to dismantle dominant discourse, as in Gloria Anzaldúa's *Borderlands,* while others may attempt to be part of it, as in Richard Rodriguez's *Hunger of Memory.*[35] For the most part, first wave Chicana writers offer a politics of what I term "prophetic revision."

THE POSTCOLONIAL CONDITION AND RESISTANCE

Like other disenfranchised groups in the United States, Chicano efforts have occurred largely through political as well as cultural resistance. According to Edward Said, "cultural resistance" causes an insistence on the right to see the community's history as a whole, coherent, and integral part of the larger culture. Furthermore, resistance is not exclusively a reaction to imperialism but "an alternative way of conceiving human history." Alternative reconceptions of history serve to break down barriers between cultures through a "conscious effort to enter into the discourse of Europe and the West, to mix with it, transform it, to make it acknowledge the marginalized or suppressed or forgotten histories." It seems clear, then, that postcolonial first wave Chicana writers participate in cultural resistance by utilizing their cultural production to reclaim buried histories. They also resist dominant discourses by appropriating, reconfiguring, and transforming it as part of their own.[36]

Thus, for first wave Chicana writers who engage in cultural resistance and employ a politics of difference, the act of "writing back to the empire" not only involves resistance as a postcolonial subject but resolution as an empowered force. Rafael Pérez-Torres brings this idea to light when he asserts that "the notion of difference within highlights the contradictory position of all postcolonials whose identity arises from histories of oppression, exploitation, violence, erasure. Without negating the reality of these histories, postcolonials engage with their disempowered pasts, and reinvoke strategies of resistance, survival, and empowerment in that past.[37] How first wave Chicana writers re-establish their histories, reinvoke their pasts, and advance their empowerment will be discussed within a framework of postcolonial theory.

Chicanas have been negated, devalued, or omitted from two types of discourse: the larger dominant American discourse and the male Chicano discourse. The reclamation and assertion of their identity takes place through the use of strategies that allow them to reclaim their language and assert and insert their own experiences as major themes. Postcolonial theory recognizes that literature has historically been used as a tool of oppression to either erase the existence of colonized subjects, or portray them as negative and inferior.[38] Consequently, language-use figures prominently as a device, which validates life experience. According to the authors of *The Empire Writes Back*, "The seizing of the means of communication and the liberation of postcolonial writing by the appropriation of the written word becomes a crucial feature of the process of self-assertion and of the ability to *reconstruct* the world as an unfolding process."[39] The use of two strategies is important to this reconstruction: abrogation and appropriation. Through appropriation, writers may take the language of the dominant culture and replace it with their own, in some cases reconstituting it totally into a "vehicle for new meanings and adaptations of the cultural experiences of the non-privileged." Abrogation challenges or rejects the idea that there exists a correct or standardized cultural aesthetic, and denies English a position of privilege.[40]

APPROPRIATION

In *Borderlands / La Frontera: The New Mestiza*, Gloria Anzaldúa explores how "linguistic terrorism," or the punishment leveled against Mexican and Mexican Americans for speaking their native language, has been enforced through the process of colonization. For a people "who are neither Spanish nor live in a country in which Spanish is the first language; for a people who live in a country in which English is the reigning tongue, but who are not Anglo, for a people who cannot entirely identify with either standard Spanish nor standard English, what recourse is left to them but to create their own language?" Anzaldúa's own use of language includes code switching "from English to Castillian Spanish to the North Mexican dialect to Tex-Mex to a sprinkling of Nahuatl to a mixture of all of these, reflects "my language, a new language—the language of the Borderlands."[41] Anzaldúa's rejection of standard U.S. language forms seems clear. She creatively and defiantly employs a strategy of appropriation by taking the dominant language and changing it to reflect her own language experience.

Biliteral text, or code switching, is a form of language variance common to postcolonial writing.[42] The appropriation of language in first wave Chicana writing takes the form of code switching, using untranslated words, or writing texts exclusively in Spanish. Thus, English becomes decentered. I now offer a few representations. The following poem, written by Cordelia Candelaria, exemplifies the metnomyic device created through code switching.

Haciendo tamales mi mama wouldn't compromise
no m.f.t. chili, no u.s.d.a. carne
nomas handgrown y home-raised, todo.
oregano had to be wildly grown
in brown earth 'bajo la sombra.
Tamale wrappers had to be hojas
dried from last year's corn
nurtured by sweat—como no¿ . . .
Entonces, como su mama antes y su abuelita
she made her tamales from memory / cada sabor nuevo
como el calor del Westinghouse where
she cooked them with gas under G.E. light
bien original to the max![43]

In this piece language variance becomes pivotal to the poem's meaning, for more than switching between codes, the poet constructs a dialectic relationship between two cultures. Cultural memory is maintained in Spanish, while the poet works in English in order to create a linkage between tradition and modernity. The linguistic situation of the poet becomes directly parallel to the contextual situation of the mother who carries on the traditions of her foremothers through the use and incorporation of modern technology (a decidedly postcolonial condition). Thus the poem utilizes code switching to illuminate a historical process whereby old and new traditions among Mexican and Chicana women become selected, maintained, and transformed.

The use of untranslated language functions to inscribe difference, since it makes the non-Spanish speaker the "other." In postcolonial writing, the use of untranslated words is a political act. "The use of english inserts itself as a political discourse . . . and the use of english variants captures the metonymic moment between the indigenous culture and the dominant one."[44] Untranslated Spanish strengthens the desire to inscribe difference in prose and poetry such as in the poetry of Lucha Corpi. Her book *Palabras de Mediodía* provides translations. The following poem, "Marina Madre," provides an interpretation of La Malinche.

> *Humeda de tradición, mistica / y muda fue vendida de mano en mano, noche a noche, / negada y desecrada, esperando el alba / y el canto de la lechuza / que nunca llegaban. / Su vientre robado de su fruto / hecha un puño de polvo seco su alma. / Tu no la querias ya y el la negaba / y aquel que cuando nino mama! le gritaba / cuando crecio le puso por nombre "la chingada."*[45]

Only through Spanish can the utterance "la chingada" reflect the full force of her condemnation. Postcolonial writers sometimes choose their language(s) based on the need to preserve an authentic sense of meaning regardless of whether it can be understood by "others." For a people who have suffered the loss of language through colonization, this clearly becomes a political act of reclamation. After a period of serving the linguistic and thematic ideas of Anglos, first wave Chicana writers reclaim their language, which may force the dominant English speaker into the role of "other."

ABROGATION

A major postcolonial theme common to first wave Chicana writers proves to be that of place and displacement. Understandably, a history of conquest and the historical and current waves of Mexican immigration provide significant themes for first wave Chicanas to explore. According to D. E. S. Maxwell the crisis of displacement often causes a postcolonial crisis of identity. Experiences of migration, enslavement, indentured labor, and cultural denigration create a need for the postcolonial writer to recover a viable relationship between self and place.[46] For example, the poem "The Unwanted Emigrants," by Phyllis López, describes Mexican immigrants as pawns of American capitalism.

> *To the deserts / of the southwest they come, only to find that they are quickly labeled / "THE UNWANTED EMIGRANTS" "the illegal aliens" / ridiculed for not / speaking English / scorned for being culturally different, condemned to an impoverished existence where deportation is a constant fear . . .*[47]

López offers an abbreviated history of the life of immigrant workers in the Southwest. Hard labor, fear, ridicule, uncertainty, and displacement underline the writer's recognition that race is an essential element in the family's social and economic predicament. The poet covers the major characteristics of their disenfranchised state: racism, poverty, low pay, and fear of deportation.

The model of grandmother serves another function of postcolonial writing. First wave Chicana writers tend to surface models of influence and inspiration as a way to insert their own images in spaces that have rendered them passive at best and invisible at worst. Grandmothers, mothers, aunts, bohemian women, strong, active women who take charge and do more than survive—they successfully challenge oppression and injustice—are but a few characters first wave writers insert into the heart of their poems and stories. With regard to grandmothers, María Herrera-Sobek paints a portrait of an amazing woman. "In Grandmother and Pancho Villa," Herrera-Sobek describes the heroic deeds of her grandmother:

> *fearless soldadera / You saddled your horse*
> *and left / To retrieve / Those horses / Pancho Villa*
> *Borrowed / You said / Unequivocally / Firmly, / Loudly:*
> *"I have come to take our horses back." /*
> *And Pancho Villa laughed. / At your audacity /*
> *At your temerity / A mere wisp of a girl / Four feet ten /*
> *. . . And you returned / Triumphant / Reins in hand*
> *Obedient horse / Galloping behind you / A mere wisp*
> *of a woman. Standing up / Against / The patriarchal law*
> *Of a ravished / Land.*[48]

Herrera-Sobek's grandmother becomes larger-than-life, defying her stature and size. While the grandmother defies Pancho Villa, María defies the constraints of Chicano nationalism. In this poem, Pancho Villa is stripped of his heroic role in the center of Chicano nationalism and is exposed as another manifestation of patriarchy. In the process a patriarchal hero is debunked and replaced by a courageous woman. This is a common decentering device employed in first wave Chicana cultural production.

The adverse effects of patriarchy on women represent another major issue in first wave Chicana writing. There exist two major responses—one to the patriarchy of the dominant culture and one to the patriarchy of the Mexican culture. Patriarchy is an arm of conquest and colonization in which men subordinate women. Women become objectified as property and are often subjected to sexual aggression. Referring to Anzaldúa's poem "We Call Them Greasers," Sonia Saldívar-Hull notes that Anzaldúa underscores a history of violence against Tejanas: "This history includes rape as institutionalized strategy in the war to disempower Chicano men.[49]

> *She lay under me whimpering / I plowed into her*
> *hard / kept thrusting and thrusting / felt him*
> *watching from the mesquite tree / heard him*
> *keening like a wild animal / in that instance*

I felt such contempt for her / round face
and beady black eyes like an Indian's.[50]

In this poem, Anzaldúa brings to light a part of Texas history avoided or neglected by traditional Chicano Texas historians. Saldívar-Hull notes that Chicano (male) historians "have been reluctant to voice the perhaps unspeakable violence against Tejanas." The simultaneous rape of the woman, and the captivity of her mate who is powerless to intervene, captures the cruel power of the "conqueror": to simultaneously sublimate men and women. "Within the hierarchy of powerlessness the woman occupies a position below the already inferior brown man."[51] She is not only subject to death, but also to the violation/torture of her body through rape. Through this poem, Anzaldúa provides a powerful interpretation of the politics of rape, and a legacy of sexual subjugation in the United States.

The second form of patriarchy is a form of cultural sexism which Chicanas endure as part of traditionally constructed gender roles for Mexican women. Lorna Dee Cervantes explores Chicano patriarchy in "You Cramp My Style Baby."

You cramp my style baby / when you roll on top of me
shouting, "Viva la Raza" / at the top of your prick
you want me como un taco / dripping with grease
or squeezing masa through my legs / making tamales
for you and my daughters. / You "mija" / "mija" me /
until I scream / and then you tell me, "Esa,
I LOVE / this revolution! / come on Malinche /
gimme some more![52]

This poem shows how males sexualize Chicanas and devalue their role as social activists. "Malinche-baiting" proved to be a strategy of intimidation utilized by Chicanos who felt threatened by Chicana political power. This poem exposes a male strategy that rationalized an attempt to sexually "conquer" Chicanas for the sake of the "revolution." The proverbial paradox is described. Whether women "give in" to sex or refuse—they will be considered "Malinches." They are forced to either serve as "whores" or be perceived as "vendidas" for not supporting their men in revolution. Yet the poem serves as a direct challenge to Chicano patriarchy, thus advancing personal and political empowerment for many Chicanas. With this poem, Cervantes establishes herself as a feminist and activist who engages in a "forbidden" theme to prove her point. Thus, sexuality becomes paramount to Chicana postcolonial writing.

Ramon Gutiérrez suggests that "[i]f the aim of the Chicano movement had been to decolonize the mind, as the novelist Tomás Rivera proposed, the Chicana movement decolonized the body."[53] As first wave Chicana writers began to explore their sexuality in prose and poetry, they not only entered forbidden waters, they dismantled the subject that trapped them in silence. Through sexuality, issues were raised that linked sex to themes of pleasure, liberation, identity, and exploitation. Issues of sexuality, especially homosexuality, often shake the foundations of cultural traditions that serve to maintain specific gender roles.

Themes that encompass sexual pleasure for women are rare due to traditions that place pressure on women to serve as "moral" pillars for their families and communities. These "forbidden" subjects became new vistas for first wave Chicana poets to explore. For example, sexual pleasure is central to Pat Mora's poem, "Mielvirgen":

> *in the shade watching the bees / remembering sweet*
> *evenings / of dipping her fingers into warm / honey,*
> *smoothing it on his lips, licking it slowly with*
> *her tongue, hearing him laugh / then breathe harder*
> *slowly unbuttoning her blouse, rubbing his tongue /*
> *on her sweet skin, / lips, honey, breasts / buzzing . . .* [54]

The poem is a celebration in which sex and innocence are connected to elements of nature.

The often taboo subject of lesbianism also made its mark as a result of the exploration of sexuality initiated by first wave Chicana writers. Gloria Anzaldúa's "Nightvoice" presents images of love between women.

> *When we met I fell / into her eyes like falling*
> *into warm rock / blurting out everything . . .*
> *I stood at the door / of the heaven I thought*
> *out of reach / When I touched her I could barely*
> *breathe and the smell of her: / toasted almonds*
> *and yeast . . .* [55]

By "violating" such cultural taboos, Chicana writers show that decolonization of the mind *is* the decolonization of the body. Ownership of one's sexuality is a powerful element of self-autonomy. These initial movements into sexuality set the tone for contemporary explorations of sexuality by more recent Chicana writers. Tey Diana Rebolledo and Eliana Rivero affirm that "[a]ll these transgressions on cultural taboos constitute a sort of guerilla warfare. The new sexuality is definitely a political ideology on the part of Chicana writers, an ideology that shreds the silences and arrives at new oneness.[56]

Among the major characteristics that established first wave Chicana literature as part of postcolonial writing is a global perspective that reflects a larger consciousness connecting the historical and socioeconomic conditions of women of color in the United States to those in Third World countries. Sonia Saldívar-Hull notes how some Chicana writers no longer "limit the feminist agenda to issues of race, class, ethnicity, and sexual orientation." Inherent in much of their literature is a need to express "solidarity with the Third World people struggling against the hegemony of the United States." Saldívar-Hull encourages an examination of a First versus Third World dichotomy, in order to explore how women of both worlds "articulate their feminisms in nontraditional ways and forms."[57] Understanding the common experiences of women from both worlds becomes a crucial implement to achieve this end. María Helena Viramontes explores these types of dichotomies in her short story, "The Cariboo Cafe."

> They arrived in the secrecy of night, as displaced people often do, stopping over for a week, a month, eventually staying a lifetime. The plan was simple. Mother would work too until they saved enough to move into a finer future where the toilet was one's own and the children needn't be frightened. In the meantime, they played in the back alleys, among the broken glass, wise to the ways of the streets.[58]

Viramontes addresses the hemispheric issue of Latin American immigration. She engages a woman of color feminist discourse by focusing the action of her story on a Salvadoran immigrant mother whose young son is a "desaparecido," (disappeared political abductee) in her country. According to Saldívar-Hull, "Through his voice we hear the articulation of the dominant race's rationale for excluding brown races from integration into the U.S. society. Because immigrants of different skin color belie the melting-pot myth, it is harder for them to be accepted in the same way that European emigrants have been accepted in the history of U.S. colonization."[59] In the course of the story, Viramontes not only accentuates the injustice and cruelty foisted on "illegal aliens," she criticizes U.S. immigration policies that create and perpetuate oppression and displacement.

INTERPRETING THE FUTURE

First wave Chicana literature is conceived in a desire for personal transformation and sustained in a political consciousness gained through social action that challenges dominant discourses. The sociopolitical and cultural elements of the historiography of first wave Chicana literature appear synonymous with the larger history of Mexican women in the United States, making it a unique and dynamic component of modern U.S. history and literature.

In the struggle to find a voice, first wave Chicana writers became interpreters for their culture. For the descendants of America's first interpreter—the new "hijas de la Malinche"—the work of social activism and creativity presents a formidable challenge for the future. Will the postmodern world, described by Ramon Gutíerrez as a series of fragmentations, break apart the bridge first wave Chicana writers constructed between their political activism and their cultural production?[60]

On another level, will the recycled injustices that seem to circulate throughout the Chicano population decade after decade ensure a pool of postcolonial writers, those who "write back" to the dominant structure and demand to be recognized on their own terms, demand justice, and the right to their creative expression? Perhaps first wave Chicana writers are the tip of the iceberg for what may come. Scholars and artists who may dispense guidance to a younger generation entangled in postmodern complexity express clues to this potential. Cornel West provides an option for artists of color who desire to engage in a cultural politics of difference. He suggests that they become "Critical Organic Catalysts," attuned to the positive elements of the mainstream and grounded in structures of criticism. Artists of color "should be exemplars of what it means to be intellectual freedom fighters, that is, cultural workers who simultaneously position themselves with (or alongside) the mainstream while clearly aligned with groups who vow to keep alive potent traditions of critique and resistance. . . . Openness to others—including the mainstream—does not entail wholesale co-optation, and group autonomy is not group insularity.[61] West maintains a belief in the power of the cultural workers but updates that role by encouraging openness to the mainstream rather than blind confrontation.

Another challenge for Chicana writers appears to be providing visions of unity in a world growing more disorderly. Gutíerrez perceives that the major ideological frameworks of the Chicano movement—cultural nationalism, Marxism, and feminism—have fragmented under the pressures of a postmodern age and "fractured all of this into bits, exploded the categories, and left a disorder and disordering vision of the past and future." Gutíerrez wonders what can be done with a political vision of postmodernisn "with its emphasis on alienation, despair, confusion, and the layer upon layer of splintering and fractures?[62] For Chicana writers, despair and alienation, which are by-products of injustice, provide the fuel and the tension not only for the creation of art, but for the transcendence of one's own social, political, economic, and personal limitations. Within this context, the dangers of postmodernism can offer alternatives. Francisco Lomelí recognizes that the work of Chicana writers of the postmodern period "does not aim to be therapeutic or cosmetic but rather a real proposition for alternatives, thus delving deeper into undervalued women narratives and identity."[63] Delving deeper is not a metaphor for sinking deeper. Chicana writers may choose to take the fragments and reconstruct new visions, new worlds. Or they may see the social and spiritual vacuums caused by alienation as space that can be filled with their stories, their poetry, and their voices. Thus there is a healing quality to first wave Chicana literature.

In her discussion about how Chicana writers heal, Tey Diana Rebolledo states: "They may be wounded by history and society, but the very act of resisting their injuries and healing their wounds through writing becomes an act of triumph. At times the triumph is winged and grand, at times it is quiet and waiting, but always it represents a singing (and its echo) in the snow."[64] Chicana writers often serve as vessels for creating alternative perspectives and self-perceptions that insert personal experience for the purpose of transcending oppression.

Through the process of writing, La Malinche becomes a redefined symbol of women at the crossroads of change. No longer a figure to be scorned or vilified, her role as first interpreter can be perceived as courageous. Like Malinche, first wave Chicana writers take risks that their voices may either disturb sleeping monsters or herald the call for struggle and liberation. Either way, the literature of the "hijas de Malinche" serves to lift an ancient curse, and in the process, first wave Chicana writers reclaim more than language, they reclaim their identities as well.

NOTES

1. Naomi Quiñonez. *Sueno de Colibri / Hummingbird Dream* (Albuquerque, N.Mex.: West End Press, 1985), 2.

2. For a comprehensive listing of Chicana writers that includes many of the first wave, see Teresa Cordova, "Roots and Resistance: The Emergent Writings of Twenty Years of Chicana Feminist Struggle," in *Handbook of Hispanic Cultures in the United States*, ed. Felix Padilla (Houston: Arte Publico Press, 1994).

3. "The Art of the Chicano Movement, and the Movement of Chicano Art," in *Aztlan*, ed. Luis Valdez and Stan Steiner (New York: Vintage Press, 1972), 272.

4. Jose Armas, "Role of Artist and Critic in the Literature of a Developing Pueblo," in *De Colores: Journal of Chicano Expression and Thought, Chicano Literature and Criticism*, ed. Jose Armas, Donaldo W. Urioste, and Francisco A. Lomelí (Albuquerque, N.Mex.: Pajarito Publications, 1977), 5–11.

5. Jose E. Limon, *Mexican Ballads, Chicano Poems: History and Influence in Mexican American Social Poetry* (Berkeley: University of California Press, 1992), 83.

6. Tomas Ybarra-Frausto, "Alurista's Poetic: The Oral, the Bilingual, the Pre-Columbian," in *Modern Chicano Writers*, ed. Joseph Sommers and Tomas Ybarra-Frausto (Englewood Cliffs, N.J.: Prentice-Hall, 1979), 118.

7. Bruce-Novoa, *Chicano Poetry: A Response to Chaos* (Austin: University of Texas Press, 1982), 71.

8. Max Martínez, "Prolegomena for a Study of Chicano Literature," in *De Colores: Chicano Literature and Criticism* (Albuquerque, N.Mex.: Pajarito Publications, 1977), 12.

9. Tomas Rivera, "Chicano Literature: The Establishment of Community," in *A Decade of Chicano Literature (1970–1979): Critical Essays and Bibliography*, ed. Luis Leal et al. (Santa Barbara, Calif.: Editorial la Causa, 1982), 10.

10. Ibid.

11. Teresa Cordova, "Roots and Resistance."

12. Quiñonez, 2

13. See introduction to *Infinite Divisions: An Anthology of Chicana Literature*, ed. Tey Diana Rebolledo and Eliana S. Rivero (Tucson: University of Arizona Press, 1993), 1–33.

14. Adaljiza Sosa-Riddell, "Como Duele," in *Chicanas en la Literatura y el Arte*, ed. Octavio I. Romano-V. and Herminio Rios (Berkeley, Calif.: Quinto Sol Publications, 1973).

15. "Beneath the Shadow of the Freeway," by Lorna Dee Cervantes, in *Mango* (San Jose, 1977), 24–27.

16. Tey Diana Rebolledo, *Women Singing in the Snow: A Cultural Analysis of Chicana Literature* (Tucson: University of Arizona Press, 1995), 49.

17. Ibid., 77.

18. Angie Chabram-Dernersesian, "I Throw Punches for My Race, but I Don't Want to Be a Man: Writing Us—Chica-nos (Girl, Us) / Chicanas—into the Movement Script," in *Cultural Studies*, ed. Lawrence Grossberg, Cary Nelson, and Paul Reichler (New York: Routledge Press, 1992), 81–84.

19. Ibid., 83.

20. Ibid., 82.

21. Ibid., 83.

22. *Chicanas en la Literatura y el Arte*, ed. Octavio I Romano-V and Herminio Rios (Berkeley, Calif.: Quinto Sol Publications, 1973).

23. Asuncio Horno-Delgado, Eliana Ortega, Nina M. Scott, and Nancy Saporta Sternbach, eds., *Breaking Boundaries: Latina Writings and Critical Readings* (Amherst: University of Massachusetts Press, 1989).

24. Elizabeth J. Ordóñez, "The Concept of Cultural Identity in Chicana Poetry," in *Third Woman*, ed. Norma Alarcón (Bloomington, Ind.: Third Woman Press, 1984), 75; and Norma Alarcón, "What Kind of Lover Have You Made Me Mother?: Towards a Theory of Chicanas' Feminism and Cultural Identity through Poetry," in *Women of Color: Perspectives on Feminism and Identity*, ed. Audrey T. McCloskey (Women's Studies Program Occasional Papers Series, Indiana University, vol. 1, no. 1, 1988).

25. Cordelia Candelaria, "La Malinche, Feminist Prototype," in *Frontiers: A Journal of Women Studies* 5, no. 2 (Summer 1980), 6.

26. Bill Ashcroft, Gareth Griffiths, and Helen Tiffin, *The Empire Writes Back: Theory and Practice in Post-Colonial Literatures* (New York: Routledge Press, 1991), 78–81; Tzvetan Todorov, *The Conquest of America* (New York: Harper & Row, 1982), 101.

27. Ashcroft, Griffiths, and Tiffin, 80.

28. Candelaria; Adelaida del Castillo, "Malintzin Tenepal: A Preliminary Look into a New Perspective," in *Essays on La Mujer*, ed. Rosaura Sanchez and Rosa Martínez Cruz (Los Angeles: Chicano Studies Center Publications, 1977), 124–146; Sandra Messinger Cypress, *La Malinche in Mexican Literature: From History to Myth* (Austin: University of Texas Press, 1991), 48.

29. Candelaria, 2–4; del Castillo; Messenger Cypress, chapter 3; Tzvetan Todorov, *The Conquest of America: The Question of the Other* (New York: Harper & Row, 1982), 100–103.

30. This aspect of Malinche's image is discussed by Octavio Paz, "The Sons of La Malinche," in *Labyrinth of Solitude: Life and Thought in Mexico* (New York: Grove Press, 1961), and by Adelaida del Castillo.

31. Chicana feminist revisions of Malinche include the works of Adelaida del Castillo, Cordelia Candelaria, and Deena J. Gonzalez, "Malinche as Lesbian: A Reconfiguration of 500 Years of Resistance," in *California Sociologist: A Journal of Sociology and Social Work* 14, no. 1–2 (Winter/Summer 1991): 93–95.

32. Ashcroft, Griffiths, and Tiffin, 80.

33. Todorov, 101.

34. Chinua Achebe, *Morning Yet on Creation Day* (New York: Doubleday, 1975), 67.

35. *Hunger of Memory* has been highly criticized for the stand Richard Rodriguez takes against bilingual education, and his advocacy for assimilation.

36. Edward Said, *Culture and Imperialism* (New York: Alfred A. Knopf, 1993), xii.

37. Rafael Pérez-Torres, *Movements in Chicano Poetry: Against Myths, against Margins* (Cambridge: Cambridge University Press, 1995), 29.

38. Ibid., 16–18.

39. Ashcroft, Griffiths, and Tiffin, 38.

40. Ibid.

41. Gloria Anzaldúa, *Borderlands / La Frontera: The New Mestiza* (San Francisco: Spinsters / Aunt Lute Book Co., 1987), 40.

42. Ashcroft, Griffiths, and Tiffin, 39–40.

43. Cordelia Candelaria, "Haciendo tamales," in *Ojo de la cueva* (Colorado Springs, Colo.: Maize Press, 1984).

44. Ashcroft, Griffiths, and Tiffin, 54.

45. Lucha Corpi, *Palabras de Mediodía,* trans. Catherine Rodriguez-Nieto (Berkeley, Calif.: El Fuego de Aztlan Publications, 1980), 119. English translation: Steeped in tradition, mystic / and mute, she was sold / from hand to hand, night to night, / denied and desecrated, waiting for the dawn / and for the owl's song / that would never come; / her womb sacked of its fruit, / her soul thinned to a handful of dust. / You no longer loved her, the elders denied her, / and the child who cried out to her "mama!" / grew up and called her "whore."

46. D. E. S. Maxwell, "Landscape and Theme," in *Commonwealth Literature,* ed. John Press (London: Heinemann, 1965), 82–89.

47. Phyllis López, "The Unwanted Emigrants," in *Comadre* (San Jose, Calif.: M'Liss Garzaa, 1976), 3.

48. María Herrera-Sobek, "Grandmother and Pancho Villa," in *CrossRoads,* ed. Arnold Garcia (Oakland, Calif.: Institute for Social and Economic Studies, May 1993), 6.

49. Sonia Saldívar-Hull, "Feminism on the Border: From Gender Politics to Geopolitics," in *Criticism in the Borderlands,* ed. Hector Calderon and Jose David Saldívar (Durham, N.C.: Duke University Press, 1991), 215.

50. Gloria Anzaldúa, *Borderlands / La Frontera,* 21.

51. Saldívar-Hull, 215.

52. Lorna Cervantes, "You Cramp My Style Baby," in Elizabeth J. Ordóñez, "The Concept of Cultural Identity in Chicana Poetry," in *Third Woman,* ed. Norma Alarcón (Bloomington, Ind.: Third Woman Press, 1984), 79.

53. Ramon A. Gutíerrez, "Community, Patriarchy and Individualism: The Politics of Chicano History and the Dream of Equality," *American Quarterly* 45, no. 1 (March 1993): 55.

54. Pat Mora, "Spring Tonic," in *Infinite Divisions,* ed. Tey Diana Rebolledo and Eliana S. Rivero (Tucson: University of Arizona Press, 1993), 352.

55. Gloria Anzaldúa, "Nightvoice," in *Chicana Lesbians: The Girls Our Mothers Warned Us About,* ed. Carla Trujillo (Berkeley, Calif.: Third Woman Press, 1991), 64.

56. Introduction, *Infinite Divisions: An Anthology of Chicana Literature,* ed. Tey Diana Rebolledo and Eliana S. Rivero (Tucson: University of Arizona Press), 30.

57. Saldívar-Hull, 208.

58. María Helena Viramontes, "The Cariboo Cafe," in *The Moths and Other Stories* (Houston: Arte Publico Press, 1985), 61.

59. Saldívar-Hull, 219.

60. Gutíerrez, 65.

61. Cornel West, *Keeping Faith: Philosophy and Race in America* (New York: Routledge, 1993), 27.

62. Gutíerrez, 66.

63. Francisco A. Lomelí, "Ars Cominatoria," in Naomi Quiñonez, "From Trobadora to Anti-World Synthesizer," in *Confrontations et Metissages,* ed. Elyette Benjamin-Labarth et al. (Bordeaux: Université Michel de Montaigne—Bordeaux III, 1994), 262.

64. Rebolledo, *Women Singing in the Snow,* 170.

8 HOW THE BORDER LIES: SOME HISTORICAL REFLECTIONS

Patricia Penn-Hilden

ASKED ABOUT the borders that separate Mexico and the United States, Carlos Fuentes replied: "A big difference, I think, is memory. I have . . . called the U.S. the United States of Amnesia. They tend to forget their own history. So when I am speaking about a Protestant republic, a republic based on democratic principles of self-government, let me not forget that it is also a republic founded on violence. That it is also a republic founded on the exclusion of important . . . groups. That in the foundation of the United States, in its Constitution, in the Declaration of Independence, there is no place for . . . blacks and Indians and Hispanics, and even women are excluded from the body politic" (Szanto: 153). So: "violence" and "exclusion," the unholy twins upon which United States identity rests.

I

"We, the People" were born in the 1620s when groups of English "Pilgrims" landed and the origin tale began to be written. Violence was in their luggage, wrapped in the Protestant Bible with its language of forgetting. An example: On the night of June 5, 1637, John Mason led English troops to attack a sleeping village of Pequot Indians, purportedly as punishment for the deaths of two English adventurers.[1] As the Pequots awoke inside their wood and straw houses, Mason and his men set everything on fire, shooting or hacking to death those who tried to flee. In one hour, at least four hundred people (Cotton Mather estimated five or six hundred) were burnt to death or slaughtered as they ran from their burning homes (Stannard: 114).[2] Later, Mason justified the killing: God, he explained, had "laughed his Enemies and the Enemies of his People to scorn, making them as a fiery oven. . . . Thus did the Lord judge among the heathen, filling the place with dead Bodies!" (113–114). William Bradford's account was more colorful: "It was a fearful sight to see them thus frying in the fire and the streams of blood quenching the same, and horrible was the stink and scent thereof, but the victory seemed a sweet sacrifice, and [the Englishmen] gave praise to god who had wrought so wonderfully for them" (Bradford: 296).

There *were* dissenters. The Puritans' Narragansett scouts protested. "Our Indians," Roger Underhill wrote, "cried 'Mach it, mach it': that is,

'It is naught, it is naught because it is too furious and slays too many people!'" They were distraught, Underhill explained, because Indians did not fight "to conquer and subdue enemies" but rather "only for sport" (Jennings: 223). The English, however, loved another kind of "sport": only a few months later, Capt. Israel Stoughton together with 120 Massachusetts militiamen again crossed the borders of the Pequot nation. Although most Pequots had been exterminated, they still hoped to discover a few refugees. Narragansett scouts again guided the Englishmen. In a swamp near the mouth of the Pequot River, where some hundred survivors had taken refuge after the nighttime massacre of their fellows, the English found their victims. "For sport" Stoughton captured these hapless refugees, then turned them over to John Gallop. Quickly binding the hands and feet of twenty captives, Gallop threw them into the sea, a terrible warning to the rest. He then sent captive women and children to the Massachusetts Bay Colony, where most were enslaved (Drinnon: 44–45).

The Englishmen's sporting adventure did not end there, however. Joined by John Mason with forty more militiamen, Stoughton set off after more Pequots, who, Mason later explained smugly, "could make but little haste. by reason of their Children and want of Provision: being forced to dig for clams and to procure such other things as the Wilderness afforded" (Stannard: 114–115). Three hundred more Pequots were quickly captured and most were killed, some after what John Winthrop described blandly as "torture." "Hard by a most hideous swamp, so thick with bushes and so quagmirey as men could hardly crowd into it," Winthrop gloated later, "they were all gotten" (Winthrop: 220). The survivors provided more "servants" for the colonists. Thomas Endicott wanted both a girl and a boy. Roger Williams wrote Winthrop that he "had fixed mine eye on this little one with the red about his neck" (Drinnon, 47).[3]

Thus was born a quickly forgotten colonial practice. Although this story too is lost in most narratives of American slavery, Indians were, in fact, the first slaves in North America, captured by all the invading Europeans and kept either in the colonies or sold into the transatlantic or Caribbean slave trades.[4]

This, then, is the violence out of which our United States was born, resting on the exclusion—by race—of the first in what has become a large group of U.S. "others."

II

I should like next to suggest, via a series of interwoven "theses on borders," that this mirror making, this building of distances between the "them's" and the "us's," are part of "our" unacknowledged past, part of the total absence of historical memory that has created and maintained "borders." These theses not only protect "We, the People" from the corruption of "others." More insidiously, they also fence the minds of the "others." Often unmarked, such borders are built from the detritus of postcolonialist struggles over the tiny pieces of power left when the "we's" vacate their spaces of authority.

Thus do groups of those marginalized by the racialized fantasies of Europeans and their descendants turn on each other, turn on themselves. Turf wars, blood wars: Chicanos against Indians, Chicanos against Latinos, Indians against Indians. Such contemporary internal walls are as divisive as the work of fanatical missionaries, or governmental divide-and-conquer policies of earlier eras. Such self-created ethnic mirrors, grounded in essentialist versions of the viewer and the viewed, constructed by one group of othered, colonized people to distort or oppose the activities of another, produce only little images, the kind seen in those warped tin mirrors handed out so profligately by Anglo invaders as payment for stolen Indian land. Nevertheless, their edges are sharp enough to cut; divided among themselves, people of color cannot challenge the real structures and purveyors of power. In the reflections produced by such tawdry, useless mirrors, moreover, interethnic stereotypes multiply. Chicanos re-create North America's indigenous peoples in their desired images, Natives whose lands they, like Europeans before them, now inhabit. Indians, in their turn, fight back, inventing narratives of nefarious plots in which Chicano/a warriors steal unbidden onto Indian land, occupy its historic centers, build monuments to their conquering heroes, appropriate ceremonies, histories, and spaces with as much avidity as their European precursors.[5] Ironically, all through this Chicano/Indian quarrel, each side claims its particular "Indianness" (Aztec on the one hand, nineteenth-century Plains warrior on the other), each more essentialized than the most nationalistic denizen of an unchallenged Aztlán would take as his/her Chicana/o identity, or any Indian claim when alone among other Indians.

La Nueva Edad

University of California, Berkeley. Spring, 1998. A day-long Latina conference, created by seven Latina and Indian graduate students. A large room, filled with some two hundred people, mostly women. Arriving early, I sat near the back of the semicircle of chairs, next to two friends and colleagues, one Chicana, one Puerto Rican.

The day began when a visiting Chicana performance artist, kneeling on a mat in the center of the circle, lit some sage, waving its smoke around her body, her space, the room. She explained that this was a ceremony of purification, learned from Frank LaPena, her professor at Sacramento State University and a well-known Maidu artist. Next she spoke an autobiographical "border" monologue, a life lived in Gloria Anzaldúa's "frontera." This was familiar terrain and my mind wandered. Suddenly, I was startled back to attention: "*Gerónimo,* our hero of the border wars, our fighter for freedom and independence from the Anglos. . . . " Already a little disconcerted by the faux Plains Indian purification ceremony, I was truly stunned by this whimsical rewriting of history, this curious appropriation of a Native hero. Repronouncing his name, I whispered to my friends: "Geronimo?! He hated Mexicans, loathed Mexicans, much more, in fact, than he hated the Americans! Mexicans killed his family. Mexicans drove him to take up war. How can this woman appropriate him for her own historical narrative like this?" But my comments elicited no response. My companions, steeped in a postmodern tolerance of historically preposterous inventions, remained unmoved. My historian's sensibilities offended, I tried again: "How can she rename him in the language he most hated—translating him into a Catholic saint, Jerome, patron of Lisbon slavers who bought and sold Indians in a lucrative trade that peopled the world with North American natives? The language of those who slaughtered his wife and children?" Again, disinterest. The look both friends turned toward me was mirrored later by other faculty colleagues, and even by the conference organizers. Amnesia, indeed.

And in the past five years, all over the Southwest, tour groups of Chicanos visit the Pueblos, the Navajo nation, the Apache nations. Everywhere they are carrying their children to view "our heritage." These visits, while not very different from the Anglo tourism that has afflicted the peoples of the Southwest for a hundred years, remain fairly anodyne. So, too, the increased assertions of their "Indianness" by Chicana/o undergraduates at the University of California (feelings that bring large numbers of Chicana/o students into Native American studies courses and draw increasing numbers to Intertribal Student Council events, further complicating the "blood purity" identity politics that cut through every Native American collectivity). But such shifts in identity assertions, however progressive in a Chicano world that once shunned any suggestion of "Indio" heritage, nevertheless disguise the existence of real quarrels grounded in real history, effectively promoting still more of the collective amnesia that maintains the borders and protects power. Until that real history comes back into view, such shifts smack more of spiritual tourism and obfuscatory hybridization than of historically grounded identification.

Remembering

Milan Kundera: "The struggle of men against power is the struggle of memory against forgetting."

Simon Ortiz: "The most immediate . . . responsibility that Pueblo and other Native Americans in New Mexico have faced in their struggle for . . . continuance in 1998 has been to counter the Cuartocentenario, . . . an audacious celebration of four hundred years of colonization . . . of Pueblo lands, people, and native culture that began in 1598." (Ortiz, "First Nations, First Peoples, First Voices for Hope and Continuance": 1)

That year, Juán de Oñate, sent by the governor of New Spain, invaded what is now New Mexico. Shortly thereafter, thirty-one of his soldiers, led by

Oñate's nephew, an officer called Zaldívar, stopped off at Acoma Pueblo to seize provisions for his troops' continued march up the valley of what *they* named the Big River.

Simon Ortiz: "U.S. and New Mexico maps and tourist bureaus do not know the Aacqumeh hanoh's name for the local community. It is Deetseyamah—The North Door. Looking northward from Aacqu and the tall rock monolith on which the mother pueblo sits, there is an opening, like a gateway, between two mesas. Looking northward, too, from Aacqu, one can see Kaweshtima—'Snow Peaked'—a dark blue misted mother mountain. Those Aacqumeh names do not appear anywhere except in the people's hearts and souls and history and oral tradition, and in their love. But you will find the easy labels: Mt. Taylor, Elevation 11,950 ft, and Acoma: The Sky City." (Ortiz, *Woven Stone:* 337–338)

Leslie Marmon Silko: "All of creation suddenly had two names: an Indian name and a white name. . . . And there would be no peace and the people would have no rest until the entanglement had been unwound to the source." (Silko, *Ceremony:* 53)

This legacy, and the subsequent translations into a third colonizers' language, scarred the land and the people.

In keeping with ancient Pueblo tradition, the people of Acoma welcomed Zaldívar's soldiers with food and clothing. (Ortiz: "They must have felt like kings, even godlike, instead of the mercenaries, errand boys, and mystics that they were" [*Woven Stone:* 341]). The Spaniards demanded more and promised to return. When they came back for their booty, some decided to steal some sacred turkeys. Still others raped at least one Acoma girl. Outraged Acoma warriors, women and men together, attacked and killed Zaldívar and twelve of his soldiers, driving the rest to flee, back to Oñate.

Oñate immediately sent a heavily armed expedition to punish the people of Acoma. Very quickly seventy Spanish soldiers killed eight hundred Indian women, men, and children. Eighty men and five hundred women and children were captured for trial. The results of the trial, according to Ramón Gutiérrez, were these:

> All men and women over 12 were condemned to 20 years of slavery among New Mexico's settlers; . . . all men over 25 had one of their feet severed. Children under the age of 12 were distributed as servants to monasteries and Spanish households. Two Hopi Indians captured at Acoma each lost their right hands and were dispatched home as testaments of the Christians' wrath. (Gutiérrez: 54)

Legacies

Ortiz, again: "When I was a boy . . . on the Acoma Pueblo reservation, I . . . never heard a specific . . . account of the destruction of Acoma in January of 1599. I've racked my memory trying to recall if there was any mention of it among many other stories told about 'the old days' of Acoma . . . , but no, there were no oral stories about this terrible knowledge. And it was not until I was in college that I came across . . . references to it in one or two books. . . . For years I wondered why Acoma people never talked openly about the destruction . . . almost as if it had never happened, almost as if the people felt it was their fault, almost as if they were burdened by an immense guilt. Now, I realize, it is because this historical truth was purposely and deliberately dismissed . . . and better left unheard and forgotten. Sadly, the result is that we do not have a truthful, honest account of ourselves as a Pueblo Indian people. And as a further result, we are diminished as an indigenous people" ("First Nations, First Peoples . . . ": 1).

Others know these silences, hybrids born of the shame of survivors, the horror of the truth, the fear of the personal and collective consequences of acknowledging the enormity of human cruelty, of the collective tragedy. Primo Levi has limned these borders in his terrible memoirs of the German camps. More recently, at the dedication of the Angel Island Immigration Station as a National Monument, its founder, Paul Chow, noted that at last "the stories of Angel Island could be told without fear, without shame." Angel Island Immigration Station, San Francisco's Ellis Island, will mark the year 2000 with an exhibit by Flo Ow Wong. She calls her work "made in usa: Angel Island Shhh."

Ortiz reclaims Acoma history for all Southwestern Native people: "It is our responsibility, to dedicat[e] . . . ourselves to . . . acknowledging the historical background of the 1998 Cuartocentenario . . . to . . . realize ourselves in terms of our struggle, hope, and continuance as First Nations, First Peoples, First Voices" ("First Nations, First Peoples . . . ": 1).

But it isn't easy. First the Spaniards rewrote the story of their invasion. Then came the Anglos. The narrative of their conquest of the U.S. Southwest, bolstered by the English-invented "Black Legend" which demonized their Spanish predecessors, created yet another cast of characters. In Anglo stories, the violent, angry Pueblo peoples were transformed yet again, their "savage" resistance forgotten. In Anglo eyes, they were ancient, peaceable, nonviolent people, tillers of the soil, gentle potters, architects of quaint little hillside cities. Their image contrasted sharply with that circulated about their still-unconquered neighbors, the Apaches and Navajos.

The Anglos did not stop at rewriting their narrative of rescue of helpless people from the horrors of Spanish (and Mexican) occupiers. As time passed and as the remaining "dangerous" Indians were conquered, the Southwest began to assume yet another image. This desert land, "opened" by the coming of the railroads, began to attract rapacious Eastern tourists, led, as always, by artifact-collecting, career-pursuing anthropologists. Tour brochures and anthropological freak shows, the results of dozens of "expeditions" into the desert, not only circulated the stereotypes launched by the first Anglos but offered them an even wider audience. The image of a peaceable, slightly stupid Pueblo people spread.

Headlines

March 6, 1886: *The Illustrated Police News*

> Cowed by a Woman
> A Craven Red Devil Weakens in the Face of a Resolute White Heroine—Exciting Adventure in an Indian Village in Arizona.

THE STORY:

At Oraibi, an ancient Hopi town, an anthropologist, Mathilda Coxe Stevenson, together with her husband, Col. James Stevenson, and eight Indians (four "friendly Moquis" and four Navajos), decided to investigate Hopi religious practices by climbing into a ceremonial space. With the arrogance she and her sister anthropologists carried in their vast, artifact-hiding handbags, Mathilda Stevenson asked no permission. Indeed, none of her party so much as acknowledged the watching Hopis, gathered in their distress at the whites' sudden appearance. Instead, she simply invaded the sacred space. As more people became aware of the Stevensons' activities, they gathered, circling the Anglos threateningly. When Mrs. Stevenson persisted, some demanded that all the whites be captured and, in the police reporter's words, taken to "the underground chapel of the village, and there summarily dealt with. . . . The friendly Moquis [in keeping with their stereotype] stood their ground only a few minutes and then disappeared, but the Navajos, who are made of firmer material, remained. Col. Stevenson," the reporter assured his Eastern readers, "says that while the situation was highly interesting, it was probably less alarming than it would have been to people unacquainted with the *natural timidity of the Pueblos.* Mrs. Stevenson, who has sojourned with her husband among many wild tribes and knows the Indian character well, created an opportune diversion by shaking her fist in the face of a hunchbacked savage, whose vindictive eloquence seemed to exert a most mischievous influence over his fellows, addressing to him at the same time several brief, but vigorous remarks in English and Spanish, which he was, of course, quite unable to understand. Before the man had recovered his self-possession, the strangers had backed down the ladder, and then slowly made their way, with the whole howling pack—men and women, children and dogs—at their heels, to their ponies, mounted and rode down to camp" (Babcock and Parezo: 11; emphasis added).

This sordid tale—written to disguise the ignorance, the cowardice, and the avarice of the whites in the face of organized Hopi hostility—is quoted by Barbara Babcock and Nancy J. Parezo in a catalogue celebrating a recent exhibition, "Daughters of the Desert: Women Anthropologists and the Native American Southwest, 1880–1980," held at the Arizona State Museum on the campus of the University of Arizona. Their comment on this newspaper story, p. 10, reads: "Stevenson's crusading zeal in collecting data occasionally offended her subjects. In the late 19th century, however, her field methods were unfortunately the accepted practice."

Zuni artist Phil Hughte strikes back:

> *A Zuni Artist Looks at Frank Hamilton Cushing* satirizes Cushing's stay among the Zuni people, where his depredations on behalf of the Smithsonian Institution were many and terrible and often very funny.[6] Hughte's work includes one telling portrait of Mathilda Stevenson, here trying to "invade" Zuni, the pueblo Cushing considered his own. One picture is captioned: "Yes, I *can* take a picture!" The text explains, "Cushing is telling Mathilda Coxe Stevenson not to take photographs of the Kachinas, but Mathilda was so stubborn that she had to have everything her way. Here she takes her umbrella and hits him over the head while the little Kachina Dancer is wondering what the heck this box is and is shaking his rattle at the camera." (Hughte: 92–93)

The Stevensons and others from the East worked their artifact-collecting myth-making more than a hundred years ago. But the tales they told, of brave and clever whites outwitting dumb Indians (who could not speak "civilized" languages but could, instead, only "howl" with their dogs) or "protecting" stupid, passive Puebloans from the incursions of other whites, continue to find voice. Both anthropologists and historians still retell a whitewashed past; Pueblo people still resist.[7] But over time, the clarity of the pre–First World War anthropologists' "us" and "them"—Yankee anthropologists, Southwestern Indians—blurred, assuming shapes more representative of the region's messy ethnicity.

One of the most influential (though by no means the first) to repaint the prewar Southern Pacific Railroad's tourist brochure version of the Southwest was Walter Prescott Webb, professor at the University of Texas and president of the American Historical Association. His 1935 hymn to male bonding, *The Texas Rangers*, divided the Southwest into three distinct groups: Indians (hopelessly savage, hopelessly warlike), Mexicans (cruel, addicted to horses, "gay attire," and Catholic "superstitions"), and Anglos (Protestant, straight-shooting, brave, honest). His triumphalist portrait, although focused on Texas, left no doubts in Southwestern Anglo hearts: the conquest, from the Gulf of Mexico to the Pacific, was right, was just, inevitable, and the best possible outcome for all the parties concerned. Although Webb's viciously racist characterizations of Indians prompted no criticism, his view of Mexicans was quickly challenged, first in the works of a progressive public official and journalist from Los Angeles, Carey McWilliams.

McWilliams's first work, *Factories in the Field* (1939), denounced the exploitation of Mexican migrant farmworkers. A decade later, he published the first history of Chicanos in the United States, *North from Mexico: The*

Spanish-Speaking People of the United States. This work, frequently republished (including a Spanish version, in 1968), immediately prompted warm and ongoing praise from Chicano scholars. The 1990 edition carries these accolades from George I. Sánchez, author of *Becoming Mexican American:* "Since its first appearance in 1950, I have placed a heavy reliance on this book—in my university classes, in my lectures, and in my counsel to those who would know my people. . . . *North from Mexico* is a persistent cry in a wilderness of neglect, mistreatment, and ignorance on the part of those who became dominant after the American occupation of the Southwest." "*North from Mexico,*" Tony Calderón adds, "is my bible on knowing about my heritage."

But Pueblo Indian peoples—or any of the indigenous peoples of the Americas—cannot feel any more sanguine about McWilliams than they did about Walter Prescott Webb. To Indian eyes, McWilliams's book is little more than an extended apologia for the Spanish invasion. In McWilliams's narrative, in fact, the Spaniards hardly invaded at all. Instead, like Webb's manifestly destined Anglos, McWilliams's conquistadores merely hastened a mysterious historical process already well under way when Oñate mounted his horse to ride north in 1598. "Prior to [the Spaniards'] appearance in the Southwest," McWilliams assures readers, "a great drama had been enacted of which they knew nothing and concerning which not too much is known today. It would seem, however, that the Pueblo Indians had for many years been fighting a losing battle against their hereditary enemies, the nomadic tribes. Driven out of the river bottoms and valleys, they had finally sought shelter in the nooks and crevices of the mountainous portions of the Southwest. Here, in cliff-dwellings, terraced adobes, and mountain villages, they were able to survive although in constant peril. As a result of protracted defensive warfare, their culture had begun to disintegrate and showed a marked decline in vigor at about the time the Spaniards arrived. *In fact, it is altogether probable that the Spaniards rescued and to a degree revitalized the culture of the Pueblo Indians*" (38–39, emphasis added).

I should have hoped that this effort by a Chicanophiliac Anglo writer to mute the facts of the Spanish conquest was so patently outrageous, so ridiculous, that it would elicit some criticism from George Sánchez or Tony Calderón, however heroic the book's revisionist portrait of their Mexican forebears. But alas, it did not. Worse still, McWilliams has Chicano descendants. Ramón Gutiérrez has recently joined his voice to this recuperative project. In the process, he has outraged contemporary Indians everywhere. His brilliantly written *When Jesus Came, the Corn Mothers Went Away* (1991), published to loud acclaim from intellectuals in both Spain and the United States, offers a more nuanced apology for the invasion, but one that nevertheless echoes those of his predecessors. Gutiérrez, too, blames the victims while at the same time minimizing the Spaniards' evil. His main focus in his apologetic version of the Spaniards' invasion is Pueblo women. According to Gutiérrez, "traditional" Pueblo women lived out their lives as passive, heavily sexualized servants of men. In their ancient, idyllic world women's lives unfolded naturally: "Rain fertilized seeds as men fertilized their women. . . . In the household, women gave men their love and their bodies." Indeed, "after feeding, the activity of greatest cultural import to Pueblo women was sexual intercourse." Thus was their biology their destiny. Gutiérrez concludes, "women were empowered through their sexuality" (14, 15, 17). Gutiérrez's sources for such curious observations are not Pueblo people or their histories. Rather, they are those same pre–World War I anthropologists, praised by the contemporary "screamer press," satirized by Phil Hughte. Gutiérrez's footnotes cite a notorious crew: Elsie Clews Parsons, Frank Hamilton Cushing, Mathilda Coxe Stevenson, Jesse Fewkes. Still more evidence comes from the self-serving narratives of Spanish soldiers and priests, whose admitted sexual exploitation of Pueblo women and girls (as well as men and boys) would not render them particularly reliable sources in the eyes of most historians.[8]

When Gutiérrez reports that Spanish friars killed men in order to steal their wives for sexual slavery, he not only removes agency from women whose participation in resistance to the Spaniards was violent and ongoing, but he also adds an excuse, again blaming the victims: "As we saw in Chapter 1, successful men who became caciques, as the friars in essence had done, were surrounded by secondary wives and concubines who offered their love and bodies in return for gifts and benefits for their children. . . . The Puebloans always transformed that which they deemed potently dangerous and malevolent into a beneficial force by offering it food and sexual intercourse. Just as the Spanish soldiers *had fallen into the loving arms of Indian women,* so too eventually did the friars, though undoubtedly nagged by pangs of guilt" (123; emphasis added). Reading these words, I am reminded of those Hollywood films of the post–World War II era which featured U.S. soldiers or occupation officials "falling into the loving arms" of Japanese women. The sacrificial female, charged with a distinctly non-Protestant sexuality, wears many racial masks, it seems.

Indian readers of *When Jesus Came, the Corn Mothers Went Away* not only protested the title's implication—that Pueblo religion disappeared in the face of Christianity—but they also winced at the portrait of Puebloans, especially women Puebloans, as highly sexualized people, whose every act, before or after the invasion, bore an intense sexual charge. This is, as many have noted, not only a bizarre misreading of the Pueblo world, but it is also a version of the invasion in which anything the Spaniards did—whether they were murderous *conquistadores,* fanatical priests, or thieving "settlers"—was overdetermined, mere adjustments of the social structures of the preconquest world.

Even the 1680 Pueblo Revolt undergoes "hispanization" in Gutiérrez's hands. He describes the retreat of the Spanish "colonists." As they hastened south, driven by enraged Pueblo warriors, their journey was "filled with horrors. In every village they found piles of mutilated bodies strewn amid ashes of still smoking fires. At Sandia Pueblo the mission's statues were covered with excrement. Two chalices had been discarded in a basket of manure and the paint on the altar's crucifix had been stripped off with a whip. Feces covered the holy communion table and the arms of a statue of Saint Francis had been hacked off with an ax. At every mission along their route they reported the most unspeakable profanations of Christian sacra." (Rudy Giuliani could not be more outraged.) Still, Gutiérrez nods in the direction of fairness though with an equivocal gesture that equates the Pueblo resistence and the Spanish invasion of their homes: "Though the Christians were aghast at how the Pueblo Indians manifested their anger, one only has to recall the massive desecration of katsina masks, kivas, and other native sacra that occurred during the Spanish conquest to understand why the Indians retaliated so exactly during the Pueblo Revolt. The tables were now turned in this contest of cultures. The Indians had learned well from their overlords the function of iconoclasm in political spectacle" (134, 135). "Contest of cultures"? "Iconoclasm in political spectacle"? What of murder, rape, torture, enslavement, theft? The Spaniards' destruction of the Pueblos, their mutilation and murder of Pueblo people fall well behind these racing abstractions, running toward an entirely metaphysical finish line.

Many among the "peaceable" Puebloans, angered by Gutiérrez's work, articulated their concerns. Of Gutiérrez's claims that his work "gives vision to the blind and gives voice to the mute and silent," that it demonstrates that "the conquest of America was not a monologue but a dialogue between cultures," Evelina Zuni Lucero (from Isleta and San Juan Pueblos) replied, "How can citations of a few Pueblo stories and reliance on data recorded by non-Pueblos possessing a vastly different worldview constitute a Pueblo view, a Pueblo voice? I find an unexplainable contradiction between Gutiérrez's claim that there was a historical dialogue that included the Pueblos and his statement that he could find 'no way around' using what he admits is European-biased information because 'there are no Pueblo Indian records of the seventeenth, eighteenth, and nineteenth century . . . ' A dialogue between cultures, at least one that includes Pueblos, cannot occur if Pueblos continue to be spoken for by 'others' but are not heard from directly" (*American Indian Culture and Research Journal:* 175).

Gutiérrez seemed surprised that Pueblo people were not among his many fans. Responding to criticism, he claimed that he had received a letter from the "All Pueblo Council" [*sic*] thanking him "for writing about the history of the Pueblo Indians and for bringing attention to their historical plight." At this, Simon Ortiz, who had been involved in the New Mexico conference, again weighed in: "Because Gutiérrez pointedly says that the All Indian Pueblo Council 'wrote' to 'thank' him 'for writing about the history of the Pueblo Indians,' I asked Herman Agoyo about it. Mr. Agoyo's reply was that it was 'highly unlikely that AIPC would write such a letter.' As an Acoma Pueblo citizen, I have to say that scholars and academics cannot dismiss our orally transmitted historical knowledge which is carried from the past to the present." (h-amindian, discussion threads: n.p.) Gutiérrez's work, though participant in the ongoing rewriting of a prouder Chicano history, once again silences the Native peoples of this land. It must be said, however, that he has attained at least one of his primary goals: to generate "a sustained discussion of the painful history of race relations in New Mexico that goes beyond the silly romanticism of harmonious pluralism" (h-amindian: n.p.).

III

Simon Ortiz tells a very different Pueblo history in his poems. "Our Homeland, a National Sacrifice Area" is his epic of the invasion (*Woven Stone:* 337–363). It begins:

> *It was only the second day,*
> *and I was on my way home*
> *from being with Srhakaiya.*
> *It is the mountain west*
> *of Aacqu.*
> *I was sick,*
> *feeling a sense of "otherness."*
> *How can I describe it?*
> *An electric current*
> *coursing in ghost waves through me?*
> *"Otherness."*

Otherness: inflicted by the overculture's re-creation of a Pueblo Indian man; prompted by the alienation of this land of the Aacqumeh hanoh, Ortiz's land, now a trash dump, a poisoned well, a (radioactive) tourist attraction.

"'Otherness.' / I can't describe it / and perhaps there is / such a sensation. / I had drunk some water the evening before / on the northside of Srhakaiya. / The spring was scummed over. / A Garden Deluxe wine empty lay nearby.

"Years ago, in the 1950s, / when I was a boy of 9 or 10, / I'd come with my father / and the sheep we herded . . . / . . . we drank from the spring. / The clear cold water was covered / with heavy plank boards / and the pool was fed by the seep / from the shale rock. / The pool had a stone lining." . . . . /

"Pueblo Bonito in Chaco Canyon / is maintained by the U.S. Park Service. / Northwards, 65 miles away, / is Aztec National Monument. / To the northwest, another 85 miles, / is Mesa Verde National Park. / The park service has guided tours, / printed brochures, clean rest rooms, / and the staff is friendly, polite, / and very helpful. / You couldn't find a better example / of Americanhood anywhere. / the monuments, or ruins / as they are called, are very well kept / by the latest technology / in preserving antiquity. /. . . .

"At Mesa Verde, not long ago, / they had Esther in a glass case. / She was a child, born / from a woman / 1000 years ago. / The U.S. Park Service / was reluctant to let her go / when some Indian people / demanded her freedom. / *Government bureaucrats / said Indians were insensitive / to U.S. heritage* / For years they sold / postcards of Esther. / Maybe they still do. / By pushing buttons, thousands of yearly tourists to these places can get an audio-taped narration. /. . . . See Museum for More Information" (emphasis added).

IV

First Peoples' First Struggle

COLONIZATION:

I read from the Anglo newspaper: *The New York Times,* Monday, February 9, 1998:

> Conquistador Statue Stirs Hispanic Pride and Indian Rage
> By James Brooke
>
> "Espanola, New Mexico.—One moonless night in early January, just as Hispanic New Mexicans were starting to celebrate the 400th anniversary of the first Spanish settlement in the American West, an Indian commando group stealthily approached a bronze statue . . . of the first conquistador, Don Juan de Oñate. With an electric saw, the group slowly severed his right foot—boot, stirrup, star-shaped spur and all."

SO: "WHO STOLE OÑATE'S FOOT?"

Michael Lacapa

"My grandmothers and grandfathers stole the foot. For it was Oñate himself who ordered hands and feet to be cut off Native Americans after defeating the Acoma Pueblo in 1599. It was our grandmas and grandpas that had to go through life without hands to touch and feel the future. Yes, my grandparents stole his foot.

. . . .

"We the Native American people took his foot and ground it up into a powder and threw it into the wind. Then we took our sacred cornmeal and made four lines on the ground, so this foot will not be able to return and harm us again. We did this so we can claim our right to be as every person, a human being.

Because now you see, today Oñate, he is defeated." (Ortiz, "First Nations, First Peoples . . . ": 32)

The *New York Times* article, together with its large photograph, writes a different scenario, one seen from the Anglo center, written in the voice of white, male privilege. Here, in the Southwest, site of generations of Anglo tourist dreams, two of the United States's subjugated "others" are quaintly at each other's throats. Brooke explains, "Below the bland, homogenized landscape of franchise motels and restaurants, ancient history [*sic*!] is exerting a powerful, subterranean pull." Like some mysterious ophiolatrous sea creatures, Brooke continues, "Hispanic residents are clinging to Oñate out of insecurities over losing their language, culture and political . . . dominance. . . . Spanish," Brooke claims, "no longer echoes around Santa Fe as the 10th generation of Spanish descendants has assimilated to the point of losing its ancestral language."

Such ignorant observations of Santa Fe's recent Anglo-ization position Brooke firmly in his all-white world, where the language spoken by those who cleaned his hotel rooms, cooked the food he ate, ran the tourist offices and guide services, was a silent one, although the same silent language spoken all across the *Times*'s home city. Still, Brooke's dubious portrait relegates Santa Fe's Latino population to Euro-America's standard location for Others, that historical reservation long occupied by the ever-vanishing Indians. There, behind the barbed wire of white ignorance, the ethnics quarrel among themselves. But the quarrel is very real. Commemorating Juan de Oñate four hundred years after his ride north was an act sure to awaken every latent tension between Chicanos and Indians. The midnight theft of Oñate's foot from the 1992 statue erected in Alcalde, New Mexico, was the first shot in what grew into a vigorous, three-pronged battle. When Albuquerque officials proposed their own statue for the Cuarto Centenario, war broke out in earnest. Unlike Anglos, Indians and Chicanos remember.

Conroy Chino, TV newsman from Acoma Pueblo: "He inflicted tremendous pain and suffering, death and destruction, especially among the Acoma people."

John Kessell, Spanish colonial historian: "Consider that something happened and it brought people together and that's something to examine."

Herman Agoyo, San Juan Pueblo Tribal Council: "From our viewpoint, we would prefer that it never did happen" (Linthiuim: n.p.).

Renaldo "Sonny" Rivera, sculptor of mutilated statue: "He is the father of New Mexico. I think he was a hell of a man" (*Albuquerque Journal:* n.p.).

Recounting a dispute between one Acoma woman and Hispanic supporters of another *cuarto centenario* Oñate statue in Albuquerque, Brooke quotes Darva Chino's plea to the city council: "Don't dishonor those Acoma families who have chosen to live in this city." But her plea fell on hostile ears: "Millie Santillanes, a Hispanic organizer of the Oñate festivities, *shot back,* 'Acoma has no place in *our* memorial.'"

In Albuquerque, the more numerous "Hispanic" citizens won, though it was not all a matter of numbers, nor did they gain a heroic, unmediated hero figure such as the one in Alcalde which "lost" its foot. Their memorial, representing "Spain's contribution to New Mexico—representing Oñate and the Indians before and after the colonization, will be designed by three local artists, one Chicano, one Puebloan, and one Anglo. Together, they will attempt to bridge the distance yawning between supporters of Oñate and those who decry the invasion, who agree with Adres Lauriano, a former governor of Sandia Pueblo: 'Oñate was a ruthless killer, a man motivated by greed'" (Associated Press Archive, *Albuquerque Journal* Archives: n.p.). Moreover, this collectively produced memorial is shortly to be joined by an uncontroversial Holocaust memorial sponsored by the 1 percent of the Albuquerque population that is Jewish.

Why memorialize the holocaust that is *not* ours rather than the one that *is* ours? Surely the answer here has less to do with the Spanish descendants' local dominance and more to do with how the United States racializes its exclusions? A Nazi Holocaust memorial in virtually every major city of the United States (some cities have two or more) while history books whisper nothing about the violent histories of the United States? Amnesia, indeed.

That James Brooke's article offers *Times* readers a view from the center to the touristy non-Anglo peripheries is underscored by its conclusion. In their behalf, Brooke has located an authoritative voice to mediate among the fractious ethnics. It is that of Marc Simmons, Anglo biographer of Oñate, who offers both Indians and Latinos satisfyingly American reasons why the conquistador should be honored by "us": "In what is now the Western U.S.," Simmons tells Brooke, "he was the founder of the livestock industry, the mining industry, and he opened the first major road. . . . He brought Christianity and Western Culture."

Oh, good: cattle have eaten the plains and are in the process of destroying the desert. Mining and roads have poisoned both the Indians who have dug the coal and uranium and copper and the air they breathe. And as for the "civilization" brought to the savages, well, I can only think of Gandhi's (possibly apocryphal) reply when he was asked what he thought of Western civilization. "I think it would be a good idea," he said.

So the *New York Times* judges: Oñate is to be honored. But the story's photograph tells an additional story. Oñate is the noble—*but vanished*—past of the "Hispanic" population of the Southwest, a glorious past to be sure, one which will provide the stooped and bowed living figure, as well as other parents and grandparents of assimilated English-speaking children, *some* pride, because Anglos have honored their entrepreneurial ancestor, if not them. In a process all too familiar to Natives, the conquistador's statue freezes Chicanos' positive images in the past, here cloaked in what is recognizably European *and military* regalia.

V

It's All about Land

Joke: In the 1960s, NASA set up a moon landing practice area in the Arizona desert. One day the astronauts and NASA officials noticed two Dine sheepherders, watching intently. Curious, one of the NASA men approached the two men to explain that this was practice for a landing on the moon. The older Navajo regarded him silently for a few seconds, then he turned to his companion and said, in Navajo, "Ask them if I can send a message to the moon." When the younger man translated the request, the NASA official was quick in his enthusiasm. "Of course we will carry a Navajo message to the moon," he told them, handing the old man a paper and pen. The old man wrote only one line. Then he handed the paper solemnly to the white man. "What does it say?" the NASA man asked. "Oh, I can't tell you that," the younger Navajo said. Frustrated, NASA tried for several days to find a willing translator in the Navajo Nation. Everyone approached took the paper, read the message, laughed, and handed it back without telling them what it said. Only later, in Phoenix, did the frustrated officials find a translator. "Watch out for these guys," the message read, "they come to steal your land."

And they did. In a process many Native people call "Trick or Treaty," the invaders from Europe, together with their descendants, mapped the borders between the hundreds of Native nations in North America. Then they eliminated them one by one, shrinking Indian land into smaller and smaller parcels. Finally, when reservations still held land whites desired, they sold it out from under Native feet. It was quite blatant. Posters plastered all across the Eastern United States trumpeted the possibilities:

INDIAN LAND FOR SALE

Get a Home Perfect Title

Of *

Your own (photograph of a Plains chief)

* Possession

EASY PAYMENTS Within 30 Days

FINE LANDS IN THE WEST

IRRIGATED GRAZING AGRICULTURAL

IRRIGABLE DRY FARMING

IN 1910 THE DEPARTMENT OF THE INTERIOR

SOLD UNDER SEALED BIDS ALLOTTED

INDIAN LAND AS FOLLOWS:

Location Acres Average price per acre (Library of Congress)[9]

which brings me to:

VI

Building Borders

How does exclusion work? Where are borders built? How are they are maintained? Within the borders of the United States of Amnesia live many languages of forgetting, all of which shape discourses that themselves become borders. Out West, we have the revered pioneer's tale. Here is Thomas J. Farnham, who carefully recorded the manifestation of his destiny in "An 1839 Wagon Train Journal." His text employs several of the mechanisms of historical forgetting. Here is the male Yankee pioneer map of North America. Its axis moves from East to West. Behind lies civilization, ahead, untamed wilderness.

Farnham and his companions reached the "border of the Indian domains . . . anxious . . . to . . . linger over every object that reminded us we were still on the confines of that civilization which we had inherited from a thousand generations: a vast and imperishable legacy of civil and social happiness. It was painful to approach the *last* frontier enclosure—the *last* habitation of the white man—the *last* semblance of home. . . . We drank at the well and traveled on. It was now behind us" (6; emphasis added).

Still, that "civilization's" discontents had driven Farnham and his companions to seek relief. They found it immediately. Though "indeed beyond the sanctuaries of society . . . the spirit of the Red Man, wild and careless as the storms he buffets, began to come over us: and we shouldered our rifles and galloped away for a deer in the lines of timber that threaded the western horizon. Our first hunt in the depths of the beautiful and dreadful wilderness!" (6).

Like today's New Agers, these invaders wanted only spirit, not reality. *Real* Indians, flesh and blood Indians, were to be dispossessed, killed. Thus they deserved the white man's conquest. "The savages" in Farnham's text are only semihuman, nearly inarticulate: "Our savage visitors seized . . . [a pair of discarded boots] with the greatest eagerness, and in their pantomimic language, aided by harsh, guttural grunts, congratulated themselves upon becoming the possessors of so much wealth" (7). But how did Farnham know what the grunts and signs meant? No matter: his blithe assumption of authority to speak for others marked that vast sense of privilege, carried in the saddlebags, tucked into covered wagons, that marched West across countless Indian borders, taking, renaming, "taming" the "dreadful wilderness."[10]

Pioneer arrogance included excuses for the massive dislocation of Indian peoples across North America that made way for white conquest. Here is how Farnham explained the dozens of infamous "removals," all those "trails of tears" that forced so many Native nations from their homes to the "Indian Territory" designated for them:

> And various and numerous were the efforts [whites] made to raise and ameliorate [the Indians'] condition in their old haunts within the precincts of the States. But total or partial failure followed them all. . . . All experience tended to prove that [the Indians'] proximity to the whites induced among them more vice than virtue; . . . both the welfare of the Indians and the duty of the Government [thus] urged their colonization in a portion of the western domain where, freed from all questions of conflicting sovereignties, and under the protection of the Union . . . , they might find a refuge from those influences which threatened the annihilation of their race. (7)

Such a self-servingly false tale demanded obfuscation. In this—and other invaders'—texts, writers employed both abstractions as agents—here "influences"—and the passive voice to hide white responsibility.

That was 1839. Lest we imagine that the amnesia has lifted, here is part of the entry called "Sioux Indians" from the recent *New Encyclopedia of the American West.* Note the obfuscatory passive voice here, too: "By the 1880s, increasing pressure for Sioux lands led to the division of the Great Sioux Reservation into five reservations. This policy of allotment and assimilation was accompanied by an all-out program of *cultural modification*" (304).[11]

"Who-Whose-Whom?" Cries Lenin's Ghost

Note, too, the accompanying illustration chosen by the *New York Times* to illustrate its review of this book. It is an Indian version of Oñate's statue, a familiar photograph of the vanishing, but still noble savage. There he stands, still proud in his ragged blanket, Sitting Bull, great Lakota leader, vanquished. This is a memorial photograph, celebrating white victory, remembering an opponent once worthy of white conquest. This is Kevin Costner's Sioux chief, just after the white lieutenant abandons him to the cavalry.

V

Caring for Borders

It's tough. Here's Newt Gingrich:

> From the Jamestown Colony and the Pilgrims, through de Tocqueville's 'Democracy in America,' up to the Norman Rockwell paintings of the 1940s and 1950s, there was a clear sense of what it meant to be an American. . . . Go and look at *The Saturday Evening Post* from around 1955," he commanded. (Lind: 3)

I did: countless clever freckled white kids, grinning white-maned, whistle-whittling granddads, turkey-toting, rosy-cheeked grandmothers, side by side with their brave pioneer forebears who, week after week, in the magazine's serialized novels, battled war-whooping, grunting, painted savages. *The Saturday Evening Post*'s 1950s version of the conquest soon spread as John Ford and John Huston brought these heroic fictions to the silver screen.[12]

The mechanisms that continue to maintain racial and gender hegemonies are many and complicated. But I'd like to suggest that perspective—the location of "us" and "them"—is inculcated early on until dozens of little-questioned assumptions veil both practice and theorizing about the quotidian acts of exclusion.

VI

Two Opposing Views; Or, "Woody Guthrie vs. Los Tigres del Norte"

First, Guthrie.

"Deportee," written in the 1930s to condemn the forced expulsion of Mexican farmworkers, captures the songwriter's indignation in the farm laborers' loss of name—though here the names are only first names, and of course it is only the whites, the deporters, who "lose" the farmworkers' names. (Like Bartleby, they know who they are.)

The refrain:

> Goodbye to my Juan / Goodbye Rosalita. / Adios, mis amigos / Jésus y Maria. / You won't have a name / When you ride the big airplane / All they will call you will be . . . deportee.

The song's effects—anger at the government for kicking people out of the United States, pity for the deportees—depend upon a familiar U.S. assumption, one that became increasingly dominant as the Cold War wore on. Everyone in the whole world (all those tired and poor, we learned in school) wants more than anything else to live in this golden (money *and* sunshine) land, to become "one of us," or—and this is rarely said—to become "white."

But no *corridos*—sung by "'my' Juan," or "Rosalita"—sing of this desire. Instead, countless songs describe terrible loss, of home, of place, of family, of community, of the values that differentiate a Mexican world from "ours." Yet, like Farnham in the presence of Kaw Indians, few Norteamericanos listen. They see instead only thousands of poor inhabitants of dusty pueblos, heading north, dreaming of the day when they will hop into a big new Jeep Cherokee, drive three blocks to a giant Wal-Mart and spend an hour deciding which of the forty-three different brands of shampoo is just right for *their* hair.[13]

It is a rather different view of "us" than that provided in dozens of *corridos.* Here is a bit of Los Tigres del Norte's 1988 "Jaula de Oro," or "The Gilded Cage," cited (and translated) by Timothy Brennan (123):

> In order to earn some money I am like a prisoner in this huge country. / When I remember Mexico I'm at the point of tears / And although this is a cage of gold, / it hasn't stopped being a prison.

VII

> José Juárez, a Honduran on his way to the United States, interviewed as he rode a freight train over the Mexican border heading for work in the U.S., told Ginger Thompson, a *Times* reporter, "This has to be the most sad experience a person could live, leaving your children. There are no words to describe that kind of pain." (*New York Times*, Monday, Jan. 18, 1999: 1)

Melting the Pot; Or, "So You Want to Cross the Border?"

1896: *Plessy v. Ferguson.* The Supreme Court tries to close one route of crossing over: "Petitioner was a citizen of the U.S. and a resident of . . . Louisiana of mixed descent, in the proportion of seven eighths Caucasian and one eighth African blood; [because] the mixture of colored blood was not discernible in him, . . . he [argued that he] was entitled to every recognition, right, privilege and immunity secured to the citizens of the United States of the white race by its Constitution and laws . . . Thereupon [he had] entered a passenger train and [taken] possession of a vacant seat in a coach where passengers of the white race were accommodated" (Harris: 276). Plessy's one-eighth was too much for the Court, as you all know. The Court decided that he had to ride with other people of color, though their coaches were supposed to be as "equal" as they were "separate."

Nevertheless, some did slip across the border. The key was a sufficient quantity of the privilege-granting whiteness that gained citizenship. But they paid a high price. Cheryl Harris describes her grandmother's "passing" in order to get a job as a clerk in a Chicago department store: "Every day my grandmother rose from her bed in her house in a black enclave on the southside . . . , sent her children off to a black school, boarded a bus full of black passengers, and rode to work. No one at her job ever asked if she was black; the question was unthinkable. . . . Each evening, my grandmother, tired and worn, retraced her steps home, laid aside her mask, and reentered herself. Day in and day out, she made herself invisible, then visible again" (276).

The belief that all people *want* to "pass" is, of course, another form of the universalist assumption that "we-ness" is something everyone desires. It is not, of course. The man whites renamed Chief Joseph put it differently: "Let me be a free man—free to travel, free to stop, free to work, free to trade where I choose, free to choose my own teachers, free to follow the religion of my fathers, free to think and talk and act for myself" (Chief Joseph: 44).

VIII

Joseph, again: "That All People May Be One People, Send Rain to Wash the Face of the Earth" (44).

A Cleansing

Recently, I was invited to address a conference held at the University of Oregon. Titled "Where the Border Lies: Race and Citizenship in Theory and Practice," the conference intended to explore issues related to these subjects. After I looked at the list of speakers, I decided to end my talk with the following:

> Borders, then, are sticky and long-lasting, much less permeable than California's recent governor, who tried to exclude "illegal aliens" or "undocumented Mexicans" from the state, would have us believe. They are everywhere, even here, in this conference. In a spirit of provocation, I should like to suggest a new title for this conference: "Academic Women of Color: An Exhibition." This re-naming is an effort to point out the unstated assumptions of today's program. We, the speakers, are all inhabitants of bordered worlds—born into zones constructed for us by others. We know the fences; we recognize the border patrols. What is missing from this program are representatives of these latter, the people born across the border, the people with the privileges protected by border patrols of all kinds. The conference has selected us to "introduce the theoretical constructs around highly contested matters of race and identity in the academy and race and citizenship in the political realm." But I'd like to ask, instead, and once again, "Who/Whom?" *Who* contests "matters of race and identity in the academy"? *Who* contests "race and citizenship in the political realm"? Again I refer you to "We, the People," all white, all male.[14]

NOTES

1. I should like to thank Timothy J. Reiss and Shari M. Huhndorf for their helpful readings of this text.

2. How effective their ruthless surprise attack, their superior weapons, was obvious: only two Englishmen died. Twenty more went home wounded.

3. Winthrop's journals for the period from 1630 to 1649 document the constant theft of Indian crops and goods—all supported by arms, every episode accompanied by the murder of one or more Indians, the burning of their homes, the destruction of their boats, and so on. He writes of all this with bland self-assurance, as though the Native peoples deserved only to serve the English by allowing them to steal everything they had and kill any Indians they wanted to kill. They also tortured any Indians they captured

(and "kept" any "squaws" they wanted). Paying bounties for Pequot body parts, they managed to collect dozens of hands and heads from other Indians and from whites who killed Indians for sport. (How it was decided that the hands and other body parts offered for pay were those of Pequot Indians one doesn't know from reading Winthrop's smug accounts.) If read from a Native perspective, the journals are terrifying and angering reading. It is also quite telling that Winthrop's status as a "founding father" is certified by Harvard University, which published these scary journals under its rare book imprint, edited by three prominent scholars, none of whom, judging from the footnotes and other text, has the least sympathy for the Native peoples invaded and killed by the Puritans. Instead, they see the whole history as that written by whites, and that as narrating a "cultural conflict" or "encounter" or merely "difference"—which made the armed and greedy English unable to understand the Native peoples whose land and goods and human beings they were stealing, enslaving, torturing, and so on.

4. Most colonial historians writing about the period make some brief mention of Indian slavery. Jack Forbes and Caroline Foreman have considered it in more detail, as has Robert Usner. The subject has recently formed the basis of my own research, the first fruits of which will appear in "'Til Indian Voices Wake Us . . . ," in Reiss and Cobham, forthcoming.

5. One of the most vociferous opponents of what he has referred to as "the Chicano take-over" is Gerald Vizenor. See a rather muddled expression of his view of himself as victim in "Transethnic Anthropologism: Comparative Ethnic Studies at Berkeley."

6. Cushing's most (in)famous act was to dress up as an Indian and have himself photographed. Although this picture is funny enough, his portrait, painted by Thomas Eakins in 1895, which presently hangs in the Gilcrease Museum in Tulsa, shows him dressed as a mixture of mountain man and Indian. Together with bow and arrows, fringed leather and feathers, he sports a rifle and the aggressive attitude of a white man.

7. See Leah Dilworth's thumbnail sketch of Southwestern history, which acknowledges a more complicated history but nonetheless reiterates the stereotypes.

8. There is a separate analysis to be written of the discursive regimes into which Gutiérrez places his portraits of Pueblo women. It is that created by the contemporary women's movement, which, beginning in the late 1960s, has undertaken countless revisions of women's history and the history of the Western family. Many of these sources, particularly those produced by feminist historians of the European Middle Ages and Renaissance (Caroline Bynum, Judith Brown, Marina Warner), lie in the footnotes, evidence of the behavior and attitudes of women a world away from their subjects. The second discourse that bolsters this work is that of contemporary anthropology. Evidence for all kinds of Pueblo activity was located by the author in works by anthropologists researching the South Pacific (Marshall Sahlins), women in general (Rayna Rapp and Sherry Ortner), rural France (Martine Segalen), and so on. Although historians might readily borrow techniques and concepts from anthropologists, evidence for behavior must surely at least emerge from documents relating to the people and place and time under investigation? Gutiérrez's work is creative, but that creativity, in the eyes of this historian, at least, ought not to include the evidence.

9. I am grateful to Gerald Johnson for bringing this advertisement to me.

10. Here was expressed, again, what Edouard Glissant describes as "the hierarchical division into written and oral languages . . . The latter were crude, unsuited to conceptualization and the acquisition of learning" (104).

11. Such grammatical passivity is de rigueur when speaking of things Native: A recent *New York Times* article, brought to me by a student (without the paper's date) explained how L.A.'s Southwest Museum was virtually forced to collect thousands of Native artifacts and ceremonial objects (and bodies): "Many of these items were acquired near the turn of the century when experts realized that Indian tribes *were moving inexorably to reservations,* and that this was the opportunity for preserving artifacts from the old way of life" (emphasis added).

12. Jane Tompkins has studied these works in *West of Everything: The Inner Life of Westerns.* This oddly self-indulgent book includes Tompkins's weird confession that because she hadn't noticed the relative absence of Native Americans in the objects of her study, movie Westerns, she didn't notice that her book similarly neglected to mention them. When someone pointed this out to her she rationalized her blindness: "My unbelief at the travesty of native peoples that Western films afford kept me from scrutinizing what was there. I didn't want to see,. . . . I stubbornly expected the genre to be better than it was and when it wasn't, I dropped the subject. . . . I never cried at anything I saw in a Western, but I cried when I realized this: that after the Indians had been decimated by disease, removal, and conquest, and after they had been caricatured and degraded in Western movies, I had ignored them too. . . . " Well, *we cry,* we "caricatured and degraded" native peoples cry at Western movies. At the same time, we are considerably less moved by Jane Tompkins's crocodile tears, especially after she informs her readers, "one movie has appeared that represents Native Americans in a serious, sympathetic way. Kevin Costner's *Dances with Wolves* (1990). Here the Lakota Sioux (played by themselves) are attractive and believable." Well, Lakotas are "real Lakotas," many of them "attractive" and all of them "believable." Alas, however, none of the Native stars of the film (Costner is, needless to say, the real star) is Lakota. The Lakota people—as Victor Masayesva's film "Imagining Indians," which tells the "behind the scenes" story about the making of *Dances,* demonstrates—appear as "colorful," authenticity-creating background extras. Of course Tompkins isn't worried about serious research or even truth. Instead, like Thomas Farnham in the early nineteenth century, like the spiritual tourists of her 1960s (white) generation, she only wanted these "authentic" movie actors' Indian "spirits": for her the nineteenth-century Lakotas depicted in the film's plot are "the family you never had, the community you never belonged to" (10). A second "startling" element of this work is the absence of any citation of the popular, mass-circulation journals, including *The Saturday Evening Post,* in which many of the films' stories were serialized. Research, evidently, was limited to Tompkins's Saturday afternoons at her local Brooklyn movie theater's matinees, another personal detail included in the book's introduction.

13. There are other views. In 1922, the U.S. Secretary of Labor complained that "the psychology of the average Mexican alien unskilled worker . . . is that when he enters in any manner into the U.S. . . . he is only on a visit to an unknown portion of his own country. He is independent and does not consider he is an immigrant alien, but rather in what is termed the U.S. by right of birth and possession, the country of his forebears. . . . To him, there is no real or imaginary line" (Sanchez: 15). Shortly thereafter, a merchant in Mexico, interviewed by a North American sociologist, insisted ("with intense emotion") that the United States "will be Mexico again, not now, but in hundreds, or a thousand years" (35–36).

14. Unfortunately, the following views are shared by much of the group presently representing itself as "We, the People." It is articulated by Robert Patterson, a columnist for the paper of Trent Lott and Bob Barr and Jesse Helms's Council of Conservative Citizens. Echoing John Winthrop and his colleagues, Patterson tells "us": "Western civilization, with all its might and glory, would never have achieved its greatness without the directing hand of God and the creative genius of the white race. Any effort to destroy the race by a mixture of black blood is an effort to destroy western civilization itself" (*New York Times,* Friday, January 15, 1999).

WORKS CITED

Associated Press Archive. *Albuquerque Journal.* Jan. 17, 1998.

Babcock, Barbara and Nancy Parezo. *Daughters of the Desert.* Albuquerque: University of New Mexico Press, 1988.

Bradford, William. *Of Plymouth Plantation, 1620–1647*. Ed. Samuel Eliot Morison. New York: A. A. Knopf, 1952.

Brennan, Timothy. *At Home in the World: Cosmopolitanism Now.* Cambridge: Harvard University Press, 1997.

Chief Joseph. *That All People May Be One People, Send Rain to Wash the Face of the Earth.* Sitka, Alaska, 1995.

"Commentary." *American Indian Culture and Research Journal* 17, no. 3 (1993): 141–178.

Corrin, Lisa G., ed. *Mining the Museum.* New York: New Press, 1994.

Dilworth, Leah. *Imagining Indians in the Southwest: Persistent Visions of a Primitive Past.* Washington, D.C.: Smithsonian Institution Press, 1996.

Drinnon, Richard. *Facing West: The Metaphysics of Indian Hating and Empire Building.* Minneapolis: University of Minnesota Press, 1980.

Farnham, John. *An 1839 Wagon Train Journal: Travels in the Great Western Prairie, the Anahuac and Rocky Mountains and in the Oregon Territory.* 1843. Monroe, Ore.: Northwest Interpretive Association, 1983.

Fuentes, Carlos. *The Crystal Frontier.* Trans. Alfred Mac Adam. New York: Farrar, Straus, and Giroux, 1997.

Glissant, Edouard. *Poetique de la relation.* Paris: Gallimard, 1990.

Gutiérrez, Ramón. *When Jesus Came, the Corn Mothers Went Away: Marriage, Sexuality, and Power in New Mexico, 1500–1846.* Stanford, Calif.: Stanford University Press, 1991.

H-amindian:thread12.htm. November 4, 1997; November 10, 1997.

Harris, Cheryl. "Whiteness as Property." In *Critical Race Theory: The Key Writings That Formed the Movement,* ed. Kimberle Crenshaw, Neil Gotanda, Gary Peller, and Kendall Thomas, 276–291. New York: New Press, 1995.

Hughte, Phil. *A Zuni Artist Looks at Frank Hamilton Cushing.* Zuni: Pueblo of Zuni, 1994.

Jennings, Francis. *The Invasion of America: Indians, Colonialism, and the Cant of Conquest.* New York: W. W. Norton, 1976.

Kundera, Milan. *The Book of Laughter and Forgetting.* Trans. from the Czech by Michael Henry Heim. New York: A. A. Knopf, 1980.

Lamar, Howard, ed. *The New Encyclopedia of the American West.* New Haven, Conn.: Yale University Press, 1998.

Library of Congress. Advertisement #001-002-5.17.

Lind, Michael. "Drums along the Potomac." *New York Times Book Review,* July 12, 1995.

Linthiuim, Leslie. "Crown, Cross, and Conquest." *Albuquerque Journal,* January 9, 1998, January 17, 1998, and January 18, 1998.

McWilliams, Carey. *North from Mexico: The Spanish-Speaking People of the United States.* 1948. Reprint, New York: Praeger, 1990.

New York Times. Feb. 9, 1998; Sept. 12, 1998; Jan. 15, 1999; Monday, Jan. 18, 1999, 1.

Ortiz, Simon. "First Nations, First Peoples, First Voices for Hope and Continuance." *Native Roots and Rhythms* 1, no. 1 (1999): 1

——. *Woven Stone.* Tucson: University of Arizona Press, 1992.

Reiss, Timothy, and Rhonda Cobham, eds. *New Approaches to Kamau Brathwaite: For the Geography of a Soul.* Trenton, N.J.: Africa World Press, forthcoming 2000.

Sanchez, George I. *Becoming Mexican-American: Ethnicity, Culture and Identity in Chicano Los Angeles, 1900–1945.* New York: Oxford University Press, 1993.

Silko, Leslie Marmon. *Ceremony.* New York: Viking Press, 1977.

Stannard, David. *American Holocaust: The Conquest of the New World.* New York: Oxford University Press, 1992.

Szanto, George. *Inside the Statues of Saints: Mexican Writers on Culture and Corruption, Politics and Daily Life.* Montreal: Véhicule Press, 1996.

Tompkins, Jane. *West of Everything: The Inner Life of Westerns.* New York: Oxford University Press, 1992.

Vizenor, Gerald. "Transethnic Anthropologism: Comparative Ethnic Studies at Berkeley." *SAIL* 7, no. 4 (Winter 1995): 3–8.

Winthrop, John. *The Journal of John Winthrop, 1630–1649.* Ed. Richard Dunn, James Savage, and Laetitia Yeandle. Cambridge: Belknap Press of Harvard University Press, 1996.

9 "SEE HOW I AM RECEIVED": NATIONALISM, RACE, AND GENDER IN *WHO WOULD HAVE THOUGHT IT?*

Amelia María de la Luz Montes

> It was the anniversary of some great day in New England when the Misses Norval were to make their farewell appearance in church before leaving for Europe—some great day in which the Pilgrim fathers had done one of their wonderful deeds. They had either embarked, or landed, or burnt a witch, or whipped a woman at the pillory, on just such a day. The reverend gentlemen of our acquaintance were to hold forth to their respective congregations, who idolized them, and would have mobbed and lynched anyone daring to hint that the two divines solaced themselves with a jug of whisky after those edifying sermons; that it was "John Barleycorn, and not John the Baptist," Mr. Hackwell said he liked to consult after church. They did not know how many puns the witty Hackwell had made on Demi-John, and Saint John, and Jolly-John, which last was himself.
>
> —*Who Would Have Thought It?* (62)[1]

> Must I always be a listener only, never hit back?
>
> —*Juvenal, The Satires* 1.1

IN María Amparo Ruiz de Burton's novel *Who Would Have Thought It?*, the reader is transported to a New England which is in the throes of the Civil War. Within this historical background, the novel parodies and satirizes New England's religious and political life through Ruiz de Burton's Mexican American perspective. Indeed, Mexican and American religion (Protestant and Catholic) and politics (American civil unrest and French colonization of Mexico) are intertwined in this novel. The quotation above encapsulates Ruiz de Burton's dislike for Protestant hypocrisy. Her description of the "great anniversary day" portrays the revered "Puritan fathers" as misogynistic caricatures. The only women mentioned within this historical illustration are either branded witches or women scourged at the pillory.[2] Historically, men were also punished at the pillory, but Ruiz de Burton's careful placement of women at the pillory and men as fathers or reverends emphasizes her critical opinion of women's subject position in New England. Ruiz de Burton furthers the parody by illustrating the real man-behind-the-scenes: Reverend Hackwell as a drinking insouciant rather than a solemn holy man. Despite the irreverence of Reverend John Hackwell's "Jolly-John" and "John Barleycorn" titles, these are tame parodies compared to the reality of his actions later in the novel, which slowly descend into a web of lasciviousness and insatiable greed.[3] I begin with this excerpt because in many ways it serves as a reference point on which to embark upon my argument for this essay.

First, however, I turn to early-nineteenth-century Anglo writer Lydia Maria Child, whose book *Hobomok* departs from traditional novels of that time and highlights social and class concerns which Ruiz de Burton later takes up in the 1870s. Child's work positions the American Indian and the Anglo-American together within the domestic sphere.[4] This was unheard of in the 1820s. Carolyn Karcher, who recovered and edited Child's writings, has said:

> Child founded both a female countertradition of American literature and an alternative vision of race and gender relations in one of our earliest fictional genres, the American historical novel. A genre created specifically to forge a nationalist consciousness and cultural identity in the newly independent United States, the American historical novel inevitably exhibited the same central contradiction as American history itself—the contradiction between an ideology based on the premise that all men are created equal and a political structure based on the assumption that people of color and white women do not fall under the rubric "men." (xv)

I use Karcher's words as a preface to my argument because Ruiz de Burton shares in the idea of a "female countertradition." Karcher says that the American historical novel reveals "contradictions" inherent in the American political and social framework. Child's work opens discussions of race and gender, specifically in regard to the American Indian and Anglo-American woman. I follow Karcher's line of argument and broaden it by integrating a discussion of the Mexican American woman in nineteenth-century Anglo-American society.

I argue that Ruiz de Burton's *Who Would Have Thought It?* unravels the inherent contradictions of American ideology in regard to the Mexican American. Her use of satire and parody unmasks the rhetoric of Manifest Destiny and displays the hypocrisy among New Englanders who espouse piety and condemn the South's alliance with slavery, yet demonstrate the opposite through their actions. Unlike her *The Squatter and the Don,* which solely concentrates on issues of disenfranchisement on California lands, *Who Would Have Thought It?* transports the reader to New England, the ancestral home of the Puritans. Within the act of fiction, Ruiz de Burton invades Anglo-American territory in order to indict their culture, which has disrespected and violated hers. Indeed, *Who Would Have Thought It?* answers the question Juvenal poses: "Must I always be a listener only, never hit back?" Ruiz de Burton "hits back" in this novel with a satirical vengeance. When the Mexican American character, Lola, appears at Mrs. Norval's doorstep, she is greeted as an untouchable. Yet the

Norval family to which she temporarily belongs is known in the community as a staunch abolitionist and religious family. They call Lola a "specimen," and throughout the novel they treat her as an object and as a means to gratify their insatiable greed for lust and money. Another character Ruiz de Burton uses to reveal New England hypocrisy and racism is Lucinda, the Quadroon Belle.[5] Lucinda is mistress to the opportunist, Le Grand Gunn, as well as the object of affection from other men of authority who objectify her and use her for their own purposes. These are negative characteristics within New England which Ruiz de Burton magnifies in order to continually reveal the inherent contradiction within the Anglo-American system of power. It is important to note, however, that Ruiz de Burton does not create a novel filled with antagonistic New Englanders. Her intent is not to stereotype and demonize all New Englanders. As in *The Squatter and the Don,* where a number of Anglo-Americans are portrayed in a benevolent light, Ruiz de Burton also includes Anglo-American protagonists in *Who Would Have Thought It?* Again, I believe her intent not only further illustrates her wish to see both sides of an issue (what I call a "double vision") but also, stylistically, reveals her experimentations with the mode of realism.

Yet, Ruiz de Burton's satirical depiction of New England Yankees implicates her as well. The novel, then, reveals an interesting paradox. I believe *Who Would Have Thought It?* uncovers the racism and gendered oppression in which all Americans participate.[6] Ruiz de Burton works toward unraveling the Anglo-American system of beliefs which set an environment of oppression in place. Her novel reveals that it is more than difficult to extricate oneself from a system of power relations because all Americans inherit this system and are imbedded within it. The racism in which Ruiz de Burton participates arises from her inheritance of the power structures of Mexican aristocracy and its stringent class distinctions. I believe it is important to investigate Ruiz de Burton's brand of racism in order to understand its variant forms. The novel reveals Ruiz de Burton's unabashed prejudice against the Indian and the Black and her alliance to an imperialist Mexico (Maximilian). Those scenes and sections which are clearly racist have placed Ruiz de Burton in a complicated position within contemporary Chicana and American literature because she is both the colonized and the colonizer. Some Chicana and Chicano critics do not want to claim her for this reason. However, it is this complexity which mirrors contemporary Chicanos in American society today.[7] I believe this work helps readers explore the intricate dynamics of prejudice in which we are all participants. It especially addresses these issues and expands our American literary canon as well as our notions of the racist legacy we carry in the United States.

A good example of this legacy is Ruiz de Burton's rendering of her character Lucinda, the Quadroon Belle. Ruiz de Burton's Lucinda is in keeping with an archetype and a mode of protest writing in the nineteenth century. Quadroon Belles were American Southern women of mixed blood, educated and raised to be graceful, intellectual beauties. Southern law prohibited these women from marriage. Instead, they would forever live as long-term mistresses or prostitutes. They were also sold into slavery. There was much outcry against the treatment of Quadroon Belles in the South even before the Civil War. Nineteenth-century writer Lydia Maria Child wrote "The Quadroons" (1842) to protest the South's practice. Harriet Beecher Stowe and William Wells Brown also used what became "the archetype of the 'tragic quadroon'" (xiv). In Child's "The Quadroons," Rosalie and her daughter Xarifa suffer the agonizing abandonment of lovers and fathers. Edward and Rosalie spend ten happy years together until Edward feels he must marry. Rosalie is left alone to raise Xarifa. She dies soon after of grief and Xarifa is sold into slavery. At the end of the story, Child writes,

> In a few months more, poor Xarifa was a raving maniac. That pure temple was desecrated; that loving heart was broken; and that beautiful head fractured against the wall in the frenzy of despair. Her master cursed the useless expense she had cost him; the slaves buried her; and no one wept at the grave of her who had been so carefully cherished, and so tenderly beloved. Reader, do you complain that I have written fiction? Believe me, scenes like these are of no unfrequent occurrence at the South. The world does not afford such materials for tragic romance, as the history of the Quadroons. (5)

Note the break in narrative and direct address to the reader. Child's motive is a political one. Ruiz de Burton expands on Child's indictment. Ruiz de Burton does not place Lucinda in the South or even mention the South when Lucinda appears in the novel. Instead, Ruiz de Burton places Lucinda in the heart of Northern abolitionist politics: within the Senate chambers of Le Grand Gunn. Gunn, Isaac Sprig, and Aeschylus Wagg all chase after Lucinda and make her the object of their affections while they are espousing abolitionist rhetoric in their allegiance to the North and participating in a bloodbath with the South. This is Ruiz de Burton's protest.

Uncovering obfuscation and lies is at the heart of Ruiz de Burton's *Who Would Have Thought It?* The presence of Lucinda, then, is a blatant accusation of Northerners who create propaganda which seeks to isolate racist prejudice below the Southern borders and which constructs the North as an angelic benevolent savior to the slaves. I believe that Ruiz de Burton wants desperately to uncover these lies because of the racial marginalization and erasure she suffered in California at the hands of Anglo-Americans who professed allegiance to a nation that constructed the idea of Manifest Destiny.

In Ruiz de Burton's novel, Lucinda could be the twin sister of Child's character Rosalie in "The Quadroons." Lucinda is beautiful and intelligent. The reader first meets her during a struggle of affection between the

Honorable Le Grand Gunn (note "honorable") and Isaac Sprig, who becomes one of the heroes in the novel. Ruiz de Burton writes:

> Isaac had the audacity to admire a lady of the demimonde whom a distinguished member of Congress also admired. One night when he, the Hon. Le Grand Gunn, was visiting the fair Lucinda, Isaac and his friend Julius Caesar Cackle, who were the boarders of the house, went into the parlor and made themselves at home. To make matters more aggravating to the Hon. M. C., Isaac absorbed the attention, smiles, and sweet glances of the charming Lucinda until the infuriated Gunn rushed out of the house in a rage. Lucinda laughed aloud while the Hon. was yet within hearing, whereupon that gentleman, forgetful of his distinguished public position, came back to ask, in a very insulting manner, if Sprig had laughed at him. Sprig colored with anger, but said he had not, whereupon Mr. Gunn, shaking his finger at him, said, "You had better not."
>
> "I did not laugh, but you are certainly laughable," said Isaac, "and I think you will make me laugh if you don't go soon."
>
> The Hon. ordered Sprig out of the house, and Sprig told him to go himself. And from words they came to blows, and had a most ignominious fistfight in the presence of the quadroon belle.
>
> Sprig came out victorious. Cackle had to go for a hack to convey Mr. Le Grand Gunn to his lodgings, as the Hon. gentleman was not able to walk because he could not see out of his swollen eyes. His bloody nose, lacerated to a large size, gave Lucinda great desire to laugh, but that inclination this time she held in check until the distinguished politician was well out of hearing. (58–59)

Ruiz de Burton's portrayal of Lucinda differs radically from the innocent, romantic rendering Child gives to Rosalie and Xarifa in "The Quadroons." Rosalie and Xarifa are helpless pawns in their incarcerated circumstances. Lucinda is incarcerated as well. Her circumstances are no less demeaning, but Ruiz de Burton fleshes her out into a more human character who wields power (albeit in a small way, but it is power nonetheless) from her oppressed position. Lucinda flirts with Isaac, then laughs loudly "while the Hon. was yet within hearing." The fight ensues to her delight. Although she does not have the power to physically attack Gunn for all he has done to her, she is symbolically performing the feat through the fists of Isaac Sprig. When the deed is done, Gunn's face is a mess and Lucinda has a "great desire to laugh, but that inclination this time she held in check until the distinguished politician was well out of hearing" (59). This second time, her laugh would have implicated her.

I especially note these differences among the characters of Rosalie, Xarifa, and Lucinda because they reveal very important aspects about Ruiz de Burton as a writer. Lydia Maria Child is writing from an Anglo-

American woman's perspective. She has never experienced racial marginalization and therefore is not familiar with acts of resistance or a consciousness that has developed oppositional methods of survival.[8] Therefore, her rendering of Rosalie and Xarifa are stereotyped and romantic. This juxtaposition makes Child, the Anglo-American writer, a benevolent patronizing voice at the end of "The Quadroons." In contrast, Ruiz de Burton's more multidimensional characters tend to be the marginalized ones while the dominant group, Anglo-American New Englanders, exhibit the uniform dimensions of bumbling, duplicitous fops. This is not to say that Child's work against Southern racial prejudice is any less worthy. My point is that how these authors create their characters reveals their position within American society.

Ruiz de Burton's character Mina is another case in point. Although Mina is a maid (and Mrs. Norval insists on calling her a "servant girl"), she finds a way to wield power, so much so that she is a key figure in the downfall of the corrupt Reverend Hackwell. Her means to power occurs when she attracts the attention of Lieutenant Sophy Head, assistant to Hackwell. Later in the novel, Mina is able to acquire information through Head and Skroo (note the silly names) which will implicate Hackwell's participation in committing fraud against the government and embezzling money. Ruiz de Burton portrays Mina in this fashion:

> To do Miss Mina justice, I must say that she did not wish to entrap Sophy into matrimony. Nor had she any idea of being a poor man's wife. Not she. She had a great deal nicer time as a rich lady's maid, and meant to stay so until she could marry some rich grocer or retired shoemaker who would adore her and give her all the ribbons and laces she wanted. She, therefore, did not mourn for the loss of Sophy, only she did not like the way it was brought about, and swore she would revenge herself on the major [Hackwell] for calling her a "grisette" and a "servant" before her devoted admirer, and she would punish Sophy for deserting her so meanly afterwards. But how could she do this? She had no other means than Sophy himself. Yes, she would find out about the major's mode of spending his days, and she would make Sophy tell her all, and then she would, perhaps, find a way of paying them off together. The first step was to get hold of Sophy, and Sophy came no more. As the mountain would not come, Miss Mina wisely foresaw that she would have to go to the mountain. And she went. (260–261)

Like Lucinda, Mina also has developed a consciousness of resistance that places her in a position of power, albeit from the confines of the place she has been given in Anglo-American society. She is not blind to her marginalized position but quite aware and insightful in her methods of politically resisting her oppressive state.

Lola is the more problematic of the three and this is because she is closest to Ruiz de Burton. Lola, the "painted" Mexican girl whose skin was dyed black, must negotiate within the Norval household, which espouses abolitionist rhetoric but begrudges the black-skinned Lola within its domestic sphere. I believe Lola is a problematic character because Ruiz de Burton's position is more complex than her characterization of Lucinda and Mina. Ruiz de Burton's position in Anglo-American society is as a marginalized class. She is also positioned within the dominant Mexican elite. Here lies Lola's and Ruiz de Burton's burden of difference and here is where, because of this complicated paradox, the novel collapses into sections that reveal blatant racism against the Native Indian and the Black.

Ruiz de Burton cannot be praised enthusiastically for the defense of minorities, especially when there are multiple scenes in the novel where her disregard of the Native Indian is reprehensible. Her efforts to eradicate racism are apparent in such characters as Mina and Lucinda. However, her participation within the Anglo-American system of power is apparent as well. When Julian professes his undying love to Lola, she says, "I was an object of aversion because my skin was black. And yet I was too proud to tell you that the blackness of my skin would wear off . . . I hated to think that you might suppose I was Indian or black" (100). Lola insists she really is white and equal to all of New England. Because she cares most for Julian, she feels that the only way she can be worthy of his love is to be white. When I say "white" I am referring to the "white" *Californios* of California. This is an important historical point. During the California Constitutional Convention of 1849, legislators were concerned with the controversy of suffrage. A discussion ensued about whether or not the vote should be solely given to the white man. A delegate to the convention, Sr. Noriega de la Guerra, debated the use of the term "white":

> Mr. Noriega desired that it should be perfectly understood in the first place what is the true significance of the word "white." Many citizens of California have received from nature a very dark skin; nevertheless, there are among them men who have heretofore been allowed to vote, and not only that, but to fill the highest public offices. It would be very unjust to deprive them of the privilege of citizens merely because nature had not made them white. But if, by the word "white" it was intended to exclude the African race, then it was correct and satisfactory. (Heizer and Almquist: 98)

Another delegate, Mr. Botts, responded to Noriega's comment. He pointed out that he had

> no objection to color, except so far as it indicated the inferior races of mankind. He would be perfectly willing to use any words which would exclude the African and Indian races. It was in this sense the word white had been understood and used—not objectionable for their color, but for what that color indicates. (98)

These blatant racist discussions did not remain inside the convention house. The California Constitutional Convention of 1849 had a deep impact upon the consciousness of the *Californio.* Census reports between 1849 and 1859 list a majority of families and individuals with Spanish surnames as "white." The end of Ruiz de Burton's *The Squatter and the Don* reflects this thinking. She writes:

> Our representatives in Congress, and in the State Legislature, knowing full well the will of the people, ought to legislate accordingly. If they do not, then we shall—as Channing said, "kiss the foot that tramples us!" and "in anguish of spirit" must wait and pray for a Redeemer who will emancipate the white slaves of California.[9] (372)

So what, then, were the *Californios* if not "white," as Ruiz de Burton would like us to believe? In her essay, "The Political Economy of Nineteenth Century Stereotypes of Californianas," Antonia I. Castañeda explains that the proliferation of Anglo-American publications (newspapers, travel journals, popular historical texts and novels) encouraged stereotypes of *Californianas* and created an image that contributed to a *Californio* class/race consciousness.

> The positive image portraying Mexican women as aristocratic, virtuous Spanish ladies directly contradicted the negative view of Californianas—but it did so by singling out elite Californianas, denying their racial identity . . . With few exceptions, women in California, including women of the elite "ranchero" class, were neither Spanish nor aristocratic by birth. They, like their male counterparts, were of mixed-blood or "mestizo" origin. Whether of military or "poblador" (settler) families, their grandparents or parents migrated to California from the impoverished classes of Mexico's Northern frontier provinces. . . . In this literature, while the women were transformed into Spanish ladies the men remained Mexicans . . . the stereotypes it presents reflected an ideology which not only excluded non-whites from American principles and institutions, but that the stereotypes of women, which represent the intersection of sex, race and class, functioned as instruments of imperialism, conquest and subordination. (225)

Ruiz de Burton fell into this imperialist construction of power. Her failure to recognize the inherent racism in her closing words to a book that seeks justice against the rhetoric of Manifest Destiny is sorely disappointing, but at the same time, to the astute reader, it reveals the intricate web of racism. By unraveling this web, the reader can begin to understand contemporary systems of power which denigrate and oppress people based on difference. Toward the second half of Ruiz de Burton's *Who Would Have Thought It?,* Isaac Sprig is in Mexico in search of Lola's father, Don Luis

Medina. When he meets him, he gives Don Luis the letter that his late wife wrote to him. In the letter, Doña Theresa recounts her sad ten-year captivity with the Indians. Don Luis breaks down and cries. Ruiz de Burton interrupts the narrative and addresses the reader directly:

> Misery is, undoubtedly, "the lot of mortals," but there is no doubt, either, that in some countries certain kinds of evils are impossible. If Mexico were well governed, if her frontiers were well protected, the fate of Doña Theresa would have been next to an impossibility. When it is a well-known fact that savages will devastate towns that are not well guarded, is there any excuse for a government that will neglect to provide sufficient protection? Does a plea of economy counterbalance an appeal for life? How fearful is the responsibility of lawgivers and law executors. (201)

Ruiz de Burton's prejudice is a distinctly Ibero-Hispanic class consciousness in that it stratifies individuals from the day they are born into types or classes from which they cannot escape. Lola's black skin serves to contrast Mrs. Norval's hypocrisy and the hypocrisy of New Englanders. However, Lola also implicates herself by insisting that she is white. Yet, it is important to understand the distinctions of racial prejudice here because Mrs. Norval's prejudice comes from the historical site of slavery and Puritan rhetoric which demonizes those of other races. In Mexico, a rigid class system exists, keeping minorities (specifically the Indians) in a subaltern class. Indeed, Ruiz de Burton's adherence to a stringent class structure, which seeks to segregate the Mexican from the Native Indian, only reflects the contradictions within her own efforts to gain equality in Anglo-American society.

Because of these contradictions, some critics have hesitated to consider Ruiz de Burton after reading her works because they inevitably find her upper-class aristocratic viewpoints at times racist and arrogant. I argue that it is especially because of these complex aspects concerning her character and writing that we need to read and discuss Ruiz de Burton. In her essay "Nineteenth-Century Californio Narratives," Rosaura Sánchez emphasizes the need to recover and investigate nineteenth-century Mexican American writing. She says:

> This period also marks the beginning of our (Mexican American) production as a marginal ethnic group. If we hope to prepare for the future, as well as to grasp the present better, we will have to understand the past. But even more importantly, if we hope to make ourselves heard, we will have to enable previously silenced voices to speak. (291)

Sánchez points to the nineteenth century as the beginning of Mexican oppression in the United States. However, it is important to recognize the complexity within that statement. Indeed, when we focus upon the sections in Ruiz de Burton's writings which uncover the inequities of women in American society, she becomes for Chicana writers today (and for all women) a prophetic voice from the nineteenth century. Her complexity is apparent in her failure to recognize the Indigena, the brown skin as her own. Ruiz de Burton does not hide the fact that she comes from an upper-class background. In a personal letter (1855), she reveals her class-conscious identity when she includes her workers in a gracious and familial manner. She is careful to place the family and workers in order of importance. She says:

> [T]odos estamos buenos . . . empezando por el Capitan, mi mamá, yo, Federico, Nelly, Harry, los indios en el rancho, las bacas, beceros [*sic*], [etc].
>
> [W]e are all fine . . . beginning with the Captain, my mother, myself, Federico, Nelly, Harry, the indians on the ranch, the cows, calves, [etc.]. (Letter to Mariano Guadalupe Vallejo, November 3, 1855)

Not only is the word "Indians" written in lowercase, but it is important to note the physical representation of the word "Indians." Indians are placed on the ranch next to the animals on Ruiz de Burton's property. In *The Squatter and the Don,* when Don Alamar tells the squatters that they might be better off raising cattle, Mathews replies, "[W]hat do I know about whirling a lariat?" (94). Alamar answers him, "You can hire an Indian boy to do that part" (94). Hired help for Ruiz de Burton is cheap labor—reserved for a marginalized class. Ruiz de Burton's cultural ambivalence and adherence to a class structure produce a body of writing full of complexities. I support an exploration of these contradictions because they resist what American literary canons and nineteenth-century constructions of the Mexicans have been doing—marginalizing, stereotyping, creating a one-dimensional caricature of the Mexican, thereby erasing her. By reading Ruiz de Burton as well as other Mexican American writers and individuals who have contributed to a written and oral history, we receive a multidimensional view of the *Californio* and of western history.

Our own complex relationships to power cross ethnic, gender, and racial borderlines. By conceptually unraveling these intricate relationships to power in Ruiz de Burton's writings, as well as those from various cultures and positions, we take the necessary step of confronting the very systems in which we participate today.[10] We have seen how Ruiz de Burton seeks to eradicate the prejudice she experiences, yet cannot free herself from her own. Reading texts that dare to reveal and portray the complexities of power relations brings us face to face with our own implication in racial and political power structures today. Such readings encourage public conversations about how we are all embedded in these relations, which then helps to develop a consciousness of power relations with a goal of making concrete change. This is why someone like Ruiz de Burton is useful to read and discuss: she was trying to contribute to public conversations about different kinds of power and she was self-consciously trying to contribute to the kinds of power she recognized. Equally interesting is how she reveals (unwittingly) her own complicity within power relations. Those aspects inherent in her works must be not ignored but fully discussed. Why? We cannot divorce ourselves from the political ideology of our own age. In all literatures and public discourse, we cannot think or imagine ourselves out of being implicated in power, and a good example is our twentieth century ability or inability to discuss conflicts within the Anglo community, the Chicano community, and other communities—concerning class issues, sexism, gender, or sexual orientation. Even as Chicanas, we are situated differently in more than one position concerning identity.

To dismiss and exclude Ruiz de Burton as a precursor to Chicana/o literature would be, as scholar Tey Diana Rebolledo has pointed out, to dismiss voices of Hispanic nineteenth-century women who, because of their economic privilege, had the means to speak and create for themselves a literary space within a primarily male Mexican and American literary landscape. Not only does Rebolledo note Ruiz de Burton's elite status which gave her the means to write, she also reminds readers that Ruiz de Burton "explores and documents the clash of two different legal systems, two different ways of doing business, two different cultures" (126). Scholar Erlinda Gonzales-Berry notes that Ruiz de Burton's "posture toward *las clases populares* is offensive yet therein lies her position in the matrix of 'difference' " (130). For these reasons, not only do I place her as a foremother of Chicana literature, but I also see an aspect of her literary inheritance as mestiza. This is a controversial point that I want to carefully discuss.

First, I want to point out how Latin American definitions of "mestizaje" and contemporary Chicana feminist theories of "mestizaje" differ. I recognize those critics who insist upon the historicity of "mestizaje" coming from the Ibero-Hispano, peninsular, Hispano-American countries. Venezuelan scholar Arturo Uslar Pietri, for example, sees the formation of the mestizo as a historical cultural process. The mestizo is a collective (the Spanish, Indian, and Black) that forms a consciousness, an identity called "mestizaje." Pietri also points out that this mestizo collective passed

> a América y en ella han empezado a caminar tropezando hacia nuevas formas de mestizaje universal.
>
> [to America, and there has begun walking, stumbling upon new forms of a universal mestizaje]. (121–125)

Pietri's historical look at the evolution of "mestizaje" is important because it serves as a counterpoint for Chicana feminist theorists. Writers such as

Gloria Anzaldúa and Chéla Sandoval write of a resistant mestizaje: one that rejects a universal consciousness.[11] Sandoval, especially, is looking at "mestizaje" in terms of how oppressed peoples, after years of domination, have created their own survival skills to combat imperialist domination. Sandoval believes that "[C]olonized peoples of the Americas have already developed the cyborg skills required for survival under techno-human conditions as a requisite for survival under domination over the last three hundred years" ("New Sciences: Cyborg Feminism and the Methodology of the Oppressed": 408).

Interestingly, the cyborg image fits Ruiz de Burton's constant immersion in technological advances (the railroad, the telegraph, the growth of cities, and the coming industrial revolution) which led her to further alienation and destitution. Within this fast-moving nineteenth-century milieu, Ruiz de Burton does not submit. She writes, she speaks with legislators, discusses issues with Vallejo, works with Anglo friends who she knows are influential. In this Anglo society which places her in a marginalized category, she acquires skills of survival that she never would have had to acquire had she remained in an aristocratic Mexican culture. Given the topic of resistance within her novels, perhaps she would not have written in a world where she was not challenged. As a displaced *Californiana,* Ruiz de Burton is forced to enter what Donna Haraway calls "a place for the different social subject" (95). This idea is at the forefront of contemporary feminist theory. In the past, feminist theory's only perspective was primarily Anglo-American. Scholars such as Chéla Sandoval, Donna Haraway, Deena González, and Norma Alarcón challenge contemporary feminist theory to include women of color from all backgrounds—women who have experienced a multitude of displacements.

In contrast, Pietri's universal mestizaje does not take into consideration North American historical racial inheritances which are political and not solely cultural. "The Chicano," as scholar Lora Romero points out, "is the result of over a century of political organizing in response to an even longer history of social, economic, and cultural violence. The word 'Chicano' does not refer to race in any simple sense—which is why most progressives use 'Chicano' in place of 'Mexican-American'" (121). Keeping these definitions in mind, we are aware of the complex racial and political history Chicanas and Chicanos inherit. Ruiz de Burton's body of work (private letters and public writings) reveals a writer who infused Anglo, French, Black, and Indian as well as *Californio* Mexican cultural traits in her literary landscape. I see Ruiz de Burton as an ancestor to our contemporary Chicana identity. In Gloria Anzaldúa's landmark work, *Borderlands / La Frontera: The New Mestiza,* she calls for the mestiza to understand her roots in order to be able to transcend the borders which limit her identity and her potential. Anzaldúa says:

> Her [La Mestiza's] first step is to take inventory. Despojando, desgranando, quitando paja. Just what did she inherit from her ancestors? This weight on her back—which is the baggage from the In-

> dian mother, which the baggage from the Spanish father, which the baggage from the Anglo? (82)

In many ways, Anzaldúa's words encourage us to understand Ruiz de Burton as our ancestor—from the Spanish father. In her own time, Ruiz de Burton's inheritance was an upper-class military elite background which disregarded the Indian. She was complicit in power relations which subordinated the position of the Indigena/o and yet culturally she comes from an Indigena inheritance. Her inheritances are also historical. Ruiz de Burton comes to us with the following. First, she experienced the Mexican American War, whose aftermath transformed her into a subordinate in an Anglo-American society. Secondly, her inheritance involves France's imperial occupation in Mexico for four years. She was also swept into an American society in the throes of establishing its nationhood, which compelled her to decide where her loyalties lay. Finally, during the Civil War, the question of slavery and Black prejudice was also her inheritance. Anzaldúa writes of the mestiza:

> [T]he future will belong to the mestiza. Because the future depends on the breaking down of paradigms, it depends on the straddling of two or more cultures. By creating a new mythos—that is a change in the way we perceive reality, the way we see ourselves, and the ways we behave—*la mestiza* creates a new consciousness. (80)

The ways in which Ruiz de Burton battled her own marginalization brought her to a new consciousness that she was able to articulate in her two novels and in her drama.

Ruiz de Burton is not what we would hope our ancestor to be like: a voice for the indigenous peoples. She cannot speak to us from that vantage point. However, she provides another look into our mestizaje which makes us conscious of power relations and how we are embedded within them because we inherit them. If we read Ruiz de Burton, we become conscious of the ways in which our progenitors complied within power structures.

In her book *The Last Generation,* Cherríe Moraga faces the fact that her Chicana heritage is not only one of the "Indigena" but also of the "Conquistador." She has inherited both the colonized and the colonizer.[12] "Most Mexicans can claim the same," Moraga says, "but my claim is more 'explorer' than not. And yes, most days I am deathly ashamed" (122). From this shameful heritage, Moraga recognizes that in order to grow and imagine a new world, "we must open the wound to make it heal, purify ourselves with the prick of Maguey thorns" (192). To look at Ruiz de Burton fully—in all her complexities—is to understand the humanness inherent in her body of work and to better understand yet another aspect of a heritage from which Chicana writers have come. What we learn from reading Ruiz de Burton is that American literature is rich with voices, and rich with a multifaceted history. Ruiz de Burton is just one writer from a large group of silenced writers whose works provide the opportunity to expand our understanding of American and Chicana literary history. She brings to both our present Chicano literary history as well as Anglo-American literary history a voice which complicates the definition of what it means to be an American in this country. To give Ruiz de Burton's writings a space for discussion and criticism in the twentieth century is to contribute to a much larger project of creating a pluralistic perspective of American literary history. "¡Mucho hay que ver!" "There is much to consider" says Ruiz de Burton in her letter dated June 23, 1860. It is up to us today to take up this larger project and see ourselves within it—not apart from it.

NOTES

1. The following is the footnote to this paragraph written by Rosaura Sánchez and Beatrice Pita, editors.

"A 'Demi-John' is a small barrel used to contain wine or another liquor. Ruiz de Burton here has the scoundrel reverends make ironic post-sermon plays on their being 'saints' and 'jolly' with their glasses of whiskey and cigars at hand" (62).

In the novel, Reverend John Hackwell actually favors a meerschaum pipe instead of a cigar. "Meerschaum is a hydrated magnesium silicate mineral which forms fine, fibrous masses like white clay and is easily carved. It is porous when dry, and is used for pipe bowls" (Crystal, *The Cambridge Encyclopedia*). Meerchaum is primarily gathered, carved, and imported from Turkey (Asia Minor). The soft porous material allows artists to produce intricately carved and ornate pipes. Hackwell favors all things that denote wealth and position. The pipe, then, is another prop for Ruiz de Burton to use in her illustration of Hackwell's greed and hypocrisy.

2. The pillory was a wooden frame with holes for the head and hands. This frame held the person in place, allowing him or her to be publicly ridiculed or whipped.

3. John Barleycorn is a personification of the barley grain from which malt liquor is made.

4. Although I look at how the American Indian is still subsumed by the end of the novel, Child's work is still remarkable for its time because of its underlying premise that supports intermarriage between Indians and Anglo-Americans.

5. At that time, a quadroon was the offspring of a white person and a mulatto or one who was a quarter African. In the South (specifically New Orleans) Quadroon Belles, as they were called, served as courtesans. I will explain more in another part of the chapter when I introduce the character of Lucinda.

6. I say this with caution, knowing that Ruiz de Burton presents a quandary to scholars concerning her rightful place in Chicana/o canon lists. But I defend my stance because it is the illegal Indigena coming across the border today, the green-card-carrying immigrant who is the oppressed and voiceless within this American system of power. The rest of us (including myself) need to recognize our participation within this system in order to move toward radical changes in U.S. power relations. Ruiz de Burton's own complicity within power relations serves as a cautionary note for us all.

7. When I participated in the Nineteenth-Century Women Writing Group in the fall of 1997, Ruiz de Burton was the topic of discussion. A number of established scholars quickly focused only on her racist views. They wanted a counterargument as to why they should have to read such racism. What they didn't realize was that they were regarding Ruiz de Burton only on Anglo-American terms. They were not looking at her work in historical or cultural terms. Also, by distancing Ruiz de Burton's work from their discussion, they were distancing themselves from looking at racial systems today and how these systems relate to nineteenth-century constructions of power.

8. I am invoking the term that Chicana scholar and feminist Chela Sandoval created. "Oppositional Consciousness" is a form of thinking "in reaction to U.S. social

hierarchy" (Sandoval). I mention it here because Ruiz de Burton's perspective is in many ways an "Oppositional Consciousness," that is, she continually reacts against and with the duplicitous constructions of nationhood in American society. See bibliographic notation to Chela Sandoval's dissertation, "Oppositional Consciousness in the Postmodern World: U.S. Third World Feminism, Semiotics, and the Methodology of the Oppressed."

9. The Channing reference is William Ellery Channing (1780–1842), American clergyman (Unitarian and Transcendentalist)

10. I am indebted to Barbara Schulman (Clark University, Massachusetts), whose work on gendered violence has greatly influenced my thinking here.

11. See bibliographical note for Chéla Sandoval's essay, "New Sciences: Cyborg Feminism and the Methodology of the Oppressed."

12. In her essay, "The Breakdown of the Bicultural Mind," Moraga looks at her mixed-blood identity. She says her "individual story" is "the marriage of my U.S. born Mexican mother of Sonora roots to my San Francisco born French and British-Canadian father" (114). This essay appears in her work, *The Last Generation: Prose and Poetry.* See bibliographic notation.

WORKS CITED

Abrams, M. H., ed. *The Norton Anthology of English Literature.* 3rd ed. Vol. 1. New York: W. W. Norton & Co., 1974.

Anzaldúa, Gloria. *Borderlands / La Frontera: The New Mestiza.* San Francisco: Spinsters / Aunt Lute, 1987.

Aranda, José F., Jr. "Contradictory Impulses: María Amparo Ruiz de Burton, Resistance Theory, and the Politics of Chicano/a Studies." *American Literature* 70 (1998): 551–579.

Arrom, Silvia Marina. *The Women of Mexico City, 1790–1857.* Stanford, Calif.: Stanford University Press, 1985.

Arteaga, Alfred. *Chicano Poetics: Heterotexts and Hybridities.* Cambridge: Cambridge University Press, 1997.

Bakhtin, M. M. *The Dialogic Imagination: Four Essays.* Ed. Michael Holquist. Austin: University of Texas Press, 1994.

Bancroft, Hubert Howe. *History of California.* 7 vols. San Francisco: The History Company, 1884–1889.

———. *Literary Industries.* San Francisco: The History Company, 1890.

———. *Pastoral California.* San Francisco: The History Company, 1888.

Barlow, Samuel Latham Mitchell. *A Private Citizen's Proposal for the Settlement of All Differences between the Northern and Southern States.* Ms. 216157. The Huntington Library, San Marino.

———. Huntington Library Quarterly. "Summary Report of the Samuel Latham Mitchell Barlow Papers." The Huntington Library.

Bercovitch, Sacvan, ed. *Rites of Assent: Transformations in the Symbolic Construction of America.* New York: Routledge, 1993.

Bhabha, Homi K. *The Location of Culture.* London: Routledge, 1994.

Bradford, William. *Of Plymouth Plantation, 1620–1647.* New York: The Modern Library, 1981.

Castañeda, Antonia I. "The Political Economy of Nineteenth Century Stereotypes of Californianas." In *Between Borders: Essays on Mexicana/Chicana History,* ed. Adelaida R. Del Castillo. Encino, Calif.: Floricanto Press, 1990.

Child, Lydia Maria. *Hobomok and Other Writings on Indians.* Ed. Carolyn L. Karcher. New Brunswick, N.J.: Rutgers University Press, 1988.

———. "Prejudices against People of Color, and Our Duties in Relation to This Subject." In *A Lydia Maria Child Reader,* ed. Carolyn Karcher. Durham, N.C.: Duke University Press, 1997.

——. "The Quadroons." Ed. Glynis Carr. The Online Archive of Nineteenth-Century U.S. Women's Writings. Internet. February 2, 1999.

Crèvecoeur, J. Hector St. John de. *Letters from an American Farmer and Sketches of Eighteenth-Century America.* Ed. Albert E. Stone. New York: Penguin Books, 1986.

Crystal, David, ed. *The Cambridge Encyclopedia.* New York: Cambridge University Press, 1990.

Ellis, Joseph J. *American Sphinx: The Character of Thomas Jefferson.* New York: Alfred A. Knopf, 1997.

Franklin, Benjamin. *The Autobiography.* In *The Norton Anthology of American Literature,* vol. 1, ed. Nina Baym. 3rd ed. New York: W. W. Norton & Co., 1989.

Goldman, Anne E. "'Who Ever Heard of a Blue-Eyed Mexican?': Satire and Sentimentality in María Amparo Ruiz de Burton's *Who Would Have Thought It?*" In *Recovering the U.S. Hispanic Literary Heritage,* vol. 2, ed. Erlinda Gonzales-Berry and Chuck Tatum. Houston: Arte Público Press, 1996.

Haraway, Donna J. *Modest—Witness@Second—Millennium.Female Man Meets OncoMouse: Feminism and Technoscience.* New York: Routledge, 1997.

Heizer, Robert F., and Alan J. Almquist. *The Other Californians: Prejudice and Discrimination under Spain, Mexico, and the United States to 1920.* Berkeley: University of California Press, 1977.

Jefferson, Thomas. *Notes on the State of Virginia.* In *The Norton Anthology of American Literature,* vol. 1, ed. Nina Baym. 3rd ed. New York: W. W. Norton & Co., 1989.

Karcher, Carolyn, ed. Introduction. In *Hobomok and Other Writings on Indians,* by Lydia Maria Child. New Brunswick, N.J.: Rutgers University Press, 1988.

Mather, Cotton. "A People of God in the Devil's Territories." The Wonders of the Invisible World. In *The Norton Anthology of American Literature,* vol. 1, ed. Nina Baym. 3rd ed. New York: W. W. Norton & Co., 1989.

——. "Galeacius Secundus: The Life of William Bradford, Esq., Governor of Plymouth Colony" (From *Magnalia Christi Americana*). In *The Norton Anthology of American Literature,* vol. 1, ed. Nina Baym. 3rd ed. New York: W. W. Norton & Co., 1989.

——. "Article XXV. A Notable Exploit; Dux Faemina Facti." *Magnalia Christi Americana; or, The Ecclesiastical History of New England, from its First Planting, in the Year 1620, Unto the Year of Our Lord 1698.* Ed. the Rev. Thomas Robbins, D.D. 7 vols. Hartford, Conn.: Silas Andrus & Son, 1855.

Melville, Margarita B., ed. Introduction. In *Twice a Minority: Mexican American Women.* St. Louis: C. V. Mosby, 1980.

Moraga, Cherríe. *The Last Generation: Prose and Poetry.* Boston: South End Press, 1993.

Pietri, Arturo Uslar. "Otra Historia." In *De Una a Otra Venezuela.* Caracas: Monte Avila Editores, 1992.

Rebolledo, Tey Diana. *Women Singing in the Snow: A Cultural Analysis of Chicana Literature.* Tucson: University of Arizona Press, 1995.

Rebolledo, Tey Diana, and Eliana S. Rivero. *Infinite Divisions: An Anthology of Chicana Literature.* Tucson: University of Arizona Press, 1993.

Romero, Lora. "'When Something Goes Queer': Familiarity, Formalism, and Minority Intellectuals in the 1980's." *The Yale Journal of Criticism* 6 (1993): 121.

Ruiz de Burton, María Amparo. Letter to Hubert H. Bancroft. Savage documents, 2: 121–123. The Bancroft Library, Berkeley.

——. Letter to Mariano Guadalupe Vallejo. October 10 (year unknown). The De La Guerra Papers. The Huntington Library, San Marino, California.

——. Letter to William Rich Hutton. February 17, 1851. Helen Long Collection. The Huntington Library, San Marino.

——. Letter to Mariano Guadalupe Vallejo. November 23, 1851. De La Guerra Papers. The Huntington Library, San Marino.

——. Letter to William Rich Hutton. November 27, 1852. Helen Long Collection. The Huntington Library, San Marino.

——. Letter to Mariano Guadalupe Vallejo. MS. FAC667(1135). November 3, 1855. De La Guerra Papers, The Huntington Library, San Marino.
——. Letter to William Rich Hutton. November 1855. Helen Long Collection. The Huntington Library, San Marino.
——. Letter to Mariano Guadalupe Vallejo. MS. FAC667(1135). March 8, 1860[1]. De La Guerra Papers, The Huntington Library, San Marino.
——. Letter to Mariano Guadalupe Vallejo. MS. FAC667(1135). June 23, 1860. De La Guerra Papers, The Huntington Library, San Marino.
——. Letter to Mariano Guadalupe Vallejo. August 26, 1867. The De La Guerra Papers. The Huntington Library, San Marino.
——. Letter to Mariano Guadalupe Vallejo. May 2, 1868. De la Guerra Papers. The Huntington Library, San Marino.
——. Letter to Mariano Guadalupe Vallejo. February 15, 1869. De La Guerra Papers. The Huntington Library, San Marino.
——. Letter to Samuel Barlow. March 27, 1869. Samuel Barlow Papers. The Huntington Library, San Marino.
——. Letter to Mariano Guadalupe Vallejo. MS. FAC667(1135). August 12, 1869. De La Guerra Papers, The Huntington Library, San Marino.
——. Letter to Mariano Guadalupe Vallejo. September 14, 1869. De La Guerra Collection. The Huntington Library.
——. Letter to Mariano Guadalupe Vallejo. October 11, 1869. De La Guerra Papers, The Huntington Library, San Marino.
——. Letter to Mariano Guadalupe Vallejo. November 23, 1869. De La Guerra Papers. The Huntington Library, San Marino.
——. Letter to Mariano Guadalupe Vallejo. May 7, 1870. De La Guerra Papers. The Huntington Library, San Marino.
——. Letter to Mariano Guadalupe Vallejo. July 27, 1870. De La Guerra Papers. The Huntington Library, San Marino.
——. Letter to Mariano Guadalupe Vallejo. July 1, 1871 (from San Francisco/Grand Hotel). De La Guerra Papers. The Huntington Library, San Marino.
——. Letter to Mariano Guadalupe Vallejo. July 21, 1871 (from San Francisco/Grand Hotel). De La Guerra Papers. The Huntington Library, San Marino.
——. Letter to Mariano Guadalupe Vallejo. August 5, 1872. De La Guerra Papers, The Huntington Library, San Marino.
——. Letter to Samuel Barlow. September 9, 1872. Samuel Barlow Papers. The Huntington Library, San Marino.
——. Letter to Mariano Guadalupe Vallejo. December 20, 1873 (from San Francisco/ Grand Hotel). De La Guerra Papers. The Huntington Library, San Marino.
——. Letter to Mariano Guadalupe Vallejo. January 15, 1874 (from San Diego/Horton House). De La Guerra Papers. The Huntington Library, San Marino.
——. Letter to Samuel Barlow. November 30, 1874. Samuel Barlow Papers. The Huntington Library, San Marino.
——. Letter to Mariano Guadalupe Vallejo. July 15, 1875 (from Jamul). De La Guerra Papers. The Huntington Library, San Marino.
——. Letter to Mariano Guadalupe Vallejo. October 10, 1876. De La Guerra Papers. The Huntington Library, San Marino.
——. Letter to Mariano Guadalupe Vallejo. May 4, 1877 (from San Francisco/Lick House). De La Guerra Papers. The Huntington Library, San Marino.
——. Letter to Mariano Guadalupe Vallejo. May 18, 1878. The De La Guerra Papers. The Huntington Library, San Marino.
——. Letter to Samuel Barlow. September 5, 1883. Samuel Barlow Papers. The Huntington Library, San Marino.
——. Letter to George Davidson. July 7, 1890. The Bancroft Library. Berkeley, California.

——. Letter to Mariano Guadalupe Vallejo. July 7, 1890. De La Guerra Papers, The Huntington Library, San Marino.

——. *The Squatter and the Don.* Ed. Rosaura Sánchez and Beatrice Pita. Houston: Arte Público Press, 1992.

——. *Who Would Have Thought It?* Ed. Rosaura Sánchez and Beatrice Pita. Houston: Arte Público Press, 1995.

Saldívar, José David. *Border Matters: Remapping American Cultural Studies.* Berkeley: University of California Press, 1997.

Sánchez, Rosaura, Beatrice Pita, and Bárbara Reyes, eds. "Nineteenth Century Californio Testimonials." *Critica: A Journal of Critical Essays* (Spring 1994). University of California–San Diego.

Sánchez, Rosaura. "Nineteenth-Century Californio Narratives: The Hubert H. Bancroft Collection." In *Recovering the U.S. Hispanic Literary Heritage,* ed. Ramón Gutiérrez and Genaro Padilla. Houston: Arte Público Press, 1993.

——. *Telling Identities: The Californio Testimonios.* Minneapolis: University of Minnesota Press, 1995.

Sandoval, Chéla. "New Sciences: Cyborg Feminism and the Methodology of the Oppressed." In *The Cyborg Handbook,* ed. Chris Hables Gray. New York: Routledge, 1995.

——. "Oppositional Consciousness in the Postmodern World: U.S. Third World Feminism, Semiotics, and the Methodology of the Oppressed." Dissertation, University of California–Santa Cruz, 1993.

Santamaria, Francisco J. *Diccionario de Mejicanismos.* Mexico: Editorial, Porrua S.A., 1959.

Schulman, Barbara. "The Anatomy of Atrocity." *The Women's Review of Books* 16, no. 5 (February 1999): 28–30.

Stowe, Harriet Beecher. *Uncle Tom's Cabin or, Life among the Lowly.* Ed. Ann Douglas. New York: Penguin Books, 1983.

Whitman, Walt. Editorial. *The Eagle.* Brooklyn, New York, May 1846.

10 ENGENDERING RE/SOLUTIONS: THE (FEMINIST) LEGACY OF ESTELA PORTILLO TRAMBLEY

Cordelia Candelaria

WHEN SHE died in 1998, Estela Portillo Trambley, a native of El Paso, Texas, left a public legacy of writing, storytelling, and several decades of teaching influence that I admire greatly and find solid as *cuentos* and important as cultural artifacts. At the same time I find her literary legacy ideologically complicated and complicating, as important legacies often are.[1] It is this tension between respect for Trambley's *obra* and my struggle with some of the thematics and signification of some of her representations that in part first drew me to this collection's theme of "millennial anxieties" for, after nearly three decades of working to promote appreciation for *raza* letters, I find that the notional possibilities associated with "The Millennium" *as an idea* offer a timely opening for the kind of reconsiderations and appraisals that are associated with the genre of homages, which is one aim of this essay. Intrinsic to the idea of The Millennium and, especially, to *writing* about that idea is *retro*spective reflection as a strategy for *pro*spective thinking. In other words, the millennial idea is a trope that demands a backward glance in order to see forward. Ultimately, The Millennium simultaneously symbolizes the end of an era and the beginning of another, even as it is but a continuation. In the Bergsonian sense of the "real time" of memory and experience[2] The Millennium is, of course, a manufactured marker of duration just like the Chinese, Jewish, and Mayan calendars, to name three which do not mark the end of the second millennium as in the Western Gregorian tradition.

Accordingly, my essay converges with this anthology's timely interrogation of Chicana/o cultural studies within the cusp "between" centuries through its examination of the work of a woman who personified the lived experience of border crossing as an originary, original, and originating personal and material practice. In this I think she is a genuine cultural foremother. This collection's concern with millennial issues of transition parallels my concern with situating and, more precisely, with appreciating (i.e., both valuing *and* understanding) the body of her work in the broader field of U.S. Latina/o and feminist thought, particularly since Trambley died in the *postererías del siglo XXI.*[3] Further, my title's opening phrase, "engendering re/solutions," also addresses the idea that Trambley's writing emerged out of the temporal and spatial precipice of the Chicano Movement—what Velez Ibanez calls "The Great Chicano Cultural Convulsive Transition Movement" (128–136)—with its attendant anxieties concerning material and cultural pasts. The ideological preoccupation with political dogma, identity formation, and their effective expression underlie Trambley's drama and fiction.

In this essay I propose that Trambley's work, like the movement itself, exhibited a concomitant utopian interest with *engender*ing solutions to problems of political exclusion, socioeconomic abjection, and canonical erasure. My title pushes the pun of "en*gender*" to *de*note the process of conceiving, birthing, and creating and also to *con*note the semiotics of gender inflection. The title similarly exploits the pun embedded in "re/solution" as referring at the same time to something resolved and resolute and also to something that needs to be *re*-solved or *re*-addressed. Importantly, depending on context and usage, the noun "resolution" can signify a formal, public declaration (e.g., the resolutions averred in the Declaration of Independence) and a private promise (e.g., a self-improvement program like a New Year's resolution), as well as a collective commitment to heal the wounds of discord (e.g., many NACCS [National Association for Chicana and Chicano Studies] resolutions).

This essay examines the nature, and problematic, of Trambley's "feminist legacy," particularly in terms of her pioneering presence as a woman *of* the Chicano Renaissance. In my view, Trambley's combined work comprises a significant number of enduring short stories (including the celebrated tale of feminist coming of age, "Paris Gown" [1973]); several full-length dramas that have seen stage production in the United States and abroad (including the controversial, lesbian-themed *The Day of the Swallows* [1971] and *Sor Juana* [1983]); the novel *Trini* (1986), and other writings. As the first female recipient of the Premio Quinto Sol awarded by the germinally influential *El Grito* and (to my knowledge) as the first Chicana to dramatize lesbianism for the stage, her intellectual impact was at least in part strongly sociological and historical (Lukens: 697). But first, I think, it was *literary.* Certainly, in terms of her representations of gender, sexuality, and ethnicity/race and their intersection with the related material issues and nodes of social class and power, Trambley inscribed her point of view in unflinching and memorable tracings of one woman's Chicana imaginary. Characterized by a hybrid consciousness of Mexican-Texan biculturality, Spanish-English bilingualism, and resistance to the entrenched vestiges of conquest and colonialism, Trambley expresses the mestizaje of her imaginary through a pointed and unflinching concern with gender relations in the full compound meaning of the term, i.e., sex roles, sexuality, orientation, and identity; patriarchy, personhood, and power, etc.

Crucial to Trambley's representations of gender/race/class identity markers is her situating of her fiction within specifically identifiable geographies like, for example, contemporary Mexican and North American villages, Tex-Mex border towns, Paris, and colonial Mexico, as well as within a variety of recognizable everyday spaces like family dwellings of middle class, poor, and rich, as well as in cantinas, industry settings, and outdoor garden and nature landscapes. Despite her meticulous attention to the details of locale and physical space, Trambley places the portrayal of fully dimensioned characters at the center of her stories (Dewey: 55; Gonzalez: 318–320). The dramatic conflicts and stresses of daily life compressed in her vivid characterizations dominate the front stage of her narrative fiction, thereby voicing her comprehension of the sexualized and gendered *tangle* of personal motivations and *tango* of social behaviors that make up human relations (or what Cixous describes as the project of *l'écriture feminine,* the resisting of the phallocentrism of closed binary structures ["The Laugh of the Medusa": 15]). Like Cixous, Portillo Trambley challenged through her work and what we know of her life the received notion that necessarily binds logocentrism, the language-centered capacity for self-expression, in an inseparable yoke with phallocentrism, the male-identified *and* masculinist imperatives of "Western Civilization" (Cixous, "Laugh": 15–21). Whether in the tragedy of *The Day of the Swallows* or the stories in the first edition of *Rain of Scorpions and Other Writings* (1975), Trambley represents the social practices associated with desire, love, courtship, and sexuality as an agonistic contest of conflicting desires which, in the *frontera* of her imaginary, are fired by the narrowest of masculinist norms (cf. Alarcón: 55; Butler, *Bodies That Matter*: 123–124) She suggests that the conventions and language of love and romance have been so inf(l)ected by the conflict that women and men of whatever identity and orientation face that they are constrained to express feeling and passion within the narrowest vocabulary of macho-dominant/hembra-subordinate terms (cf. Pérez: 69; Butler, *Bodies That Matter*: 67–88; Marcus: 263–265). Similarly in her novel, *Trini,* and her completely revised second edition of *Rain of Scorpions and Other Stories* (1993), she explores the effects of such a narrow lexicon of *inter*course in all its meanings on personal human relations and society as the basis of authentic community, or what Anzaldúa calls the new consciousness of "la mestiza" (765–770).

At the center of her plots Trambley constructs protagonists struggling to express the actual experience of their material lives within society's suffocating grammar of gender relations and who, in that struggle, discover their creative individuality.[4] Ultimately, the creativity and individuality of her protagonists provide new wor(l)ds of self-reflecting power which usually eventually lead to reintegration into their family, neighborhood, village, and/or social matrix *on their own terms.* In this, I see Trambley situating the plot and thematics of her stories in the border zone of received gender dichotomies. For instance, Clotilde in "The Paris Gown" and Beatriz in "If It Weren't for the Honeysuckle . . . " personify the heroics of Trambley's protagonists. The action of her stories typically generates another zone of expression outside the codes of orthodoxy to voice the author's concern with constructing textured mestiza/o worlds of self-reflecting power as in, for example, Refugio and Chucho's relationship in "Pay the Criers" and the ecopoetic theme of "Rain of Scorpions" (Eagar: 3–7, 57) It is this other expressive zone, or counterdiscourse, that I suggest forms another zone of potential human connectedness, *una frontera de Yo-soy-porque-Somos* to challenge, resist, deflect, defy, denounce, distort, and, perhaps especially, explode the received patterns of gender rigidities forced upon women and men from the moment of the first natal cry.[5]

To deploy this hypothesis more fully in this essay, I examine one of Trambley's thus far largely ignored short stories, "La Yonfantayn,"[6] first published in 1985 and later revised for inclusion in the 1993 edition of *Rain of Scorpions.* That is, I read the narrative for its representation of desire and sexuality and how the characters respond to the gender inflections of conventional courtship, love, and romance. I am specifically interested in decoding the author's use of mimicry and minstrelsy in this narrative. By "mimicry" I refer to imitation for comedic purposes, especially of a parodic and caricaturing nature; by "minstrelsy" I refer to the use of a form of *blackface*—the disguises by non–African Americans intended to caricature, lampoon, and stereotype African Americans, their origins, and their culture (as in the well-known denigrations of "Amos 'n' Andy," to name one example). By analogy, as a critical concept for interrogating signs and codes of cultural iconography, "minstrelsy" refers as well to other disguises of ethnoracially different groups for parody and/or derision (Lott, 230). Familiar examples of this non-blackface form include Carmen Miranda as Latina bimbo, Gilbert Roland as Latin lover, Marilyn Monroe as dumb blonde, and Flip Wilson's Geraldine as airhead female and/or drag queen. These representations share one important feature: they typically depict the subjects they are portraying by exaggerating one *gender-specific* and/or *ethnicity- or race-specific* characteristic into an extreme caricature that distorts the complex multiple dimensions of their subjects into a flattened stereotype. They also share another key feature: an audience united by what writer Richard Wright describes as "the tradition which was forced upon the Negro in the theater, that is the minstrel technique that makes the 'white folks' laugh" (251) The "white folks" in the case of this essay refers to any self-identified person or group that does not or cannot identify with, show empathy for, or respect the full humanity of (in the respective examples cited above) Latinas and Latinos, women generally and blond women specifically, or gay men.

The central question I pursue in this reading of "La Yonfantayn" is, does the mimicry in the story constitute a form of minstrelsy that negatively stereotypes the main characters and their culture? In considering this, I necessarily discuss the terms and problematic of Trambley's deployment of ethnic, gender, and class markers with particular emphasis on how the characters negotiate what Trambley represents as the constricting grammar of gender relations. My focus is on her use of exaggerated stereotypes of conventional gendered femininity and masculinity in her portrayal of the story's two main characters, the Mexican American Alicia and the immigrant Mexican Buti.

"La Yonfantayn" recounts the meeting and courtship of forty-two-year-old Alicia Flores, an overweight property-owning Mexican American widow of independent means, who becomes infatuated with Buti, a womanizing heavy-drinking immigrant from Chihuahua, Mexico, who has decided it is time to quit a life of macho philandering and to settle down, especially if he can do so with a wealthy widow. In personality, Alicia is an assertive task-oriented actor who, at least on the surface of first reading, appears vain and self-absorbed, partly because of her obsession with the old romantic movies she watches on television and with the glamorous movie stars she tries to emulate. These old-fashioned movies from the 1940s and '50s offer her both an escape from the reality of her unexciting middle-aged life as a plump, quickly fading sexual persona and a template of sophisticated conduct for her to imitate as a means of improving what she sees as the dull material facts of her lived experience. Likewise, Buti's personality reveals a self-centered pleasure-seeking middle-aged bachelor who is still trying to make his mark in a capitalistic world that perceives him to be a somewhat ridiculous junk seller when, in his overly optimistic, even Panglossian mind, he prefers to think of himself as an entrepreneur engaged in a legitimate "antique business" (Portillo Trambley, *Rain of Scorpions and Other Stories:* 104).

The plot of this simple boy-meets-girl tale of romantic pursuit is complicated in several crucial ways, however. First, it actually reverses the familiar conventional outline by presenting instead the plot of girl connives to meet boy, girl pursues boy, he resists, she insists, and after upheaval and conflict, they in the end finally unite sexually as a couple. This reversal contributes to the story's dramatic conflict by placing Alicia in the dominant position of romantic pursuer and Buti in the subordinate place of the desired prey. Nevertheless, since at first he wants to marry her to fulfill his gold-digging greed, he only pretends coyness to ensure that her desire for him will be whetted. For example, to her *carpe diem* demand on their first date that they quit wasting time on false chivalry and just go to bed with each other, he insists, "Our love is sacred. It must be sanctified by marriage" (106). This heightens the tension between them because Alicia is not accustomed to being rejected when she plays her Chicana femme fatale game of sexual pursuit. After this hard-to-get role playing as foreplay, Buti suddenly realizes that he wasn't really "playing a game anymore. . . . [She was] the kind of woman he would want to spend the rest of his life with" (107).

Also complicating the standard boy-meets-girl plot is the extent to which Alicia lives a virtual life (Rodriguez, "Introduction": 5) as an obsessive consumer of old romance movies. Sealed within her fantasy existence she identifies with Hollywood's leading ladies to such a degree that she even absorbs scenes from the silver screen into her everyday life in a way that blurs the boundaries between the materially *real* and the manufactured *experienced-as-real* (cf. Williams: 202–204; Bourdieu: 360). For example, snippets from film dialogue continually enter her thoughts and conversation, as when she subjects herself to the trouble and inconvenience of wearing false eyelashes because she "remember[s] Lana Turner with her head on Clark Gable's shoulder, her eyelashes sweeping against her cheeks. Max Factor's finest, Alicia was sure of that" (Portillo Trambley, *Rain of Scorpions and Other Stories:* 100). Or, in a pivotal moment in the story, she is inspired "to forgive" Buti *because of* a scene from a late-night movie in which Joan Fontaine goes "to Clark [Gable] to ask forgiveness, [and] to say she was wrong" (108). With causal effectuality, Fontaine's meekness on the screen turns Gable into "a bowl of jelly," suddenly causing Alicia to realize the efficacy of "[a]ll that feminine submissiveness" (108) and to reconsider her desire—as she suggestively puts it—"to always be on top." It is at this point that she reverses her solely self-serving demands and dominant position by electing to run to Buti in the middle of the night and fling her contriteness at him with scripted "[w]ords straight from the movie" (109).[7]

This summary of the text's dramatic conflict and ensuing complications serve to link the key forms of mimicry in the story to this essay's consideration of whether it and the story's other elements of humor constitute a form of "brownface" minstrelsy. Some argue that the imitative parodies of mimicry and minstrelsy are damaging because they constitute a form of "cultural malpractice" that *mis*represents the markers of gender, ethnic, and race identities and their intersecting nodes (Lott: 231; Williams: 210–212). Accordingly, my reading of "La Yonfantayn" detects in it two major kinds of mimicry: imitation *by the characters* of dominant culture Euro-American gender and ethnic stereotypes, and imitation *by the author* of ethnic and racial stereotypes. The first category, mimicry *by the characters* of dominant culture traits, which they regard as ideals, divides naturally into those portrayed through the Alicia persona and those through Buti's persona.

As the plot summary indicates, Alicia defines herself in relation to the Hollywood movies that obsess her and also in relation to the cosmetics industry that provides her only means of imitating the movie stars on the screen. For example, the very first glance the reader has into her personal imaginary is in the third sentence in the story: "She wanted to be pencil thin like a movie star. She would leaf through movie magazines, imagining herself in the place of the immaculately made-up beauties that stared back at her" (Portillo Trambley, *Rain of Scorpions and Other Stories:* 99). Alicia pursues her girlish fantasy of transformation into a beautiful princess for her charming prince by imitating an extreme commercial stylization of femme fatale beauty. This manufactured image of perfect external beauty is based largely on retrograde aristocratic standards that emerged from a caste system that allowed, for instance, The Queen—or whoever was considered the state's highest ranking female authority—the wealth and privilege of being idle and unmarked by the imperatives of quotidian work and sweat (Kolbenschlag). Related to this example of Alicia's mimicry are her notions of love and romance, which she also squeezes out of the tube of Hollywood movie scripts. In other words, her personal imaginary of feminine and sexual identity take the form of dominant culture norms as presented in 1940s and 1950s Hollywood scripts which themselves are corrupted variations of the already corrupt social *doxa* of the "Pretty Woman" as "Queen." Their cartoon versions of physical beauty, *un*spontaneous courtship, and sublimation of erotic sensuality teach Alicia a mechanics of social intercourse that her fantasies elevate into a flawed ideal standard of personal identity.

A related example of dominant culture mimicry occurs through the use of lines of motion picture dialogue to replace actual spontaneous conversation.[8] Both Alicia and Buti borrow lines of dialogue in two key scenes. In the first, Alicia is so excessively moved by a sentimental scene of contrition featuring Joan Fontaine begging "forgiveness" from Clark Gable that she rushes out of her house in her nightclothes to throw herself at Buti and beg his forgiveness. She says to him. "'I want to be forgiven. How could I have doubted you? I'm so ashamed . . .' Words straight from the movie" (109). He recovers from his surprise and eventually enters her virtual Hollywood reality (i.e., fantasy) by literally sweeping her off her feet with one of the screen's most famous lines ever: "'Frankly, my dear, I don't give a damn!' He winked at her and threw her on the bed" (110). The well-paced theatrics of this doubly climactic moment in the plot disclose the author's adroit skills as a dramatist, her first calling as a writer (e.g., in *The Day of the Swallows* and later in *Sor Juana and Other Plays*). They also reveal Portillo Trambley's desire to expose both the effects *and* the efficacy of Hollywood's virtuality as a public curriculum of instruction on physical beauty, gender roles, and sexual relations—described elsewhere in this essay as the *tangle* and *tango* of private and public interactions (cf. Cortes: 24–32; Keller: 34–58; McLuhan: 5–15).

Portillo Trambley's skills and literary aims connect to the second broad category of mimicry identified earlier, that is, the imitation of ethnic, racial, and gender stereotypes *by the author.* Since the story and all the characterizations are constructed and propelled by Estela Portillo Trambley, there clearly is a degree of irony in even making this distinction. My point in doing so is that readers with "suspended disbelief" usually begin the *first* reading of any fictional narrative by engaging the narrative on its own terms. This requires that the characters' motives and actions be considered first within their fictive words and worlds *within the story* before attempting to decode them through the filter of the world of material experience that I share with the author (and, of course, with you, the reader of this essay), for this would remove them from their only (virtual, or fictive) actuality. But there are elements in any given fiction that are not filtered through characterization and that therefore, during the first stage of reception, reading, and critical inquiry, can only be attributed to their creator's agency. These include such elements as setting, point of view, figurative imagery and tropes, and the like. It is in these that I am interrogating the underlying premises of the author's mimicry of ethnic and racial cultural stereotypes. (Crucially important here is recognizing that issues of mis/representation are perceptual—like beauty and humor—

for their underlying assumptions reside in the eyes and minds of the beholders. Thus, the interpreter—in this essay, I, the reader—has the burden of proof regarding whether a given work or performance constitutes minstrelsy.)

Examples of potentially ethnocentric minstrelsy in this group include Trambley's representation of the Chicano and Mexican males as either "a yard boy," in the case of Rico; as tequila-guzzling machos in the case of Buti and Don Rafael; or as crooked "federales" types in the case of the police who throw Buti and Don Rafael in jail. Rico's name, of course, can only be interpreted as providing ironic humor since, as Alicia's hired help, he's anything but *"rico."* Concerning Buti's name Alicia laments that it's "a ridiculous name" even as she drools that he's "a gorgeous hunk of a man" (Portillo Trambley, *Rain of Scorpions and Other Stories:* 100). Adding to the parody is Buti's occupation as a junk seller with pretensions of grandeur, a self-described antique dealer, an awareness that calls to mind his name's English homophone, "booty" meaning a storehouse of loot and treasure.[9] In Spanish, "Buti" calls to mind the vulgar buffoonery of *butifarra,* i.e., pork sausage, and *butiondo,* an "obscene" something or someone. Only the truly wealthy landowners, Alicia and Don Rafael, are spared the diminished authority and, by extension, the diluted dignity implied by the use of diminutive nicknames. Trambley characterizes Buti's persona by the way he's perceived at his favorite cantina, El Dedo Gordo. "At the Fat Finger everybody knew Buti. That's where he did the important things in his life—play poker, start fights, pick up girls, and . . . drink until all hours of the morning" (101). Taken together and in isolation, these examples suggest an *at least* patronizing tone toward Buti and Alicia and their pathetic circumstances and, *at worse,* a defaming depiction of minstrelsy.

But the reader discovers that the stereotypes are not all there is to these droll protagonists. The author's pointed use of language in the title underscores the complex way that Portillo Trambley challenges conventional sex and gender roles and, thereby, hybridizes consciousness. It also represents the most singular and prominent usage of mimicry in the story. Drawn from the story's penultimate scene, the title itself can serve as a gloss for decoding the use of mimicry and minstrelsy in the entire tale.

> Buti's eyes began to shine. She was beginning to sound like the Alicia he knew and loved. "Why should I be like some dumb old movie star?"
>
> "Don't you see?" she held her breath in desperation. "It's life . . . "
>
> "The late late show?" He finally caught on—the dame on television.
>
> "You were watching it too!" She accused him, not without surprise.
>
> "Had nothing else to do. They're stupid you know." . . .

"That proves to me what a brute you are, you insensitive animal!" She kicked his shin.

"Well, the woman, she was kind of nice."

"Joan Fontaine . . . "

"Yonfantayn?"

"That's her name. You're not going to marry her, are you?" There was real concern in her voice.

"Yonfantayn?" He could not keep up with her madness.

"No—that woman up in Raton [New Mexico]." (109)

By entitling her story with the character Buti's mispronunciation of the Hollywood actor's name, Portillo Trambley immediately signals readers to take note of the story's multiple border and border-crossing realities. The scene stresses Buti as a heavily accented Spanish/English Mexican bilingual, and Alicia as an unaccented English/Spanish Chicana bilingual. As indicated in the introduction of this essay, Trambley lived on the *frontera* and her accumulation of writings embodies borders and border crossing as an originary (i.e., primal), original (i.e., fresh and innovative), and originating (i.e., from the root sources) *lived* experience. Thus, what might appear as defaming mimicry within one narrow North American attitude or narrow Mexican attitude proffers an alternative reading if it is decoded as part of the materially real *frontera* phenomena of more plural, authentically transcultural, transnational, and certainly multilingual border experiences. Consequently, even though the story presents social behaviors and self-images in Alicia and Buti that sometimes, at least on the surface, appear as caricatures, the narrative also, importantly, depicts the perversions and shallowness of social norms and Hollywood movies, both of which are driven by commercial desires and objectives.

What saves "La Yonfantayn" from ethnocentric minstrelsy is that the objects of parody, Alicia and Buti, remain only superficially "whitewashed," for their characterizations are balanced with other central facets of character and conduct, while oppositely, the objects of derision in the story—i.e., unbridled money making, Hollywood, the hypocrisy of monocultural "American Dream" values—are emphatic and unredeemed. Ultimately, Buti is revealed to be more than the sum of the parodic parts of macho minstrelsy and certainly greater than the cartoon which emerges from first reading. Buti possesses a personal imaginary too, but unlike Alicia's, which emerges from the curriculum of filmic popular culture (Cortes: 24–25), his arises from conformity to the majority patriarchal culture. For instance, his dreams of success as a rich businessman reflect a personal desire perverted by the mythic American Dream and the attendant requirements of his new homeland's culture of conspicuous consumption. "Buti . . . tried so hard to become a capitalist in the land of plenty to no avail" (Portillo Trambley, *Rain of Scorpions and Other Stories:* 102). His lack of success in his view is not because he lacks the talents and skill. He declares that he "know[s] the principles of good business—contacts, capital, and a shrewd mind. But where in the hell do I get the contacts and the capital?" (102).

Similarly, Alicia is more than the sum of her cosmetic parts, from painted toenails to false eyelashes. She, for example, does not identify with the minor characters or males in the movies, but with those leading "ladies" who land the objects of their desires, whether career, wealth, or romantic partner. Because the young Alicia worked hard to marry well and to invest and manage her sufficiency and wealth after widowhood, she will not jeopardize her independence or security—even for the "gorgeous" Buti. Thus, the irony is that Alicia doesn't alter or disguise her sense of femininity even as she enacts her manifest role as a genuinely confident, tough, and independent achiever.

In the same way, although Buti doesn't have to seek role models on television because patriarchal realities surround him with successful men (e.g., Rico, Don Rafael, the policeman), like Alicia he does subscribe to aspects of the American Dream myth in his goal to be a rich capitalist. But also like her he elects to identify with a resourceful Chicano entrepreneur, Don Rafael, and to work hard (as the piñon-picking episode in Raton, New Mexico, attests) instead of abandoning all traces of his Mexican selfhood. Nor does Buti change his sense of personal identity as a macho even as he performs his reversed role as the pursued and not, in this case, pursuer. Trapped by orthodox gender imagery and patriarchal iconography, both characters manage to negotiate a space of mutuality and authenticity that defies their "game" of courtship (107) and create new rules of engagement in both the military *and* the romantic sense. The conclusion is constructed to underscore that the outcome of their romance is inspired by authentic passion and desire, even if their style of courtship reflects the ubiquitous (popular) culture around them, and despite the uncertainty of not knowing whether their stagey clinch at the end represents the artifice of a happy Hollywood ending.

In "La Yonfantayn," then, Trambley in the early 1980s tackled head-on some of the most painful, anxiety-producing aspects of gender relations, just as she had in the earliest stages of her writing career. By not avoiding machismo and sexuality she strode onto the stage of *raza* creative literature and found it to be a temporal and spatial precipice of the Chicano Movement with its own anxieties—or, at least, its own distinctive intracultural, transnational perturbations—of politics and identity. She wrote her unique expressive zone, or border discourse, as a means of suggesting another zone of potential human connectedness, *una frontera de Yo-soy-porque-Somos.* In this story like many of her others, Portillo Trambley engenders the seeds of her distinctive re/solutions to some of the generic problems of female inequality, political exclusion, socioeconomic abjection, and canonical erasure. Through the techniques of role reversal, humor based on parody and satire, and the destabilizing effects of a *raza mestizaje* that is simultaneously entwined with and resistant of dominant society's social curricula of popular culture, she generates fresh inflections of class, ethnicity, gender, and sexuality and thereby ruptures reductionist versions of Chicana/o identity from the literalism of patriarchal monotheism. This as much as anything in Trambley's impressive *obra* constitutes an unignorable feminist legacy for the millennial mestizaje of the twenty-first century.

NOTES

1. Examples are legion of the paradoxical nature of literary artistic accomplishment that (seemingly incongruously) unites extraordinary insight and skill with (seemingly) antithetical personal qualities, especially when considered in distant hindsight. Extreme examples of the paradox include Edith Wharton and Ezra Pound as anti-Semitic, Ernest Hemingway and Oscar Zeta Acosta as sexist, Gertrude Stein and Robert Frost as abusive spouses, Richard Rodriguez and Linda Chavez as mestizo-bashers, et al.

2. Henri Bergson, the French philosopher and 1927 Nobelist in literature whose theories were absorbed by Joyce, Proust, Faulkner, Stein, Picasso, Borges, Paz, García Márquez, and others, distinguishes between the common apprehension of time as measurements of duration—what he labels *"le temps scientifique,"* or scientific time—and the intuited apprehension of time which is experienced and remembered—what he calls *"le temps réèlle"* or real time (see *Time and Free Will,* 1971, and *The Creative Mind,* 1945).

3. Trambley's birthdate is variably recorded, but 1936 is most often used. Two well-known Chicano literary scholars who knew her well and respected her accomplishment have told me that she was at least a decade older, a point that may be relevant in contextualizing her *obra* generationally and culturally.

4. Compare such similar antinomian characters as Emma Bovary, Jane Eyre, the doctor's wife in Charlotte Perkins Gilman's "The Yellow Wallpaper," the housewife in Rosario Ferré's "La muñeca menor" [The Youngest Doll], and, perhaps quintessentially, the historical personage, Sor Juana Inés de la Cruz [Asbaje y Ramirez de Santillana: 1651–1695].

5. I identify this (in unpublished poetry) as our individual *(g)rito de dolores de partir* (not *de "parto,"* i.e., pain of childbirth), a play on words about the pain of psychological and political estrangement.

6. "La Yonfantayn" was first published in *Revista Chicana-riqueño* (1985), but it was revised for the second edition of *Rain of Scorpions* (Bilingual Review Press, 1993), the text I am citing here.

7. Compare Sedgwick's useful intergenre intertextual reading of gender as represented in *Gone with the Wind,* novel and movie, and the distortion and erasure of the material experience of race and class in the central plot treatment of desire and sexuality (in "Gender Asymmetry and Erotic Triangles").

8. This very common borrowing from filmic icons of popular culture has contributed many new idioms to the repertoire of American English. For example, "I'll make you an offer you can't refuse" or "Okay, go ahead, make my day" or "Sorry, Toto, this ain't Kansas," ad infinitum.

9. Compare Redd Foxx's television sitcom character or Lucille Ball's and Carol Burnett's portrayals of janitors, and in a much earlier prototype, Charlie Chaplin's silent-film version. This comedic type, the menial picaro with dreams of wealth and glory, reflects an ostensibly "past" classism that resonates in the present because of the residual caste stratifications and practices that divide social classes.

WORKS CITED

Alarcón, Norma. "Traddutora, Traditora: A Paradigmatic Figure of Chicana Feminism." In *An Introduction to Women Studies,* ed. J. W. Cochran, D. Langston, and C. Woodward. Dubuque, Iowa: Kendall-Hunt, 1988.

Anzaldúa, Gloria. *Borderlands / La Frontera: The New Mestiza.* San Francisco: Spinsters / Aunt Lute, 1987.

Bergson, Henri. *The Creative Mind* [orig. *L'energie spirituelle,* 1919]. Trans. Mabelle L. Andison. New York: Philosophical Library, 1946.

——. *Time and Free Will* [orig. *Essai sur les données immediates de la conscience,* 1889]. Authorized trans. Frank L. Pogson. New York: Humanities Press, 1971.

Bourdieu, Pierre. "Sport and Social Class." In *Rethinking Popular Culture: Contemporary Perspectives in Cultural Studies,* 357–373. Berkeley: University of California Press, 1991.

Butler, Judith. *Bodies That Matter: On the Discursive Limits of "Sex."* New York and London: Routledge, 1993.

——. *Gender Trouble: Feminism and the Subversion of Identity.* New York: Routledge, 1990.

Christian, Barbara. "The Highs and Lows of Black Feminist Criticism" [1989]. In *Feminisms: An Anthology of Literary Theory and Criticism,* ed. Robyn R. Warhol and Diane Price Herndl, 51–56. 2nd ed. New Brunswick, N.J.: Rutgers University Press, 1997.

Cixous, Helene. "The Laugh of the Medusa" [1975]. Trans. Keith Cohen and Paula Cohen. In *Feminisms: An Anthology of Literary Theory and Criticism,* ed. Robyn R. Warhol and Diane Price Herndl, 347–362. 2nd ed. New Brunswick, N.J.: Rutgers University Press, 1997.

——. *Three Steps on the Ladder of Writing.* Trans. Sarah Cornell and Susan Sellers. New York: Columbia University Press, 1993.

Cortes, Carlos E. "The Societal Curriculum: Implications for Multiethnic Education." In *Education in the 80's: Multiethnic Education,* 24–32. Washington, D.C.: NEA, 1981.

Dewey, Janet. "Dona Josefa: Bloodpulse of Transition and Change." In *Breaking Boundaries: Latina Writings and Critical Readings,* ed. Asuncion Horno-Delgado, Eliana Ortega, Nina M. Scott, and Nancy Saporta Sternbach. Amherst: University of Massachusetts Press, 1989.

Eagar, George D. "The Chicana Female Hero and the Search for Paradise: Estela Portillo-Trambley's Archetypal Discourse on Liberation," Ph.D. dissertation, Arizona State University, 1996.

Gonzalez, Laverne. "Portillo Trambley, Estela." In *Chicano Literature: A Reference Guide,* ed. Julio Martinez and Francisco Lomeli, 316–322. Westport, Conn.: Greenwood, 1984.

Keller, Gary D., ed. *Chicano Cinema: Research, Reviews, and Resources.* Binghamton, N.Y.: Bilingual Review Press, 1985.

Kolbenschlag, Madonna. *Kiss Sleeping Beauty Good-bye: Breaking the Spell of Feminine Myths and Models* [1979]. 2nd ed. San Francisco: Perennial Library, 1988.

Lott, Tommy L. "Black Vernacular, Representation, and Cultural Malpractice." In *Multiculturalism: A Critical Reader,* ed. David Theo Goldberg, 230–258. Cambridge, Mass.: Blackwell, 1994.

Lukens, Margaret A. "Estela Portillo-Trambley." In *The Oxford Companion to Women's Writing in the United States,* ed. Cathy N. Davidson, Linda Wagner-Martin, et al. New York: Oxford University Press, 1995.

Marcus, Jane. "Storming the Toolshed." In *Feminisms: An Anthology of Literary Theory and Criticism,* ed. Robyn R. Warhol and Diane Price Herndl, 263–279. New Brunswick, N.J.: Rutgers University Press.

McLuhan, Marshall. *Understanding Media: The Extensions of Man.* New York: McGraw-Hill, 1964.

Pérez, Emma. "Sexuality and Discourse: Notes from a Chicana Survivor." In *Chicana Lesbians: The Girls Our Mothers Warned Us About,* ed. Carla Trujillo. Berkeley, Calif.: Third Woman Press, 1991.

Portillo Trambley, Estela. *The Day of the Swallows.* In *Contemporary Chicano Theatre,* ed. Roberto Garza. Notre Dame, Ind.: University of Notre Dame Press, 1976.

——. *Rain of Scorpions and Other Stories.* Tempe, Ariz.: Bilingual Press/ Editorial Bilingue, c. 1993.

——. *Rain of Scorpions and Other Writings.* Berkeley, Calif.: Tonatiuh International, 1975.

——. *Sor Juana and Other Plays.* Ypsilanti, Mich.: Bilingual Press/Editorial Bilingue, 1983.

——. *Trini.* Binghamton, N.Y.: Bilingual Press/Editorial Bilingue, 1986.

Rodriguez, Clara, ed. *Latin Looks: Images of Latinas and Latinos in the U.S. Media.* Boulder, Colo.: Westview, 1997

Sedgwick, Eve Kosofsky. "Gender Asymmetry and Erotic Triangles" [1985]. In *Feminisms: An Anthology of Literary Theory and Criticism,* ed. Robyn R. Warhol and Diane Price Herndl, 507–532. New Brunswick, N.J.: Rutgers University Press.

Vallejos, Tomas. "Estela Portillo Trambley's Fictive Search for Paradise." *Frontiers: A Journal of Women Studies* 5, no. 2 (1980): 54–58.

Vélez-Ibáñez, Carlos G. *Border Visions: Mexican Cultures of the Southwest United States.* Tucson: University of Arizona Press, 1996.

Williams, Rosalind. "The Dream World of Mass Consumption." In *Rethinking Popular Culture: Contemporary Perspectives in Cultural Studies,* 198–235. Berkeley: University of California Press, 1991.

Wright, Richard. "How 'Bigger' Was Born." Epilogue to *Native Son* [1940]. New York: HarperCollins / Perennial Classics edition, 1998.

11 *UNIR LOS LAZOS:* BRAIDING CHICANA AND *MEXICANA* SUBJECTIVITIES[1]

Anna M. Sandoval

MY INTEREST in comparing Mexican women's literature and Chicana literature began during a year of study at the Universidad Nacional Autónoma de México, (UNAM) in Mexico City in 1990. As a Chicana from a working-class background, my attraction to living and studying in Mexico was based not only on my respect and scholarly interest in the work, but also on my lived experience as a Chicana. Although I did not spend summers and vacations with family in Mexico like many of my friends (my roots are in Colorado and New Mexico), similar to others who self-identify as Chicana/o, I understood my historical and cultural connection to the land that my ancestors knew as Mexico. The experience of living in a place where I was not visibly the other would turn out to be one of the most empowering experiences of my life.

My initial intention was to review the scholarship on Chicanos written by Mexican scholars, but as a student in *filosofía y letras,* I was enrolled exclusively in literature courses. During one such course in *literatura femenina,* I began my exploration of Mexican women's literature. Reading about the *Mexicana* experience, then building alliances and developing relationships with *Mexicanas* made me realize the connections that finally needed to be systematically discussed. Because my emphasis in U.S. literature is on Chicana writers, a comparative literary study of *Mexicanas* and Chicanas seemed natural and, to be sure, necessary—not much work having been done in this area.[2]

A comparative analysis of *Mexicana* and Chicana subjectivities, this essay examines oppositional discourses that these writers present in their work. By reformulating cultural symbols and offering nontraditional constructions of culturally relevant themes, Chicanas and *Mexicanas* are responding to systems of patriarchy. Having a shared cultural history, Chicanas and *Mexicanas* critique similar issues. Interesting differences in their literature, however, due to the writers' unique subject positions in their respective communities, their different experiences with colonization by the United States, and other unique aspects of their lives, also lead to enhanced understandings of their voices.[3]

To begin my study of *Mexicana* and Chicana writers, I examine new currents in scholarship and in the theoretical approaches to several related areas. The increased interest in critical literary studies in Chicano literature both by Chicanas/os and non-Chicanas/os reflects the increased literary production by Chicanas. The work of the past fifteen years has been invigorating; it has also been "women's work." Men, of course, are still publishing, but their literature does not seem to be enjoying the same popularity as women's literature.

Anyone who is teaching courses on Chicano literature has a much larger body of texts from which to select than they did ten years ago. No longer is it necessary to read *only* Rudolfo Anaya, José Antonio Villarreal, Rodolfo González, Ernesto Galarza, and other male authors once seen as the first authors of Chicano literature. Furthermore, with the recovery projects of some Chicana critics like Clara Lomas, Rosaura Sánchez, and María Herrera-Sobek, the point of departure for the contemporary study of Chicano literature has become the women's voices of the early nineteenth century in the southwestern United States.[4] This new scholarship will indeed change the field of Chicano literature. Along with those of other Chicanas in various disciplines who are giving sorely needed attention to issues of race, class, gender, and sexuality, the voices of Chicana literature will seed the field of Chicano studies, as well as other disciplines such as U.S. history and American studies.

HISTORICAL OVERVIEW

In the field of literary criticism, Norma Alarcón's several essays make important contributions. "Chicana Feminism: In the Tracks of the Native Woman" (1990) gives attention to the issue of Chicana subjectivity. Literary critic Rosaura Sánchez gives a postmodern reading to Chicano literature, yet does not include women in the debate in her essay "Postmodernism and Chicano Literature" (1987). Anthropologist Renato Rosaldo enters the literary discussion through a study of the "warrior hero" in his text *Culture and Truth: The Remaking of Social Analysis* (1989). Sonia Saldívar-Hull begins to articulate a theory of international feminism in her study "Feminism on the Border: From Gender Politics to Geopolitics" (1991). Angie Chabram-Dernersesian, in "I'll Throw Punches for My Race, but I Don't Want to Be a Man" (1990), critiques the way in which women were given a subordinate role in the Chicano Movement and examines how some Chicanas are rewriting Chicano nationalism. Carl Gutiérrez-Jones examines Chicana and Chicano literature through the lens of critical legal studies in *Rethinking the Borderlands: Between Chicano Culture and Legal Discourse* (1995). Ramón Saldívar's text *Chicano Narrative: The Dialectics of Difference* (1990) places the theoretical debates surrounding the field into a chronological context, beginning with the folk-based narrative, the *corrido,* and continuing into contemporary Chicana narrative. Using a poststructuralist approach, Saldívar develops a model for reading Chicano literature, a model that he calls a "dialectics of difference."[5]

As we can see, the theoretical debates that these critics cover are wide-ranging and cross several disciplinary boundaries. The present work enters the debate by offering a comparative model for reading Chicana and *Mexicana* literature that describes how these two literatures inform each other.[6]

This work belongs to a new area of studies that is opening up the discussion among the many Americas, an inclusive area that ideally would address issues of North, Central, and South America.[7] A mere handful of critical works were published between 1986 and 1992 on comparative literatures of the Americas. One of the first texts to attempt this type of analysis is *Reinventing the Americas: Comparative Studies of Literature of the U.S. and Spanish America* (1986), edited by Bell Chevigny and Gari Laguardia. This text is key to my work, initiating the larger dialogue from which my study stems. Addressing questions about the canon of American literature, Chevigny and Laguardia discuss the need for its redefinition. They do not, however, specifically address Chicano literature. Other provocative new discussions place comparative American studies in the foreground. Among these are Lois Parkinson Zamora's *Writing the Apocalypse: Historical Vision in Contemporary U.S. and Latin American Fiction* (1989); Gustavo Pérez-Firmat's *Do the Americas Have a Common Literature?* (1990); and José Saldívar's *The Dialectics of Our America* (1991).

Pérez-Firmat's work examines the "contact and perhaps the clash between some of the cultures of the Americas" (Pérez-Firmat: 1). He begins his discussion by pointing to the novelty of such a study, reminding us that literary comparison most often refers to studies that run east to west. In the introduction to this work, he states:

> [S]cholars of North American literature, while they have been much concerned with the "Americanness" of their domain, have usually neglected to consider this notion in anything other than the narrow nationalistic and anglophone sense, where America becomes a synonym for the United States. On the other hand, students of Latin American literature have for the most part not looked northward in search of significant contexts for their texts. (2–3)

The essays aim to "couple the literatures and cultures of this hemisphere —particularly their North American and Latin American sectors—in order to find regions of agreement or communality" (1–2). Pérez-Firmat states that he chooses to work toward strengthening commonality, instead of crystallizing difference. He realizes that many scholars may find problems in the intention of his work and in the book's title. Certainly, many would answer the title's question, "Do the Americas have a common literature?" with an emphatic "No!" Roberto Fernández Retamar argues, for example, that the "histories of the United States and the rest of the hemisphere are so unlike that the corresponding literatures are therefore incommensurable" (Pérez-Firmat, 5). Pérez-Firmat, while agreeing that the difference in historical and political position between Spanish America and the United States is huge, makes the point that "historical position is not always identical with cultural position" (5).

José Saldívar's study *The Dialectics of Our America: Genealogy, Cultural Critique, and Literary History* (1991) not only presents a critical framework for discussing U.S. and Latin American fiction and culture and the canon of American literature, but also "questions the notion of America itself" (xii). He states in his preface:

> *The Dialectics of Our America* thus charts an array of oppositional critical and creative processes that aim to articulate a new, trans-geographical conception of American culture—one more responsive to the hemisphere's geographical ties and political crosscurrents than to narrow national ideologies. (xi)

Referring to José Martí's term "Nuestra América," Saldívar critically examines "Martí's conviction of a profound gap between our America and the other America, which is not ours" (Saldívar: 7). The present project adds to this body of literature by examining the historiographic debates of previous decades and by focusing on women's writing and feminist critique.

Closer to my specific area of study on women is *Talking Back: Toward a Latin American Feminist Literary Criticism* (1992) by Debra Castillo. Castillo's project is not intended to create "an overarching theory" of Latin American feminism, but rather to explore critical issues and strategies of a "hispanic feminist literary practice" (Castillo: 2):[8]

> Latin American feminisms are developing in multiple directions not always compatible with directions taken by Anglo-European feminisms and frequently in discord with one another. It would be premature to try to invent an overarching theory to account for these developments; rather, I hope to offer a continually self-questioning theorizing anchored in specific texts. (xxii)[9]

Castillo's study includes *Mexicanas,* Chicanas, and other Latin American women and is essential for the study of comparative American literature. Pérez-Firmat mentions the lack of inter-American comparative studies; so too is there an absence of the critical study of Latin American women. Castillo's study makes an attempt to fill this gap. Although many of these texts provide useful approaches in the area of "hemispheric comparative inquiry," the texts most helpful to a comparative literature by Chicanas and *Mexicanas* have been the anthologies produced from the conference sponsored by el Colegio de México, el Colegio de la Frontera Norte, the University of California–San Diego, and San Diego State University entitled *Mujer y literatura mexicana y chicana: Culturas en contacto* (1988 and 1990).[10] Prior to these anthologies, no academic journal had compiled these critics' work. The first of these invaluable anthologies carries the epigraph: *"Con el deseo de unir los lazos entre las mujeres chicanas y Mexicanas"* (With the Hope of Binding the Ties between *Mexicanas* and Chicanas). The organizers of the conference understood the role that literature plays in producing cultural exchange: literature is a means by which people, sometimes from very distinct worlds, can communicate. The worlds of Chicanas and *Mexicanas* are distinct, yet their strong cultural ties make exchange of ideas, experience, and information imperative. The anthologies offer a starting point for readers of literature who are interested in the relations of Chicanas and *Mexicanas.* The editors state their goal in the introduction:

> . . . para experimentar el intercambio intenso de la *Mexicana* de este lado y la chicana de aquel. . . . lo que esperamos sea una aportación al conocimiento de las culturas que la nutren; los tópicos que maneja, los silencios que hacen presente aquello que no se menciona, el tipo de lenguaje utilizado, la palabra escrita que nos habla del trabajo de las mujeres que tradicionalmente son hacedoras silenciosos de la cultura. (12)

The anthology's essays provide individual analyses of various works, yet no in-depth comparative study of the two national literatures is included in either edition.[11] Nonetheless, the work initiates an important dialogue between *Mexicanas* and Chicanas because it offers them and their respective nations a better understanding of their shared historical and cultural experience.

Beyond the issue of "cultural contact" between *Mexicanas* and Chicanas through literature, no one theme is central within the anthologies; the content is wide-ranging because the conference addressed new areas of study. By examining specific literary texts, critics address identity issues, feminist discourse, colonialism, difference, sexuality, and marginality, issues relevant to all national literatures. However, the narratives that are being viewed through these many discourses articulate a particular *Mexicana* and Chicana experience. The second volume of *Mujer y literatura mexicana y chicana: Culturas en contacto* (1990), while recognizing the text as only a starting point for further investigation, stresses the importance of viewing *Mexicana* and Chicana literature in a shared context. In the introduction, Aralia López González states:

> . . . ya es posible plantear algunos resultados que aún siendo generales y tentativos, permiten perfilar ciertos rasgos afines y también diferenciar entre produccíones literarias que teniendo raíces comunes, se han conformado en procesos históricos diferentes; y, asimismo, partiendo del hecho de que se trata de una producción escrita por mujeres, sin renunciar a la posible caracterización

> de una poética femenina, revelan la necesidad de contextualizar el género como categoría de análisis si quiere evitar las muchas veces estériles totalizaciones abstractas. (11)

With this in mind, my study continues this exchange through a comparative look at the multiple contexts of cultural, historical, and geographical borders for *Mexicanas* and Chicanas. Both redefine nationalism in their respective cultures: Chicanas are looking at the roots of the Chicano Movement and demonstrating how the movement has been rooted in sexism; *Mexicanas* are examining and challenging their patriarchal culture. I propose a comparative framework for looking at recent developments in Chicana and *Mexicana* literature.

Similar to Chicana writers, *Mexicana* writers in the past ten years have had their own literary boom. Jean Franco in *Plotting Women: Gender and Representation in Mexico* (1989) discusses the development in her critical study of *Mexicana* literature. A great deal of Mexican women's literature includes a "repudiation of nation and family": national myths, for example, are parodied, and writers such as Poniatowska, Boullosa, and Mastretta find creative means to undermine the patriarchy. Also prevalent in recent texts produced by Mexican women are themes of adolescence, sexuality, domestic violence, and, through these, a call for the creation of women-centered communities.[12] Poniatowska also gives the reader female revolutionaries and rebels—such as her character Jesusa in the testimonial novel *Hasta no verte, Jesús mío* (1969). *Mexicana* literature, then, is representing a historical reality, breaking the patriarchal stranglehold of the Mexican male literature that portrays women as weak and powerless.

Following is an overview of the common thematics of *Mexicana* and Chicana writers, an examination of how their discursive positions differ, and how they articulate their political and theoretical positions by challenging dominant ideologies.

COMPARING FEMINISMS

My starting point is an examination of the subject position of each group. I argue that while *Mexicanas* have the privilege of writing against a national discourse that at least includes them, Chicanas write against a national discourse that does not recognize them. For the Chicana, her national identity is often challenged.

Mexicanas, while clearly included in the nation, albeit many times as second-class citizens, are similarly talking back to the systems of patriarchy in Mexico.[13] Most *Mexicana* and Chicana writers have been university educated, although in many cases distinct class differences separate the two groups. Despite the unique circumstances of each group, the common experiences with cultural institutions in a patriarchal society lead them to a common literary expression, both formally and thematically.

Beginning with a look at thematics, talking back to dominant ideologies is in itself a highly subversive act. One result of talking back is the redefinition of family or cultural symbols. Chicanas have different ways of expressing this strategy. "Making familia from scratch" is how Cherríe Moraga describes it; "familia de mujeres" is Denise Chávez's term; "border feminism" is how Sonia Saldívar-Hull and others express the particularities of the development of women-centered spaces in Chicana literature. Though *Mexicanas'* and Chicanas' positions differ in their respective nations, their narratives take on similar experimental forms as well as a similar thematics. The shared experience of the influence of the Catholic church, for example, accounts for many common thematic responses in their literature. Refuting the Catholic church is viewed as highly subversive in both cultures, as are references to other shared themes such as sexuality, domestic violence, and incest. I argue that within the narratives of *Mexicanas* and Chicanas are embedded their political and theoretical agendas, which challenge dominant ideologies.[14]

Another central issue that the present comparison addresses is how Chicanas and *Mexicanas* articulate their political and theoretical positions through representations of various figures of resistance, often revisionings of traditional cultural symbols. Chicana writers often appear to be more critical than *Mexicanas,* in their literature, of traditional cultural symbols such as La Llorona, La Virgen de Guadalupe, and La Malinche.

Chicana and *Mexicana* feminisms have developed from very different circumstances and have gone in very different directions in their respective countries. Mexico has a long history of struggle for women's liberation. Beginning with the seventeenth-century Mexican nun Sor Juana Inéz de la Cruz, who chose the convent in order to follow her intellectual pursuits, to the women who fought for women's suffrage, to the organizers of the first women's congress in Yucatán, to the writer and ambassador of modern Mexico Rosario Castellanos, Mexico has seen in its long history as a nation many leaders, intellectuals, stateswomen, writers, and other women who have been intimately involved in all areas of Mexico's development.[15] Despite this, surprisingly little has been written on the history of feminist movement in Mexico. One of the first and few texts that outlines this development is *Against All Odds: The Feminist Movement in Mexico to 1940* by Anna Macías (1982).[16] Much of the feminist critique which comes out of Mexico is published in journals and newspaper supplements such as *Fem* and the supplement to the daily paper *La Jornada,* cleverly titled "*La Doble Jornada*" and dedicated to women's lives. A major contribution to Mexican feminist studies is the extensive bibliography of Rosario Castellanos. Her *La mujer que sabe latín* (1984) presents a series of essays that critique Mexican culture as well as several intellectuals and celebrities. The essay that opens the text, "La mujer y su imagen," makes an important contribution to critical studies on Mexican women and to feminist studies in general. Another recent study that looks at Mexican feminism in relation to other feminisms is "Feminisms in Latin America: From Bogotá to San Bernardo" by Nancy Saporta Sternbach et al. (1992).

Until 1848, Chicanas and *Mexicanas* shared feminist movements.[17] Other scholarly studies are attempting to find a defining point that names the beginning of Chicana/o culture. With the "discovery" of journals, serial novels, and other writing by women from the nineteenth century, many questions will be answered and new light will be shed on issues of identity, politics, and popular culture of the time. If one takes the historical date, Chicana culture begins with the annexation of Mexico's land by the United States in 1848.[18] Since that time, women have played an active role in all aspects of political, economical, and cultural life. Nonetheless, men's role in history has been the one portrayed as most critical. An early historical study is Marta Cotera's *Diosa y Hembra: The History and Heritage of Chicanas in the U.S.* (1976).[19] Other crucial works are Adelaida Del Castillo's *The Mexican Woman in the U.S.* (1990), and Rosaura Sánchez's *Essays on La Mujer* (1977). One of the first texts that looks at the history and development of Chicana feminism is Marta Cotera's *The Chicana Feminist* (1977); also significant is Alma García's essay "The Development of Chicana Feminist Discourse, 1970–1980" (1989). Some of the more recent scholarship includes an edited text by Adela De La Torre and Beatriz M. Pesquera, *Building with Our Hands: Directions in Chicana Studies* (1993). Ana Castillo introduces the term "Xicanisma" in opposition to the U.S. feminist movement, which has often ignored the woman of color's struggle. Her collection of essays *Massacre of the Dreamers: Essays on Xicanisma* (1994) adds to the development of literature which brings the Chicana's experience to the forefront. Tey Diana Rebolledo's text *Women Singing in the Snow: A Cultural Analysis of Chicana Literature* (1995) acts as a theoretical base for *Infinite Divisions: An Anthology of Chicana Literature* (1993), and is the first analysis of its kind in which the development of a Chicana literary tradition is traced from its roots in 1848 to the present.

Just as *Mexicana* feminism is often viewed in the context of a larger Latin American feminist discourse, so too is Chicana feminism viewed in the context of a larger U.S. Third World Women's feminist discourse. One of the first key texts that offers a discussion of U.S. Third World feminism is *This Bridge Called My Back: Writings by Radical Women of Color,* edited by Gloria Anzaldúa and Cherríe Moraga (1981). The text which acts as a second volume to *Bridge* is *Making Face, Making Soul / Haciendo Caras* edited by Gloria Anzaldúa (1990). Chela Sandoval's "U.S. Third World Feminism: The Theory and Method of Oppositional Consciousness in the Postmodern World" (1991) also contributes to this area. In my larger project from which this essay stems, I call upon the work of Chandra Mohanty et al. for their discussion of Third World feminism in *Third World Women and the Politics of Feminism* (1991). This work offers a starting point for viewing international feminisms.

Bringing together Chicana and *Mexicana* feminism presents a tremendous challenge. For the reasons explained above, the two histories have been disconnected in a various ways for over a hundred years. Yet, as part of an international feminist community, and particularly a Third World feminist community, the two have shared in the same larger struggle for liberation, "not only individual liberation but [one] of social justice and democratization" (Franco: 187). The shared history creates strong ties, ties evident in the contemporary literary expressions of both groups. One important entrance into the literature is by way of the representations of cultural symbols and the mythologies that Chicanas and *Mexicanas* share.

MYTHOLOGIES

The revisioning of myths, legends, and cultural symbols has always been a significant feature of the literature of Chicanas and *Mexicanas.* Several cultural symbols have derived from these myths, the most significant ones dating back to the Spanish Conquest of the fifteenth and sixteenth centuries, later adapting to include contemporary events such as the indirect colonization of Mexico and other Latin American countries by the United States, or the internal colonization of Mexicans in the United States. The trilogy of La Virgen de Guadalupe, La Malinche (also called Malintzín or Marina), and La Llorona has long been present in the literature of Latin America and the Latino United States. As Chicanas and *Mexicanas* write their experience into history, this corrected history also reflects in their literature. No longer are these figures of the trilogy the only ones drawn from; no longer are these figures the chaste virgin mother, the traitor to *la raza,* or the hysterical murderess of children.

Feminist rereadings of these cultural symbols give these figures agency and often rewrite them as heroines. Of the three figures, La Malinche is the one most grounded in actual Mexican history.[20] She becomes a mythical figure, however, in the patriarchal discourse and is seen as a traitor to her race, the cause of pain and suffering of all generations of Mexicans. Yet, women writers are reclaiming her image, placing Malintzín in her proper historical context and accurately viewing her as a figure of resistance.[21] Norma Alarcón in "Chicanas' Feminist Literature: A Re-Vision through Malintzín / or Malintzín: Putting Flesh Back on the Object" (1981) begins her argument by stating:

> In our patriarchal mythological pantheon, there exists even now a woman who was once real. Her historicity, her experience, her true flesh and blood were discarded. A Kantian, dualistic male consciousness stole her and placed her on the throne of evil, like Dante's upside down frozen Judas, doomed to moan and bemoan. The woman is interchangeably called by three names: Malintzin, Malinche, Marina. Malintzin's excruciating life in bondage was of no account,

> and continues to be of no account. Her almost half century of mythic existence, until recent times mostly in the oral traditions, had turned her into a handy reference point not only for controlling, interpreting or visualizing women, but also to wage a domestic battle of stifling proportions. (Alarcón, 1981: 182)

Alarcón, in this essay, gives a critique of how the historical figure of Malintzín has turned into a mythical figure that works toward the continued subjugation of women, only, however, if women themselves continue to internalize the myth—certainly true to now. Several Chicana writers, however—Alarcón points to two in particular—do refute the myth and restore the symbol of La Malinche to a woman with agency. While Alarcón critiques the patriarchal system which made La Malinche a slave, she recognizes how women have internalized that myth:

> Because the myth of Malintzin pervades not only male thought ours too as it seeps into our own consciousness in the cradle through their [male] eyes as well as our mothers', who are entrusted with the transmission of culture, we may come to believe that indeed our very sexuality condemns us to enslavement. An enslavement which is subsequently manifested in self-hatred. (183)

In Chicana literature, Alarcón and others argue that La Malinche is the cultural symbol most often called forth and, as such, is the most useful representative for women's rebellion.

The figure of La Llorona, though more prevalent in popular culture than La Malinche, does not always carry the same historical significance, although many view her legend as an adaptation of the myth of La Malinche.[22] La Llorona is a character in Chicano and Mexican folk legend who, in a supposed moment of insanity, drowns her own children. She wanders the rivers at night searching and calling for them. As is the nature of folk legends, this story has many adaptations, in almost all of which La Llorona is represented as a passive character. Yet, one can also read this story as a cautionary tale, one told to keep children, women, and men "in their place." The figure of La Llorona, her history, and the strong cultural significance of her legend are complex. As in the cases with other cultural symbols such as La Malinche and La Virgen de Guadalupe, the symbol of La Llorona is being transformed and reread through the experience of Chicanas and *Mexicanas.*

José Limón, in his essay "*La Llorona,* The Third Legend of Greater Mexico: Cultural Symbols, Women, and the Political Unconscious" (1989), indicates that prior to his work La Llorona "[had] received precious little close analytical, interpretive attention in relationship to Greater Mexican society and culture" (69). Limón cites various studies which have been attempted, demonstrating that these studies do not fully acknowledge the usefulness of La Llorona in feminist interpretation, that they "fall short of a contestative and critical understanding and offer only historically limited, localized interpretations" (73). Quoting the work of Alfredo Mirandé and Evangelina Enríquez, Limón adds:

> [La Llorona is] a female who strayed from her proper role as mother, wife, mistress, lover, or patriot . . . a woman who regrets her transgression or bemoans having been denied the fulfillment of her role. . . . *La Llorona* persists as an image of a woman who willingly or unwillingly fails to comply with feminine imperatives. As such, a moral light is cast on her, and she again reflects a cultural heritage that is relentless in its expectations of feminine roles. (70)

Limón, indeed, sees this Mirandé and Enríquez reading as passive and offers what he believes to be a more accurate reading. In comparing La Llorona to La Malinche and La Virgen de Guadalupe, Limón sees her as a "critical contestative performance in the everyday lives of the ordinary women of Greater Mexico," one who "shows her relationship to all of the folk masses of greater Mexico" (79). Limón's ethnographic work critiques the vital importance of La Llorona, but it lacks a comprehensive understanding of what he claims are "feminist misreadings" of the La Llorona legend. Norma Alarcón responds to Limón in her essay "*Traddutora, Traditora:* A Paradigmatic Figure of Chicana Feminism" (1989):

> José Limón has argued that La Llorona would make a more effective feminist cultural symbol for women of Mexican descent. In fact, he argues that Chicanas have failed to recognize her potential feminist political importance [Limón: 77–78]. In my view, La Llorona fails to meet some of the modern and secularizing factors that Chicanas have felt they need in order to speak for themselves. The so-called second wave of global feminism forces contemporary women to deal with the notion of the self and subjectivity that previous feminisms have often bypassed in favor of women's rights on the basis of being wives and mothers. The current debate on La Malinche goes beyond that. (Alarcón, 1989: 77–78)

Giving one cultural symbol precedence over another does not help us toward better understanding. Nonetheless the work of both critics is important, as important as the work of contemporary poets, novelists, and short story writers who interrogate, appropriate, and revise these cultural symbols so that they become a part of a female interpretation interrupting and disrupting traditional patriarchal modes of thinking.

The third cultural symbol discussed in the present study is the patron saint of Mexico and Latin America, La Virgen de Guadalupe. In poetic form, Gloria Anzaldúa retells the story of La Virgen's divine appearance:

> El nueve de diciembre del año 1531 / a las cuatro de la madrugada / un pobre indio que se llamaba Juan Diego / iba cruzando el cerro de Tepeyac / cuando oyó un canto de pájaro. / Alzó al cabeza vio que en la cima del cerro / estaba cubierta con una brillante nube blanca. / Parada en frente del sol / sobre una luna creciente / sostenida por un ángel / estaba una azteca / vestida en ropa de india. / Nuestra Señora María de Coatlalopeuh / se le apareció / "Juan Diegito, El-que-habla-como-un-águila," / La Virgen le dijo en el lenguaje azteca. / "Para hacer mi altar este cerro eligo. / Dile a tu gente que yo soy la madre de Dios, / a los indios yo les ayudaré." / Estó se lo contó a Juan Zumarraga / pero el obispo no le creyo. / Juan Diego volvió, lleno su tilma / con rosas de castilla / creciendo milagrosamente en la nieve. / Se las llevó al obispo, / y cuando abrió su tilma / el retrato de *La Virgen* / ahí estaba pintado. (Anzaldúa: 28)

Although in patriarchal culture La Virgen de Guadalupe has been viewed as the other figure in the virgin/whore dichotomy, women have seen her as a symbol of resistance and cultural survival. During the conquest, when the native people of Mexico were supposedly being Christianized, they were still seen as "savages" not worthy of full membership in the church. Yet, La Virgen de Guadalupe appeared to an Indian man, Juan Diego, to express her and God's servitude to his people. A brown virgin represented acceptance of the native peoples by their newly adopted God. Some theorists, however, speculate that La Virgen was fundamentally an adaptation by the indigenous tribe of their earth goddess, Tonantzín. In this reading, La Virgen would be a symbol of resistance to the conqueror's religion. The case of syncretism is evident throughout history as the Catholic Church tried and continues to try to impose its Christian religion on the people of America. As we enter the new millennium, *Mexicana* and Chicana cultural critics and writers are highly invested in claiming a space in the rewriting and reconstruction of history. It is a necessary bond that must continue to be formed and maintained between those who embody the geographical border.

NOTES

1. See the epigraph in Aralia López González, Amalia Malagamba, and Elena Urrutia, eds., *Mujer y literatura mexicana y chicana: Culturas en contacto,* 2 vols. (Mexico, D.F.: Colegio de México, Programa Interdisciplinario de Estudios de la Mujer; Tijuana, B.C., Mexico: Colegio de la Frontera Norte, 1988, 1990). It reads: "Con el deseo de unir los lazos entre las mujeres chicanas y *Mexicanas*" (With the hope of binding the ties between Chicanas and *Mexicana*s).

2. In my work, I am making a distinction between the terms "*Mexicana*" and "Chicana." Often, the two are collapsed into each other, both by the United States and by the groups themselves. However, these acts of homogenization are being done for

two very different reasons. For the U.S. government, the merging of the two terms is much like their imposition of the term "Hispanic," a device used to erase or homogenize the many different groups throughout Latin America. Yet, for the groups themselves, the connection of the two terms, separated only by a slash, is a statement pointing to political and cultural solidarity that attempts to unite the groups in order to bring a closer understanding of both worlds—not as a form of governmental erasure. Also, it is only Chicanas who would make this gesture of joining the two terms since a Chicana always has the *Mexicana* in her, but the *Mexicana* does not necessarily have the Chicana in her.

3. See Benedict Anderson, *Imagined Communities: Reflections on the Origin and Spread of Nationalism* (New York: Verso, 1991).

4. See Tey Diana Rebolledo and Eliana S. Rivero, ed., *Infinite Divisions: An Anthology of Chicana Literature* (Tucson: University of Arizona Press, 1993).

5. Ramón Saldívar explains in his introduction: "This narrative strategy for demystifying the relations between minority cultures and the dominant culture is the process I term 'the dialectics of difference' of Chicano literature. In the course of my discussion, I will show how the dialectical form of narratives by Chicano men and women is an authentic way of grappling with a reality that seems always to transcend representation, a reality into which the subject of the narrative's action seeks to enter, all the while learning the lesson of its own ideological closure, and of history's resistance to the symbolic structures in which subjectivity itself is formed." See Ramón Saldívar, *Chicano Narrative: The Dialectics of Difference* (Madison: University of Wisconsin Press, 1990).

6. See the following unpublished dissertations: Roselyn Constantino, "Resistant Creativity: Interpretative Strategies and Gender Representation in Contemporary Women's Writing in Mexico" (Arizona State University, 1992), and Helga Winkler, "Selected *Mexicana* and Chicana Fiction: New Perspectives on History, Culture and Society" (University of Texas, 1992).

7. What I am calling comparative American studies refers to the United States and Latin America. I realize, however, that as I am trying to be as inclusive as I can in my discussion, that Canada, part of this hemisphere as well, does not enter my discussion at any point. I think that further comparative American studies needs to address Canadian literature as well.

8. For a discussion of Latin American feminisms by Latin American feminists, see Nancy Saporta Sternbach, "Feminisms in Latin America: From Bogotá to San Bernardo," *Signs: Journal of Women in Culture & Society* 17, no. 2 (1992): 393–433.

9. Studies by Anglo women such as Castillo give an interesting viewpoint of Chicana, Latina, and Latin American feminist discourse which offers a very different representation of these feminisms than the analysis by those groups themselves.

10. Here, I use Gustavo Pérez-Firmat's term to refer to inter-American comparative studies.

11. The most recent colloquia essay, however, is one by Norma Alarcón entitled "Cognitive Desires: An Allegory of/for Chicana Critics," forthcoming, in which she gives a critique of the relationship between Chicana and *Mexicana* cultural production.

12. This parallels thematic developments in African-American women's literature.

13. For an examination of feminist theory and the contributions of women of color, see bell hooks, *Talking Back: Thinking Feminist, Thinking Black* (Boston: South End Press, 1989). Also, see Debra Castillo, *Talking Back: Toward a Latin American Feminist Literary Criticism* (Ithaca, N.Y.: Cornell University Press, 1992). I use it similarly to refer to *Mexicanas* and Chicanas talking back from the margins to the dominant systems of patriarchy in their respective countries.

14. See Rosario Castellanos, "La mujer y su imagen," *Mujer que sabe latín* (Mexico: Fondo de Cultura Económica, 1984), 7–21. Castellanos suggests that "one is not born a *Mexicana*." I suggest that neither is one born a Chicana. Both are self-identified terms

which assume a certain political ideology. See Norma Alarcón, "Chicana Feminism: In the Tracks of the Native Woman," *Cultural Studies* 4, no. 3 (1990): 248–256.

15. As Deena González suggests, La Malinche can be viewed as the forerunner of Mexican women's liberation struggles. See Deena González, "Encountering Columbus," in *Chicano Studies: Critical Connection between Research and Community* (National Association of Chicano Studies, 1992).

16. Also see Berta Hidalgo, *Movimiento femenino en México* (Mexico, D.F.: Editores Asociados Mexicanos, S.A., 1980); Pablo Tuñes, *Mujeres en México: Una historia olvidada* (Mexico, D.F.: Planeta, 1987); Emma Perez, "Yucatecan Feminist Congress, 1917–18" (dissertation, University of California–Los Angeles, 1988).

17. In 1848, with the annexation of large portions of the Mexican nation, Mexican-born citizens became U.S. citizens literally overnight. For an important historical study, see Adelaida Del Castillo, *Between Borders: Essays on Mexicana/Chicana History* (Encino, Calif.: Floricanto Press, 1990).

18. Some historians however, argue that the starting point for a particular Chicana/o history begins with the conquest of the Americas.

19. Again, here I refer mostly to historical studies. In other parts of the manuscript, other area studies which look at Chicana issues are cited. The bibliography of Chicana studies is extensive and continues to grow rapidly.

20. I will refer to the figure of La Malinche, the symbol, and to Malintzín, the actual historical figure, depending on the context of my discussion. Her Nahuatl birth name is Malintzín; in other contexts she is referred to as Malinal or Doña Marina, her Christian name.

21. See Gloria Anzaldúa, *Borderlands / La Frontera: The New Mestiza* (San Francisco: Spinsters/Aunt Lute, 1987). Here, Anzaldúa gives her interpretation of La Malinche in "Not me betrayed my people, by they me," and she reads La Malinche as the woman who for reasons of survival acted as the interpreter for Hernán Cortés.

22. The La Llorona legend is more prevalent than La Malinche in popular culture; La Llorona is more adaptable than La Malinche for a children's tale. There may be a subconscious understanding of the figure of La Malinche in the tales of La Llorona. As adults, and especially during the Chicano Movement of the 1960s, *malinchista* became the familiar term for a woman who was viewed as a traitor to the cause if she dared not to submit to the sexism of the movement.

WORKS CITED

Alarcón, Norma. "Chicanas' Feminist Literature: A Re-Vision through Malintzín / or Malintzín: Putting Flesh Back on the Object." In *This Bridge Called My Back: Writings by Radical Women of Color,* ed. Cherríe Moraga and Gloria Anzaldúa, 182–190. Watertown, Mass.: Persephone Press, 1981.

———. "*Traddutora, Traditora:* A Paradigmatic Figure of Chicana Feminism." *Cultural Critique* (Fall 1989): 57–87.

Anzaldúa, Gloria. *Borderlands / La Frontera: The New Mestiza.* San Francisco: Spinsters/Aunt Lute, 1987.

Chevigny, Bell Gale, and Gari Laguardia, eds. *Reinventing the Americas: Comparative Studies of Literature of the U.S. and Spanish America.* New York and Cambridge: Cambridge University Press, 1986.

Franco, Jean. *Plotting Women: Gender and Representation in Mexico.* New York: Columbia University Press, 1989.

Limón, José. "*La Llorona,* The Third Legend of Greater Mexico: Cultural Symbols, Women, and the Political Unconscious." In *Between Borders: Essays on Mexicana/ Chicana History,* ed. Edelaida R. Del Castillo, 399–432. Encino, Calif.: Floricanto Press, 1990.

Pérez-Firmat, Gustavo. *Do the Americas Have a Common Literature?* Durham, N.C.: Duke University Press, 1990.

Saldívar, José. *The Dialectics of Our America: Genealogy, Cultural Critique, and Literary History.* Durham, N.C.: Duke University Press, 1991.

Sternbach, Nancy Saporta, et al. "Feminisms in Latin America: From Bogotá to San Bernardo." In *The Making of Social Movements in Latin American Identity, Strategy, and Democracy,* ed. Arturo Escobar and Sonia E. Alvarez. Boulder, Colo.: Westview Press, 1992.

12 BORDERS, FEMINISM, AND SPIRITUALITY: MOVEMENTS IN CHICANA AESTHETIC REVISIONING

Sarah Ramirez

Cultural transformation requires an expansion of aesthetic language.
—*Amalia Mesa-Bains*

Vision is not just a perception of what is possible, it is a window to the knowledge of what has happened and what is happening.
—*Beth Brant*

THIS ESSAY addresses the "possession and ownership" of an ideological Chicana aesthetic space interpreted through the digital photography of Alma López (Harlan: 7). The aesthetic space inhabited by Alma López's visual voice, agent of her own oppositional gaze, is based on the examination of "new aesthetic opportunities" which deconstructs and lays out "alternative perspective(s) that represent [a Chicana] social quandary" (Quintana: 21). A Chicana aesthetic space, suggests Laura Pérez (1998), participates in community empowerment through *curandera* (healer) work, which expresses the concern for social, global, and environmental justice as well as engages in the processes of recovery and transformation. This *curandera* work, Pérez argues, reclaims and reformulates a spiritual worldview that empowers the artist as woman, but also interrupts "the reproduction of gendered, raced, and sexed politics of spirituality and of art" (42). As such, close attention will be given to the way López foregrounds a female-centered indigenous/spiritual space and builds from Chicana feminist practices to embody a revolutionary praxis that functions for individual and community healing, while at the same time altering traditional perceptions of spirituality as passive into an overt political and cultural negotiated production. From this respect my analysis of Alma López's work asks: How does this Chicana aesthetic space reintegrate spirituality as a politically significant cultural marker? How does it address the postcolonial project which recuperates an indigenous/spiritual consciousness? How does this space redefine and reconstruct nationalist symbols, images, icons, and spirituality that can negotiate issues of identity and community, and more fully represent a Chicana feminist social and spiritual quandary?

SEARCHING FOR A NATION

Realizing that colonialism distorts, disfigures, and destroys the past and effectively transforms the present and future of oppressed people, Frantz Fanon argues that the process toward decolonization involves the creation of a national consciousness (1979: 210). Beyond rehabilitating the people, he argues that a nationalist consciousness engaged in the recuperation of the past becomes an act of resistance and self-determination that destabilizes and releases the colonized subject from the minds of subjugated communities. Understanding its position within the United States as neocolonial, the recuperation of an indigenous past was one of the influential aspects of the Chicano Movement.[1] This indigenous recuperation, as well as the other qualities Benedict Anderson (1991) identifies as providing a foundation for national consciousness, gave the appearance that Chicano nationalism was an extension of unchosen "natural ties" (143). As a result, Chicano nationalists reveal their construction of community and nationalism on the basis of shared cultural indigenous heritage, common language, connection to a land base, and a political, social, and historical disenfranchisement.

While not the only document verbalizing Chicano nationalist ideologies, the 1969 *Plan Espiritual de Aztlán* was perhaps one of the most influential motivating manifestos for the Chicano Movement. It articulates many of the ideologies Anderson describes as the basis of national consciousness, or, in Fanon's case, a decolonizing consciousness. As a unifying concept and the base for nationalist discourse, "Aztlán" was a signifier intended to develop pride and self-awareness among Chicanos through the creation of a distinct culturally mestizo or mixed-blood identity. It also served to legitimize and document a historical Chicano presence within the borders of the United States. Claiming that "cultural values" would strengthen Chicano identity and function as the "moral back bone of the movement," the cultural politics and unification outlined in the *Plan* shaped nationalist discourse, leaving indelible impressions which remain a fixed presence on contemporary Chicana/o cultural productions and popular culture.[2]

Moreover, saying the word "Aztlán" also became a source of spiritual inspiration toward recognizing and accepting indigenous heritage as part of the Chicano reality. As a result, Aztlán was seen as both a "vital element of [Chicano] cultural heritage and political ideology" (Pina: 17). Aztlán provided a spiritual liberation, whose myths, spiritual concepts, and symbols Chicano nationalists utilized to unearth a Chicano collective history, an "umbilical cord" to a Mesoamerican heritage (Anaya: 234). Guillermo Lux and Maurilio Vigil (1991) also insist that philosophies of the Chicano Movement inspired and may have "indirectly resulted in the regeneration of interest in our Indian origins" (93).

Although Chicano nationalism attempted to recuperate an indigenous identity and, in some cases, create a humanizing praxis based on indigenous philosophies, the "imagined" Chicano nation served to subjugate, define, and control Chicanas, revealing a contradiction between ideology and praxis.[3] As demonstrated in Lux and Vigil's quote below, the attempts to encourage revival and pride in indigenous cultures simultaneously asserted patriarchal structures and did not offer alternative visions to the subjugation of Indian or Chicana/Mestiza women:

> [I]nfluences of our Indian past on Mexican and Mexican American culture may have been more covert or gone unnoticed because they were generally consistent with Hispanic cultural traits. Among these are the patriarchal tradition in which the father is the unchallenged head of the family. In Indian cultures the woman walks behind the man and generally performs most of the chores. (105)

When contextualized within a larger nationalist project, these examples reveal how Chicano nationalism and the indigenous past are (re)constructed to subjugate Chicanas. Cherríe Moraga (1993) succinctly summarizes the contradiction:

> [Chicano] nationalist leaders used a kind of *selective* memory, drawing exclusively from those aspects of Mexican and Native cultures that served the interests of male heterosexuals. At times, they took the worst of Mexican machismo and Aztec warrior bravado, combined it with some of the most oppressive male-conceived idealizations . . . and called that cultural integrity. (156–157)

Furthermore, Lara Medina (1998) claims, "What appears as indigneous spirituality through the uncritical appropriation of popular images becomes a way to encourage patriarchy, cultism, and cultural nationalism" (200). While the indigenous consciousness was said "to be located in the deepest layers of consciousness of every Chicano" and posited an essential monolithic *male* identity, it also replicated a nationalist aesthetic production whose rhetoric of an idealized past suppresses and omits female experiences (Chabram-Dernersesian and Fregoso: 204; Quintana: 19–21).

Though Anderson argues that an integral component to imaging the nation includes the essentialist characteristics that serve to assimilate internal cultural differences and create a "uniform" identity, the uncritical duplication of the *Plan*'s rhetoric in aesthetic productions failed to recognize that cultural identities, "subject to the continuous 'play' of history, culture, and power," produce and reproduce themselves through transformation and difference (Anderson: 143; Hall: 70). Furthermore, the obscuring of gender issues within a postcolonial indigenous context of Chicano nationalism specifically demonstrates the ways in which "[m]en displaced from power or made insecure by a sorry present can derive solace from a romantically magnified past" (Lowenthal: 335).

Such practices, as well as the continuation of these practices within Chicana/o cultural productions, have prompted Chicana critics to look for the roots of machismo beyond the Chicano Movement and into pre-Columbian society. This Chicana analysis and critique demonstrates how the alterations to pre-Columbian foundational myths and their transformation into a Chicano male-centered society reveal a simultaneous historical denigration of women's power and value.[4] In effect, an understanding of this process and its continued reproduction within popular culture exposes what Foucault would describe as an overlapping blueprint of control and domination applied to Chicanas within the context of larger Chicano nationalist discourse (138).

Asserting a living Chicana theory:[5] a theoretical discourse that considers the intersections of race, class, gender, sexuality, and religion, among other factors, Chicana feminism integrates these complex intersections of the Chicana social quandary, creating alternative spaces to the controlling images and spaces of ethnocentric, ethnonostalgic, and patriarchal nationalist discourses. While also drawing from indigenous cultures and philosophies, Chicana aesthetic productions employ its revisionist critique and create empowering images of personal and communal self-identity. The inclusion of indigenous worldviews as well as historical events and representations reveals the various diasporic histories that make up the Chicana social quandary and reality.

If Chicano nationalism used neoindigenism to create a "transcendental Chicano subject" that privileged patriarchy, the visual language of Alma López emerges, reflects, and bears witness to an alternative female-centered aesthetic. Unlike the intersections within Chicano nationalism's gender politics and indigenous recuperation, the artistic work of Alma López reveals the way in which spirituality, particularly a female-centered indigenous spirituality, expands the perceptions of nationhood and engages in a process of social activism for Chicana/o empowerment. Although particular characteristics emerge in her cultural productions, López needs to be situated within a larger indigenous feminist consciousness expressed by other Chicana and Native women artists and writers.[6] López's images respond to social injustices as well as to nationalist male aesthetics and also redefine spirituality on feminist terms. Her artistic productions reflect a spirituality which, drawing on indigenous philosophies, has political, social, and cultural implications and sets a framework for feminist liberation/revolutionary praxis. Such an *indígena* feminist worldview, what is characterized as mestiza spirituality and/or Xicanisma,[7] is an everyday *lived* spirituality that does not separate the spiritual from the political or the theoretical from the practical.

Reflecting what Víctor Zamudio Taylor describes as an aesthetic of fragmentation, a common trait in Latino arts, López incorporates fragments of personal, border, spiritual, and historical images into her digital photography. This artistic technique allows López to historically contextualize her images with present-day relevance in order to address social, political, and cultural issues pertinent to the Chicana/o community. The process of fragmentation, affirms Zamudio Taylor, reveals a "quest to unearth another version of both a personal and collective history" (Zamudio Taylor: 15). The artistic negotiation of individual and community identity also reveals what Native scholar Jace Weaver describes as "communitism," a combination of community and activism. According to Weaver, a communitist aesthetic provides a medium through which fractured communities "rendered dysfunctional by the effects of more than 500 years of colonialism . . . participate in the healing of the grief and sense of exile" experienced by these individuals and communities (Weaver, 1997: 43). Furthermore, communitist values depict a "post-colonial we-hermeneutic" in which community and building community stands at the center of interpretive systems (Weaver, 1998: 22). Addressing the ramifications of the border, history, violence, and spirituality on individuals and community, the we-hermeneutic in López's art engages in a communal project of cultural (re)signification that raises questions about the intersections between gender, sexuality, class, ethnicity, and spiritual belief and practices.[8]

The series *Lupe and Sirena* is a collection of nine images.[9] In line with Lopez's Chicana aesthetic, the lead image "Ixta" (1999) (fig. 1) is a feminist digital reinterpretation of Mexican artist Jesús Helguerra's reappropriated Ixtacihuatl and Popocatepetl myth *"Leyenda de Amor,"* or "Legend of Love." The significance of Helguerra's images lies in the fact that his *almanaques*/almanacs have, primarily since the Chicano Movement, become images of popular and youth cultures and are coded with Chicano nationalist ideologies.[10] While originally adorning *almanaques* or calendars, Helguerra's images *"Leyenda de Amor," "Amor Indio," "Gesto Azteca,"* and *"Grandeza Azteca"* now appear in some productions on the back of Chicana/o T-shirts, on calendars, low riders, posters, CD jacket covers, or movies.

The original lithograph images, produced during and after the 1930s, are interpretations of Mexican historical events; however, many of the most popularly duplicated images depict pre-Columbian myths. The resonance of these romantic and utopian images has continued since Helguerra's death in 1971 and, as noted in the 1999 exhibit "La Patria Portatil: 100 years of Mexican Chromo Art Calendars," his images have become "identity symbols of the everyday citizen in Mexico and of the Chicano/Mexican in the United States."[11] Considered a response to powerlessness, these images are perceived as forms of revival, recuperation, and pride in a Mexican indigenous heritage that helps "reinforce the theme of Chicano self-determination" (Goldman: 130). Within Chicana/o artistic productions, Helguerra's images have been recontextualized and reconstructed, appearing on new mediums and often accompanied with the word "Aztlán" or the phrase "Brown and Proud."[12] In its totality, the recontextualized image symbolically reflects a microcosm of Chicano aesthetics, cultural na-

Figure 12.1. "Ixta" (1999), by Alma López. Courtesy of the artist.

tionalist consciousness, and imagination. Unfortunately, their popularization also replicates and maintains racial and gendered semiotics consistent with other Chicano nationalist ideologies and practices.

A greater appreciation of López's reinterpretation in the lead image is based on the knowledge of the original story. Having heard erroneous rumors of the warrior Popocatepetl's death, his betrothed Ixtacihuatl kills herself. The former is grief-stricken upon finding Ixtacihuatl dead. He carries her up to the highest mountains in the Valley of Mexico and guards her body; they become transformed into the twin volcanoes that to this day bear their names. The myth of Ixtacihuatl's tragic death, motivated by the loss of her true love, ideologically codes Ixtacihuatl as a disempowered woman with her identity and apparent survival both dependent on male identification.

Having grown up with pervasive male indigenous images López chooses to reinterpret *"Leyenda de Amor"* and names her work "Ixta." No longer the central text, Helguerra's own male-centered image serves as a backdrop in "Ixta" and its overpowering feminist reinterpretation reminds the viewer of the male cultural baggage which the original legend and its marked death of the native woman implies. Similar to other Chicana artworks, López's evocation and displacement of Helguerra's Ixtacihuatl and Popocatepetl image does not serve to glorify or recuperate male mythic memory; rather, it signifies a revision that challenges male Chicano nationalist memory and constructions of Chicano his-story. As many Chicana writers and scholars have previously exposed, the successful elevation of patriarchy and female subjugation within the Mesoamerican and/or Chicano nations required an appropriation of female power and a transformation of foundational myths which confined and controlled women.[13]

Keenly aware of the patriarchal heterosexual subjugation of women, López photographically reinterprets Helguerra's image, which is loaded with such cultural baggage, in "Ixta." Rather than reify patriarchal tradition, she locates a female body over the U.S.-Mexican border, rescuing any woman's death from the male confined nationalist imagination and an idealized romantic past. Through this symbolic liberation López also provides a contemporary narrative of death that reflects Chicana social and geopolitical realities. In her new interpretation of the Popocatepetl and Ixtacihuatl myth, death is located right on top and across the U.S.-Mexican border, suggesting that imperialist aggression and fragmentation of identities, land base, and culture also cause death. López conceptualizes and codes the U.S.-Mexican border described by Gloria Anzaldúa as an "open wound . . . where the Third World grates against the First and bleeds" (Anzaldúa: 3), as a primary example of colonialist expansion and a source of community fragmentation. In fact, Mexican, Chicano, and Native communities continue to intimately feel along the border the effects of fragmentation and colonialist experience.[14] Despite using the female body across the border to imagine a new death, López also locates another young woman in a pseudo-Christ-like position and crouched as if guarding or resurrecting the sleeping maiden. In such context, death is not finite; rather, the image instills a message of women saving and healing other women. Though resurrection and survival will be discussed in relation to spirituality, I want to address the image "Ixta" in terms of borders plus theory and its ramifications on Chicana/o community themes further developed in López's work *1848*.

López's series *1848* goes into greater depth and engages in a discussion on border discourse. "California Fashion Slaves" (1997), the lead image in this series, contextualizes visually the present-day participation of Mexican women in the garment industry as part of a long history of Mexican industrial workers since the 1930s. Attempting to capture issues of the working poor, the image "California Fashion Slaves" recuperates women's participation in the Los Angeles garment industry, which, like other low-paying industrial trades, survives by exploiting an ethnic niche sustained through a pool of immigrant Latina and Asian working women (Soldatenko, 1991: 78). López depicts this timeline of Mexican garment workers through a sequence of photographs, moving from the earlier black-and-white photos to a more contemporary color image closer to the surface.

Figure 12.2. "187" (1998), by Alma López. Courtesy of the artist.

In the image "187" (1998) (fig. 2) López provides a visual interpretation of California's Proposition 187, which was passed by California voters in 1994. Considered the first in a series of anti-equal-human-rights initiatives, 187 preceded Proposition 209 (the Civil Rights Initiative passed in 1996) and Proposition 227 (the English for the Children Initiative passed in 1998), both of which are also referenced in the image now under discussion. Proposition 187 was considered anti-immigrant legislation that targeted primarily Mexican immigrants in California. Its stated purpose was that California would "provide for cooperation between [the] agencies of state and local government with the federal government, and . . . establish a system of required notification by and between such agencies to prevent illegal aliens in the United States from receiving benefits or public services in the State of California."

The image "187" explores the ramifications of all of the above mentioned laws on the lives of children. In a haunting image, López places a young girl, execution style, sitting on the U.S.-Mexican border. The young girl is blindfolded with a piece of the U.S. flag and the numbers 187 written across the blindfold in a bloody red. Unquestionably, the legal ramifications mean certain death to Mexican/Chicano children.

In both "California Fashion Slaves" and "187," the central figures are layered over the Los Angeles skyline and a map of the Southwest. The icon

Figure 12.3. "December 12" (1999), by Alma López. Courtesy of the artist.

of a state-enforced patrol car pursuing a man running across the map's landscape, phrases such as "Manifest Destiny" plus "English only," and the date 1848 are integrated into visual elements which provide further historical and social evidence of an imperialist legacy that continues to manifest itself in anti-immigrant and dehumanizing practices. The border becomes the dividing line that separates the territories north of the border from the territory to the south. By foregrounding these diverse icons and issues, the visual elements negotiate between complex related issues of social injustice, geopolitical space, and identity.

While increased attention to globalization and transnational migration has promoted among writers and critics an interest in border theory and the practice of dismantling multiple ideological, spiritual, and physical borders, little attention is given to understanding the ramifications of theoretical border crossings on the lives of individuals intimately affected by the actual and physical border crossing. In fact, Chicano scholar Arturo Aldama (1998) calls attention to border discourse and construction and argues that, in some critical analyses, the U.S.-Mexican border has become misappropriated as a mere metaphor or a "universalized model that moves beyond historical understandings of subaltern Latina/o 'border-crossers' as 'real people' responding to 'real' geo-political social realities" (43).

Through the combination of the various images in the series *1848*, López reinserts this forsaken body and self relationship into her image as a reminder of the real exploitative and violent forces present in border issues (Aldama: 48). The combination of images is not utilized as an empty recuperation of historical memory, but as a social critique through which López resists the erasure of the social, historical, and geopolitical realities on the lives of women and children. Taken in totality, López's images in the series *1848* engage in a U.S.-Mexico border aesthetics that according to José Saldívar (1997) "does not merely extend the canon but radically reframes and topospatially reconceptualizes what it means to be 'worldly,' 'cosmopolitan,' and 'regional'" (91). Furthermore, in calling attention to historical events and social injustices López reflects the border feminism Sonia Saldívar-Hull (1991) identifies as a theory and method in which Chicanas utilize history to transform the future (220).

SPIRTUAL MOVEMENTS, *FRUTO DE NUESTRO VIENTRE*

The following excerpt by Tey Diana Rebolledo effectively describes and interprets the various processes involved in Chicana feminist transformations of Chicana/o and Mexican mythology:

> If, however, the existing mythology (as defined by patriarchy) is unable to fulfill the increasing demand for women as active, energetic and positive figures, then women writers may choose myths and archetypes, historical and cultural heroines, that are different from the traditional ones. They may create new role models for themselves or choose existing models but imbue them with different (sometimes radically different) traits and characteristics. (49)

Similar to other postcolonial efforts of Third World self-determination, Chicanas also engage in the process of recuperating disavowed histories through the transformation of existing female myths and archetypes. However, the primary ones rescued are often used to construct an indigenous, feminist-centered spirituality that addresses the issues of oppression, activism, and women's liberation.

For López, spirituality becomes a pivotal source from which to recuperate a feminist voice and "attain knowledge of self and purpose" (López, personal correspondence). As a result, many of López's images in the series *1848* and the series *Lupe and Sirena* include both the traditional image of La Virgen de Guadalupe and the re-interpreted Guadalupe of lesbian desire. Along with the digital mural projects, both series include images of pre-Columbian feminine deities. Observing and studying López's work reveals the "undercurrent of spirituality" which, Castillo writes, "is the unspoken key to [the mestiza's] strength and endurance as a female" (95). Spirituality becomes a foundation from which mediation of identity, experiences, and survival in sometimes antagonistic and hostile environments can be addressed.

La Virgen de Guadalupe continues to be, as Gloria Anzaldúa claims, "the single most potent religious, political, and cultural image of the Chicano/Mexicano" (30). However, as a symbol Guadalupe has multiple meanings and messages. Similar to Marina Warner's analysis (1976) of the Virgin Mary, La Virgen de Guadalupe is considered by some a symbol of ideal womanhood embodying opposing traits as an unselfish, giving mother, with a repressed female sexuality.[15] The contradictory veneration of a mythic figure, both virgin and mother, as the embodiment of "goodness" and ideal womanhood contributes to a self-perpetuating misogynist web that constrains female sexuality as sin (Warner: 337). Her passive and complacent qualities, more than representing an image of ideal womanhood, sometimes take on a political context in which Guadalupe also reflects failure, that is, the inability to intercede on behalf of her people (Rodríguez: 53).

Since Guadalupe intertwines both Christian and Indian religious symbolism, many feel that the belief in her acknowledges Indian values as well (Guerrero: 107). Guadalupe-Tonantzín is the Empress of the Americas and patron saint of Chicanos and Mexicanos who have enshrined her in countless popular culture productions; she also represents a subversive image in the struggle for liberation. Though there are disagreements, Guadalupe-Tonantzín remains a symbol of both Chicana/o consciousness and the social, spiritual, and political Chicana/o reality, as well as a symbol of justice, empowerment, and hope in the struggle to survive.[16] In fact, during their labor strikes in the mid-1960s the United Farm Workers carried her banner alongside their own UFW flag. Unlike the Virgin Mary, who, Warner claims, cannot be transformed into the New Woman without dredging up centuries of prejudice, recognizing Guadalupe's indigenous roots allows a space for new womanhood (338).

Chicana feminists value the indigenous roots of Tonantzín and other female sacred beings because such knowledge shatters and transforms Catholic-imposed patriarchal perceptions of femininity inscribed on La Virgen and on Chicanas as well. As a result, they transform the "natural" cultural understanding and limitations of Guadalupe as a sign coded from a Chicano male perspective. Similar to Anzaldúa's use of Coatlicue,[17] through recuperation these indigenous icons become personal empowering embodiments of the Chicana self. As Sandra Cisneros writes, "Coatlicue, Tlazolteotl, Tonantzín, la Virgen de Guadalupe. They are each telescoped into the other, into who I am" (Cisneros: 50). Personalizing and viewing her from a 1990s perspective, La Virgen de Guadalupe becomes "sex goddess," "a woman enraged, a woman as tempest . . . *La Lupe as cabrona.* Not silent and passive, but silently gathering force" (Cisneros: 50).

Constructing an image more like her Chicana self, Alma López personalizes La Virgen de Guadalupe and participates in the process of her (re)signification. In the series *Lupe and Sirena,* López unmasks the restrictive patriarchal interpretations of La Virgen. Instead of remaining hidden under her traditional dress and gown, Guadalupe, in the image "Our Lady" (1999), reveals her body and is depicted, in lieu of traditional images of La Virgen de Guadalupe, as a corporeal sexual being. Images such as "December 12" (1999), "Retablo" (1999), and "Lupe and Sirena in Love" (1999) display La Sirena, or the mermaid image from the *lotería* or bingo game, and La Virgen de Guadalupe embracing one another.

In the image "December 12" (fig. 3), López evocatively unfolds and reconstructs a new vision of the historical event that occurred on December 12, 1531. In this image, López's body is positioned with reverence: her hands open and out and her head inclined. The image of an embracing Lupe and Sirena appears imprinted on López's dress. Continuing a contemporary Chicana feminist practice of indigenous recuperation, López incorporates Coyolxauhqui into the background of this image. Artists and critics such as Cherríe Moraga have symbolically (re)membered Coyolxauhqui's mutilated image and history. In Moraga's reinterpretation, Coyolxauhqui is reclaimed by Chicana lesbians as a symbol of the *fuerza femenina* and is incarnated in the rebellious daughter who is unwilling to submit to patriarchal/machista values (74). Since Coyolxauhqui resisted patriarchal constructions, her appearance in the background of the López's image "December 12" signifies an approval of the new union between women.

Lesbian desire is a theme López incorporates as well into the other images in the series *Lupe and Sirena.* Self-reflexively, López becomes not unlike Juan Diego, the bearer of the new Virgen's messages. No longer confined to the patriarchal heterosexual imagination, the reconstructed Guadalupe-Tonantzín image validates sexuality and the existence of Chicana lesbian desire (Trujillo: 226).

These new interpretations of La Virgen de Guadalupe not only serve to liberate those who emulate her but to validate *lesbianas* and other women who claim her as part of a self-representation (226). López's iconographic transformation of Guadalupe shatters predefined images, disengages the aura of passivity her traditional image brings forth, and creates the possibility of sexual agency (226). La Virgen de Guadalupe, asserts Carla Trujillo, "is as much ours, as Chicana Lesbians, as anyone else's" (227). The re-interpretation of Guadalupe demonstrates how the visual transformation of mythic icons creates empowering new narratives that more fully represent the Chicana social quandary.

Recontextualizing Guadalupe-Tonantzín, Coatlicue, or Coyolxauhqui into her images of contemporary life and environment, López transposes an indigenous ancestral memory into a living present within feminist liberationist parameters. The reappropriation of these old legends and myths emphasizes their connection to a lived reality and conveys the idea that their stories are alive and have the power to heal and protect (Silko: 152).

Figure 12.4. "Juan Soldado" (1997), by Alma López. Courtesy of the artist.

The re-incorporation of ancestral memory on today's society does not simply provide an alternative space for resistance. Through her recovery and transformation of the indigenous legends or myths, López contributes to a process of feminist empowerment and healing. Images traditionally used to control and restrict Mexicana/Chicana social practices are reconciled with a female-centered worldview and imbued with personally empowering feminine traits. Spirituality, then, does not seem like abstract folklore, often attached to indigenous/mythic recuperation; it participates at personal and communal levels within human cultural systems. López's visual art reveals the qualities Medina identifies as mestiza spirituality, where actions result "from the desire to create expression for [Chicana's] spirituality rooted in a quest for self determination and the liberation of their communities" (206).

However, this mestiza indigenous feminist consciousness extends beyond the feminine and personal. It utilizes spirituality in addressing social, political, and cultural conditions of the Chicana/o community—female and male, lesbian and heterosexual. López not only displaces conventional religious beliefs, but also reinterprets traditional images of La Virgen de Guadalupe within the series *1848*. Except for the image "California Fashion Slaves," the traditional representations of Guadalupe are not the central focus of the image, nor are they placed in a position of veneration.

In the series *1848*, Guadalupe is reduced and placed on the U.S.-Mexican border icon. Though La Virgen represents a unifying spirituality to Mexicanos/Chicanos on both sides of the border, Guadalupe, placed on the border with the phrases "Manifest Destiny" or the date "1848" across or near her image, forces the recognition of the other unnatural imperialist forces that forged her restricted image. By including Guadalupe in these images, López creates a space from which to examine and explore the relationship between the physical imperialist Manifest Destiny and the expanding imperialism of patriarchy. Combining traditional and contemporary aspects, the series *1848* also addresses issues of spirituality. In fact, this combination significantly contributes to our understanding of spirituality as a mechanism for survival.

As images, both "Juan Soldado" (1997) (fig. 4) and "Santa Niña de Mochis" (1999) stand out as primary examples of the role spirituality plays in Chicana/o survival. Juan Soldado is the name given to the historical and legendary figure Juan Castillo Morales, who is considered within the Chicano/Mexicano community an unofficial patron saint and protector of undocumented immigrants. In her artist statement, López recounts the legend of Juan Soldado:

> Morales was a soldier in Tijuana executed in 1938. He claimed he was framed by a superior who actually committed the crime. According to the legend, he swore that he was innocent, and his innocence would be proven when miracles were asked and granted in his name. He is not recognized by the church, and is therefore an illegal saint of "illegal" immigrants. (López, personal correspondence)

This explanation magnifies the way in which the image "Juan Soldado" engages in the social and geopolitical realities of border discourse, but it documents how a people's faith and spirituality have converted his tombstone into an altar. López incorporates into the digital image the imagery of the actual altar that is adorned with candles, photos, letters, and personal effects. According to López, the devotee's letters ask or give "thanks for miracles received relating with either crossing the border safely, or successfully filing for permanent U.S. residency or citizenship" (López, personal correspondence). Both the description and the image "Juan Soldado" ethnographically and artistically document a contemporary manifestation of the *exvoto* religious folk art tradition.[18] Revealing enduring qualities of spiritual and religious traditions, "Juan Soldado" digitally collapses three-dimensional sacred space into a photographic *nicho* or *caja*, box, which is a traditionally mixed-media enclosure that utilizes a combination of personal elements with religious iconography to reveal autobiographical or cultural narratives as well as faith and devotion (Ybarra Frausto, 1988: 152).

Another altarlike photographic representation, the image "Santa Niña de Mochis" gives homage to a young female saint that López herself creates from a photograph of a young girl. The image had its genesis during a stay in Mexico for the 1997 observance of the *Día de los Muertos* (Day of the Dead), when López visited her maternal grandmother's gravesite in Los Mochis, Sinaloa.[19] López recounts, "At the time I was going through a life conflict and . . . being there with my grandmother helped me make a difficult decision. So this work is to give honor to my grandmother's memory, to give thanks for her guidance, and to create an image of a girl saint that is my own" (López, personal correspondence).

In "Santa Niña de Mochis" López foregrounds her saint: an image of a young girl with the wings of a viceroy butterfly. The artist utilizes the viceroy butterfly, which closely resembles the monarch butterfly, to evoke the monarch's scientific narrative of genetic memory and natural border crossings between Mexico and the United States. Juxtaposing the butterfly with border imagery re-emphasizes the unnaturalness of a border whose purpose is to impede human movement. López also utilizes the viceroy butterfly as a symbol of survival, which, she states, "mirrors parallel and intersecting histories of being different or 'other' even within our own communities."[20] In general, López's images artistically reveal the way in which spirituality, memory, and migration bridge territories north and south of the border. Considering the continuation of native beliefs regardless of the syncretism from a colonizing religion, the image "Santa Niña de Mochis" reveals the reconciliation and creation of personal spirituality. The common themes in all of López's images depict memory and migration as key functions in Chicana/o survival and continued existence. The young Mexican/Chicana saint stands as living testimony and as a negotiated spiritual site where memory and social issues collide.

CONCLUSIONS

Beyond nationalistic concepts, the work of López highlights a subversive act in which the artist and her visual productions participate in disintegrating multiple forms of hegemonic borders. Rather than directly address nationalism, López's visual voice bears witness to a hybridized negotiated spirituality that considers the process of decolonization, community, healing, and personal experience, and collapses traditional understanding of nationalist, spiritual, and border constructions. In addressing issues of justice, her art reveals an indigenous quality marked with social responsibility, activism, and spirituality. Revealing what Chela Sandoval identifies as a method and theory of mestizaje, the art of Alma López shows how the acutely personal, spiritual, political, and social intersections are never far removed from one another.[21]

López's artistic recuperation of the indigenous portion of the mestiza past also represents a collective Chicana experience that, according to Norma Alarcón (1998), brings into focus the "cultural and psychic dismemberment linked to imperialist racist and sexist practices" (375). Moreover, Alarcón adds that the "strategic invocation and recodification of 'the' native woman in the present has the effect of conjoining the historical repression of the 'non-civilized' dark woman . . . with the present moment of speech that counters such repression" (375). As such, the inclusion of both memory and history in López's visual narratives forges connections with diasporic historical realities in order to expand our understanding of history, spirituality, and nation. However, rather than locking "history" or "memory" in presubscribed meanings, López's art provides a fruitful space where Chicanas can examine the way meanings are constructed and employed to inform the audience of specific uses of this history and memory in the struggle for Chicana/o empowerment. This indigenous feminist-centered consciousness and spirituality are articulations of empowerment and resistance that become part of the "whole body of efforts made by a people in the sphere of thought to describe, justify and praise the action through which that people has created itself and keeps itself in existence" (Fanon: 233).

Though some may view the remembering, recycling, and construction of a hybridized indigenous feminist-centered spirituality as having roots in Fanonian constructs, it is a politically significant cultural perspective that many Chicana and Native women draw from their indigenous worldviews. Laguna scholar Paula Gunn Allen (1986) addresses the importance of memory for a holistic sense of self.

> We must remember our origins, our cultures, our histories, our mothers and grandmothers, for without that memory which implies continuance rather than nostalgia, we are doomed to engulfment by a paradigm that is fundamentally inimical to the vitality, autonomy, and self-empowerment essential for satisfying, high-quality of life. (214)

Based on such perspectives, feminist-centered spirituality has political implications which, so affirms Alarcón, "must not be underestimated, but refocused for feminist change" (375).

NOTES

1. For the study of Chicano colonialism and neocolonialism, see Tomás Almaguer's "Toward the Study of Chicano Colonialism," *Aztlán* 2, no. 1 (1971); Raoul Contreras, "The Ideology of the Political Movement for Chicano Studies" (diss., UCLA, 1993); and Manuel de Jesús Hernández-G., *El Colonialismo interno en al narrative Chicana: el Barrio el Anti-Barrio, y el Esterior* (Tempe, Ariz.: Bilingual Press, 1994).

2. Looking through any newspaper or magazine, especially in areas such as Los Angeles, one can find references to stores with names such as Premiere Aztlán and Tolteca Productions, among others.

3. The intersections between nationalist aesthetics, gender politics, and the indigenous/spiritual worldview are more clearly identified in Yolanda Broyles-González's 1994 study of El Teatro Campesino. Particularly, Broyles-González examines El Teatro Campesino's model for Theater of the Sphere, which is rooted in the indigenous/spiritual worldview of the Americas. In analyzing the model, she examines the way in which

Theater of the Sphere expressed a decolonized Chicana/o aesthetic model of human liberation indispensable to the larger social struggle. Though she does agree that this socio-spiritual model—Theater of the Sphere—created an alternative pedagogy for humanity, her comprehensive analysis of El Teatro Campesino also reveals how gender politics, limited and defined roles serving to subordinate women, existed simultaneously within a context of postcolonial liberational praxis.

4. See Norma Alarcón, "Traddutora, Traditora: A Paradigmatic Figure of Chicana Feminism," *Cultural Critique* (Fall 1989), 57–87; Gloria Anzaldúa, *Borderlands / La Frontera: The New Mestiza* (San Francisco: Spinsters/Aunt Lute, 1987); Marta Cotera, *Diosa y Hembra: The History and Heritage of Chicanas in the U.S.* (Austin: University of Texas Mexican American Library Project, 1976); Ana Castillo, *Massacre of the Dreamers: Essays on Xicanisma* (New York: Penguin Books 1995); Cherríe Moraga, *The Last Generation* (Boston: South End Press, 1993); and Elizabeth Salas, *Soldaderas in the Mexican Military: Myth and History* (Austin: University of Texas Press, 1990).

5. This is, in fact, the phrase used as a title in a recent publication edited by Carla Trujillo. The book features an interdisciplinary analysis applied to Chicana realities. *Living Chicana Theory*, ed. Carla Trujillo (Berkeley, Calif.: Third Woman Press, 1998).

6. These artists and musicians include but are not limited to Celia Rodríguez, Santa Barraza, Irene Pérez, Hulleah Tsinhnahjinnie, Buffy St. Marie, and Ullali.

7. This perspective is what Ana Castillo describes as a "Xicanista philosophy." See *Massacre of the Dreamers: Essays on Xicanisma* (New York: Penguin Books 1995).

8. Weaver describes "communitism" as a communal project which is not just a projection of author intent that recovers and recreates Indian identity and culture; it includes how the community receives the text. He states, "It is part of a shared quest for belonging, a search for community." See *That the People Might Live: Native American Literatures and Native American Community* (New York: Oxford Press, 1997), 45.

9. The images in the series are "Ixta," "Tattoo," "Our Lady," "Heaven," "Pix," "Diego," "December 12," "Retablo," and "Lupe and Sirena in Love."

10. See Dorie Goldman, "Down for la Raza: Barrio Art T-Shirts, Cultural Pride, and Cultural Resistance" *Journal of American Folklore Research* 34, no. 2 (May 1997); Shifra Goldman and Tomás Ybarra Frausto, "The Political and Social Contexts of Chicano Art," in *Chicano Art Resistance and Affirmation 1965–1985*, ed. Richard Griswold de Castillo, Teresa McKenna, and Yvonne Yarbo Bejarano (Los Angeles: Wright Art Gallery, University of California, Los Angeles, 1991)

11. This quote is from the catalogue to the exhibition "La Patria Portatil: 100 years of Mexican Chromo Art Calendars" at the Latino Museum of History, Art, and Culture in Los Angeles. The exhibition is now touring various other galleries and museums in California.

12. It is not uncommon to find Helguerra's recontextualized Chicano images at local swap meets, low-rider exhibits, or even national Chicana/o events.

13. See Norma Alarcón, "Traddutora, Traditora: A Paradigmatic Figure of Chicana Feminism," *Cultural Critique* (Fall 1989), 57–87; Gloria Anzaldúa, *Borderlands / La Frontera: The New Mestiza* (San Francisco: Spinsters/Aunt Lute, 1987); Marta Cotera, *Diosa y Hembra: The History and Heritage of Chicanas in the U.S.* (Austin: University of Texas Mexican American Library Project, 1976); Ana Castillo, *Massacre of the Dreamers: Essays on Xicanisma* (New York: Penguin Books 1995); Cherríe Moraga, *The Last Generation* (Boston: South End Press, 1993); and Elizabeth Salas, *Soldaderas in the Mexican Military: Myth and History* (Austin: University of Texas Press, 1990).

14. Prior to 1848, the region considered the Southwest in the United States was part of Mexico. This region included the states of California, Arizona, Colorado, Texas, and New Mexico. The border separated thousands of Mexicans nationals living north of the Rio Grande from their national origins. It has also had a significant impact on Native communities, including the Tohono O'Odham and the Yoeme communities; their territory was also divided by the border.

15. See Sandra Cisneros, "Guadalupe the Sex Goddess," in *Goddess of the Ameri-*

cas: Writings on the Virgen of Guadalupe, ed. Ana Castillo (New York: Riverhead Books, 1996); Tey Diana Rebolledo, *Women Singing in the Snow: A Cultural Analysis of Chicana Literature* (Tucson: University of Arizona Press, 1995); Carla Trujillo, "La Virgen de Guadalupe and Her Reconstruction in Chicana Lesbian Desire," in *Living Chicana Theory,* ed. Carla Trujillo (Berkeley, Calif.: Third Woman Press, 1998); and Marina Warner, *Alone of All Her Sex: The Myth and the Cult of the Virgin Mary* (New York: Knopf, 1976).

16. See Andrés Guerrero, *A Chicano Theology* (New York: Orbis Books, 1987); *Goddess of the Americas: Writings on the Virgen of Guadalupe,* ed. Ana Castillo (New York: Riverhead Books, 1996); Carla Trujillo, "La Virgen de Guadalupe and Her Reconstruction in Chicana Lesbian Desire," in *Living Chicana Theory,* ed. Carla Trujillo (Berkeley, Calif.: Third Woman Press, 1998).

17. In her groundbreaking work *Borderlands / La Frontera: The New Mestiza* (1987), Gloria Anzaldúa delineates the importance of spirituality as part of the mestiza consciousness. In fact, she draws on the image of Coatlicue to describe the manifestation of mestiza consciousness as a personal psychological process of rebirth; it is a consciousness which transforms rage and opposition into activism and agency.

18. *Exvotos* are small paintings on tin that are usually hung in a church or chapel to give thanks for the miraculous answering of a prayer. Devotees also petition for deliverance from some grave and present danger. The devotees illustrate the received miracle in a very simple fashion along with a depiction of to whoever is given credit for the miracle: the saint, the Virgin, or Christ. The event and details leading up to it are described in writing. Dates are usually included. While most *exvotos* found today are on tin (increasing their durability), they can also be found using other materials.

19. *Día de los Muertos* is a tradition whose roots stretch back to pre-Columbian Mexico. It is believed to be the day that ancestor spirits are given the opportunity to return to visit friends and relatives on Earth. While the Day of the Dead is a Mexican Indigenous/Mexican/Chicano tradition, there are other Native traditions which have similar celebrations to those of the Day of the Dead.

20. According to López, she uses the viceroy butterfly in place of the monarch butterfly. The viceroy butterfly is known for its mimicry of the monarch. Monarch butterflies are poisonous to predators while the viceroy is not. The viceroy survives, in part, because of its similar appearance to the monarch.

21. See Chela Sandoval, "Mestizaje as Method: Feminists of Color Challenge the Canon," in *Living Chicana Theory,* ed. Carla Trujillo (Berkeley, Calif.: Third Woman Press, 1998).

WORKS CITED

Alarcón, Norma. "Chicana Feminism: On Tracks of the Native Woman." In *Living Chicana Theory,* ed. Carla Trujillo. Berkeley: Third Woman Press, 1998.

Aldama, Arturo. "Millennial Anxieties: Borders, Violence, and the Struggle for Chicana/o Subjectivity." *Journal of Hispanic Cultural Studies* 2 (1998).

Allen, Paula Gunn. *The Sacred Hoop: Recovering the Feminine in American Indian Traditions.* Boston: Beacon Press, 1986.

Anaya, Rudolfo. "Aztlán: A Homeland without Boundaries." In *Aztlán: Essays on the Homeland,* ed. Rudolfo Anaya and Francisco Lomelí. Albuquerque: University of New Mexico Press, 1991.

Anderson, Benedict. *Imagined Communities: Reflections on the Origin and Spread of Nationalism.* Rev. ed. New York: Verso, 1991.

Anzaldúa, Gloria. *Borderlands / La Frontera: The New Mestiza.* San Francisco: Spinsters / Aunt Lute, 1987.

Castillo, Ana. *Massacre of the Dreamers: Essays on Xicanisma.* New York: Penguin Books, 1995.

Chabram-Dernersesian, Angie, and Rosa Linda Fregoso. "Chicana/o Cultural Representations: Reframing Alternative Critical Discourses." *Cultural Studies* 4 (1990).
Chicano Youth Liberation Conference. *El Plan Espiritual de Atzlán.* In *Atzlán: Essays on the Homeland,* ed. Rudolfo Anaya and Francisco Lomelí. Albuquerque: University of New Mexico Press, 1991.
Cisneros, Sandra. "Guadalupe the Sex Goddess." In *Goddess of the Americas: Writings on the Virgen of Guadalupe,* ed. Ana Castillo. New York: Riverhead Books, 1996.
Fanon, Frantz. *The Wretched of the Earth: The Handbook for the Black Revolution That Is Changing the Shape of the World.* Trans. Constance Farrington. New York: Grove Press, 1979.
Foucault, Michel. *Discipline and Punish: The Birth of the Prison.* New York: Vintage Books, 1979.
Goldman, Dorie. "Down for la Raza: Barrio Art T-Shirts, Cultural Pride, and Cultural Resistance." *Journal of American Folklore Research* 34, no. 2 (May 1997).
Guerrero, Andrés. *A Chicano Theology.* New York: Orbis Books, 1987.
Freire, Paulo. *Pedagogy of the Oppressed.* 3rd ed. New York: Continuum, 1996.
Hall, Stuart. "Cultural Identity and Cinematic Representation." *Framework* 36 (1989).
Harlan, Theresa. "To Watch, to Remember, and to Survive." Curatorial statement of the exhibit *Watchful Eyes* presented at the Heard Museum, Phoenix, Arizona, 1994.
Hernández-Avila, Inés. "Open Letter to Chicanas." In *Without Discovery: A Native Response to Columbus,* ed. Ray González. Seattle, Wash.: Broken Moon Press, 1992.
———. "Relocations upon Relocations: Home Language, and Native Women's Writings." *American Indian Quarterly* 19, no. 4 (Fall 1995).
López, Alma. Artist's statements and personal correspondence. September 1999.
Lowenthal, David. *The Past Is a Foreign Country.* Cambridge: Cambridge University Press, 1985.
Lux, Guillermo, and Vigil, Maurilio. "Return to Aztlán: The Chicano Rediscovers His Indian Past." In *Aztlán: Essays on the Homeland,* ed. Rudolfo Anaya and Francisco Lomelí. Albuquerque: University of New Mexico Press, 1991.
Medina, Lara. "Los Espíritus Siguen Hablando: Chicana Spiritualities." In *Living Chicana Theory,* ed. Carla Trujillo. Berkeley, Calif.: Third Woman Press, 1998.
Moraga, Cherríe. *The Last Generation.* Boston: South End Press, 1993.
Pérez, Laura. "Spirit Glyphs: Reimagining Art and Artists in the Work of Chicana Tlamatinime." *Modern Fiction Studies* 44, no. 1 (1998).
Pina, Michael. "The Archaic, Historical, and Mythecized Dimensions of Aztlán." In *Aztlán: Essays on the Homeland,* ed. Rudolfo Anaya and Francisco Lomelí. Albuquerque: University of New Mexico Press, 1991.
Quintana, Alvina. *Home Girls: Chicana Literary Voices.* Philadelphia: Temple University Press, 1996.
Rebolledo, Tey Diana. *Women Singing in the Snow: A Cultural Analysis of Chicana Literature.* Tucson: University of Arizona Press, 1995.
Rodríguez, Jeanette. *Our Lady of Guadalupe: Faith and Empowerment among Mexican-American Women.* Austin: University of Texas Press, 1994.
Saldívar, José David. *Border Matters: Remapping American Cultural Studies.* Berkeley: University of California Press, 1997.
Saldívar-Hull, Sonia. "Feminism on the Border: From Gender Politics to Geopolitics." In *Criticism in the Borderlands: Studies in Chicano Literature, Culture, and Ideology,* ed. Héctor Calderón and José David Salívar. Durham, N.C.: Duke University Press, 1991.
Silko, Leslie Marmon. *Yellow Woman and the Beauty of Spirit: Essays on Native American Life Today.* New York: Touchstone, 1997.
Soldatenko, María Angelina. "Organizing Latina Garment Workers in Los Angeles." *Aztlán* 20, no. 1–2 (Spring/Fall 1991).
———. "Summary of Issues Affecting Indigenous Women." Drafted at the Fourth World Conference on Women in Beijing, China.

Trujillo, Carla. "La Virgen de Guadalupe and Her Reconstruction in Chicana Lesbian Desire." In *Living Chicana Theory,* ed. Carla Trujillo. Berkeley, Calif.: Third Woman Press, 1998.

Warner, Marina. *Alone of All Her Sex: The Myth and the Cult of the Virgin Mary.* New York: Knopf, 1976.

Weaver, Jace. *That the People Might Live: Native American Literatures and Native American Community.* New York: Oxford Press, 1997.

——. "From I-Hermeneutics to We-Hermeneutics: Native Americans and the Post-Colonial." In *Native American Religious Identity: Unforgotten Gods,* ed. Jace Weaver. New York: Orbis Books, 1998.

Ybarra Frausto, Tomás. "Cultural Context." From the catalogue to the exhibit *Ceremony of Memory,* Center for Contemporary Arts of Santa Fe, New Mexico, 1988.

Zamudio Taylor, Víctor. "Contemporary Commentary." From the catalogue for the exhibit *Ceremony of Memory,* Center for Contemporary Arts of Santa Fe, New Mexico, 1988.

PART III

MAPPING SPACE AND RECLAIMING PLACE

13 BORDER/TRANSFORMATIVE PEDAGOGIES AT THE END OF THE MILLENNIUM: CHICANA/O CULTURAL STUDIES AND EDUCATION

Alejandra Elenes

In July 1997 the police of Chandler, Arizona, assisted the INS in a sweep of undocumented immigrants. The main criterion for stopping, questioning and eventually arresting "undocumented" individuals was the color of their skin; legal immigrants and US citizens were questioned. Many of those harassed by the Chandler police, and their supporters in the larger Phoenix metropolitan area, organized the Chandler Coalition for Civil Rights and sued the City. The case was settled for $400,000.
—Jim Walsh, "Illegals Target of Crackdown by Chandler Police," *Arizona Republic*, July 31, 1997.

During the spring of 1999 in the Sunny Slope district in Phoenix, Arizona, the INS arrested undocumented workers in the neighborhood grocery store near an elementary school. Parents, fearful that their children might be deported, or just simply harassed by the INS, kept them out of school for a few days.
—Julie Amparano and Becky Ramsdell, "Border Patrol Sweep Angers Parents," *The Arizona Republic*, March 3, 1999.

Recently, Ray Borane, Mayor of Douglas, Arizona, in an op-ed piece in the *Arizona Republic* expressed his views on the undocumented thusly, that those who hire "illegal immigrants" force the elderly "to live in constant fear because of the *marauding hordes* who trespass their homes and properties every night, all night, and who are growing more aggressive in creating more disturbances."
—Ray Borane, "Immigrant Supply, Demand Create Unbearable Situation," *The Arizona Republic*, July 27, 1999.[1]

IN THEIR introduction to *Border Theory* (1997), David E. Johnson and Scott Michaelsen propose that border theories elaborated by Gloria Anzaldúa, Emily Hicks, and Héctor Calderón and José David Saldívar offer "essentialist" constructions of Chicana/o identity based on exclusionary, "stereotypical," repressive, and even colonial mores. By negating or vehemently arguing against the political constitution of Chicana/o identity, Johnson and Michaelsen foreclose the possibility of engaging in any project based on race, class, gender, and sexual orientation identities. Instead they endorse the suggestion that Benjamin Alire Sáenz makes in his contribution to their volume to rethink Chicano identity as "an identity that waits for the day that it is no longer necessary" (20). Chicana/o identity, like all identities, is co-constructed and reflects a multiplicity of layers and tensions. By claiming that the struggle for Chicana/o identity should focus on an utopian future when it would no longer be necessary, Johnson and Michaelsen are proposing the same type of ahistorical politics that has given way to the above quoted events and anti-immigrant sentiments, and to the passage of Propositions 187, 209, and 227 in California. Their ultimate goal will maintain whiteness as the universal model and basis of a homogenous identity. For many years, Chicana/o and other people of color have called this process *"assimilation."* Moreover, this construction of Chicana/o identity would only claim an identity that is always already defined in opposition to the normative. Ultimately, this notion of identity denies Chicanas/os any sense of agency and undermines the political struggles of the Chicana/o Movement.

California's propositions, based on the hysteria manifested by constructions of immigrants, Chicanas/os, and other minorities as criminals and/or as undeserving of certain rights, are manifestations of anxieties over the "browning of America." The policies advocated through these ballot initiatives deny some of the most basic rights of modern civil societies: access to education and health care. Indeed, Chicana education scholar Dolores Delgado Bernal states in her essay "Chicana/o Education from the Civil Rights Era to the Present" (1999) that "[m]any of today's most important educational issues are similar to those voiced in Mexican communities before the 1950s" (101). If we are to scrutinize essentialist tendencies, then, I propose that we look at those that are constructing static images of Latina/o communities. What is at stake here are not only philosophical and theoretical arguments (as interesting and intellectually stimulating as they are), but access to basic material human needs such as health care and education. Much of the so-called women of color identity politics movements based on feminist ideals are struggles against policies that affect the material well-being of the communities of women of color, as well as their own experiences of oppression and marginalization.

In this chapter, I am proposing that border/transformative pedagogies informed by Chicana/o cultural studies and feminist theory can serve as a space of critical scrutiny that offer alternatives to essentialist construction of Chicana/o identity and subjectivity, and to conservative educational discourses. Just as Chicana/o cultural critics have significantly contributed to cultural studies scholarship, it is necessary to apply similar theoretical perspectives to interrogate educational policies and pedagogies that hinder the educational progress of the Chicana/o communities. Therefore, I argue that it is necessary to maintain a dialogue among Chicana/o educators and Chicana/o cultural studies proponents, and to propose pedagogical alternatives.

MILLENNIAL ANXIETIES AND WHITENESS

Anti-immigrant sentiments, attacks on bilingual and multicultural education, and affirmative action are expressions of anxieties created by the cultural changes brought about the New Left movements of the '60s and '70s. Sociologist Howard Winant in *Racial Conditions* (1994) argues that racially based movements transformed the meaning of American culture; "they made identity, difference, the 'personal,' and language itself political issues in very new ways. They made mainstream society—that is, white people—take notice of 'difference'; they created awareness not only of different racial identities, but also of the multiple differences inherent in U.S. culture and society" (25–26). These racially based movements put into question the ideological core by which "American" culture and identity have been historically constructed. Racial difference could no longer be contained within the traditional discourses; therefore, "it became necessary, from the late 1960s onward, to rearticulate these ideas in a conservative ideological framework of competition, individualism, and homogeneity" (26). Indeed, Winant argues that

> [c]ultural debates are dominated by the right's *rejection* of difference and "otherness" (whether racial, gender-based, sexual, or anything else). The right's strong defense of "traditional values," of individualism, and of mainstream culture, its discourse about family, nation, our "proud heritage of freedom," and so forth betokens intense resistance to the very idea of a polyvalent racial culture. (27)

The emphasis of racially based movements, including the Chicana/o Movement, to reconstitute identities that were heretofore defined through negative adjectives to an empowering signification, resulted in making visible the normative registrars "white," "heterosexual," and "male." David Wellman, in his essay "Minstrel Shows, Affirmative Action Talk, and Angry White Men: Marking Racial Otherness in the 1990s" (1997), proposes that it is precisely the visibility and markedness of whiteness at a time when the political-economic landscape is reconfigured that racialized what are class grievances (321). Moreover, these cultural and political changes reconfigured white/male identities in ways that were not expected by those who embody these subject positions. The normativity of their unmarked identity camouflaged their privilege. Thus, in Wellman's words, "The taken-for-granted world of white, male Americans, then, was their normalcy, not their whiteness or their gender. As a result, the privileges that came with whiteness and masculinity were experienced as 'normal,' not advantages" (321). By every statistical account on employment (particularly high-status positions), college and university enrollment, wages, and the like, white males have not lost ground. However, ideologically and psychologically there is a perception that whites (both men and women) are losing their hegemonic position, or that they are expendable.

It is difficult to understand the level of anxiety that the growth of Latina/o communities in the United States produces in individuals who as a group yield much more power and can exercise much more privilege. Yet many arguments against identity-based programs are articulated through such anxieties. Undocumented immigrants are such visible signs that they bring these white fears to the open. Mexican and Central American immigrants' presence in the United States fuels the anxiety of certain white communities about losing ground, or, worse, becoming a *minority*. The demographic changes in California based on the growth of Latino communities and the decline of whites make this scenario very real and frightening to dominant groups. In *Revolutionary Multiculturalism* (1997) Peter McLaren analyzes this phenomenon in relation to Proposition 187:

> I remember the bestial hate mongering among whites after the anti-Proposition 187 march in East Los Angeles in 1994. The size of the crowd—approximately 100,000 protesters by some estimates—instilled such a fear of a brown planet that many white Angelenos fervently took to the streets in anti-immigration demonstrations. Too much "difference effect" resulting from the borderization phenomenon has created among previously stable white constituencies a type of fibrillation of subjectivity—a discursive quivering that eventually leads to a state of identity collapse. Wreaking havoc on the social landscape by creating a spectacular demonology around African American and Latino/a gang members, welfare queens, undocumented workers, and gays and lesbians, members of professional-managerial class made up primarily of cosmopolitan whites have tried to convince white America that its identity is threatened and that white people now constitute the "new" oppressed. Can anyone take this claim seriously, coming as it is from the most privileged group in history? (9–10)

The definition of "America" first codified in the Declaration of Independence and now articulated through the doctrine of family values, meritocracy, Protestant work ethic, and so on historically has constructed a narrow definition of citizenship. In such dominant discourses, social groups are divided into those who deserve certain privileges (read "rights") and those who do not. Civil rights legislation and the programs aimed at remedying "past discrimination" are seen as un-American because they confer group rights that are not gained through individual merit. For example, the argument against welfare is that resources are given to those who do not deserve them and thus promote irresponsibility (the fact that the ones who receive these resources are children is lost in this argument). Similarly, the implementation of bilingual and multicultural education in schools, as well as Chicana/o and women's studies in higher education, puts into question the tradition of monoculturalism so basic for the construction of "American" identity. These programs also debunk the transparency of whiteness and its universalizing tendencies. As Renato Rosaldo established well in *Culture and Truth* (1989), cultural visibility and invisibility are mapped into the spatial organization of certain societies such as the United States, where "full citizenship and cultural visibility appear to be inversely related. When one increases the other decreases. Full citizens lack culture, and those most culturally endowed lack full citizenship" (198).

Multicultural education, Chicana/o studies, and women's studies, for example, are seen as programs that address specific identities that leave white folks out, notably white men. This mentality provokes a feeling of marginalization to which members of the dominant culture are not accustomed, that is, the "me too" cry "how come we don't have white studies or men's studies?" which unwittingly recognizes the paradox in the normativeness of whiteness: what seems to be a universal category is also a particular one. The problem with these manifestations is that they are not offering a struggle against normalizing proclivities, but a desire to maintain such normalization, universalization, and the privilege that it grants.

Given these anxieties and the public policies they provoke, it is imperative to develop educational discourses and policies that are capable of critically engaging a multicultural world that decenters Eurocentric thought. It is necessary to engross students in a critical dialogue where various subjectivities can be explored. In the words of Peter McLaren, "to know ourselves as revolutionary agents is more than the act of understanding who we are; it is the act of reinventing ourselves out of our overlapping cultural identifications and social practices so that we can relate them to the materiality of social life and power relations that structure and sustain them" (1997: 12–13).

CULTURAL STUDIES' INTERVENTIONS

Angie Chabram-Dernersesian in her introduction to the recent *Cultural Studies* (1999) special issue asserts that Chicana/o cultural studies have flourished, incorporated, and intervened in new cultural practices that inscribe conversations with various forms of feminism (e.g., Chicana, women of color, African American), other forms of cultural studies (e.g., indigenous, Mexican, Boricua), ethnic studies, women's studies, American studies, and cultural studies. Chabram-Dernesesian proposes that these "critical interventions" are stable: "here to stay" (173). Herman Gray makes a similar point in his essay "Is Cultural Studies Inflated? The Cultural Economy of Cultural Studies in the United States" (1996) when he argues that "since much of the work in cultural studies focuses on the intersections between race, class, gender, sexuality, and their relationship to cultural meanings and social practices of everyday life, its trans-disciplinary emphasis also places cultural studies in dialogue with (and suspicion from) a group of recent intellectual and political projects that I will, somewhat unconventionally, call area studies" (204).[2]

Lawrence Grossberg in *Bringing It All Back Home* (1997) conceptualizes cultural studies as radical contextualism. Rejecting the belief that equates cultural studies with either theories of ideology, representation, identity, subjectivity, and communication (although it has intervened in all of these elements), Grossberg argues that what is significant about this movement is that its problematics are always shifting. For, Grossberg argues, cultural studies refuses, or should refuse, to take its theory or politics for granted. We cannot assume our positionings in advance. It is not about discovering what we already know even though it might be significant. The point of cultural studies, as I see it, is to understand the struggles over meanings, and the complexities such dynamics might invoke. Cultural studies, then, "is about finding theoretical resources that allow you to redescribe the context that has posed a political challenge. The fact that the context may be part of the United States, or the United States itself, or even the region of the Americas does not guarantee that a theory that has been locally articulated will provide the best resources" (291). For Grossberg theory is "cheap" and politics "expensive" (291).

What, then, are the particular interventions that Chicana/o cultural studies offers? José David Saldívar in *Border Matters* (1997) proposes that "Chicana/o cultural studies offers the loose group of tendencies, issues, and questions in the larger cultural studies orbits in Britain and the United States is the theorization of the U.S.-Mexico borderlands—literal, figurative, material, and militarized—and the deconstruction of the discourse of boundaries" (25). Ultimately, Saldívar proposes that Chicana/o cultural studies has yet to write "the people's histories" that the cultural studies movement in the Centre for Contemporary Cultural Studies (CCCS) produced (34). Although Saldívar recognizes the work of Chicana/o cultural studies scholars, he indicates that "if Chicana/o cultural studies is to flourish in the next century, it must begin to place a greater research emphasis on the ways in which our lived memory and popular culture are linked—on how the postmodernist shocks of electronic mass media create a crisis for 'absolutist' paradigms of national culture and collective memory frames the production and reception of commercial culture" (35). Chabram-Dernesesian hopes that "these [Chicana/o Latina/o] cultural studies formations . . . 'push the dialogues' of both traditions (Chicana/o studies and cultural studies) into uncharted territories of resistance and contestation" (178). Thus it is worth quoting her at length:

> Ultimately, the formation of a conjunctural relationship with cultural studies depends on how cultural studies (in the plural) inflects intellectual resources into "specific contextual politics" that are "expensive," and thus engages a variety of contemporary dynamics, including, for example, the social, symbolic material effects of the recent political, economic, racial and linguistic assault on people of

> colour, women and immigrants; the fate of racialized and gendered workers in the transnational, global economy; the lack of access to higher education and the high drop-out rates; the hopelessness of the youth and the elderly; the upsurge in racial, sexual, linguistic and domestic violence; the widespread incidence of environmental toxicity; the inordinately high levels of incarceration of Chicana/o youth; the Eurocentric bent of educational programmes; and the silencing of the liberatory discourses of women—particularly women of colour and feminists—within political narratives referencing the struggles against the new racism and global capitalism. (182)

The crucial point that Chabram-Dernesesian makes is that Chicana/o cultural studies is, as Grossberg would have it, anti-essentialist. Its anti-essentialism is based not in the sense that it avoids any conceptualization of identity and subjectivity. Rather, Chicana/o cultural studies works against any type of narrow positioning, whether it be Chicana/o nationalism; racist policies against Chicanas/os and other people of color, including immigrants; rigid intellectual positions; theoretical stultification; and so forth. Therefore, cultural studies proposes "expensive" politics to challenge essentialist constructions of Mexican and Chicana/o subjectivity invoked in contemporary public policy.

CULTURAL STUDIES AND EDUCATION

The cultural studies movement provides theoretical frameworks through which we can critically interrogate contemporary educational and public policies. Giroux in his essay "Is There a Place for Cultural Studies in Colleges of Education?" (1996) proposes that "educational theorists can make a major contribution to how cultural studies is taken up by deepening and expanding some important considerations central to the intersection of pedagogy, cultural studies and a project for political change" (52). For Giroux, cultural studies can become the theoretical matrix for producing teachers at the forefront of interdisciplinary, critically engaged work in six different interventions: (1) by making culture a central construct in the classroom and curricula, cultural studies can inform the production of curriculum knowledge and pedagogy that provide a narrative space for understanding multiple histories, experiences, and cultures, as well as offering a critical analysis of these; (2) by placing a major emphasis on the study of language and power; (3) by linking the curriculum to the experiences that students bring to legitimated school knowledge; (4) through a commitment to studying the production, reception, and situated use of varied texts, and how they structure social relations, values, particular notions of community, the future, and diverse definitions of self; (5) by analyzing history as a series of ruptures and displacements; and (6) by expanding the definition of pedagogy in order to move beyond a limited emphasis on the mastery of techniques and methodologies.

As Giroux makes clear, a significant intervention that cultural studies can make for education and pedagogy is to make culture central to their practices. Unfortunately, scholars in colleges of education are reluctant to follow the cultural studies movement. This is ironic, given that in the United States, according to Lawrence Grossberg, one of the first academic spaces open for cultural studies was education. Part of this problematic is the tendency of colleges of education to emphasize efficiency and applied learning. What is "lost from this reductionistic emphasis on the practical," according to Giroux, "is any broader sense of vision, meaning, or motivation regarding the role that colleges of education might play in expanding the 'scope of democracy and democratic institutions'" (47).

CHICANAS/OS AND CRITICAL PEDAGOGY

The history of Chicana/o education is one of marginalization, neglect, and segregation. Although discursively educational policy aimed at Chicanas/os has been premised on the hope of their assimilation, the reality has been that the purpose of education is to socialize Chicana/o youth to their subordinate position in the social order. This is exemplified in a "chilling example" presented by Rubén Donato in *The Other Struggle for Equal Schools* (1997), where he quotes from Theodore Parsons Jr.'s doctoral dissertation an incident in which a white boy was observed leading five Mexican students out of a classroom: "the teacher replied that '[his] father owns one of the big farms in the area and . . . one day he will have to know how to handle the Mexicans'" (4–5). Though this event occurred sometime in the early '60s, it is an illustration of the social and economic reproduction function of schools, for both white and Chicana/o students. It is not surprising, then, that the Chicano Movement recognized the important role of educational reform for the progress of the community. I have argued in "Reclaiming the Borderlands" (1997) that the Chicano Movement's struggle to reform education was the first time that Chicanas/os articulated educational reform in a clearly anti-assimilationist perspective. "For the Chicano movement, access to education meant not only the literal access of bodies into the classroom, but also to a curriculum where Chicana/o history, culture, politics, and identity were central" (361).

Peter McLaren believes that "critical pedagogy . . . remains committed to the practical realization of self-determination and creativity on a collective social scale" (1997, 13). I have no doubt that progressive Chicana/o educators share this vision. While critical pedagogy (especially that articulated by Henry Giroux and Peter McLaren) has proposed the notion of a border pedagogy, there are very few Chicana/o educators who are producing work on transformative pedagogy.[3] (At the same time critical pedagogy has paid scant attention to Chicana/o cultural practices.) In *Teaching to Transgress* (1994), bell hooks has also discussed the underrepresentation of people of color producing scholarship on pedagogy. She writes:

> The scholarly field of critical pedagogy and/or feminist pedagogy continues to be primarily a discourse engaged by white women and men. Freire, too, in conversation with me, as in much of his written work, has always acknowledged that he occupies the location of white maleness, particularly in this country. But the work on various thinkers on radical pedagogy (I use this term to include critical and/or feminist perspectives) has in recent years truly included a recognition of differences—those determined by class, race, sexual practice, nationality, and so on. Yet this movement forward does not seem to coincide with any significant increase in black or other nonwhite voices joining discussions about radical pedagogical practices. (9–10)

The reason for this paucity is that, for the most part, educational research tends to be atheoretical and positivistic. Recently, there has also been a move in colleges of education to focus on classroom management and practical/pragmatic issues at the expense of cultural and area content studies. Research on bilingual education, for example, follows such perspectives because it has been necessary to develop methods for research and teaching. Additionally, the field of Chicana/o education has had to fill many gaps such as writing the histories of education. In higher education, Chicana/o studies has not engaged in pedagogical questions in the ways that women's studies has. Yet Chicana/o studies has intervened in curriculum transformation and canonical revisions. Although these are pedagogical interventions, they are usually thought of as separate. Yet transformative pedagogy like critical pedagogy believes in pedagogy engaged in the construction of knowledge, not only its transmission by an all-knowing teacher to passive students.

Recently, Enrique Trueba in *Latinos Unidos* (1999) proposed a pedagogy of hope. For Trueba, "the praxis that accompanies a pedagogy of hope is clearly a conscious detachment from 'whiteness' and from a rigid, dogmatic, and monolithic defense of a Western or North American way of life, schooling codes, and interactional patterns" (161). Moreover, this pedagogy of hope requires a daily praxis; "[an] open interaction with immigrant children starts from the assumption that these children can learn and they deserve to become empowered with knowledge" (161). Antonia Darder, in "Creating the Conditions for Cultural Democracy in the Classroom" (1996), proposed an emancipatory pedagogy for bicultural students. Like Trueba, Darder uses the language of hope and proposes a vision for democracy and schooling for bicultural students. In Darder's emancipatory pedagogy, "students are encouraged to question the conflicts, contradictions, disjunctions, and partiality of standardized knowledge forms in their own lives. Consistently, liberatory educators support and challenge bicultural students to struggle together so that they may come to know all the possibilities that might be available to them as free citizens" (350). Adriana Hernández, in her book *Pedagogy, Democracy and Feminism: Re-*

thinking the Public Sphere (1997), has pointed at a feminist transformative pedagogy which "address[es] difference in all its possibilities within power relations in a constant process of contestation against concrete oppressive practices" (19). Moreover, Hernández's pedagogy recognizes not only multiple positions but also the tensions among them, particularly for women of color (19).

I suggest that given the aforementioned policies against Chicanas/os and immigrants, we need to create a pedagogical project that takes into account the multiple social positions that these subjectivities entail. I have named such project border/transformative pedagogy because it cuts across the boundaries of critical/feminist/multicultural/queer pedagogy. Border/transformative pedagogy is an activity that, precisely because it is centering on Chicana/o cultural practices and subjectivities, recognizes its praxis cannot be conducted by isolating any form of representation. Doing so contributes to the sexist, heterosexist, racist, and classist practices of conservative and some liberal educational discourses that universalize white maleness. These constructions are precisely what gave political impetus to the passage of California Propositions 187, 209, and 227.

Border/transformative pedagogy proposes that in order to adequately account for the multiple subject positions encountered in contemporary classrooms a relational theory of difference is necessary (Yarbro-Bejarano: 1999). According to Yvonne Yarbro-Bejarano in "Sexuality and Chicana/o Studies: Toward a Theoretical Paradigm for the Twenty-First Century," a relational theory of difference examines "the formation of identity in the dynamic interpenetration of gender, race, sexuality, class and nation" (340). As Chandra Talpade Mohanty points out in her essay "Cartographies of Struggle" (1991) gender and race are relational terms. Therefore, in Mohanty's words "to define feminism in purely gendered terms assumes that our consciousness of being 'women' has nothing to do with race, class, nation, or sexuality, just with gender" (12). A similar issue can be encountered with pedagogical practices whose foci are on a single axis of analysis.

The problematic with many pedagogical discourses is not necessarily that they have not taken into account differences of race, class, gender, and sexuality. The difficulty resides in the undertheorization of historically unmarked categories such as "white," "male," "heterosexual," and "middle class." What is necessary is to recognize the unmarked categories as relational as well.[4] In the words of Yvonne Yarbro-Bejarano, this means that "the theory is also relational within each binary set, for example, a man lives his masculinity through his cultural, sexual and class identifications, but also in relation to a certain construction of femininity which for the man is essential to his manhood" (430). Democratic pedagogical discourses need to theorize all subject positions, dominant and subaltern, and mark its registers. Moreover, it is necessary to decenter the hegemony of the white, middle-class, heterosexual, male subject as normative, and to recognize the multiple marginality of people of color and those with hybrid identities.

As Theresa Martínez explains in "Toward a Chicana Feminist Epistemological Standpoint" (1996), border/transformative pedagogies recognize that "Chicanas are inhabitants of the borderlands—the lands on the U.S.-Mexican border, as well as the crossroads between cultures. They themselves inhabit multiple spaces between cultures, ethnicities, genders, and classes. They are outsiders and insiders; they inhabit the center and the margin; they are self and other; they are subject and object" (116). It is precisely this borderland existence of Chicanas/os in institutional settings such as schools, media, and cultural centers that has marginalized them. For Chicanas/os presence in such institutions is a paradoxical state of "belonging" and "not-belonging."

Border/transformative pedagogies seek to remap pedagogical discourses by recognizing that the borderlands characteristics of Chicanas/os are paradigmatic of the subject positions of people of color in the United States. The language of the borderlands, with its flexible notion of identity, helps decenter the dominant subject. Whether dealing with classroom practices or cultural practices, the multicultural realities of the United States attest to the need to recognize the multiple levels of difference that we encounter in any variety of pedagogical practices.

BORDER/TRANSFORMATIVE PEDAGOGY AND FEMINISM

Like other democratic and visionary pedagogical practices, Chicana feminist/transformative pedagogies are rooted in liberation politics and in struggles for survival and voice. There is an agreement with Peter McLaren, who writes in his recent article "The Pedagogy of Che Guevara: Critical Pedagogy and Globalization Thirty Years after Che," (1998) that "Critical Pedagogy is a way of thinking about, negotiating, and transforming the relationship among classroom teaching, the production of knowledge, the institutional structures of the school, and the social and material relations of the wider community, society, and nation state" (45). Border/transformative pedagogies are informed by Chicana feminist theorists' and cultural workers' engagement in a process of self-renewal that constructs alternative identities than those imposed by Anglo-American and Chicano patriarchies (e.g. Alarcón, Anzaldúa, Chabram-Dernersesian, Candelaria, Castillo, Trujillo, Cisneros). These new visions of Chicana cultural identities are anchored in their everyday experience within an oppressive system. The cultural politics engaged by Chicanas are struggles against oppressive policies that limit Chicanas' educational opportunities and are the legacy of decades of struggle of farmworkers, cannery workers, welfare rights activists, students, mothers, and professionals. Chicana feminist theorist Aida Hurtado, in her article "Relations to Privilege: Seduction and

Rejection in the Subordination of White Women and Women of Color" (1989), writes that "socially stigmatized groups have reclaimed their history by taking previously denigrated characteristics and turning them into positive affirmation of self" (846). Accordingly, Chela Sandoval in her essay "U.S. Third World Feminism: The Theory and Method of Oppositional Consciousness in the Postmodern World" (1992) proposes that U.S. Third World women have developed an oppositional consciousness from everyday strategies of survival (3).

One's experiences of oppression and marginalization influence how one makes sense of the world. Chicana cultural workers and scholars who are committed to the liberation of the Chicana/o community bring their own experiences in their creative and scholarly endeavors as part of the politics of social change. In her essay "Using a Chicana Feminist Epistemology in Educational Research" (1998), Dolores Delgado Bernal argues that Chicana scholars who have challenged the historical representation of Chicanas and relocated them into a central position are creating a Chicana feminist epistemology (559). For Delgado Bernal, Chicana feminist epistemology is concerned with knowledge about Chicanas that generates an understanding of their experiences and the political manipulation over the legitimization or illegitimization of that knowledge. Chicanas, thus, become agents of knowledge who participate in an intellectual discourse that links experience, research, community, and social change (560). Similarly, I have argued in "Chicana Feminist Narratives and the Politics of the Self" (1999) that Chicana autobiographical texts help explain how particular Chicanas make sense of their social positioning. Thus, these narratives offer unique pedagogical strategies, given that autobiographical texts are ways of constructing knowledge and theory building that is oppositional and situational. Inés Hernández-Avila has made a comparable argument in her essay "Relocations upon Relocations: Home, Language, and Native American Women's Writings" (1995) when she writes that

> [Native women's] historical cultural identities are contextualized within the personal and collective historical processes that we have undergone and the cultural pedagogies that have sustained us and our families and communities, not without suffering or grievous loss, but with courage, beauty, and dignity as well. The experience of invasion, genocide, dispossession, colonization, relocation, and ethnocide is marked at different historical moments by singular imperial, then governmental policies. (495)

The unique characteristics of Chicana feminist epistemologies, according to Delgado Bernal, are the engagement with issues such as immigration, generational status, bilingualism, limited English proficiency, and the contradictions of Catholicism (561). Moreover, she bases her epistemology on Anzaldúa's *mestiza consciousness*, which, according to Delgado

Bernal, is a new form of awareness that straddles cultures, races, languages, nations, sexualities, and spirituality (561). Chicanas and other marginalized peoples have a strength that comes from their borderland experiences. These are experiences that although clearly marked in the "specificities" of race, class, and gender exploitation form part of the construction of multiply layered identities.

Sofia Villenas in her fine article "The Colonizer/Colonized Chicana Ethnographer: Identity, Marginalization, and Co-optation in the Field" (1996) proposes that "[w]e scholars/activists of color need to understand the ways in which we manipulate our multiple, fluid, clashing, and colonized identities and how our identities are manipulated and marginalized in the midst of oppressive discourses" (728). These multiple identities and social positions are present in the classroom, museums, and other cultural institutions. Chicana/o teachers/professors must contend with students, administrators, and colleagues that "other" them and construct their identities in subordinate ways. At the same time, Chicanas/os bring into their teaching practices their own epistemology, which is rooted in their own marginalized experience. Whether a Chicana teacher/professor believes she is assimilated or not, much of her pedagogical efforts must contend with deconstructing hegemonic definitions of Chicana womanhood.

If we follow Johnson and Michaelsen's admonitions on Chicana/o identity, then, the pedagogical strategies that I have presented here are essentialist. However, as Norma Alarcón states in her essay "Conjugating Subjects in the Age of Multiculturalism" (1996) in relation to the critiques of Gloria Anzaldúa's and Frantz Fanon's constructions of identity, we must think of essentialism in different ways. Thus she writes,

> If to "ontologize difference" in the pursuit of identity and meaning as modes of resistance to domination entails essentializing by relying on the concept of an *authentic core* that remains hidden to one's consciousness and that requires the elimination of all that is considered foreign or not true to the self, then neither Anzaldúa nor Fanon is essentialist at all. Both are quite clear that the pursuit of identity through "psychobiological syncretism" is one engaged through the racial difference imputed to them as stigma that is now revalorized through reconstruction in historical terms. (133; my emphasis)

Chicana feminist theory, pedagogies, and epistemologies, as well as many cultural productions, are an engagement with a process of self-renewal and rebirth. Chicanas employ a process of decolonization that through a critique of material conditions has constructed an oppositional speaking subject. Therefore, following Alarcón, border/transformative pedagogies and Chicana feminist epistemologies are not essentialist but empowering. It is precisely the empowering characteristics of these practices that are dangerous and provoke "millennial anxieties." The critique of essentialism can be a veiled attempt to invite Chicanas/os to continue to constitute ourselves as colonial subjects, by constructing an identity that is counter to our own interests.

CONCLUSION

The claiming of a national unity in terms of culture, language, race, and gender invoked through the passage of Propositions 187, 209, and 227 represent a challenge to democratic principles that give rights to all members of the society. To become a truly democratic nation, it is necessary to recognize that the diversity of the United States is not a problem that must be solved or celebrated, but the result of colonial/neocolonial practices that resulted in the slavery, conquest, deterritorialization, and displacement of peoples from all around the globe. To recognize these power relations as such involves multicultural educational discourses where the various dimensions of race, class, gender, and sexuality are central, and where these dimensions do not only became the marked categories of people of color, women, and gays and lesbians. As Ernesto Laclau has written in "Universalism, Particularism, and the Question of Identity" (1992), this is a precondition of democracy:

> The unresolved tension between universalism and particularism allows a movement away from Western Eurocentrism, through what we could call a systematic decentering of the West . . . Eurocentrism was the result of a discourse that did not differentiate between the universal values that the West was advocating and the concrete historical actors that were incarnating them. Now, however, we can separate these two aspects. If the social struggles show that the concrete practices of our society restrict the universalism of our dimension while widening the spheres of its application—which, in turn, will redefine the concrete contents of such a universality. Through this process, universalism as a horizon is expanded at the same time as its necessary attachment to any particular content is broken. The opposite policy—that of rejecting universalism in toto as the particular content of the West—can only lead to a political blind alley. (90)

A cultural studies practice that takes seriously "expensive" politics offers a space where we can scrutinize contemporary public policy and educational policies that are detrimental to the economic, social, and political advancement of the Chicana/o and Latina/o communities. Chicana feminist theorists and cultural workers provide a theoretical and practical basis for the constitution of pedagogical practices that seek to undermine hegemonic discourses. I have argued here that it is precisely when Chicanas and Chicanos became speaking subjects who are politically engaged, naming their own realities, and offering truly democratic alternatives that we become dangerous. Whether it is academics veiled under certain theoretical positions or conservative politicians proposing policies that are unconstitutional, these groups ultimately deny Chicanas/os the right to name their own identity and analysis of their "lived realities."

NOTES

1. Borane's tone in his op-ed piece is aggressive against undocumented workers, no doubt. However, I would like to point out that he does recognize the inhumane and dangerous conditions suffered by undocumented immigrants at the hands of unscrupulous *coyotes.* I'm not so sure he is worried about the economic exploitation suffered by undocumented workers.

2. Gray includes within the area studies nomenclature African American atudies, gay and lesbian studies, Asian American studies, Chicano/a studies, ethnic studies, postcolonial studies, diasporic studies, and women's studies.

3. By transformative pedagogy I mean the various types of pedagogical discourses, such as critical, feminist, radical, and/or queer. For the most part these different pedagogical discourses share a vision for social change where "macro" and "micro" issues of schooling are interrelated. Influenced by the late Brazilian educator Paulo Freire, these discourses understand pedagogy as the construction of knowledge, not the transmission of knowledge by an all-knowing teacher to passive students. There are Chicana education scholars who are engaging in pedagogical work, among them Francisca González, Dolores Delgado Bernal, and Sofia Villenas.

4. Recently there has been some work on the construction of whiteness and educational research. See for example, Michelle Fine et al., eds., *Off White: Readings on Race, Power, and Society* (New York: Routledge, 1997); Leslie Roman, "White Is a Color! White Defensiveness, Postmodernism, and Anti-Racist Pedagogy," in *Race, Identity and Representation in Education,* ed. Cameron McCarthy and Warren Crichlow (New York: Routledge, 1993), 71–88; and Peter McLaren, *Revolutionary Multiculturalism* (Boulder, Colo.: Westview Press, 1997), 237–293.

WORKS CITED

Alarcón, Norma. "Conjugating Subjects in the Age of Multiculturalism." In *Mapping Multiculturalism,* ed. Avery F. Gordon and Christopher Newfield, 127–148. Minneapolis: University of Minnesota Press, 1996.

Borane, Ray. "Immigrant Supply, Demand Create Unbearable Situation." *The Arizona Republic,* July 27, 1999, Final Edition, B7.

Chabram-Dernersesian, Angie. "Introduction" to *Chicana/o Latina/o Cultural Studies: Transnational and Transdisciplinary Movements. Cultural Studies* 13, no. 2 (1999): 173–194.

Darder, Antonia. "Creating the Conditions for Cultural Democracy in the Classroom." In *Latinos and Education: A Critical Reader,* ed. Antonia Darder, Rodolfo D. Torres, and Henry Gutiérrez, 331–350. New York: Routledge, 1997.

Delgado Bernal, Dolores. "Chicana/o Education from the Civil Rights Era to the Present." In *The Elusive Quest for Equality: 150 Years of Chicano/Chicana Education,* ed. José F. Moreno, 77–108. Cambridge, Mass.: Harvard Educational Review, 1999.

———. "Using a Chicana Feminist Epistemology in Educational Research." *Harvard Educational Review* 68, no. 4 (Winter 1998): 555–579.

Donato, Rubén. *The Other Struggle for Equal Schools: Mexican Americans during the Civil Rights Era.* Albany: SUNY Press, 1997.

Elenes, C. Alejandra. "Chicana Feminist Narratives and the Politics of the Self." *Frontiers: A Journal of Women Studies* 21, no. 3: 105–123.

———. "Reclaiming the Borderlands: Chicana/o Identity, Difference, and Critical Pedagogy." *Educational Theory* 47, no. 3 (1997): 359–375.

Giroux, Henry A. "Is There a Place for Cultural Studies in Colleges of Education?" In *Counternarratives: Cultural Studies and Critical Pedagogies in Postmodern Spaces,* ed. Henry A. Giroux, Colin Lankshear, Peter McLaren, and Michael Peters, 41–58. New York: Routledge, 1996.

Gray, Herman. "Is Cultural Studies Inflated? The Cultural Economy of Cultural Studies in the United States." In *Disciplinarity and Dissent in Cultural Studies,* ed. Cary Nelson and Dilip Parameshwar Gaonkar, 203–216. New York: Routledge, 1996.

Grossberg, Lawrence. *Bringing It All Back Home: Essays on Cultural Studies.* Durham, N.C.: Duke University Press, 1997.

Hernández, Adriana. *Pedagogy, Democracy and Feminism: Rethinking the Public Sphere.* Albany: SUNY Press, 1997.

Hernández-Avila, Inés. "Relocations upon Relocations: Home, Language, and Native American Women's Writings." *American Indian Quarterly* 19, no. 4 (Fall 1995): 491–507.

hooks, bell. *Teaching to Transgress: Education as the Practice of Freedom.* New York: Routledge, 1994.

Hurtado, Aida. "Relations to Privilege: Seduction and Rejection in the Subordination of White Women and Women of Color." *Signs: Journal of Women in Culture and Society* 14, no. 4 (1989): 833–855.

Johnson, David E., and Scott Michaelsen. "Border Secrets: An Introduction." In *Border Theory: The Limits of Cultural Politics,* ed. Scott Michaelsen and David E. Johnson, 1–39. Minneapolis: University of Minnesota Press, 1997.

Laclau, Ernesto. "Universalism, Particularism, and the Question of Identity." *October* 61 (1992): 83–90.

Martínez, Theresa A. "Toward a Chicana Feminist Epistemological Standpoint: Theory at the Intersection of Race, Class, and Gender." *Race, Gender & Class* 3, no. 3 (1996): 107–128.

McLaren, Peter. "The Pedagogy of Che Guevara: Critical Pedagogy and Globalization Thirty Years after Che." *Cultural Circles* 3 (Summer 1998): 29–103.

———. *Revolutionary Multiculturalism: Pedagogies of Dissent for the New Millennium.* Boulder, Colo.: Westview Press, 1997.

Mohanty, Chandra T. "Introduction: Cartographies of Struggle—Third World Women and the Politics of Feminism." In *Third World Women and the Politics of Feminism,* ed. Chandra T. Mohanty, Ann Russo, and Lourdes Torres, 1–47. Bloomington: Indiana University Press, 1991.

Rosaldo, Renato. *Culture and Truth: The Remaking of Social Analysis.* Boston: Beacon Press, 1989.

Saldívar, José David. *Border Matters: Remapping American Cultural Studies.* Berkeley and Los Angeles: University of California Press, 1997.

Sandoval, Chela. "U.S. Third World Feminism: The Theory and Method of Oppositional Consciousness in the Postmodern World." *Genders* 10 (Spring 1992): 1–24.

Trueba, Enrique T. *Latinos Unidos: From Cultural Diversity to the Politics of Solidarity.* Boulder, Colo.: Rowman & Littlefield, 1999.

Villenas, Sofia. "The Colonizer/Colonized Chicana Ethnographer: Identity, Marginalization, and Co-optation in the Field." *Harvard Educational Review* 66, no. 4 (Winter 1996): 711–731.

Wellman, David. "Minstrel Shows, Affirmative Action Talk, and Angry White Men: Making Racial Otherness in the 1990s." In *Displacing Whiteness: Essays in Social and Cultural Criticism*, ed. Ruth Frankenberg, 311–331. Durham, N.C.: Duke University Press, 1997.

Winant, Howard. *Racial Conditions: Politics, Theory, Comparisons.* Minneapolis: University of Minnesota Press, 1994.

Yarbro-Bejarano, Yvonne. "Sexuality and Chicana/o Studies: Toward a Theoretical Paradigm for the Twenty-First Century." *Cultural Studies* 13, no. 2 (1999): 335–345.

14 ON THE BAD EDGE OF *LA FRONTERA*

José David Saldívar

Where the transmission of "national" traditions was once the major theme of world literature, perhaps we can now suggest that transnational histories of migrants, the colonized, or political refugees—these border and frontier conditions—may be the terrains of world literature.

—Homi Bhabha, "The World and the Home" (1992)

IN AN influential manifesto published in *La Línea Quebrada / The Broken Line* (1986), Guillermo Gómez-Peña theorized the *transfrontera* urban galaxy of San Diego and Tijuana as a new social space filled with multicultural symbologies—sent out in polyglot codes (Spanish, English, *caló,* and Spanglish).[1] Though perhaps too steeped in poststructuralist playfulness (at the expense of critical multicultural work), Gómez-Peña nevertheless hit upon one of the central truths of our extended U.S.-Mexico Border culture: the *Frontera* culture stretching from the shanty barrios of Tijuana and San Diego to the rich surf and turf of Santa Barbara (dominated by the megaspace of Los Angeles in the middle) is an enormous "desiring machine."[2] Starting from Deleuze and Guattari's famous concept of the machine in their *Anti-Oedipus: Capitalism and Schizophrenia* (1977), Gómez-Peña envisioned a radical re-reading of the U.S.-Mexico border as a conjunction of desiring machines brought together. Such a notion of the *Frontera* as a real machine with flows and interruptions, crossings and deportations, liminal transitions and reaggregations, is fundamental to my reading of the extended U.S.-Mexico Borderland cultural texts of Los Angeles, for it will permit us to travel along different routes and paths other than the "Sunshine or Noir" and "Black or White" master dialectics thematized in Mike Davis's *City of Quartz: Excavating the Future in Los Angeles* (1990).

The two-thousand-mile-long U.S.-Mexico border, without doubt, produces millions of undocumented workers from Central America and Mexico who are essential to North American agriculture's, tourism's, and *maquiladora*'s economic machines. The U.S.-Mexico border thus not only produces masses of agricultural farmworkers, low-tech laborers (mostly women), dishwashers, gardeners, and maids, but a military-like machine of low-intensity conflict (Dunn 1996)—INS helicopters, Border patrol agents with infrared camera equipment used to track and capture the border crossers from the South, and detention centers and jails designed to protect the Anglocentric minority in California who fear and even loathe these scores of *indocumentados.* Moreover, this desiring machine also comprises an enormous bureaucratic, political, cultural, and legal machine of *coyotes* (border crossing guides for hire), *pollos* (pursued undocumented border crossers), *fayuqueros* (peddlers of food), *sacadineros* (border swindlers), *cholos/as* (Chicano/a urban youth), notary publics, public interest lawyers, public health workers, a huge "juridical-administrative-therapeutic state apparatus" (JAT) [1989, 154]—to use Nancy Fraser's unruly coinage.[3]

The only thing that matters here for our purposes is that the U.S.-Mexico border machine constructs the subject-positions exclusively for the benefits of the North American JAT machine: juridically, it positions the migrant border crossers vis-à-vis the U.S. legal system by denying them their human rights and by designating them as "illegal aliens"; administratively, the migrant border crossers who desire amnesty must petition a bureaucratic institution created under the 1986 Immigration Reform and Control Act (IRCA) to receive identification papers (including a social security card); and, finally, therapeutically, migrant border crossers in their shantytowns in canyons throughout California have to grapple with various county Health Departments and the Environmental Health Services offices. For instance, at one shantytown called El Valle Verde (Green Valley) in San Diego County, the Environmental Health Services' director shut down the migrant border crossers' camp "for violations dealing with lack of potable water for drinking, building-code violations, [and] fecal material on the ground" (quoted in Chávez 1992, 108).

This analysis of the U.S.-Mexico border as a "juridical-administrative-therapeutic state apparatus" can allow us to see that migrant border crossers from the South into the North are largely disempowered by the denial of cultural and legal citizenship.[4] The JAT border machine, moreover, positions its subjects in ways that do not humanize them. It often personalizes them as "illegal aliens," "cases," "dirty," "amoral," and "disease-ridden," and so militates against their collective identity. As Nancy Fraser says about the JAT welfare system, the JAT border machine "imposes monological, administrative definitions of situation and need and so preempts dialogically achieved self-definition and self-determination" (155). To be sure, the identities and needs that the JAT border machine fashions for migrant border crossers are "interpreted" identities and needs. Further, they are highly political interpretations and are therefore subject to dispute. In what follows, I will analyze the Los Angeles *Frontera* social texts of Helena Viramontes, John Rechy, Los Illegals, and (Kid) Frost as liminal culture critiques and analyses of the interpreted identities and needs of Latinas/os in California, for Viramontes's "The Cariboo Cafe" (1985), Rechy's *The Miraculous Day of Amalia Gómez* (1991), Los Illegals' "El Lay" (1983), and (Kid) Frost's *East Side Story* (1992) have been more accurate and politically perceptive (than the mainline postmodern realists and urban planners) in representing what Mike Davis calls "the programmed hardening of the urban surface" (1990, 223) in the extended *Frontera* of Southern California.

If "all machines have their mastercodes" (1992, 17), as Antonio Benítez-Rojo suggested in a different context, what are the codebooks to the cultural machines of these four U.S.-Mexico Border writers? What networks of subcodes hold together these autonomous works of art? What are the central rituals, ceremonies, and ideologies in the texts of the transfrontier "contact zone" (Pratt 1992)? And finally, what are the benefits of examining U.S.-Mexico Border texts as cultural practices with institutional implications for cultural and critical legal studies?

To begin answering some of these questions, I want to examine a liminal short story, "The Cariboo Cafe," from *The Moths and Other Stories* by Helena María Viramontes, coordinator of the Los Angeles Latino/a Writers Association and former literary editor of *XhismeArte* magazine. I emphasize Viramontes's institutional grounding as a former coordinator and editor in Los Angeles because it is an unsettling fact that all too often U.S. Latino/a writers are omitted from intellectual surveys and literary histories. Even sympathetic New Left surveys exploring the role played by waves of migrations of intellectuals to Los Angeles—from Charles F. Lummis and Theodor Adorno to Ornette Coleman and the gangster rap group NWA—such as Mike Davis's superb *City of Quartz* (1990)—schematizes this intellectual history in exclusively racialized black and white terms, or in linear East and West global mappings.[5] Like the scores of brown maids and gardeners with their brooms and blowers working all over California, isn't it about time that we sweep away once and for all this Manichaean construction? Might not a sweeping, even crude, transnational South-North mapping (using the interpretive power of liminality) be more appropriate?

While Viramontes's richly provocative "The Cariboo Cafe" has elicited rigorous ideological, Chicana feminist, and semiotic, gendered readings by literary critics such as Sonia Saldívar-Hull, Barbara Harlow, and Debra Castillo, who convincingly read the story as what Saldívar-Hull suggests is a local Chicana feminist text with "an internationalist agenda" (1990, 193), or what Harlow calls "a site of confrontation between popular and official interpretations of the historical narrative" (1991, 152), and what Castillo sees as a "tortured dystopia" (1992, 94), my view is that not enough attention has been drawn to the diverse manifestations of "liminality" in the story, or to the explicitly migrant border-crossing phenomena of the "unhomely" that, in Victor Turner's terms, fall "betwixt and between the positions assigned and arrayed by law, custom, convention, and ceremonial" (1969, 95). Using insights from anthropologists such as Turner, among others, I propose to elaborate less a manifesto of U.S.-Mexico border liminality than to use the interpretive force of this concept to tell us something about Viramontes's "The Cariboo Cafe" and the rites of passage migrant border crossers from the South into the North generally share.

Anthropological discussion of migrant border crossers as "liminals" can be said to begin with Leo Chávez's experimental ethnography, *Shadowed Lives: Undocumented Immigrants in American Society* (1992), where he describes migrant border crossing as "transitional" phases in the three-step process of ritual initiation. Relying and elaborating on Arnold van Gennep's *Rites of Passage* (1909) and Victor Turner's *The Ritual Process* (1969), Chávez traces the interstitial stages migrant border crossers from both Mexico and Central America make in their journeys to the U.S.-Mexico Borderlands. While Chávez, perhaps, overemphasizes "the transition people undergo as they leave the migrant life and instead settle in the United States" (4), we could indeed extend his sensitive reading of liminality by adding a synchronic dimension to the concept of liminality as Victor Turner suggested. For Turner (as put forth by Gustavo Pérez-Firmat), "liminality should be looked upon not only as a transition between states but as a state in itself, for there exist individuals, groups, or social categories for which the 'liminal' moment turns into a permanent condition" (1986, xiii–xiv).

A liminal reading of Viramontes's "The Cariboo Cafe" thematizing the ritual process thus would emphasize both van Gennep's and Chávez's temporal, processual view with Turner's topo-spatial supplementation. Liminality in Viramontes's hands (as Turner himself said) is "a semantic molecule with many components" (1969, 103). Seen in this light, "The Cariboo Cafe" is built upon a series of multiple border crossings and multilayered transitions an undocumented migrant washerwoman undergoes as she moves from the South into the North. Foremost among the transitions thematized in Viramontes's story are the actual border crossings the washerwoman makes, for crossing both the *frontera del sur* in Central America and the U.S.-Mexico border without documentation is what anthropologist Chávez sees as the "monumental event" (4) of many migrant border crossers' lives.

Like many undocumented migrants, the washerwoman in Viramontes's text gathers resources and funding from her family and extended community (her nephew Tavo sells his car to send her the money for a bus ticket to Juárez, Mexico), for crossing the JAT border machine with its extended machines of *coyotes, sacadineros,* and *fayuqueros* is a financially exorbitant undertaking. Fundamentally, "The Cariboo Cafe" allegorizes hemispheric South-North border crossing in terms anthropologists such as Chávez see as emblematic of undocumented border crossers in general: "a territorial passage that marks the transition from one way of life to another" (4). As an exemplary border crossing tale, then, we can initially map "The Cariboo Cafe" in Chávez's temporal, ritualistic terms: it moves (in a non-linear narrative) through the interstitial phases of separation, liminality, and (deadly) reincorporation. Let me hasten to add that Viramontes throughout her disjunctive narrative privileges the everyday experiences (the rituals of separation and liminality) the washerwoman must face as she travels from her appointments with legal authorities in Central America (guerrillas have "disappeared" her five-year-old son) to the actual border crossings and to her final searches (together with two Mexican migrant undocumented children, Sonya and Macky) for sanctuary at The Cariboo Cafe. The cafe sign symbolically reads as the "oo Cafe," for "the paint's peeled off" (1985, 64) except for the "two o's."[6] In other words, while anthropologists such as Chávez see the U.S.-Mexico border "limen" as threshold, for Viramontes it is a lived socially symbolic space.

But why does Viramontes represent the U.S.-Mexico border limen in "The Cariboo Cafe" as position and not as threshold? The reasons for this are complex, but one reason is that the washerwoman, like the majority of undocumented migrants in the U.S., never acquires what Leo Chávez calls "links of incorporation—secure employment, family formation, the establishment of credit, capital accumulation, competency in English" (5) which will allow her to come into full cultural and legal citizenship. Not surprisingly, the washerwoman in the story remains a "marginal" character whom the Anglo-American manager and cook of the "zero zero" cafe crudely describes as "short," "bad news," "street," "round face," "burnt toast color," and "black hair that hangs like straight rope" (65). Given such racist synecdochic views of undocumented migrant border crossers as "otherness machines" (Suleri 1989, 105), blocked from ever attaining full cultural and legal citizenship, why did the Central American washerwoman migrate to the U.S.-Mexico Borderlands? What narrative strategies did Viramontes use to represent the washerwoman's shifting and shifty migrations?

The first question is easier to answer than the second. While the majority of undocumented border crossers from Mexico migrate to the U.S. for economic reasons and a desire for economic mobility (often doing so for generations and thus seeing migration as family history[7]), migration from Central America as Leo Chávez emphasizes is a "relatively recent" phenomenon and is closely related to the Reagan-Bush war machine in support of "contras" in El Salvador, Nicaragua, and Guatemala. Viramontes's washerwoman thus migrates from her unnamed *pueblo* in Central America to escape from the political strife waged on Amerindians and mestizos/as, and more phantasmatically (given her post-traumatic stress syndrome) to continue searching among the unhomely for her five-year-old son:

> These four walls are no longer my house, the earth beneath it, no longer my home. Weeds have replaced all good crops. The irrigation ditches are clodded with bodies. No matter where we turn . . . we try to live . . . under the rule of men who rape women, then rip their bellies. . . . [T]hese men are babes farted out from the Devil's ass. (71)

Displaced by civil war, defeated by debilitating patriarchy (what Viramontes straightforwardly sees as "the rule of men" who have been "farted out from the Devil's ass"), and deranged by the murder of her son, the washerwoman migrates, in stages, to the U.S. extended *frontera* to flee from guerrilla activity. Once across the U.S.-Mexico border, she will work "illegally" at jobs that, for the most part, legal Americans disdain: "The machines, their speed and dust," she says, "make me ill. But I can clean. I clean toilets, dump trash cans, sweep. Disinfect the sinks" (72).

These multiple border crossing rites of passage, however, are not narrated in a traditional realist fashion. Rather the totality of Viramontes's story is scrambled in three separate sections, with each narrating the washerwoman's and the two undocumented Mexican children's shifting, interstitial experiences. The decentered aesthetic structure of Viramontes's text has elicited fanciful attention from literary critics. Sonia Saldívar-Hull, for example, suggests that Viramontes "crafts a fractured narrative to reflect the disorientation that the immigrant workers feel when they are subjected to life in a country that controls their labor but does not value their existence as human beings" (223). Likewise, Barbara Harlow elegantly argues that the political content of Viramontes's text merges (in strong dialectical fashion) with the tale's aesthetic form: "Much as these refugees transgress national boundaries, victims of political persecution who by their very international mobility challenge the ideology of national borders and its agenda of depoliticization in the interest of hegemony, so too the story refuses to respect the boundaries and conventions of literary critical time and space and their disciplining of plot genre" (152). In other words, for Saldívar-Hull and Harlow, Viramontes's experimental "The Cariboo Cafe" challenges both the arbitrariness of the nation-state's borders and the institutionalized mobilizations of literary conventions such as plot structure, space and time.

In contrast, Debra Castillo presents a diametrically opposed reading of Viramontes's experimental narrative (a narrative bereft of traditional transitions between sections and without markers indicating breaks and shifts in time and place). For Castillo, "The story presents itself as a colonialist narrative that is obviously, unambiguously, at least doubly (more accurately, multiply) voiced" (79). The challenge of "The Cariboo Cafe" for Viramontes as Castillo sees it is rather complicated; on the one hand, Viramontes must "giv[e] voice to the silent refugees, as well as to such minimally articulate people as the other urban dwellers" (80). On the other hand, Viramontes must further "balance" in the story "two very different constituencies: those who read, who speak, who enjoy freedom of speech, and those who are illiterate, who dare not speak" (80). In short, donning the class-conditioned 1960s perspective of a Sartrean reader, Castillo criticizes Viramontes's experimental aesthetics as follows: "the Sartrean critic might legitimately address the propriety of [Viramontes] writing a complex work in English about (and partially for) people who cannot speak, much less read, even the simplest phrase" (80).

Although it isn't entirely clear why Castillo questions the propriety of Viramontes's experimental aesthetic practices (perhaps she desires an orderly realist tale done in the various appropriate *telenovela* [Televisa] Spanish languages and styles), she does succeed in posing one of the text's central questions: "Who speaks . . . in this story? What is his/her language, sex, age . . . ?" (80) Provocatively, Castillo answers that "readers alternately [speak]. . . . We, who speak for them, who give voice to their unexpressed longings, their inchoate thoughts, their emptied selves" (81) necessarily speak from the dominant perspective of what Castillo (quoting de Certeau) calls "a primarily repressive" and "learned culture" (81). Castillo then suggests that our reading practices are mobilizations, for "Ours is a police action: separating out the voices, bringing law and order, soliciting confessions" (82).

Given the transgressive border crossings (both aesthetic and political) in "The Cariboo Cafe," isn't there a possibility for a non-instrumentalized view of the nature of Chicana resistance literature, reading practices, cultural critique, and philosophical and literary production? Might not Theodor Adorno's aesthetic philosophy of "non-identity" and "negative dialectics" be more appropriate than a 1960s Sartrean philosophy of engagement? "Adorno," Fredric Jameson writes, "was surely not the philosopher of the thirties . . . ; nor the philosopher of the fifties; nor even the thinker of the sixties—those are called Sartre and Marcuse; and I have said that . . . his old-fashioned dialectical discourse was incompatible with the seventies. But there is some chance that he may turn out to have been the analyst of our own [postmodernist] period" (1991, 5).

Perhaps there should be nothing scandalous in reading Viramontes's autonomous "The Cariboo Cafe" in Adornean aesthetic and political fashion for both writers shared more than their local addresses in Los Angeles. (Theodor Adorno, we might recall, like scores of Central Europe's most celebrated intellectuals such as Brecht and Horkheimer, sought political sanctuary in Los Angeles during the fascist terror). As Mike Davis notes, it was in "Los Angeles where Adorno and Horkheimer accumulated their 'data,' [and] the exiles . . . allowed their image of first sight to become its own myth: Los Angeles as the crystal ball of capitalism's future" (48). Though ignorant, of course, of what Davis calls "the peculiar historical dialectic that had shaped Southern California" (48), Adorno's rousing critique of Hollywood, of North American consumerism, the "Culture Industry" and so on clearly allies him with Viramontes's cultural critique where she vividly represents in "The Cariboo Cafe" the harrowing underside of the glossy Los Angeles postmodernist culture. In other words, for Viramontes the postmodern such as it is in Los Angeles—a "crystal ball of capitalism's future"—is a fully planned strategy, the social and psychic effects of which are historical dislocation and cultural relocation.

Further, Adorno's conception of the experimental work of art as something radically different might allow us to view Viramontes's narrative practices in terms other than Sartre's philosophy of engagement. To begin with, the work of art, as Adorno stressed in his *Aesthetic Theory*, "obeys immanent laws which are related to those that prevail in the society outside. Social forces of production and social relations of production return in the very form of the work" (qtd. in Jameson 1991, 187). Briefly stated, for Adorno, "the most authentic works of art are those that give themselves over to their historical raw materials without reservation and without any pretense to floating above it somewhere" (qtd. in Jameson 187). Foreshadowing Fredric Jameson's well-known notion of the "political unconscious," Adorno theorizes the work of art as "unconsciously the historiography of [its] own epoch." Thus envisaged, "The Cariboo Cafe" offers not Sartrean engagement (or even Brechtean praxis), for "praxis," Adorno writes, "does not lie in the effects of the work of art, but rather encapsulated in its truth content" (qtd. in Jameson 188). This then means that the complex aesthetic experiences contained in Viramontes's text always lead us back to history—to the history of undocumented migrant border crossing, to the history of postmodernism in Los Angeles, and to the constellation of class contradictions from which the work of art emerged. It would therefore be justifiable to say that if Viramontes's text leads us back to history, this means in Adornean terms that for works of art the "non-identical" is society.

The vital relationship of Viramontes's experimental U.S.-Mexico border aesthetics to her political thinking about culture in Los Angeles involves more than the content of her thinking about undocumented migrant border crossers, but (as Saldívar-Hull and Harlow suggested above) it significantly also lies in the fractured form of the story itself. The phantasmatic story of the Central American washerwoman's crossing multiple borders to search for her son leads her to come into contact with two Mexican undocumented children, Sonya and Macky, thus establishing a new transnational family.[8] Multiple Border zones thus diametrically criss-cross in the tale, allowing us to begin a complicated re-reading involving historical, political, and cultural simultaneity in the Américas.

If disjunctive separation, liminality, and reaggregation are the central cultural rituals performed in "The Cariboo Cafe," then it is hardly surprising that rhetorically and tropologically Viramontes relies heavily on prolepsis (flashforwards) and analepsis (flashbacks) to structure the tale. It begins *in medias res* with a near-omniscient narrator situating readers about the realities of migrant border crossing separation: "They arrived in the secrecy of the night, as displaced people often do, stopping over for a week, a month, eventually staying a lifetime" (61). From the very beginning, liminality is thematized not as a temporary condition of the displaced but as a permanent social reality.

Given that both of Macky and Sonya's parents work (undocumented workers are rarely on welfare[9]), the children are instructed to follow three simple rules in their urban galaxy: "never talk to strangers"; avoid what their father calls the "polie," for the police he warned them "was La Migra in disguise"; and keep your key with you at all times—the four walls of the apartment were the only protection against the street" (61). But Sonya, the young *indocumentada*, loses her apartment key. Unable to find their way to a baby-sitter's house, Sonya and Macky begin their harrowing encounter and orbit with the unhomely's urban galaxy, what Viramontes lyrically describes as "a maze of alleys and dead ends, the long, abandoned warehouses shadowing any light[;] . . . boarded up boxcars [and] rows of rusted rails" (63). Looming across the shadowed barrioscape, "like a beacon light," the children see the double zero cafe sign.

Without any traditional transitional markers, section two tells in a working-class (albeit bigoted) vernacular of an Anglo-American cook the lurid story of the unhomely's experiences at the Cariboo cafe, especially those of the washerwoman, Sonya, and Macky. Situated in the midst of garment warehouse factories where many of the undocumented border crossers labor, the zero zero cafe functions as sanctuary where many of the workers can get away from the mean streets of Los Angeles. On an initial reading, however, it isn't at all clear how the brave, new transnational family of the washerwoman, Sonya, and Macky met, or why they are now together at the cafe. All we know is reflected through the crude nativist testimonial narrative of the manager: "I'm standing behind the counter staring at the short woman. Already I know that she's bad news because she looks street to me. . . . Funny thing, but I didn't see the two kids 'til I got to the booth. All of a sudden I see the big eyes looking over the table's edge at me. It shook me up" (65–66).

Viramontes, of course, shakes things up a bit more by describing another of the unhomely's predicament of culture, Paulie's overdose at the cafe: he "O.D.'s" in the cafe's "crapper; vomit and shit are all over . . . the fuckin' walls" (67). Not surprisingly, the immense U.S.-Mexico border machine shifts into high gear: "Cops," the cook says, are "looking up my ass for stash" (67), and later on "green vans roll up across the street . . . I see all these illegals running out of the factory to hide . . . three of them run[ning] into the Cariboo" (67). Given the events of the day, section two ends with the cook telling us: "I was all confused" (68).

Having moved through separation and liminality in the first sections, Viramontes's denouement (section three) provides readers with what we may call a phantasmatic folktale of (deadly) reincorporation. Slipping in and out of stream of consciousness shell shock, the narrator explains: "For you see, they took Geraldo. By mistake, of course. It was my fault. I shouldn't have sent him out to fetch me a mango" (68). Eventually the washerwoman fills in the gaps to the earlier sections: when Geraldo failed to return, she is hurled into the spatiality-time of night, for "the darkness becomes a serpent tongue, swallowing us whole. It is the night of La Llorona" (68).

With this reference to La Llorona, readers familiar with one of Greater Mexico's most powerful folktales can begin to make sense of the tale's freakish entanglements. Though the washerwoman tells us in her own fraught logic how she "finds" Geraldo in Macky ("I jumped the curb, dashed out into the street . . . [,] [and] grab[bed] him because the earth is crumbling beneath us" [72]), readers acquainted with the legend of La Llorona know even as they don't know that the wailing washerwoman will surely find her children at the Cariboo cafe. Thus using and revising La Llorona legend to produce cultural simultaneity in the Américas (uniting Central American and North American Borderland history), Viramontes allows us also to hear the deep stirrings of the unhomely wailing woman. Capturing something that the inhabitants of the Américas share—a legacy of 500 years of Spanish conquest and resistance—the legend of La Llorona creeps into the zero zero place of Chicana/o Fiction: "The cook huddles behind the counter, frightened, trembling . . . and she begins screaming enough for all the women of murdered children, screaming, pleading for help" (74). But why is the cook so frightened? Why do males "tremble" in La Llorona's presence?

As anthropologist José E. Limón suggests, La Llorona, "the legendary female figure" that dominates the cultures of Greater Mexico, is a "distinct relative of the Medea story and . . . a syncretism of European and indigenous cultural forms" (1986, 59). While various interpreters of La Llorona have not accorded her a resistive, utopian, and liminal history (viewing her as a passive and ahistorical creature), Limón systematically takes us through what he calls the "genesis and formal definition of this legend," arguing that "La Llorona as a symbol . . . speaks to the course of Greater Mexican history and does so for women in particular" (74).

As far back as Fray Bernardino de Sahagún's chronicle of the New World, *Historia general de las cosas de Nueva España,* La Llorona, Limón writes, "appeared in the night crying out for her dead children" (68). Let me hasten to add that another Spanish chronicler, the foot soldier Bernal Díaz del Castillo, likewise collected and recorded indigenous Amerindians' narrations telling her tale of loss: "At night, in the wind, a woman's voice was heard. 'Oh my children, we are now lost!' Sometimes she said, 'Oh my children, where shall I take you?' " (Castillo qtd. in Castañeda Shular 1972, 98) In later colonial versions (as reported by Frances Toor), the legend incorporates other forms: a lower-class woman is betrayed by an upper-class lover who has fathered her children. She then kills the children and walks crying in the night.[10]

In Limón's utopian reading, La Llorona's "insane infanticide" can be said to be a "temporary insanity *produced historically by those who socially dominate*" (his emphasis; 86). Seen in this historical light, that Viramontes's wailing washerwoman grieves and searches for her lost child (finding Geraldo in her kidnapping of Macky) is not something that is produced inherently but rather produced by the history which begins with Cortés's conquest of Mexico. If all children of loss in the Américas (produced by Euro-imperialism) are also children of need, they are also what Limón sees as potentially "grieving, haunting mothers reaching for their children *across fluid boundaries*" (my emphasis; 87). We may now be in a better position to understand why the manager of the Cariboo Cafe is so frightened by the washerwoman/La Llorona. In her act of infanticide, La Llorona "symbolically destroys" what Limón argues is "the familial basis for patriarchy" (76).

Nevertheless, in Viramontes's hands, La Llorona/washerwoman offers her readers a startling paradox: while her folktale in section three always suggests the symbolic destruction of patriarchy—represented in the washerwoman's fight to the death with the police at the story's end—there also remains the washerwoman's utopian desire to fulfill the last stage of her territorial rite of passage, namely, her dream of incorporation, or better yet, what Debra Castillo calls the washerwoman's "project[ed] . . . dream of re-incorporation, of returning her newborn/reborn infant to her womb" (91). Viramontes writes:

> She wants to conceal him in her body again, return him to her belly so that they will not castrate him and hang his small, blue penis on her door, not crush his face so that he is unrecognizable, not bury him among the heaps of bones, of ears, and teeth, and jaws, because no one, but she, cared to know that he cried. For years he cried and she could hear him day and night. (74)

Like Rigoberta Menchú, the exiled Quiché Indian who was awarded the Nobel Peace Prize in 1992, the washerwoman (even in her abject solitude) finally becomes an eloquent symbol for indigenous peoples and victims of government repression on both sides of the South-North border. When confronted in the zero zero cafe by the Los Angeles Police, "with their guns taut and cold like steel erections" (74), the washerwoman resists them to the bitter end rather than unplug her dream of an incorporated, transnational family: "I will fight you all because you're all farted out of the Devil's ass . . . and then I hear something crunching like broken glass against my forehead and I am blinded by the liquid darkness" (75).

Our subject here has been the intercultural and transnational experiences of migrant border crossers from the South into the North represented as a complex series of traversing and mixing, syncretizing and hybridizing. As both Leo Chávez and Helena Viramontes emphasize in their narratives, migrant U.S.-Mexico Border crossing cultures are often formed under powerful economic and political constraints. Like the Black British diasporic cultures of Stuart Hall and Paul Gilroy, U.S.-Mexico Border cultures share what James Clifford has described as a "two-sidedness, expressing a deep dystopic/utopian tension. They are constituted by displacement (under varying degrees of coercion, often extreme" (1992, 6). And as Chávez and Viramontes adamantly argue, migrant U.S.-Mexico Border crossing cultures represent alternative interpretive communities where folkloric and postnational experimental narratives can be enunciated. What is finally remarkable about Viramontes's "The Cariboo Cafe" is that borders—as Barbara Harlow writes—"become bonds among peoples, rather than the articulation of national differences and the basis for exclusion by the collaboration of the United States and [Central American] regimes" (152). In other words, in Viramontes's "zero zero place" a worlding of world historical events has erupted—from Cortés's Euro-imperialism to Reagan-Bush's wars in Central America—and their coming to the Américas was embodied in the haunting, resisting figure of La Llorona. This is a story to pass on, to pass through the fluid borders of world literature.

No less important than the complex migrant border crossings explored in Viramontes's "The Cariboo Cafe" are the post-national dramatizations of Hollywood (The American Dream) as another multicultural carceral neighborhood, complete with high-tech Los Angeles Police Department mobilizations, INS raids of undocumented workers in downtown sweat shops, drive-by gang shootings, skinhead street hate-crimes against gays and people of color, chauvinist "Seal the Border" campaigns, and soap-opera fabulations rendered in John Rechy's *The Miraculous Day of Amalia Gómez.* If Mike Davis is right about Los Angeles's culture being conjured as either "sunshine" or "*noir,*"[11] or as being historically structured around rich and privileged boosters such as the Owen and Chandler families to the current Republican mayoral administration contrasted against the radicalized debunkers from Carey McWilliams to the recent multiracial and trans-class participants of the Rodney King uprising, how can we begin to situate critical work about Los Angeles by Chicanos/as such as Viramontes, Rechy, Los Illegals, and (Kid) Frost? Do their cultural critiques add nuances to the revival of Southern California *noir*—a revival Davis notes has been made up of "writers and directors [who] revitalized the anti-myth of [Los Angeles] and elaborated it fictionally into a new comprehensive history"? (44)

My view is that analyzing Rechy's Hollywood fiction within Davis's megaspatial view of Los Angeles as it "actually exists" (23) can help us begin to understand how Los Angeles—once "the most *Waspish* of big cities in the 1960s" (104)—now contains more multicultural diversity than New York. If demographers are on target that Latinos/as now make up one-quarter of California's population, and the number is expected to grow from 5.8 million in 1985 to 15 million in 2020 (tripling in size), isn't it crucial for intellectuals to take seriously what Chicano/a writers are imaginatively saying about this exceptionally growing population?

Paradoxically, Rechy's cultural interventions—from his lyrical *City of Night* (1963), *Numbers* (1967), *This Day's Death* (1969), *The Vampires* (1971), or his controversial *The Sexual Outlaw* (1977) to his defiant Los Angeles fiction *Bodies and Souls* (1983) and *The Miraculous Day of Amalia Gómez* (1991)—have yet to be interpreted by his mainline or his subcultural critics as texts emerging from and responding to his Mexican-American background in El Paso, Texas, or as cultural critiques inspired by and contained by his extended Southern California Borderlands consciousness. The reasons for this are complex. On the one hand, as Juan Bruce-Novoa emphasizes, Chicano proto-nationalist critics have largely ignored Rechy because he is an openly gay Chicano writer;[12] on the other hand, even as savvy a cultural critic as Jonathan Dollimore, who, though superb in exploring Rechy's "rages against oppression" and his attributing "extraordinary political potential to transgressive sexuality" (1991, 214), seems hardly to have a clue about the author's U.S.-Mexico Borderlands past. Don't these biographical referents inform Rechy's insistence in seeing himself as a "defiant outlaw"?

As early as 1958, in his autoenthographic essay, "El Paso del Norte" (first published in *The Evergreen Review*), Rechy has been representing what many Chicano/a lesbian and gay writers such as Gloria Anzaldúa, Cherríe Moraga, and Arturo Islas call their "bridge" consciousness, a consciousness which allows them to explore and exploit their double-vision as both participant and observer, and as displaced subjects across multiple discourses.[13] Not surprisingly, for Rechy, his "U.S.-Mexico border consciousness" includes both El Paso and Ciudad Juárez for "the Rio Grande, which in the Southwest is a river only part of the time and usually just a strait of sand along the banks . . . divides the United States from Mexico. Only geographically" (qtd. in Castañeda Shular et al. 158). Culturally, of course, "The Mexican people of El Paso," he continues, "more than half the population . . . are all and always completely Mexican. . . . They speak only Spanish to each other and when they say Capital they mean Mexico DF" (158).

Written partly as a U.S.-Mexico Borderland hipster's response to a xenophobic and historically misguided 1950s *Time* magazine feature story describing Mexican *braceros* as a "line of desperate ants" and "of mustached, strawhatted men, braceros invading America," Rechy's "El Paso del Norte" can be read as a powerful cultural intervention, questioning the dominant Anglocentric's view of Mexican migration to the United States. Looming behind Rechy's U.S.-Mexico Borderlands raging, moreover, is his vivid memory as a teenager in El Paso of seeing a dead *bracero* in the Rio Grande, a haunting memory that, as we will see below, he returns to years later *in The Miraculous Day of Amalia Gómez:* "I remember a dead *bracero* near the bank of the Rio Grande, face down drowned in the shallow water, the water around him red, red, red. Officially he had drowned and was found, of course, by the Border Patrol. And his wife will go on thinking forever he made it with a beautiful blonde Georgia woman—loaded with toothpaste" (1991, 160).

Satirizing the nativist Anglocentric view that said "well, isn't it natural, those wetbacks wanting to come into America?—Christ, they heard about sweet-tasting toothpaste" (159), Rechy, in a perversely tragic-comic narrative, rebuts the magazine's conventional "push-pull" view of Mexican migration. In this view, Mexican workers are pushed from their country by their destitute living conditions and lured into the United States by the promise of the American Dream, what the mainline magazine article called "sweet-tasting toothpaste." But the reality of Mexican migration as

Rechy suggests and legal scholar Gerald López argues is something very different, for the United States "actively promoted migration" through its legal treaty with Mexico (the 1942 Bracero program) "encourag[ing] Mexican workers to fill lower echelon jobs in the country" (1981, 642).

Although Rechy is generally silent on the politics of sexual transgression in "El Paso del Norte," his "defiant outlaw" sensibility can already be seen in strong formation, created from both the hypocrisy of the Catholic Church (priests are depicted in "bright drag") and the terms of his racial oppression in the white supremacist state of Texas:

> In Balmorhea, with its giant outdoor swimming pool (where that summer the two blond tigers and I went swimming, climbed over the wall and into the rancid-looking night water) there were signs in the two-bit restaurant, in Balmorhea-town then, that said *We do not serve mexicans, niggers or dogs.* That night we went to the hick movie, and the man taking the tickets said, You boys be sure and sit on the right side, the left is for spiks. So I said I was on the wrong side and walked out. (His emphasis, 161)

Later that evening at the home of his friend's aunt, Rechy again encounters nativist white supremacy in Texas head on: "the aunt waited until the Mexican servant walked out and then said, miserably, Ah jaist caint even eat when they are around. And because earlier had made me feel suddenly a Crusader and it was easy now, I walked out of the diningroom and said well I shouldnt be here to louse up your dinner lady" (161).

Rechy's U.S.-Mexico "crusader" radicalism, what Dollimore mistakenly calls a radicalism "trapped in romantic/tragic self-glorification inseparable from naive fantasies of revolutionary omnipotence" (214) (especially in *The Sexual Outlaw*), of course, has to be contextualized and read against the author's earlier battles against bigotry in Texas. Lest I overemphasize Rechy as seeing the culture of the U.S.-Mexico Borderlands in exclusively binary ethno-racial terms, "El Paso del Norte," like *The Miraculous Day of Amalia Gómez,* mocks the family romance of Mexican-American patriarchal culture, especially in his description of how Mexican-American men "really love Mothers" while most "Americans dont." "I dont," Rechy writes, "have a single American acquaintance whose mother faints everytime he comes home and again when he leaves. Mine does. The Mexican mother-love has nothing to do with sex, either. . . . [C]an you imagine making it with your mother if she wears a Black Shawl, and, even if she doesn't, if she acts all the time like she is wearing one?" (163).

Some thirty years later, Rechy returns to this U.S.-Mexico border sensibility to tell the engrossing tale of a Mexican-American mother and maid who migrates in stages from El Paso, Texas, to Southern California, and who, one day, finds herself in the midst of a "decaying" neighborhood off Hollywood Boulevard, gazing out of her barred bungalow window, and seeing "a large silver cross in the sky" (1991, 3).

While Rechy's post-national fable, *The Miraculous Day of Amalia Gómez,* tells us much about the incredulous terror and the remarkable hope among the unhomely migrant border-crossers in Los Angeles, and he imaginatively thematizes what Homi K. Bhabha sees as the post-contemporary "terrains of world literature"—transnational histories of migrants, the colonized and so on—mainline reviewers and critics by and large refused to acknowledge (much less attempt to comprehend) the centrality of this emergent U.S.-Mexico Borderlands fable-making, dismissing it as unremarkable and as invisible as the scores of Amalia Gómezes in our midst. For instance, in a *New York Times Book Review* article, Karen Brailsford wrote that Rechy's novel was "not so remarkable" after all, and claimed that his narrative about Amalia Gómez contained "an unbelievable denouement that's as awkward as the novel's title" (1992, 16). Capable of such parochial and chauvinist remarks one wonders what the reviewer would say about magic realist fables such as Gabriel García Márquez's "Balthazar's Marvelous Afternoon," or how she would explain former Los Angeles Police Department's Chief Daryl F. Gates's brutal militarization of Los Angeles that, in turn, led to the thousand fires of rage that consumed Los Angeles on April 30–May 2, 1992! At any rate, the highbrow reviewer completely misses the fundamental irony of Rechy's *fabula:* that the Hollywood of movie fantasy has become the Hollywood of all-too-real violence and racial unrest.

My own view is that Rechy's socially symbolic *fabula* about how Amalia Gómez and her three children survive and die in Southern California can metaphorically convey a great deal about whom we actually live with in our communities, and how our communities either fail to live up to, or have fallen short of, what used to be called the American Dream. As the novel begins, Amalia Gómez works hard as a housekeeper in Los Angeles, for "she liked being in pretty apartments in California, and she was paid in cash, without deductions, and that was essential to her day-to-day survival" (42). And she works equally hard as a mother, a cook, a part-time seamstress, and an avid consumer of mass-mediated culture in the extended U.S.-Mexico *Frontera,* especially the romantic Pedro Infante *mariachi* songs on the radio, Hollywood movies such as *The Song of Bernadette,* starring a smashing Jennifer Jones, and the *telenovela* (soap opera) passions on local Spanish TV. Rechy's hypothesis about his Mexican-American heroine is that the invisible Amalia Gómezes in our communities are essential to the economy, indispensable to middle-class everyday life, and even intimately connected to the American ideological consensus. Paraphrasing Ralph Ellison, Rechy pointedly asks: Who knows but that, on lower frequencies, Amalia Gómez and her children speak for us?[14]

If readers—like the *New York Times Book Review* writer—think that Rechy is exaggerating all that confronts Amalia Gómez and her family, let's take a brief view of Amalia Gómez's life as represented through Rechy's displaced fable. Born in El Paso, Texas, trained by her mother to believe in the mysteries of the Blessed Holy Mary, raped at fourteen, and later forced by her parents to marry the young man, Salvador, who assaulted her, and then after another brutally unlucky marriage to a U.S. Latino Vietnam veteran, Gabriel, Amalia Gómez migrates from West Texas to Hollywood hoping to fashion a better life. Like thousands upon thousands of other "solas" with children, she works her way to Southern California cleaning houses and sewing in downtown sweat shop garment factories, surviving on the day laborer's jobs that pervade what economists call the secondary labor market. When she still cannot make do with these jobs, Amalia "occasionally took in piecework to do at home. Her children would help. Gloria would adjust the expensive labels, Juan would then glue them on the garment, and Amalia would sew them" (56).

Throughout her migrations in California, Amalia flees barrio after barrio in East Los Angeles "to keep [Juan] and Gloria from drugs and killings and gangs that had taken Manny" (8). When she finally settles in a rented stucco bungalow in Hollywood, Amalia finds herself in the midst of "cars left mounted on bricks [and] everywhere . . . iron bars on windows" (6). More by force of habit than anything else, Amalia Gómez, a "legal" Mexican-American, keeps afloat by hustling as a housekeeper but more often than not she feels "some anxiety about her regular workdays because "new illegals"—Guatemalans, Salvadorans, Nicaraguans without papers—were willing to work for hardly anything at all" (6).

Twice divorced from U.S. Latino men with good Catholic names—Salvador and Gabriel (who are hardly saviors)—Amalia is more and more consumed by her desire to find a hard-working and nonabusive husband and a father for her three children, a task made all the more problematic by her propensity for U.S. Latino "men with holy names." Though mostly stuck in her work as a maid, her everyday experiences often take her beyond the edge: "Worries about Juan!—handsomer each day and each day more secretive, no longer a happy young man, but a moody one. . . . And who wouldn't worry about Gloria? So very pretty, and wearing more and more make-up" (8). Manny, "her beloved firstborn," hangs himself at the Los Angeles County jail.

As if her everyday family life were not remarkable enough, Amalia's best friends, Milagro (Miracle) and Rosario (Rosary), each find themselves consumed by the Southern California Borderland's culture: Milagro, who can't cope with her incorrigible gang-banging son, survives by spinning "accounts of the romantic travails in her serials" (77) to her factory coworkers, and Rosario becomes entangled in the murder of an INS agent who has violently abused scores of undocumented workers:

"Jorge killed a *migra*. . . . [He] paid a *coyote* to bring his youngest son with his wife across the border and they had to take the dangerous route across the hill because the migra now . . . flood the border with lights. . . . Hundreds of people from San Diego drive there each night to add their car lights, shout their support, while desperate people are netted rushing the border—and now snipers wait for them. Yesterday a twelve-year-old boy was killed" (176). In scenes such as these, Rechy dramatizes how the government's militarized "low-intensity conflict" doctrine (Dunn 1996) spills over into the lives of everyday people.

There are, however, some rewarding—albeit fleeting—moments in Rechy's fable, for "Amalia liked watching the 'parades'" (44) which took place "every Saturday night on Whittier Boulevard [where] the young men of East Los Angeles would display their 'customized' cars, growling machines worked on constantly, often prized '50s 'Cheveez'; cars silver-sprinkled red, green, blue; purple birds or fiery flames painted on the sides and hoods" (43–44). If barrio "parades" of lowriders suggest how Chicanos/as (situated between a rock and Gates's Operation Hammer) elaborate a sense of what Tomás Ybarra-Frausto sees as "a communal consciousness of allegiance" (qtd. in Castañeda Shular 1972, 152–153), and the special *cholo/la* (youth culture) calligraphy and their inner-city cross-word graffiti are examples of an alternative expressive culture,[15] Rechy reminds us how these cultural counter-practices are routinely smashed by search-and-destroy missions of the Los Angeles Police Department:

> Police helicopters hovered over the unofficial parade. Suddenly light poured down in a white pit. Squad cars rushed to block the side exits off the boulevards. Police motorcycles tangled in and out of lanes. Young Mexicans rushed out of cars. Some were pushed to the ground. There were screams. The police pulled out their guns. (44)

Scenes such as these are hardly unbelievable, for as Mike Davis has painstakingly recorded in *City of Quartz,* the Los Angeles Police Department (especially under former Chief Gates [RIP]) saturated the barrios of South Central and East Los Angeles with Vietnam-inspired offensives such as Operation Hammer, "jacking up thousands of local teenagers at random like so many surprised peasants" (268).

If Rechy rages against the militarization of Southern California through Reagan, Gates, and Bush's doctrine of low-intensity conflict, his fable is deeply rooted in actual search-and-destroy missions such as the astonishing one that took place in August 1988: "Only a short time ago," Rechy writes, "cops had raided and smashed houses randomly in south central Los Angeles, and amid the wreckage they created in search of unfound drugs in the neighborhood suddenly under double siege, they had spray-painted their own *placas,* their own insignia: Los Angeles Police Rule" (114). Thus, under the "double siege" of the gang crack cocaine blizzard and the out-of-control Los Angeles Police Department, Amalia and her children become prisoners in their own backyards.

These scenes in Rechy's post-national Chicano fable, of course, only begin to tell the lurid story of the "programmed urban hardening" in Southern California. Mike Davis's summary survey in *City of Quartz* of Gates's sustained raids on non-Anglos in Los Angeles must be congratulated for documenting what all too-many Chicanos/as and African Americans have known for years: that the mostly whitemale police are liars and extreme fabulators. For years and years, Chief Gates with his Gang Related Active Trafficker Suppression program (GRATS) conducted regular sweeps through barrio neighborhoods to curtail intracommunity gang fighting. Often on the perverse evidence of high-five greetings, or colors of clothing, for instance, Davis records how on one particular mission, Gates's "Blue Machine" "mounted nine sweeps, impounded five hundred cars and nearly fifteen hundred arrests" (272). Moreover, Rechy's brief allusion to the Los Angeles Police Department as gang-bangers (with their own graffiti *placas*) is scandalously elaborated on by *The Los Angeles Times:*

> Residents . . . said they were punched and kicked by officers during what those arrested called an "orgy of violence." Residents reported the officers spraypainted walls with slogans, such as 'LAPD Rules!'
>
> . . .
>
> Damages to the apartments was so extensive that the Red Cross offered disaster assistance and temporary shelter to displaced residents—a service normally provided in the wake of major fires, floods, earthquakes or other natural disasters. (Qtd. in Davis 276)

If, for residents of the Dalton Street apartments, Gates's raid, as Davis writes, was "not quite the My Lai of the war against the underclass," it nevertheless signaled "a grim portent of what 'unleashing the police' really means" (275).

If Los Angeles *"es una fabula"* (is a fable)—as a mural in Rechy's novel graphically puts it—then the author's hyperbolic representation of everyday life becomes more comprehensible, for a fable, as defined by the *OED*, is a narrative "relating to supernatural or extraordinary persons or an incident." In Rechy's fable, (complete with animal characters—*coyotes* and *pollos*—and a scathing moral) the supernatural high-tech LAPD's raids are therefore the stuff of postmodern myth, and its "extraordinary" leader's actions are patently unreal, for who would actually believe that ex-Chief Gates could tacitly approve of his officers forcing the thirty-two prisoners of the Dalton Street raid "to whistle the theme of the 1960s Andy Grifith [*sic*] TV show . . . while they ran a gauntlet of cops beating them with fists and long steel flashlights" (276)?

In any case, when the dust finally settled, the police, Davis notes, "found neither wanted gang members nor weapons, just a small quantity of dope belonging to two non-resident teenagers" (276). What for years Gates and his predecessors William Parker and Ed Davis had been able to deny—that reports of police violence on non-Anglo citizens were pure fables—the 1988 Dalton Street raid confirmed the cops as gang-bangers in their own right, and demonstrated that non-Anglo citizens (such as Rechy's characters, Amalia, Gloria, Juan, and Manny) are often forced to live under de facto apartheid in Los Angeles.[16]

At a time when many middle-class intellectuals of color are tacitly supporting the exterminist rhetoric and practices of the LAPD (calling for more draconian curfews and police raids on their multicultural communities) it is heartening to see that "defiant outlaws" such as Rechy are refusing to join in the grim foreboding. If Hollywood—the terrain of the American Dream—no longer affords the democratic design for freedom, and Los Angeles has itself become an armed fortress, what Davis calls a "fragmented, paranoid spatiality" (238), Rechy maintains throughout his text that power is fundamentally a mechanism of State, Church, patriarchy, class, and compulsory heterosexual interests whose work is to silence and oppress dominated groups.

While Rechy is justly famous for narrating how gay males confront and transgress the laws of society ("The law tells us we're criminals so we've become defiant outlaws. . . . Religion insists we're sinners and so we've become soulful sensualists"), in *The Miraculous Day of Amalia Gómez* he insists on throwing considerable light on how Chicanas/os are "discriminated against more than most people imagine" (1992, 28). Not surprisingly, he is "outraged by any kind of injustice, whether against homosexuals, against women, against Chicanos, against Jews, against whomever" (28). This then leads him to be especially critical of patriarchal and homophobic practices within traditional Chicano male culture.

Although Amalia is fascinated by "the murals scattered about the area . . . paintings as colorful as those on calendars, sprawled on whole walls" (45), she is haunted and befuddled by one depicting a "tall, plumed Aztec [holding] a bleeding, dying city boy in his arms" (56). Though Rechy's heroine intuitively grasps in the murals of East Los Angeles what art historians Shifra Goldman and Tomás Ybarra-Frausto call "a high idealism" (1991, 83) emphasizing the "community oriented" and "public art forms" of the 1960s, she nevertheless is troubled by the exclusion of women as historical agents.

To understand how this 1960s Chicano liberatory idealism was at best limited, we only would have to recall that many Chicano murals of the period reflected the male utopian youth, "carnalismo" philosophy contained in manifesto's such as "El Plan espiritual de Aztlán" (The Spiritual Plan of Aztlán). Separatist in nature, the manifesto adopted at the 1969 Chicano Youth Conference in Denver advocated the re-claiming of Mexican lands lost to U.S. empire (the Southwest), a privileging of Amerindian (male) consciousness, and an emphasis on Chicano studies and multiculturalism in higher education. Proclaiming that Aztlán "belongs to those that plant the seeds, waters the fields, and gather the crops, and not to foreign Europeans" (qtd. in Castañeda Shular et. al. 84), the "spiritual plan" grounded us not only in the social philosophy of the Chicano Movement, but also, as Goldman and Ybarra-Frausto emphasize, in "the themes of Chicano art and letters" (1991, 84).

Rechy's cultural critique of murals celebrating Aztlán and Mexican patriarchy (taken together with his raging against gang violence and the

"Blue Machine" killings by the Los Angeles Police Department) is therefore illuminating:

> A muscular Aztec prince, amber-gold-faced, in lordly feathers, stood with others as proud as he. They gazed toward the distance. Behind them on a hill pale armed men mounted on horses watched them. At the opposite end of the painting brown-faced, Muslim-clothed men stared into a bright horizon. They were the ones whom the Aztecs were facing defiantly. (45)

If "Aztlán es una fabula," it is partly so because its Chicano youth philosophy glorifying Aztec warriors while at the same time excluding women is itself a deceiving story. That the mural depicts "The *conquistadores* [who] are about to subdue the Indians with weapons," and juxtaposes that image with the Mexican "*revolucionarios* who will triumph and bring about Aztlán, our promised land of justice" (45), Rechy presents Amalia's respectful but critical response to the work: "There were no women. Where were they? Had they survived?" (45).

Fundamentally, Rechy's fable focuses on that May day when she apparently sees "a large silver cross in the sky" (3). But is this sign the miraculous sign that she's been praying for—the miracle that will solve her family's tragic life in Hollywood? Will Guadalupe, the Holy Mother, appear before "a twice-divorced woman with grown, rebellious children . . . ?" (3)

As Amalia moves into the day—full of flashbacks to her turbulent childhood in El Paso and flashforwards to police and gangs rampaging through her urban galaxy in Hollywood—she is encouraged by two other hopeful signs: a rose bush with new blossoms "had managed to squeeze through a large crack in the cement" (109) and two hilarious "espiritualistas/shamans" assure her that "something big" will occur in her tragic life. Thus encouraged, Amalia represses all that has been happening around her, for amid what must appear as nirvana for the white youth culture in Los Angeles, Manny, Juan, and Gloria remain trapped in either low-wage employment, County jail, or succumb to the underground economy, where over one thousand Latino and African-American gangs license what Mike Davis calls "crack-dealing franchises."[17]

While Amalia stands at the corner of Sunset and Western rereading Manny's last letter from County jail, she decides to walk over to a neighborhood health *clinica* where she can have her "blood pressure checked" (137). Afterwards, she walks briskly down Sunset Avenue, deciding to visit Milagro's housing project near MacArthur Park, where she hopes to get Rosario's address.

Once on the mean streets of what Rechy describes as "the other Hollywood," Amalia encounters a series of eccentric characters—some comical and others emotionally challenged. The first deals with Amalia's attempt to confess to a priest her previous night's peccadillos with a Salvadoran man named Angel who, not surprisingly, is not very angelic at all—a *coyote* who sexually humiliates and abuses her. As the scene unravels, Rechy wryly shows how the Roman Catholic priest ends up masturbating to Amalia's sexually explicit confession:

> I cannot grant you absolution unless—Did he touch you?
> . . . Yes, she whispered.
> When he had already removed your intimate clothes?
> Yes. . . .
> How many times did he touch you?
> Twice . . . Three times. . . .
> Between your legs . . . ? With his tongue? (156–157)

In a Michel Foucault–like precision, Rechy examines how the Roman Catholic Church uses and abuses the confession ritual for having the subject of sex spoken about. Rechy here is in complete agreement with Foucault's thesis that "the Christian pastoral always presented [sex] as the disquieting enigma: not a thing which stubbornly shows itself, but one which always hides, the insidious presence. . . . It is . . . a fable that is indispensable to the endlessly proliferating economy of the discourses of sex. What is peculiar to modern societies . . . is not that they consigned sex to a shadow existence, but that they dedicated themselves to speaking of it *ad infinitum,* while exploiting it as *the* secret" (his emphasis 1980, 35).

Thus blocked from appeasing her religious guilt, she decides to visit two "*espiritualistas*" (spiritualists) for what she hopes will be a "*limpieza*" —a folk ritual cleansing. But here again Amalia is victimized by her own folk, leading readers to see how Rechy's heroine (who as we've seen is devoutly if not conventionally Catholic) can only find salvation from within the confines of the church. As Rechy noted in one of his numerous interviews, "For [Amalia] to liberate herself . . . she has to do it through the very instrument that oppresses her" (1992, 28). In other words, as we will see below in the novel's ending, after being rejected by the male-centered Roman Catholic Church—with its entrenchment of machismo and its oppressive attitudes toward divorce and abortion—Amalia has very little recourse but to believe that she cannot help her children to survive unless she has the power to hope.

While Amalia "search[es] for signs of resurrection everywhere" (191), she only finds a bench on Sunset Boulevard "with a picture of Marilyn Monroe" (199). She then steps into a bus that takes her to a "huge shopping complex at the edge of Beverly Hills" (199). Just as the washerwoman's ending in Viramontes's "The Cariboo Cafe," Amalia's ending is as bloodied and nightmarish as the Los Angeles *noir* Davis explicated in *City of Quartz.* Amalia ends up in a panopticon-like mall with video cameras and "sturdy middle-aged" men tracking her every step in "stores with names that were impressive, no matter what they meant" (200).

Amid all these extraordinarily well-policed stores, Rechy's heroine is taken hostage by a man "with crazed eyes" (204). Pressing a gun against her temple, the man is surrounded by scores of uniformed men crushed by their cars and motorcycles. When she finally "thrust[s] the man away from her" (205), bullets rip and are hurled out of their chambers at an astonishing pace. Like Viramontes's lyrical denouement in "The Cariboo Cafe," Rechy poetically writes that "Amalia saw a beautiful spatter of blue shards that glinted and gleamed like shooting stars as they fell on splotches of red like huge blossoms, red roses" (205).

In Amalia's wanderings through Hollywood and Beverly Hills, we also see the principle of simultaneous events happening to a variety of ethno-racial groups in different parts of the same place, thus thematizing the national mappings that theorists of the novel insist is so key to the genre of the novel. All of Rechy's *The Miraculous Day of Amalia Gómez* seemingly is narrated as a blistering urban realism. But Amalia's circulation around the apparatuses of late capitalist Hollywood signals a different signifying system. Amalia's wanderings around Hollywood, like Joyce's Bloom's wanderings around the colonial capital of Dublin in *Ulysses,* maps a different mass-mediated imperialist capital of culture. Wandering Amalia sees all the glossy advertising hoardings at the tony mall and she meets not only her working-class peers on the streets but also encounters the intense police and INS presence as well. Amalia's *flânerie,* in this light, signals her attempt to escape from the panoptic surveillance of the border-patrolled state.

On another level, Rechy—a brilliant student trained in the critical philosophy of the New School for Social Research in New York—has his fable escape the textuality of engaged "realist" art through its own splendid destruction of the "real." To pursue this negative dialectical reading, we must not only see the fastidious realism of Amalia's beatings, rapes, and humiliations but also understand how Amalia's oppressions and humilations serve as an analogy to the oppressed and misunderstood artist Rechy himself.

In other words, Amalia's life struggle and circulations in Hollywood concretize Rechy's critical philosophical views about the insurrectionary power thematized through the very form of his genre—the novel. When Amalia has a gun pointed at her head by the man with "crazed eyes," or earlier when Rosario informs Amalia that "For all the destitute people [in the U.S.-Mexico borderlands], it's like having a loaded gun held to your head" (77), we grasp Rechy's splendid allusion to Theodor Adorno's famous response in an essay entitled "Commitment" to the Sartrean "engaged literature" thesis: "It is not the office of art to spotlight alternatives, but to resist by its form alone the course of the world, which permanently puts a pistol to men's heads" (1982, 305). Rechy's New School for Social Science–inspired fable, we might say, does not so much destroy "realism" as attempt to destroy the destroyer's concept of positivism and realism. In so doing, Rechy explodes from within the form of the novel itself, and negates Hollywood realism. Rechy emphasizes this philosophical point in a *Diacritics* interview when he says: "In all my novels, I extend 'realism' into metaphor for deeper meaning. . . . In *The Miraculous Day of Amalia Gómez,* I extend the book into surrealism, and then fable" (1995, 119).

If intellectuals have dramatized a *noir* history of Los Angeles's past and future—which as Davis argues "actually has come to function as a surrogate public history" (44)—Rechy's grand achievement *The Miraculous Day of Amalia Gómez* captures, from the standpoint of a Chicana housekeeper, the image of the city proliferating in endless repressions in social space. While many post-contemporary urban theorists have facilely celebrated the postmodern spaces of the new urban "hypercrowd," they have also been what Davis calls "strangely silent about the militarization of city life so grimly visible at street level" (223). Rechy's Hollywood fable, together with Viramontes's "The Cariboo Cafe," thus openly challenge this silence by providing readers with their own Chicana/o *noir.*

It is, therefore, hardly surprising that Rechy's denouement takes place in a Beverly Hills tony mall, a mall full of unsubtle signs warning off the Amalia Gómezes of the world:

> Within a huge circular plastic column, an elevator rose. . . . Amalia stared up, at the arched ceiling of the mall. It had translucent brightness like that of an eternally perfect day. Over the railings on upper floors, shoppers peered down onto the spill of shops. For a moment, she felt dizzy, dazed. Then she saw a sturdy middle-aged man looking at her.
>
> . . .
>
> She hurried into a jewelry store. She was admiring a display of wedding rings when she noticed there was a guard there. . . . (201–202)

In scenes such as these, Rechy does not turn a blind eye—like many postmodernist architectural critics—to the obvious fact that tony malls such as the one Amalia finds herself in reinforce urban apartheid. Amalia Gómez, like other pariahs, however, reads all too clearly the meaning of such practices: "She stood in the middle of the mall, aware of herself in this glistening palace. So many people. . . . Did they see her? Yes, they saw a woman who looked out of place, tired, perspiring" (202).

Despite being forced to see herself as an "othering machine," despite her imprisonment as a maid in the secondary level job market, and despite her living in what once used to be the demi-paradise of Hollywood, Amalia survives her hostage-taking but not before seeing what Rechy lyrically and beautifully describes as "a dazzling white radiance enclosed in a gleam of blue and within it hovering on a gathering of red roses stood. The Blessed Mother with her arms outstretched to her" (206). In other words, Rechy, like Adorno before him, remains convinced that autonomous art contains a utopian moment that points toward a future sociocultural transformation.

The language here in Rechy's denouement is, of course, familiar to Chicanos/as: folkloric and religious. "The Blessed Mother" who appears to

Amalia is Guadalupe—the Mexican people's version of the Virgin Mary who, as Norma Alarcón suggests, "substituted for the Aztec goddess Tonantzin" (1989, 58). To argue over whether or not Rechy's denouement is "unbelievable" is downright silly, and misses the social message of the author's fable-making, for Guadalupe—as anthropologist Eric Wolf taught us—always represents in Mexican folktales: "Mother, food, hope, life; supernatural salvation from oppression" (1958, 38). Additionally, as Jeanette Rodriguez emphasizes, unlike "other Marian apparitions only Our Lady of Guadalupe comes, not to make a request, but make an offering, and stays. . . . And the people truly believe that she is alive and present for them" (1994, 128). Understandably, then, Roman Catholic oppression and supernatural liberation are from Rechy's standpoint not mutually contradictory but mutually reinforcing. Amalia Gómez suffers and is victimized by the Roman Catholic Church and in the process paradoxically becomes liberated through Guadalupe.

In the end, Amalia's constructive, if brief, insight of the convergence of ethno-race and oppression and ethno-race and homosexuality occurs as well in the author's phantasmatic denouement. While Amalia continually rationalizes (given Los Angeles's conscious policy of social disinvestment in its youth) that Juan has more than likely entered the crack cocaine underground economy in order to survive, at the novel's end, she admits to herself that something very different has happened, for Juan has, in fact, decided to make do by homosexual hustling with a young Salvadoran boy: "I sent away that boy Juan brought to live in the garage. I saw his sad young eyes. I knew what I was doing was cruel. But I also knew what was really involved between him and my son" (197).

Given that the complexities which arise at the intersection of ethnorace and sexuality which most U.S. Latinos/as simply repress, it is important to emphasize that Amalia is finally prepared to acknowledge a convergence of ethno-racial formation, homosexuality, and maybe even queer theory. All the more remarkable, perhaps, is that Rechy's attempt to show the literal alliance between Juan and his Salvadoran comrade occurs at the very historical moment in Los Angeles when the Salvadorans of Mara Salvatrucha (near MacArthur Park) were waging what Mike Davis describes as "a bloody war against the established power of the 18th Street Gang—the largest and fastest growing Chicano gang which threatens to become the Crips of East L.A." (316). What we therefore learn from John Rechy's displaced fable, *The Miraculous Day of Amalia Gómez,* among other things, is that a conventionally understood class liberation which ignores gender, sexuality and ethno-race will be disastrous.

If the culture of the extended U.S.-Mexico Borderlands and transnational migrant history are inextricably linked in Viramontes's "The Cariboo Cafe" and Rechy's *The Miraculous Day of Amalia Gómez*—grounding overtly global formulations of hybridity, syncretism, and the postcolonial condition—there are still other complex "soundings" of mass media texts critiquing and complicating the dominant culture's linear lines of immigration, the American *bildung*, ethno-race, and the nation.[18] I refer, of course, to the mass media *rolas* by U.S. Latino (punk) rockers and hip-hoppers such as Los Illegals and (Kid) Frost, among others.

In his justly famous "Cruising around the Historical Bloc," George Lipsitz argued that from the 1940s to the late 1980s "Chicano rock and roll music from Los Angeles transformed a specific ethnic culture rooted in common experiences into more than just a novelty to be appropriated by uncomprehending outsiders" (1990, 149). Drawing upon both "residual" and "emergent" elements in their barrios, mass cultural musicians and cultural activists from Ritchie Valens to Los Lobos "w[o]n some measure of participation," Lipsitz noted, "in the creation and dissemination of mass popular culture" (149).

The underground emergence of Los Illegals as a significant punk rock band, for example, provides us with still another remarkable illustration of the US-Mexico's *Frontera*'s persistent cultural clash of migrations, deportations, and INS raids. Mixing the shocking multiple realities of undocumented border crossers with New Wave/punk sensibilities, Los Illegals were one of the first Chicano bands to stand in between *Frontera* culture and mass culture, performing a frenzied and overwhelming electric-guitar music that seemed on the surface as if it were a CD recording played at quadro speed.[19] Willie Herrón claims that he started his punk band "to talk about the experience of being a *cholo*, a low rider, of being in gangs, all of it" (qtd. in Lipsitz 155). In their transnational anthem, "El Lay (L. A., the Law)"—from their *Internal Exile* (1983) album—co-written in vernacular Chicano Spanish by Herrón and po-mo artist Gronk, Los Illegals represent Los Angeles as it actually is for the millions of *indocumentados/as* and unhomely:

Parado en la esquina
Sin rumbo sin fin
Estoy in El Lay,
No tengo donde ir
Un hombre se acercó,
Mi nombre preguntó
Al no saber su lengua,
Con el me llevó
Esto es el precio
Que pagamos
Cuando llegamos
A este lado?
Jalamos y pagamos impuestos
Migra llega y nos da unos fregasos
El Lay, L. A.
El Lay, L. A.
El Lay, L. A.

El Lay, L. A.
El Lay, L. A.
En un camión,
Sin vuelta me pusieron
Por lavar platos en El Lay me deportaban
Mirar por el cristal,
Sentí pertenecer
Un millión ilegales, no podemos fallar
Esto es el precio
Que pagamos
Cuando llegamos
A este lado¿
Y porque no—podemos quedar
Que Gronk, no borro la frontera¿
El Lay, L. A.
Manos fijadas,
Al fin en la frontera
Lo dije que quería,
Mejorar la vida
Familia sin futuro, falta de respeto
Adonde fue,
La libertad y justicia¿
(Qtd. in Loza 1993, 231–232)

(Standing on the corner / Got nowhere to go / I'm here in El Lay, Got no place to stay / A man came up to me / And he asked me my name / Couldn't speak his language so he took me away / Is this the price / You have to pay / When you come / To the USA? / We come to work, we pay our taxes / Migra comes and they kick us on our asses / El Lay L. A. / He threw me on the bus / That headed one way / I was being deported, for washing dishes in El Lay / Looking out the window, / I felt I belonged / A million illegals, we can't all be wrong / Is this the price / You have to pay / When you came / To the USA / I don't know why, we cannot stay / Didn't Gronk erase the border yesterday? / We ended at the border, / Hands above my head / I told him all I wanted, / Was a chance to get ahead / No future for my family, can't even get respect / What happened to the liberty / And the justice that we get?)

"The texture of 'El Lay,'" as Steven Loza writes, "is one of unifying forms." "The text," he continues, "conceived through jagged contours of metaphor, satire, and symbolic contradiction, unites itself stylistically with the dissonant harmonic framework and the abrasive, hard-driving rhythmic structure" (1993, 232). On a different register, presenting the traditional push-pull view of Mexican migration to the United States that we saw above in Rechy's "El Paso del Norte," "El Lay" sums up a complex view of U.S.-Mexico migrant border crossing in moral and historical terms, exhorting the listener to answer the following questions: Hasn't the United States government actively promoted Mexican migration since 1942 with the Bracero treaty? Haven't millions of undocumented laborers built up unreasonable expectations that their employment as dishwashers and their presence as taxpayers will continue? Should residency be the only route to legal and cultural citizenship? And what are the moral obligations of the destination country which arise from these dedicated workers' involvement in our communities?

By exposing the moral hypocrisy of Los Angeles—which hyped itself in the late 1980s as "A City for a Future"—Los Illegals produced a musical style of crisis emphasizing their defiant outlawed and "illegal" politics, for even the band's very nomenclature suggested the new face of U.S. Latino/a youth subculture in Southern California. Much as these young *indocumentados/as* themselves, the punk musical style in "El Lay" is angry, sharp, and loud: the Spanish vernacular lyrics are shouted by Herrón in an exaggerated voice, supported, and, on first listening, blasted away, by a barrage of over-amplified electric guitars and dizzying Afro-Cuban drumming. "El Lay," as music critic Iain Chambers might very well have put it, is a "rude blast" (1986, 172) directed against "the pretentious domain" of mainline pop music.

Moreover, Los Illegals' cryptic reference to "Gronk" and his "erasing the border yesterday" needs some elaboration, for "El Lay's" self-conscious and irreverent musical quotations and ironic poses (The Clash and Rock Against Racism) also offer listeners an ear-filled "presentation of actualities" of U.S.-Mexico migrant culture, deconstructing Herrón's and Gronk's earlier utopian attempts as members of the urban ASCO collective to "erase the border" in their urban performance art pieces. While Herrón and Gronk (together with video/photo artists Patssi Valdez, Marisela Norte, and Harry Gamboa, Jr.) were all *veteranos/as* of the "blow outs" at Garfield High School in the late 1960s and early 1970s, and though their ASCO performance art "happenings" such as their memorable "Walking Mural" (1972) in which the members gathered on Whittier Boulevard "intent on transforming muralism from a static to a performance medium" (1991, 124)—as Gamboa himself wrote—Los Illegals' self-conscious and playful riff also has a critical edge to it, warning against the postmodern collapsing of history into theoretical wish-fulfillment.

In brief, the musical "chaos" that Los Illegals performed in their transnational anthem "El Lay" forces a stark reappraisal of pop music's own politics and cultural soundings. As Chambers said of British punk in general, "El Lay" disrupts the distinction "between mainstream and margin, between avant-garde and popular, and between music and 'noise'" (172). We might also note that Los Illegals set aside a monocultural and monological sound and replaced it with a multiply layered, bilingual sounding of their own.

If 1980s British punk offered Los Illegals and other Chicano bands such as The Brat and Los Cruzados a more democratic and dialogic vernacular form for exploring and transforming the everyday life border deportations of the *indocumentado/a* in Los Angeles, 1990s gangster rap, hip hop, and Black British jungle (often in wild combinations) are the privileged expressive forms appropriated in (Kid) Frost's *East Side Story* (1992). From the very title of his work, (Kid) Frost (Arturo Molina) attempts to talk back to Hollywood's mass cultural constructions in which U.S. Latino/a gang life is used to libidinally entertain audiences. The intertextual reference here, of course, is to Hollywood's *West Side Story,* a film depicting gang life in the 1950s. As Martín Sánchez Jankowski says of Hollywood's representation of gangs, films such as *West Side Story, Fort Apache/The Bronx,* and *Colors* "depict gangs as composed of poor or working-class males who lack the skills and desire to be upwardly mobile and productive citizens. Essentially, they are not only "losers" but "losers" who are also primitive and brutally violent. Their values are painted as both anathema to the values held by the society as a whole and a threat to them (society's values)" (1991, 300).

Moderating his earlier romanticized and misogynist rap persona in his debut *hispanic causing panic* (1990), and deconstructing attempts to essentialize rap as the "authentic" black noise of the U.S. Northeastern 'hood, (Kid) Frost responds to Hollywood's typically colonial symbology in hybrid rap songs such as "I Got Pulled Over," "Penitentiary," and "Chaos on the Streets of East Los Angeles," all of which feature sirens, gunshots, and racist LAPD radio conversations among whitemale cops as "backdrops" to the out-of-control gangbanging and drive-by shootings in East Los Angeles. While occasionally presenting uncritical hymns of Chicano proto-nationalism in songs with titles such as "Another Firme Rola (Bad Cause I'm Brown)," and offering his listeners lurid fantasies of teenage *cholo* male violence (he recalls how at fourteen he relished his first .32 Beretta handgun), (Kid) Frost resists outright mistranslation and appropriation by the hegemonic mass media in songs such as "Mi Vida Loca," "Home Boyz," and "These Stories Have to Be Told." Here in this interlingual hip hop song, the Chicano rapper begins to rehearse for us a variety of mestizo/a identifications and social relations not yet permissible in the urban U.S.-Mexico *frontera:*

> *. . . and this little cholito who got himself in a mess*
> *his plaqueazo was güero,*
> *and everywhere daddy went*
> *the batos quieren pedo.*
> *So as the tiempo went on,*
> *the hatred for güero just got more strong.*
> *So güero started packing the filero*
> *cuz the guys in the barrio, the block, the ghetoo*
> *were all trying to get him.*

He wanted out, to forget his past,
but they won't let him.
So he moved out of state and changed his name . . .
I know this story's getting kinda old,
but it has to be told. (1992)

Although Mike Davis might justly see (Kid) Frost's interventions as merely another Hollywood attempt "to mime Los Angeles's barrios and ghettoes for every last lurid image of self-destruction and community holocaust" (87), I prefer historian George Lipsitz's apt observations in "Crusing around the Historical Bloc" that when Los Angeles's expressive culture's forms (gangster rap, hip hop, *caló*, reggae) rub together they are not concessions to the pressures and demands of Anglocentric Hollywood but attempts to use vernacular forms most likely to appeal to masses of hip hop audiences across the Américas. Likewise, I am persuaded by historian Robin D. G. Kelley's graceful insights in *Race Rebels* (1994) that West Coast hip hop, in many ways, anticipated and prophesied the 1992 trans-class upheaval in Los Angeles. Kelley's provocative reading of gangster rap overlaps with John Rechy's riffs on Hollywood in *The Miraculous Day of Amalia Gómez* (as we saw above), for both cultural critics thematize everyday events in the extended *Frontera* of Southern California as grounded in the "rap sheets" of their male protagonists.

Thus envisaged, West Coast gangster rap, in Kelley's words, opens "a window into, and a critique of, the criminalization" (1994, 187) of youths of color. Moreover, (Kid) Frost's hip hop songs, like Ice T's songs, take on in their form and content what Kelley describes as "a sort of street ethnography of racist institutions and racial practices" (190). Heard and read collectively, Chicano/a punk, *conjunto*, polka, *technobanda*, and hip hop songs speak to what social theorists call the "deindustrialization" of North America. Paraphrasing Marx, we might rightly conclude in listening to Los Illegals, Los Tigres del Norte (see Introduction[1]) and (Kid) Frost, among others, that young documented and undocumented men and women make their own history but not under circumstances of their own choosing.

(Kid) Frost's excursions, moreover, into a material hybrid reggae/hip hop/*caló* sound as in "Home Boyz," or a phat jazz *mestizaje* as in "La Raza" pushes the logic of his project to its anti-essentialist conclusions by fusing local soundings with pop forms rooted in the borders and diasporas of the Américas. Frost's "La Raza," for example, thematizes collective memory in its lyrics and sounding samples (from El Chicano's classic "Viva Tirado") to construct what on the surface appears to be a Chicano protonationalism for the *fin de siglo*. Nevertheless, in the act of declaring himself "brown and proud," he consciously echoes James Brown's 1968 song, "I'm Black and I'm Proud," thus grounding an inter-cultural mass-mediated alliance with the African American community. Frost then brings the soundings full circle by using a vocal style innovated by the OG hip-hopper, Ice T, paying tribute to the cut and mixings established within the Southern California hip hop tradition. One last comment is in order here to emphasize the complexities of (Kid) Frost's "La Raza." In sampling El Chicano's wonderful "Viva Tirado," arguably one of the most famous "authentic" Chicano soundings of the Chicano Youth Power social movement, he acknowledges that "Viva Tirado" was first written and performed by the African American jazz composer Gerald Wilson. "Music and its rituals," as Paul Gilroy writes in *The Black Atlantic,* "can [therefore] be used to create a model whereby identity can be understood neither as fixed essence nor as a vague and utterly contingent construction . . . " (1993, 102). Thus envisaged, (Kid) Frost's Southern California *frontera* identification remains the outcome of what Gilroy calls "practical activity: language, gesture, bodily significations, desires" (102). "[T]hese significations," Gilroy continues, "are condensed in musical performance by acting on the body through the specific mechanisms of identification and recognition that are produced in the intimate inter-action of performer and crowd" (102).

This examination of U.S.-Mexico border culture—from Helena Viramontes, John Rechy, and Los Illegals to (Kid) Frost—shows something of the richness of cultural critique in and around (trans)national identity and demonstrates also the dimensions of an emergent Chicano/a oppositional practice. The cultural forms examined above—the short story, the fable, punk and hip hop music—are simultaneously sites of ethno-race, class, gender, sexuality, and trans-national identity. Further, I think it bears some repeating that these sites are not interchangeable. As Viramontes, Rechy, Los Illegals, and (Kid) Frost demonstrate again and again in their works, cultural forms can no longer be exclusively located within the border-patrolled boundaries of the nation-state. Chicano/a America therefore defines itself as a central part of an extended *Frontera.* Its cultures draw revitalization through a "re-Hispanization" of migratory populations from Mexico and Central America.

Fundamentally, as the texts by Viramontes, Rechy, Los Illegals, and (Kid) Frost suggest, the cultures and politics (Central and North American) of the extended Borderlands have become the very material for hybrid imaginative processes which are redefining what it means to be a Chicano/a and U.S. Latino/a. As Juan Flores and George Yúdice emphasize, "The fact is that [U.S.] Latinos, that very heterogeneous medley of races and nationalities, are different from both the older and the new ethnicities" (1993, 199); moreover, U.S. Latinos/as constitute a new powerful and demographically rich social movement. Thus envisaged, *la Frontera* of the U.S. and Mexico may very well turn out to be another alternative to what Paul Gilroy described as "the different varieties of absolutism which would confine culture in 'racial,' ethnic, or national essences" (1991b, 155). U.S.-Mexico Border culture is always already localized and global, and this is why our monocultural national categories are not the most sensible structures for understanding these emergent expressive cultural practices.

POSTCRIPT

> A firestorm of rage and destruction is consuming Los Angeles' inner city, but Downtown itself is an eerily quiet ghost town. . . . Thanks to riot television coverage, hundreds of thousands of white Southern Californians are visiting Southcentral L.A. for the first time in their lives. . . . Because of television's monomanaical insistence on "black rage," most will also miss the significance of the participation of thousands of poor Latinos in what may be modern America's first multi-ethnic riot.
>
> —Mike Davis, "The L.A. Inferno" (1992, 59)

Will the politics of backlash and the Reagan-Bush-Clinton's "low-intensity conflict doctrine" (Dunn 1996) target new and old U.S. Latino/a ethno-racial populations in California? Will an ugly and chauvinistic "Light Up the Border" campaign and nativist Proposition 187s continue to go unchecked, like a weed, along the U.S.-Mexico *Frontera*? Will California Sheriff deputies (who were caught on videotape in April 1, 1996) keep clubbing with their erect batons defenseless undocumented border-crossers like Alicia Sotero, Enrique Funes, and José Pedroza? Will our own home-grown *intifada* (intimated in Viramontes's, Rechy's, Los Illegal's, and [Kid] Frost's cultural work), as Mike Davis notes, "be fueled by a generation's collapsing hopes in the future"? (1992, 59)

NOTES

1. For more on Guillermo Gómez-Peña's career and performance border art, see Claire F. Fox's excellent essay, "The Portable Border: Site-Specificity, Art, and the US-Mexico Frontier," *Social Text* 41 (Winter 1994): 61–82.

2. In *Border Writing: The Multidimensional Text* (Minneapolis: University of Minnesota Press, 1991), Emily Hicks supplements Gómez-Peña's use of Deleuze and Guattari's desiring machine to explore postmodernism.

3. Nancy Fraser's term, "juridical-administrative-state apparatus," of course, echoes Louis Althusser's phrase "ideological state apparatus," in "Ideology and Ideological State Apparatuses: Notes towards an Investigation." In general Fraser's JAT can be understood as a subclass of an Althusserian Institutional State Apparatus (ISA), and this is how I am using it in this chapter.

4. For more on this cultural and legal re-definition of citizenship, see Renato Rosaldo's "Cultural Citizenship: Attempting to Enfranchise Latinos," *La Nueva Visión*, Stanford Center for Chicano Research, no. 1/2 (Summer 1992): 7. Rosaldo uses cultural citizenship "both in the legal sense (one either does or does not have a document) and also in the familiar sense of the spectrum from full citizenship to second-class citizenship" (7); he uses the term cultural "to emphasize the local people's own descriptions of what goes into being fully enfranchised" (7). Also relevant here is Gerald P. López's "The Work We Know So Little About," *Stanford Law Review*, 42/1 (1989): 1–13.

5. Even at the mass-mediated level, the national press rarely mentions Latinos/as when discussing ethno-race relations and urban problems. As Gerald P. López writes, "when people visualize the goings-on in this country they most often don't even seem to see the 25 million or so Latinos who live here." Thus, it is hardly surprising, López notes, that "we Latinos haven't made it onto some list of nationally prominent folks—in this case, it's '*The Newsweek* 100' of cultural elite. . . . Having no Latinos on the *News-*

week list might not get under our skin were it not so utterly familiar." See López's "My Turn," in *Newsweek*, November 2, 1992: 12.

6. According to Debra Castillo, "What tends to drop out of sight . . . is . . . the *Carib*, the indigenous element that waits, another hidden layer of writing on the scratched surface of the palimpsest, the unrecognized other half of the backdrop against which the transients shuffle, and suffer, and die. What remains undefined is the nameless act of violence that has suppressed the *Carib*, as well as the outline of the form the history of its repression might take" (81). See Castillo's splendid *Talking Back: Towards a Latin American Feminist Criticism* (Ithaca, N.Y.: Cornell University Press, 1992).

7. In 1942, the United States government negotiated a treaty with Mexico popularly known as the Bracero Program which provided the destination country with the use of Mexicans as temporary workers. When the treaty expired in 1964, generations of Mexicans had "legally" migrated to the United States.

8. As Leo Chávez suggests, "While migrants may not sever family ties, those ties are stretched across time, space, and national boundaries" (119). See Chávez's *Shadowed Lives: Undocumented Immigrants in American Society* (New York: Harcourt Brace Jovanovich, 1992).

9. According to legal scholar Gerald López, "Data strongly suggest that only one to four percent of undocumented Mexicans take advantage of public services such as welfare, unemployment benefits, food stamps, AFDC benefits and the like; that eight to ten percent pay Social Security and income taxes; that the majority do not file for income tax refunds; that all contribute to sales taxes; and that at least some contribute to property taxes" (636). See López's superb monograph, "Undocumented Mexican Migration: In Search of a Just Immigration Law and Policy," *UCLA Law Review* 28/4 (April 1981): 616–714.

10. Frances Toor, *A Treasury of Mexican Folkways* (New York: Bonanza Books, 1985), 532.

11. According to Mike Davis, *noir* as a genre refers to the Southern California writers and film directors—from James Cain to the rap group NWA—who "repainted the image of Los Angeles as a deracinated urban hell" (37). See Davis's *City of Quartz: Excavating the Future in Los Angeles* (London: Verso, 1990).

12. See Juan Bruce-Novoa's "The Space of Chicano Literature Update: 1978," in *Retrospace: Collected Essays on Chicano Literature* (Houston: Arte Público Press, 1990): 93–113. See also B. Satterfield's "John Rechy's Tormented World," *Southwest Review* 67 (Winter 1982): 78–85, and Didier Jaén's "John Rechy," in *Dictionary of Literary Biography*, vol. 122: *Chicano Writers*, Second Series, ed. Francisco Lomelí and Carl Shirley (Detroit: Gale Research, 1992), 212–219.

13. For more on the U.S.-Mexico Borderland's "bridge" consciousness, see *This Bridge Called My Back: Writings by Radical Women of Color*, ed. Cherríe Moraga and Gloria Anzaldúa (New York: Kitchen Table Press, 1983). According to Norma Alarcón, "The writer in *Bridge* was aware of the displacement of her subjectivity across a multiplicity of discourses: feminist/lesbian, nationalist, racial, and socioeconomic. The peculiarity of her displacement implied a multiplicity of positions from which she was driven to grasp or understand herself and her relations with the real" (28). See Alarcón's incisive "The Theoretical Subject(s) of *This Bridge Called My Back* and Anglo-American Feminism," in *Criticism in the Borderlands: Studies in Chicano Literature, Culture, and Ideology*, ed. Héctor Calderón and José David Saldívar (Durham, N.C.: Duke University Press, 1991), 28–39.

14. See Ralph Ellison's *Invisible Man* (New York: Random House, 1982), 439. Early in the novel, John Rechy writes: "They just don't see us, Amalia knew" (67).

15. See Brenda Bright's "The Meaning of Roles and the Role of Showing: Houston's Low Riders," unpublished ms.

16. For more on Daryl F. Gates's use and abuse of the Los Angeles Police Department, see Mike Rothmiller's and Ivan Goldman's *L.A. Secret Police: Inside the LAPD Elite Spy Network* (New York: Pocket Books, 1992). "Unbeknownst to both friends and

enemies of the LAPD," the authors write, "[Gates's secret unit, OCID,] maintained secret, Stalinesque dossiers" (9) on the shakers and movers of Southern California. This unit's attitude towards non-Anglos, of course, was not a positive one, for "Racism was expected, part of the group's persona. Shrink from it and you were an odd duck, perhaps a pink one" (30).

17. Needless to say, Manny's "entrepreneurial spirit" as a "defiant individualist" in East Los Angeles/Hollywood has to be understood within Martín Sánchez Jankowski's reading of gang business in general: "[G]ang members' entrepreneurial spirit," he argues, "is both stimulated and reinforced by the desire to resist what they perceive to be their parents' resignation to poverty and failure" (108). See Martín Sánchez Jankowski's excellent *Islands in the Streets: Gangs and American Urban Society* (Berkeley: University of California Press, 1991).

18. I have profited from Ella Shohat's sharp critique of the rather loose and ahistorical use of the terms, "postcolonial," "hybridity," and "syncretism," in her "Notes on the Post-Colonial" in *Social Text* 31/32 (1992): 99–113. Also relevant here is James Clifford's call in "Borders and Diasporas" (unpublished manuscript, 1992) for "close attention to discrepant hybridities, with attention to the power relations producing various syncretic forms" (4).

19. Other Chicano New Wave and punk bands in Los Angeles include The Brat and The Plugz. As Steven Loza writes, "[The Brat's and The Plugz's] style has relied on the punk and new wave formations, although certain musical nuances and literary styles still relate to aspects of the historically unique Chicano/Mexican musical tradition" (110). See Steven Loza's exhaustive *Barrio Rhythm: Mexican American Music in Los Angeles* (Urbana: University of Illinois Press, 1993).

WORKS CITED

Adorno, Theodor. "Commitment." In *The Essential Frankfurt School Reader*, ed. Andrew Arato and Eike Gebhardt, 300–318. New York: Continuum, 1982.

Alarcón, Norma. "Traddutora, Traditora: A Paradigmatic Figure of Chicana Feminism." *Cultural Critique* 13 (Fall 1989): 57–87.

Benítez-Rojo, Antonio. *The Repeating Island: The Caribbean and the Postmodern Perspective*. Trans. James E. Maraniss. Durham, N.C.: Duke University Press, 1992.

Bhabha, Homi. "The World and the Home." *Social Text* 31/32 (1992): 141–153.

Brailsford, Karen. Review of John Rechy's *The Miraculous Day of Amalia Gómez*. *New York Times Book Review*, May 10, 1992.

Castañeda Shular, Antonia, Tomás Ybarra-Frausto, and Joseph Sommer, eds. *Literatura Chicana: Texto y contexto*. Englewood Cliffs, N.J.: Prentice-Hall, 1972.

Castillo, Debra. "An Interview with John Rechy." *Diacritics* 25, no 1 (Spring 1995): 113–125.

——. *Talking Back: Towards a Latin American Feminist Criticism*. Ithaca, N.Y.: Cornell University Press, 1992.

Chambers, Iain. *Popular Culture: The Metropolitan Experience*. London: Methuen, 1986.

Chávez, Leo. *Shadowed Lives: Undocumented Immigrants in American Society*. New York: Harcourt Brace Jovanovich, 1992.

Clifford, James. *Person and Myth: Maurice Leenhardt in the Melanesian World*. Durham, N.C.: Duke University Press, 1992.

Davis, Mike. *City of Quartz: Excavating the Future in Los Angeles*. London: Verso, 1990.

——. "The L.A. Inferno." *Socialist Review* 1/2 (1992): 57–80.

Deleuze, Gilles, and Félix Guattari. *Anti-Oedipus: Capitalism and Schizophrenia*. Trans. Robert Hurley, Mark Seem, and Helen R. Lane. New York: Viking Press, 1977.

Dollimore, Jonathan. *Sexual Dissidence: Augustine to Wilde, Freud to Foucault*. Oxford: Clarendon Press, 1991.

Dunn, Timothy J. *The Militarization of the U.S.-Mexico Border, 1978–1992: Low-Intensity Conflict Doctrine Comes Home.* Austin: University of Texas, 1996.

Flores, Juan, and George Yúdice. "Living Borders / Buscando America: Languages of Latino Self-Formation." In *Divided Borders: Essays on Puerto Rican Identity,* ed. Juan Flores, 199–252. Houston: Arte Público Press, 1993.

Foucault, Michel. *The History of Sexuality.* Vol. 1: *An Introduction.* Trans. Robert Hurley. New York: Vintage Books.

Fraser, Nancy. *Unruly Practices: Power, Discourse, and Gender in Contemporary Social Theory.* Minneapolis: University of Minnesota Press, 1989.

Frost, Kid. *East Side Story.* Virgin Records, 1992.

Gamboa, Harry. "In the City of Angels, Chameleons, and Phantoms: Asco, a Case Study of Chicano Art in Urban Tones (or Asco Was a Four-Member Word)." In *Chicano Art, Resistance and Affirmation: An Interpretive Exhibition of the Chicano Art Movement, 1965–1985,* ed. Richard Griswold del Castillo, Teresa McKenna, and Yvonne Yarbro-Bejarano, 121–130. Los Angeles: Wright Art Gallery, 1991.

Gilroy, Paul. *The Black Atlantic: Modernity and Double Consciousness.* Cambridge: Harvard University Press, 1993.

———. *There Ain't No Black in the Union Jack: The Cultural Politics of Race and Nation.* Chicago: University of Chicago Press, 1991.

Goldman, Shifra, and Tomás Ybarra-Frausto. "The Political and Social Contexts of Chicago Art." In *Chicano Art, Resistance and Affirmation: An Interpretive Exhibition of the Chicano Art Movement, 1965–1985,* ed. Richard Griswold del Castillo, Teresa McKenna, and Yvonne Yarbro-Bejarano, 83–96. Los Angeles: Wright Art Gallery, 1991.

Gómez-Peña, Guillermo. "Border Culture: A Process of Negotiation toward Utopia." *La Línea Quebrada / The Broken Line* 1 (1986): 1–6.

Harlow, Barbara. "Sites of Struggle: Immigration, Deportation, and Prison." In *Criticism in the Borderlands: Studies in Chicano Literature, Culture, and Ideology,* ed. Héctor Calderón and José David Saldívar, 149–163. Durham, N.C.: Duke University Press, 1991.

Jameson, Fredric. *Postmodernism, or, The Logic of Late Capitalism.* Durham, N.C.: Duke University Press, 1991.

Kelley, Robin D. G. *Race Rebels: Culture, Politics, and the Black Working Class.* New York: Free Press, 1994.

Limón, José E. "La Llorona, the Third Legend of Greater Mexico: Cultural Symbols, Women, and the Political Unconscious." In *Renato Rosaldo Lecture Series Monograph* 2, ed. Ignacio M. García, 59–93. Tucson: University of Arizona, Department of Chicano Studies, 1986.

Lipsitz, George. *Time Passages: Collective Memory and American Popular Culture.* Minneapolis: University of Minnesota Press, 1990.

López, Gerald. "Undocumented Mexican Migration: In Search of a Just Immigration Law and Policy," *UCLA Law Review* 28, no. 4 (April 1981): 616–714.

Los Illegals. "El Lay." *Internal Exiles* (A & M Records, 1983).

Loza, Steven. *Barrio Rhythm: Mexican American Music in Los Angeles* (Urbana: University of Illinois Press, 1993.

Pérez-Firmat, Gustavo. *Literature and Liminality: Festive Readings in the Hispanic Tradition.* Durham, N.C.: Duke University Press, 1986.

Pratt, Mary Louise. *Imperial Eyes: Travel Writing and Transculturation.* London: Routledge, 1992.

Rechy, John. *The Miraculous Day of Amalia Gómez.* New York: Arcade/ Little, Brown, 1991.

———. "El Paso del Norte." In *Literatura Chicana: Texto y contexto,* ed. Antonia Castañeda Shular, Tomás Ybarra-Frausto, and Joseph Sommer, 158–164. Englewood Cliffs, N.J.: Prentice-Hall, 1972.

Rodriguez, Jeanette. *Our Lady of Guadalupe: Faith and Empowerment among Mexican-American Women.* Austin: University of Texas Press, 1994.
Saldívar-Hull, Sonia. "Feminism on the Border: From Gender Politics to Geopolitics." Ph.D. dissertation, University of Texas, 1990.
Sánchez Jankowski, Martín. *Islands in the Streets: Gangs and American Urban Society.* Berkeley: University of California Press, 1991.
Suleri, Sara. *Meatless Days.* Chicago: University of Chicago Press, 1989.
Turner, Victor. *The Ritual Process: Structure and Anti-Structure.* Chicago: Aldine, 1969.
Van Gennep, Arnold. *Rites of Passage.* Trans. Monika B. Vizedom and Gabrielle L. Caffee. Chicago: University of Chicago Press, 1960 [1909].
Viramontes, Helena María. "The Cariboo Café." In *The Moths and Other Stories.* Houston: Arte Público Press, 1985.
Wolf, Eric. "The Virgén de Guadalupe: A Mexican National Symbol." *Journal of American Folklore* 71 (1958): 34–39.

15 "HERE IS SOMETHING YOU CAN'T UNDERSTAND . . . ": CHICANO RAP AND THE CRITIQUE OF GLOBALIZATION

Pancho McFarland

> Truth sparks revolution and is therefore labeled violent.
> —*Psycho Realm, "Lost Cities" (1997)*

THE YEAR "Two G" is finally here and the consequences of the capitalist project of globalization are becoming apparent. Scholars and activists from all over the globe and throughout the political spectrum have spilled gallons of ink and killed hectares of trees in their attempts to understand (and, for some, to halt) the effects of late capitalism (neoliberalism) and its primary vehicle, globalization. Many, including this author, have turned their gaze southward to Chiapas or elsewhere in the "underdeveloped" world to analyze the structures, ideologies, and practices of the global free trade project sponsored by governments and multinational corporations in the North and their supranational institutions, e.g., the World Trade Organization, the World Bank, and the International Monetary Fund. Some have even turned their gaze inward and focused on "third world" populations in the United States[1] in order to better understand the devastating consequences of globalization and economic restructuring for the "social majorities"[2] of this world. With few exceptions their analyses have relied on traditional socioeconomic indicators, e.g., poverty rates, unemployment, housing, income, and wages.

Rarely do scholars analyze the theorizing of the social majorities. A brief look at grassroots struggles from environmental justice movements to indigenous and land struggles indicates that many of the seemingly most destitute among us are theorizing and practicing new ways of living while critiquing and resisting the intrusion of the global market into their homes and communities.[3] This essay analyzes one effort to survive in the "new world order." I read the lyrics and structures developed by the rap community in order to suggest an alternative route to understanding globalization and its impacts on the social majorities in the United States. Due to the vastness and heterogeneity of the rap/hip-hop community I will focus on a few relatively well-known Chicano rappers from Southern California. Before I turn to an analysis of the poetics of young, brown urban America, I discuss the context out of which Chicana/o youth have forged a culture and a critique.

THE MAKING OF THE WORLD IN CAPITALISM'S IMAGE

It seems to me that the single most important trend facing Chicanas and Chicanos today (not to mention the rest of the world's two-thirds majority) is the recent change in the form of capitalism from a nationalist-based, protectionist variety to a transnational capitalism. That is, prior to the 1970s, capitalist accumulation was primarily structured along nation-state lines with the bourgeoisie of each nation competing with one another for ever greater shares of labor, resources, means of production, and, of course, capital. Thus, conflict was centered between nations based on the national bourgeoisie's needs and desires for increasing accumulation. Today, more than ever before in history, national bourgeoisies are aligning themselves not against each other but against the rest of the world, disregarding nationalist ideals and practices which ultimately constrain their godlike attempts to make the world in capitalism's image. Barriers to free trade such as taxes, tariffs, import restrictions, and environmental regulations have, along with the Berlin Wall, been hacked away at and dissolved.[4] This neoliberal cooperation between elites (known as transnationalism) has further subjugated the world's poor, leading to exponential increases in the numbers of people living in poverty or extreme poverty.[5]

An important aspect of the globalization process that I should comment on here is the continued subordination of the South to the North. While national bourgeoisies in southern countries have embraced the free trade logic of globalization, they have done this as junior partners. They have been coerced and cajoled by international financial institutions such as the World Bank (WB) and the International Monetary Fund (IMF) to accept an economic strategy that includes austere public spending, lowering of trade barriers, privatization of industry, and changes to property laws and other codes that would allow for multinational control over ever greater portions of the country's land and human resources. The loss of indigenous land to multinational corporations and subsequent proletarianization of the indigenous and other peasantry, the dismantling of the social safety net (decreased welfare and other public spending), and increased unemployment in southern cities has led to the dislocation, disenfranchisement, and, ultimately, immigration to the North for millions of the world's poor.[6] As the next section of this essay illustrates, the fate of the poor, especially people of color, in both the North and the South is linked through globalization.

ECONOMIC RESTRUCTURING IN LATINA/O U.S.A.

In their important introduction to *In the Barrios: Latinos and the Underclass Debate,*[7] Moore and Pinderhughes define economic restructuring as "changes in the global economy that led to deindustrialization, loss and relocation of jobs and a decline in the number of middle-level jobs."[8] These changes have negatively impacted the experiences of Latinas/os in the United States. Furthermore, given that most people do not accept such changes in their livelihood without resistance, policing in our society has undergone a transformation that limits the effectiveness of rebellion. Policing agencies in urban areas and along the Mexico-U.S. border have become militarized and their role as enforcer of elite economic policy has been solidified while their stated goal, "to serve and protect," has devolved into a darkly ironic cliché.[9]

Most indicators reveal that the economic situation of Latinas/os has been steadily declining since the beginning of the globalization process in the 1970s.[10] For example, while Chicanos and Chicanas have high rates of labor force participation (LFPR) their "high levels of work effort . . . [do] not translate into high occupational or income achievement relative to other groups."[11] An important cause of low income for Chicanas/os is underemployment, which for Mexican-origin men was twice that of non-Hispanic white men in 1987.[12] Unemployment has, of course, also been a concern for the Latina/o community, whose rates of unemployment have historically been much higher than the rates for non-Hispanic whites.[13] Thus, Chicano earnings are well below those of non-Hispanic white men and Chicana earnings were lower than those of their non-Hispanic white counterparts.[14] Further illustration of this trend is provided by median family income, which for Chicanas/os was $23,240 versus $36,334 for non-Hispanic white families in 1992. Due to this low median family income "the 1990 U.S. census identified one in four Chicano families as poor, versus 9.5 percent of non-Hispanic white families"; in addition, one in three Chicana/o children and one in eight non-Hispanic white children lived in poverty in 1990.[15]

Especially troubling for the Chicana/o and greater Latina/o population in the United States is our relationship to the criminal justice system. Rates of incarceration, percentage of new admissions, percentage of new admissions for drug offenses, length of sentences, recidivism rates, juvenile detention rates, and many other indicators of criminal activity and contact with law enforcement agencies reveal that Latinas/os interact with the criminal justice system at levels disproportionate to their percentage of the United States population. The National Criminal Justice Commission (NCJC) reports that while the African American prison population far outnumbers that of non-Hispanic whites and Latinas/os, Latinas/os were the "fastest growing minority group in prison from 1980 to 1993."[16] If these trends continue unabated, 25 percent of "Hispanic" men between the ages of eighteen and thirty-four will be imprisoned by 2020, creating an overall "Hispanic" male prison population of 2.4 million.[17] Given new legislation, tougher sentencing, charging juveniles as adults, mandatory minimums, "three-strikes" laws, and drug policies, as well as the aforementioned economic trends, we can expect that without a revolutionary revisioning of criminal justice the NCJC projections for Latina/o incarceration in the coming decades will be met or even surpassed.

I contend, and it is a goal of this essay to argue, that the disproportionate number of negative interactions with the criminal justice system for Latinas/os and Chicanas/os, especially our youth, results directly from the consequences of globalization. The economic policy making of the transnational bourgeoisie has deftly used racial, ethnic, and gender ideology inherited from their colonial forefathers to divide and conquer the world's two-thirds majority. In order to deflect attention from the causes of increased poverty and marginalization due to globalization, the transnational bourgeoisie has utilized deeply entrenched racialized and gendered ideologies and the existing stratification based on them to drive deeper wedges between the working classes and between men and women. The result for workers and the poor in the United States has been increased racial stratification and animosity leading to xenophobia and racialized conflict.[18]

CHICANA/O YOUTH NARRATIVES OF THE CONSEQUENCES OF GLOBALIZATION

Gustavo Esteva and Madhu Prakash (1998), in their pathbreaking work *Grassroots Postmodernism,* focus our attention on the fact that while most people in the world toil under the yoke of globalization they have not given up hope and are resisting the dehumanizing affects of neoliberalism and struggling to advance alternatives to it. Stories from numerous places throughout the world suggest an emergent "grassroots postmodernism" through which the world's marginalized resist the logic, structures, and behaviors associated with globalization and the "new world order" and construct alternative institutions based on the cultural logic of their local traditions and customs. Esteva and Prakash contend that we must listen to these voices and engage in dialogue with them if we hope to stem the tidal wave of globalization and survive the coming decades of globalization. In agreeing with them I assert that the voices of Chicana/o youth present a particular, localized critique of globalization through the narration of their experiences in urban "America." Chicano rappers have taken the lead in presenting this critique to the rest of us through recorded stories (both "real" and "imagined") of inner-city life that if read carefully can contribute to our understanding of the effects of globalization, especially those concerned with violence, xenophobia, and economic powerlessness.

As a result of the rappers' synthesis and representation of the primary concerns of many Chicana/o and Latina/o youth, I want to suggest that these young Chicanos serve as an organic intellectual class for the young, brown, urban disenfranchised.[19] Chicano rappers represent the cares, concerns, desires, hopes, dreams, and problems of young inner-city Chicanas/os through their poetics rapped over the aggressive, transgressive rhythms conceived in the smoke-filled rooms[20] of recording studios and private dwellings of the musicians. The following is a discussion of a sample of this Chicana/o poetics.

"HERE IS SOMETHING YOU CAN'T UNDERSTAND / HOW I COULD JUST KILL A MAN"[21]: URBAN VIOLENCE AS A CONSEQUENCE OF GLOBALIZATION

Much of "America" consumes the world of gang-bangin' brown youth through media images and the endless refrain of the criminal justice system's discourse that we need more cops and prisons, more military technology and logic, to contain the threat posed by gangs. News stories, yellow television journalism, and the gang genre in film render the horrors of inner-city living, which has the propagandistic effect of creating an enemy, an Other, out of our youth of color. State and federal legislative bodies increasingly pass draconian legislation which disregards the human and civil rights of urban youth with the approval of members of middle-class "America," who lock themselves behind walled communities with neighborhood patrols and purchase the latest surveillance and deterrence equipment to protect themselves from the new "Brown Scourge."[22]

Of course, left out of this hyperreal depiction of the gang threat is the fact that most youth of color, including most inner-city Chicanas/os, are not members of a gang, nor do they participate in its violent subculture or in an analysis of globalization or economic restructuring. But propaganda is never intended to present the facts. The role of propaganda is to establish the legitimacy of those in power and their acts of violence (physical, economic, symbolic, or other); to illustrate the righteousness and benevolence of "our side" and the evil of the enemy.[23] So, it is left to the organic intellectuals, the urban poets, of the barrios to include an analysis of globalization and illegitimate violence on the part of the state in our imaginary of urban warfare.

> They keep order by making street corners gang borders / Beating down King and setting the theme for riot starters / Cop quarters can't maintain the disorder / So they call the National Guard to come strike harder / Rolling deep headed for Florence and Nor-

> mandy where all you see / Buildings on fire chaos on Roman streets / Hope is cheap sold by the local thief relief from the common grief / Served on a platter shatter your smallest dreams / Pig chiefs are referees on gladiator fields / We're too busy dodging the sword truth stays unrevealed / Sealed all filled in the federal cabinets / Classified order through chaos for world inhabitants / . . . / We go to the streets at night / And fight in the sick-ass side show of mine / We play the government role / And straight up fuckin' smoke the rival.[24]

The three Chicano members of Psycho Realm (Jacken, Duke, and B-Real) spit these words with vengeance on their second release, *A War Story* (2000). These Los Angeles youth claim the barrios of Pico-Union and the Rampart District as their 'hoods. Since their arrival onto the hip hop scene in 1997 with their self-titled debut, *The Psycho Realm*, they have focused their poetics on the violent environments found in the concrete jungles of Los Angeles. They pull no punches in making testaments to violence in the barrios and locating the cause of that violence in illegitimate state policies.

Their song "Order through Chaos" analyzes the multiethnic Los Angeles Rebellion that followed the 1991 verdict in the case of the police beating of Rodney King. The members of Psycho Realm locate the violence associated with the uprising as well as that of everyday violence in many L.A. barrios in the state strategies of containment of poor people of color. In stating "they keep order by making street corners gang borders" the authors offer a firsthand critique of the police practice of exacerbating neighborhood tensions.[25] They go on to state "we play the government role and straight up fuckin' smoke the rival." Psycho Realm presents a vivid critique of how the powerful use the divide-and-conquer strategy to undermine potential revolt by focusing people's angst on one another. The divide-and-conquer strategy has the added benefit of causing people to be "too busy dodging the sword" to see the "truth," thus maintaining the elite's claim to legitimate rule. Psycho Realm suggests that in busying themselves with fighting each other, many barrio residents remain uninformed of the true nature of their oppression at the hands of the state and the transnational bourgeoisie. In another song from the same album, "Enemy of the State," they rap even more strongly that

> We're killing family tragically / The enemy dividing those fighting against it / Weakening our infantry / We caught on to your big plan / Separate us into street gangs / Infiltrate the sets[26] put some battles in effect / To distract from your dirty outfit, yeah.[27]

Finally, they assert that the propagandistic function of the media furthers intra-ethnic violence and masks damaging state policies. From "Order through Chaos" they rap:

> Chaos serves as smoke repeated hoax to screen / We lose control confused in the midst of staged scenes / Media invented unrelented reports presented / Often enough to make us think our world's tormented / Sentenced by momentous news of feuds we side and choose / Use weapons and step in the trap we lose . . . / All because the broadcast flashed ghetto stars / How much television you watch you tube whores? . . . / Through TV set nonsense / We sit and fit as the face of violence[28]

In "Order through Chaos" the Psycho Realm reveal another common theme in Chicano rappers' analysis of urban violence: animosity toward and conflict with "the pig." Many barrio residents have had negative interactions with law enforcement agents including unwarranted stops, searches and seizures, harassment, "planting" of evidence, physical abuse, and even murder. Increasingly we hear reports of police officers stopping and harassing Latinas/os for infractions such as "driving while brown" and talking with friends. Repressive legislation and police policies have been used to deal with the young "Brown Scourge," including the proliferation of gang databases and a 1997 court order that placed a curfew on "members" of the 18th Street Gang in Los Angeles and made it illegal for more than two identified "gangmembers" to congregate together even though some of the supposed "gangmembers" were family members who lived in the same house. Such measures have promoted further animosity between Chicana/o youth and police officers. No one theme, save for perhaps songs dedicated to marijuana use, has been discussed in Chicano rap as much as young Chicanas/os' animosity toward "the pig."

> This pig harassed the whole neighborhood / Well this pig worked at the station / This pig he killed my homeboy / So the fuckin' pig went on vacation / This pig he is the chief / Got a brother pig, Captain O'Malley / He's got a son that's a pig too / He's collectin' payoffs from a dark alley . . . / An' it's about breakin' off sausage / Do ya feel sorry for the poor little swine? / Niggas wanna do him in the ass / Just ta pay his ass back / So they're standing in line / That fuckin' pig / Look what he got himself into / Now they're gonna make some pigs feet outta the little punk / Anybody like pork chops? / How 'bout a ham sandwich?

The song "Pigs" is off the 1991 album *Cypress Hill,* by the pioneering multiethnic rap group Cypress Hill. Cypress Hill's members include a Cuban, Sen Dog; a Chicano-Afro-Cuban, B-Real; and an Italian, DJ Muggs. While some might argue that their multiethnic makeup would disqualify them as Chicano rappers, I believe it appropriate to discuss Cypress Hill as organic intellectuals for the young, brown urban class and their lyrical analysis as rooted in a young, Chicana/o urban reality. The lyrics are penned mostly by B-Real, a Chicano from Los Angeles, with Sen Dog, a Cuban raised in Chicana/o Los Angeles, providing additional writing. They have consciously decided to rap about what they see and experience on Cypress Avenue (the street where Sen Dog lived), located in a Chicana/o barrio in the town of Southgate.

"Pigs" reflects two common themes associated with young Chicana/o barrio dwellers' understanding of the police: (1) police harassment of Chicana/o barrios and (2) police violence directed at Chicana/o youth. Further, this song plays out a violent fantasy of some Chicana/o youth who wish to retaliate against their oppressors. For many barrio youth their most immediate oppressor and symbol for all oppressors is the "pig." In this song Cypress Hill tells of a police officer who gets convicted of drug trafficking (another common theme in lore about the role of police in barrios) and gets sent to prison where he will not have his "gang" (other police officers) to protect him, nor will he have the protection of the state. Cypress Hill raps "'Cos once he gets to the Pen / They won't provide the little pig with a bullet-proof vest / To protect him from some mad nigga / Who he shot in the chest and placed under arrest." The fantasy continues as they discuss paying the "pig" back for crimes he has committed against barrio and ghetto youth. They liken their revenge to the cutting up of a pig into pig's feet, pork chops, sausage, and ham. As well, they mention what is perceived in some violent subcultures to be the ultimate act of vengeance, rape, when they say, "Niggas wanna do him in the ass."[29]

This song introduces the next theme associated with the relationship between Chicana/o barrio youth and police officers: the criminality of cops. First, they suggest that cops are murderers and then go on to discuss their role as drug traffickers: "He's collectin' payoffs from a dark alley . . . / This pig works for the mafia / Makin' some money off crack." In another song from their album *IV* (1998), they discuss the dark world of the police officer. "Looking through the Eye of a Pig" presents the ravings of a fictional cop who in his twenty years on the force has become "worse than some of these motherfuckers I put away." Cypress Hill talk about what they believe is the tendency for many cops to use cocaine for the purposes of getting "wired" enough to meet barrio streets with a battle mentality: "Bad dreams all up in my head / No lie / Sometimes I got to take a sniff so I could get by." They also accuse cops of alcohol, as well as drug abuse, rapping in this song from the point of view of their fictional cop: "Fuck I need a drink and I'm almost off / At the precinct it's like an AA meeting all gone wrong." Moreover, Cypress Hill understands the cops' criminality and drug use/abuse to be sanctioned by the state and sees cops as a tight-knit group, or "gang," that protects one another either from external enemies such as "criminals" and "gang members" or from the law. Following barrio wisdom about the police, Cypress Hill raps in this song: "I'm in the biggest gang you ever saw / Above the law / Looking through the eyes of a pig / I see it all . . . / I.A. got an eye on my close friend, Guy / For takin' supply from evidence / A bust on a buy / That doesn't concern me / We never rat on each other / We went through the academy / Just like frat brothers." "I.A." refers to police Internal Affairs office whose mandate is to investigate the criminal activities of police officers, and the "supply" they mention is drugs stolen from police evidence rooms.

The song ends with the police officer pulling over a truck because it has been modified, customized, in the low-rider style popular with Chicana/o youth. Again, this formerly illegal practice of "illegal searches and seizures" has become increasingly common in ghettos and barrios. As it turns out the victim of "driving while brown" is Cypress Hill rapper B-Real, who gets "framed" by the criminal cop. They end the song rapping:

> What's this a dark green truck / Tinted windows / Dually modified / Probably a drug dealer / "Pull over to the curb / Take your key out of the ignition / Raise your hands out the windows / Get 'em in a high position / Don't move or I'll blast your fuckin' head off / Don't give me that bullshit / I've heard about your raps / All you're talkin' about is slangin' and shooting off your straps / Okay Mr. B-Real get the fuck out of the truck / I love it how all you fuckin' rappers think you're so tough / Get your ass out / I don't need no probable cause / You got a big sack of coke / So take a pause."

This ending illustrates a common problem for Chicana/o youth who participate in a subculture characterized by their style—baggy jeans, baseball hats, wearing hair short or shaved, low-rider cars and trucks, tattoos, and hip-hop music. The song suggests that the vehicle occupants are innocent and are pulled over and framed simply because they are barrio youth. Cypress Hill connects drug use by police officers with police brutality and harassment of Chicana/o youth. In the song "Earthquake Weather" (2000), Psycho Realm takes a step further in their analysis of the connection between police cocaine abuse and their violence as they rap, "Split second in time life becomes short / Courtesy of LAPD psycho / Inhaling white coke straight snort."

"MOVING THE REVOLUTION THROUGH USING / ALL KINDS OF MUSICAL FORMS OF CONFUSION"[30]: UNIFYING THE SOCIAL MAJORITIES

Rap artists and enthusiasts have consciously banded together as a community with a unique culture and worldview. They call themselves members of the Hip-Hop Nation. This nation is multiethnic and multiracial, as are the roots of hip-hop.[31] Chicano rappers have been concerned with making multiracial and international connections with like-minded people resisting the same forces of globalization. Chicano rappers, Cypress Hill, Funky Aztecs, and others have operationalized Laura Pulido's notion of the "people of color" identity.[32] Pulido notes that within the environmental justice movement in the Southwest Chicanas/os, African Americans, and American Indians are developing a movement based on a common identity as people of color. While many grassroots movements that use identity as a catalyst for social change are exclusive and limit the possibilities for a broad-based multiethnic movement, the environmental justice movement has been successful in creating an inclusive identity, "people of color," that has the power to unite people of various ethnic and/or racial groups for the purpose of challenging environmental racism at the regional or national level. However, Pulido, like Chicana/o rappers, believes that "people of color" identity does not preclude the use of one's own particular racial, ethnic, or other identity; one need not lose oneself in order to become part of a multiracial alliance. Further, we can extend the idea of a "people of color" identity to include all of the two-thirds majority and like-minded whites. Chicano rappers have enacted a broad-based multiracial identity through expanding their audience beyond Chicanas/os and blacks and, especially, by reaching out to Mexicans and Mexican immigrants in the United States.

Members of Cypress Hill exemplify the unifying project of hip-hop as they have reached out to those who might have a sense of *carnalismo* with them. Soon after Cypress Hill released their debut album in 1991 they joined the alternative rock tour, Lollapalooza, and began to reach "hippies, stoners and Gen X alternarockers"[33] with their discourse of marijuana smoking and critiques of gang and state-sponsored violence. Moreover, Cypress Hill has been active in critiquing Chicana/o nationalism that overemphasizes Chicana/o solidarity at the expense of a broader working-class and youth solidarity.[34] In a 1994 interview the members of Cypress Hill began a public debate with Chicano rapper (Kid) Frost over this issue. They claim that Frost errs when he focuses too much on "la raza," screaming "Brown Pride" while ignoring other youth who might benefit from hip-hop solidarity.[35]

On the flip side, others, including editors of the hip-hop magazine *The Source,* accused Cypress Hill of "selling out" as a result of their touring with alternative rock bands and marketing their music to white kids. B-Real responded to this critique by stating:

> You can't stop people from buying your shit. If it's good and it's what you feel, that ain't sellin' out, man. You gotta figure that's introducing your shit to new people, it's making rap bigger. So what if white people like it or not, big fucking deal. If they can relate to it, it's a part of their lives. They always make this cop out that rap is for us, solely for us. Music is for everybody, no matter what color . . . It ain't about black or white, not for me.[36]

This does not mean that Cypress Hill does not emphasize their Latina/o roots in their music or that they ignore Latina/o youth. On the contrary, they celebrate their Latina/o culture and language (see the song "Latin Lingo," from their *Cypress Hill* album) and address issues pertinent to urban Latinas/os. In 1999 they reached out further to the Latina/o audience, especially those "South of the Border," releasing an album of their most important and well-received songs totally in Spanish. The album, titled *Los Grandes Exitos en Español,* features the Mexican rap group Control Machete, whose hardcore sound owes much to the trailblazing of Cypress Hill.

Other Chicano rappers who have focused their attention on Mexicans and Mexican immigrants in the United States include the Funky Aztecs. Their two albums, *Chicano Blues* and *Day of the Dead,* discuss the everyday violence in California barrios and pay homage to "partying" and marijuana use but also implore Mexicans (both U.S. citizens and noncitizens) to critique the United States government and white supremacy ("Amerikkkan" and "Prop 187") and to organize themselves to take action ("Organize" and "Nation of Funk").

> A Message to the Coconut / No matter how much you switch / Here is what they think about you / Cactus frying, long distance running, soccer playing, shank having, tortilla flipping, refried bean eating, border crossing, fruit picking, piñata breaking, lowrider driving, dope dealing, Tres Flores wearing, green card having, illiterate gangmember, go the fuck back to Mexico (Funky Aztecs, 1995, "Prop 187" from *Day of the Dead,* Raging Bull Records).

The narrator urges people of Mexican descent who try to "act white" and invest in the white, middle-class "American Dream" to recognize that "Amerika" and white "Amerikans" do not want them; that no matter how much you attempt to assimilate and become good, upstanding, middle-class Americans, if you are of Mexican descent, you are stigmatized and discriminated against.

Further, they link the narratives of Chicana/o experiences discussed throughout their album to the fate and experiences of Mexicans. The song continues with the menacing refrain "Secure the Border," repeated over news reports reproducing the new nativism that led to the passage of Proposition 187 in California. If upheld, Proposition 187, which was passed in 1994, would have essentially undermined a fundamental aspect of the founding of the United States, birthright citizenship, by denying citizenship to U.S.-born children of undocumented immigrants and denying undocumented immigrants and their children access to public services such as health clinics and public schools.[37] The authors in the excellent anthology *Immigrants Out!* write that during hard economic times people search for a scapegoat. The initial years of globalization have created uncertain and difficult economic times for most U.S. citizens. Propaganda from think tanks, universities, public officials, and the media has placed much of the blame on members of powerless groups such as undocumented immigrants, welfare mothers, and gangbangers. This propaganda has led to the dismantling of public assistance programs, legislation increasing prison sentences, prison development, numbers of police officers, and use of military technology by inner-city police forces and the Border Patrol.[38] The Funky Aztecs, aware of the damage caused by the xenophobia and racism directed at people of Mexican descent, reproduce recordings of newscasters, white citizens, and others claiming that immigrants are a drain on resources and that we taxpaying citizens should not have "to pay to educate those children and their healthcare." The FAs predict the outcome of Proposition 187 and increased racism by repeating "Proposition 187" followed by a gunshot. They end the song discussing news from Mexico, including the two major political assassinations in 1994 and the uprising in Chiapas. We could read this ending any number of ways: as a critique of further propaganda aimed at Mexicans; a recognition of the link between globalization, Mexican political instability, and Mexican immigration to the United States; a call to arms for Mexican (American) peoples and a threat to U.S. elites. I believe that the Funky Aztecs probably intend to suggest all of these and more.

As discussed at the beginning of this section, the hip-hop community has always been multiracial and continues to forge a multiracial alliance in building their "Hip-Hop Nation." This act of multiracial community formation resists globalizing forces that undermine multiracial solidarity through fostering xenophobia and racism. Increasingly, rappers are looking internationally for sources of *carnalismo* to increase the ranks of their cultural movement. Chicano rappers have naturally looked southward to Mexico to create bridges over the border in attempts to transnationalize the hip-hop community. As William Robinson suggests, countering transnational capitalism (globalization) requires building "a transnational class consciousness and a concomitant global political protagonism and strategies that link the local to the national and the national to the global."[39] Chicana/o rappers have done this through linking globalization, political instability in the United States and Mexico, racial stereotypes, nativism, and violence and repressive legislation aimed at people of Mexican descent, and reaching out to broader Latina/o and non-Latina/o audiences.[40]

However, we should be aware that within the Hip-Hop Nation women are marginalized and often represented in rap lyrics in extremely negative ways. First, female rappers have had a very difficult time breaking into the "game," and when they do get a record deal their lyrical content, image, and success are heavily monitored, mediated, and controlled by record executives. In a 1997 interview pioneering female rappers Salt-n-Pepa, MC Lyte, Mia X, and others discussed the trials and tribulations of women trying to break into the rap game.[41] Mia X, commenting on how male rappers have made it difficult for females, stated, "I've never had a problem with a sister that I've met that's rhyming, but I've had problems with men, always men, writing this and saying that about our lyrics." Asked about having to compromise themselves "in entering the male-dominated hip-hop industry" the female MCs agreed that record labels try to control their image, appearance, lyrics, and music.[42]

In addition, rap lyrics and videos often present women as mere sex objects. For evidence of this problem in rap, one need only tune into Black Entertainment Television (BET) on any weekday afternoon to see images of scantily clad black women dancing as "video 'hos." Rarely are women depicted as protagonists in rap videos. Rather, they exist in the videos as titillation and to further aggrandize the male rappers who demonstrate their prowess through their association with these unrealistically sexualized women. As rap has become more corporatized (transitions from ghetto streets to Wall Street) and an increasingly important part of the global entertainment industry, these images of women become increasingly devoid of substance and unidimensional. Once again, globalization has taken deeply entrenched notions of race and sex and turned them into a profit. The music industry has taken the battle of the sexes within minority communities, combined it with old Anglo-European notions of the "Jezebel" or "Latin spitfire,"[43] updated it with a dance beat, and packaged it for international consumption.[44]

This analysis of rap does not intend to let the young black and brown MCs off the hook for presenting tales of conquering women and explicit discussions of women as mere whores. Certainly, the young men must analyze their own sexism if they are to be truly revolutionary in their rhetoric and behaviors. However, I believe that there are openings in rap for such self-reflection. Many young men have rethought their understanding of women and posed challenges to other male rappers in their lyrics.[45] Another important opening for challenging the phallocentrism of rap and the sexist images in its lyrics comes from a new wave of female MCs who have projected positive, multifaceted images of women in their videos and songs. Female rappers have taken the discursive and everyday resistance of women of color to the patriarchy and critiqued their brothers in the Hip-Hop Nation and the misogyny of Western society that they often emulate.[46]

As with many male-dominated liberation movements such as the Black Power Movement or the Chicana/o Movement,[47] men within the Hip-Hop Nation have marginalized women. They exhibit in their lyrics and behaviors a use and abuse of the male privilege afforded them in a sexist society. Such a stance seems hardly revolutionary to women who lose privilege and are harmed as a result of black and brown men accepting from greater U.S. society an uncritical, sexist definition of masculinity. So, it is hoped that while the Hip-Hop Nation continues to define itself in the face of globalization and the co-optation of its culture by corporate America, its ideology and gender analysis will evolve beyond its current "parroting" of the sexist norm in U.S. society.

"LA ORDEN DEL NUEVO MUNDO, NO, NUNCA!"[48]: CHICANO RAP'S "GREAT REFUSAL"

Chicano rap narratives vividly illustrate the consequences of urban decay resulting from globalization. Their stories of violence, murder, drug use and trafficking, police repression, and poverty contribute to a theorization of globalization from barrio streets. Their narration of urban dystopia puts brown faces on statistics concerning urban neglect, decreased job opportunities, and hopelessness in Chicana/o U.S.A. Their "armed-with-words" response to the war waged by the transnational bourgeoisie and their conscious rejection of the middle-class lifestyle reflects a Great Refusal[49] shouted by many throughout the two-thirds world.[50]

In the place of globalization and the violence attending it, Chicana/o rappers and other members of the Hip-Hop Nation are building a multiracial community based on love for one another and free expression. This utopic model is, of course, not always followed by practitioners and enthusiasts of hip-hop. Rappers have often illustrated racism and vehement hatred toward other members of the Hip-Hop Nation, resulting in a few isolated acts of violence. Further, the pervasive sexism and homophobia in rap turns the utopic Hip-Hop Nation upside down for women and gays and lesbians. Nevertheless, Chicano rappers[51] (who have mostly stayed away from sexist and homophobic images in their music) have begun to illustrate ways in which to unify "people of color" and other marginalized people through "love for the 'hood."

NOTES

1. W. J. Wilson, *The Truly Disadvantaged: The Inner City, the Underclass, and Public Policy* (Chicago: University of Chicago Press, 1987); L. R. Chavez, *Shadowed Lives: Undocumented Immigrants in American Society* (Fort Worth, Texas: Harcourt Brace College Publishers, 1992); J. Moore and R. Pinderhughes, eds., *In the Barrios: Latinos and the Underclass Debate* (New York: Sage Foundation, 1993).

2. G. Esteva and M. S. Prakash, in *Grassroots Postmodernism: Remaking the Soil of Cultures* (London: Zed, 1998), p. 16, prefer the term "social majorities" to describe the majority of people in the world who "have no regular access to most of the goods and services defining the average 'standard of living' in the industrial countries. Their definitions of 'a good life,' shaped by their local traditions, reflect their capacities to flourish outside the 'help' offered by 'global forces.'" They compare the social majorities (or the Two-thirds World) to the "social minorities" of "both the North and South that share homogeneous ways of modern (western) life all over the world."

3. Esteva and Prakash, *Grassroots Postmodernism*; L. McFarland, "A New Democracy: A Genealogy of Zapatista Autonomy" (dissertation, University of Texas, 1999).

4. This new free trade regime, or neoliberalism, is exemplified in treaties such as the North American Free Trade Agreement (NAFTA), the General Agreement on Tariffs and Trade (GATT), and the Multi-Lateral Agreement on Investment (MAI) which formalize economic cooperation between national bourgeoisies, especially those of the North.

5. William I. Robinson, "Globalisation: Nine Theses on Our Epoch," *Race and Class* 38, no. 2 (1996): 22, reports the following United Nations figures on global poverty:

Between 1990 and 1995 Latin American poverty increased from 183 million to 230 million people; the percentage of poor people in Latin America increased from 40 percent in 1980 to 48 percent in 1995; across the globe 1.3 billion people live in absolute poverty. Commenting on the growing gap between the global rich and the global poor, Robinson concludes that "the ratio of inequality between the global rich and the global poor . . . was 1:150."

6. For more detailed discussions of the affects of globalization in Latin America see Robinson, "Latin America and Global Capitalism," *Race and Class* 40, no. 2–3 (1998): 111–131; for its effects in Mexico, see McFarland, "A New Democracy."

7. Moore and Pinderhughes, *In the Barrios*, xiii.

8. These changes began in the early 1980s and in the United States include the following: weakening of union power (inaugurated and exemplified by the Reagan government's defeat of the Professional Air Traffic Controllers' Organization, PATCO, in 1981); the change from a manufacturing to a service economy; the trend toward increasing reliance on part-time and temporary workers; the internationalization of production, leading to the export of well-paying manufacturing jobs; technological developments that replaced workers with machines or computers; deregulation of the workplace (halting or rolling back workplace safety standards, environmental regulations, worker benefits, etc.); changes in the tax code that place a larger percentage of the burden on workers; and changes in government spending that shifted a greater percentage of the nation's tax base to business and military subsidies and away from an investment in human capital (education and job training, health care and welfare).

9. T. Dunn, *The Militarization of the U.S.-Mexico Border, 1978–1992: Low-Intensity Conflict Doctrine Comes Home* (Austin, Texas: Center for Mexican American Studies Books, 1996); M. Davis, *City of Quartz: Excavating the Future in Los Angeles* (New York: Vintage Books, 1990).

10. A. Aguirre and J. H. Turner, in *American Ethnicity: The Dynamics and Consequences of Discrimination*, 2nd ed. (Boston: McGraw-Hill, 1998), using Bureau of the Census data, show that economic restructuring has had a disproportionately negative effect on Latinas/os, as indicated by the following data: (1) the 1994 poverty rate for Mexican Americans was 31.8% (more than twice the rate for non-Hispanic whites, 12.2%), up from 1970, 1980, and 1990 rates, and (2) in 1994 few Mexican Americans labored in high-wage, high-prestige managerial or professional occupations (10.9%), and they were disproportionately represented in the ranks of the low-wage, unstable service industry (33.9%) and farmer/laborer sector (32.5%). Moreover, in 1990 in every occupational category (except "craftsmen") Latinas/os earned less than their non-Hispanic white colleagues did (M. Avalos, "Economic Restructuring and Young Latino Workers in the 1980s," in R. M. De Anda, ed., *Chicanas and Chicanos in Contemporary Society* [Boston: Allyn and Bacon, 1996], p. 35).

11. Chicano and Chicana LFPR in 1991 were 80% and 51%, respectively, compared to 74% and 57% for non-Hispanic white males and females, respectively. S. Gonzalez-Baker, "Demographic Trends in the Chicana/o Population: Policy Implications for the Twenty-first Century," in D. R. Maciel and I. D. Ortiz, eds., *Chicanas/Chicanos at the Crossroads: Social, Economic, and Political Change* (Tucson: University of Arizona Press, 1996), p. 13.

12. R. M. De Anda, "Falling Back: Mexican-Origin Men and Women in the U.S. Economy," in De Anda, *Chicanas and Chicanos in Contemporary Society*, pp. 44–47.

13. D. S. Eitzen and M. B. Zinn report that in 1995 the Latina/o unemployment rate was 9.4% while the rates for African Americans and non-Hispanic whites were 10% and 4.8%, respectively (in *In Conflict and Order: Understanding Society*, 8th ed. [Boston: Allyn and Bacon, 1998], p. 303).

14. Median income in 1991 was $12,894 for Chicanos, $22,207 for non-Hispanic white men, $9,286 for Chicanas and $12,438 for non-Hispanic white women (Gonzalez-Baker, "Demographic Trends in the Chicana/o Population," 15).

15. Gonzalez-Baker, "Demographic Trends in the Chicana/o Population," 15.

16. The "Hispanic" imprisonment rate during this period rose "from 163 to 529 prison inmates per 100,000 "Hispanic" residents." S. R. Donziger, ed., *The Real War on Crime: The Report of the National Criminal Justice Commission* (New York: HarperPerennial, 1996), 104.

17. S. R. Donziger, ed., *The Real War on Crime*, 104.

18. For a discussion of the increased xenophobia and nativism directed at Latina/o immigrants in the United States see J. F. Perea, ed., *Immigrants Out! The New Nativism and the Anti-Immigrant Impulse in the United States* (New York: NYU Press, 1997), and for a discussion of ethnic conflict in the United States as a result of increasing poverty and stratification see R. Gooding-Williams, ed., *Reading Rodney King, Reading Urban Uprising* (New York: Routledge, 1993).

19. In theorizing the concept of "organic intellectual" in contrast to the "traditional intellectual," Gramsci writes that "[e]very social group, coming into existence on the original terrain of an essential function in the world of economic production, creates together with itself, one or more strata of intellectuals which give it homogeneity and an awareness of its own function not only in the economic but also in the social and political fields" (*Selections from the Prison Notebooks* [New York: International Publishers, 1971], 6). Excepting the vanguardist role that Gramsci reserves for the organic intellectual, this concept can be useful for understanding the role that rappers play in their community. That is, Chicano rappers serve the function of solidifying a self-understanding for Chicana/o youth in urban "America." I use the term "solidifying self-understanding" as opposed to the Gramscian-like construction of "giving an awareness to" because I contend that the intellectual material from which rappers or any other organic intellectual develops her/his knowledge of the world results from an embeddedness in her/his community and interactions and an interdependency with her/his community's customs and traditions (its epistemology, ontology, and social structures). While rappers may present new understandings that serve a pedagogical function for their constituency, their cultural production owes a great deal to the community wisdom in which the rappers were socialized. Moreover, Gramsci's concept is apt given that the aforementioned discussion of Chicana/o youth's role in the international economy allows us to conceive of urban Chicana/o youth as a class with a specific, unique, and "essential function in the world of economic production."

20. The use of marijuana in rap and hip-hop culture is well-known and celebrated in songs too numerous to mention here. A cursory look at the lyrical content of the rappers discussed in this essay reveals several "cuts" devoted to the pleasures and politics of marijuana consumption. It is beyond the scope of this essay to detail the use of marijuana and the uses to which it is put in the hip-hop community. Suffice it to say that we cannot underestimate the importance of marijuana to the evolution of this form of cultural production.

21. These well-known lyrics come from the group Cypress Hill. The song title is "How I Could Just Kill a Man," from their debut album, *Cypress Hill* (1991).

22. Davis, *City of Quartz*.

23. S. E. Pease, *PSYWAR: Psychological Warfare in Korea, 1950–1953* (Harrisburg, Pa.: Stackpole Books, 1992).

24. Cypress Hill lyrics used by permission of BMG Music Publishing. All Rights Reserved.

These lyrics are posted on the World Wide Web at http://www.angelfire.com/mi2/cypress2/prii21.htm. The Web has been an important site for the development of hip-hop culture. Besides downloading the lyrics for thousands of songs, rap enthusiasts can discuss their favorite artists (including the politics of their lyrics), read or write biographies of artists, and read about contemporary issues pertinent to the existence and survival of hip-hop culture, including legislation, recent public debate on music, and insights into the recording industry.

25. The fine documentary *The Fire This Time* (R. Holland, Rhino Home Video, 1995) offers a similar critique of state practices which contribute to inner-city fratricide through exacerbating gang difference, allowing for and encouraging weapons distribution, and the government's role in the crack cocaine trade. See also P. D. Scott and J. Marshall, *Cocaine Politics: Drugs, Armies and the CIA in Central America* (Berkeley: University of California Press, 1998). Along the lines of *The Fire This Time, Cocaine Politics* and Mario Van Peebles' critique of the Counter Intelligence Program (COINTELPRO) abuses against the Black Panther Party (BPP) in the movie *Panther* (1995; see also Ward Churchill and Jim Vander Wall, *Agents of Repression: The FBI's Secret Wars against the Black Panther Party and the American Indian Movement* [Boston: South End Press, 1988]), Psycho Realm offers the following in "Conspiracy Theories": "The masterplan don't include us so they shoot us / Supply weapons, coke, crack and buddha / Keep track of who took the bait through computers / Enslave and regulate the 'hoods through the *juras* / We're all victims as the plot thickens / Better recognize the big plan the clock's ticking." "Buddha" is hip-hop slang for marijuana. The reference to computer surveillance alludes to the practice of authoritarian states to continuously monitor its citizens, especially rebels and "criminals." In the barrios of the United States this takes the form of gang databases and a sophisticated national FBI data center. "*Jura*" is Chicana/o slang for the police.

26. "Sets" is another term for gang.

27. Psycho Realm lyrics used by permission of Sick Jack Gonzales of Psycho Realm.

28. This analysis of the propagandistic function of the media which causes people to believe that "the face of violence" is a young and brown one is illustrated in the following lines from the Chicano rappers Funky Aztecs in their song "Nation of Funk" (*Day of the Dead,* 1995): "Ever since you saw *American Me* / You're scared of me."

29. I must note here that this form of domination stems from a deep homophobia and sexism in Chicana/o and Black American culture. The reason that this is seen as the ultimate act of vengeance is because the person committing the rape turns the raped into either "his bitch" or a "fag." In our sexist, homophobic society it becomes the ultimate expression of heterosexual male superiority through symbolically creating an inferior woman or homosexual out of the victim.

30. These lyrics are from Psycho Realm's song "Moving through Streets" (2000).

31. See D. Hebdige, *Cut 'n Mix: Culture, Identity and Caribbean Music* (New York: Methuen, 1987).

32. L. Pulido, "Development of the 'People of Color' Identity in the Environmental Justice Movement of the Southwestern United States," *Socialist Review* 26, no. 3–4 (1996): 145–180.

33. R. Trakin, "In the Temple with Cypress Hill," *Cover Story* (Web magazine, n.d.).

34. Their practices and critiques echo an important discussion in Chicana/o studies about the continued reliance on outdated cultural nationalist models that cause researchers to study Chicana/o history and contemporary experiences in a vacuum as if Chicanas/os have not had contact with any other marginalized and/or working-class peoples. This type of Chicanocentrism has distorted history and has been detrimental to the formation of interethnic alliances between Chicanas/os and other social groups that constitute the social majorities. Furthermore, Chicana/o parochialism limits even our ability to fully understand Chicana/o experiences because without an analysis of globalization and the location of Chicanas/os in the new world order vis-à-vis groups throughout the world we are unable to accurately assess the ideologies, structures, and policies that negatively impact Chicanas/os. See A. Darder and R. D. Torres, "Latinos and Society: Culture, Politics, and Class," in Darder and Torres, eds., *The Latino Studies Reader: Culture, Economy and Society* (Oxford: Blackwell Publishers, 1998), pp. 3–26.

35. This interview appears in B. Cross, *It's Not about a Salary: Rap, Race and Resistance in Los Angeles* (Berkeley: University of California Press, 1994). Frost (formerly

[Kid] Frost) has been described as the "Godfather of Latin Hip Hop" by Brown Pride Online (<www.brownpride.com>). Frost had the first Chicano rap hit with "*La Raza*" (1989, *Hispanic Causing Panic*).

36. Dumisani Ndlovu, "Back with a Boom: Cypress Hill" (Cypress Hill homepage, n.d.).

37. For a detailed account of Proposition 187 and the causes, effects, and consequences of the "new nativism," see the various chapters in Perea, *Immigrants Out!*

38. Dunn, *The Militarization of the U.S.-Mexico Border*; Davis, *City of Quartz*.

39. Robinson, "Globalisation," 27.

40. An important critique of hip-hop as a revolutionary social movement argues that the methods and much of the ideology of these young people are steeped in patriarchy and patriarchal notions of masculinity and sexuality. Often the violence discussed in rap songs celebrates armed defense (and offense) as a solution to problems attending globalization. Many women and peace advocates would challenge this masculinist solution. It is important to note, however, that most of violence discussed in rap is a critique of intraracial violence and state violence and that rappers are involved in a grassroots "stop the violence" campaign. Finally, the promotion of consumerism and the fact that rap music is part of global music industry are certainly not revolutionary and, in fact, may be exactly what the fight against globalization is all about. Further, one must question the degree to which corporate control mediates the politics of rap music. Again, the hip-hop community is challenging the global circuits of cultural diffusion and commodity exchange through grassroots entrepreneurship and "underground" promotion and organization of the Hip-Hop Nation.

41. Few Latinas have been successful as rap artists. The current most notable Latina MC is Hurricane G., a *Puertorriqueña* from New York.

42. T. McGregor, "Mothers of the Culture," *The Source* 97 (October 1997): 115–122.

43. Patricia Hill Collins, in her excellent article "Mammies, Matriarchs, and Other Controlling Images" (in *Black Feminist Thought* [Boston: Unwin Hyman, 1990], 67), theorizes that "portraying African-American women as stereotypical mammies, matriarchs, welfare recipients, and hot mommas has been essential to the political economy of domination fostering Black women's oppression." For a discussion of Latina images in film see R. L. Fregoso, *The Bronze Screen: Chicana and Chicano Film Culture* (Minneapolis: University of Minnesota Press, 1993); C. Noreiga, ed., *Chicanos and Film: Essays on Chicano Representation and Resistance* (New York: Garland, 1992); A. L. Wool, "Bandits and Lovers: Hispanic Images in American Film," in R. M. Miller, ed., *The Kaleidoscope Lens: How Hollywood Views Ethnic Groups* (Englewood Cliffs, N.J.: J. S. Ozer, 1980), pp. 54–72.

44. In December, 1999 as I watched BET's "100 Greatest Videos of the Millennium" I noticed that while women were marginalized and sometimes presented as sex objects in the rap videos and lyrics of my childhood they were not commodified in the same way as they are in today's corporate rap industry. The few women presented in early rap videos were women just like any we might find in our neighborhoods. The central problem in early rap was the lack of female representation. Today, nearly every rap video requires women with unrealistically large breasts strutting or, more often, dancing seductively for the pleasure of the male rappers and the adolescents watching on the television screen. While I have found no direct causal evidence between the increasing corporatization of rap and the increasingly pornographic images found in rap videos, I suspect at least an indirect relationship between the two.

45. For such an interesting transformation see the later recordings of Tupac Shakur (*Makaveli, Killuminati: The Seven Day Theory*, and songs such as "Keep Your Head Up," "Dear Mama," and "Baby, Don't Cry") and Goodie Mob ("Beautiful Skin").

46. An analysis of the themes of female rappers is beyond the scope of this essay. However, many of the female rappers mentioned earlier and new rappers such as Lauryn Hill, Solé, Rah Digga, and Eve have taken on themes of domestic violence, rape, and

sexual and economic powerlessness. Others have, of course, capitulated to corporate greed and teenage desire for sexual images through presenting themselves and other women as sex objects.

47. See works by Chicana feminists who discuss the battle of the sexes during the Chicana/o Movement. G. Anzaldúa, ed., *Making Face, Making Soul / Haciendo Caras* (San Francisco: Aunt Lute, 1990); Y. Broyles-González, *El Teatro Campesino: Theater in the Chicano Movement* (Austin: University of Texas Press, 1994); A. M. García, ed., *Chicana Feminist Thought: The Basic Historical Writings* (New York: Routledge, 1997).

48. These lyrics come from the Psycho Realm song "Premonitions" (1997, Ruffhouse Records).

49. H. Marcuse, *One-Dimensional Man: Studies in the Ideology of Advanced Industrial Society* (Boston: Beacon Press, 1964). Marcuse suggests that an important aspect of a revolutionary social movement is the rejection of capitalist society and its logic. He notes that art (including rap?) in its most "advanced" and political form serves as an important catalyst for this form of social protest.

50. Esteva and Prakash, *Grassroots Postmodernism*; McFarland, "A New Democracy."

51. I have concentrated on a few relatively well-known Chicano rappers from California. For a list and discussion of dozens of Chicano rappers see the "Brown Pride Online" homepage at <www.brownpride.com>.

16 A SIFTING OF CENTURIES: AFRO-CHICANO INTERACTION AND POPULAR MUSICAL CULTURE IN CALIFORNIA, 1960–2000

Gaye T. M. Johnson

THIS ESSAY moves toward an understanding of the politics of Afro-Chicano culture in contemporary California. It builds from an assumption that the realms of culture, politics, and economy are inseparable.[1] In this post-industrial moment, the deleterious effects of deindustrialization, the evisceration of the welfare state, and a massive influx of Asian and Latin American workers has created new urban identities for African American and Chicano populations. Egregious manipulations of immigration and labor laws in the interest of free trade have made collective action in the United States very difficult to engage in, especially among black and Latino populations, who in California have suffered more from the effects of capital flight and the reorganization of work than any other groups.

This essay offers a musical depiction of an historical pattern: for as long as they have occupied common living and working spaces, African American and Chicano working-class communities have had continuous interactions around civil rights struggles, union activism, and demographic changes. But there have been several obstacles to building community between these populations in Los Angeles. This may seem ironic when one considers the tremendous influence that Chicano and black musicians have had on each other's musical cultures: to hear the manifestation of that interaction in musical form, one need only listen to the sounds of L.A. musicians Chuck Higgins, Richard Berry, and Ritchie Valens in the 1950s; in the 1960s and 70s, WAR, Los Lobos, and Cannibal and the Headhunters; and presently Ozomatli, the Red Hot Chili Peppers, and Rage Against the Machine. Yet strong anecdotal evidence of the tensions between these groups exists.[2]

As we enter a third decade of MTV, music continues to play a vital role in people's political awareness and cultural realities. Now it is informed not only by inter- and intracommunity politics and subjectivities, but also by translocal and transnational politics of economy and culture. Writing about cooperation and solidarity, then, means writing at the same time about rejection and mistrust (Douglas, 1986). Increased competition for scarce resources and the trap of racial chauvinism have too often positioned workers of different races in opposition to each other, a phenomenon that is as much about globalization as it is about the changing meaning of all socio-racial identities in the current historical moment.[3] Perhaps the occasional triumph of mistrust over the spirit of solidarity is a symptom of the lack of awareness of the historical links between these communities.

This essay tells a story which builds on the past to understand the interlaced subject positions of African Americans and Chicanos in the present, as well as their common future amid the rapid mobility of culture, capital, and populations across the globe. I will broadly sketch a history of cultural and political interaction through the lens of music, from the 1960s to the present. Today, a successful interethnic movement for social change must work for equality in a language understood by its constituents: popular musical culture is often that language.

My emphasis on popular music supports the contentions of ethnic studies scholars who see cultural production not only as an integral part of oppositional politics, but as an "important register" of social and political change (Lipsitz: 213). This is particularly important in California today: it has become a majority-minority state, that is, a state in which no racial or ethnic group represents over 50 percent of the total population. We continue to occupy center stage in national immigration policies and international politics, important since California's 52-person delegation to the US Congress and its 54 Electoral College votes make the state a central player in determining the outcome of national politics.[4] And we have led the nation in passing legislation that denies immigrants access to basic social services like education and medical treatment, eradicating affirmative action, and all but outlawing bilingual education. States such as Michigan, Texas, and Florida have endeavored to follow in the educational and immigration policy footsteps of California, demonstrating Chester Himes's concise observation in the early 1960 that: "as the west coast goes, so the nation goes."[5]

California legislative actions have carried within them overlapping and even contradictory distinctions about citizenship, ethnicity, border geography, and race. Because the state has been the terrain over which some of the most highly publicized debates have been fought about race, labor, education, and immigration, the cultural and political commonalities as well as the interactions of African Americans and Chicanos in California deserve particular attention. Cultural and historical studies of California have been written to reflect discrete racial and cultural categories, making this state appear as if it is a space inhabited by individualized, distinct groups. This is an inaccurate portrayal of California as a cultural and social space: labor, racial, and educational policies as well as cultural practices have resulted in both interethnic antagonisms and a rich history of intercultural interaction. Recasting California in this way illumines a dynamic legacy of conflict and cooperation, one which gives us a history to draw from when faced with California's national leadership in passing discriminatory educational and immigration policies.

Sociohistorical linkages between Chicanos and African-Americans in the area now known as California began long before the United States appropriated that territory from Mexico. Because many were excluded in various ways from the privileges that citizenship should have afforded them, these groups formed alternative strategies to assert their entitlements. Often, this was in the realm of popular musical culture. It is this site which yields some of the most dynamic and mutual interchanges between black and Chicano populations, neighborhoods, and musical cultures: the past forty years of this history of exchange and interaction is the subject of this essay.

"MAKING WAR ON THE WARS"

The War on Poverty, the Vietnam War, and the governmental war on nationalist and civil rights movements were just a few of the several wars witnessed during the 1960s and '70s in America. But WAR, the Compton-based African American and Danish band with Chicano influences, was waging, as they put it, a "war on the wars," one informed by "our conception of what was going on in the world at that time." WAR traces its roots back to 1962, when guitarist Howard Scott and drummer Harold Brown were high school students in the Compton/South Central Los Angeles area. Together they launched an R&B club group, The Creators. By 1965, the band had added Lonnie Jordan, bassist B. B. Dickerson, and saxophonist Charles Miller, all of whom would eventually become members of WAR. "What made us different," said Howard Scott, "was the Latin influence we picked up in the Compton area . . . Compton was an amazing place to grow up—we were so intermingled with the Spanish-speaking people that it came out naturally in our music and our rhythms." Jordan agrees: "We mixed and mingled everything, even mariachi music. We were trying to imitate what we heard, but it came out being something else."

The mixing and mingling Jordan speaks of was the result of several demographic changes. In Los Angeles as a whole, the combination of the opening of new shipyards and aircraft assembly plants in the 1930s and '40s, severe housing shortages, and housing covenants produced unprecedented interethnic mixing. Official segregation slowly gave way as Chicanos and European ethnics worked together in Boyle Heights and Lincoln Park, while blacks and Chicanos lived in close proximity to each other in Watts and in the San Fernando Valley suburb of Pacoima. This was the social and cultural climate which produced musician Ricardo Valenzuela, whom we know as Ritchie Valens.

The notion that California was a state unburdened by racial differences was a myth built to epic proportions by the media. Mike Davis's superb *City of Quartz* shows how Los Angeles had a mystique that hid its faults. California's government, major universities, and corporations prided themselves on being models of fairness, and a laboratory of racial equality. Yet the reality of the California's "racial utopia," at the time of WAR's emergence in the mid-sixties, was the virulent racism of the Los

Angeles Police Department, racist hiring practices, housing discrimination, and lack of adequate schools for ethnic minorities. These are the realities which led Martin Luther King Jr., after his visit to Watts in 1965, to interpret the Watts riots as a crisis of disjuncture between the affluence of whites and the distance of blacks from that luxury: "Los Angeles could have expected riots because it is the luxurious symbol of luxurious living for whites. Watts is closer to it and yet further from it than any other Negro community in the country" (Wyatt: 210).

By the time WAR's syncretic style emerged, complicated demographic conditions had made Compton and Watts the multiracial area that it became. Originally part of a large Mexican land grant, the area that became Watts was first subdivided in the 1880s. During this time, Mexican laborers moved into the area to work on the Southern Pacific Railroad, forming the village of Tujuata. Incorporated in 1907, Watts developed as a grid of small residential lots without the significant industrial base enjoyed by neighboring Compton. Blacks who moved into the area settled in a district called Mudtown, which, as part of Watts, was annexed by Los Angeles in 1926. Until World War II, Watts remained pretty racially balanced between whites, blacks, and Mexican Americans. With the migrations sparked by the war, Watts became a primarily black city. It offered low-cost housing and was largely free of the deed restrictions that limited black access to other areas of Los Angeles. Between 1950 and 1960, Compton's white population declined by 18.5 percent, while the number of nonwhites was increasing by 165 percent. By 1966, the "minority group," as the papers called it, had become Compton's majority. Between 1940 and 1960, the black population of Watts increased eightfold (Wyatt: 210). By 1970, more than 50,000 Latinos lived in the traditionally black south-central area of Los Angeles; by 1980 that figure had doubled, with Chicanos alone making up 21 percent of the total population of the south-central area. With an area of two and half square miles, Watts had the highest population density of any city in Los Angeles County (Wyatt: 210).

By 1968, the group that was to become WAR was reorganized as The Nightshift, and recruited Papa Dee Allen, an East Coast percussionist who had years of experience with Dizzy Gillespie and other jazz greats. The final addition to the group was Lee Oskar, a Danish harp and harmonica player. It was this group which became WAR. Their songs, according to many music critics at the time of their second album's release in 1971, were in tune with the urban America of the early '70s, striking the right balance between hope, fear, and frustration. Pianist Lonnie Jordan commented on "our battle to make our instruments shoot out notes instead of bullets." Combining black, white, and brown musical traditions, WAR found common ground during an era of conflict, and disappointment over the repression of struggles for social justice. Other groups, musical and political, were attempting to do the same.

Other Afro-Chicana/o collaborations in California at this time included the peace pact between Reies López Tijerina and Black Power groups, the joint meeting of the California Conference of Black Elected Officials and the Legislative Conference of Spanish-Speaking Organizations in Sacramento in February 1968, the working relationship between La Raza groups and the Black Congress in Los Angeles, and the joint leadership of blacks and browns during the Poor People's March on Sacramento and on Washington, D.C., in 1968. Importantly, these marches were preceded by black and brown women's coalition work and marches in the area of welfare rights. The intersecting political agendas which brought Corky González and Ralph Abernathy together to unite blacks and Chicanos during the Poor People's Campaign had a lengthy history. For example, in his autobiography, César Chávez credits Ernesto Galarza with teaching him how to organize and build coalitions among Mexican farmworkers in Northern California. But Galarza, who had a history of organizing farmworkers around the country, had learned these organizing strategies from both the Communist Party and black sharecroppers in Alabama and Mississippi during the 1930s (Chávez: 60).

These interchanges are not always easy coalitions: they were complex ideological, political, and cultural relationships that were not always mutual admirations, either during the height of WAR's musical popularity or in the present. Demographic changes have often exacerbated this as well, as they did in the 1980s.

Blacks and Latinos are the majority in a number of L.A. central-city districts where new Latino immigrants have been arriving in large numbers. According to polls, all ethnic groups in Los Angeles believe that most discrimination is directed against Latinos and blacks.[6] Some of the tensions between these groups are grounded in specific developments in late-twentieth-century capitalism.

For working-class Latinas/os and blacks, economic problems have been a crucial source of conflict. The economic downturn of the late 1980s ended a short-lived era of upward mobility via blue-collar work for blacks. But by 1990, black family income had fallen by 50 percent from 1965, and black youth unemployment quadrupled. During the 1980s, many Latina/o immigrants flocked to Los Angeles service and garment industry jobs, which many blacks and U.S.-born Latinas/os had managed to rise beyond during the preceding decade. However, the 1982 recession rescinded important gains that many of these workers had won in the 1970s when the economic restructuring eliminated jobs in heavy industry. It was here and in the area of durable consumer goods, traditionally the strongholds of high-wage organized labor, that manufacturers either abandoned factories to imports or shifted overseas or to areas where organized labor was weakest; service jobs became one of the only alternatives, particularly for blacks. This often caused tension, and many African American Angelenos bought into national beliefs about immigrants stealing jobs which belonged to U.S. citizens. Simultaneously, Mexican and Latino service workers guarded hard-won gains from their struggles to unionize, which had brought higher wages and benefits.

Employers in a postindustrial economy have restructured work to cut labor costs by shedding in-house, long-term union employees and adopting flexible work schedules using subcontracted, part-time nonunion employees, a term one can almost equate, in L.A., with Latinas. Economic restructuring within Los Angeles meant that many of the plants closed during the height of deindustrialization in the 1980s were located in predominately African American communities. For African Americans, this has certainly effected a shift in available jobs, but importantly, capital flight and economic restructuring have left few remaining options apart from low-paid, unskilled work which is increasingly done by immigrant laborers. Changes in the economy and structure of work have had dire significance for Latino populations in Los Angeles as well: the movement to Los Angeles of low-wage workers from Mexico has meant little protection from employer mistreatment, Immigration and Naturalization Service harassment, or even vigilante violence.[7] At the same time, over the past two decades the infrastructure in traditionally Mexican and African American areas of L.A. has declined under the impact of deindustrialization and economic restructuring. As businesses closed and city residents left for other jobs, municipal tax bases suffered. The less mobile population remaining in cities often were members of groups that placed greater demands on municipal services—poorer individuals, larger families, and more recent immigrants. This combination of a diminished tax base and higher expenditure needs contributed to municipal fiscal problems. In an effort to counter these trends, local governments increased their emphasis on economic development policies, despite the fact that many of the factors driving the restructuring were outside local control.[8] Under the press of immigration, diminishing job opportunities, and media demonization of both groups, Latinos and African Americans have sometimes identified each other as impediments to their own community's progress.

Rodolfo Acuña's important work recounts how Chicano political leaders proposed to increase their numbers in office when they discovered that a Chicano could be elected in the Seventh Congressional District in the San Fernando Valley and another by shifting the boundaries of Rita Walters's Ninth Congressional District. The ninth district's African American population had declined from 56 percent to 36 percent during the 1980s, and its Latino population had increased from 36 percent to 61 percent. But redistricting the area to reflect these changes meant that Walters would have to give up downtown Los Angeles, and the black community was unwilling to do this in a time when blacks were losing political and economic power in Los Angeles. Councilman Mike Hernández and others accused African Americans of making sure that Latinos remained politically disadvantaged. And conservative blacks raised the specter of "illegal immigrants," saying that many of the people in the community would not be able to vote anyway. This specter was a chilling precursor of the kinds of politics Pete Wilson and others exploited during their campaign for Propositions 187 and 209, in which African American support was garnered against Latinos in the case of the former, and Chicano and Mexican American support was garnered for Proposition 209, which abolished affirmative action.

It was in the midst of these discouraging politics in the 1980s that Los Lobos, a band from East Los Angeles, came to be known internationally after they signed a recording contract with Slash Records. This band was formed in 1974 in East Los Angles by Louie Pérez, César Rosas, Conrad Lozano, and David Hidalgo. Their neighborhoods, which used to be one barrio, were separated by a freeway, reflective of the kinds of structural choices many U.S. cities make. Their band members pay homage to, and their style often reflects, the influence of blues guitarist Albert Collins. Collins, born to an African American sharecropping family in Texas, moved to Houston as a child; although he began his career playing the piano, Collins's cousin Lightnin' Hopkins taught him to play the guitar, and was responsible in large part for what became Collins's trademark: tuning his guitar to a minor key. Louie Pérez remembers carefully listening to Collins play with Big Mama Thornton, Little Richard, and the Imperials, and he taught himself to play guitar listening to soul music and buying the sheet music of artists like Sam and Dave and Aretha Franklin. Pérez's first musical gigs were playing Tower of Power and James Brown hits for Chicano audiences. So by 1975, as Los Lobos was beginning to enjoy a wide Los Angeles following, these blues and soul styles permeated their music, which they performed at weddings, block parties, and high schools. They became known for being a "Chicano" band, emphasizing the ranchera, Tex-Mex, and mariachi styles they had heard as children in their homes. In 1975, aware of the struggles occurring in the Chicano Movement, they contributed to the album *Si Se Puede* (It Can Be Done) in support of the United Farm Workers. *The Neighborhood,* recorded in 1986, captures the syncretic style associated with their urban background, but also addresses some of the demoralization in urban neighborhoods in the 1980s. Los Lobos, not a political band in terms of their lyrics or activism, nevertheless tremendously influenced the kind of music young people identified with, and redefined "Mexican" music in East Los Angeles in the 1980s. They brought African American and later Japanese influence into play with instruments reflective of Tex-Mex and other Latin American styles, like the accordion, guitarrón, vihuela, jarana, and charango. At a time of discouraging political events in the 1980s, Los Lobos showed that coalitions and multidirectional influences could still be meaningful and make sense.

Since the 1990s, in the wake of the abandonment of the most privileged stratum of the working class (organized manufacturing labor), California has been in the process of ending subsidies to the poor, racial minorities, children, and the elderly—rolling back hard-won, if temporary, gains of the civil rights era. However, important coalitions continue to be made.

At the Democratic national convention protests in August 2000, the Bus Riders' Union and Justice for Janitors used music and street theater to inspire their constituents. As the Bus Riders Union marched, they chose songs in lieu of chants to convey their agenda. The ethnic and immigrant realities of work in Los Angeles, especially in the industries like janitorial work, made it appropriate that the songs were sung in Spanish, by a Latina woman. In Los Angeles, economic restructuring has meant that the janitorial industry could switch from union janitors to nonunion janitors in the 1980s as building owners contracted with the lowest-bidding cleaning companies, enabling Latina immigrants to move into what had previously been a job dominated by African American males. Globalization and massive immigration to Los Angeles over the past ten years have made women (particularly those from Latin America and Asia) the new proletariat in an international division of labor: this means that in all ethnic groups they are an important register of the effects of globalization on their communities as a whole. Yet the restructuring of janitorial work has generated an unintended consequence: Latina immigrants are struggling to reunionize Los Angeles janitors. As promising as this seems, the fact remains that common experience of worker's-rights violations does not ensure common interest in class coalitions; in fact, it sometimes exacerbates existing tensions between communities of color. Justice for Janitors organizers continue to negotiate long-standing tensions between Salvadoran and Mexican immigrant workers. At the 2000 Justice for Janitors and Bus Riders Union marches during the Democratic national convention and at other important moments in the collective activism of interethnic movements in Los Angeles, these tensions succumbed to a spirit of solidarity and understanding about the common positionality of various populations marginalized by the climate of free trade and deindustrialization.

Rage Against the Machine, a multi-ethnic band from Los Angeles featuring Chicano lead singer Zack de la Rocha and Kenyan-born African-American guitarist Tom Morello, gave a free concert at the convention, and their first song was a cover of the MC-5's "Kick Out the Jams." When the MC-5 performed this song during the Democratic national convention in 1968, they characterized it as an opportunity to "testify" and to "use to music to hold us together." Drummer John Sinclair told listeners that rock and roll was the resensifier that listeners needed to build a gathering —or else, he warned, "you're dead and gone." Sinclair urged the audience to "stay alive with the MC-5!" which was what concertgoers were trying to do when the LAPD attacked protesters at an L.A. protest. When the L.A. band Ozomatli followed Rage Against the Machine onstage, the LAPD demonstrated their recognition of music's role in social protest by disconnecting the band's microphones from the speakers and rehooking their own microphone. After declaring the protest an unlawful assembly, they deployed more than two hundred officers to disperse the crowd, most of whom were gathered to watch the performance. Ozomatli already knew that their musical politics were a threat to the kinds of messages imparted just across the street at the convention. They had been born out of an interethnic working-class struggle.

In mid-March 1995, twenty-three workers began a sit-in at the 4th

Street office of the Los Angeles Conservation Corps. The corps, a nonprofit organization whose annual budget at the time was $6.5 million, was government- and privately funded, and paid its workers from $4.25 to $6.25 an hour to plant trees, remove graffiti, clean up after disasters, and paint murals at elementary schools and other buildings. Like most of its sister programs under the Corporation for National Service, the LACC paid its members minimum wage, but did not provide enough work hours for workers to qualify for medical benefits. LACC workers had tried unsuccessfully to unionize the corps, but their endeavors were foiled by managers, who told workers at other sites that the organizers were a rebellious group trying to ruin things for everyone. By March, what began as a protest when one of the union organizers, Carmelo Alvarez, was placed on administrative leave, grew into concerns about broader issues. The protesters complained that these low-paying jobs demeaned the minority workers, and their demands included higher pay, health benefits, and advancement to management jobs. Wil-Dog Abers, a corps worker who was paid $4.25 per hour, remarked to the *Los Angeles Times*, "It's slave labor. Some of these women have two children. How are they going to pay for those children on minimum wage?" Abers continued, "We're getting paid minimum wage and they keep our hours beneath the legal max where they have to give you benefits. Of course, the upper management is getting full benefits and rental cars." On March 22, corps officials, eager to avoid the bad publicity of forcibly removing the workers, began a mediation process.

Wil-Dog Abers's characterization of his and others' salaries as "slave wages" reflected a national pattern. According to political economist Holly Sklar, the minimum wage has become a poverty wage. By 1998 the minimum wage was 19 percent lower than in 1979, adjusting for inflation. The minimum wage, which formerly brought a family of three with one full-time worker above the official poverty line, now will not allow one full-time worker with one child above that line (Sklar: 31). For many working-class families of color in Los Angeles, these conditions were brought into sharp relief in the events leading up to and as a result of the 1992 riots after the acquittal of the LAPD officers who beat Rodney King. In the tradition of government remedies in times of crisis, Clinton signed the National and Community Service Trust Act in 1993, creating AmeriCorps and the Corporation for National Service.

The LACC, which was formed two decades before, followed a tradition of American national service programs since the early twentith century, like the Civilian Conservation Corps (CCC), created by Franklin Delano Roosevelt in 1933; John F. Kennedy's Peace Corps, approved by Congress in 1961; and Lyndon Johnson's VISTA program, established in 1964. What these and other service programs have in common is that they were created in response to economic crisis in order to build national infrastructure. Notably, we witness this directly after the Depression, in the creation of the Works Projects Administration and Roosevelt's CCC, and again during the Civil Rights Era. Clinton's plan in 1993 came after a major economic recession whose official end was March 1991. In the opinion of Sklar, however, one would never have known that this was the official end, since the poverty rate of two-parent young families more than doubled between 1973 and 1994. As Wil-Dog Abers observed, LACC management received full benefits while LACC workers received only minimum wage. This disparity is part of a rising trend. The average CEO in *Business Week*'s annual survey in 1997 made 326 times the pay of factory workers in 1997, compared to 1980, when CEOs made 42 times as much. The reality for families like Abers's at the time of the sit-in in 1995, not just in Los Angeles but nationwide, was that because of employment, housing, insurance, and other discrimination, the homeownership rate among black and Latino families was 47 percent for blacks and 44 percent for Latinos, about two-thirds the rate for white households (69 percent). In 1995, the median Latino household had a net worth of only $5,000 (just 8 percent of whites) and the median black household had a net worth of just $7,400.

The experience of failed unionization efforts and subsequent firing recounted by Carmelo Alvarez, Wil-Dog Abers, and their co-workers was likewise part of a nationwide trend. In 1994, *Business Week* reported that "over the past dozen years, the U.S. has conducted one of the most successful anti-union wars ever, illegally firing thousands of workers for exercising their right to organize."

In the midst of this crisis for young urban would-be workers, the Corporation for National Service happily reported by 1998, "when faced with challenges, our nation has always relied on the dedication and action of citizens." The creation of corps of young workers is therefore imagined as being reflective of what historian David Noble has called "the deep fraternity of the people," and is often successful in co-opting would-be leaders of grassroots movements, engaging them instead in "national service."

Wil-Dog Abers, who in 1995 called the Los Angeles Conservation Corps "slave labor," in 1998 went a little further, calling it a "poverty-pimp program," adding that politicians set up these kinds of jobs for inner-city youth to secure positive statistics for voting time. With this kind of truth serum floating among the workers, the LACC was eager to avoid both bad publicity and the contamination of other workers. They reached, finally, a settlement with the protesters: the workers lost their jobs, but were granted the use of the building for the rest of the year to engage in their own projects. These workers used the building to open a cultural community center dedicated to the arts of inner-city Los Angeles youth.

This seeming end to the story is more accurately characterized as the beginning: Wil-Dog Abers and longtime friend and co-worker José Espinosa had begun to collaborate on musical ideas, and decided to put together a band to raise money for the youth center. After they hired friends and other musicians around Los Angeles to participate, this new band had nine members, hailing from African American, Cuban, Chicano, Japanese, and Jewish cultural backgrounds. What resulted inspired the *San Jose Mercury News* to remark, "If Afrika Bambaata's cosmic utopia—Planet Rock—had a house band, this would be it." *Jam Magazine* characterized them as "Santana meets Wu-Tang Clan on a runaway party bus driven by the Tower of Power horns." Wil-Dog, Espinosa, and the others decided to give their band a Nahuatl name, after the Aztec god of dance: Ozomatli.

Arguably, more than any other musical group on the market at this time, Ozomatli's music reflects the fluidity of national borders engendered by technology free trade agreements. Their latest album, on which one can hear such diverse percussive instruments as tablas, congas, and turtle drums, is reflective of what George Lipsitz has termed "diasporic intimacy." He illustrates that as the machinations of global capital bring the world closer together, artists, activists, and intellectuals often find cultural forms and social movements from countries they've never been to more relevant to their experiences than those in their own countries. In addition to using a combination of African, Caribbean, and Mexican instruments and musical patterns, Ozomatli's performances and music videos include portraits of Che Guevara, Malcolm X, La Virgen de Guadalupe, and Mumia Abu-Jamal, suggesting a complex system of political, cultural, and religious influences which reflect not only the changing demographics of urban areas in California, but also the movement of culture and capital across what are increasingly fluid national boundaries. The fluidity of these boundaries in the popular sense is contradicted by the newest forms of rigidity employed by the state to control the makeup and activities of the national citizenry. Ozomatli captures this contradiction in its demands for public rights and recognition, directly engaging local public policy through urban popular music. Additionally, Ozomatli addresses local topics like police brutality, political prisoners, women's rights, censorship, and nonviolence; these topics are often as diverse as the musical patterns they employ: for example, "Superbowl Sundae" highlights the percussive talent of Jiro Yamaguchi on tabla, and manipulates a nine-string fretless guitar to sound like a sitar.

The fact that Ozomatli was formed out of a political event is important, because it has determined the kind of politics the group maintains. Ozomatli can be heard at Mumia rallies, college campuses whose student organizations they often affiliate with, and fund-raisers for various political organizations. The creation of the youth center that they were largely responsible for had a positive impact on the community, providing a space where young people could become involved in the arts. So inspired was Rage Against the Machine's Zack de la Rocha that he opened a similar space in East Los Angeles, the People's Resource Center.

In 1997, *Rolling Stone* called Ozomatli "a multiracial, neighborhood-spanning product of post-riot Los Angeles." Yet this is a flawed characterization for two reasons: it is tempting to see interethnic coalition politics like the cultural production of Ozomatli as a celebratory, utopic, and natural end to a period of unrest that many journalists, scholars, and L.A.

residents are eager to fix in space and time. But the truth is that Ozomatli was formed three years after the riots, not as a direct result of them. Additionally, this characterization of Ozomatli as "post-riot" is confounded by evidence that this political and musical style is not a recent phenomenon. There is a scholarly convention in the historiography of California which implies discrete racial and cultural categories, making this state appear as if it is a space inhabited by individualized, distinct groups. While important to reclaiming otherwise erased histories, this convention has often missed the complexities of racial and cultural multidirectional influences, both locally and diasporically. This leaves broad questions unanswered not only about the seeming "hermetically sealed histories," but about the future of alternative sites of struggle and contestation.

To their credit, some recent scholars have begun to explore the relationship of racialized minorities to each other in creating communities here, but most have only marginally addressed a dynamic history of cultural, political, and social interactions of a diversity of populations in California. That is, there is a crisis of historical memory which becomes institutionalized and perpetuated on a variety of levels, too often keeping us operating as if we have hermetically sealed cultural and political agendas, complicating opposition to the racist policies which George Lipsitz has identified as symptomatic of a "possessive investment in whiteness." The struggles over affirmative action and immigration occurring in California at this time, in tandem with a new era of global economic restructuring, demand this practice in our scholarship, in our pedagogy, and in our politics.

Fredric Jameson has argued that unlike previous moments of social drama, social movements now face a "new and historically original dilemma" for which adequate or cognitive maps do not exist.[9]

Protest music isn't always resistant, and its messages are sometimes detrimental to communities and movements. A given individual can be both oppressed and privileged in varying degrees and in different contexts:[10] gains made by one group might come at the expense of another aggrieved community. Ozomatli has been criticized for capitalizing on an iconic value of Che Guevara, Subcomandante Marcos, and Mumia Abu-Jamal: the band leads people to question, but sometimes, that's all it does. But across what Arjun Appadurai has called "the ethnnoscapes"[11] of Los Angeles, these groups have sometimes secured both literal and symbolic victories, providing a "new and historically original" map. In the absence of true national membership, excluded populations create alternative communities of allegiance. They are shifting and unstable but often meaningful enough to effect change and set an example for future formations.

In this postindustrial, transnational age, successful resistance is found in movements like the Justice for Janitors campaign and the Bus Riders Union, but it's also found in the music of bands like Quetzal, Ozomatli, and Rage Against the Machine. Today, youth culture has been nearly convinced of the fiction that collective action does not work. A successful movement must be open to accommodating shifting identities, and its musical culture must move across lines of race, gender, and geography to make sense of those shifts.

Perhaps by paying more attention to the links that already exist between populations like African Americans and Chicanos we will be able to see that new links are not needed between our communities: they are already there.

NOTES

I would like to thank the Center for Black Studies at the University of California–Santa Barbara for the invaluable resources and time which went into completing this work.

1. Lisa Lowe and David Lloyd have argued for the equal importance of sites of struggle that do not privilege the nation and are not necessarily defined by class consciousness. They argue that the critical displacement of "modern" modes of opposition (like Western Marxism) permits us to see how feminist, antiracist, and subaltern struggles provide an affirmative inventory of the survival of alternatives in many locales worldwide.

2. *Los Angeles Times*, August 21, 1994, A33; March 25, 1995, B3.

3. This is a force evoked well by George Lipsitz: "the influx of hundreds of thousands of Central Americans over the past decade has changed what it means to be Chicano for the nearly 3,000,000 people of Mexican origin in the city, while the migration of nearly 200,000 Koreans reconfigures the contours of the area's Asian American population. Immigration has changed cultural networks, the color of low-wage jobs, and increased competition for scarce resources." George Lipsitz, "World Cities and World Beat: Low-Wage Labor and Transnational Culture," *Pacific Historical Review* 68, no. 2 (May 1999): 213.

4. Mark Baldassare, *California in the New Millennium: The Changing Social and Political Landscape* (Berkeley and Los Angeles: University of California Press, 2000), 17.

5. Chester Himes, *Lonely Crusade* (New York: Grove Press, 1969), 17

6. *Los Angeles Times* poll, November 16, 1992, JJ5.

7. Maxine Waters, "Testimony before Senate Banking Committee," in Don Hazen, ed., *Inside the L.A. Riots* (New York: Institute for Alternative Journalism, 1992), 26.

8. Annette Steinacker, "Economic Restructuring of Cities, Suburbs, and Nonmetropolitan Areas, 1977–1992," in *Urban Affairs Review* 34, no. 2 (November 1998): 212 (29).

9. Frederic Jameson, "Cognitive Mapping," in Cary Nelson and Lawrence Grossbert, eds., *Marxism and the Interpretation of Culture* (Urbana: University of Illinois Press, 1988): 351; Jeanne Colleran and Jenny S. Spencer, eds., *Staging Resistance: Essays on Political Theater* (Ann Arbor: University of Michigan Press, 1998).

10. Maxine Baca Zinn and Bonnie Thornton Dill, "Theorizing Difference from Multiracial Feminism," *Feminist Studies* 22 (vol. 2): 321–331.

11. Arjun Appadurai's concept of ethnoscapes, which purports to release ethnicity like "a genie [previously] contained in the bottle of some sort of locality," is helpful to understanding the ways in which these changes have affected the identities and movements of those within the cities. Arjun Appadurai, *Modernity at Large: Cultural Dimensions of Globalization* (Minneapolis: University of Minnesota Press, 1996), 15.

WORKS CITED

Chavez, César. *César Chavez: Autobiography of La Causa.* New York: Norton, 1975.

Cruz, Jon, and Justin Lewis, eds. *Viewing, Reading, Listening: Audiences and Cultural Reception.* Boulder, Colo.: Westview Press, 1994.

Douglas, Mary *How Institutions Think.* Syracuse, N.Y.: Syracuse University Press, 1986.

Gilroy, Paul. *The Black Atlantic: Modernity and Double Consciousness.* Cambridge: Harvard University Press, 1993.

Jones, LeRoi. *Black Music.* New York: Quill Books, 1967.

Lipsitz, George. *Time Passages: Collective Memory and American Popular Culture.* Minneapolis: University of Minnesota Press, 1990

———. "World Cities and World Beat: Low-Wage Labor and Transnational Culture." *Pacific Historical Review* 68, no. 2 (May 1999).

Manley, Michael. *Jamaica: Struggle in the Periphery.* London: Third World Media, 1982.

Neal, Lawrence P. "Black Power in the International Context." In *Black Power Revolt,* ed. Floyd B. Barbour. Boston: Horizon Books, 1968

Roberts, John Storm. *The Latin Tinge: The Impact of Latin American Music on the United States.* New York: Praeger, 1977.

———. *Black Music of Two Worlds: African, Caribbean, Latin, and African-American Traditions.* 2nd ed. New York: Schirmer Books, 1998.

Said, Edward W. *Culture and Imperialism.* New York: Random House, 1993.

Sher, Chuck, ed. *The Latin Real Book: The Best Contemporary and Classic Salsa, Brazilian Music, and Latin Jazz.* Petaluma, Calif.: Sher Music Co., 1997.

Sklar, Holly. *Shifting Fortunes: The Perils of the Growing American Wealth Gap.* Boston: United for a Fair Economy and Holly Sklar, 1999.

Wade, Peter. "Black Music and Cultural Syncretism in Colombia." In *Slavery and Beyond: The African Impact on Latin America and the Caribbean,* ed. Darién J. Davis. Wilmington, Del.: Scholarly Resources Books, 1995.

Wyatt, David. *Five Fires: Race, Catastrophe, and the Shaping of California.* Reading, Mass.: Addison-Wesley, 1997.

17 NARRATIVES OF UNDOCUMENTED MEXICAN IMMIGRATION AS CHICANA/O ACTS OF INTELLECTUAL AND POLITICAL RESPONSIBILITY

Alberto Ledesma

INTRODUCTION: A QUESTION

Even though Noam Chomsky does not directly deal with issues of Mexican immigration and subalternity in the United States, his book *Powers and Prospects* (1996) calls attention to the need for academics to assume a responsibility toward social justice. In one of the chapters of this book, "Writers and Intellectual Responsibility,"[1] Chomsky notes that "[t]he responsibility of the writer as *a moral agent* is to try to bring the truth about *matters of human significance* to *an audience that can do something about them*" (56; his italics). Although, in my estimation, Chomsky has not paid enough attention to the specific problems of people of color, women, or gays and lesbians, I have long admired his analyses of the methods by which class oppression, social antagonisms, and political apathy are manufactured and maintained by a vast media apparatus that is at the service of powerful American corporations and cultural elites. He is one of this country's most prominent dissident voices, someone who—in a Gramscian sense—works against the subalternization of the masses precisely because of the organic and informational substance of his analyses.

I was thus interested in what Chomsky had to say about the practice of socially responsible writing because that is something that I think I do. More significantly, I became interested in what Chomsky could suggest is the political responsibility of Chicano writers because I have often wondered why it seems that, at least according to the majority of contemporary Chicano/a literary cultural critics that I have read, there are so few Chicana/o authors who have chosen to write and to tell the truths they perceive about such significant issues as undocumented immigration. Though undocumented immigration is an experience that I have some personal knowledge about, given that my family has lived it, and though I have read a good number of sociology books on the topic, this is not an experience that I have seen widely addressed in the pages of Chicano literary criticism, especially during a time when Mexican undocumented immigration has become such a heated political topic.

It seems striking to me that very little critical analysis of how Chicana/o writers have represented undocumented immigrant themes or figures has been offered by literary and cultural studies scholars during these last few years and precisely during a time when California voters passed Proposition 187. Out of such major works as Carl Gutíerrez-Jones's *Rethinking the Borderlands: Between Chicano Culture and Legal Discourse* (1995), Teresa McKenna's *Migrant Song: Politics and Process in Contemporary Chicano Literature* (1997), Tey Diana Rebolledo's *Women Singing in the Snow: A Cultural Analysis of Chicana Literature* (1995), José David Saldívar's *Border Matters: Remapping American Cultural Studies* (1997), and Ilan Stavans's *The Hispanic Condition: Reflections of Culture and Identity in America* (1995), only Saldívar's *Border Matters* devotes sustained and significant analytical attention to Mexican undocumented immigration as a Chicana/o subject. Indeed, Saldívar's book stands out as an exception in the way that it addresses the following questions:

> Is it possible today to imagine new cultural affiliations and negotiations in American studies more dialogically, in terms of multifaceted migrations across borders? How do musicians, writers, and painters communicate their "dangerous crossings" to us? How do undocumented and documented migrants in the U.S.-Mexico borderlands secure spaces of survival and self-respect in light of the government's doctrine of low-intensity conflict in regions undergoing what social theorists call "deindustrialization"—the decline of traditional manufacturing? (1)

Saldívar's questions echo my own concerns. And in his book, he goes a long way in addressing those "dangerous crossings" that undocumented-immigrant narratives relate. By citing numerous works by Chicana and Chicano writers, musicians, performance artists, and painters who codify Mexican (im)migrant borderness into their works, Saldívar proves his hypothesis that "[t]he history of migration, of forced dispersal in the Américas as represented in vernacular border cultures, challenges us to delve into the specific calculus of the U.S.-Mexico border-crossing condition" (197). And yet, while Saldívar's work is exemplary in the way that it does this, the subaltern undocumented immigrant subject remains but a peripheral figure and not an active agent within the material being analyzed. That is, the limit of Saldívar's book is in its scope. It focuses much more on the border, as most contemporary borderland studies do, and not enough on the "border conditions" that undocumented immigrants are challenged by once they move beyond the border's proximity. Still, this is a minor concern given the issues that the book seeks to put into question. After all, this is, as far as I know, the only study of its kind to substantively examine undocumented immigration as a fundamental Chicano issue. But, what about the other critics?

Is not undocumented immigration one of those constitutive elements that make up what is collectively referred to as the Chicana/o experience? Is there in the minds of readers, writers, and/or critics a list of criteria that must be fulfilled in order for Mexican immigrant subjects to be considered valid protagonists of Chicano/a stories? I have particularly become concerned about this question in recent years because of the way that anti-immigrant initiatives such as Proposition 187 have surfaced throughout the United States, very often as thinly disguised voter propositions that are policies, really, of demographic control. These policies, as most Chicano/a sociologists and immigration scholars, such as David G. Gutiérrez, Leo Chávez, and Pierrete Hogdagneu-Sotelo have observed, have had detrimental impacts on both recently arrived Mexican immigrants and long-time Mexican American citizens living in the United States. If there are no stories chronicling Mexican undocumented immigrant experiences out there, is this because, as Chomsky would suggest, not many authors have deemed the issue a pertinent Chicano "matter of significance"? Or, can it be that Chicano/a critics, those academically privileged interpreters who wield the power to decide what counts or does not count as meritorious creative craft and content, have chosen to not count these stories as part of the experiential base that informs what Chicana/o literature is about? In short, do these stories deal with thematic concerns unrelated to the aims of Chicano literature as perceived by its critical interpreters?

It is important to note, of course, that Chomsky's reference to "responsible writing" mostly alludes to American foreign policy journalism and that his reference to "telling the truth" chiefly refers to the unbiased reporting of political conflicts. Also, in fairness to Chicana/o literary critics, it seems crucial to keep in mind that one may not easily reduce an entire set of legally bound, historically conditioned, and culturally mediated Mexican immigrant experiences such as undocumented immigration into one representative mode. One, of course, cannot do this without engaging in some serious essentializing. Despite these caveats, writing that deals with undocumented immigrant narratives provides Chicana/o readers with opportunities to, as Gayatri Spivak has suggested, employ "strategic essentialisms," to focus on those fundamental commonalities that are shared by all undocumented subalterns and that might be the basis on which a social movement can be formed on their behalf (183). Furthermore, because Chomsky's argument about the moral responsibility of writers assumes that writing can and should be employed as a tool for creating meaningful social change, it is my view that his observations are strongly relevant to the purposes of Chicana and Chicano narratives. This is, after all, what Chicana/o narratives seek to do according to Ramón Saldívar's *Chicano Narrative: The Dialectics of Difference* (1990). In his book, Saldívar has argued that "the task of contemporary Chicano narrative is to deflect, deform, and thus transform reality by revealing the dialectical structures that form the base of human experience" (7). In other words, Saldívar suggests that "the function of Chicano narrative" is "to produce creative structures of knowledge to allow its readers to see, to feel, and to understand their social reality" (7).

The uniqueness of Chicano narrative, according to Ramón Saldívar, is not only that it tells the truth about Mexican American historical experience, but also that, as a result of its consciousness-raising function, it seeks to create social change, to "transform" the "social reality" Chicanos have known over the years. While I agree with Saldívar that Chicana and Chicano narratives do enable readers to envision possibilities for positive social change, I also believe that this change only happens when a critical mass of readers is able to understand and register a course of action connoted by the compelling "truths" that these narratives relate. And because critics have collectively analyzed few Chicana/o stories of undocumented immigration, it would seem that there is a scarcity of significant messages that these stories have related. Indeed, the fact that, up until this moment, there have been few literary critics who have read and/or presented interpretive theories about undocumented-immigrant stories, would suggest that the issue is not an important one for Chicanos, that stories about undocumented immigration have been unable to represent, as Ramón Saldívar might state, sound Chicano "creative structure[s] of knowledge."[2]

I am convinced, however, that narratives of undocumented immigration have always acted as essential "creative structures of knowledge." Inter- and intraethnic antagonisms, to borrow Edna Bonacich's concepts, exist within a split labor force in order serve this very purpose.[3] That Chicanas/os have felt personally attacked by the politics of California's Proposition 187, for example, only goes to show that non-Chicanos have had a difficult time making distinctions between recently arrived Mexicans and established Chicanos who have been in the United States for many generations—though David Gutiérrez has argued that "[a]s increasing numbers of Mexican immigrants entered their communities, Mexican Americans were compelled to reconsider the criteria by which they defined themselves" (67). And yet, why have those interconnections, real or imagined, between Mexican undocumented immigrants and Chicanos not been extensively theorized and/or analyzed in any significant fashion by the interpreters of a literature that purports to give voice to the experiences of Mexican-origin people who have lived and continue to live in the United States since 1848?

When sensitive stories of Mexican documented and undocumented immigration are told and when these stories are read because of the intrinsic value found in them, those pseudoracist stereotypes employed by anti-immigrant political pundits are resisted and challenged. What has happened to the English-language stories that undocumented immigrants have had to tell about their lives in the United States, however, has been the opposite of the way these narratives have been greeted in Mexico. While these stories have been prolific in Mexican creative production,[4] where do these stories get told once undocumented immigrants become "permanent" settlers in the United States? Although their experiences might be present, explicitly or implicitly, in a notable number of Chicana/o stories, it is only those critics who view undocumented immigration as a constituent element of the Chicano condition who write about it.

In this essay, I will argue that the reason that the vast number of interpreters of Chicana/o stories have not sought to interpret or represent undocumented immigrant themes and figures as constitutive components of a larger corpus of Chicano/a stories is due to the fact that they occupy, as a rule, a different epistemological position than the undocumented subalterns who are the literal and figurative agents of these stories. This difference in agency, an epistemological positionality if you will, prevents those who have shaped what Chicana/o literature is and how it should be defined from attaining more than a narrow understanding of the way that *indocumentado*-subaltern experiences, perspectives, and sensibilities constitute meaningful Chicana/o stories. That is, I hold that the act of decoding and writing about *indocumentado*-Chicano discourses of power, which have been strategically encoded into a good number of Chicano stories, is not an easy endeavor. It requires that a new definition of Chicano narrated experience—of Chicano literature itself—be formulated, one which affirms that Chicano/a experience can and should be understood as that which is also lived by those who are not yet, and may possibly never be, official American citizens. Not taking this step, consequently, prevents an understanding of the relevant Chicano "structures of knowledge" that *indocumentado* narratives have to offer readers.

PARADOXICAL REPRESENTATIONS

An interesting example of a Mexican American writer who has attempted to offer a sustained and accountable exploration of undocumented immigrants in his recent work is Richard Rodriguez.[5] Although the collection of autobiographical essays that Richard Rodriguez has published during the last thirteen years cannot be strictly referred to as "Chicano narratives," his work has certainly reverberated among readers since *Hunger of Memory* was first published in 1982. In *The Hispanic Condition: Reflections of Culture and Identity in America,* Ilan Stavans has observed, as have several cultural commentators, that "ironically enough, [Rodriguez's *Hunger of Memory*] has become something of a minor American classic, required reading in universities and high schools" (157). Indeed, Rodriguez has been considered such "a darling of a certain segment of the white intelligentsia" (M. Rodriguez: 13) that he has been widely anthologized in mainstream college composition readers as an example of a Mexican American who has achieved educational success in spite of his cultural origins. To most Chicana and Chicano readers, however, Rodriguez's testimony of his childhood and success as an adult has been less than representative of the lives of most Mexican Americans.

Readers may be surprised to find that Richard Rodriguez's *Days of Obligation: An Argument with My Mexican Father* (1992) is, as I see it, more sensitive in its depiction of Mexican undocumented immigrant experiences than they suspected. Given that for almost two decades Rodriguez's work has been viewed by Chicana and Chicano critics as nothing less than a betrayal of what it has meant to live as a Mexican American in the

United States,[6] the idea that his work sensitively portrays Mexican experience runs counter to what has been generally attributed to him. Critics tend to focus on Rodriguez's championing of assimilation as a strategy for succeeding in American society so much that they have come to regard him as someone "who considers himself first a *gringo* and then a Mexican" (Stavans: 159).

While Richard Rodriguez has been regarded, in the words of Marcelo Rodriguez, as "a man who would deny and betray his blood" (13), the portrayal that Rodriguez has offered of Mexican immigrants, both documented and undocumented, has been as multilayered and perceptive as Ramón Pérez's. In his works, and especially in his more recent material, Rodriguez has depicted Mexican undocumented immigrants not purely as marginalized and powerless individuals who operate invisibly in the fringes of American society. Rather, he has registered, more sympathetically at some times than others, the constraints under which undocumented immigrants have lived and the dilemmas that such constraints entail. It might be argued that Rodriguez has shown, in effect, an understanding of the "liminality"[7] that Mexican undocumented immigrants experience as they negotiate their lives in "limbo"—the space that exists, according to them (Chávez: 41–61), "between" their willingness to take on one of many undesirable jobs in the United States and "betwixt" their unemployment and poverty in Mexico. But the liminality that Rodriguez registers is not just physical. Rodriguez also acknowledges that Mexican undocumented immigrants possess a common epistemological point of view, a pattern of knowing that is unique to *indocumentados,* that influences their outlook on life and how others perceive them. For Rodriguez, the dual-liminality that Mexican undocumented immigrants live denotes a condition that is usually not articulated in verbal speech, but in the eloquence of silent actions, in the subtlety of gestures. Indeed, the assumptions that Rodriguez draws in order to determine what undocumented immigrant experience entails are not explicitly articulated in his work. Rather, these are only made evident with an analysis of his collective references to immigrants.

Undocumented immigrants appear in two ways in Rodriguez's work: as an "imagined mass" of impoverished Mexican immigrants he calls *"los pobres"* and as symbolic "individual" young men and women with dark faces and long names who race across the border seeking jobs that most American citizens do not want. More specifically, in *Days of Obligation* undocumented immigrants are represented as individual *pollos,* naïve Mexican travelers who heed the beckoning lights of American cities like San Diego, Los Angeles, San Antonio, and El Paso.

Rodriguez's representation of Mexican immigrants illustrates the challenges that Mexican American authors face when trying to write about the undocumented. Although Rodriguez, as an author, is able to capture important aspects of what it means to be an undocumented immigrant in his accounts, his work suggests that understanding the marginality that *indocumentados* live is not an easy task to accomplish. In fact, Rodriguez's sensitive representation of undocumented immigrants seems to occur only when he empathizes with relative aspects of the undocumented immigrant's condition of oppression, only when he recognizes that the forces that silence *indocumentados* affect him also.

In short, Richard Rodriguez addresses the undocumented in a way that most other Chicana and Chicano authors do not. Whereas such authors as Tomás Rivera, Estela Portillo Trambley, and Victor Villaseñor offer portrayals of undocumented immigrants that can be generally typified as "realist,"[8] Rodriguez seeks to explore the existential and epistemological perspectives of undocumented immigrants. Much of the difference in approach may be due to the fact that Rodriguez's narrative is not undocumented. His narrative, rather, is composed of personal essays, chronicles that tend to highlight a meditative perspective. Given the many politically oriented criticisms of his critics, however, one must wonder what it is that Rodriguez finds of interest in the undocumented immigrant's worldview—whether or not he is seeking to represent them as part of a open-ended "dialogue" or merely using them toward some political gain. Indeed, why would an author who supposedly cares so little about the history of the Chicana and Chicano people, who supposedly cares little about initiating dialogue among segments of *la raza,* want to explore undocumented Mexican immigrant experiences without some ulterior political motive? Of course, only Rodriguez knows the answer to this question. Readers, however, can profit from an interrogation of this issue in his work and by carefully exploring how the accounts that Rodriguez relates of Mexican immigrants are rhetorically crafted. By focusing on the stories and the language that Rodriguez uses in *Days of Obligation* to relate immigrant experiences, his interest in the immigrant subject can be understood.

Rodriguez does not really hear voices whispering to him as he develops his theory of what the voices of undocumented immigrants must sound like. Indeed, it is probable that no undocumented immigrant could literally "speak" to Rodriguez about his/her experience as an *indocumentado* without risking deportation. The imbalances in power are too great. We can safely presume, then, that the undocumented speak to Rodriguez mostly in a figurative sense, through the symbolism of their actions, or through what we may refer to as a semiotic language of manifested actions that Rodriguez is able to perceive as "voice" and then represent as "text."

Of course it should be noted that Leopoldo Rodriguez and Victoria Moran Rodriguez[9] are the first Mexican immigrants that Rodriguez came to know. However, they are unlike any other Mexican immigrants that Rodriguez discusses in his creative nonfiction. Both of Rodriguez's parents represent immigrants who came to the United States looking for a better life and found it, his mother as a secretary for a California governor and his father as a dental technician. Rodriguez notes in the last chapter of *Days of Obligation* that "[m]y mother, my father, they were different in California from what history had in store for them in Mexico. We breathed the air, we ate the cereal, we drank the soda, we swam in the pools" (217). In other words, they were "not bad off" when Rodriguez was growing up in 1950s Sacramento; as he states in *Hunger of Memory,* "They were nobody's victims" (12). As immigrants, Rodriguez's parents were not at all like *los pobres,* those countless immigrants who crossed the border as economic refugees and never managed to rise out of their poverty. Instead, his parents saw the United States not as a temporary location but as the permanent home in which they would build their lives, socially and physically.

Rodriguez's recognition of the differences that distinguish him from *los pobres,* the undocumented, represents a key and cathartic moment in *Hunger of Memory.* It is by recognizing the class position that *los pobres* occupy that Rodriguez begins to understand his own privilege. However, he tries to reduce material differences that distinguish him from *los pobres* to philosophy instead of class. In one of the book's key and often-cited passages he states, "That summer I worked in the sun may have made me physically indistinguishable from the Mexican working nearby. (My skin was actually darker because, unlike them, I worked without wearing a shirt. By late August my hands were probably as tough as theirs.) But I was not one of *los pobres.* What made me different from them was an attitude of *mind,* my imagination of myself" (138). There is great significance in Rodriguez's recognition that "[w]hat made me different from them was an attitude of *mind.*" Though he seems to be aware that the workers he has been laboring with don't have their papers, that they are legally prohibited from public participation in the society Rodriguez celebrates so much, he claims that the only matter of difference that exists between the immigrants and himself is "an attitude of *mind.*" Clearly, Rodriguez does not seem to be aware of the structural impediments—judicial and economic—that prevent undocumented immigrants from reaching the same success he has. Though he might be aware of their marginality, he does not seem to recognize it as something that cannot be easily overcome through education.

Indeed, it is only because of his education that Rodriguez believes that he is different from *los pobres.* With certainty, he asserts that if placed in a similar situation as the Mexican workers he observed above, events would proceed differently:

> If tomorrow I worked at some kind of factory, it would go differently for me. My long education would favor me. I could act as a public person—able to defend my interests, to unionize, to petition, to speak up—to challenge and demand. (I will never know what real work is.) I will never know what the Mexicans knew, gathering their shovels and ladders and saws. (138)

Of course Rodriguez is absolutely right that he will never know what undocumented immigrants know; he cannot easily undo the constitutional privilege that allows him to be a citizen of American society. And yet, if Rodriguez were to be placed in a similar situation as the undocumented immigrants, if he were to be declared "illegal" and barred from pursuing educational opportunities, he would find that many of his accomplishments would be nearly impossible to achieve. He would find, as Leo Chávez has stated, that "[f]irst and foremost, undocumented immigrants are constantly aware that at any moment they could be apprehended and deported from the country" (157). Instead of academic success, he would find innumerable obstacles limiting a full public manifestation of his intellectual abilities. Questions about whether or not he is a "permanent" member of American society would arise as issues to be dealt with. Eventually, he would discover that it is wiser to remain inconspicuous, invisible to the guardian agents of society; for, as Leo Chávez states, "Questions about residency are important because they point to the basic assumption that 'outsiders' should not enjoy the same societal benefits as 'insiders,' or citizens. As a consequence, the larger society excludes, or attempts to exclude undocumented immigrants from public goods such as taxpayer-financed health care, education, housing, and so on" (185). Thus, what Rodriguez does not seem to initially acknowledge is that his education has been precisely enabled by an agency that he and his parents have exercised which undocumented immigrants can never exercise as long as they remain undocumented.

And yet, even though he is aware of a profound difference that separates him from the undocumented workers he meets, there still seems to be a haunting connection that Rodriguez feels with them. More than their labor exploitation or their economic marginality, it is the undocumented immigrant's lack of a socially recognized voice with which he most attunes himself. Indeed, Rodriguez considers that it is only the silence of undocumented immigrants that limits their social condition. He observes:

> . . . Their silence stays with me now. The wages those Mexicans received for their labor were only a measure of their disadvantaged condition. Their silence is more telling. They lack a public identity. They remain profoundly alien. Persons apart. People lacking a union obviously, people without grounds. They depend upon the relative good will or fairness of their employers each day. For such people, lacking a better alternative, it is not such an unreasonable risk.
>
> . . . Their silence stays with me. I have taken these many words to describe its impact. Only: the quiet. Something uncanny about it. Its compliance. Vulnerability. Pathos. As I heard their truck rumbling away, I shuddered, my face mirrored with sweat. I had finally come face to face with *los pobres.* (138–139)

It seems that it is only the immigrants' silence, their "quiet," which interests Rodriguez—not so much the social and historical factors that explain the powerless nature of their marginality. Though Rodriguez finds the undocumented immigrants' silence "uncanny," needing to devote "many words to describe its impact," he does not seem to understand that the silence that these Mexican immigrants exhibit is not of their own choosing. He cannot see that more than a manifestation of being uneducated, their silence is an articulation of structural disenfranchisement. There is a price to pay when a worker who has no legal "right" to do so "demands, unionizes, or asserts a need"; that is precisely why they don't do it. Rodriguez does not seem to grasp how undocumented immigrants willingly suffer exploitation. Because they do not enjoy the luxury of American citizenship that Rodriguez does, they do not mythify education as the idyllic solution to their problems. They understand that no matter how much education *indocumentados* may have attained, as long as they remain undocumented, they must remain silent and undemanding lest they be deported. For Rodriguez, it is his educational achievements that define consciousness as an American citizen.

Rodriguez has continued to compare and contrast what he shares with the undocumented in many of the works he has written since *Hunger of Memory* was first published. In the four essays about Mexican immigration that he presents in *Days of Obligation* and in numerous pieces on the topic of immigration that he has published in various magazines and newspapers, Rodriguez has consistently juxtaposed his experience with that of Mexican immigrants. For example, in "Mexico's Children," an important essay that Rodriguez includes in *Days of Obligation,*[10] he seems to identify himself with Mexican immigrants. He writes:

> Mexico, mad mother. She still does not know what to make of our leaving. For most of this century Mexico has seen her children flee the house of memory. During the Revolution 10 percent of the population picked up and moved to the United States; in the decades following the Revolution, Mexico has watched many more of her children cast their lots with the future; head north for work, for wages; north for life. Bad enough so many left, worse that so many left her for the gringo. (52)

Rodriguez's use of the attributive adjective "our" in his statement that Mexico "does not know what to make of our leaving" would suggest that he considers himself an immigrant of sorts, another Mexican who at a moment's notice packed and left country and home. Yet, as noted before, he is not like other Mexicans. He is a Mexican American, a person who although having been born of Mexican immigrant parents has been reared under a different kind of social and constitutional relationships with the American society than his mother or father.

Though he distinguishes himself as an American citizen, Rodriguez's particular identification with Mexican undocumented immigrants seems clear, if not obvious. In the places that he has written about them since

Hunger of Memory it has been evident that he has been fascinated by what they represent culturally in American society, especially in contrast to Chicanos. For example, in an essay published in the winter 1995 edition of the *New Perspectives Quarterly,* he defines undocumented immigrants in the following way: "Illegals are an embarrassment to Mexico's government. They are an outrage to suburbanites in San Diego who each night see the Third World running through their rose garden. They are often adolescent, often desperate and reckless. They are disrespectful of American custom and law. They are also among the most modern people in the world" (61–62). It seems that for Rodriguez the undocumented are not just disenfranchised laborers, they are also enigmatic representatives of a new social paradigm—what he calls "prophets." At the same time that the undocumented represent "embarrassment to Mexico" they are also "the most modern people in the world." As if admiring the traits that constitute who "illegals" are, Rodriguez seems to suggest that there is something to be desired about being undocumented, that in spite of their "illegal" existence, something about what undocumented immigrants do is vanguard.

It is because of the broadly social and legal significance of their actions that Rodriguez considers the undocumented to be at the forefront of a new kind of society. And by presenting undocumented immigrants in both positive and negative terms, Rodriguez's treatment of Mexican immigrants becomes very different than what most Chicano authors have offered. The single most significant difference is that Rodriguez does not assume Mexican immigrants to be faithful to a specific cultural ideal; they are at the same time an "embarrassment to Mexico" and "an outrage to suburbanites in San Diego." For Rodriguez, undocumented immigrants are not defined by their cultural or national affiliation, but, rather, by the actions that reveal their philosophy of life—to survive at whatever the cost, "often desperate and reckless." Unlike Arturo Madrid, who has argued in his essay "Alambristas, Braceros, Mojados, Norteños: Aliens in Aztlán—An Interpretative Essay" that undocumented immigrants are "*mexicanos* on their way to becoming Chicanos" (28), Rodriguez considers the undocumented people without borders, or better yet, people without a country—an interpretation of Mexican immigration that cryptically echoes Ernesto Galarza's assertion in *Merchants of Labor* (1964) that "[m]igration is the failure of roots" (17).

For Rodriguez, the social condition of Mexican undocumented immigrants differs from Chicanos precisely because in his view the undocumented do not contemplate their departure from Mexico romantically, as a tragic event, but because they see their entrance into the United States optimistically, with an eye toward the future. Note these two paragraphs from *Days of Obligation:*

> Mexican Americans of the generation of the sixties had no myth of themselves as Americans. So that when Mexican Americans won national notoriety, we could only refer the public gaze to

> the past. We are people of the land, we told ourselves. Middle-class college students took to wearing farmer-in-the-dell overalls and they took, as well, a rural slang to name themselves. Chicanos.
>
> *Chicanismo* blended nostalgia with grievance to reinvent the mythic northern kingdom of Atzlán [*sic*] as corresponding to the Southwestern American desert. Just as Mexico would only celebrate her Indian half, Chicanos determined to portray themselves as Indians in America. (65–66)

Notice that while Rodriguez uses the pronoun "we" when referring to "Mexican Americans of the generation of the sixties," by also using the pronoun "they," he distances himself from "[m]iddle-class college students" who began to call themselves "Chicanos." He ascribes to Chicanos a certain philosophical perspective—"*Chicanismo*"—to which he attributes esoteric properties, "nostalgia," and "myth."

In comparison to Chicanos, the "illegal immigrants" that Rodriguez defines are characterized not by a sentimental viewpoint, but rather by physical affirmations. Rodriguez elaborates:

> The illegal immigrant is the bravest among us. The most modern among us. The prophet.
>
> "The border, señor?" the illegal immigrant sighs. The border is an inconvenience, surely. A danger in the dark. But the border does not hold. The peasant knows the reality of our world decades before the California suburbanite will ever get the point. (62)

Instead of being victims of nostalgic illusions like Chicanos, Rodriguez would suggest, undocumented immigrants know what it takes to survive in the real world. Rodriguez's conceptualization of undocumented immigrants above focuses more on the actions of immigrants than on their emotional state. Yet, while Rodriguez believes that the undocumented know how to negotiate "the reality of our world," he is not quite certain about what "the peasant," as he calls him, is feeling as he crosses the border.

No matter what traits *indocumentados* may have represented for Rodriguez when he wrote *Hunger of Memory*, it seems clear that in his more recent material he has increasingly become more aware of the complex characteristics associated with being undocumented. Again, "Mexico's Children" provides us with an interesting representation when it states that

> [t]o enter America, which is invisible, Mexicans must become invisible. Tonight, a summer night, five hundred Mexicans will become invisible at 8:34 P.M. While they wait, they do not discuss Tom Paine or Thomas Jefferson or the Bill of Rights. Someone has an uncle in Los Angeles who knows a peach farmer near Tracy who always hires this time of year. (51)

In referring to immigrants who must remain "invisible," Rodriguez seems to suggest that he can perceive them, that he is attuned with the shadowed lives of the undocumented. Rodriguez seems to recognize that as long as Mexican immigrants remain undocumented their success in American society is determined by their ability to remain unperceived, to stay silent. But they do not have to be silent with each other. Other undocumented immigrants are allies and function as a support system. In fact, Leo Chávez has observed that "[h]aving a trusted amigo de confianza can serve as an important resource. Indeed, having a trusted friend or relative with more experience dealing with institutions of the larger society is an important survival strategy found among undocumented immigrants" (137).

It is this relationship between the undocumented immigrants' need for silence and their need to form survival networks that Rodriguez considers being the essence of their "modern" outlook. Although Rodriguez may not personally understand the fundamental nature of the undocumented immigrant's experience, in "Illegal Immigrants: Prophets of a Borderless World" he recognizes that

> Before the professors in business schools were talking about global economics, the illegal knew all about it. Before fax machines punctured the Iron Curtain, coyotes knew the most efficient way to infiltrate Southern California. Before businessmen flew into Mexico City to sign big deals, the illegal was picking peaches in the fields of California or flipping pancakes at the roadside diner. (62)

Undocumented immigrants, according to Rodriguez, know about "global economics," "infiltration," and "big deals" because they learn it from each other. They, according to Chávez,

> create layers of resources and strategies for dealing with the larger society. These levels are based on the individual, on the family, and on a social network of *parientes* (relatives), *camaradas* (comrades), *paisanos* (fellow countryfolk), *amigos de confianza* (trusted friends), and *vecinos* (neighbors). By forming a network of family and friends in an area, undocumented immigrants increase the numbers of people that can be turned to for help during times of unemployment and when other crises strike. (135)

In his reflections on the undocumented, then, Rodriguez seems to demonstrate the understanding that although the undocumented are "invisible" to most of the American society, they are not alone. This is not what one would expect from him. His understanding of the undocumented immigrant experience seems consistent with the work of academics that have researched the subject. But why does he understand immigrants this way?

In *Days of Obligation,* Richard Rodriguez discusses the undocumented in five chapters. Yet, he essentially juxtaposes his experience to theirs in only two of those five chapters: "Mexico's Children," and "In Athens Once." Unlike in *Hunger of Memory,* in the chapters that make up *Days of Obligation* (most of which he published beforehand), Rodriguez attempts to imagine the thoughts and feelings of undocumented immigrants. Particularly in "Mexico's Children," Rodriguez imagines the voice of what seems to be a hypothetical immigrant crossing the border. This is no ordinary voice. It is a voice that is usually not heard, a voice that is usually silent and invisible to the majority of American society. The voice focuses on an immigrant narrator telling his tale as the events he is describing are happening—the journey from Mexico to the United States. Told in the second person singular voice, the tale allows the reader to place him or herself in conversation with the Mexican immigrant who is about to make the undocumented passage. Rodriguez writes:

> *You stand around. You smoke. You spit. You are wearing your two shirts, two pants, two underpants. Jesús says, if they chase you throw that bag down. Your plastic bag is your mama, all you have left; the yellow cheese she wrapped has formed a translucent rind; the laminated scapular of the Sacred Heart nestles flame in its cleft. Put it in your pocket. The last hour of Mexico is twilight, the shuffling of feet. A fog is beginning to cover the ground. Jesús says they are able to see in the dark. The have X-rays and helicopters and searchlights. Jesús says wait, just wait, till he says. You can feel the hand of Jesús clamp your shoulder, fingers cold as ice.* Venga, corre. *You run. All the rest happens without words. Your feet are tearing dry grass, your heart is lashed like a mare. You trip, you fall. You are now in the United States of America. You are a boy from a Mexican village. You have come into the country on your knees with your head down. You are a man.* (77–78; his italics)

There is an obvious existential quality in the scene narrated above, especially given Rodriguez's use of the pronoun "you." This is what immigrant life is about in Rodriguez's mind. Yet, this scene he imagines is not without significant subtextual meaning. Rodriguez's use of Jesús, an anonymous immigrant who shares his advice with the crosser, appears to represent his attempt to have the reader understand how it is that Mexico is "losing its children." The religious connotation in having Jesús act as the veteran counsel to the young immigrant about to cross the border is unmistakable. What is more subtle in Rodriguez's conception of the undocumented immigrant passage above is his suggestion that such an experience constitutes a skewed coming-of-age ritual in which Mexican boys find their manhood "on their knees," "with their heads down," and in silence—that becoming an undocumented immigrant means accepting degradation. Not as obvious is Rodriguez's suggestion that language defines the undocumented immigrant condition. In Mexican villages, the

United States exists only as a myth, a story shared by those who have already made the crossing. Would-be immigrants ready themselves for the passage on the basis of these stories, on the basis of what veteran immigrants like "Jesús" tell them about the United States: "Jesús says, if they chase you throw that bag down"; "Jesús says that they are able to see in the dark"; "Jesús says wait." Once across the border the undocumented immigrant experiences the United States not as an imaginary possibility, but literally as action: "You run. All the rest happens without words."

Of course, Rodriguez is absolutely right that Mexico is losing its "children" to America's lures. In *Return to Aztlan: The Social Process of International Migration from Western Mexico* (1987), Douglas Massey, Rafael Alarcón, Jorge Durand, and Humberto González observe that since 1964 "both legal and undocumented immigration have continued to grow" (43). In fact, they point out, "Between 1960 and 1980, a minimum of 1.1 million undocumented immigrants and an equal number of documented immigrants entered the United States from Mexico" (43–44). But that's not the point here. Rather, Rodriguez seems interested in rendering an epistemological perspective that is not usually acknowledged—a conversation between Mexican undocumented immigrants who are at the border's threshold that exists only in his imagination. And the significance of this imaginary position is that Rodriguez hears the immigrant's voice when so many others do not seem to do so. Where other authors hear silences, Rodriguez fleshes out the hidden narrative.

In the recent work that Rodriguez has written about Mexican undocumented immigrants he certainly seems to identify with aspects of their subaltern marginality, particularly their silence. A close reading of this work reveals that what he seems to be most sensitive to is their silent liminality, the undocumented immigrant's condition of being caught between two worlds—the public and the private—and not being able to say anything about this. In a sense, however, undocumented immigrants represent something that Rodriguez has known. While they can only exist in their own private world, necessarily hidden from the probing forces of public society, Rodriguez's sensibility to this liminality is that he has also been subjected to such probing forces of public society; indeed, he has achieved public success in spite of these forces, even though for a good number of years he had to retain a part of his identity as a secret—his homosexuality.

Only recently has Rodriguez himself publicly acknowledged that he is "a gay man."[11] As David L. Kirp noted in his article "The Many Masks of Richard Rodriguez," there have been many readers who recognized Rodriguez's gay experience. Kirp states:

> The real attraction of those shirtless men he describes [the undocumented] is not their poetic lives but their muscled bodies. But this he cannot—at least he will not—say. Fittingly, the final chapter of *Hunger of Memory* is called "Mr. Secrets." The well-crafted mask, the intellectual's Mardi Gras costume, kept this part of Richard

> Rodriguez's identity hidden from his straight audience. But gay readers knew how to read between the lines in order to find the beads of identity being dropped. (16)

Rodriguez's exploration of his gay self-consciousness is such, as Ilan Stavans has recognized, that "[h]is contribution is akin to that of James Baldwin, perhaps because the two have so much in common: their homosexuality, their deeply felt voyage from the periphery of culture to center stage, and their strong religiosity and sense of sacredness" (159). Yet Rodriguez's homosexuality has been more than just codified experience articulated in various essays—it has been a strong element of the worldview by which he has come to theorize others. More importantly, his homosexuality has constituted the kind of "liminal" condition analogous to the undocumented immigrant's for no other reason than the fact that he has kept it invisible for so long from public society. Indeed, in a society that still sees homosexuality as a form of deviance, it is difficult for Rodriguez not to fully disclose his sexual identity without paying a price. This is what Cherrié Moraga noted in *Loving in the War Years* (1984). She said: "Male homosexuality has always been a 'tolerated' aspect of Mexican/Chicano society, as long as it remains 'fringe'" (111). In fact, Moraga specifically offers the following commentary about Richard Rodriguez in *The Last Generation* (1993):

> with so much death surrounding him, [he] has recently begun to publicly address the subject of homosexuality; and yet, even ten years ago we all knew "Mr. Secrets" was gay from his assimilationist *Hunger of Memory.* Had he "come out" in 1982, the white establishment would have been far less willing to promote him as the "Hispanic" anti-affirmative action spokesperson. He would have lost a lot of validity . . . and opportunity. (163)

Thus, in order to remain "fringe," Richard Rodriguez has had to obscure his sexual identity and render it invisible to those who might object. Rather than clearly confessing his "secret," he silences it and codifies it lest he violate the expectations of those who afford him his power and privilege.

In *Hunger of Memory* Rodriguez states that his public success came at too high a price—the "private" life that he enjoyed. The significance of this statement can only be appreciated if one understands that in choosing to succeed publicly, according to the dominant expectations of what was considered acceptable in society during the '60s and '70s, Rodriguez had to silence an important aspect of his identity. Much more so, when we note that Rodriguez's success was appropriated by right-wing politicians to argue against progressive policies, it is clear that if Rodriguez wanted to remain successful, he had no choice but to remain silent about his sexual identity. It is in this way that Rodriguez presents those of us who study the representation of undocumented immigrant experience in the humanities with interesting questions: What is it that is necessary for the interpreters of Chicana and Chicano literature to have experienced if they are to represent undocumented immigrant stories sensitively? How many of us who interpret Chicano literature are subjected to circumstances which prevent us from addressing unpalatable issues directly? What cost is there to pay if we propose representations of "Mexico's children" that go against the convention?

The answers are not clear. Yet what seems to be obvious is that we need to open up a discursive space in Chicano and Chicana literary criticism where an honest discussion of Mexican and Chicano culture can be offered without having to suffer the wrath of the righteous. As Moraga notes, "To be critical of one's culture is not to betray that culture" (108). I am not suggesting here that Chicanos who have not theorized undocumented subjects have not been critical of the culture. What I am saying is that it will be difficult for Chicana and Chicano critics to rise above the current discursive approaches that privilege Chicano cultural citizenship and put forward readings of our stories that do not re-edify the silences that society already imposes. We cannot dismiss the fact that Rodriguez's work lent itself so freely to such reactionary forces as the ones behind California's English-only campaign of the late 1980s—a campaign whose members have figured prominently in the ranks of those who favored Proposition 187. Yet, this recognition only reinforces the need for further understanding of the profound heterogeneity that characterizes the Mexican heritage population living in the United States. Although it could be argued that the arguments presented by Rodriguez are directly linked to the anti-immigrant sentiments so popular today in the Southwest, the fact is that lately Rodriguez has now become a powerful voice reminding all his readers that Mexican immigrants are here to stay and that they form a thread in the fabric of our society. When a truckload of undocumented immigrants ran past an immigration checkpoint in Southern California and two sheriff's deputies beat two of the immigrants they caught, for example, Rodriguez commented: "The Mexicans took the blows, literally. They would have the bruises to show for it. But those sheriff's deputies were beating away last Monday at something less fleshy, as well. Call it an old American idea, a lofty dream of nationhood—based on soil" ("Soil and Water").

The old American idea that Rodriguez refers to—that the immigrant is to be subordinate—has also been an old idea among some Chicanos. But now a change is in order. And what Rodriguez reminds his readers is that those undocumented immigrants in our midst are also Americans of sorts; they have traveled long and far in search of a better life. And so Rodriguez, in spite of the political opportunism on which he capitalized before, reminds us that although undocumented immigrants are silent figures, they are not ghosts—that they will not disappear no matter how much we may try to exorcise them.

Richard Rodriguez has indeed written extensively on the plight of the undocumented since he first published his infamous *Hunger of Memory* in 1982. He has published numerous essays contemplating the meaning of undocumented immigration in a post-187 society. In such essays as "Will We Still Embrace Immigrants Rushing to Citizenship?" "The New Native Americans," and "Illegal Immigrants: Prophets of a Border-less World," Rodriguez has commented so much on the issue that Peter Brimelow, author of the highly reactionary *Alien Nation* (1994), attacked him for defending immigrants. And yet, Rodriguez's famed role as the darling of the very forces that are now pushing for limits on immigration has made it difficult for Chicanos to listen to what he has to say now.

A Chicana who has recently authored a compelling story about the undocumented is Demetria Martínez. In her novel *Mother Tongue* (1994), Martínez offers a dramatic story of a Chicana activist who actually participates in helping a Salvadoran political refugee find sanctuary in the United States. Besides the fact that the novel is very artfully written, the book is notable because of the way that it compares to the life experience of the author herself. In her novel, Martínez chronicles the story of María, a young Chicana activist who falls in love with José Luis Romero, a *Salvadoreño* seminary student who has had to escape his country after being tortured and threatened. The novel recounts the multiple emotions María feels as she tries to win José Luis's love. José Luis's trouble is that he is still haunted by the violent memories of his life in El Salvador, that he cannot maintain a healthy relationship. In the end, he abandons María when, during a moment of passion, the violence of his past makes him violently hurt her.

Again, *Mother Tongue* is significant for me because the author, a Chicana, actually lived some of the experience she cites. In the last page of her book, there is a passage that states: "In 1987 Martínez was indicted on charges related to smuggling Central American refugees into the United States. A jury later acquitted her on First Amendment grounds" (195). Yet, though *Mother Tongue* does deal with undocumented immigration, it is important to note that the plot of the book centers more on the sanctuary movement of the early 1980s. This was not the primary kind of "illegal immigration" that Proposition 187 meant to discourage. More importantly, it is quite revealing that the book makes very little mention of the historical relationships between Chicanos and the undocumented. That nexus remains at the periphery.

AN INTERESTING CASE

I believe that the most significant narrative of undocumented immigration published in the last four years, since California's approval of Prop 187, is a narrative published by a non-Latino: *Illegals* (1996), by J. P. Bone.[12]

Illegals is an important book for me because it tries to live up to Chomsky's definition of what socially responsible writing ought to do.

The book tells the tale of a group of undocumented immigrant shoe-factory workers who attempt to create a labor union but are thwarted by the Border Patrol, a corrupt union boss, and a duplicitous employer. The story revolves around the experiences of Antonio, a young Chicano labor organizer, and Don José, Felipe, and Sonia, undocumented immigrant workers whom he has trained to be organizers themselves. The story also relates the experiences of Ana and Manuel, a pair of Salvadoran cousins who are making the risky trek, first across Mexico, and then across the United States, all in the process of escaping the violence and terror of El Salvador in 1980. In the end, Ana and Manuel make it to the United States, where they, too, join the rest of the immigrants in the labor struggle. Unfortunately for them and the rest of their comrades, the union drive they have initiated fails. Yet all is not lost. What the immigrants come to understand after their ordeal is that they do have some power, that by uniting their voices—silenced as they may be—they can actually stand up and affirm their rights.

I must tell you that I was a bit skeptical of the book when I first read it. Initially, I felt that the characters and the plot were guided by too many stereotypical frames of reference. Antonio, the young Chicano hero, seemed too much like a *cholo*-gone-good cliché, a labor activist cut straight out of the pages of *Lowrider Magazine.* Ana and Manuel, the Salvadoran refugees, also seemed too familiar, almost carbon copies of the protagonists, Rosa and Enrique, of Gregory Nava's *El Norte.* And yet, something about the book made me read it more than once, something made me pay attention to it.

Maybe what attracted me about the book was that it hit too close to home, that it told the kind of "true" undocumented immigrant life experience that I and my parents once knew. One thing the book does effectively is chronicle the fear that undocumented immigrants feel whenever the police are around, the fear that undocumented immigrant children feel when their parents don't return home at just the right time, the fear that immigrant workers feel when, though they might be fired (or, worse, deported), they still speak up about the injustices they face at work. This is a fear my family has known.

Indeed, I became so curious about the book that I decided to do something that I had never done before: to actually talk to the writer, to call and find out why he had written the book in the first place. It was very difficult getting in touch with the author. There was no one by the name of "J. P. Bone" listed in the Los Angeles telephone directory, or in Berkeley's for that matter, the town where the book's publisher has its office. Yet, one day, while surfing the Web, I found the address to a page that had contact information to get in touch with the author. What I found out impressed me, and also motivated me to write the words you are reading today. J. P. Bone had his phone number listed on that page.

After I found out J. P. Bone's number I called him. When he answered the phone, I introduced myself, told him about the kind of work I do, and asked if I could talk to him about his book. He seemed excited, and after some small conversation, he invited me to dinner. It turned out that he lived in the San Francisco Bay Area. All I had to do was cross the bridge. Before he hung up the phone, however, he told me in a deep and somber voice, "You should know that I'm not Chicano—I'm a gringo." I went anyway.

Dinner at Bone's was pleasant. When I arrived I was greeted at the door by the author, a tall, clean-shaven blue-eyed man, wearing wire-rimmed glasses, worn Levi jeans, and working boots. Inside, his wife and mother-in-law greeted me with Salvadoran *pollo asado* and black beans. The author's wife, it turned out, had helped him with much of the book. Some of her own experiences, her flight from El Salvador, were included in its pages. The author's mother-in-law, like my own abuelita, all dressed in black, listened while her daughter and J.P. told me about the challenges that they had had in getting the book published.

What struck me most about the conversation that I had with J.P. occurred when he told me that he had not intended to write the book for a Chicano or Latino audience. He had actually meant for the book to be read by a general audience. He told me that he had been writing the book for many years—that he was "obsessed by it." Having been a labor organizer himself, he had felt it important to tell the truth about the things *indocumentados* had accomplished when they actually organized, that it was a myth that the undocumented were indeed powerless. He had written the book as an organizing manual of sorts, a story that showed how even undocumented immigrants could have a worker's revolution.

In fact, he said, he was actually surprised that most of the readers for his book were Latinos. He told me that since its publication, the book has been primarily sold by Latino bookstores. Moreover, he said, because a press that he had created, Mindfield Publications, published the book, he knew that most of the books had reached largely Latino audiences in East L.A., in San Francisco's Mission District, and in the East Bay. He had even been invited to speak by a number of Latino organizations, including the UFW's own Radio Bilingüe, which is located in Fresno. Everyone always seemed to be surprised that he was not a Chicano author.

Even more dramatic, it seemed to me, was how Bone had chosen to advertise the book. Not only had he created a Web page for it, he had tried selling it in the streets of downtown L.A. In fact, he said, he and his wife had worked closely to prepare a one-page flyer containing a short chapter of the book in Spanish. He thought it was interesting that when he tried to hand out the flyers in L.A.—which had the Spanish title of the book emblazoned in large print—many of the passersby whom to he handed the flyer seemed reticent. "There I was, in the middle of the sidewalk, handing the flyer out, not knowing what would happen." As it turned out, he said, many of the passersby, having walked several steps past him, immediately turned around and asked him where they could get the book advertised by the flyer. They had read the excerpt and wanted to read more. He ran out of leaflets in less than an hour, and he was able to sell a good number of books in spite of the fact that the books he sold were in English and had not yet been fully translated into Spanish.

Bone also told me about the many phone calls that he has received from readers, young and old, all of them having done detective work like me in order to find him. They had all read his book in one venue or another and had generally called to thank him for writing the book. I had no reason to doubt him, for here I was. One woman had even called to thank Bone because her daughter, who had picked up the book from a friend, had finally been able to understand something of that undocumented immigrant experience that her mother had been so reluctant to speak about. "Now I understand what you went through, mamá." This is what she had said to her mother and what the mother said to Bone.

Before I left, Bone handed me a local newspaper, the April 4, 1997, edition of *The Express: The East Bay's Free Weekly,* wherein his book was being advertised. It read:

> Pete Wilson Would Burn This Book
> After conducting a vicious campaign against undocumented workers, Wilson and his ilk don't want people to read anything that tells the immigrant's side of the story. But someone finally has. (3)

Underneath this caption, a blurb by noted historian Howard Zinn further elaborated:

> J. P. Bone's novel *Illegals* is a rarity in contemporary literature—a story which boldly and vividly presents a piece of contemporary history, told through characters who cannot fail to move you with their anguish and their courage. I am reminded of Upton Sinclair and John Steinbeck, who did not hesitate to confront the most urgent issues of their day through their fiction. *Illegals* is a political novel that touches the heart. I hope that it is widely read. (3)

The probability, of course, is that as long as major literary critics do not choose to read and review Bone's work, most Chicano readers will not get to hear the message of a novel like *Illegals.* Such a message is unlikely to reach most of its intended or unintended audience, but it is surely being read by many Latino readers who have access to it. In Chomsky's terms, these readers have found value in the meaningful truths that the work has articulated and, in so doing, have made it apparent that there is a need for more of this kind of work. These truths, of course, are diametrically opposed to the malignant stereotypes that politicians have used in order to exploit the immigration issue. Bone's work is valuable because it seeks to empower. What I wonder is who is going to promote the value of such work? Whose responsibility is it to promote the honest representation of a class of people who by definition cannot represent themselves?

NOTES

1. It should be noted that Chomsky's "Writers and Intellectual Responsibility" itself makes indirect reference to the first influential political essay that he wrote. Published in the February 23, 1967, edition of *The New York Review of Books,* that essay was titled "The Responsibility of Intellectuals," and it argued that "[[i]t is the responsibility of intellectuals to speak the truth and to expose lies."

2. Among the early literary critics who developed an integrated theory of Chicana/o literature is Arturo Madrid. He is one of the few scholars who made reference to undocumented immigrants in his interpretations of the literature. The essay he published in the spring of 1975 edition of *Aztlán,* "Alambristas, Braceros, Mojados, Norteños: Aliens in Aztlán—An Interpretative Essay," remains one of the only widely disseminated critical studies of undocumented immigrants to date by Chicano/a literary scholars.

3. For a definitive discussion of this concept see Edna Bonacich's essay "A Theory of Ethnic Antagonism: The Split Labor Market," *American Sociological Review* 37, no. 5 (October 1972): 547–559.

4. For a more extensive discussion of the way that undocumented immigration has been prolifically presented by Mexican authors in such creative forms as *corridos* and cinema, I invite the reader to look at María Herrera-Sobek's *Northward Bound: The Mexican Immigrant Experience in Ballad and Song* (1993) and David R. Maciel and María Rosa García-Acevedo's "The Celluloid Immigrant: The Narrative Films of Mexican Immigration."

5. Though I am only discussing Rodriguez in this section the reader should note that a close examination of Chicana/o literature clearly shows that narratives relating undocumented immigrant experience have always been thematically present in Chicana/o novels, short stories, and creative nonfiction. In my essay "Undocumented Crossings: Narratives of Mexican Immigration to the United States" (1996) and my doctoral dissertation, "Undocumented Immigrant Representations in Chicano/a Narratives" (1996), I showed this and argued that "[o]nly by reading and understanding how Mexican immigrants, whether documented or not, have been represented in Chicano narratives, can Chicano literary critics prevent the establishment of ideas that, in effect, divide 'Americans of Mexican descent' from 'newly arrived Mexicans'" (57). In these works I also reviewed how, but for a few notable works by such critics as José David Saldívar, María Herrera-Sobek, and Genaro Padilla, recent literary criticism has failed to account for an unessentialized depiction of Mexican immigrant experience in its collective analysis. This present essay does not allow me to extensively review the way that Chicana and Chicano literary scholars have interpreted undocumented immigrant themes and figures. For that purpose, I invite readers to peruse one of my previous works.

6. Richard Rodriguez's narrative commentaries have long been seen as antithetical to Mexican American cultural pride. This point is well articulated by none other than Tomás Rivera. In an essay that he titled "*Hunger of Memory* as Humanistic Antithesis," published posthumously in *MELUS* 11, no. 4 (Winter 1984): 5–13, Rivera notes that "[t]his book has been controversial for the Hispanic in general and in particular to the Mexican American or Chicano" (5), because, as he goes on to discuss, "[t]he only positive cultural attributes which [Rodriguez] signals throughout his book are those relative to the English-speaking world" (p. 13). More recently, in an article published by the *San Francisco Examiner's Image Magazine,* David L. Kirp observed that "many Latinos and leftists angrily denounced *Hunger of Memory* as a neurotic's tale and a sellout's story. To the generation of militant Latinos who have come after him, whose voices now de-

liver lectures in Chicano Studies classes and from political podiums, Richard Rodriguez stands accused as *Tío Tom*—a traitor to his people, his family and himself" (12).

7. I base my use of the term "liminality" on Leo Chávez's *Shadowed Lives: Undocumented Immigrants in American Society* (Fort Worth, Texas: Harcourt Brace Jovanovich College Publishers, 1992). In *Shadowed Lives*, Chávez himself credits the concept to Victor Turner and defines it as "when an individual is no longer in the Old World but has not yet moved into, or been accepted into, the new world." Chávez further observes that "[t]his liminal period is typically a time of ambiguity, apprehensiveness, and fear. The participant does not know what the outcome of the migratory experience will be, nor the trials and obstacles he or she will have to endure" (41).

8. I use quotation marks in referring to "realism" deliberately in order to recognize the problems that are implicit in using it as a category of literary genres. As *The Penguin Dictionary of Literary Terms and Literary Theory*, edited by J. A. Cuddon (New York: Penguin Books, 1991), points out, "Realism" is "[a]n exceptionally elastic critical term, often ambivalent and equivocal, which has acquired far too many qualifying (but seldom clarifying) adjectives" (772).

9. For the specific identification of Rodriguez's parents' names and brief bibliographic data I used Richard D. Woods's short essay "Richard Rodriguez," in the *Dictionary of Literary Biography: Chicano Writers*, ed. Francisco A. Lomelí and Carl R. Shirley (Detroit: Bruccoli Clark Layman, 1989), pp. 214–216.

10. "Mexico's Children" is, indeed, a significant essay when one considers where it fits in what Rodriguez has written over the years. Besides being one of the first major expositions about Mexico and Mexican Americans, it is the essay wherein Rodriguez has discussed Mexican American and Mexican immigrant identity the most. First printed in *The American Scholar* (published by Phi Beta Kappa, 161–177) in 1986, "Mexico's Children," the essay, assumed the title of what Rodriguez had advertised would be his next book after *Hunger of Memory.* First announced as a forthcoming book when Rodriguez published "Across the Borders of History" in March of 1987, in *Harper's Magazine, Mexico's Children* was later re-advertised as Rodiguez's next book by *Mother Jones* magazine in November of 1988 when he published "I Will Send for You or I Will Come Home Rich." In June 1990, when Rodriguez published his essay "Sodom: Reflections of a Stereotype," *Mexico's Children* was again identified by the editors of the *San Francisco Examiner*'s *Image* magazine as the title of an upcoming "novel." More recently, in the November 1991 edition of *Harper's Magazine*, when he published "Mixed Blood" (five years after he had published the first draft of the essay), *Mexico's Children* was represented as the title of a book that Viking Press would publish for Rodriguez in 1992. In 1992 Viking Press did publish a book for Richard Rodriguez; however, *Days of Obligation* is the title of the book and "Mexico's Children" is an essay included in it.

11. Although he had made hints about his sexuality in previous work, including *Hunger of Memory*, it was in a commentary that Rodriguez wrote on a Supreme Court decision that Rodriguez referred to himself "As a gay man." The commentary, "Scalia Scores Gays for America's Sexual Meltdown," was released on May 21, 1996, at 9 A.M. by the Pacific News Service, where Rodriguez serves as editor.

12. The name J. P. Bone is a pseudonym. The author, a journalist of European American heritage, worked for many years as a labor organizer in Los Angeles. He is married to a Salvadoran woman. She, along with many of the workers that he helped organize, inspired much of the novel's premise (Bone interview).

WORKS CITED

Bone, J. P. *Illegals.* Berkeley, Calif.: Mindfield Publications, 1996.

——. Personal interview. November 18, 1999.

Chávez, Leo R. *Shadowed Lives: Undocumented Immigrants in American Society.* Case

Studies in Cultural Anthropology, ed. George and Louise Spindler. San Diego, Calif.: Harcourt Brace Jovanovich College Publishers, 1992.

Chomsky, Noam. *Powers and Prospects: Reflections on Human Nature and the Social Order.* Boston: South End Press, 1996.

——. "The Responsibility of Intellectuals." *New York Review of Books,* February 23, 1967. Reprinted in *The Chomsky Reader,* ed. James Peck, 59–120. New York: Pantheon, 1987.

Galarza, Ernesto. *Merchants of Labor.* Charlotte, N.C.: McNally and Loftin, 1964.

Herrera-Sobek, María. *Northward Bound: The Mexican Immigrant Experience in Ballad and Song.* Bloomington: Indiana University Press, 1993.

Hondagneu-Sotelo, Pierrete. *Gendered Transitions: Mexican Experiences of Immigration.* Berkeley: University of California Press, 1994.

Illegals. Advertisement. "Pete Wilson Would Burn This Book." *Express: The East Bay's Free Weekly,* April 4, 1997, 3.

Kirp, David L. "The Many Masks of Richard Rodriguez." *Image. San Francisco Examiner,* November 15, 1992, 11–16, 35.

Ledesma, Alberto. "Undocumented Crossings: Narratives of Mexican Immigration to the United States." In *Culture across Borders,* ed. David R. Maciel and María Herrera-Sobek, 67–98. Tucson: University of Arizona Press, 1996.

——. "Undocumented Immigrant Representation in Chicano Narrative: The Dialectics of Silence and Subterfuge." Dissertation, University of California at Berkeley, 1996.

Maciel, David R., and María Rosa García-Acevedo. "The Celluloid Immigrant: The Narrative Films of Mexican Immigration." In *Culture across Borders,* ed. David R. Maciel and María Herrera-Sobek, 149–202. Tucson: University of Arizona Press, 1996.

Madrid, Arturo. "Alambristas, Braceros, Mojados, Norteños: Aliens in Aztlán—An Interpretative Essay." *Aztlán: A Journal of Chicano Studies* 6, no. 1 (1975): 41.

Martínez, Demetria. *Mother Tongue.* New York: One World, 1994.

Massey, Douglas, Rafael Alarcón, Jorge Durand, and Humberto González. *Return to Aztlan: The Social Process of International Migration from Western Mexico.* Berkeley: University of California Press, 1987.

Moraga, Cherríe. *The Last Generation.* Boston: South End Press, 1993.

——. *Loving in the War Years.* Boston: South End Press, 1983.

Pérez, Ramón. "Tianguis." In *Diary of an Undocumented Immigrant,* trans. Dick J. Reavis. Houston: Arte Publico Press, 1991.

Rivera, Tomás. "*Hunger of Memory* as Humanistic Antithesis." *MELUS* 11, no. 4 (Winter 1984): 5–13.

Rodriguez, Marcelo. "HUNGER of reality." *SF Weekly,* September 30, 1992, 13–14.

Rodriguez, Richard. *Hunger of Memory: The Education of Richard Rodriguez.* New York: Bantam Books, 1982.

——. *Days of Obligation: An Argument with My Mexican Father.* New York: Viking, 1992.

——. "Illegal Immigrants: Prophets of a Borderless World." *New Perspectives Quarterly* (Winter 1995): 61.

——. "Sodom: Reflections on a Stereotype." *Image. San Francisco Examiner,* June 10, 1990, 11–12, 15–16.

——. "Mexico's Children." *The American Scholar.* Phi Beta Kappan (Spring 1986): 161–177.

——. "I Will Send for You or I Will Come Home Rich." *Mother Jones* 13, no. 9 (November 1988): 26–33, 56.

——. "Mixed Blood: Columbus' Legacy—A World Made *Mestizo.*" *Harper's Magazine* (November 1991): 47–56.

——. "Across the Borders of History." *Harper's Magazine* (March 1987): 42–53.

Saldívar, José David. *Border Matters: Remapping American Cultural Studies.* American

Crossroads, ed. George Lipsitz, Earl Lewis, Peggy Pascoe, George Sánchez, and Dana Takagi. Berkeley: University of California Press, 1997.

Saldívar, Ramón. *Chicano Narrative: The Dialectics of Difference.* Madison: University of Wisconsin Press, 1990.

Spivak, Gayatri Chakravorti. "Criticism, Feminism, and the Institution." Interview with Elizabeth Gross. *Thesis Eleven* 10/11 (November/March 1984–85): 175–187.

Stavans, Ilan. *The Hispanic Condition: Reflections on Culture and Identity in America.* New York: HarperCollins Publishers, 1995.

Woods, Richard D. "Richard Rodriguez." In *Dictionary of Literary Biography: Chicano Writers—First Series,* ed. Francisco A. Lomelí and Carl R. Shirley, 214–216. Detroit: Bruccoli Clark Layman, 1989.

18 *TEKI LENGUAS DEL YOLLOTZÍN* (CUT TONGUES FROM THE HEART): COLONIALISM, BORDERS, AND THE POLITICS OF SPACE

Delberto Dario Ruiz

> I accept the assumption that "all relations are relations of power" (Touraine 1981), and am therefore analytically compelled to understand the dynamics of social relations as relations of power.
>
> —Teresa Córdova, "Power and Knowledge: Colonialism in the Academy" (1994)

> Far from the blinding light of Europe's Enlightenment, among people who wear the scars of modern violence as a second skin, it becomes difficult to clear from sight or to displace onto foreign Others the barbarous underside of modern civilization.
>
> —Fernando Coronil, *The Magical State* (1997)

> . . . as history constantly teaches us, discourse is not simply that which translates struggles or systems of domination, but is the thing for which and by which there is struggle.
>
> —Michel Foucault, "The Order of Discourse" (1981)

AS A Yaqui/Huichol/Xicano, the realities of a cut tongue are especially disturbing. When I was young, my great-grandmother, Rita Cubedo (later "cut" to Diaz as a stratagem for surviving the inquisition against Yaquis in the late 1900s), would speak to me in our native Yaqui language. Though quite young, I nonetheless retain vivid recollections of those interactions. One image I remember in particular is of my great-grandmother and me speaking to each other in Yaqui, Mexican Spanish, and bits of English while she made tortillas on a wood-burning stove. After I enrolled in school, I learned to leave such stories and language skills behind. Tongues were cut from my heart.

"Speak English, you are in America now!" is a statement forever embedded in my psyche. Such utterances can be heard throughout pedagogical practices across the United States, functioning to occlude anyone and anything deemed outside of mainstream discourse. My project thus implicates colonialism and its machinations: the theft of lands, the demonization of native inhabitants, and the creation of borders. Foremost for this essay, *"Teki Lenguas del Yollotzín,"* my project reclaims cut tongues and offers an analysis of how dominant discourses and languages relegate Xicanas/os to lives with "cut tongues." Such domination contributes to the displacement of a people, their cultures and languages. I show how subaltern cultural practices create alternative discourses and serve to counter Eurocentric intellectual and cultural hegemony. The heterotextual and hybrid literatures created by writers such as Gloria Anzaldúa, Alfred Arteaga, Francisco Alarcón, Lorna Dee Cervantes, and José Montoya challenge, I argue, the hegemonic critical apparatus which silences and buries Xicana/o concepts, languages, and cultural productions. These authors speak to the varying ways *gente de las Américas* (people of Latin American ancestry) create identities in opposition to colonialism and borders by articulating alternate political spaces. By interweaving analysis of border cultures, pedagogical and juridical systems, and examples of subaltern productions, my essay reveals alternative modes for reading the oppressive nature of Western modernity.

Colonial powers, first Spain and then the various nations that followed, controlled institutions, while legitimizing subordination under the guise of a "natural ordering" of the universe. One of the darker sides of this colonialist "natural ordering" has been the psychological effects on colonized people, embedding in them a subordinate and submissive sense of being and place. The violent psychological and cultural imperialism of colonial domination is difficult to gauge. However, Jean Paul Sartre's preface to Frantz Fanon's *The Wretched of the Earth* (1963) summarizes the how the colonial balance of power operates: "Not so long ago, the earth numbered two thousand million inhabitants; five hundred million men, and one thousand five hundred million natives. The former had the World; the other had the use of it."[1]

Alfred Arteaga, professor of ethnic studies at the University of California-Berkeley, opens his work, *Chicano Poetics: Heterotexts and Hybridities,* by referring to a few lines in his poem "Cantos":

> *Another Island*
> *A continent*
> *A line, half water, half metal.*

The last line, "A line, half water, half metal" reads to him in two ways. "[O]n the one hand, [the line serves] to point to the intersection of the personal and the social and, on the other, to point to something else" (6). For Arteaga the line not only signifies borders metaphorically, "but the actual physical and political borderline" demarcating the United States from Mexico, "which is, after all, Rio Grande water that runs from the Gulf of Mexico to Juaréz / El Paso and a metal fence from there to the Pacific Ocean" (6). The border establishes a wedge between his family's histories and forms a limiting sense of tolerance by Anglos for "my kind." Arteaga writes, "[I]t is a line that crosses the personal and the social in me in profound ways" (6). Indeed, it is a line that has crossed the personal in many whose lives are marked by borders. A line that crossed those who have died and those who perish while attempting to "illegally" cross. The border line crosses the crossed, their relatives, friends, and acquaintances. Whether through *antepasados* (ancestors) now living in the spirit world or in connection to those living in this world, the border crosses over and over, as do many of the humans who find themselves separated from families on opposite sides of the U.S.-Mexican "herida abierta" (Anzaldúa). Sadly, the border also works to ascribe to these humans vicious signifiers such as aliens, mojados, wetbacks, welfare-parasites, and scum. The borders do not end here, however. They can be located throughout the discourses and institutions that seek to maintain the myth of a "desired" citizen at the expense of others.

Returning to Arteaga's poetry line that cast the border "half water, half metal," in "Cantos" we are able to witness how the line serves to locate Arteaga's work in relation to what can only be described as indigenous thinking rooted in indigenous philosophy, or more specifically in this case a Náhuatl worldview. As such, the line reclaims that which the colonizers hoped to destroy. Arteaga's endeavor to evoke the border in a union of two seemingly contrary elements, metal and water, is an attempt to employ a trope characteristic of Náhuatl poetry and a general feature of Náhuatl language and thought. Arteaga relies on Angel María Garibay's concept of *difrasismo* as defined in her work *Llave del Náhuatl* (1970). *Difrasismo* allows for the representational coupling of two elements.[2] Arteaga in his line of water and metal uses notions of *difrasismo* as a means of embedding the character of difrasismo through imagery in "Cantos." *Difrasismo* for Arteaga is thus a characteristic feature of how his poetry comes to meaning and how one may choose to articulate what it means being Xicana or Xicano—notions of interconnectedness become central.

For Arteaga, a poem connects the private and public, "Cantos" and Xicana/o poetry and concepts in general allow for such links—as well as others. His attempt in "a line, half water, half metal" is to address the significance of the border, and to illumine a way of Mexican-Indian thinking that is similar to how other Xicana/o poets articulate a sense of "Indianness." Examples range from how Gloria Anzaldúa invokes/is invoked by Coatlicue, Lorna Dee Cervantes's encounter with the god Mescalito, José Montoya's parody of identity politics, and Francisco Alarcón's reconfigurations and restatements of Náhuatl incantations.

However, these linkages are far more complex than a superficial gaze allows. These examples do more than merely point to *Indios*. Each in different ways provides insight into how an Indian presence affects the act of being Xicana/o. When Gloria Anzaldúa, in "The Coatlicue State," and Lorna Dee Cervantes, in "Meeting Mescalito at Oak Hill Cemetery," cite Mexican indigenous deities, they present an alternate consciousness. Coatlicue is the goddess of a feminine subjectivity and Mescalito is the god of the heightened spiritual sensory of the vision-inducing sacred peyote. Coatlicue represents the changeable. In Anzaldúa's motif, Coatlicue embodies a mixture of antipodean: "the eagle and the serpent, heaven and the underworld, life and death, mobility and immobility, beauty and horror" (Anzaldúa: 47). Anzaldúa argues that because Xicanas/os have long practiced the art of cultural blending, "we" now stand in a position to become vanguards in articulating new forms of hybrid cultural identities. Herein lies the healing of the cut tongues—the suturing, if you will, of *teki lenguas* and hearts. This performance thus allows for the crossing from heart to tongue, and back again—in this, the journey for reclaiming, reinventing, and healing reveals its crossing.

Cervantes's poem, while situated in an English book, "crosses" through the book's title, *Emplumada* (1981), which speaks to the trope of the text. *Emplumada* allows for multiple sites of representations, in one instance a feather, pen, or plumage—or all three at once, much like her depiction of the sacred peyote when she says, " . . . in my palm-Mescalito / was a true god" (10). Is she referring to Mescalito as an *antepasado*, a god, or a plant, a combination thereof, or all three at once? Cervantes invokes a certain metaphorical ambivalence, allows several possibilities to co-exist. Moreover, these modes of expression allow for alternative discourses and sites of representation that give voice to the lives of the crossed.

José Montoya creates a third site of representation when he parodies the politics of racial identities in "Hispanic Nightlife at Luna's Cafe When th' Mexicans Came to Visit th' Chicanos in Califas"; Montoya divides "La Raza" into the Casindio, in one instance, and "Casipano," "also pronounced with a Castillian Spanish lisp Cathipano" in another. Montoya speaks to the interstices created by notions of mixed bloods—neither "this" nor "that" but something "different." In Montoya's poem, "El Louie" (1972), he depicts the protagonist as a pachuco who dances both mambo and boogie, thereby conflating cultures split by a mythical border (173–176). "El Louie" mixes languages in the style of popular Chicano utterances.[3] "Hoy enterraron al Louie / and San Pedro o sanpinche / are in for it . . . " (loosely translated: "Today they buried Louie / and heaven or hell / are in for it . . . "). Montoya's work emerges as an alternative voice to the legacies of imperialism and its consequences in the day-to-day lives of Xicanas/os. To live on the street is to read correctly—to misread could cost you your life. Montoya's poetry inspires thinking from a space only the violated know: "Ponte trucha, ese! [Be alert!] / So, let 'em kill me, pinches / mocosos! / And the streets screamed aloud," he shouts. Going further Montoya laments: "And they walk only on / Certain violent streets / Of the inner city / Until they die / Of the irony / Since on any other street / They would obviously perish / So much sooner."[4] Walking while brown in Anytown USA could get you deported, detained, or, worse, dead. Political spaces, as such, thus become another daily reminder of the dominant discourses that perpetuate and maintain the borders that relegate the lives of subalterns.

Montoya expresses a hybridization of Mexican Spanish, Southwest English, and *caló*, creating alternative spaces for the articulation of border creations. *Border Matters: Remapping American Cultural Studies* (1997), by José David Saldívar, argues that the border is a site of historical and intercultural *transfrontera* contact zones which produces "new relations, hybrid cultures and multiple voiced aesthetics" of cultural productions (12–13). In similar terms, distinguished anthropologist Renato Rosaldo argues that border maps a space whereby "creative processes of transculturation center themselves along," in, and through "literal and figurative borders where the 'person' is crisscrossed by multiple sites of identities" (216).

Francisco X. Alarcón's *Snake Poems* (1992) translates Náhuatl incantations which in turn serve to create a rhythm of Xicano poetry. Alarcón's ability to intermix Azteca and mestizo consciousness into contemporary Xicano concepts is exemplified in the following poem, "Mestizo": "my name is not Francisco / there is an Arab within me / who prays three times a day / behind my Roman nose / there is a Phoenician smiling / my eyes still see Sevilla / but my mouth is Olmec / my dark hands are Toltec / my cheekbones fierce Chichimec / my feet recognize no border / no rule no code no lord / for this wanderer's heart" (14–15).

For Alarcón, his poetry is very much alive: Mesoamerican consciousness survives not only in the collective memory, but also in the living words of the descendants of the original Indian authors. "So while the poem 'Mestizo' celebrates the many strands that meet and hybridize in New World people, the epigraph by Agueda Martínez grounds identity very clearly, 'ya que seamos hispanos, mexicanos; seamos más indios': more than Hispanics or Mexicans, we are Indians." Alarcón's stanzas are short and direct and work to elicit and evoke the millennial expressions of life they speak. His poetry reveals the persistence and profundity of ancestral worldviews and their significance to the reinvigorated wakefulness of contemporary indigenous peoples seeking and practicing balance in the present with teachings of the past and experiences of the immediate.

Here, Alarcón, Anzaldúa, Arteaga, Cervantes, and Montoya expose and negotiate a third space, an alternative oppositional consciousness and subjectivity. The work of these writers, in ways as diverse as the writers themselves, asseverates particular connections between Indian thought and Xicana/o identity by the incorporation of *difrasismo.* It is a way of writing or, rather, conceptualizing and articulating that allows for the voice of the native. Hence, we witness cultural identities emerging from the resistive efforts lodged against colonial silencing processes which discount and subjugate peoples who have always possessed the creative faculties necessary to persevere against all odds. Anzaldúa's and Alarcón's languaging interweaves Spanish, English, and Náhuatl. Their languaging invokes two kinds of writing (Mignolo: 1995): "alphabetic writing of the metropolitan center and pictographic writing of pre-Columbian Mexican and Mesoamerican civilizations" (181). The languages and concepts contribute to the creation of something new. Under the current fervor of "English-only laws" such innovations would surely suffer.

The colonial imposition of language and writing systems by the nation-state hegemony achieved a double subalternization of writing (Mignolo: 1995): first, by promoting alphabetic writing as a pinnacle of civility, and second, by maintaining a gender division in writing practices. These so-called "men of letters" ruled the literacy within the state apparatus; "textile" production, a form of symbolic communication, stayed in the hands of women and became viewed as folkloric. By resurrecting "the path of the red and the black ink"—in other words, ancient systems for writing—Gloria Anzaldúa "restores the conceptualization of writing and text, and makes possible the rethinking of "hegemonic complicities that exist among texts, empires, nations and cultural scholarships" (viii–xiii).

Her work directly addresses the *Teki Lenguas del Yollotzín.* It is through languaging that Gloria Anzaldúa, Alfred Arteaga, Lorna Dee Cervantes, José Montoya, and Francisco X. Alarcón allow us to accentuate the importance of moving away from the idea that language is a fact (e.g., a system of syntactic, semantic, and phonetic rules) and acknowledging that speaking and writing are discourses that orient and manipulate social interaction. The linguistic conceptualization and literary practices of Alarcón et al. create fractures within languages (Náhuatl, *caló,* Mexican Spanish, Spanish, and English—and combinations thereof) and between languages (Spanish on the Iberian Peninsula "bumping" with Spanish "dialects" and in Mexico "bumping" with "Amerindian languages"; English in America and Mexico, and in the differential times and spaces where *caló* is spoken), revealing the colonial aspects of linguistic, literary, and cultural landscapes. To read Anzaldúa's *Borderlands* is to read three languages and three literatures together, creating an innovative way of languaging—the practice of combining different tongues. Cultural creations, in this sense, emerge from the heart, carrying the messages from the *antepasados,* the stories passed down through generations, and the ability to imagine one's self-identity within the context of lived experiences. The vinculum Anzaldúa constitutes between language and identity creates spaces for transposing geocultural notions such as "Their America" and "Our America." These spaces are sites where languages (Náhuatl, Mexican Spanish, English, *caló*) and the fluidity of gender generate in-between-spaces-in-between that allow one to talk about a hybrid thinking-space of Amerindian and Spanish/Latin American cultural legacies and neocolonial struggles.

Cherríe Moraga also draws from a discursive genealogy that emanates from dual *memorias* and makes one ask: Is there room for bi[poly]-languaging from the spaces of such languages as Spanish and Quechua, Yaqui and Spanish? How does poly-languaging work with my friend William Underbaggage, who skillfully flows and navigates between Náhuatl, Mexican Spanish, English, and Lakota? Is it possible for Underbaggage, a cultural activist for indigenous rights in the Américas, who was born and raised on the Pine Ridge Lakota reservation in South Dakota, studied in Mexico, and moved to the Bay Area, to be accorded a space?

The border, immigration regulations, and restrictions on naturalization and citizenship contribute to the construction of racialized and gendered Xicanas/os. The racialization of Xicanas/os in relationship to the state positions Xicana/o culture into a "something" that is easily cultivated into an "other" political subject. As such, the Xicana/o has been historically cast into an "alien-ated" relation to the category of citizenship. The division positions the Xicana/o political subject not only in critical apposition to the "desired" classification of a U.S. citizen, but also in contrast to the political realm of representative democracy that the "ideal" notion of the citizen ostensibly signifies. The "culling" of Xicana/o immigrants from the national citizenry is inscribed not only politically, but culturally as well: recast through recollections, accounts, and representations immersed, fragmented, and pieced together in a historical "unconscious." These, in turn, become reconfigured in Xicana/o culture through the development of discretionary, oppositional, and alternative identities and practices. However, it is important to note that the emergence of alternative identities and practices in and of themselves has a long history. Xicanas/os derived their "existence" from their ancestors—ancestors who were accustomed to traveling well-established corridors between what are now Mexico and the United States. Many of these ancestors lived in what is now the United States. Included in these migrating practices, once again, were those who traveled back and forth maintaining relationships on both sides of what is now the U.S.-Mexican border. These journeys afforded the travelers opportunities to come in contact with other cultures throughout the Américas; as a result, different cultural forms emerged. It was not until the imposition of borders that travel became constricted and extensively monitored. The border coupled with the Anglo's xenophobias (both emanating from a Eurocentric colonialist discourse) served to further demonize the original inhabitants of the Américas.

As such, Xicanas and Xicanos have been ascribed a life that through differential social, juridical, political, and economic institutions confine them to multiple sites of marginality that prey on the physical, cognitive, and spiritual aspects of their lives. In short, the inspiration, opportunity, and freedom to create are denied. According to John Guillory in "Canonical and Non-Canonical: A Critique of the Current Debate," schools, like courts, maintain social inequalities but more accurately "succeed by taking as their first object not the reproduction of social relations but [rather] the reproduction of the institution itself" (Guillory, 1987; as cited in Gutiérrez-Jones, 1995: 11). Interrogating such interconnected processes reveals that the power institutions exhibit over time rests on discourses which silence potentially disruptive rhetorical options by formally prohibiting them. For that reason, certain "eternal verities"—often articulated from a position of (Eurocentric) values—take a defensive stance against rhetorical strategies recognizing historical change. Both pedagogical systems and the courts produce means of accessing the traditions of culture and law; however, these institutions perpetuate specific relations which differ for different people (depending on, for instance, race, ethnicity, class, gender, and sexuality). Xicanas/os recognize this precise state of affairs or rather "master narratives" when they protest for equitable educational programs and solutions for addressing declining graduation rates, when they champion civil rights activism, and when they exhibit fear about legal and other institutions.

Resistance and challenge to the more than five-hundred-year legacy of Eurocentric and institutional practices across the Américas has been an ongoing battle since the first European washed ashore. While a modicum of gains were made during the 1960s and 1970s, much work remains. In fact, many of the gains were severely hampered and many were eradicated during the Reagan-Bush era. Some thirty years after the resistive cries and actions by members of the "original" third world Liberation Front which led to the creation of ethnic studies at Berkeley, students of color, radical critics, creative writers, and feminists once again felt compelled to stand up and fight for an intellectual space. A space that allows for the production of alternative intellectual property, funding, recruitment and retention of professors, and the necessary institutional support for articulating their/our distinct and unique imaginary—their different ways of conceptualizing and articulating the world and its inhabitants. On April 14, 1999, and extending into May 1999 at the University of California at Berkeley, undergraduate and graduate students, professors, and community members rallied in an effort to again reiterate the importance of maintaining a space for disenfranchised populations at universities and colleges. Public interest in the grievances of the students was heightened when students occupied a building. Subsequently, police forcibly removed and cited forty-eight students; six students were jailed. One of the student demonstrators, Michael Lamb, required hospitalization after his neck was severely traumatized and left ear partially detached as a direct result of police brutality. The student demonstrations at Berkeley quickly garnered public support both on and off the campus, locally and globally—which solidified and expanded the students' protest movement. These initial actions were followed by weeks of demonstrations. A week after the struggle began, eight members of the movement, termed the third world Liberation Front (twLF), began a hunger strike in a concerted effort to bring attention to the systemic neglect and atrophying policies directed against the ethnic studies department at UC-Berkeley. Healing cut tongues, unfortunately, at times entails committing oneself to the ultimate sacrifice—dying.

The aforementioned literary examples and actions of anticolonial conceptualizations/articulations actively challenge a hegemonic process that has served for much too long to violently relegate disenfranchised populations to a status of subaltern. Members of society who, without deserved recognition, respect, and dignity, continue to be violated and viewed as nothing more than "the wretched of the earth." An urgency exists for the production of works for and by people of all social classes and racial/ethnic backgrounds. Works which also take into account differences of gender and sexuality. Projects which create alternative narratives and accounts—and thereby assist in contributing to other humans the ability to use one's understanding of the past to inspire, legitimize, and account for one's actions in the present. The violence will stop when the violations perpetrated by the violators stop.

NOTES

1. From a passage in Angelina Villafañe's essay "The Failure or Possibility of Puerto Rican Independence," in *The Berkeley McNair Journal.*

2. Arteaga's footnote on page 157 offers Garibay's definition of *difrasismo:* "Llamo así a un procedimiento que consiste en expresar una misma idea por medio de dos vocablos que se completan en el sentido, ya por ser sinónimos, ya por ser adyacentes." *Llave de Náhuatl* (Mexico: Porrua, 1970), 115.

3. José Montoya, "El Louie," in *Literatura Chicana, Texto y Contexto,* ed. Antonia Castañeda et al. (Englewood Cliffs, N.J.: Prentice Hall, 1972), 173–176.

4. For a seminal discussion of "El Louie," see Arturo Madrid-Barela, "In Search of the Authentic Pachuco: An Interpretive Essay," *Aztlán* 4, no. 1 (1973): 31–59.

WORKS CITED

Alarcón, Francisco X. *Snake Poems: An Aztec Invocation.* San Francisco: Chronicle Books, 1992.

Anzaldúa, Gloria. *Borderlands / La Frontera: The New Mestiza.* San Francisco: Spinsters/Aunt Lute, 1987.

Arteaga, Alfred. *Chicano Poetics: Heterotexts and Hybridities.* Cambridge: Cambridge University Press, 1997.

Ashcroft, Bill, and Gareth Griffins. *Key Concepts in Post-Colonial Studies.* London: Routledge, 1998.

Bakhtin, M. M. *The Dialogical Imagination: Four Essays.* 1975. Ed. Michael Holquist. Trans. Caryl Emerson and Michael Holquist. Austin: University of Texas Press, 1994.

Belnap, Jeffrey, and Raúl Fernández, eds. *José Martí's "Our America."* Durham, N.C.: Duke University Press, 1998.

Bender, Thomas, and Carl E. Schorske, eds. *American Academic Culture in Transformation.* Princeton, N.J.: Princeton University Press, 1998.

Butler, Judith. *The Psychic Life of Power.* Stanford, Calif.: Stanford University Press, 1997.

Carroll, John B. *Language, Thought and Reality: Selected Writings of Benjamin Lee Whorf.* Cambridge: MIT Press, 1956.

Cervantes, Lorna Dee. *Enplumada.* Pittsburgh: University of Pittsburgh Press, 1981.

Christian, Barbara. "The Race for Theory." 1987. In *The Post-Colonial Studies Reader,* ed. Bill Ashcroft, Gareth Griffiths, and Helen Tiffin, 457–460. London: Routledge, 1995.

Córdova, Teresa. "Power and Knowledge: Colonialism in the Academy." 1994. In *Living Chicana Theory,* ed. Carla Trujillo, 17–45. Berkeley, Calif.: Third Woman Press, 1998.

Coronil, Fernando. *The Magical State: Nature, Money and Modernity in Venezuela.* Chicago: University of Chicago Press, 1997.

Dussel, Enrique. "Beyond Eurocentrism: The World-System and the Limits of Modernity." In *The Cultures of Globalization,* ed. Fredric Jameson and Masao Miyoshi. Durham, N.C.: Duke University Press, 1998.

Fanon, Frantz. *The Wretched of the Earth.* New York: Grove Press, 1963.

Flores, William V., and Benmayor Rina. *Latino Cultural Citizenship,* Boston: Beacon Press, 1997.

Foucault, Michel. "The Order of Discourse." *Untying the Text: A Poststructuralist Reader.* Ed. Robert Young. London: Routledge & Kegan Paul, 1981.

Freire, Paulo. *Pedagogy of the Oppressed.* New York: Continuum, 1970.

Garibay, Angel María. *Llave del náhuatl.* México: Porrúa, 1970.

Gates, Henry Louis, Jr., and Cornel West. *The Future of the Race.* New York: Vintage Books, 1996.

Gramsci, Antonio. *Selections from the Prison Notebooks of Antonio Gramsci.* Ed. and trans. Quintin Hoare and Geoffrey Nowell Smith. New York: International, 1971.

Guillory, John. "Canonical and Non-Canonical: A Critique of the Current Debate." *English Literary History* 54 (1987): 483–527.

Gutiérrez-Jones, Carl. *Rethinking the Borderlands: Between Chicano Cultures and Legal Discourse.* Berkeley: University of California Press, 1995.

JanMohamed, Abdul R. "The Economy of Manichean Allegory." 1985. In *The Post-Colonial Studies Reader,* ed. Bill Ashcroft, Gareth Griffiths, and Helen Tiffin. London: Routledge, 1995.

Laclau, Ernesto, and Chantal Mouffe. *Hegemony and Socialist Strategy.* New York: Verso, 1987.

Loewen, James W. *Lies My Teacher Told Me: Everything Your American History Textbook Got Wrong.* New York: Touchstone Books, 1995.

López, Ian F. Haney. *White by Law.* New York: New York University Press, 1996.

Lotringer, Syvere, and Lysa Hochroth. *The Politics of Truth: Michel Foucault.* New York: Semiotext(e), 1997.

Lowe, Lisa. *Immigrant Acts.* Durham, N.C.: Duke University Press, 1996.

Lowe, Lisa, and David Lloyd. *The Politics of Culture in the Shadow of Capital.* Durham, N.C.: Duke University Press, 1997.

Mignolo, Water D. *Local Histories/Global Designs: Coloniality Subaltern Knowledges and Border Thinking.* Princeton, N.J.: Princeton University Press, 2000.

———. "Globalization, Civilization Processes, and the Relocation of Languages and Cultures." In *The Cultures of Globalization,* ed. Fredric Jameson and Masao Miyoshi. Durham, N.C.: Duke University Press, 1998.

———. *The Darker Side of the Renaissance.* Ann Arbor: University of Michigan Press, 1995.

Mills, Sarah. *Discourse.* London: Routledge, 1997.

Montoya, José. *In Formation: Twenty Years of Joda.* San José, Calif.: Chusma House, 1992.

Ngúgí wa Thiong'o. *Decolonizing the Mind.* Portsmouth, N.H.: Heinemann, 1986/1997.

———. *Moving the Center.* Portsmouth, N.H.: Heinemann, 1993.

Omi, Michael, and Howard Winant. *Racial Formation in the United States: From the 1960s to the 90s.* London: Routledge, 1994.

Payne, Michael, ed. *A Dictionary of Cultural and Critical Theory.* Malden, Mass.: Blackwell Publishers, 1996.

Quijano, Anibal. "Modernity, Identity and Utopia in Latin America." In *The Postmodernism Debate in Latin America,* ed. John Beverly, José Oviedo, and Michael Aronna. Durham, N.C.: Duke University Press, 1995.

Rosaldo, Renato. *Culture and Truth: The Remaking of Social Analysis.* Boston: Beacon Press, 1989/1993.

Said, Edward W. *Culture and Imperialism.* New York: Vintage Books, 1994.

Saldívar, José David. *Border Matters: Remapping American Cultural Studies.* Berkeley: University of California Press, 1997.

Todorov, Tzvetan. "Mikhail Bakhtin: The Dialogical Principle." In *Theory of Modern Literature,* vol. 13. Minneapolis: University of Minnesota Press, 1984.

Villafañe, Angelina. "The Failure or Possibility of Puerto Rican Independence." *The Berkeley McNair Journal* 6 (Winter 1998). Berkeley: University of California McNair Scholars Program.

19 THE ALAMO, SLAVERY, AND THE POLITICS OF MEMORY

Rolando J. Romero

> The Alamo serves as the most salient and ambiguous symbol of Texas. Its semantic imprint dominates the social landscape between Texans and Mexicans, even as its full disclosure reveals deep racial and class fissures between the two.
>
> —Richard Flores (1996)

> Sisters, brothers, know too well
> what memories can do.
> Climbin' up when you're down
> from the West Side of Town.
>
> —Tish Hinojosa, "West Side of Town"

> I want to allow her [Adina de Zavala's] embedded critical discourse to remind us that keeping Mexicans in line has been a central plot of the Alamo all along.
>
> —Richard Flores (1996)

SOME TIME ago I was invited to participate in a panel in an international conference of world English that purported to address the issues facing the English language in the twenty-first century. While working on the presentation, my mind kept racing back to my own very personal introduction to issues of power, of voice, of determination and agency, enveloped in the classic coming-of-age story, in which language awareness serves as the primary catalyst for notions of self. For discovering the English language as a thirteen-year-old immigrant entailed also discovering accompanying hierarchies. It is in this primal moment that the colonial condition teaches people to either cry uncle or become subject to borderline psychosis. The semantic space of my reflections took me back to a barrio school appropriately named David Crockett, situated in the middle of the San Antonio, Texas, neighborhood that provides the local color to Sandra Cisneros's *Woman Hollering Creek.* This neighborhood lived in the shadow of the Alamo, a constant reminder to tourists of a colonial condition of families like my own who lived within walking distance of the old San Antonio de Valero mission. There was a thirteen-year-old avid reader at the David Crockett Elementary School, who mixed in the same bundle such books as *Mary Poppins, Peter Pan, War and Peace,* and *Los bandidos*

Figure 19.1. Pilgrimage to the Alamo, April 22, 1968. Copyright © San Antonio Express-News. Used with permission.

de Río Frío, a bright child who had graduated at the top of his class in a Mexican elementary school but who nonetheless had to start elementary school over in the first grade in Texas because of an inability to speak English. In this school, the crossing guards were fittingly named Davy Crocketts. In a ceremony to celebrate the opening of Fiesta Week, on April 22, 1968, the organizers invited the crossing guards, dressed in their Davy Crockett buckskins and raccoon caps, to participate. A *San Antonio Express* photographer took a picture. On a recent visit, I discovered the photo on one of the pamphlets that circulate throughout the tourist venues of the city (see fig. 19.1). The photographer must have been behind all the Davy Crockett look-alikes, who faced the entrance to the building, with their backs toward the photographer. The reader will not be able to identify any one child individually, since clearly the Alamo itself is the central image in this photograph. The caption reads:

> Pilgrimage to the Alamo, April 22, 1968, with Crockett Elementary School students clad in Davy Crockett buckskins and raccoon caps. Officially opening a week of Fiesta, students, organizations and clubs from throughout the State march quietly through the streets of San Antonio to lay flower wreaths at the Alamo in memory of the heroes who died there in 1836. (Noonan Guerra: n.p.)

I was surprised to see this picture that was taken more than thirty years ago. As a U.S. Latino scholar with a focus on Mexico and Mexico-U.S. interactions and a professor in one of the top ten universities of the Midwest, I felt that I had placed myself as subject and object of the critical eye. As much as I tried to distance myself from my own personal knowledge of the Alamo, these memories kept providing the filter that allowed for the critical introspection of my memory. For I think that it was not coincidental that the school teachers made an immigrant child from Mexico, unable to speak English, stand in front of a building that was then projecting two different memories: one national, which has served the Anglo-American as the creation myth of the Texas republic; the other personal, albeit one that mirrored the acculturation process through education in the very site of the battle that gestated the U.S. plunder of Mexico. The battle of the Alamo, as popular myth has it, led to the battle of San Jacinto, in which the U.S. army took Santa Anna prisoner. Santa Anna negotiated his release with the recognition of Texas independence. The U.S. annexation of Texas ten years later led to the U.S.-Mexican War, initiated with the pretext of the invasion of the United States by Mexico.[1] The popular press recast the cry of "Remember the Alamo" in the Spanish-American War of 1898 as "Remember the Maine." U.S. hegemony over the peoples of Caribbean and Mexican descent in fact started over the battle of the Alamo.

This battle for the memory of Texas has been a subject of debate. Mexico, as Griswold del Castillo has pointed out, forgot the territory, and rarely disputed the violations of the Treaty of Guadalupe Hidalgo. Mexico archived the rights and guarantees of this first civil rights document for the people of Mexican descent. The National Museum of History at the Palacio de Chapultepec does not overtly record the loss of the U.S. Southwest in the nineteenth century. Mexico allegorizes the loss of the territory through narratives of the U.S. invasion of Mexico, and the myth of the Niños Héroes celebrated on September 13. Though the history does not record it officially in the wing of the nineteenth century at the Palacio de Chapultepec, the whole site itself reminds the public of the U.S. invasion, for it was in this very place that the last of the Niños Héroes purportedly jumped to his death wrapped in the Mexican flag, a suitable metaphor for national innocence. Mexico's historical conscience has used the myth of the Niños Héroes as its own counter-Alamo narrative. Tibol describes the monument at Chapultepec:

> La patria adolorida se ve cubierta por las alas del águila, teniendo a los lados nopales, mientras el todo descansa sobre la serpiente enroscada. En el gran pedestal cuatro figuras de adolescentes simbolizan el sacrificio supremo, la desesperación en la defensa, la lucha desigual y la epopeya. (Tibol: 82)
>
> (The wings of the eagle cover the wounded motherland, flanked by some cacti, while everything rests on the coiled serpent. In the

> great pedestal, four adolescent figures symbolize supreme sacrifice, desperation in defense, the uneven battle and the epic.)

The Chicano memory in the United States has also had a hard time finding a suitable frame for remembering the Alamo. Rosa Linda Fregoso characterizes Chicano emplotments of the period as "me-too" attempts at historical revision. She entitles her essay on the film *Seguín* "The Same Side of the Alamo," arguing that the focus on a Chicano serving the cause of Texas independence simply exposes the ideological gaps of the Mexican criollo elite of the time. A contemporary ethnic reading of the battle fails to expose the issues of class. Timothy M. Matovina exemplifies this attitude in his introduction to *The Alamo Remembered: Tejano Accounts and Perspectives.* Matovina argues that most of the documents that have allowed historians to reconstruct the history of the battle were generated as

> petitions and depositions filed in land claim cases for heirs of the Alamo defenders. The majority of these documents are sworn testimony that a particular Tejano died in the Alamo fighting on the Texan side. Thus they are an early Tejano rebuttal to depictions of the Alamo defenders as a homogeneous Anglo-American group. (3)

Richard Flores engages in a similar strategy when he writes:

> The Texas nationalist discourse surrounding the Alamo claims this was a battle between Texans and Mexicans. This is not correct. . . . The portrayal of the Battle of the Alamo as a clearly demarcated zone of interests between Texans and Mexicans is clearly unwarranted. Prominent Mexican citizens fought on both sides, dividing their allegiance along lines of political and ideological interests, and not along the ethnically or nationally circumscribed positions that have been fabricated by the custodians of the Alamo and popularized at various levels through collective memory. (x)

This position has been textualized, as in the recent Discovery Channel documentary, as a battle between brothers. Francisco Esparza, who fought with Santa Anna's forces, buried his brother Gregorio, who fought with the Texan rebels and was killed at the siege. Francisco Esparza petitioned Santa Anna to have his brother properly buried.[2] The Discovery Channel program on the battle not only engages all the myth making of national construction, but also has tried to include this "Mexicanos-too" strategy with which Fregoso disagrees.

Adina de Zavala's text on the Alamo, recently published by the Recovering the U.S. Hispanic Literary Heritage Project of Arte Público Press, best examplifies this "me-too" strategy. Though Flores's reading attempts to circumscribe the production of the narrative within the general historical and sociological events of the beginning of the century—best textualized in *With His Pistol in His Hand* by Américo Paredes—the fact remains that Adina de Zavala was interested in preserving the memory of her grandfather, Lorenzo de Zavala, the first vice president of the Republic of Texas. Flores attempts to read Adina de Zavala's narratives against the grain, akin to Rosaura Sánchez's reading of Amparo Ruiz de Burton.[3] Adina de Zavala will in fact attempt to construct a historical memory that is based on more than the Anglo-American presence in the area, in which the Mexicano serves as the abject for the construction of the state. Her narratives include not only the details of the battle, and details of the layout of the mission grounds, but also details of the first arrivals and colonization of the area by the original settlers from the Islas Canarias. These narratives and accounts, which de Zavala quotes at length, are really not at all dissimilar to other accounts ideologically designed to convert the Native Americans of the region to Catholicism. From the Pastorelas to other accounts of miracles happening at the area, it is hard not to be critical of the hidden agenda of the stories told by the Franciscans to the native populations.

One such story is that of the apparition of María de Jesús Coronel, Sor María de Agreda. Fray Damián Manzanet had been given specific instructions to look for the tribes that Sor María de Agreda had visited in her religious ecstasy. The Franciscan found the tribes in Texas, and

> Manzanet and his companions were joyfully and kindly received and shown every consideration. The Governor, or Chief, of the Tejas Indians one day asked Manzanet for some blue baize in which to bury his grandmother when she died.
>
> Manzanet asked him why he desired it blue. The Chief replied that it was because a beautiful woman who had come often to visit their tribe and whom they reverenced wore blue, and they wished to be like her on passing to the other world . . . she had promised them teachers, and now that Manzanet and his companions had come, the "high priest" or medicine man of the tribe had told them that these were the true teachers who had been expected.
>
> The strange part of the story is that Mary de Agreda had never really been in Texas or the New World in person, but during her state of intense longing and continued prayer, she must have dreamt or visited them in ecstasy. . . . She conversed with these dream people and promised them teachers which she finally caused to be sent as we have seen. Numerous were her writings descriptive of these people, their country, customs, and names of tribes, and it was afterwards found to be correct and true. (de Zavala, 101–102)

As we can see, this Chicano me-too narrative hardly contradicts the dominant narrative of national construction; its only redemption is the feminist reading attempted by scholars such as Tey Diana Rebolledo, who read these narratives in the context of the Reformation in Spain. While society did not allow women to participate in public, "rational" state discourse, the church accepted mysticism because it considered it a "more intuitive direct form of knowledge." "In dreams and visions" writes Rebolledo, "these women went beyond their cells and convents, flying across time and space: they at times went to hell and viewed life and the dangers (as well as the seductions) of purgatory" (10). Jean Franco believes that "[t]his flight was the feminine equivalent of the heroic journey of self-transformation, with the difference that it met no obstacles and was less a narrative than an epiphany" (16).

Ironically de Zavala's zeal to preserve the Mexicano/Chicano memory of the Alamo may in fact be responsible for the dominant narrative to which every tourist is exposed. Adina de Zavala formed an organization called the De Zavala Daughters, "a group of women dedicated to the preservation of Texas history and historical sites" (Flores: xii). The organization changed its status to a chapter of the Daughters of the Republic of Texas in 1893. The Alamo at the time belonged to commercial interests, and Adina de Zavala, through her chapter, initiated the negotiations that would lead to the building's purchase and preservation. When the building was finally purchased, the Daughters of the Republic of Texas attempted to take control of the building. This second "battle of the Alamo" was a fight for the "final historical portrait of the Alamo" (xv), since the Daughters of the Republic of Texas, not knowing enough about the building and its history, wanted to demolish the commercial building constructed on the original Alamo structure in order to build a park and a monument. De Zavala argued that the walls of the commercial building were the original walls of the mission and should not be destroyed. Taking possession of the keys, de Zavala barricaded herself in the building while trying to negotiate with the authorities. She was dubbed as a "defender of the Alamo," no doubt facetiously, by contemporary newspaper accounts. The myopic vision of the Daughters of the Republic of Texas prevailed. Richard Flores has argued that the de facto original downtown of the San Antonio—which, like that of most Hispanic cities consists of the plaza, the church, and the seat of government—has been literally transferred to the Alamo grounds, now surrounded by a hotel complex, a mall, the Ripley's Believe It or Not, and the Plaza Wax Museum. The river, which by orders of Santa Anna carried the corpses of the Mexican soldiers killed in the battle, now carries the barges with tourists dining on Mexican food. The myopic vision of the Daughters of the Republic of Texas explains the gigantic size of the Imax Theater's screen on which "Alamo: The Price of Freedom" shows at the mall.

The publication of the *Diary of José Enrique de la Peña* recently put to the test the dominant 1950s narrative on the myth of the Alamo. De la Peña gives a first-person account of the battle. The passage that created much controversy follows:

> Shortly before Santa Anna's speech, an unpleasant episode had taken place, which, since it occurred after the end of the skirmish,

> was looked upon as base murder and which contributed greatly to the coolness that was noted. Some seven men had survived the general carnage and, under the protection of General Castrillón, they were brought before Santa Anna. Among them was one of great stature, well proportioned, with regular features, in whose face there was the imprint of adversity, but in whom one also noticed a degree of resignation and nobility that did him honor. He was the naturalist David Crockett, well known in North America for his unusual adventures, who had undertaken to explore the country and who, finding himself in Béjar at the very moment of surprise, had taken refuge in the Alamo, fearing that his status as a foreigner might not be respected. Santa Anna answered Castrillón's intervention in Crockett's behalf with a gesture of indignation and, addressing himself to the sappers, the troops closest to him, ordered his execution. The commanders and officers were outraged at this action and did not support the order, hoping that once the fury of the moment had blown over these men would be spared, but several officers who were around the president and who, perhaps, had not been present during the moment of danger, became noteworthy by an infamous deed, surpassing the soldiers in cruelty. They thrust themselves forward, in order to flatter the commander, and with swords in hand, fell upon these unfortunate, defenseless men just as a tiger leaps upon his prey. Though tortured before they were killed, these unfortunates died without complaining and without humiliating themselves before their torturers. (de la Peña: 53)

The fact that a soldier had witnessed the death of Davy Crockett not on the field of battle, but surrendering or being made a prisoner by Santa Anna, had the potential to destroy the Alamo legend. A controversy quickly arose, led by Bill Groneman, a self-described arson investigator for the New York City Fire Department, who labeled the diary a forgery. He pointed to the evidence that de la Peña's 1836 diary included a citation of General Urrea's 1838 *Diary.* James Crisp has determined, by another document written by José Enrique de la Peña in prison, that de la Peña was still working on his diary in 1839, laying to rest the purported discrepancies in de la Peña's account. Ironically, most of the controversy seems to ensue from purported faulty translations of the original document. Llerena Friend echoes the lackadaisical nature of much of the scholarship in a 1975 comment: "I wish . . . I were a literary sleuth with a command of Spanish and a mañana temperament" (de la Peña: xi). Ironically none of the scholars take responsibility for their inability to speak and read Spanish, and read the diary in its original language. Instead, they project their own inefficiencies as scholars onto the people entrusted to help in the readings of the documents. The general tone of the controversy (ironically much of it not carried on by university-trained scholars), as well as the title of Bill Groneman's book, *Death of a Legend,* which implies both the death of

Davy Crockett and the death of the myth brought about by de la Peña's diary, signals that the narrative of the Alamo is ready for a historical revision.

There are several indications that the piece of the puzzle that is missing has to do with the relationship of the Texas war for independence and the issue of slavery. Richard Flores writes:

> . . . in an effort to curb the growing immigration from the United States, they [the Mexican government] passed an emancipation proclamation in 1829 forbidding slavery. While slavery was not a practice in Mexico, this law was aimed at the growing number of U.S. citizens holding slaves in the Mexican province of Texas. (viii–ix)

A scant seven years later, in 1836, when Santa Anna discarded the Constitution of 1824, Texas declared its independence. The Texas rebels, both Tejanos and Texans alike, were purportedly fighting for the restoration of the 1824 Mexican constitution. It may have been, in fact, that by voiding the 1824 constitution, Santa Anna also did away with the right of the state of Texas to allow slavery. This view circulated in the Mexican analyses of the time. Like Abraham Lincoln afterwards, Santa Anna moved to squelch the rebellion, but was not able to put the country back together; Texas remained an independent republic until it was annexed by the United States on December 29, 1845.

Henry David Thoreau's "Resistance to Civil Government," widely circulated also under the title "Civil Disobedience," expressed just these views. Thoreau had written the essay, according to Philip Van Doren Stern, "to protest against taxes levied to support slavery and to finance the war with Mexico that many Northerners felt was being waged to benefit the slave states and extend their territory" (453). Thoreau wrote in "Resistance to Civil Government":

> Witness the present Mexican war, the work of comparatively a few individuals using the standing government as their tool; for, in the outset, the people would not have consented to this measure. (455)

> Practically speaking, the opponents to a reform in Massachusetts are not a hundred thousand politicians at the South, but a hundred thousand merchants and farmers here, who are more interested in commerce and agriculture than are in humanity, and are not prepared to do justice to the slave and to Mexico, *cost what it may.* (459)

> There are thousands who are *in opinion* opposed to slavery and to the war, who yet in effect do nothing to put an end to them; who, esteeming themselves children of Washington and Franklin, sit down with their hands in their pockets, and say that they know not what to do, and do nothing; who even postpone the question of

> freedom to the question of free trade, and quietly read the prices-current along with the latest advice from Mexico, after dinner, and, it may be, fall asleep over them both. (460)
>
> It is there [in prison] that the fugitive slave, and the Mexican prisoner on parole, and the Indian come to plead the wrongs of his race, should find them, on that separate, but more free and honorable ground, where the State places those who are not *with* her, but *against* her,—the only house in a slave State in which a free man can abide with honor. (465)

Though it was widely believed that Thoreau had gone to jail for refusing to pay his taxes to support the war with Mexico, the case may have been a simpler one, of Thoreau simply using the war with Mexico as an example of why citizens had the right to refuse to pay taxes when ideologically opposed to the war.

The issue of slavery lies just below the surface in several narratives. For example, Martha Anne Turner's *The Yellow Rose of Texas: Her Saga and Her Song* blames Santa Anna's defeat at the battle of San Jacinto on the "twenty-year-old mulatto slave girl, Emily Morgan, who Turner believes is the true 'Yellow Rose of Texas.'" Turner details the legend of the young woman entertaining Santa Anna in his tent to the point of the general not paying attention to what was going on in the battle:

> Not only did Emily's dalliance with Santa Anna at San Jacinto keep him occupied and cement the victory of the sixteenth decisive battle of the world, it validated an empire—the Republic of Texas—that flourished for a decade. Moreover, the victory at San Jacinto not only brought Texas into the United States but also added the future states of New Mexico, Arizona, California, Utah, Colorado, Wyoming, Kansas, and Oklahoma—a million square miles of territory that more than doubled the size of the American nation at the time. Even for a most generous ladies' man, this real estate, in terms of intrinsic nineteenth-century values, had to be an all-time record as a fee for the companionship of Emily for a period of less than two days and nights. As payment by the hour for that brief time, the fee approximated a world-shattering record. The fortunes paid by the crowned heads of Europe for the favors of Madame de Pompadour and her successor, the Comtesse Du Barry, became paltry sums by comparison. (39)

More recent scholarship, like Marcus Embry's, contends that issues like slavery have not been looked upon more carefully because readers have not integrated Anglo-American canonical literature with the Latina/Latino traditions. The myth of the Texas Republic rings so untrue because it has not layered the different accounts into a comprehensive history that makes sense for everybody: Anglo-Americans, Chicanas/Chicanos, and African Americans alike.

The complete narrative of the Alamo has in fact already surfaced in literature. Tino Villanueva's *Scene from the Movie "Giant"* concentrates on the Rock Hudson–Elizabeth Taylor allegory of the King Ranch. "Mrs. R. J. Kleberg and her family at the King Ranch were, according to the Mexican folklore of the day, responsible for the social and economic demise of Mexicans in Texas" (Flores, xxviii). Ironically it may be this film, starring James Dean and Dennis Hopper, that holds the real memory of the Alamo. The matriarch East Coaster marries the Texas millionaire because of her opinions about the Alamo, and the Mexicans keep moving from the background to center stage, in several episodes of the film, until they manage to become the central plotline. The demise of the family represented the new reality for Texas, one in which the discovery of oil made the old ranch hands as obsolete as the landed gentry. And it is that scene that Tino Villanueva makes famous, as the young man remembers the showing of the film in South Texas. In this battle of good and evil, a foundational moment for the construction of a boy's identity, a song plays in the background. The viewer does not hear the lyrics, but in the final irony of the film, the jukebox plays "The Yellow Rose of Texas," the Texas national anthem, purportedly standing for the old order of white supremacy. The sergeant does not know that in the 1835 original lyrics, it is a black lover singing to her black beloved. She is a "sweetest rose of color," with bright-moist eyes more beautiful than any southern belle. His sweetheart walks along the Río Grande, waiting for her beloved, who has promised to return:

> *There's a yellow rose in Texas*
> *That I am going to see*
> *No other darky knows her*
> *No one only me*
> . . .
> *Where the Río Grande is flowing*
> *And the starry skies are bright*
> *She walks along the river*
> *In the quite [sic]* summer night. (Quoted in Turner)

It may just be that the real story of the Alamo can be heard behind multicultural voices that contributed to the formation of the state.

NOTES

1. Mexico recognized the Nueces River as the southern border of Texas. After the annexation, the U.S. claimed the Río Bravo/Río Grande, farther south than the Nueces,

divided Texas from Mexico. When the Mexican Army stationed troops between the Nueces and the Río Bravo/Río Grande, the United States claimed Mexico had invaded its territory. The United States used this pretext to declare the war with Mexico.

2. Santa Anna ordered that the people killed at the Alamo be cremated in a funeral pyre. He ordered one of his soldiers to dispose of the Mexican bodies. Since so many people had been killed, the order was not strictly carried out; many of the bodies were simply dumped in the San Antonio River.

3. See the introduction to Amparo Ruiz de Burton's *The Squatter and the Don.*

WORKS CITED

de Zavala, Adina. *History and Legends of the Alamo and Other Missions in and around San Antonio.* Ed. Richard Flores. Houston: Arte Público Press, 1996.

Embry, Marcus. "The Shadow of Latinidad in U.S. Literature." *Discourse* 21, no. 3 (Fall 1999): 77–94.

Flores, Richard. "Adina de Zavala and the Politics of Restoration." Introduction to *History and Legends of the Alamo and Other Missions in and around San Antonio,* by Adina de Zavala, ed. Richard Flores. Houston: Arte Público Press, 1996.

Franco, Jean. *Plotting Women: Gender and Representation in Mexico.* New York: Columbia University Press, 1989.

Fregoso, Rosa Linda. "*Seguín:* The Same Side of the Alamo." In *Chicano Cinema: Research, Reviews and Resources,* ed. Gary Keller, 146–152. Tempe, Ariz.: Bilingual Review Press, 1993.

Fuentes, Carlos. *La frontera de cristal.* México: Alfaguara, 1995.

González, Jovita, and Eve Raleigh. *Caballero: A Historical Novel.* Ed. José Limón and María Cotera. College Station: Texas A&M University Press, 1996.

Griswald del Castillo, Richard. *The Treaty of Guadalupe Hidalgo: A Legacy of Conflict.* Norman: University of Oklahoma Press, 1990.

Groneman, Bill. *Death of a Legend: The Myth and Mystery Surrounding the Death of Davy Crockett.* Plano, Texas: Republic of Texas Press, 1999.

Hardin, Stephen L. *Texian Iliad: A Military History of the Texas Revolution.* Austin: University of Texas Press, 1994.

Hinojosa, Tish. *Homeland.* A&M Records, 1989.

Holland, Cecilia. "Two Dreams of California." *Harper's Magazine,* June 2000, 122–126.

Limón, José. *Dancing with the Devil: Society and Cultural Poetics in Mexican-American South Texas.* Madison: University of Wisconsin Press, 1994.

Matovina, Timothy M., ed. *The Alamo Remembered: Tejano Accounts and Perspectives.* Austin: University of Texas Press, 1995.

Noonan Guerra. *The Alamo.* San Antonio, Texas: Alamo Press, 1996.

Peña, José Enrique de la. *With Santa Anna in Texas: A Personal Narrative of the Revolution.* Trans. Carmen Perry. Introduction James E. Crisp. College Station: Texas A&M University Press, 1997.

Rebolledo, Tey Diana. "Imágenes de las primeras pobladoras: 1582–1680: Images of the First Female Colonists." In *Nuestras Mujeres/Hispanas of New Mexico: Their Images and Their Lives, 1582–1992,* ed. Tey Diana Rebolledo, 5–12. Albuquerque, N.Mex.: El Norte Publications, 1992.

Sánchez, Rosaura, and Beatriz Pita. "Introduction." In *The Squatter and the Don,* by Amparo Ruiz de Burton. Houston: Arte Público Press, 1992.

Seguín, Juan N. *A Revolution Remembered: The Memoirs and Selected Correspondence of Juan N. Segúin.* Ed. Jesús F. de la Teja. Austin, Texas: State House Press, 1991.

Serna, Enrique. *El seductor de la patria.* México: Joaquín Mortiz, 1999.

Texas History Movies. 1928. Text by John Rosefiled, Jr. Illustrations by Jack Patton. Dallas: MJM Publishers, 1928. Reprint, abridged version, Texas Historical Foundation, 1974.

Thoreau, Henry David. "Civil Disobedience." In *A Yankee in Canada with Anti-Slavery and Reform Papers.* Boston: Ticknor and Fields, 1866. Reprint of "Resistance to Civil Government." 1849. *Heath Anthology of American Literature,* vol. 1, 2015–2029. Lexington, Mass.: D.C. Heath and Company, 1994.

Tibol, Raquel. "Monumento a los Niños Héroes, de Ignacio Asúnsolo, Escultor, y Luis Macgregor, Arquitecto." In *Tesoros del Museo Nacional de Historia,* 81–84. México: Instituto Nacional de Antropología e Historia, 1994.

Tinkle, John. *13 Days to Glory: The Siege of the Alamo.* College Station: Texas A&M, 1985.

Turner, Martha Ann. *The Yellow Rose of Texas: Her Saga and her Song.* Austin, Texas: Eakin Press, 1986.

Wagner, Paul, dir. *Battle of the Alamo.* Discovery Communications, 1996.

20 COLOR CODED: REFLECTIONS AT THE MILLENNIUM

Vicki L. Ruiz

THIRTEEN YEARS ago, I arrived at the El Paso airport after facilitating an oral history workshop for community groups sponsored by New Mexico State in nearby Las Cruces. As I passed security and strode toward my gate, I noticed that I was matching my pace with an impeccably dressed young blonde whose hair was styled in an elegant chignon. I then spied an individual in uniform walking toward us—he was *la migra.* He let the blonde pass but stopped me. He inquired as to my citizenship, to which I replied "U.S." Satisfied with my answer, he permitted me to pass. I caught up with the young woman as I had quickened my steps to reach the boarding area. The blonde turned and gave me a small smile. "Me alegro de que no me piedieron los papeles." ("I'm glad he didn't ask me for my papers.")

Color judgments appear with such regularity as to escape notice. Color as code permeates popular conceptions and preconceptions as evidenced by this letter in an Ann Landers column. The writer laments her loss to a "Mexican" in a "most suntanned legs contest." "I had sunbathed five days a week for two to three months, four hours a day. . . . The winner didn't even have to step outside to get her color." Landers writes, "If the facts are as you describe them, the decision was unjust. The only way such a contest could be fair would be to limit the contestants to Caucasians."[1] To her, Mexicans constitute a racialized ethnicity, people who do not qualify as white.

Color is also a cue in nativist rhetoric surrounding immigration. Color and "illegality" went hand in hand during Operation Restoration (no decoder ring needed here). In July 1997, Chandler, Arizona, law enforcement and the INS took to the streets, entering supermarkets and private residences, even stopping two young girls, ages seven and ten, threatening "to ship them to Mexico because they weren't carrying birth certificates."[2] There emerged a tremendous public outcry against Operation Restoration and in February 1999, the city of Chandler agreed to a $400,000 out-of-court settlement with the Chandler Coalition for Human Rights, a group that had sued the city for its police involvement.[3]

Interestingly, given the popular imaginary of the "Old West" that permeates Arizona, the local press consistently referred to the July raids as a "round-up." Defending the actions of the Chandler police for their participation in the controversial July 1997 raids, raids that resulted in the harassment of Mexicanos and Mexican Americans alike, Karen Calvert expressed the following opinion to the *Arizona Republic:* "If your skin is brown, this is a probable cause and a police officer may assume you are breaking the law until proved differently."[4]

In a language reminiscent of rhetoric directed at Mexicans, Asians, and European immigrants during the early decades of the twentieth century,[5] nativists craft an iconography of fear rooted in perceived threats to economic, physical, and cultural well-being. In 1995, as a registered California voter, I received a survey from the California group American Immigration Control, a program of a nonprofit organization called "We the People," that asked respondents to name the social ills associated with immigration. Boxes to be checked included the following: terrorism, welfare fraud, taxpayer burdens, AIDS, drugs, riots, and bilingual education. Perhaps following the example of Pete Wilson, then governor of California, some local politicians sounded a nativist call in their campaign literature. Conservative businessman Bill Hoge's flyer read in part: "The flood of illegal aliens crossing our border is overwhelming our society. They pour into our overcrowded classrooms and hospitals. And, fill our jails, too. They consume precious resources that are needed to help those who legally live in our country. Just last year alone, Los Angles spent 163 million on health care for illegal aliens. That money could have done a lot to help teach our children, feed our poor and care for our sick."[6]

How widespread is this rhetoric? Have I selected only the most egregious examples? Political scientist Lisa Magaña and psychologist Robert Short have recently completed a content analysis of remarks made by political candidates on the topic of Mexican immigration that appeared in their canvass of fifty-three major newspapers representing a national sample, over a five-year period (1993–1998). Magaña and Short found that 63 percent of candidate quotes characterized Mexican immigrants as "illegal"; 32 percent as "welfare burdens"; and an astounding 30 percent as indicative of a "Border Invasion."[7] Using immigration as a political ploy requires neither statistical precision nor logic. As perennial presidential hopeful Pat Buchanan stated, "There is an invasion of illegal aliens with one, two, three million people walking across our borders every year."[8]

What do these representations convey? Latin American historian Stefan Rinke contends that "[i]mages function like a filter that determines not only what we see, but also the way we see it." What's behind the iconography of fear? Pointing only to racism an all-encompassing construct ignores white privilege and its shortsighted historical memory. Such imagery also involves the acceptance of what I term "suburban legends."[9]

Many of us are familiar with urban legends specific to African American and Latino inner-city communities, such as the story that a famous fashion designer X (identified variously as Liz Claiborne or, more recently, Tommy Hilfiger) made such outrageous statements about people of color on the *Oprah Winfrey Show* that Oprah ordered the offensive celebrity to leave. In her path-breaking monograph, *I Heard It through the Grapevine,* folklorist Patricia Turner underscores the economic and cultural roots behind rumors popular in African American urban communities.[10]

Perhaps, operating in a similar fashion, suburban legends are situated narratives within the locus of bedroom communities or small towns, predominately Euro-American in population. Certainly suburban legends resonate with their intended audience. An ad for a new middle-income subdivision in Loma Linda, a small town within an hour's drive of downtown Los Angeles, speaks volumes about notions of race and social location. Purchasing a home in Windsor Crest, according to the advertisement, promises "safety, security, and peace of mind." "You can take a walk without carrying Mace, or pack a picnic without packing a gun. . . . The only gangs you'll see are the Scouts, 4-H Club, baseball, and soccer teams."[11] Suburban legends are also a function of class. Many middle-class and affluent Latinos, African Americans, and Asian Americans also embrace the motif of "security"—physical, cultural, and economic—proffered by suburban developers.

Nativist-tinged suburban legends have wound their way into cultural iconography and political discourse. The selling of Proposition 187 ("the Save Our State" initiative) was particularly virulent. Passed by a margin of 59 percent of ballots cast in November 1994, it purports to deny undocumented workers all public services, except for emergency health care, and requires doctors and teachers to report to the INS people they suspect are undocumented.[12]

One full year before the public debate on Proposition 187 ensued, Pete Knight, a first-term Republican in the state assembly, circulated his own suburban legend to the Republican Caucus of the California Assembly, a bit of doggerel mailed to him by a constituent. Entitled "I Love America," this "poem" encapsulates every coarse stereotype aimed at Latino immigrants. A single snippet should suffice:

> *WE HAVE A HOBBY, ITS CALLED BREEDING*
> *WELFARE PAY FOR BABY FEEDING*[13]

As the verse reached the media, Knight at first appeared unapologetic. "Take it wrong? . . . It's an interesting poem. One person's point of view." To their credit, his Republican peers publicly distanced themselves from Knight. An editorial in the *Los Angeles Times,* however, commented that "it must be noted that these condemnations came after the meeting and after, we presume, the poem was obtained by reporters. . . . We would like to know why no one stood up and demanded to know immediately who had circulated it, and why Knight was not upbraided at the time."[14]

Historical memory and historical entitlement figure prominently in nativist thought, factors that historian George Lipsitz refers to as "the possessive investment in whiteness.[15] I witnessed this in the privacy of my home as I watched the eleven o'clock news during an autumn evening in 1994. A reporter covered a ladies' luncheon in Orange County; the featured speaker was former INS commissioner Harold Ezzell, who had come to urge support for Proposition 187, a measure he co-authored. He asked the women in the attendance, elegant blue-haired matrons as far as the camera panned, to take out pictures of their grandchildren and hold them up in the air. Displaying photos of his own grandchildren, he declared, "California is for them." With pride, he expressed how Proposition 187 would "save" California, the birthright of his grandchildren and the grandchildren of his audience.

Proposition 187 appealed to a certain cross-section of the California electorate. Although the measure passed by a 59 percent margin, support varied by ethnicity. As economist and political commentator Adela de la Torre noted, "Latinos overwhelmingly rejected the initiative (only thirty percent of Latino voters supported it). Similarly, the majority of Asian American, Jewish, and African American voters also rejected it."[16]

What are the dimensions of immigration? Do studies exist that counter nativist suburban legends? The scenario of faceless people scurrying across the border remains a popular media/political image, but 77 percent of the undocumented population enter the United States by the front door with legal visas in hand.[17] Visa overstays, not dangerous border crossings, are the preferred means of arrival. How many undocumented immigrants live in the United States? According to Magaña and Short, "the best and most generous estimates are somewhere around 400,000 illegal entries per year." The total number of undocumented people range from three to five million, representing less than 2 percent of the nation's population.[18]

Other sound-bite findings include the following:

1. Undocumented newcomers represent less than 30 percent of total immigration to the United States.
2. Of total legal immigrants who arrived between 1981 and 1990, 12 percent are from Mexico, 26 percent from other Latin American countries, 45 percent from Asia, and 17 percent from other nations (primarily Europe and Canada).
3. The proportion of the foreign-born population in the United States is lower today than it was ninety years ago (8 percent compared to 15 percent).
4. Immigrants pay $133 billion dollars annually in local, state, and federal taxes.
5. Immigrants generate an annual net surplus (taxes to services) in the range of 25 to 30 billion dollars.[19]

While representations of contemporary immigrants, such as suburban legends, offer one window into the dynamics of racialization, the material realities—especially those that are job-related—faced by immigrants redirect the discussion to lived experiences. The segmentation of the Mexican population in the United States into low-paying, low-status jobs has characterized southwestern labor markets since the late nineteenth century, a pattern that has persisted to the present. According to 1980 census reports, blue-collar, service, and farm labor occupations, when taken together, account for approximately 75 percent of Mexicano/Chicano workers and for 50 percent of their wage-earning sisters.[20] Little change occurred in the 1980s, "the Decade of the Hispanic." In 1990, 71 percent of Latino (men) workers nationally fell into the three categories of blue-collar, service, and farm labor. For Mexican working women in the Southwest, over 40 percent could be located in service, factory, and agricultural jobs; in California, this figure is 48 percent.[21]

Mexican women with blue-collar jobs face the triple obstacles of gender, nationality, and class. For recent immigrants, lack of citizenship poses an additional barrier. They are overworked and underpaid, often struggling to support themselves and their families on less than minimum wage. Garment and other forms of factory work means putting up with production speed-ups, sexual harassment, hazardous conditions, and substandard pay for fear that plants will downsize or mechanize, or pack up shop entirely and move "off shore" to Mexico, Costa Rica, or Honduras. As Tejana apparel operatives laid off from Levi's explained, "In the end, we saw that they treated the machines better than us." "No tenemos hambre de comida, tenemos hambre de justicia—we are hungry for justice, not food."[22]

To many Americans, sweatshops are factories that exist in other nations, not our own. Homegrown garment sweatshops, however, did not disappear with Progressive Era reforms or New Deal legislation. Sociologist María Soldatenko has poignantly documented the exploitation of undocumented people in Los Angeles garment shops. Managers and subcontractors intimidate workers from complaining about back pay or contract fraud by threatening to report them to the INS.[23] The pay scales, especially for homeworkers under the subcontracting system, seem reminiscent of the going rate during the Great Depression. One *costurera* was paid $3.75 for an intricately sewn cocktail dress. A 1994 survey of 69 California garment plants indicated that 93 percent violated health and safety standards and more than 50 percent violated minimum wage and overtime laws. Reminiscent of the Triangle Shirtwaist factory in New York City in the early twentieth century, some managers had locked or barricaded the exits, and in two shops children "as young as 13 [were] working nine hour days." In 1999, piecework rates continue to be abysmal with apparel operatives earning "as little as $150 for a 50 hour week."[24]

Understandably, workers are fearful of voicing their complaints. Recognizing the limits of their education and employment background, some value job security above all other considerations. El Paso native and former apparel worker Elsa Chávez poignantly described the mind-set of these factory women:

> A lot of them couldn't even read or write and they were so scared to lose their jobs because they didn't know how to work at another place. They didn't know how to look for a job, so they were really scared. They just wanted to stay there at Farah. And the same thing happened . . . at Mann Manufacturing. . . . I was working there after I had lost my job at Farah—one day, I went over and there were some ladies crying and I asked them why. And some of them had worked their whole lives at the same factory, at the same place, at the same machine. They did not know how to do anything else. And when Mann sold the factory to Billy the Kid, they were all afraid that they were going to be fired because they were so old, and they did not know how to go look for a job.[25]

Fear of deportation also looms large in the minds of undocumented workers, and INS raids play into the cycle of exploitation. According to a 1990 issue of *California Lawyer,* "the garment industry depends more heavily on undocumented workers than any other—even more than agriculture or restaurant industries. One reporter wryly commented, "Think of LA fashion and you think less of twirling runway models than of immigrant agents raiding sweatshops."[26]

What about education? What are the responsibilities of our universities and of ourselves? In 1990, only 5 percent of Mexican women workers in the Southwest had four or more years of college.[27] What programs exist that address disparities in education by gender, race, nationality, and class? As an advisory board member and workshop facilitator, I am proud of my affiliation with Arizona State University's Hispanic Mother-Daughter Program (HMDP). Founded in 1984, the project recruits young women and their mothers to a program of workshops, field trips, interactive activities, and individual mentoring designed to motivate and prepare them for higher education. HMDP requires a five-year commitment that begins in the eighth grade and continues through high school. Daughters who attend Arizona State also have HMDP-related activities, including peer advising of younger teens. The curriculum for each grade level integrates academic and personal issues. Participants learn how to apply for financial aid, how to study for the SAT, and how to write a personal statement. Moreover, they attend structured workshops on pragmatic life decisions—managing money, avoiding friendship violence, and discussing the consequences of unplanned pregnancy. Directed by long-time community activist Rosie López, the Hispanic Mother-Daughter Program also imparts basic civic lessons—following a bill through the state legislature and staging a mock trial at the law school. Teens even interview their mothers as part of a Latina history and culture component.[28]

The program has enjoyed remarkable success. "Since 1988, over 80% of the daughters who began the program in eighth grade have graduated from high school and 63% have enrolled in college." In 1997–98, of the daughters who attended Arizona State (n=92), 45% have grade point averages of 3.0 or higher and only 6% withdrew or were disqualified. In 1998, out of 106 HMDP seniors, 89 graduated from high school and 82 (77 percent) were college bound. During the same year, furthermore, the program's teen pregnancy rate was only 3 percent. The Hispanic Mother-Daughter Program is not a small-scale endeavor. In 1997–98, 1,198 mothers and daughters proved active participants (284 in the eighth-grade cluster, 822 at the high school level, and 92 at ASU).[29] Mothers are also encouraged to pursue their education and since 1988, "over one-third of the mothers report that they have continued their own education." Raquel Hidalgo, for instance, is becoming a nurse as the result of participating in the program with her three daughters.[30] In May 1996, the Hispanic Mother-Daughter Program reached a milestone: the first mother/daughter team graduated from Arizona State University. Lucy and Monica Orozco both majored in bilingual education. Mother Lucy "graduated with a 3.8 grade point average from the Honors College" while daughter Monica trailed with a 3.2.[31] In Lucy's words:

> I'm too old not to try hard. . . . I had never even dreamed of coming to college. I knew this world existed but it was like a different planet. I didn't know what business I'd ever have coming here. The people in the program let us know it was possible.[32]

Community counts. As George Lipsitz reminds us, "We do not choose our color, but we do choose our commitments. We do not choose our parents, but we do choose our politics."[33] In my mind, the future of race is intertwined not only with the usual suspects of class, gender, and sexuality, but also with community, especially at the grassroots. Our obligations as teachers and scholars do not end at the university parking lot. It is a matter of partnership, not outreach. In the words of the mentor of César Chávez, the legendary California organizer Fred Ross, "[Y]ou work with people where they are—not where you are."[34] This is the first step in building tactical coalitions predicated on strategies of empowerment.

In shifting through the (mis)representations, I remember Carmen, a Mexicana immigrant who came of age in El Paso's Segundo Barrio. As a student in my Chicano history class at the University of Texas–El Paso more than seventeen years ago, she penned an autoethnography, and in bridging class materials and lived experiences (her own), she claimed an authorial voice as she crafted a manifesto for immigrant rights.

> The daily struggles for survival of the immigrant are known only to the immigrant. Books can expose details and experiences but never thoughts and intensity of feelings. Endurance and its reasons are hard to convey. It isn't easy to give up a homeland and set out to conquer the unknown, so the immigrants must have superior qualities and tolerance unknown to the so-called "native" Americans. The determination of our people to endure . . . change in an

> effort to upgrade a lifestyle and educate their children calls for admiration (not deportation).[35]

Given the challenges of representation, segmentation, and tactical coalitions, let us be engaged citizens, not disengaged cynics. Or as Cornel West so eloquently puts it, "I remain a prisoner of hope."

NOTES

I would like to acknowledge my hard-working graduate research assistants, Timothy Hodgdon, Laura Muñoz, and Mary Ann Villarreal. I also thank Valerie Matsumoto for her care packages of articles from the *Los Angeles Times* during the five years I have lived in Arizona and to Matthew García, Anne Larson, Rosie López, Lisa Magaña, Stefan Rinke, Howard Shorr, and Robert Short for graciously sharing published and unpublished materials with me. And to Victor Becerra, who believes.

1. *Visalia Times Delta*, October 24, 1986, In fairness, Ann Landers expressed her distaste for "such guidelines" and for contests in general.
2. *Arizona Republic*, November 25, 1997; *Arizona Republic*, January 11, 1998.
3. *Arizona Republic*, February 14, 1999. City officials also promulgated a policy whereby law enforcement would no longer act "as an auxiliary to the Border Patrol." A local columnist further noted, "Of the 432 undocumented immigrants . . . deported in the Chandler round-up, none was charged with any other crimes" (ibid.).
4. *Arizona Republic*, January 5, 1999. Other letters followed that chastised not only Calvert for her "Jim Crow mentality" but also the *Arizona Republic* for printing Calvert's letter in the first place. (See, for example, *Arizona Republic*, January 10, 1999.)
5. See Robert McLean, *That Mexican! As He Is, North and South of the Rio Grande* (New York: Fleming H. Revell, 1928); Roy L. Garis, "The Mexican Invasion," *Saturday Evening Post*, April 19, 1930, 43–44; and Alan Kraut, *Silent Travelers: Germs, Genes, and the "Immigrant Menace"* (New York: Basic Books, 1994).
6. "U.S. Citizen Opinion Poll on America's Illegal Alien Crisis" by American Immigration Control, a project of "We the People" (1995); flyer for Bill Hoge (in author's possession).
7. Lisa Magaña and Robert Short, "The Social Construction of Mexican Immigrants by Politicians" (unpublished paper, courtesy of the authors).
8. Magaña and Short, 9.
9. Stefan Rinke, "'The Fear of the Vampire Woman': Engendering the Image of the Yankee Girl in Chile, 1918–1932" (unpublished paper, courtesy of the author).
10. Patricia A. Turner, *I Heard It through the Grapevine: Rumor in African-American Culture* (Berkeley: University of California Press, 1993), 213–214, 224–226; "Tommy Who?" e-mail communication I received on February 19, 1999 (print copy in author's possession). Note: This e-mail had made its way through several e-mail lists before I received it.
11. *Valley Life*, June 7, 1993.
12. Philip Martin, "Immigration to the United States: Journey to an Uncertain Destination," in *Immigration and Ethnic Communities: A Focus on Latinos*, ed. Refugio Rochín (East Lansing: Julian Samora Institute, Michigan State University, 1996), 53; Adela de la Torre, "Proposition 187 and Its Aftermath: Will The Tidal Wave Continue?" in *Immigration and Ethnic Communities*, 105–106; Anne Larson, "A Comparative Analysis of Proposition 187 and the Immigration Act of 1924" (seminar paper, Claremont Graduate School, 1994); *Los Angeles Times*, October 30, 1994; *Los Angeles Times*, March 12, 1995. Note: The only section of Proposition 187 currently enforced is the felony penalty for using or creating false documents "to obtain public benefits or employment" (Martin, "Immigration to the United States"). In a world where Proposition

187 was fully enforced, undocumented mothers could be sentenced to five years in prison for sending their children to public school.

13. "I Love America" (poem distributed by California State Assembly member Peter Knight, copy in author's possession); *Los Angeles Times,* May 19, 1993.

14. *Los Angeles Times,* May 19, 1993; *Los Angeles Times,* May 20, 1993.

15. George Lipsitz, *The Possessive Investment in Whiteness: How White People Profit from Identity Politics* (Philadelphia: Temple University Press, 1998).

16. de la Torre, "Proposition 187," 105.

17. Congressional Hispanic Caucus Report, "Fact and Fiction: Immigrants in the U.S." (October 7, 1994), 5.

18. Magaña and Short, "The Social Construction of Mexican Immigration," 10; Juan L. Gonzales, Jr., "Discrimination and Conflict: Minority Status and the Latino Community in the United States," in *Immigration and Ethnic Communities,* ed. Refugio Rochín (East Lansing: Julian Samora Institute, Michigan State University, 1996), 16.

19. Congressional Hispanic Caucus Report, "Fact and Fiction," pp. 5–6; *The Los Angeles Times,* August 2, 1994; Ruben G. Rumbaut, "Immigrants from Latin America and the Caribbean: A Socioeconomic Profile," in *Immigration and Ethnic Communities,* ed. Refugio Rochín (East Lansing: Julian Samora Institute, Michigan State University, 1996), 3; *Washington Post,* January 9, 1999; *Arizona Republic,* August 16, 1998; "Immigration: Women and Girls: Where Do They Land?" *Issues Quarterly* 1, no. 3 (1995): 2. (*Issues Quarterly* is a publication of the National Council for Research on Women.) Note: With regard to point 2, numbers and proportions vary depending on whether the researcher relies on census, INS, and/or other government statistics. Point 2 derives from INS figures reported in the *Los Angeles Times,* August 2, 1994.

20. U.S. Department of Commerce, Bureau of the Census, *1980 Census of the Population. General Social and Economic Characteristics: Arizona, California, Colorado, New Mexico, and Texas.*

21. U.S. Department of Commerce, Bureau of the Census, "We the American . . . Hispanics" (November 1993), 13; U.S. Department of Commerce, Bureau of the Census, *1990 Census of the Population. General Social and Economic Characteristics: Arizona, California, Colorado, New Mexico, and Texas,* tables 50 and 124. We must also bear in mind that undocumented workers are not usually included in these statistics and that their exclusion may affect occupational categories to different degrees.

22. For further elaboration, see William V. Flores, "Mujeres en Huelga: Cultural Citizenship and Gender Empowerment in a Cannery Strike," in *Latino Cultural Citizenship: Claiming Identity, Space, and Rights,* ed. William V. Flores and Rina Benmayor (Boston: Beacon Press, 1997), 210–254; Karen Hossfeld, "Why Aren't High-Tech Workers Organized?' Lessons in Gender, Race, and Nationality from the Silicon Valley," in *Working People in California,* ed. Daniel Cornford (Berkeley: University of California Press, 1995); María Angelina Soldatenko, "Organizing Latina Garment Workers in Los Angeles, *Aztlán* 20, no. 1–2 (1991): 73–96; Vicki L. Ruiz, "'And Miles to Go' . . . Mexican Women and Work, 1930–1985," in *Western Women: Their Land, Their Lives,* ed. Lillian Schlissel, Vicki L. Ruiz, and Janice Monk (Albuquerque: University of New Mexico Press, 1988), 127–132; Denise Segura, "Labor Market Stratification: The Chicana Experience," *Berkeley Journal of Sociology* 29 (1984): 57–91; Elizabeth Martínez, "Levi's, Button Your Fly—Your Greed Is Showing," *Z Magazine,* January 1993, 22–27 (quotes are from pp. 24 and 26, respectively).

23. Soldatenko, "Organizing Latina Garment Workers," 86.

24. *Los Angeles Times,* April 15, 1994; Thompson, "Threadbare Justice," *California Lawyer* 10 (May 1990): 28–32; *Los Angeles Times,* March 11, 1999. According to Thompson's article in *California Lawyer,* apparel companies receive "a virtual slap on the wrist" for violating child labor laws.

25. Interview with Elsa Chávez, April 19, 1983, conducted by Vicki L. Ruiz. Note: Elsa Chávez is a pseudonym used at the person's request.

26. Thompson, "Threadbare Justice," 30, 32, 84; *Los Angeles Times*, March 12, 1995; *Los Angeles Times*, June 7, 1996.

27. U.S. Department of Commerce, Bureau of the Census, *1990 Census of the Population. General Social and Economic Characteristics: Arizona, California, Colorado, New Mexico, and Texas*, tables 47 and 120.

28. "Generations Two: Hispanic Mother-Daughter Program" (pamphlet published by ASU Student Life, ca. 1997); 1998–1999 Workshop Schedules for 8th Grade, High School, and College Levels for the Hispanic Mother-Daughter Program; *Arizona Republic*, November 5, 1998; personal experiences and observations of the author.

29. "Generations Two"; Rosie Marie López, "1997–98 Annual Report, Hispanic-Mother Daughter Program, Arizona State University" (July 1, 1998), 5–6. Note: The graduates' college choices are as follows: 26 headed for ASU; 52 opted for the local community colleges; 3 elected other Arizona universities; and 1 ventured to a school in Texas.

30. "Hispanic Mother-Daughter Program Pregnancy Rates" (in-house document, courtesy of Rosie López); "1997–98 Annual Report," HMDP, 6.

31. "Generations Two"; *Arizona Republic*, November 5, 1998.

32. *ASU Insight*, May 17, 1996.

33. Lipsitz, *The Possessive Investment in Whiteness*, vii.

34. Fred Ross Papers, M812, Box 2, Folder 15, Department of Special Collections, Green Library, Stanford University, p. 1. (Gracias a Matthew García for this citation.)

35. "Carmen's Story" (author's personal files).

CONTRIBUTORS

NORMA ALARCÓN is Chair of Women's Studies and Professor of Ethnic Studies at the University of California–Berkeley. She is the founder of Third Woman Press, now in its twentieth year. Her recent publications include "The Theoretical Subject(s) of *This Bridge Called My Back* and Anglo-American Feminism," in *Criticism in the Borderlands;* "Traddutora, Traditora: A Paradigmatic Figure of Chicana Feminism," in *Cultural Critique;* and *The Sexuality of Latinas* with Ana Castillo and Cherríe Moraga.

ARTURO J. ALDAMA is Associate Professor in the Department of Chicana/o Studies, Arizona State University. He is the author of *Disrupting Savagism: Intersecting Chicana/o, Mexicana/o, and Native American Struggles for Representation* (forthcoming), as well as several articles in Chicana/o and Native American cultural, literary, and filmic studies.

FREDERICK LUIS ALDAMA is Assistant Professor in the Department of English at the University of Colorado, Boulder. He is the author of more than a dozen refereed articles in Chicana/o, Asian American, African American, and British postcolonial literary, cultural, and filmic studies in such publications as *Genre, Nepantla, Lucero, Literature Interpretation Theory,* and *Callaloo.* His *Dancing with Ghosts,* a critical biography of the late Arturo Islas, is forthcoming. He is a recipient of several awards, including the Ford and the Stanford Humanities Center.

CORDELIA CANDELARIA has been Professor at Arizona State University in the Department of English since 1992, and in the Department of Chicana and Chicano Studies since 1998. Her works include *Seeking the Perfect Game: Baseball in American Literature* (1989) and *Chicano Poetry: A Critical Introduction* (1986), as well as the poetry collections *Arroyos to the Heart* (1993) and *Ojo de la Cueva / Cave Springs* (1984). Works that she has edited or co-edited include *The Legacy of the Mexican and Spanish-American Wars: Legal, Literary, and Historical Perspectives* (2000); *Women Poets of the Americas: Toward a Panamerican Gathering* (1999); *Multiethnic Literature of the United States: Critical*

Introductions and Classroom Resources (1989); and *Estudios Chicanos and the Politics of Community* (1989).

ALEJANDRA ELENES is Associate Professor in the Department of Women's Studies, Arizona State University-West. She has published several refereed articles on Chicana critical issues, multicultural pedagogy, feminism, and cultural studies and is the author of a forthcoming book on feminism and U.S.-México border pedagogy.

RAMÓN GARCIA is Assistant Professor of Cultural, Filmic, and Literary Studies in the Department of Chicana/o Studies, Cal State–Northridge. He received his Ph.D. in Literature at the University of California–San Diego. Garcia is the author of several essays in Chicana artistic and cultural studies, as well as a forthcoming collection of short stories.

MARÍA HERRERA-SOBEK holds the Luis Leal Endowed Chair in the Department of Chicano Studies, University of California–Santa Barbara. Her publications include *The Bracero Experience: Elite Lore versus Folklore; Northward Bound: The Mexican Immigrant Experience in Ballad and Song* (Indiana University Press); and *The Mexican Corrido: A Feminist Analysis* (Indiana University Press). She has edited several volumes, including *Chicana Creativity and Criticism; Culture across Borders; Mexican Immigration and Popular Culture; Chicana Writers on Word and Film; Saga de Mexico;* and *Reconstructing a Hispanic/ Chicano Literary Heritage.*

GAYE T. M. JOHNSON is the recipient of the UC Presidents Postdoctoral Fellowship in the Department of Black Studies, University of California–Santa Barbara. She is completing a book manuscript on the history and cultural politics of musical collaborations between Latinas/os and African Americans in the twentieth century.

ALBERTO LEDESMA is Assistant Professor in the Division of Human Communications, Cal State–Monterey Bay, and Visiting Professor in the Ethnic Studies program at the University of California–Berkeley. He is the author of several essays in Chicana/o literary studies with a specific focus on immigration, as well as a forthcoming collection of short stories.

PANCHO MCFARLAND is a first-generation college graduate from Raton, New Mexico. He earned his Ph.D. at the University of Texas at Austin. He currently teaches Chicana/o expressive culture and community learning courses in the Southwest Studies Department at the Colorado College.

AMELIA MARÍA DE LA LUZ MONTES is Assistant Professor in the Department of English at the University of Nebraska–Lincoln and affiliate faculty of the Institute for Ethnic Studies. Among her publications are "'Es Necesario Mirar Bien': The Letters of María Amparo Ruiz de Burton," in *Recovering the U.S. Hispanic Literary Heritage,* vol. 3 (2000), and "María Amparo Ruiz de Burton Negotiates American Literary Politics and Culture," in *Challenging Boundaries: Gender and Periodization* (2000). In addition to critical publications, her fiction has appeared in *HERS 3: Brilliant New Fiction by Lesbian Writers* (1999) and *Chicana Literary and Artistic Expressions: Culture and Society in Dialogue* (2000). She is currently finishing a critical book on Ruiz de Burton.

PATRICIA PENN-HILDEN is Professor of Ethnic Studies/Native American Studies at the University of California, Berkeley. Her publications include *Working Women and Socialist Politics in France* (1986); *Women, Work, and Politics: Belgium* (1993); and *When Nickels Were Indians* (1995). She is currently co-editing a collection of essays, *Topographies of Race and Gender* (with Shari M. Huhndorf), and is completing a fourth book, called *Racing the West.* Her articles have appeared in such scholarly journals as *Social Identities, American Literary History, TDR/ The Drama Review,* and *The Historical Journal.*

LAURA E. PÉREZ is Assistant Professor in the departments of Ethnic Studies, Spanish, and Portuguese at the University of California–Berkeley. Her teaching and publications are in contemporary U.S. Latina and Latin American women's writing, Chicana/o literature and visual arts, and contemporary cultural theory.

NAOMI H. QUIÑONEZ is Assistant Professor in the Department of Chicana and Chicano Studies at California State–Fullerton. A widely anthologized poet, she is the author of *Hummingbird Dreams/Sueño de Colibri* and *The Smoking Mirror* (1998) and the editor of *Invocation L.A.: Urban Multicultural Poetry.* She is currently completing a book on "First Wave" Chicana writers and activists.

SARAH RAMIREZ is the first in a farmworker family to pursue higher education. She is completing doctoral study in the Department of Modern Thought and Literature, Stanford University. Her areas of research include Chicana and Native American feminism, visual arts, music, and popular culture. She has received several academic awards and distinctions and has presented her work at scholarly conferences.

ROLANDO J. ROMERO is Associate Professor in the Department of Spanish, Italian, and Portuguese at the University of Illinois–Urbana-Champaign, where he teaches U.S. Latina/Latino and Latin American literatures. He is the founding director of the Latina/Latino Studies Program at the University of Illinois–Urbana-Champaign. He is the general editor of *Discourse: Journal in Theoretical Studies in Media and*

Culture and has published essays in *Revista de Estudios Hispánicos, Confluencia, and Revista Iberoamericana,* among others. He served as chief academic consultant for *Indigenous Always,* a documentary that explores the life of La Malinche.

Delberto Dario Ruiz (Yaqui and Chicano) is a Ford Foundation Fellow currently completing his doctoral study at the Department of Ethnic Studies, University of California–Berkeley. His scholarship and poetry focus on indigenous subaltern studies along the U.S./México border.

Vicki L. Ruiz is Chair of Chicana/o Studies and Professor of History at Arizona State University. Her publications include *From Out of the Shadows: Mexican Women in Twentieth Century America* (1997); *Cannery Women, Cannery Lives: Mexican Women, Unionization, and the California Food Processing Industry, 1930–1950* (1987); *Unequal Sisters: A Multicultural Reader in U.S. Women's History* (co-edited with Ellen Carol Dubois); and *Women on the U.S.-Mexico Border: Responses to Change* (co-edited with Susan Tiano). Professor Ruiz has recently been nominated to be on the National Endowment of Humanities.

José David Saldívar is Chair of the Department of Ethnic Studies, University of California–Berkeley. He is the author of *The Dialectics of Our America: Genealogy, Cultural Critique, and Literary History* (1991) and *Border Matters: Remapping American Cultural Studies* (1997). He edited *The Rolando Hinojosa Reader* (1985) and co-edited *Criticism in the Borderlands: Studies in Chicano Literature, Culture, and Ideology* (1991).

Anna M. Sandoval is Assistant Professor of Literature and Cultural Studies in the Department of Chicano and Latino Studies at California State University–Long Beach. She received her Ph.D. from the University of California–Santa Cruz, in 1995. She is the author of several articles in Chicana literary studies and has written a forthcoming book, *Unir los Lazos: Towards a Mexicana and Chicana Literary Study.*

Jonathan Xavier Inda teaches anthropology and global cultural studies in the Department of Chicano Studies at the University of California–Santa Barbara. He is co-editor of *Race, Identity and Citizenship: A Reader* (1999) and has published articles on globalization, race, and migration in *Educational Policy; Plurimondi; Cultural Studies: A Research Volume; Discourse; Latino Studies Journal;* and *Encyclopedia of Cultural Anthropology.* He is currently co-editing a book with Renato Rosaldo on the anthropology of globalization.

INDEX

Page numbers for illustrations are in *italic*. Initial articles (e.g., The, El) are ignored in sorting headings except for city names. Numbers and dates are sorted as spelled.